$6,00

Lot 12⁵⁰

THE PENN STATE SERIES
IN GERMAN LITERATURE

GERMAN POETRY
IN THE AGE OF
THE ENLIGHTENMENT

ROBERT M. BROWNING

GERMAN POETRY IN THE AGE OF THE ENLIGHTENMENT

From Brockes to Klopstock

The Pennsylvania State University Press

University Park and London

Library of Congress Cataloging in Publication Data

Browning, Robert Marcellus, 1911–
German poetry in the age of the Enlightenment.

  (The Penn State series in German Literature)
  Includes bibliography and index.
  1. German poetry—18th century—History and
criticism.   2. Enlightenment.   3. Germany—Intellectual
life. I   Title.   II.   Series.
PT535.B7   831'.04   77-26832
ISBN 0-271-00541-6

CONTENTS

PREFACE

In 1749, the year of Goethe's birth, the last witch was publicly executed in Germany. In 1740, the year in which Frederick the Great ascended the throne, the philosopher Christian Wolff was recalled from exile to make a triumphant entry into Halle, from which he had been expelled seventeen years before by Frederick's father for his all-too-enlightened doctrines. The reinstatement of the "teacher of the Germans" in his old university was one of the first official acts of Frederick's reign. These symbolic events mark the progress of the Enlightenment and at the same time indicate the unevenness of the road it had to travel.

Between the Baroque and the Enlightenment there is no clear break, no sudden sunrise. Rather it is like the dawn of an overcast day, when the sun may be felt but not seen. The light of reason that was struggling to break through the clouds had actually appeared on the horizon around the middle of the seventeenth century, an age of astounding scientific progress and the pivotal century between the Middle Ages and modern times. But this light was slow in penetrating the overcast, or, to change the metaphor, the peaks were aglow long before the light reached the valleys.

The watchword of the Baroque was learning, *eruditio*, and it was oriented toward Revelation. The watchword of the Enlightenment was reason, *ratio*, and it was oriented toward nature. The Baroque sought to keep its eyes fixed on the divine, conceived as absolutely transcendent; the Enlightenment sought to keep its eyes fixed on man, seen as a part of nature. With the divinization of nature, the merging of the two realms, the Enlightenment at once reached its peak and was superseded. The Here and Now is also the There and Then, each step paced off in this world at the same time a measure of immeasurableness: "Und jeder Schritt ist Unermesslichkeit."

With the centering of the universe in man, God was necessarily forced toward the periphery and His will transferred to another authority. This authority is a double one: Reason on the one hand and the State on the other. Both are absolute. Karl Barth eloquently pointed out that with the decay of the "Reichsidee," i.e., the idea governing the Holy Roman Empire with its guarantee (under God) of the rights and privileges of all classes through mutual interdependence, the absolute monarch became possible and with him the absolute antimonarchist, the revolutionary.[1] Louis XIV and Robespierre are brothers under the skin. "Die schreckliche, die kaiserlose Zeit" had begun. For the absolute state, as Hobbes tells us, arrogates all right to itself, whether this right be concentrated in the person of the ruler or the people. In both instances the individual is deprived of place and meaning.[2] The "city of man" is achieved at the cost of the bitter paradox of the depersonalization of the individual.

As a result of this development, the arts, and especially poetry, began to go underground, becoming the domain of the private, the last refuge of the individual. This led to the rise of modern artistic sensibility. It led to poetry that springs from subjective experience rather than from an objective idea, to poetry that is ego-centered rather than society-centered, that is symbolic rather than emblematic, private rather than public. The process is of course a gradual one, with its ups-and-downs, its hesitations and *repentirs*, but it is not to be stemmed. The chapters that follow, though not meant to prove or disprove any thesis, will, I think, bear this out.

Originally I had planned to treat the poetry of the eighteenth century through Sturm und Drang, but reflection convinced me that to do so would detract from the picture I wished to present of the poetry of the Enlightenment, which deserves to be viewed in its own terms. A word of explanation on the omission of Wieland, the German rococo poet *par excellence*, from my discussion: Wieland is an epic rather than a lyric writer, and my concern was primarily with the latter. One can perhaps excuse the inclusion of Gellert's *Fabeln und Erzählungen* under an extended understanding of lyric poetry but hardly *Oberon*.

The present volume was begun in the spring of 1971 as a direct continuation of my *German Baroque Poetry*, published in that year. It was completed in June 1975 with the support of a Senior Fellowship from the National Endowment for the Humanities, which allowed me a year's freedom from instructional duties. Besides my wife and personal friends, especially my colleague Otto K. Liedke, who read the manuscript with a critical eye and offered a number of valuable suggestions for improvement, I owe particular thanks to the staff of Hamilton College Library and its director, Walter Pilkington, for their cheerful and unfailing cooperation. To W. Lawrence Gulick, Dean, Hamilton College, I am deeply grateful for encouragement and the authorization of financial support to help defray publication costs in times so critical for studies in foreign languages.

This volume, like *German Baroque Poetry*, I dedicate to my students, past and present.

R.M.B.

CHAPTER ONE

DIDACTICISTS AND THE POETRY OF REFLECTION

It is customary to begin a survey of eighteenth-century German literature with a condescending glance at Johann Christoph Gottsched (1700–1766) and the state of poetics in the early Enlightenment. Gottsched's *Versuch einer critischen Dichtkunst vor* (= für) *die Deutschen* first appeared in 1729 (dated 1730) and reached its fourth, much-expanded and improved edition in 1751. It was a work not without resonance, and yet a work without real influence. With the example of the baroque before us it would be rash to maintain that no poet was ever begot by a manual of poetics, but by the eighteenth century the situation had changed, certainly as concerns those poets whose work is of primary interest here. Gottsched looks backward rather than forward; he sums up a period, that of Neoclassicism, rather than inaugurating a new one. The tendencies he typifies we have already discussed in the last chapter of *German Baroque Poetry*.

Gottsched is not interested in the poetic process as such, but in the production of a certain kind of literature according to tested formulae. Thus he is a true, if belated, son of Martin Opitz, whom he greatly admired. Gottsched's watchword is *probability* (Wahrscheinlichkeit), his guiding principle *canonicity* (the idea rather than the term). By prob-

1

ability he means that which is acceptable to common sense, that which does not fly in the face of reason and which is therefore in harmony with nature and her laws. His chief aim, however, is the establishment of a canon. Here he inevitably becomes involved in the thorny question of good taste and, like all who venture onto this terrain, finds himself forced into a circular argument: canonical works are those highly regarded by those whose taste we admire, and we admire them for regarding such works highly. It goes without saying that only works which conform to the criterion of probability are acceptable, and that wide areas of taste are ignored or rejected as barbarous. There is hardly a hint of historicity. Vico's *Scienza nuova* (1725, 1730) was being written at the same time, but Gottsched belongs to another age. Still, one cannot but regard his efforts to establish a canon—one that included German poets, of course—as laudable when one realizes that his aim was not to understand poetry but to guide the taste of his countrymen along certain narrow but safe paths, so that they might also have a voice in the choir of European song. This too is Opitz all over again, but Opitz looking backward.

Gottsched, a pupil of Christian Wolff, whose voluminous work he popularized with tremendous success, regarded himself more as a philosopher than a theorist of literature. As a philosopher he represents the viewpoint of the early Enlightenment. It is a viewpoint singularly unproductive of impressive poetry, at least in German-speaking lands, where no Pope arose to show what could be accomplished within these limited confines. The motive force of the seminal poetic works of the age springs from another source, one that conflicts with the doctrines of the Enlightenment and Neoclassicism. These works are shaped by revolt against the absolutism of the century—the absolutism of reason, the absolutism of the state and state religion, the absolutism of prescriptive poetics. Basically they have a religious motivation, though toward the end of the century this may be concealed by a tendency to secularization, which leads to the divinization of nature.

2

DIDACTICISTS AND THE POETRY OF REFLECTION

The prodigiously extensive work of Barthold Heinrich Brockes (1680–1747),[1] whose *Irdisches Vergnügen in Gott* (1721–47) runs to nine portly volumes, is in many respects a typical product of the Enlightenment and could not have been written at any other time. On a deeper level, however, it could almost be called medieval: in basic feeling and attitude Brockes belongs more in the company of Friedrich Spee and Catharina Regina von Greiffenberg than in that of Haller, Hagedorn, and Gellert. The motivation of Brockes' work is profoundly religious. Like Greiffenberg in her nature lyrics and like Spee in those parts of *Trutznachtigall* that celebrate the wonders of creation, Brockes' poetry "dances the orange" in praise of God. "Sinnlicher Gottesdienst," sensual praise of the divine, is his own characterization of his work. It is one long, never-ending *Gloria*. An apt translation of the title of his book might be "Earthly Foretaste of the Divine." In the eighteenth century *Vergnügen* had a much wider semantic range than today; it meant not only "pleasure" but also "contentment," "joy," even "bliss," as for example in Christian Wolff's words on the feeling aroused in the Maker from the contemplation of His handiwork: "Eine anschauende Erkenntnis der Vollkommenheit machet *Vergnügen*" (Entw.reihen, Aufkl. 2, 135).

Brockes is above all a man for whom the sensual world exists. God is for him the giver of sensuality ("Geber der Sinnlichkeit," *Auszug*, p. 16). Seeing, hearing, touching, tasting, smelling—these are the God-given ways of participating in the Divine. Conscious participation, participation with "betrachtendem Gemüte," is praise, refusal to do so is sin:

Dass wir nicht aufs Geschöpf, nicht auf den
Schöpfer merken,
. . . .
Ach! möchte man doch einst, dass dieses Sünde,
fassen . . .

[*Auszug*, pp. 106f.]

The intent of Brockes' work is to save us from this sin, to cure us of our saddest affliction, our habitual blindness

3

("Gewohnheit-Pest," *Auszug*, p. 179), that we may become more perfectly conscious of the earthly-divine. It is the poet's ancient task. Greiffenberg too knew that "Göttliche Wunder in allem man siehet / Wann man den Vorhang der Faulheit aufziehet" (Sonnett 227). These poets embrace the principle of plenitude or the Idea of Goodness in their praise of the divine, rather than the Idea of the Good, concepts made familiar to most of us by Arthur O. Lovejoy in *The Great Chain of Being* (1936). The Idea of the Good, Lovejoy explains, "was an apotheosis of unity, self-sufficiency, and quietude"; the Idea of Goodness, on the other hand, apotheosized "diversity, self-transcendence, and fecundity" (pp. 82 f.). It celebrated God the Creator. Those who seek the divine through and in the creation do not turn from the world but toward it, seeing the divine as its "source and informing energy."

Undeniably, the superficial reader can gain the impression that Brockes wrote not so much to glorify God as to glorify a ridiculously shallow utilitarianism. Many passages in the later parts of his works seem to exemplify this; the following is typical:

Eine Mücke legt die Eier auf das Wasser,
    draus entstehn
Kleine Würmer, welche lang in gedachtem Wasser
    leben,
Eh sie in die Luft sich heben;
Diese dienen nun zur Nahrung Krebsen,
    Wasservögeln, Fischen,
So man uns pflegt aufzutischen.
Ist es also für den Menschen auch sogar, dass
    Mücken sein.
Er verbindet aller Wesen, die man allenthalben
    spüret;
Alle zielen auf ihn ab.
              [*Dt. Nat.-Lit.* 39, 371]

But utilitarianism in a narrower sense is not Brockes' point at all. These lines are from a poem on the "Kräfte der menschlichen Vernunft," celebrating our God-given reason as the ordering and interpretive power of the universe, that is, as the organ of conscious praise. The naive manner may excite our risibility, but the underlying thought is hardly naive. The passage continues:

> . . . Seine [des Menschen] Gegenwart allein
> Ist die Stelle, wo ein Ganzes aus viel Teilen
> sich formieret;
> Er ist gleichsam ihre Seele. Ja es ist der Mensch
> nicht nur
> Der Geschöpfe Mittelpunkt, die ihn überall umringen,
> Er ist überdem ihr Priester; er ist ihrer Dankbarkeit
> Gleichsam ein getreuer Dolmetsch. Wenn sie Gott ihr
> Opfer bringen,
> Der sie ihm [= sich] zur Ehr' gemacht, wenn sie ihrem
> Herrn lobsingen,
> Schallet es durch seinen Mund. . . .

Through man, creation is raised to the realm of the spirit. We may think of Romans 8:19 ff., or we may think of Leibniz's monadism, with man playing the role of creation's central monad. Brockes' notorious "Nutzanwendungen," or practical applications, and his naive teleological explanations are primarily intended to convince the "verwildertes Gemüte" (Entw.reihen, Aufkl. 2, 269), i.e., the mind gone astray, the unbeliever, that nature is meaningful, and if meaningful, then divine, for all meaning comes from the Maker. Passages that strike us as the veriest pedantry, products of the self-satisfied Enlightenment at its most ridiculous, are actually informed with a religious sense straight out of the Middle Ages. They are akin to the old bestiaries and lapidaries. Brockes is intent on making us aware of "nature's marvelous web":

> O wunderbar Gewebe der Natur!
> Wer dich mit menschlichem Gemüth,
> Und nicht mit vieh'schen Augen, sieht;
> Der kann die Allmacht-volle Spur
> Von einem ew'gen Wunder-Wesen,
> Auf deinen Blättern, deutlich lesen.
>
> [*Auszug*, p. 103]

5

The key word in Brockes is not utility (Nutzen) but *wonder*. By wonder he does not mean that which contravenes the laws of nature but these laws themselves—the fundamental inexplicableness of all natural phenomena. "Laws" after all explain nothing, they have no epistemological value, they are only names: "Sprecht nicht," the poet says in "Betrachtung der Blätter," "Sprecht nicht: in Samen steckt die Kraft; / Es stösst sich alles fort. Die Kraft, die Eigenschaft / Ist eben das, was wir nicht fassen, / Durch deren blossen Schall wir uns verblenden lassen" (quoted after Wolff, "Brockes' Religion," p. 1131). Surrounded by wonders and a wonder himself, what is left for man but praise?

It would of course be a mistake to assume that Brockes divinizes nature in the manner of the Romantics and the pre-Romantics. He is far from identifying the Creator with His creation; the latter is only His "Bild" (*Auszug*, p. 687). Brockes' God is transcendent and unknowable, the *deus absconditus* of Luther and St. Augustine. But to disregard His earthly image is a grave sin, graver than the pardonable error of the heathen who made divinities of the sun, moon, stars, and air: "Abgötter waren sie: Hingegen viele Christen / Sind, durch der Creatur Verachtung, Atheisten" (*Auszug*, p. 687). Neither does Brockes, as is still maintained by some literary historians led astray by the theologian David Friedrich Strauss, try to prove the existence of God from His works. The *Irdisches Vergnügen* is not, as Strauss claimed, one enormous "rhymed physico-theological proof of God's existence." This view has been thoroughly discredited by Hans M. Wolff.[2] Brockes begins with God, as every believer must; he does not, like the deists, end with Him by a process of deduction:

> Durch das eine Wörtchen: Werde!
> Ward die Erde.
> Und aus dieses Wortes Kraft
> Stammt noch ihre Dau'r und Güte,
> Keimt der Same, spriesst die Blüte,
> Fliesst des Frühlings Lebens-Saft.
> [*Auszug*, p. 16]

The basic metaphor of Brockes' work is the medieval one of nature as God's book. In lines worthy of Angelus Silesius he calls the world:

> O unbegreiflichs Buch; o Wunder-ABC!
> Worin, als Leser ich, und auch als Letter, steh![3]

Nature is a poem God writes to man, and Brockes bends over it with the meticulous fervor of a bibliophile examining a rare manuscript, expatiating on its wonders, its beauties, its strangeness, its incredible detail, and its unimaginable immensity, explicating its syntax, pointing out its conceits, and always concluding with an expression of profound admiration for the Poet. God's poem is written for our delight and instruction; its Author holds with a Renaissance-Baroque poetics of *delectare et prodesse*:

> Auf, lasst uns recht mit Andacht sehn
> Die Dinge, die mit Emsigkeit
> In dieser holden Mayen-Zeit
> Zu unsrer Lust, zu unserm Nutz geschehn!
> [Quoted after Blackall, *Emergence*, p. 241]

Brockes himself holds with the same view of the ends of poetry, but there is a significant difference between him and his seventeenth-century predecessors. The typical poet of the Baroque uses nature decoratively or emblematically, as a stage-setting or to illustrate a concept. In either case he tends to degrade nature to a cliché he can manipulate at will. Nature is there to suit *his* purpose; he is little interested in its quiddity, the ensemble of conditions that determine its particularity. Now for Brockes too nature is fundamentally an emblem, and he still structures his poems according to the standard baroque scheme of *descriptio* + *applicatio*, but with him nature is no longer something to be manipulated at will, something whose quiddity may be disregarded. All natural things retain a strong personal identity; though they point beyond themselves, they are nonetheless prized in themselves. It is the *descriptio* that carries the poem, and it is the phenomenon itself that makes the poet say: "Unglaublich ist, wie sehr mich dieser Anblick rührte" ("Mondschein") and fills him with "süsses Schrecken" (Entw.reihen, Aufkl. 2, 247). The subjoined *applicatio*, though vitally important to the poet, scarcely rises by necessity out of the *descriptio*, but is added to it in an openly didactic manner: the symbolic mode is still far in the future. The joinder is all the more evident because the *descriptio* has such plasticity and is so absorbing in itself.

Attentive consideration of all earthly phenomena is one determinant of the linguistic form of Brockes' poetry, the other being praise of the divine. The former corresponds to the *descriptio*, the latter to the *applicatio*. His typical procedure is to begin with a circumstantial description of a situation in the recent past ("Ich sahe jüngst . . . ," "Indem ich jüngst . . . ," etc.), then to turn to some particular feature of nature encountered in this situation, describe it in ever more minute detail with "reverent mind" and "searching brain," which leads in turn to the discovery of new wonders and this new discovery to praise of the Maker. This turning toward nature with open senses, looking at the thing and not past it, represents both the beginning of a new kind of poetry in German and a height in descriptive nature poetry that has rarely been surpassed. (James Thomson, for example, and his German emulator, Ewald von Kleist, are almost abstract compared to Brockes.) In riveting his attention on what is actually there and in striving to make us experience it, Brockes develops an antibaroque attitude toward language and a style particularly his own, a proselike verse aiming at clarity and sobriety, though filled with tense emotion. The *vers libre* of the madrigal is the nearest relative of this prose-verse with irregular rhyme. Such is the style of the descriptive passages. In many poems ("Die Rose," Reclams UB 2105, 42 ff., is a good example) these parts are interspersed with "arias" and "ariosi," with set strophic form and more lyrical in feeling. They are devoted to praise. Such poems are thus really cantatas, the descriptive sections being the recitative.

In the fixity with which he keeps his eye on nature, and nature in a strictly scientific sense, Brockes is a true son of the Enlightenment. The new science is for him a fruitful source of a sense that had previously received scant attention in German literature: the sense of the sublime. Because of it, such poems as "Die himmlische Schrift" and "Das Firmament" add a whole new dimension to German poetry. The whole of creation, "das Grosse und Kleine" (the title of one of his poems), from the microscopic animalcule to the starry heavens, is the subject of his song. In accepting the new science Brockes is particularly innovative: he is the first German poet to incorporate into his work the Copernican view of the universe. To this theme something like eight percent of the *Irdisches Vergnügen* is devoted.[4]

The writings of Junker, Lovejoy, Nicolson, Blumenberg, and Richter have sensitized the modern reader to the issues raised for poetry by the Copernican revolution.[5] At first the reaction to the new science was, on the whole, positive and liberating. Man, who in the old cosmogony had occupied the lowest position, namely the middle—with Hell, the spot farthest from the divine, as its very center—was released from his place of ignominy and the star he inhabited was incorporated into the vast astronomical family as an integral part of creation. "The *first* effect of the Copernican reform," Blumenberg writes, "did not consist in demeaning and mortifying man but in the consciousness of his membership in the world of planets as a being who determines for himself his place in the cosmos and his share in the universe" ("Selbstverständnis," p. 347). There were, to be sure, other considerations that were to lead to new humility and even to despair, but these, as Lovejoy points out, were not a direct result of the systems of Copernicus and Kepler (pp. 99 ff.). They mainly derived from philosophical and theological premises as corollaries of the principle of plenitude (i.e., the doctrine that an infinitely fecund diety must create an infinitely "full" universe) when this principle was applied to questions of the magnitude of the stellar universe. The principal far-reaching effect, which only gradually made itself felt, was the loss of a sense of *place*. No longer was there an Above and a Below, a Right and a Left; the "four corners" of the world were gone forever. There was also a loss of a sense of position

9

in *time*. The medieval conception of history as strictly bipartite (B.C. and A.D.) stood in analogy to the cosmic scheme of Above and Below (superlunary and sublunary). The post-Copernican concept of the universe as infinite allowed no such division. No more was there an "end of days" to which man could look forward in hope and trembling. These problems, which become central in Haller, hardly arise in Brockes, who, despite his intense interest in the new cosmology, still thinks in terms of Above and Below. The universe revealed by the new science above all feeds his sense of awe and wonder and powerfully stimulates his feeling for the sublime.

This feeling, Schiller explains, is "mixed," being composed of dismay ("Wehsein") and elation ("Frohsein"), and though not really pleasurable is preferred by all finer temperaments to any possible pleasure because it offers proof of our moral freedom: that which exceeds the bounds of the imagination does not exceed the bounds of thought, and that which is physically overwhelming still cannot conquer the will.[6] Brockes does not analyze this feeling in such Kantian terms, but he too knows that its tremendous attraction lies precisely in the sense of being lifted inwardly to a godlike level, while being reduced outwardly to nothingness:

> O! welche Tieffe! Welche Höh!
> Worin, wohin ich mich auch wende,
> Ich doch kein Ende,
> Wol aber viele Billionen (eine Billione hält tausend mahl
>   tausend Millionen)
> Von Billionen Sternen seh!
> Indem ich also voll Verwunderung steh',
> Und die Unendlichkeit von dieses Raumes Höhe,
> Und die Unendlichkeit der Zahl der Sternen-Heer
> Erstaunt und halb entzücket sehe;
> Kehr ich die angespannten Blicke
> Von ungefehr
> Auf mich zurücke
> Und fand, bey diesem Raum und aller Sternen Schein,

Mich wunderbarlich gross und klein
. . . .
Ich traff zugleich, weit mehr als ich beschreiben kann,
Ein' Art von Gröss' in unsern Seelen an,
Die alle Gröss' unendlich ubersteiget,
Indem sie, in uns selbst, uns selbst was Göttlichs zeiget.
["Grösse der Seelen," quoted after Junker, p. 62]

In Schiller's words, "We willingly allow our imagination to
find its master in the realm of phenomena, for after all this is
only one sensual power triumphing over another; but the
absolutely great within us nature in its boundlessness can
never touch" ("Über das Erhabene," p. 797). Schiller speaks
of the "angenehme Bestürzung" characteristic of the experience of the sublime; Brockes employs such oxymora as "hei-
ligs Grauen," "frohe Angst," "bange Lust" ("Die himmlische
Schrift") to express his reaction. It is the experience of the
tremendum, the earthly counterpart of the awesome fear God
inspires in the saints and angels, making them shudder with
unimaginable delight at their ability to perceive and participate in the divine radiance and causing them to sing "Holy,
Holy, Holy" for evermore.

The sublime is the actual that overwhelms the imagination and Brockes is a poet of the actual. There is no fundamental distinction in sublimity between the vast cosmic
spaces and a flower or a frog. Both are beyond our imagination, both are divine wonders, both are equally important
subjects of Brockes' song. No doubt, however, we value him
most as a poet of the uniquely earthly rather than as a poet of
the cosmos. He remains, for all his moralizing, almost un-
equalled in his ability to open our eyes and all our senses to
the wonders that immediately surround us. His striving is to
make his work a mirror of the actual, as the actual is the
mirror of the divine (the mirror image occurs frequently in
his work). Exactitude, not fantasy, is his ideal, for the actual
surpasses any fantasy, becoming itself a magical realm as soon
as we truly perceive it.

His attempt to be perfectly exact explains an often-noted

11

trait of his language, namely, the constant insertion of "scheint," "fast wie," "als (ob)," etc., in introducing a similitude. For if the thing itself is more wonderful than any metaphorical description of it, then the attempt to depict it in metaphorical terms must necessarily cause a certain embarrassment—indeed, something like a crisis of language. Hence the saving particles and frequent use of "seems." In other words, Brockes is a nominalist, one who holds that only existing things are real, and he encounters the problem of every nominalist: how to describe the unique in the symbolic medium of language.[7] On the other hand, to *try* to come to terms linguistically with the unique is the poet's inescapable duty, for it is man's mission and in the end his only truly useful activity to appreciatively contemplate that which is ever being wrought by "die wirkende Natur," *natura naturans*, a phrase constantly on the poet's lips. This is the kernel from which the whole *Irdisches Vergnügen* springs. It must therefore be endless, just as nature itself is endless: the excessive length of the book reflects the immensity of its subject. In the final analysis, nature remains indescribable and unfathomable:

> Weil, wenn wir zufern es wagen,
> Das durchdringend'ste Gesicht
> Doch auf die Natur erblindet.
> Keiner leb't, der sie ergründet,
> Und wir scheinen bloss gemacht,
> Zu bewundern ihre Pracht.
> [*Auszug*, p. 529]

Examples illustrative of Brockes' loving attempt to depict the actual may be found on almost every page of his work, though his prolixity and often the interspersion of reflective passages make him somewhat awkward to quote for this purpose. The following lines are a rather rare example of organic combination of reflection and description, in which the former is used to enhance the latter:

> Der Guckguck schreyt und rufft: Guck! guck! des
> Frühlings Pracht!

Guck, in der schönen Welt des grossen Schöpfers
  Macht
Mit froher Andacht an! Wenn er sie dann beschaut,
Und, dass die Welt so wunderschön,
Nun eine Zeitlang angesehn;
Lacht er, vor Anmuth, überlaut.

                                        [Auszug, p. 8]

Can anyone who has ever heard the call of a cuckoo help
chuckling—if not laughing outright "vor Anmuth"—at this
highly successful fusion of didacticism and nature description? The reflective passage fills the pause between the first
part of the cuckoo's cry and its always surprising, delayed
conclusion, the loud burst of laughter, and at the same time
tells *why* the cuckoo laughs. The sly naïveté of offering the
reflection as the thought of the bird itself must make us smile
and then, in the last line, laugh together with it. Our own
amused reaction is, like that of the cuckoo, somewhat delayed
by the process of reflection.

The following passage describes the inner part of the
corolla of a rose:

Ein roter Schatten ohne Schwärze
Bedeckt das kleine güldne Herze,
Das in dem Mittelpunkt der holden Tiefe sitzt
Und in der balsamreichen Höhle
In purpurfarbner Dämmrung blitzt.
Der roten Farben süsser Schein
Scheint leiblich nicht, nein geistig fast zu sein,
Da er, nachdem als man die Rose drehet,
Bald von, bald nach dem Licht, entstehet und vergehet,
So dass ihr Rot und Weiss, als wie das Blau und Grün
An einem Taubenhals, sich oft zu ändern schien.
Dies ist der innre Schmuck, die kühle rote Glut,
Die in dem runden Schoss der edlen Rose ruht . . .

                               [Reclams UB 2015, 45]

Nothing in German poetry before Brockes can really be compared to a passage like this, which is representative of many in
the *Irdisches Vergnügen*. The poet's passionate involvement finds

expression in such adjectives as "süss," "hold," and "edel," but just as obvious is his concentration on the quiddity of the rose; it is from his absorption in the latter that the former arises. The thing itself, not the poet's feeling, is primary.

In the next example, from "Der weisse Schmetterling," the "painterly" element is marked—a symphony of dark greens and contrasting whites—and the hush of hot midday is also marvelously evoked. Yet here too it is the thing, the butterfly-ness of butterflies, that the poet above all wishes to capture:

> Im Garten sass ich jüngst zur schwülen Mittagszeit
> In einem dicht verwachsnen Bogen
> Voll angenehm begrünter Dunkelheit
> Und sah, wie voller Munterkeit
> Viel weisse Schmetterlinge flogen,
> Die durch die grüne Nacht mit zarten Schwingen eilten
> Und die beschatteten, gekühlten Lüfte teilten;
> Da sie denn in dem dunklen Grünen
> Wie weisse Rosenblätter schienen.
> Bald sah ich sie, vom Schwärmen gleichsam matt,
> Als wie ein von der Luft getragnes welkes Blatt,
> Schnell, doch gerade nicht zur Erde sinken,
> Bis ich sie allgemach, bald hie, bald da
> Schnell flatternd wieder steigen sah,
> Da sie, vom Sonnenstrahl gerührt, wie Funken blinken.
>
> [Reclams UB 2015, 51]

The point of this poem as a whole is didactic: the parallel between the metamorphosis of the butterfly and the immortality of the human soul, which is lamely argued in the second half, the *applicatio*. But the poetry lies in the *descriptio*, the precise observation of nature, which is poetic by its very preciseness, like a drawing by Dürer. The thing itself is poetry, part of God's poem. This is the real message of Brockes' work, much more fundamental than any "Nutzanwendung" or *applicatio*.

One more example, this time with an auditory emphasis: an apple tree in full bloom laden with nectar-gathering bees:

Auf allen Aesten scheint ein Wunder-Schnee zu liegen,
Der warm und trocken ist; die Silber-weisse Blühte
Ergetzt nicht nur das Aug', sie labt auch das Gemüthe,
Durch den Geruch, zugleich. Viel tausend Bienen
    fliegen,
Und sammeln Honig ein,
Mit schwarmendem Getös' und angenehmem Summen.
Es tön't, als wann Bassons, gedämpfet, sanfte
    brummen.
Beym zwitschernden Discant von manchem Vögelein,
Beym rauschenden Tenor der wallenden Krystallen,
Die über glatte Kiesel fallen,
Und bey dem hohen Alt, dem lispelnden Gezische
Der Bäum' und Büsche,
Scheint dieses murmelnde Geräusch der Bass zu seyn.
[Auszug, p. 92]

Though there are onomatopoetic effects in this passage, and very evocative ones, it is a far cry from the "Lautmalerei" of the Nuremberg poets. Instead of trying to create a linguistic equivalent of the object, to reproduce or replace it by language, Brockes is intent upon *describing* it as vividly as possible. A comparison with a typical passage from Harsdörffer will make this clearer:

Die lisplend- und wisplende Bächelein wudeln/
die wellen-geflügelte Fluten erstrudeln.
Najaden die baden und waten am Rand.
Die Schuppen-einwohner beleichen den strand.
[Entw.reihen, Barock 2, 150]

In Harsdörffer the world has practically become pure sound, and his sound effects are almost absolute, intransitive; while in Brockes onomatopoeia serves an end beyond itself, being meant as an aid in realizing the nature of the given. If Harsdörffer may be said to write program music, Brockes writes notes on program music, nature's program music, which is God's. Even in the following dactyls, which have a much stronger kinship to the poetry of the Nurembergers, it

15

is not so much imitation as accuracy of description that Brockes strives for:

Der schallenden Nachtigall liebliche Lieder
Bezaubern der Hörer empfindliches Herz;
Ihr künstliches Gurgeln, ihr klingender Scherz,
In feurigen fertigen richtigen Sprüngen,
Ihr gluckendes, lockendes, lachendes Singen
Kann Geister entzücken, kann Seelen bezwingen,
Dem gütigen Schöpfer ein Loblied zu bringen.
[Entw.reihen, Aufkl. 2, 248]

Not that Brockes was above playing with sound effects. The best known example is "Die auf ein starkes Ungewitter erfolgte Stille," in which, as he himself is at pains to point out, the sections describing the fine weather preceding and following the storm (eighty lines in all) contain no r's, while the 100 lines devoted to the storm contain as many as possible. This he regards, quite in the spirit of the linguistic theorists of the Baroque, as proof of the musicality of German and its richness of vocabulary.

The reader coming to Brockes for the first time will probably be attracted more by his striking similes, especially by the naively homely ones, than by his sound effects, though it seems to have been the latter that particularly charmed his contemporaries. A nightingale is "Ein Schall, ein Hauch mit Haut umgeben"; the young buds surrounding a rose in full bloom sit "recht wie Kinder um sie her"; the bumblebee is like a "kleiner Bär mit Flügeln"; the peacock's tail is compared to the train of a royal robe: "Er [der Pfau] schleppt so gar, Weit mehr als Kaiserlich,/ Den prächtigsten Talar,/ Ja gar ein Bluhmen-Feld und Garten hinter sich," and in its markings one seems to see "alle Pracht von einer hellgestirnten Nacht," "Copernici so herrlichs Stern-Gebäude"; a peach tree in blossom is itself like a "glänzender, erhabner Pfauenschwanz"; autumnal foliage and flowers are "Als wie ein Schlaff-Rock von Drap d'or [cloth of gold],/ In welchem die Natur, eh sie zur langen Ruh/ Die müden Glieder neigte,/ Annoch zu guter letzt sich halb entkleidet zeigte." This is a small sampling from Brockes' store. To reiterate, metaphor in Brockes serves exactitude, not rhetorical splendor. With loving desperation he tries to say exactly what things are like, striving to decipher God's manuscript. Far from constructing a purely poetical world of the possible, he devotes himself almost exclusively to the description of the actual, to empirical reality. We have already seen that he knows how wide he falls of the mark. God's "Gegenwurf," His earthly manifestation, remains in the end indescribable, even as it remains unfathomable: man, like the angels, was created to wonder and to praise.

Brockes largely ignores man as a direct theme of his poetry. For him the proper study of mankind is nature. Albrecht von Haller (1708–77),[8] though one of the foremost natural scientists of the century, is concerned with man to the exclusion of all other themes.

That Haller should have written poetry at all must seem at first surprising. According to his own pronouncements, he had a low opinion of poets and poetry. Like Plato and Thomas Aquinas, Haller believed that "the poets lie too much" and that both eloquence (Beredsamkeit) and poetry (Dichtkunst), which in true Baroque fashion he mentions in one breath, "ziehen vom richtigen Gebrauch der Vernunft ab," detract from the proper use of reason through that which is—again in accordance with the standard poetics of the day—their very reason for being, namely, to "clothe" thought in figurative language. Tropes are "tacit lies": "heimliche Lügen sind die Figuren" (Hirzel, p. 379). Yet Haller is regarded, and he so regarded himself, above all as a philosophical poet. In the foreword to a volume of verse by a fellow physician (Werlhof), Haller praises the author for not being "merely a poet," "a dispensable and ineffective member of society" who contributes nothing to the well-being of his fellows, but also a physician, "an instrument by means of which Providence spreads its blessings" (Hirzel, p. 392). Yet Haller, himself a renowned physician, zealously guarded his whole life long the poetic reputation he had acquired before the age of thirty, meticulously revising each successive edition of his collected poems, *Versuch Schweizerischer Gedichte*, which first appeared anonymously in 1732. He spoke deprecatingly of his weakness for verse as a "poetic sickness," but he nonetheless published its symptoms. Obviously, the man whom Kant called "the most sublime of German poets" and Goethe and Herder called "the immortal Haller" contained within himself a deep division.

This division has to do primarily with Haller's attempt to fathom man's place in creation. Neither science nor religion offered him a satisfactory answer to this most vexing of all questions; indeed, one seemed to contradict the other. Yet, as Karl S. Guthke puts it, both feed his poetry, which is, as it were, the battlefield upon which the struggle between science and religion, philosophy and theology is waged.[9] Haller's poetry is a desperate, if finally unsuccessful, attempt to come to terms with the problems raised by this conflict. Though it may give itself the air of didactic poetry conveying an *answer*, it is really a dramatic statement of the human *problem*. The poets lie too much, yes, but do they not after all paradoxically tell the truth? That a poetic "lie" may also convey a deep truth is an insight to which Haller, who regarded language merely as an "Abschrift der Gedanken" (Hirzel, p. 378), may not have consciously attained, though it was the fundamental message of the new poetics that was contemporaneously being developed by his own countrymen, Bodmer and Breitinger, and is implicit in his own practice.

With "Die Alpen" (1729) Haller gained fame as a master of descriptive poetry and as the discoverer of the Alps as a poetic subject. In Haller's day the Alps were mainly regarded as merely a hindrance to commerce and their inhabitants as little above the level of the herds they tended. "Was für eine entsetzliche, schaurige Landschaft!" cried Winckelmann, and his sentiments were undoubtedly widely shared. The Alps were an acquired taste even with Haller himself. The land-scape he instinctively appreciated was that of Holland: flat, laid out as by a geometer, entirely subjected to human ends, a *useful* landscape, where, as he noted, "kein Baum wachsst . . . aussert der Schnur und kein fussbreit Boden ist ohne Aus-beute." Here he found "alles verhoffte Vergnügen."[10] But Haller's primary interest is man, not nature, and the Alpine landscape of his poem is admired less for its own sake than for its relation to those who live in it. The discovery of its attractions, though certainly deeply experienced, is incidental to his main theme, which is the decadence of modern society.

"Die Alpen" contains forty-nine ten-line stanzas in alex-andrines rhyming abababbabcc. In stanzas 1–10 the universal corruption of the cultured world is contrasted with the virtu-ous simplicity of the Swiss mountaineers; stanzas 11–17 de-pict the recreations of these innocent people and their court-ing and marriage customs; stanzas 18–31 follow them through the round of their seasonal occupations and characterize par-ticular exemplars of mountain men; stanzas 32–44 are de-voted to the landscape itself; stanzas 45–49, the coda, return to the contrast of the opening stanzas. As our outline shows, only thirteen of the forty-nine stanzas are actually given over to depiction of the landscape.

Haller's view of the yawning inward emptiness, the "Ei-telkeit," of modern civilization is in good part no more than a development of a Renaissance commonplace, though a singu-larly engaged development. The contrast between city and country, the city representing false values, the country true ones, goes back to antiquity, to Horace, and was a favorite topos throughout the Baroque period. It is of course the basic convention of the pastoral. Opitz got good mileage out of the theme in "*Zlatna* oder Getichte von Ruhe dess Gemüthes" (1623), in "Vielguet" (1629), and in "Schäfferey von der Nimfen Hercinie" (1630). To insist upon it in the midst of the Enlightenment was, however, to swim against the stream. True, there were some strong swimmers who preferred this kind of exercise. One of the most influential was Shaftesbury, whose works were probably known to Haller when he composed "Die Alpen."[11] In a "philosophical rhapsody" in his *Characteristicks* (1711), Shaftesbury lets Theocles persuade his friend Philocles that Nature's "quiet Sanctuarys," in which one may lead a life of "thoughtful Solitude," are in every way to be preferred to the wheel of Ixion upon which the slaves of civilization are bound: "I shall no longer resist the Passion growing in me," says Philocles, amazed and convinced by Theocles' outpourings, "for Things of a *natural* kind, where neither *Art*, nor *Conceit* or *Caprice* of Man has spoiled their genuine *Order*, by breaking in upon that *primitive* State. . . . all the horrid Graces of the *Wilderness* itself, as representing NATURE more, will be more engaging, and appear with a magnificence beyond the formal Mockery of princely Gardens."[12] But the direction of the main current in the Enlightenment is probably more accurately represented by such a city man as Samuel Johnson, who loved the "wonderful immensity" of London; who maintained that "the happiness (!) of London is not conceived but by those who have not been in it"; who told Boswell: "Why, Sir, you find no man, at all intellectual, who is willing to leave London. No, Sir, when a man is tired of London, he is tired of life."[13]

We have seen that Haller himself, when it was not a question of proving a point, did not hide his enlightened prejudices but glowed with enthusiasm at the highly cultivated landscape of Holland. But in "Die Alpen" he is intent upon proving a point and therefore employs the readily available topos of unspoiled nature versus corrupt civilization. It is but one more example of the conflict within him. One cannot doubt that Haller genuinely feels that civilized man lives without living, frantically beating his wings above an abyss of hopelessness and disgust to keep from plummeting into it. Haller is one of the discoverers of the theme of *ennui, Ekel, noia* in modern European literature, a more pregnant discovery perhaps than that of the Alpine landscape. He frankly admits that he is "tired of life." His cultural pessimism and skepticism of the values promulgated by the Enlightenment are extreme. At the same time, he was continually contributing to their advancement through his own scientific achievements.

To avoid being caught in the snares of gold, honors, and sensuality, which lead only to disgust—"Der Eckel im Genuss entdeckt das innre Blöde" (Hirzel, p. 137)—man should, according to Haller, strive to follow the golden mean, that is, extirpate the passions. This is the solution offered in "Die Alpen" and other poems. But the golden mean is an ideal as easy to formulate as it is difficult to achieve. The temptations of the world are strong, usually, indeed, irresistible. Insight into their nature does not keep us from succumbing to them. "Die Alpen" show us a world in which such temptations are absent, a garden of Eden without a serpent or even a tree of knowledge. This garden is self-supporting and inaccessible, guarded by towering mountains, a veritable Shangri-La or Pays d'Eldorado, such as Voltaire depicts in *Candide*. Here, in a still golden age, life is lived according to the golden mean, and this life is held up as an example to us, the corrupt heirs of civilization.

Haller has here maneuvered himself into a corner. The ideal he holds up is completely unviable in terms of modern civilization. Nor was he really so naive as to equate primitivism with innocence. The Third Book of "Über den Ursprung des Übels" contains the following often cited passage:

> Vergebens rühmt ein Volk die Unschuld seiner Sitten,
> Es ist nur jünger schlimm und minder weit geschritten:
> Der Lappen ewig Eis, wo, allzu tief geneigt,
> Die Sonne keinen Reiz zur Üppigkeit erzeugt,
> Schliesst nicht die Laster aus, sie sind, wie wir,
> hinlässig,
> Geil, eitel, geizig, träg, missgünstig und gehässig.
> Und was liegt dann daran, bei einem bittren Zwist,
> Ob Fisch-Fett oder Gold des Zweispalts Ursach ist?
> [verses 73–80]

In presenting the life led by his Swiss peasants as an ideal for us to strive for the poet is therefore guilty of blatant disingenuousness. The paradox is that this disingenuity is also the source of the poem's artistic strength and moral persuasiveness. Though it derives from the pastoral, it does not follow

21

the pastoral convention of make-believe, but seeks to comport itself realistically. Every effort is made to make the fiction seem true, to keep us from realizing that it is merely a depiction of a land of the mind invented for the needs of the heart. The realism of the work, the details of cheese-making and cattle-raising, harvesting hay, folk sports and customs, the botanical, topographical, and geological accuracy with which the flora and physical features of the landscape are described, all these are a means of lending verisimilitude to the vision, in order to uphold its exemplary quality.

It is true that Haller's "realism" still wears the clothing of baroque diction, and the poet was quite justified in saying that one sees in it "noch viele Spuren des Lohensteinischen Geschmacks" (Hirzel, p. 20). Concrete situations, as Werner Kohlschmidt has emphasized, are idealistically stylized in a way that makes Haller's peasants a far cry from those of the nineteenth-century realist Jeremias Gotthelf.[14] An amusing example is the periphrastic description of two young people declaring their feeling for each other:

> So bald ein junger Hirt die sanfte Glut empfunden,
> Die leicht ein schmachtend Aug in muntern Geistern
> schürt,
> So wird des Schäfers Mund von keiner Furcht
> gebunden,
> Ein ungeheuchelt Wort bekennet, was ihn rührt;
> Sie hört ihn und, verdient sein Brand ihr Herz zum
> Lohne,
> So sagt sie, was sie fühlt, und thut wornach sie
> strebt . . .
> . . . .
>
> Verzüge falscher Zucht, der wahren Keuschheit Affen,
> Der Hochmut hat euch nur zu unser Qual geschaffen!
> [verses 131–40]

Here the diction is still full-dress baroque, the principle being not to say directly what can be said indirectly or figuratively: "sanfte Glut," "Brand" for sexual impulses, a "languishing eye" that "stirs the embers" of "lively spirits" for a come-hither look, a mouth "bound by no fears" for outspokenness, the personification of abstracts in the final couplet. The intent of the passage is of course to show the ideal in the real, to point out that true naturalness is an ideal condition, lost by us, the apes of false modesty.

A prime characteristic of the life of Haller's peasants is *timelessness*. Effectively shut off from the stream of history, their existence is almost plantlike. In this world

> Das Leben rinnt dahin in ungestörtem Frieden,
> Heut is wie gestern war und morgen wird wie heut.
> ....
> Der Jahre Lust und Müh ruhn stets auf gleicher Waage,
> Des Lebens Staffeln sind nichts als Geburt und Tod.
> [verses 93 ff.]

Here, Haller proclaims in the best manner of the Aufklärer, "herrschet die Vernunft, von der Natur geleitet" (verse 67). But what, after all, is the good of a reasoning plant? The radical reduction of humanity that the poet must undertake in order to present his ideal at all is itself deeply pessimistic. The force of the vision as a flail of modern society depends to a large degree upon our not becoming aware of this reduction. Hence the striving for vividness, the assurance (in the footnotes) that this or that scene is "nach der Natur gemalt," the "realism" of the whole.

It is undeniable that some passages are charmingly vivid. These lines, for example, describing cows making their eager way to pasture on a dewy morning, were widely admired:

> Dort drängt ein träger Schwarm von schwerbeleibten
>   Kühen,
> Mit freudigem Gebrüll, sich im bethauten Steg . . .
> [verses 185 f.]

Sometimes there is an air almost of faerie in the descriptions, as in these lines on flowers in an Alpine meadow:

23

> Der Blumen scheckicht Herr scheint um den Rang zu
>   kämpfen,
> Ein lichtes Himmel-blau beschämt ein nahes Gold;
> Ein ganz Gebürge scheint, gefirnisst von dem Regen,
> Ein grünender Tapet, gestickt mit Regenbögen.
>
> [verses 377–80]

Shall we say that this is not "nach der Natur gemalt"? It is painted after the second nature in the poet's eye, of course, but he has now made it our nature, enabling us also to see a flowery mountain meadow in these terms. Is this not true discovery of a landscape?

Lessing, in *Laokoon* XVII, criticizes a passage from "Die Alpen" as an example of what poetry—in contrast to painting—cannot do, i.e., present a unified image of an object made up of a number of parts. Since the poet, Lessing maintains, is forced to describe the parts one by one, we are bound to lose sight of the whole. He quotes verses 381–400 in support of his contention. I quote only verses 381–90; the reader may judge whether Lessing is right.

> Dort ragt das hohe Haupt am edlen Enziane
> Weit übern niedern Chor der Pöbel-Kräuter hin;
> Ein ganzes Blumen-Volk dient unter seiner Fahne,
> Sein blauer Bruder selbst bückt sich und ehret ihn.*
> Der Blumen helles Gold, in Strahlen umgebogen,
> Thürmt sich am Stengel auf und krönt sein grau
>   Gewand;
> Der Blätter glattes Weiss, mit tiefem Grün durchzogen,
> Bestrahlt der bunte Blitz von feuchtem Diamant;†
> Gerechtestes Gesetz! dass Kraft sich Zier vermähle;
> In einem schönen Leib wohnt eine schönre Seele.

Whatever our judgment may be as to the justice of Lessing's strictures, it is obvious that he is not reading Haller's lines in the spirit in which they were meant. Haller is not so much describing a flower as presenting a symbolic

---

*The *blauer Bruder* is another variety of gentian.
†Reference to the dew that gathers in the concave leaves.

24

exemplification of a "most just law," a reflection of the order that rules throughout his Alpine Eldorado. The stanza illustrates with exemplary clarity the fact that Haller stills tends to follow the emblematic tradition, employing the closing couplet of his stanza as a vehicle for the *applicatio*, the first eight lines forming the *descriptio*.[15] In fact, the whole poem might be said to be modeled on an emblem or to be constructed emblematically, the opening stanzas (1–10) forming the superscript, the long middle section on the customs of the mountaineers and the description of the landscape in which they live representing the emblem proper, and the final stanzas (45–49) the subscript or *applicatio*.

Haller was proud, and justly so, of having introduced a new kind of poetry into German, verse modeled on the English poetry of "wit." We recall that he visited England in 1727 after taking his degree in Leiden. He was deeply impressed by contemporary English literature and eager to emulate it. "Ihr [der Englander] Spectator, Butlers Hudibras, Rochester, Swifts und andere Sitten–und Hekelschriften [writings satirizing manners and morals] sind ganz neue und von andern Völkern nie berührte Länder," he remarks in his diary.[16] In an often-cited comparison of himself with his immediate contemporary Hagedorn, who had likewise traveled in England and admired its literature, Haller writes that they, after reading the English satirists, felt "dass man in wenigen Worten weit mehr sagen konnte, als man in Deutschland bis hieher gesagt hatte; wir sahen, dass philosophische Begriffe und Anmerkungen sich reimen liessen, und strebten beyde nach einer Stärke, dazu wir keine Urbilder gehabt hatten" (Hirzel, p. 398).

It is in imitation then of the British, especially in the poems following "Die Alpen," that Haller develops his famous terse or "difficult" style that seeks to pack as much meaning as possible into the shortest compass, not infrequently at the expense of clarity. This style is nearly the opposite of the self-consciously antibaroque compositions of a Canitz or Weise, and reminds one forcibly of Tacitus put into rhyme. The English were the school in which Haller learned to despise not only the florid manner of his earlier model Lohenstein but also the "flat" style of his sober, prosaic contemporaries. Due to his (and to a lesser degree to Hagedorn's) Anglophilia German poetry began to turn away from the French, up to then the undisputed models for the postbaroque poets who cultivated the flat style, and to look toward the English, whose influence on eighteenth-century German literature can scarcely be overestimated. One detects a note of malicious approval of the English attitude toward the French in the diary passage immediately following that just quoted: The English, Haller writes, "despise the elsewhere so highly admired French and look upon them as children who are capable of treating only trivialities." In our next poem we find Haller's "difficult" style in full flower.

"Gedanken über Vernunft, Aberglauben und Unglauben" (1729), a poem of 388 lines in alexandrine couplets, shows Haller in the role of a rather problematical modern Lucretius, whose *De rerum natura* was one of the most reliable sources of inspiration for the men of the Enlightenment in their rebellion against established religion.[17] As usual when his overt statement is not in accord with accepted doctrine, Haller attempts in his headnote and footnotes to defuse the explosiveness of his argument. It is the spectacle of Haller versus Haller that we find throughout his work. With this poem, he tells us, he hoped to prove that German was as fit a medium as English for philosophical poetry. The implication is that the work is a kind of stylistic exercise, which is true, but it is also more, namely, the treatment of themes nearest to Haller's heart. The thematic material derives from the anthropological ontology of the Enlightenment: What is man's place in creation? What must he believe? What can he know? How should he act? Lines 1–110 seek to establish man's place in the great scale of being; lines 111–288 examine the question of belief; lines 289–324 draw the conclusion that man *must* err and that the eternal metaphysical problems are insoluble; the end—lines 325–88—is resignation: the physicotheological proof must convince us that a divine being exists, but his ways are unfathomable; as to the best way to conduct our lives, the poet can only recommend the Stoic *aurea medio-critas*, the extirpation of the passions as a way to inner peace.

The image of man that emerges from the poem is not encouraging. Man is an "unselig Mittel-Ding von Engeln und Vieh" (verse 17), who uses his God-given reason only to err. It is the accepted Renaissance view of man inglorious. The implication is that man can find his true destiny, learn to know his place in the scheme of things, by studying himself. This is what the poem intends to do. It takes the form of unmasking man's inveterate tendency to err and counsels him, in effect, to retire from life in order to avoid erring. The ideal of conduct held up for emulation at the end of the poem resembles closely the idealized life of Haller's Alpine peasants:

Kein Glück verlangen wir, ein Tag soll allen gleichen,
Das Leben unvermerkt und unbekannt verstreichen . . .
[verses 383 f.]

It is hard to suppress a smile at the reversal of values by which Haller himself, a Faustian nature if one ever lived, guided his own life. Even science, his own ruling passion, is to be extirpated or at least reduced to a mere "Zeitvertreib" (verse 379). Resignation, then, and an attempt to put a good face on a hopeless situation—this is what Haller's "philosophy" amounts to. But it is not for solutions that one goes to Haller; it is for problems.

The first insight to which man must attain is that into the limitations of human reason. Lines 27–64 contain a splendid "engaged" passage on the absolutism of man's rational powers, which in a Newton may even exceed "das Ziel erschaffner Geister" (verse 51), but the end, no less than with Gryphius, though for a nontheological reason, is vanity. Underlining the heavy irony with a bizarre rhyme, the poet exclaims:

Wohl-angebrachte Müh! gelehrte Sterbliche!
Euch selbst misskennet ihr, sonst alles wisst ihr eh!
[verses 57 f.]

Without self-knowledge all knowledge is vanity.

27

The next insight to which the poet would help us is that into the self-deceptive nature of religious beliefs. This is the burden of the most Lucretian section of the poem, that on *Aberglauben* (verses 113–222), but also of that on *Unglauben* (verses 223–68). Though Haller is careful to speak of superstition, it is clear enough that superstition here equals established religion. Superstition's reign is universal: "Der Erdkreis ist sein Reich und wer drauf wohnt sein Knecht" (verse 114). The irresistible attraction of superstition lies in its appeal to the baser passions, ever the ultimate villain in Haller. Man abdicates his reason in favor of dogma, which promises richer emotional rewards, and becomes the willing victim of a cynical priesthood motivated solely by lust for power:

> Umsonst sieht die Vernunft des Glaubens Fehler ein;
> Sobald der Priester spricht, muss Irrtum Weisheit sein;
> Von dem bethörten Sinn lässt sich das Herz betrügen,
> Liebt ein beglaubtes nichts und irret mit Vergnügen:
> Ein angenommner Satz, den nichts als Glauben stützt,
> Wird bald ein Theil von uns und auch mit Blut
> beschützt.
>
> [verses 201–6]

The section ends with a translation of Lucretius' most famous line: *Quantum (Tantum) religio potuit suadere malorum*: "Was Böses ist geschehn, das nicht der Glaube tat?"[18] Voltaire himself could hardly have penned a more mordant indictment of established religion than some of the passages in this work.

But that Haller is no Voltaire, much less a Lucretius, becomes evident in the next part of the poem, that on *Unglauben. Unglaube* is just as self-seeking as *Aberglaube* and just as liable to err. The unbeliever is characterized as a kind of cynical Lucretius with a purely mechanistic view of the universe, a disbeliever in the soul's immortality and one who regards self-love as the sole motive of human actions. Reason, the unbeliever claims, is his sole arbiter, but reason, the poet points out, is itself the dupe of passion:

> O blinde Richterin! wen soll dein Spruch vergnügen,
> Die oft sich selbst betrügt und ofters lässt betrügen?

28

Wie leicht verfehlst du doch, wenn Neigung dich
    besticht!

[verses 255–57]

Here, as before, *vergnügen* rhymes with *betrügen*: Haller turns
the unbeliever's distrust in the purity of human motives
against the unbeliever himself. The "wise man," to whom
lines 269–88 are devoted, is a kind of unbeliever against his
will. His aim is the right one, self-discovery: he seeks "Beim
Lichte der Vernunft *sich* in sich selbst zu finden" (verse 272),
but his efforts end in self-doubt when he ventures upon metaphysical speculation, and self-doubt leads to doubt of a Creator: "Wer zweifelt, ob *er* ist, kann keinen Schöpfer glauben"
(verse 288). Reason, then, is not enough, no matter what
one's motives.

The upshot of Haller's examination of the human situation from the standpoint of man's ability to know both himself
and ultimate truths is utterly negative: "Wir irren allesammt,
nur jeder irret anderst" (verse 292). The final mask has been
torn off and man's desperate helplessness revealed. The conclusion is a *pis-aller*. The poet cuts the Gordian knot, proclaim-
ing in effect that we must believe in a divine being because
creation is a miracle that can be explained in no other way
(verses 325 ff.). Reason's role is radically reduced. Only divine
revelation will throw light on the ultimate mysteries, but such
revelation, it seems, will come only at the end of time:

Vernunft kann, wie der Mond, ein Trost der dunkeln
    Zeiten,
Uns durch die braune Nacht mit halbem Schimmer
    leiten;
Der Wahrheit Morgen-roth zeigt erst die wahre Welt,
Wann Gottes Sonnen-Licht durch unsre Dämmrung
    fällt.

[verses 359–62]

Neither here nor elsewhere does Haller mention the Savior or
the specifically Christian interpretation of the meaning of existence. His aim is that of Epictetus: to expose human frailty.

29

The origin of philosophy is the realization of one's own weakness and helplessness. The behavior adequate to this realization is likewise the Epictetan "endure and abstain."

The poem as a whole presents the spectacle of reason at war with itself, the Enlightenment versus the Enlightenment, Haller versus Haller. This is the source of its tension and the tension the source of its drive. Its thrust is to expose the limits of reason. Reason is a weak reed because of its susceptibility to self-deceit through the passions. This argument is exemplified through an examination of the forms of belief. The canon against which this Lucretian satire is in revolt is Lucretius' own canon, reason and science, but in the name of reason itself.

"Über den Ursprung des Übels" (1734) ostensibly deals with *the* philosophical problem of the Enlightenment: How is the evil in the world reconcilable with an almighty and loving deity? Like all theodicies it attempts to justify the ways of God to man, and like all theodicies of the Enlightenment to do so by justifying God as a reasonable being. The presence of evil is the sticking point, for it seems to contradict the idea of a reasonable deity. On the solution of this dilemma depends the salvation of the optimism of the Enlightenment.

The poem is divided into three books. Book I (162 lines) sets the problem: that God created the world out of love and for the joy of His creatures is indubitable; why then a world in which mental torment, physical pain, and sin are unavoidable? Book II (212 lines) depicts the creation of the world and the world of spirits ("Geister-Welt"), which includes both men and angels. Their distinguishing characteristic is free will, which alone makes true love of the divine possible. Book II also depicts creation's interdependent order and man's ambiguous position within it. Book III (232 lines) falls into two parts. The first tells of the fall of angels and man, the former through overweeningness, the latter through succumbing to sensuality, both through misuse of freedom of the will. The

result is universal corruption, made all the more sickening by
the realization that it is self-caused. The coda (verses 161–
232), though it sees salvation as possible for a tiny minority of
the elect, despairs at fathoming God's ways and ends in deep
resignation, the problem of evil left unsolved.

Philosophically, the poem ends in defeat, even in a kind
of retreat before the question posed in Book I (verses 139–42)
and again, almost sacrilegiously, in III, 177–82:

> O Gott voll Gnad und Recht, darf ein Geschöpfe
>   fragen:
> Wie kann mit deiner Huld sich unsre Qual vertragen?
> Vergnügt, o Vater, dich der Kinder Ungemach?
> War deine Lieb erschöpft? Ist dann die Allmacht
>   schwach?
> Und konnte keine Welt des Uebels ganz entbehren,
> Wie liessest du nicht eh ein ewig Unding währen?

Yet Haller, so he claims in his headnote, and this time we
have no reason to disbelieve him because he is now speaking
aesthetically (and not philosophically or religiously), always regarded this poem "with special affection." This can provide a
key to the truer understanding not only of this poem but also
of Haller's "philosophical" verse in general. Why was the
poet particularly satisfied with this poem? It utterly fails in
doing what it ostensibly sets out to do. The answer can only
be that the poet's intent is not to provide solutions but to
show man's existential situation. And in this he succeeds remarkably. Haller himself formulates the matter with all possible precision: "Aber ein Dichter ist kein Weltweiser [Phil-
osoph], er malt und rührt und erweiset nicht" (Hirzel, p.
118). Eduard Stäuble, who has devoted a whole book to the
explication of this poem, is determined not to believe Haller
at this crucial point. Haller, he maintains (*Ursprung des Übels*,
p. 84), differs from a philosopher only insofar as he "clothes
his thoughts in images." "Aber grundsätzlich will er durchaus
'erweisen'—beweisen und unterweisen. Mag Haller dies in
der Vorrede . . . abstreiten, wir glauben ihm nicht." But it is
precisely here that Haller is most worthy of belief, however

much we may distrust his special pleading in religious matters. When, in the foreword, he berates himself for not having taken into consideration the Christian solution, our reaction is disbelief. This is the height of disingenuousness. Why he refused to do so is obvious enough: it would have vitiated the image of man in hopeless torment, which is the whole point of the poem. Why doesn't Lear recognize Kent? Why don't Kent and Lear recognize Edgar? asks Tolstoy. The reason: there would be no play if they did.

Through misuse of freedom of the will, which Haller must posit to save his universe from mechanism and make true love of the divine possible, men and angels fell. Man, indeed, still falls continuously through wrong choice between good and evil, for reason is ever the dupe of desire. But though he cannot rely upon his reason, man is still not completely without resource. He has a *conscience*. Haller views this faculty more in the light in which Socrates viewed his *daimonion* than in the light of a Christian Wolff, for whom the conscience was only the judgment of reason based on insight into the structure of causality. For Haller, the conscience is a religious instinct and can be an infallible guide. But alas! this is seldom the case. Instead, it becomes the chief source of our torment, for we heed its voice as little as we heed the dictates of reason. Thus we are constantly haunted by "des Lasters Scheu / Und ihren Nachgeschmack, die bittre Kost der Reu" (II, 183 f.). And "Ein Geist, wo Sünde herrscht, ist ewig ohne Frieden, / Sie macht uns selbst zur Höll und wird doch nicht gemieden!" (II, 185 f.). Our existential situation is a closed system from which, after we have fallen, there is no escape. The best we can hope for is to reduce the leverage it has on us. This is the attraction of the Stoic solution. The only other solution is not to fall at all, that is, to heed the voice of conscience. But the strength to do this is given only to the elect. One detects a distinctly Calvinistic note in III, 161–64:

> O selig jene Schar, die, von der Welt verachtet,
> Der Dinge wahren Werth und nicht den Wahn
> betrachtet,

> Und, treu dem innern Ruf, der sie zum Heile schreckt,
> Sich ihre Pflicht zum Ziel von allen Thaten steckt!

Of this blessed band "man," as seen here, is not a member. His lot is the torment so eloquently depicted in III, 141–60, the torment of the spirit upon realizing that it has sold its birthright for a mess of pottage:

> Der Geist, von allem fern, womit er sich bethöret,
> Sieht sich in einer Welt, wovon ihm nichts gehöret;
> . . . .
> Die Wahrheit, deren Kraft der Welt Gewühl
>   verhindert,
> Findt nichts, das ihr Gefühl in dieser Wüste mindert;
> Ihr fressend Feur durchgräbt das innre der Natur
> Und sucht im tiefsten Mark des Uebels mindste Spur.
> Das gute, das versäumt, das böse, so begangen,
> Die Mittel, die verscherzt, sind eitel Folter-Zangen,
> Von stäter Nachreu heiss. Er leidet ohne Frist,
> Weil er gepeiniget und auch der Henker ist.

This is the general situation, but the tone of the whole poem is indication enough that it is also, indeed especially, the poet's. This situation is also a dominant theme of Haller's diaries, which are always "von stäter Nachreu heiss." It can hardly be an accident that he began keeping these diaries immediately after abandoning poetry for good. Stäuble, who insists, as we saw, upon interpreting Haller's poetry as philosophy clothed in poetic imagery, rightly regards the diaries as an expression of Haller's "Leiden an der Geschöpflichkeit" (*Ursprung des Übels*, p. 190). Our thesis is that his poetry is exactly the same thing. It is not philosophy masquerading as poetry, it is confessional poetry masquerading as philosophy. Its theme, like Günther's, is suffering. Why Haller did not give his suffering a more direct and personal expression is an interesting question. Out of shame perhaps? Out of a feeling that to do so would contravene decorum, both social and poetic? Up to his day, only a poor outcast like Günther had ventured to speak with the voice of undisguised personal confession in a public medium. Whatever the reason, the suffering of Haller the individual is elaborately depersonalized and philosophically generalized in most of his public works as the suffering of man.

The poem ends in a seemingly self-contradictory fashion. The world undeniably is "des Uebels Eigenthum" (III, 172), though God is just as undeniably omniscient and all-merciful. The best the poet can do is to offer a series of surmises on the possible meaning of evil. No firm ground is reached. Haller takes neither the Miltonic nor the Leibnizian position but leaves the question open. There is good reason for this: the question itself is a chief contributing factor to the suffering that is the essence of man's (of Haller's!) existential situation. Thus the true theme of the poem demands that the question remain unresolved—philosophical "failure" is here poetic triumph.

Perhaps Haller's most fascinating, certainly his most enigmatic, poem is "Unvollkommenes Gedicht über die Ewigkeit," which up to now has remained without adequate exegesis.[19] First published in 1743, in the third edition of the collected poems, it was apparently already present, except for the last eight lines and a significant revision of lines 17–20, approximately in the state in which it was first published by 1736, the date which Haller assigns it.

The poem contains 125 lines in mixed meters, alexandrines and lines of from two to five feet, with irregular rhyme scheme, so-called madrigal verse, a form which Haller also uses in the first sixty-four lines of "Über den Ursprung des Übels." The title, as Haller tells us in a footnote, is meant to indicate that the work is a fragment. Had he been capable of finishing it, he claims, he would have obviated the theological objections raised against it, a statement we may confidently mistrust. The fact is, as an examination will show, it is highly questionable whether the work actually is a fragment. A complete work, Baudelaire reminds us, is not necessarily finished, and a finished work not necessarily complete.

The poem may be divided into three main parts. Lines 1–30 present an image of eternity in terms of ancient Orcus—spatiality rather than temporality here images forth eternity—and characterize a recently deceased friend now held fast in "eternity's strong arms." The "I" has a presentiment of his own near end. Lines 31–93 present an entirely different image of eternity, described not in terms of ancient mythology but of modern physics poeticized. Lines 94–125 speak of the mystery of individuality and end on a note of despairful *ennui* and longing for peace.

The key to the poem lies in the two concepts of eternity, the ancient versus the modern, and in the two images of man, the recently deceased friend in contrast with the "I." That Haller himself became aware of this only some time after he had published the first version of the poem seems indicated by internal evidence, namely, by the revision of lines 17–20 and by the addition of the final eight lines. With this revision and this addition the poem may be said to be complete, whatever theological objections may be raised against it and however "unvollkommen" it may be in respect to eternity.

The first lines depict a stylized wilderness of gloomy woods and crags, barely crawling streams and stagnant swamps, barren fields and "Grausen-volle Gründe," populated only by the whirring of lonely birds, *Seelenvögel* without doubt. The features of this landscape the poet addresses thus:

> O dass ich doch bei euch des Todes Farben fünde!
> O nährt mit kaltem Schaur und schwarzem Gram mein Leid!
> Seid mir ein Bild der Ewigkeit!
>
> [verses 8–10]

That we are to be reminded of the ancient underworld or of an entrance thereto is beyond question. Once eternity was seen in these colors. The point is here that the land of eternity, for all its melancholy desolation, is localizable and imaginable. Would it *were* my image of eternity! "*Seid* mir ein Bild der Ewigkeit!"

35

It is strongly implied that it is in the arms of this eternity that the departed friend is now "held fast." We learn that "Die dicke Nacht der öden Geister-Welt / Umringt ihn jetzt mit Schrecken-vollen Schatten" (verses 21 f.) and that, like a Homeric shade, he is still attached to this world by fierce longing: "Und die Begier ist, was er noch behält / Von dem, was seine Sinnen hatten" (verses 23 f.). The friend, then, if he could go to the ancient underworld after death, must himself have been an "ancient" man? This is the undoubted implication not only of the passage just quoted but particularly of lines 17–20:

> Kein Strahl vom künftigen verstörte seine Ruh,
> Er sah dem Spiel der Welt noch heut geschäftig zu;
> Die Stunde schlägt, der Vorhang fällt,
> Und alles wird zu nichts, was ihm so würklich schien.

These are key lines and it is extremely revealing that their wording is significantly different in the earlier version:

> Noch heut war er, was ich, und sah auf gleicher Bühne,
> Dem Schauspiel dieser Welt, *wie ich*, beschäftigt zu.
> Die Stunde schlägt, und in dem gleichen Nu
> Ist alles nichts, so würklich als es schiene.
>
> [Hirzel, p. 331; emphasis added]

Though the "I" of the later version may still rhetorically ask (verses 25 ff.) if his fate will not be the same as his friend's— he already feels the approach of life's evening—this "I" is definitely not one who watches the spectacle of this world with absorbed interest, much less one untroubled by any "ray of the future." His concern is now *solely* with the future, the future under the aspect of eternity. As for the Here and Now, the final lines—added later, we must not forget—tell us that he feels utter disinterest, blackest *ennui*:

> Itzt fühlet schon mein Leib die Näherung des nichts!
> Des Lebens lange Last erdrückt die müden Glieder;
> Die Freude flieht von mir mit flatterndem Gefieder
> Der Sorgen-freien Jugend zu.

Mein Eckel, der sich mehrt, verstellt den Reiz des
   Lichts
Und streuet auf die Welt den Hoffnungs-losen
   Schatten;
Ich fühle meinen Geist in jeder Zeil ermatten
Und keinen Trieb, als nach der Ruh!
                                    [verses 118–25]

It seems clear, therefore, that Haller's intent was to characterize the "I" in direct contrast with the friend, just as he
contrasts the two views of eternity. It also appears clear that
this contrast is the result of revision and addition. Is it a new
insight into the meaning of his own poem and at the same
time its completion? One must admit that the long middle
section, lines 31–93 (or even 31–117), acts as an effective
distracter, making it rather unlikely that the comparison will
actually be made. (Stäuble, who examines the poem closely,
does not remark on it.) Precisely why Haller should play this
game of hide-and-seek is not clear. Is the poet's insight into
his own meaning after all incomplete? Is the poem merely
poorly constructed? Or is this lack of clarity only a half-con-
scious attempt to conceal both from himself and the reader
his own inability (i.e., that of the persona) to achieve the ideal
of Stoic calm predicated of the friend ("Kein Strahl vom
künftigen verstörte seine Ruh"), this being the ideal he had
previously insisted upon at the end of "Gedicht über Vernunft, Aberglauben and Unglauben" and held up for admiration in "Die Alpen"? By making the contrast between the "I"
and the friend less immediately obvious, the former's failure
to achieve the ideal is made less striking. Whatever the
answer, the pagan friend has gone to his pagan reward, to an
eternity that is almost homey in comparison with that which
awaits the "I," for it is at any rate an eternity where man is
still the measure.

The eternity that awaits the "I," who represents the man
of the Enlightenment, is the eternity of modern physics, ter-
rifying in its abstract unimaginableness. Underlying the image in the following lines, as Stäuble (*Ursprung des Übels*, p.

61) has pointed out, is the mathematical formula $\infty - a = \infty$, i.e., infinity minus the greatest possible number still equals infinity:

> Die schnellen schwingen der Gedanken,
> Wogegen Zeit und Schall und Wind
> Und selbst des Lichtes Flügel langsam sind,
> Ermüden über dir [der Ewigkeit] und hoffen keine
>   Schranken.
> Ich häufe ungeheure Zahlen,
> Gebürge Millionen auf;
> Ich welze Zeit auf Zeit und Welt auf Welten hin,
> Und wann ich auf der March [Grenze] des endlichen
>   nun bin
> Und von der fürchterlichen Höhe
> Mit Schwindeln wieder nach dir sehe,
> Ist alle Macht der Zahl, vermehrt mit tausend Malen,
> Noch nicht ein Theil von dir;
> Ich tilge sie [ziehe sie ab], und du liegst ganz von mir.
>
> [verses 63–75]

When seen in scientific terms eternity turns into infinity, that is, into an abstraction that refuses to submit to mythologizing and thus assume humanly realizable proportions—this is the horror of it. Here man, or the human soul, has no place to *be*. Kierkegaard, in his *Concluding Unscientific Postscript*, Part Two, Chapter III (trans. Swenson and Lowrie), polemicizes against the "questionable character of abstract thought" when dealing with the problem of immortality:

> This questionable character of abstract thought becomes apparent especially in connection with all existential problems, where abstract thought gets rid of the difficulty [of bringing together a "definite something and the ideality of thought"] by leaving it out, and then proceeds to boast of having explained everything. It explains immortality in general, and all goes quite smoothly, in that immortality is identified with eternity. . . . But whether an existing human being is immortal, which is the difficulty,

abstract thought does not trouble to inquire. It is disinterested; but the difficulty inherent in existence constitutes the interest of the existing individual, who is infinitely interested in existing.

In Haller's poem the problem of the existence of the individual soul is seen in terms of the question of *how*—not *whether*—immortality is possible. The answer given by abstract thought turns out to be questionable indeed. Faced with the infinite and the experience of the *tremendum*, Brockes felt sublimely elevated, he experienced man's kinship with the divine. All the insights of modern science served to intensify rather than diminish this sense of sublimity. Haller's experience of the *tremendum* is the opposite of Brockes'—instead of singing with the angels, he is filled with a deep anxiety, and the pessimism that pervades the poem is not lightened.[20]

Should it not afford comfort that eternity is grounded in the divine? One might at first think so. God is "allein des Alles Grund" and in Him "Ein einzig Itzt . . . ist Ewigkeit," which I interpret as an image of timelessness. Without God neither time nor eternity could be (verses 76 ff.). But for Haller this is only equivalent to formulating the problem another way. Man's relation to the divine—seen here, it must be remembered, out of the Christian context—is analogous to his relation to eternity. The terms are interchangeable:

> Vollkommenheit der Grösse!
> Was ist der Mensch, der gegen dich sich hält!
> Er ist ein Wurm, ein Sandkorn in der Welt;
> Die Welt ist selbst ein Punkt, wann ich an dir sie messe.
> [verses 86–89]

It is the divine that is thus addressed. And strange indeed is the negative manner in which belief in the immortality of the soul is expressed:

> Nur halb gereiftes nichts, seit gestern bin ich kaum,
> Und morgen wird ins nichts mein halbes Wesen
> kehren . . .
> [verses 90 f.]

39

"Half my being," i.e., my body, will return to nothingness and my individuality as I know it will be dissolved. By implication the soul will be in eternity, with God. But God and eternity are only two aspects of the same unimaginable otherness.

The hopelessness that pervades the poem, the black *Ekel* and longing for peace, are justified on this ground. It is an expression of religious doubt, not disbelief but the struggle to believe. "Lord, I believe, help thou mine unbelief!" is a constant refrain of Haller's diaries. The doubt concerns the viability for man of the "new" eternity revealed by modern science. Thus one can say that the theme of the poem is the conflict between science and religion. The *experience* of the poem, however, is shaken faith, with its resultant despair and *Weltmüdigkeit*, and we may safely assume that it was to give form to this experience that it was written.

"Unvolkommenes Gedicht über die Ewigkeit" is one of Haller's last serious productions or at least one of the last that we can take seriously. It shows him, at the age of twenty-eight, at the height of his poetic powers, in complete control of his linguistic medium, if not perhaps completely in control of his tectonics, though this, as we saw, is a moot question. The essential characteristic of his poetry, the fusion of intellectuality and feeling, is shown here in great purity.

It remains for us to glance at the poetry written in the name of feeling alone. That Haller should have been a favorite with the sentimentalists is not surprising. He places great emphasis on the heart and mistrusts the absolute claims of reason. His peasant maids say what they feel and do what their instincts urge: "Dann zarte Regung dient den Schönen nicht zum Hohne" ("Die Alpen," verse 137). The shepherd musician sings and plays a "neues Liedgen" inspired by "Natur und Liebe": "Sein Lehrer ist sein Herz, sein Phöbus seine Schöne, / Die Rührung macht den Vers und nicht gezählte Töne" ("Die Alpen," verses 279 f.). In Klopstock's

ode "Der Zürchersee" (1759), the party on the excursion is
enraptured when one of the company sings "Hallers Doris."
"Doris" (1730), a poem of 132 four-beat lines in six-line stanzas, must have afforded rapture for a considerable stretch of
the trip, if it was sung in its entirety. At first blush it seems a
rather strange choice for the worshipers of Klopstock, for it
appears to be a treatment of the *carpe-diem* motif completely in
the baroque manner, employing the familiar argument of
"gather ye rosebuds while ye may." But the passion sung
here "leitet zum Altar," not to the surrender of empty virtue
for mere sensual pleasure; indeed, because feeling and reason
are in harmony, pleasure is itself highly virtuous:

> Wann, nach erkannter Treu des Hirten,
> Die Tugend selbst ihn kränzt mit Myrten,
> Und die Vernunft spricht wie das Herz . . .
>   [verses 63–65]

Klopstockians could subscribe to such sentiments without
qualms. The whole remains nevertheless a bizarre mixture of
sentimentality and baroque sensuality reinforced by sly argument, as though a new attitude toward feeling were not able
to throw off the bonds of a convention invented for the expression of an older one. The conflict may be seen in the
following two stanzas. The first (verses 37–42) would be completely in place in any seventeenth-century persuasion to
sweet surrender; the second (verses 73–78) is hardly conceiv-
able except against the background of the emergent cult of
feeling:

> Mein Kind, erheitre deine Blicke,
> Ergieb dich nur in dein Geschicke,
> Dem nur die Liebe noch gefehlt.
> Was willst du dir dein Gluck missgönnen?
> Du wirst dich doch nicht retten können!
> Wer zweifelt, der hat schon gewählt.
> . . . .
> Wann sich—allein, mein Kind, ich schweige.
> Von dieser Lust, die ich dir zeige,

> Ist, was ich sage, kaum ein Traum.
> Erwünschte Wehmuth, sanft entzücken,
> Was wagt der Mund euch auszudrücken?
> Das Herz begreift euch selber kaum.

Haller's "Zwischenzeitlichkeit," his position between-the-times, is especially clear in such a poem as "Doris."

Undoubtedly the most moving of Haller's poems of feeling are those occasioned by the death of his first wife, "Trauer-Ode beim Absterben seiner geliebten Mariane" (November 1736) and "Ueber eben Dieselbe" (February 1737). These are no conventional funeral odes in the baroque manner but genuine expressions of emotion. It is true that Schiller, though a great admirer of Haller and in many respects his true disciple, insists in a well-known passage in "Über naive und sentimentalische Dichtung" that the poet of the "Trauer-Ode" does not so much express his feelings as his reflections upon his feelings. He is, Schiller says, only "ein Zuschauer seiner Rührung," a spectator of his own emotion. In spite of this, Schiller is forced to admit: "tiefrührend ist seine Klage." One may well question whether Schiller—impelled by his general argument—is not unfair to Haller. The opening lines of the "Trauer-Ode,"

> Soll ich von deinem Tode singen?
> O Mariane! welch ein Lied,
> Wann Seufzer mit den Worten ringen
> Und ein Begriff den andern flieht!

with their emphasis on "Begriff" might lead one to think that Schiller is right. But "Begriff" here has the force of "memory" rather than "concept" or perhaps of neither precisely one nor the other, but smething that includes both. This is apparent from the rest of the poem, which is largely devoted to recollection of scenes from the past. Turns like "Dein Bild in mir," "meine Seele . . . ergötzt an Trauer-Bildern," "Ich seh dich noch," "denken An jenen Tag, der dich mir gab" show that it is the memory of past intimacies, not abstract concepts, that move the poet. The latter would be, indeed, typical of Schiller, if *he* were composing such a poem, but Haller is more a poet of actual experience than Schiller.

It is a mixed feeling that Haller especially seeks to convey. The day that gave him Mariane was a supreme moment in his life, yet he cannot remember it without tears:

> Noch jetzt mischt Lust sich mit dem kränken,
> Entzückung löst mit Wehmuth ab.
>
> [verses 59 f.]

The tone of these conflicting emotions is powerfully translated into an image in lines 49–56, which describe the departure of the young couple for Göttingen:

> Dort in den bittern Abschieds-Stunden,
> Wie deine Schwester an dir hieng,
> Wie, mit dem Land gemach verschwunden,
> Sie unserm letzten Blick entgieng;
> Sprachst du zu mir mit holder Güte,
> Die mit gelassner Wehmuth stritt:
> "Ich geh mit ruhigem Gemüthe,
> Was fehlt mir? Haller kommt ja mit!"

For Haller and Mariane, we, in the callous rootlessness of modern life, must not forget, going to Germany was equivalent to exile. To a large degree such emotion has become foreign to us. This is eighteenth-century sentimentalism at its best.

There is also another strong emotional component in the "Trauer-Ode" and one most characteristic of Haller. This is the sense of *guilt*, aroused partly by the feeling that by being too happy he tempted fate, partly by the feeling that he did not love Mariane enough, and partly by the feeling that he has interfered in another's life, depriving Mariane of home and country:

> Wer riss dich aus dem Schooss der deinen?
> Du liessest sie und wähltest mich.
>
> [verses 43 f.]

43

This is the basic Haller, the one we have learned to know in his broodings on man's place and fate. Every human situation, if we fathom it to its depths, Haller's poetry implies, is a *Grenzsituation* and shows us the inevitability of suffering. It is true that in the final stanzas he takes refuge in the Christian myth of heavenly reunion, something that he has elsewhere refused to do. One can hardly help suspecting that he does this as much in the name of Mariane as his own, reducing the poem, as it were, to her level of conceptualization, though it is also his "brünstigs hoffen," if not his calm conviction:

> Vollkommenste! die ich auf Erden
> So stark und doch nicht gnug geliebt!
> Wie liebens-würdig wirst du werden,
> Nun dich ein himmlisch Licht umgiebt.
> Mich überfällt ein brünstigs hoffen,
> O! sprich zu meinem Wunsch nicht nein!
> O! halt die Arme für mich offen!
> Ich eile, ewig dein zu sein!
>
> [verses 121–28]

If we take "Der Frühling" (1749) by Ewald Christian von Kleist (1715–59)[21] at its face value, it is ostensibly descriptive verse in an idyllic vein with a moralistic intent, a work in the spirit of Haller's "Alpen." Kleist himself invokes Haller as a model for poetic landscape painting toward the close of his poem (verses 440 ff.). Like Haller, he holds up an image of joy and innocence to a saddened and corrupt modern society (verses 60 ff.; 450 ff.); like Haller, he idealizes the life of the countryman as one of self-sufficient idyllic contentment (verses 138–211). Unlike Haller, however, Kleist's theme is not the human condition as such. His moral and religious reflections are mostly banal and, from the standpoint of the impact of the poem as a whole, strictly secondary, whereas with Haller they are primary. "Der Frühling" appeared the year after the publication of the first three cantos of the *Messias*, and though written before Kleist could have been acquainted with any of Klopstock's work, it proves upon examination to be closer in spirit to Klopstock's kind of poetry than to Haller's. We shall return to this point.

The direct model for "Der Frühling" was *The Seasons*, by James Thomson, which Kleist knew in Brockes' translation (1726–30). Like most of his generation, Kleist was an ardent admirer of the English neoclassicists. The first printing of the poem contains 460 lines (the edition of 1756 has 398) in unrhymed hexameters with anacrusis. The rhythm is strongly dactylic:

> Empfangt mich, heilige Schatten! Ihr Wohnungen
> süsser Entzückung,
> Ihr hohen Gewölbe voll Laub und dunkler schlafender
> Lüfte!

From these opening lines one can already sense the meridian toward which the poem seems to be aiming. It is Dionysian in character, informed by a longing to return to some lost oneness. (Longing to return to oneness also informs Haller's "Alpen," but not Dionysian dissolution.) The imagery here is that of a primal womb; the verses vibrate with the thrilling expectation of some sweet security. There is marked euphony, emphasized by the numerous liquids and the carefully controlled rhythm (especially evident in the slow phrase in the last half of the second line). The generalized nature of the diction scarcely permits us to see anything distinctly, but calls up an image of vague, dusky openness, or duskiness and openness, the former enclosing the latter, so that there is a sense of being held ("Empfangt mich!") and at the same time being free and at ease in these "Wohnungen" and "hohen Gewölbe[n]" with their spacious, inviting "o's."

All this, it is perhaps not idle to point out, is quite unlike the opening lines of Thomson's "Spring":

> Come, gentle SPRING, ethereal Mildness come;
> And from the bosom of yon dropping cloud,
> While Music plays around, veil'd in a shower
> Of shadowing roses, on our plains descend.

The two passages are similar, to be sure, in their generalized, neoclassical diction, but they are very different in feeling. There is less sense of personal involvement in Thomson, who assumes the role of a spectator rather than that of an actor. Above all, the imagery is totally different: here, descent of the numen; there, entry into its realm.

Kleist's first seventeen lines continue to stress the imagery of entry into some holy of holies, of enclosure, shelter, nursing, union, dissolution of the ego, echo (i.e., reassurance): "Die Ihr oft einsamen Dichtern . . . azurne Thoren [i.e., Tore] eröffnet"; "empfangt mich"; "O, dass mein Lebensbach endlich . . . in Euren Gründen verflösse!"; "Führt mich in Gängen voll Nacht"; "Lehrt mich den Wilderhall reizen"; "die Wollust in mich . . . ziehen"; "Gestreckt im Schatten"; "Dass meine Töne die Gegend wie Zephyr's Lispeln erfüllen." Only when he has assured himself of Dionysian union by this long, essentially magical, invocation does Kleist begin the description proper, employing the same image of descent we find in Thomson's opening lines, but vividly activating the image of nursing which is only latent in Thomson:

> Auf rosenfarbnem Gewölk, bekränzt mit Tulpen und Lilien,
> Sank jüngst der Frühling vom Himmel. Aus seinem Busen ergoss sich
> Die Milch der Erden [*dat. sg.*] in Strömen. . . .
> [verses 18–20]

One need not be deeply versed in psychology to see what the persona of "Der Frühling" is seeking. And remembering the poet's personal situation and how he sought death on the battlefield, we can confidently say what Kleist as Kleist is seeking, for in both instances it is dissolution of the ego-role imposed by society and return to oneness. He speaks to the reader who seeks the same thing. He knew his age, and his voice, like that of other idyllists, was heard with sympathetic identification. Haller's "Alpen," Thomson's "Seasons," Kleist's "Frühling," Gessner's idylls, Voss's "Luise," even

Goethe's "Hermann und Dorothea"—these are in their basic appeal, if not in poetic quality, all of a piece. What pressures society exerted on the individual even in the eighteenth century, which seems to us so idyllic, is seen nowhere more clearly than in the cultivation of the idyll itself and the eagerness with which the public became immersed in such works. The individual, looking for a place to be, shut off from effective self-realization by the absolutism of the age (and nowhere more than in the Prussia of Frederick the Great), could withdraw in the idyll into a land of peace and harmony, where oneness with creation was the fundamental rule of being. Through his poem Kleist would let the disinherited of modern society, the despairing and the rejected, participate in a primal union, partake of the milk from Nature's breasts and be restored to wholeness:

> Ihr, deren zweifelhaft Leben gleich trüben Tagen des
>   Winters
> Ohn' Licht und Freude verfliesst, die Ihr in Höhlen des
>   Elends
> Die finstere Stunden verseufzt, betrachtet die Jugend
>   des Jahres!
> . . . .
> Ihr seid zur Freude geschaffen; der Schmerz schmipft
>   Tugend und Unschuld.
> Saugt Lust und Anmuth in Euch! . . .
> [verses 60–67]

Unlike Haller, Kleist's emphasis is only superficially moralistic, and he is not primarily interested in the human condition as such. The appeal of "Der Frühling" is not intellectual; neither does it chiefly lie in vivid nature descriptions, as in Thomson. What then is the precise nature of the participation in the feast of oneness offered by the poem? What is the poetic method employed to induce a sense of harmony and union? The answer must be that Kleist operates with musical effects. Not mere melodiousness and euphony, but rather the crescendo and decrescendo of feeling in and for itself, life rhythms in their most elemental form. And in this he is the brother of Klopstock rather than of Haller.

In a review of a collection of poems by Friedrich Matthisson published in 1794, Schiller asks how inanimate nature may become a symbol of human nature, that is, how descriptive nature poetry may be raised to a humanly meaningful level. There are, he says, two ways: either as a representation of emotions or as a representation of ideas. Emotions, he continues, are not capable of representation *contentually* (ihrem Gehalte nach), but they can be represented *formally* (ihrer Form nach). The art especially devoted to such formal representation of feeling is *music*, and insofar as landscape painting or landscape poetry affects us like music, it is a representation of feeling, an "imitation of human nature." Descriptive nature poetry can thus become an analogy of feeling. There is no doubt that this is what it is meant to be in Kleist's "Frühling." Haller's method, on the other hand, is rather to make nature express an idea, i.e., he moralizes it.

Emotional indulgence upon entry into a magical, womblike realm of security and irresponsibility—this is the fundamental pleasure Kleist offers his readers. The appeal of his poem rests mainly on its radical infantilism. If this sounds farfetched, let one examine the following passage:

> . . . Ihr dichten Lauben, von Händen
> Der Mutter der Dinge geflochten, Ihr dunkeln einsamen
> Gänge,
> Die Ihr das Denken erhellt, Irrgärten voller Entzückung
> Und Freude, seid mir gegrüsst! Was für ein angenehm
> Leiden
> Und Ruh und sanftes Gefühl durchdringet in Euch die
> Seele!

> [verses 253–57]

It would be hard to surpass the riot of emotions envisioned in these lines. One should mention that the "Denken" referred to here is also emotional, rather than intellectual, in nature. In this context it can only mean the "Gefühldenken," or "thinking with the heart," so dear to eighteenth-century sentimentalism.

48

The tone of "Der Frühling" is rhapsodic. There is no perceivable plan, no firm narrative outline. The method of composition, if one may call it that, is purely associative. Lessing, in *Laokoon* XVII, condemns it along with Haller's "Alpen." Descriptive poetry he considered a contradiction in terms and the poem's lack of plan a prime defect.

> Herr von Kleist, I know, prided himself very little on his "Spring." Had he lived he would have refashioned it altogether. He wanted to introduce some plan, and was meditating how he could best make the crowd of pictures, which seemed to have been drawn at random from the whole vast range of fresh creation, rise in some natural order and follow each other in fitting sequence. . . . He would have converted a series of pictures scantily interwoven with emotions, into a series of emotions sparingly interwoven with images. (Frothingham's translation)

This one may seriously doubt. At any rate one may be sure that if Kleist had been capable of undertaking such an operation, the resulting poem would no longer have been the "Frühling" we know and Kleist no longer Kleist. Lessing refuses to recognize what a Klopstockian like Giseke clearly comprehends: that Kleist's images of nature "arouse in us emotions which the sight of nature itself produces" (Sauer 1, 157), i.e., that such images are analogues of feeling, not merely "a series of pictures scantily interwoven with emotions (Empfindungen)." For Lessing the "Empfindungen" would seem to lie only in the overtly reflective passages, which are the weaker parts of the poem. Lessing, one may speculate, was reluctant to descend to the primitive level on which Kleist's poem achieves its main effects. He is put off by the comparative lack of ideas. Men like Klopstock and Herder, on the other hand, delighted in the work (Sauer 1, 157 f., 164) and probably overestimated its quality as seriously as Lessing misunderstood its nature.

It is rather difficult to illustrate the way Kleist's poem works without resorting to extensive quotation. Let us, how-

ever, attempt it by glancing at lines 258 ff., the passage immediately following the verses last quoted. This passage begins
softly: inviting duskiness, gentle western breezes, "visible
coolness," and in the midst of this sensuous landscape a Pan
figure:

> . . . sitzt zwischen Blumen der Geisshirt,
> Bläst auf der hellen Schalmei, hält ein und höret die
> Lieder
> Hier laut in Buchen ertönen, dort schwach und endlich
> verloren,
> Bläst und hält wiederum ein. . . .

Then a clear vignette of a he-goat, the "bearded husband" of
the she-goats, browsing the leaves of a willow:

> . . . ihr bärtiger Ehmann
> Ersteigt die über den Teich sich neigende Weide,
> beraubt sie
> Der bläulichen Blätter und schaut von oben ernsthaft
> herunter.

With the appearance of a herd of deer in swift flight the
tempo begins to quicken, then gathers still more momentum
with a spirited passage on a herd of horses "incited by the
spring to love":

> Der Boden zittert und tönt, es strotzen die Zweige der
> Adern;
> Ihr Schweif empört sich verwildert, sie schnauben
> Wollust und Hitze . . .

The horses gallop from the scene and

> . . . Jetzt eilen Stiere vorüber;
> Aus Nasen raucht Brunst, sie spalten mit Hörnern das
> Erdreich
> Und toben im Nebel von Staub.

50

With the bulls the celebration of elemental life forces reaches a climax and the passage itself a crescendo. The bulls bellow from caves (suddenly there are caves!) and plunge down precipices. Immediately there is also a swift stream rushing tumultuously into the valley, carrying with it debris and frightening the more timid wildlife. Kleist's purely associative method of composition is obvious: the bulls plunge down, the stream rushes down, and now songbirds, unable to hear their own voices, flee the vicinity. With the birds, another set of instruments is added to the orchestra, the woodwinds, as it were. A decrescendo follows in an andante passage; the birds seek "ruhige Stellen, wo sie den Gatten die Fühlung / Verliebter Schmerzen entdecken"; a "glassy brook" is admonished to "flow softly" that it may not drown out the birds' "amorous whispering." There then follows a passage (admired by Klopstock) on the birds' song, especially that of the nightingale—loud, clear, sweet, inebriating—and the build-up to another crescendo: "symphonische Töne / Durchfliehn von Eichen und Dorn des weiten Schattenthals Kammern. / Die ganze Gegend wird Schall." Occasionally there is restrained onomatopoeia, as in the phrase "Vom Ulmenbaum flötet die Amsel / In hohen Tönen den Bass," with its suggestive alternation of high and low vowels, but such devices are not especially typical of Kleist, who mainly strives to arouse a sense of rapturous identification through kinetic rather than auditory means.

"Der Frühling" is not great poetry—it is emotional license in the name of virtue and nature, essentially an escape mechanism from bonds the man of the eighteenth century must have felt to be severely onerous. Like Brockes' *Irdisches Vergnügen* it is an early expression of that "Weltfrömmigkeit" or natural piety that plays such a central role in German literature after the middle of the century. But unlike Brockes, Kleist is not an insistent moralizer, and his method is no longer emblematic, though of course he too, in his overtly reflective passages, points out that all creation is a mirror of the divine and sees God "so herrlich im Vogel, . . . als in der Feste des Himmels" (verses 338 f.). All nature praises its

Maker. And in this sense Kleist's "Frühling" is certainly a didactic poem. More important, however, is the theme of nature as a refuge for pure feeling.

If Ewald von Kleist is only incidentally a didacticist, a didacticist more out of force of convention than conviction, Christian Fürchtegott Gellert (1715–69)[22] is a didacticist by nature and conviction. In an often-quoted passage from a letter Gellert explains his purpose in writing his enormously popular *Fabeln und Erzählungen* (First Book 1746, Second Book 1748; reissued 1748 and 1751, and almost countless times thereafter):

> Mein grösster Ehrgeiz besteht darin, dass ich den Vernünftigen dienen und gefallen will und nicht den Gelehrten im engen Verstande. Ein kluges Frauenzimmer gilt mir mehr als eine gelehrte Zeitung, und der niedrigste Mann von gesundem Verstande ist mir würdig genung, seine Aufmerksamkeit zu suchen, sein Vergnügen zu befördern, und ihm in einem leicht zu behaltenden Ausdruck gute Wahrheiten zu sagen, und edle Empfindungen in seiner Seele rege zu machen.
>
> [Quoted after Pellegrini, "Krise," p. 69]

The audience that he seeks is not that of the baroque poet, the artfully learned and initiated, but the naturally intelligent and sensible of whatever station, the "kluges Frauenzimmer" and the lowly man "von gesundem Verstande." He hopes to appeal to them both intellectually and emotionally, tell them "sound truths" while "furthering their enjoyment" and arousing "noble feeling." It is the ideal of the "Popularaufklärung."

These are indeed the three main strands in Gellert's work: he seeks to amuse, to instruct, and to touch our heart. It is rare, however, that he succeeds in combining all three strands in one poem: amused we may often be and instructed not infrequently in the ways of the world and human nature, but it is seldom that the fable or tale that fulfills these aims also arouses noble feelings. There is a clear dichotomy in Gellert between feeling and worldly wisdom.

What Gellert's true view of the world and man is has long been a matter of dispute and puzzlement. On the one hand he seems sly, almost cynical, bent only on showing that man is ruled by his baser instincts; on the other he descends to the lowest depths of bathos to touch our hearts with tales purporting to show to what lengths magnanimity can go. In these latter tales he is the perfect example of a poet that can be appreciated in the spirit in which he is meant to be taken only by his own time—for us, these works are purest "camp."

It has recently been suggested by Wolfgang Martens in his essay on "Weltbild und Gattungs-Tradition bei Gellert" that the striking discrepancy in the poet's work—the cleft between the satirical and worldly-wise on the one hand and the bathetic on the other—is attributable to the coercive force of genre, which acts as a determinant of content. In cultivating the fable, Martens argues, Gellert followed the satirical tradition of the *Schwank* or *facetiae*, in which the peasant is sly, stubborn, selfish, crude, the women coquettes and gossips ruled by the spirit of contradiction, the poet or scholar an object of ridicule, etc. In short, the genre had an obligatory repertoire of subject matter, motifs, characters, techniques, as well as an obligatory attitude toward man and society. In his all-too-touching tales, on the other hand, Gellert disregards this tradition and presents a different view of human nature, one in which spiritual values are supreme and noble feelings per se are celebrated. Such tales Martens sees as an attempt to extend the limits of the genre. Whether, however, the "true" Gellert is more evident in the one type of tale than the other must remain an open question. Perhaps he is equally present in both.

Reference to the coercive force of genre is probably justified and may indeed explain a good deal, but it hardly explains everything, for after all the genre remains essentially the same (if we look at it purely from the standpoint of form) in all these productions, whether they fall into the category of the ironic-satiric or that of the touching and noble. To explain the latter as an attempt to extend the genre only leaves us with the old question in slightly different form. If genre coerces in one case, why not in another? On the whole, it would seem that we are dealing with a content-centered rather than a genre-oriented poet.

Furthermore, it is not always the case that even in the ironical-satirical poems human character is seen in the stereotyped terms Martens claims to be typical of the *facetiae*. For example, "Die Biene und die Henne," "Der gütige Besuch," "Der glückliche Dichter," and "Elpin" do not satirize the poet but rather defend him. These are balanced, to be sure, by three other fables and tales which do take a satirical attitude toward scholars and poets: "Der Polyhistor," "Die Nachtigall und die Lerche," and "Der unsterbliche Autor." But in the end the score remains even. Women come off no worse than men. "Die zärtliche Frau," who claims she is willing to die in her young husband's stead, shows Death, who comes at her call, her bedridden spouse. This is balanced by "Der zärtliche Mann," who promises his dying wife not to remarry and is then incensed when he sees that she is to be buried in her wedding gown—he will need to have a new one made! Both of these fables (from a fifteenth-century source) satirize the vanity of sentimental ideals, the very ideals for which Gellert lets his characters die of pure grief on the spot ("Das neue Ehepaar") or commit both murder and suicide ("Der Hochzeittag"). "Die Widersprecherin" is about a woman who must have the last word, but it is cleverly insinuated that her husband's sweet-tempered hypocrisy is the cause of her argumentativeness, while "Crispin und Crispine" tells of a man so overbearing that his wife's ghost haunts the sexton until he moves her body from their common grave. "Die Witwe" treats the widow of Ephesus motif, but "Der betrübte Witwer" (from Bayle's Dictionary) balances it with the story of a man who is taking no chances on his wife's returning to life a second time, and "Lisette" is a gruesome tale of male infidelity.

These tales, and others like them, may strike one as the essential Gellert—they tell us that human beings are incurably self-seeking, willful, sensual, envious, devious, foolish, little concerned with those touching ideals that rule the hearts of the magnanimous. In fact, they strongly imply that such ideals are nugatory and have nothing to do with real human relationships. But the obverse, as has been pointed out, is also conspicuously present in those pieces in which Gellert is intent upon arousing "edle Empfindungen." We should be a bit cautious about regarding these tales as examples of "German sentimentality"—the source of most of them is the English moral weeklies: the *Spectator, Tatler, Father.*

The most famous, and also the best, is "Inkle und Yariko" (from the *Spectator*), a tale treated dozens of times, usually in dramatic form, in the eighteenth century. Its popularity was no doubt due to the white man's bad conscience at his treatment of the noble American savage. Yariko is an Indian maid whom a young Englishman heartlessly sells into slavery after she has saved his life and become his mistress. Inkle puts financial gain above all demands of the heart and conscience. "Denn Handeln war sein Witz, und Rechnen seine Tugend." In this tale, Gellert succeeds in achieving all three of his stated aims: he instructs (castigates baseness), celebrates nobility of feeling, and entertains (by the masterly way in which he tells the story).

Rarely, however, was Gellert so fortunate in the choice of a subject. Ambiguous indeed, for example, is the moral lesson, if any is meant, that is to be derived from "Der Hochzeittag," whose source is the *Tatler.* A young couple has been sent to the country by the bride's father to be married in the same village and by the same minister that married him and his now deceased wife. Wantonly luxuriating in his new happiness, the young husband playfully points one of a pair of pistols at his bride, saying that he will now have revenge for her premarital severities. She tells him to go ahead and shoot. He pulls the trigger, the weapon is loaded, she falls dead. Enter the servant. The master demands:

"Wer lud mir die Pistolen?"
"Ich tat's, weil mir's zur Reise nötig schien."
"Ich habe dir's doch nicht befohlen?"
"Nein, Herr!" Und gleich erschoss er ihn.

The young widower now writes a note to his former father-in-law, explaining the miserable circumstances and closing with the words:

Ich bete noch für dich, wenn mir die Augen brechen,
Der ich für mich nicht beten kann—

He then kills himself:

Man traf ihn neben ihr durchs Schwert getötet an.

No moral is drawn. The story is told in a slice-of-life manner with little auctorial comment, though with obvious sympathy for the personages. What is Gellert telling us? Accidental homicide, murder, suicide in the name of "edle Empfindungen"? Defense of the rights of feeling in themselves? The fearful aberrations to which the human heart may succumb? A bourgeois fate tragedy? No answer seems satisfactory. Emotion is indulged, our attention held by a skillfully told tale, but art refuses to submit to any court of appeal but its own, whatever deductions it may allow about its author and the times in which it was written and appreciated.

If fate is left an ironic mystery in "Der Hochzeittag," it is explained in terms of shallowest cause-and-effect rationalism in "Das Schicksal" (drawn from the *Spectator*), which purports to show that "das, was Gott verhängt, aus weisen Gründen fliesst, Und, wenn dir's grausam scheint, gerechtes Schicksal ist." It is an *exemplum* meant to teach resignation to fate. Moses, on a mountain with the Lord, sees a horseman stop to drink at a spring in the valley. He rides away, a shepherd boy comes to drink, finds a purse the horseman has dropped, and absconds. An old man comes to drink and lies down to rest beside the spring. The horseman returns, accuses him of stealing his purse and slays him. The Lord explains to Moses:

> Hier kannst du inne werden,
> Wie in der Welt sich alles billig fügt;
> Denn wiss: es hat der Greis, der itzt im Blute liegt,
> Des Knaben Vater einst erschlagen,
> Der den verlornen Raub zuvor davon getragen.

The Lord's morality is apparently based on the principle that two wrongs make a right. A theft and a murder revenge a murder. In attempting to show that all is grounded in divine justice, Gellert rather shows that God's ways, when explained in terms comprehensible to us, are diabolical. Goethe, in the seventh book of *Dichtung und Wahrheit*, calls Gellert's writings "das Fundament der deutschen sittlichen Kultur" of his day, and many other sources confirm this judgment.

Gellert was read and read avidly as much no doubt for his style as his content. "Es war eine seltsame und in Deutschland noch unerhörte Erscheinung Verse zu lesen, wo alles so gesagt war, wie man spricht, und doch alles edel und einnehmend, und alles zugleich im Silbenmaasse und Reime richtig," wrote Christian Garve in 1771. Gellert, he says, "schien nur den Ausdruck der Gedanken zu suchen, und doch zugleich den Reim und das Metrum zu finden" (quoted after Schlingmann, p. 124). Gellert's art hides its artfulness. The baroque has been superseded by a new concept of style. Garve's characterization accords perfectly with Gellert's own formulation of the stylistic principles he promulgates in his treatise on letter-writing (*Praktische Abhandlung von dem guten Geschmacke in Briefen*, 1751), though here he of course says nothing of rhyme and meter. Naturalness is the prime criterion, to which should be joined, especially in narrative passages, vividness. The reader should feel that he is an eyewitness of the action. Above all, however, one's style should have *Anmuth* or grace, a quality which Gellert naturally cannot pin down precisely. He speaks, it is true, of certain tricks of his own fabulistic manner, but they are things which only a Gellert, a Sterne, or a La Fontaine can bring off, "nameless graces, which no methods teach":

> Man redet oft selbst im Erzählen den Andern an. . . .
> Man antwortet sich; man streut kleine Betrachtungen
> ein, die uns unser Witz oder unsre Belesenheit herge-
> ben. Alles dies am rechten Orte, mit Anständigkeit,
> nicht zu häufig, kurz, so thun, dass alles, so sehr es
> entbehrt werden kann, doch zur Anmuth der Ge-
> schichte unentbehrlich gewesen zu seyn scheint, dieses
> ist das Verdienst der Erzählung.[23]

Gellert is a born anecdotist. This is undoubtedly the true
secret of his undying popularity. We may be shocked at his
theology, regard his sentimentality as camp, even find his
moral teachings shallow, but we will find it hard, in his more
successful pieces, to resist him as a storyteller. In this he is
like Richardson, whom he prized above all contemporary
writers.[24] Let us glance at a few examples.

> Ein Bär, der lange Zeit sein Brot ertanzen müssen,
> Entrann, und wählte sich den ersten Aufenthalt.
> Die Bären grüssten ihn mit brüderlichen Küssen,
> Und brummten freudig durch den Wald.
> Und wo ein Bär den andern sah:
> So hiess es: "Petz ist wieder da!"

The identification of our feeling with that of the bears is
immediate and complete, though the bears remain bears. We
share their joy and emit throaty grunts of satisfaction.

Or consider this depiction of a magpie as a sophist who
can prove that black is white in "Der Fuchs und die Elster":

> So, wie ein weiser Arzt, der auf der Bühne steht,
> Und seine Künste rühmt, bald vor, bald rückwärts
> geht,
> Sein seidnes Schnupftuch nimmt, sich räuspert, und
> dann spricht:
> So lief die Elster auch den Ast bald auf, bald nieder,
> Und strich an einen Zweig den Schnabel hin und
> wieder,
> Und macht ein sehr gelehrt Gesicht.

One of the most successful pieces is "Die Widersprech-erin," a tale rather than a fable (the distinction is not always easy to make). The tone is ironic, but not heavily ironic. The poet uses asides and mock-heroic comparisons, telling his tale in an elaborately leisurely, worldly-wise manner. The dialogue, as always, is handled with consummate skill. Ismene, who had, "among her other gifts, this one too: she liked to contradict," and her husband are having a dinner discussion:

> Einst sass sie mit dem Mann bei Tische;
> Sie assen unter andern Fische,
> Mich deucht, es war ein grüner Hecht.
> "Mein Engel," sprach der Mann, "mein Engel, ist mir
>   recht:
> So ist der Fisch nicht gar zu blau gesotten."
> "Das," rief sie, "hab ich wohl gedacht,
> So gut man auch die Anstalt macht:
> So finden Sie doch Grund, der armen Frau zu spotten.
> Ich sag es Ihnen kurz, der Hecht ist gar zu blau."
> "Gut," sprach er, "meine liebe Frau,
> Wir wollen nicht darüber streiten,
> Was hat die Sache zu bedeuten?"

The soft answer that turneth away wrath causes Ismene to fly into rage, which leads to an elaborate mock-heroic comparison with an angry turkey. She faints when her husband, who refuses to continue the argument, leaves; nothing will revive her, not rubbing, not smelling salts, not burnt feathers held under the nose. The husband, recalled to her side, is dissolved in grief, though still duty-bound to tell the truth:

> "Du stirbst, mein Leben!
> Du stirbst? Ich armer Mann; ach, meine liebe Frau,
> Wer hiess mich dir doch widerstreben!
> Ach, der verdammte Fisch! Gott weiss, er war nicht
>   blau."
> Den Augenblick bekam sie wieder Leben.
> "Blau war er," rief sie aus, "willst du dich noch
>   nicht geben?"

Gellert ends with a wry flourish that ironizes the genre of the moralizing tale itself:

> So tat der Geist des Widerspruchs
> Mehr Wirkung, als die Kraft des heftigsten Geruchs!

Schlingmann finds three typical narrative forms in the *Fabeln und Erzählungen* (pp. 112 ff.). The first he calls "das pointierte Erzählgedicht," the second "die freie Versfabel," the third "die satirische Verserzählung." This scheme omits a fourth typical form, namely, those tales, some of which we have already discussed, that are told for their purely emotional value.

The technique common to those pieces that Schlingmann characterizes as "das pointierte Erzählgedicht" is that which Heine was later to make famous; it is, in fact, a technique widely used by circus clowns and rests upon disparity between preparation and result: the elaborate windup and the wild pitch, the huge firearm aimed with deadly accuracy and the cork that pops out of the barrel. "Die Guttat" is a bitterly amusing example:

> Wie rümlich ist's, von seinen Schätzen
> Ein Pfleger der Bedrängten sein!
> Und lieber minder sich ergetzen,
> Als arme Brüder nicht erfreun.
>
> Beaten fiel heut ein Vermögen
> Von Tonnen Golds durch Erbschaft zu.
> "Nun," sprach sie, "hab ich einen Segen,
> Von dem ich Armen Gutes tu."
>
> Sie sprach's. Gleich schlich zu seinem Glücke
> Ein siecher Alter vor ihr Haus,
> Und bat, gekrümmt auf seiner Krücke,
> Sich eine kleine Wohltat aus.
>
> Sie ward durchdrungen von Erbarmen,
> Und fühlte recht des Armen Not.
> Sie weinte, ging und gab dem Armen
> Ein grosses Stück verschimmelt Brot.

Other pieces in this mode are "Der Geheimnisvolle," "Der Selbstmord," "Der Greis." An unusually successful variation on this scheme and one that gives us a clear insight into Gellert as an antisentimentalist, a side of his being probably more important than his tearjerking sentimentality, is:

DER JÜNGLING UND DER GREIS

"Wie fang ich's an, um mich empor zu schwingen?"
Fragt einst ein Jüngling einen Greis.
"Der Mittel," fing er an, "um es recht hoch zu bringen,
Sind zwei bis drei, so viel ich weiss.
Seid tapfer! Mancher ist gestiegen,
Weil er entschlossen in Gefahr,
Ein Feind von Ruh und Vergnügen,
Und durstig nach der Ehre war.
Seid weise, Sohn! Den Niedrigsten auf Erden
Ist's oft durch Witz und durch Verstand geglückt,
Am Hofe gross, gross in der Stadt zu werden:
Zu beiden macht man sich durch Zeit und Fleiss
     geschickt.
Dies sind die Mittel grosser Seelen."
"Doch sie sind schwer. Ich will's Ihm nicht verhehlen,
Ich habe leichtere gehofft."
"Gut," sprach der Greis, "wollt Ihr ein leichteres
     wählen:
So seid ein Narr; auch Narren steigen oft."

Gellert's "freie Versfablen," to follow Schlingmann's classification, are more in the tradition of La Fontaine, though animals do not play such a large role as in the works of the delightful Frenchman. Here belong such classic pieces as "Der Maler" and "Die Geschichte von dem Hute" as well as the animal fables. The satirical verse tales are represented by such poems as "Die Widersprecherin," "Der Prozess" (a satire on pigheaded plaintiffs and sly lawyers), "Die Betschwester" (on religious hypocrisy), and "Die Bauern und der Amtmann," a humorous tale of great psychological penetration without any apparent moral.

Gellert's *Geistliche Oden und Lieder* (1757) contain some of the best known German hymns, a number of which passed into English common use (Julian's *Dictionary of Hymnology*, 1892, lists six). As a hymnist, Gellert concludes a period rather than initiating a new one. He is the last classical German hymn writer. If he has a model, it is Paul Gerhardt.

Gellert's hymns display little overheated pietistic fervor and are likewise largely free of pietistic sentimentality. In the more odelike pieces, as distinguished from the hymns (a distinction that is often hard to make), there is, it is true, considerable soul-searching, and soul-searching is certainly a pietistic trait. These poems ("Prüfung am Abend," "Das natürliche Verdenben des Menschen," "Demut" are typical examples) belong among Gellert's weakest productions. Gellert frequently appeals to reason, but he is far from being a religious rationalist: Revelation always has the final word. We must regard it as a rationalistic trait, however, that he cannot conceive of a true conflict between reason and revelation. Gellert is not one to quote "credo *quia* absurdum."

> Er [Gott] gab dir die *Vernunft*, und du verleugnest sie?
> Er sendet dir sein *Wort;* und du gehorchst ihm nie?
> ["Wider den Aufschub der Bekehrung"]

Virtue, *Tugend*, a key concept in eighteenth-century piety, Gellert regards as attainable only by following both reason and Revelation. Reason alone is a weak reed, the dupe of the passions, just as in Haller, a point made in "Der Freigeist" in the *Fabeln und Erzählungen*. But virtue for its own sake is empty of meaning. We should strive for virtue to save our immortal soul. Salvation and virtue are indissolubly connected:

> Ihn [Gott] fürchten, das ist Weisheit nur,
> Und Freiheit ist's, sie wählen.
> Ein Tier folgt Fesseln der Natur,
> Ein Mensch dem Licht der Seelen.
> Was ist des Geistes Eigentum?
> Was sein Beruf auf Erden?

Die Tugend! Was ihr Lohn ihr Ruhm?
Gott ewig ähnlich werden!
["Der Kampf der Tugend"]

Gellert knows the difficulty of belief, though he does not often stress it. His most moving formulation of this theme is found in "Trost eines schwermütigen Christen":

Zag nicht, o Christ! denn deine Schmerzen,
Sind sichre Zeugen bessrer Herzen,
Als dir das deine scheint.
Wie könntest du dich so betrüben,
Dass dir die Kraft fehlt, Gott zu lieben,
Wär nicht dein Herz mit ihm vereint?
Kein Mensch vermag Gott zu erkennen,
Noch Jesum einen Herrn zu nennen,
Als durch den heilgen Geist.
Hast du nicht diesen Geist empfangen?
Er ist's, der dich nach Gott verlangen,
Und sein Erbarmen suchen heisst.

Though he may speak as one who has himself won the struggle, the tone of compassion with the "heavy-hearted Christian" shows that he is well acquainted with its difficulties. The theme itself is thoroughly modern; it is, for example, the theme of Unamuno's *Del sentimiento trágico de la vida*, especially of Chapter VI, "En el fondo del abismo."

One of Gellert's basic and most convincingly treated themes is that of the solemnity and grandeur of creation that speaks to the human heart and mind of a great and good Creator. It is Brockes' theme, of course, and central one for the first half of the eighteenth century. Like Brockes, and unlike Haller, Gellert can read only comfort and exaltation in God's word as written in the heavens. These infinite spaces do not make his heart sink, but lift it up. The first two stanzas of his most famous hymn, "Die Ehre Gottes aus der Natur" (set to music by Beethoven), are based on the nineteenth Psalm. They stride with a majestic stateliness that admits no nay-saying:

Die Himmel rühmen des Ewigen Ehre,
Ihr Schall pflanzt seinen Namen fort.
Ihn rühmt der Erdkreis, ihn preisen die Meere;
Vernimm, o Mensch, ihr göttlich Wort!

Wer trägt der Himmel unzählbare Sterne?
Wer führt die Sonn aus ihrem Zelt?
Sie kommt und leuchtet und lacht von ferne,
Und läuft den Weg, gleich als ein Held.

In these stanzas the evidence of natural revelation is presented. The majesty of Nature praises the majesty of God. Man has only to open his eyes and his ears to be convinced. Technically, these verses show Gellert at the height of his poetic powers. The movement of the lines, their kingly stride, reflects the dominion of the Creator in His creation. The imagery of the first stanzas is auditory, that of the second visual. Alliteration and vocalism underline the harmony of the divine symphony and majestic spectacle: des *E*wigen *E*hre; Ihr Sch*a*ll pfl*a*nzt seinen N*a*men fort (the a-sound does what the lines discursively express: it "pflanzt sich fort"); *l*euchtet und *l*acht und *l*äuft. The verses describing the course of the sun, with their alliterative chain of verbs, show forth in a visual image of strong kinetic suggestiveness the striding that we have felt in the rhythm throughout—a dynamic image of creation's irresistible power that reflects the power of its Creator.

The next two stanzas, appealing first to human reason, then to feeling, are not as successful. We are called upon to reflect: "Durch wen ist alles? O gib Ihm die Ehre! Mir, ruft der Herr, sollst du vertraun." These verses lead to the final division of the poem, in which God, who has spoken only through His creation, now speaks to us directly, His own interpreter:

Mein ist die Kraft, mein ist Himmel und Erde;
An meinen Werken kennst du mich.
Ich bin's, und werde sein, der ich sein werde,
Dein Gott und Vater ewiglich.

Ich bin der Schöpfer, bin Weisheit und Güte,
Ein Gott der Ordnung und dein Heil;

> Ich bin's! Mich liebe von ganzem Gemüte,
> Und nimm an meiner Gnade teil.

The benevolent despot (*l'état, c'est moi*) has spoken and contradiction is unthinkable. *Ich* and *mein* dominate these lines. God's final word is "I am"—and without me thou art not. This is what the "Freigeist" must discover to his sorrow, what the believer knows to his salvation. When Gellert remains within the framework of the main Christian tradition, he is completely persuasive, as ridiculous as he may become when he tries to persuade by rational argument alone. He is a prime example of a poet whose wisdom is either purely worldly or purely religious, that is, traditional; it is useless to look for any other philosophy or "Weltbild" in his work.

God's absolutism is again the theme of "Gottes Macht und Vorsehung," the first stanza of which was also set by Beethoven:[25]

> Gott ist mein Lied!
> Er ist der Gott der Stärke;
> Hehr ist sein Nam, und gross sind seine Werke;
> Und alle Himmel sein Gebiet.

The form is very sophisticated: four iambic lines of four different lengths: two-, three-, five-, and four-beat. In the stanza just quoted, the first three verses have "schwebende Betonung" or hovering accent at the beginning: Gótt ìst; Ér ìst; Héhr ìst, identifying God with being, is-ness. The only verb in the stanza is *sein*. What is, is God and through Him. The second stanza, and one must agree with Schlingmann (p. 177) that it is "ungeheuer," speaks of the coincidence between the divine will and being (emphasis added):

> Er *will* und spricht's;
> So *sind* und leben Welten.
> Und er gebeut; so fallen durch sein Schelten
> Die Himmel wieder in ihr Nichts.

God is not dependent on His creation nor identical with it. He is being that can will its nonmanifestation as readily as its manifestation. The handling of the verse is a perfect reflection of this idea. The first two lines stride forcefully and are end-stopped. It seems that the phenomenal world must be grounded eternally. But that depends on God's will. At His command all phenomenality must plunge into nothingness, just as the third line into the final one. "Nichts" is an exceedingly expressive rhyme with "spricht's," for even as creation is a manifestation of the Word, so too is noncreation, nothingness. The rhyme scheme as a whole is also eloquent: abba, the enclosing a-rhymes reflecting God's constant presence, as is especially evident in the seventh stanza:

> Er ist dir nah,
> Du sitzest oder gehest;
> Ob du ans Meer, ob du gen Himmel flöhest:
> So ist er allenthalben da.

"Weihnachtslied" ("Dies ist der Tag, den Gott gemacht," Psalm 118:24), meant to be sung to the melody of Luther's "Vom Himmel hoch da komm ich her," is a reverent contemplation of the mystery of the Incarnation, simple in structure and fervent in tone. It is well suited to show Gellert's Christology. Here is no cloying pietistic sweetness nor baroque play with paradox, paradoxical as the idea of man-god in itself is. The style is rather that of the Psalms and the Prophets, reduced, as it were, to the *genus humile* of the New Testament. A cento of Old and New Testament references (Isaiah and Galatians) underlies the second stanza:

> Die Völker haben dein geharrt,
> Bis dass die Zeit erfüllet ward;
> Da sandte Gott von seinem Thron
> Das Heil der Welt, dich, seinen Sohn.

The feeling that informs the whole is one of reverent wonder and gratitude for Christ's "condescension":

> Damit der Sünder Gnad erhält,
> Erniedrigst du dich, Herr der Welt,
> Nimmst selbst an unsrer Menschheit teil,
> Erscheinst im Fleisch, und wirst uns Heil.

Sator Mundi and Pantokrator—the Christ is both, and Gellert's constant awareness of His double nature forbids familiarity. There is no cooing over the Babe in this Christmas song. If he wants to luxuriate in sentimentality, Gellert chooses other themes, preferably from the English moral weeklies.

CHAPTER TWO

HAGEDORN, GLEIM, AND THE ROCOCO LYRIC

If posterity's judgment of the relative merits of the kinds of poetry cultivated by Friedrich von Hagedorn (1708–54)[1] were in agreement with that of the poet himself, we should have discussed his work in the foregoing chapter. But Hagedorn, unlike Haller, does not live primarily because of his longer reflective poems, which he himself considered his most important productions. He lives because of his verse in a lighter vein, his *Fabeln und Erzählungen* (1738) and *Oden und Lieder* (1742), rather than his *Moralische Gedichte* (1750), which take pride of place in his collected works.

Hagedorn's personal taste was quite catholic. His correspondence shows that he reveled in the English sentimentalists, that he defended Klopstock and admired Milton, that he did not see the salvation of German literature solely in following in the footsteps of Horace, Opitz, and Pope.[2] In his own work, however, he is a thoroughgoing neoclassicist. His taste was more catholic than his practice.

Gottsched was the high priest of neoclassicism in Germany. It is revealing that Hagedorn did not side with him in his tiresome dispute with the Swiss literary theorists Bodmer and Breitinger. His private correspondence clearly shows that he was on the side of the Swiss, who saw in Milton and

Klopstock the realization of their poetic ideals, who eloquently defended the primacy of the imagination and the
nature of poetry as convincing virtuality against Gottsched's
shibboleths of "probability," "truth to nature," restraint in
metaphoric usage, and so on, in short, all the neoclassical
rules we associate with Boileau. Yet it is the doctrine of
Gottsched-Boileau rather than that of Bodmer and Breitinger
that one finds exemplified in Hagedorn's own work.

In his mature work, i.e., after the *Versuch* of 1729, which
is late baroque in tone, though antibaroque in intent, Hagedorn shows strict adherence to neoclassical aesthetics.[3] His
models, besides Horace and Pope, are such poets as Prior,
Swift, La Fontaine, and the writers of *poésie fugitive*. His
diction has a colloquial ring, but idealized, purified, as it
were, and abstracted. The guiding principles are clarity, euphony, correctness. The level is that of the *genus medium*,
neither heroic nor coarse. Reason and nature are assumed to
coincide, since nature is regarded as the true essence of things
as intuited by reason, those harmonious laws decreed by God
which govern the universe. "Follow nature!"—the slogan of
the Enlightenment to an even greater degree than *sapere
aude!*—means to follow reason, which is truth. Through this
kind of circular argument the classicist attains his unity of
view. Naturalness does not mean for him realism but clarity
and reasonableness, avoidance of excess, which is the way of
nature. This the "wise man," the ideal figure of all classicistic
writing, well knows:

> Er folget der Natur, in deren schönen Werken
> Wir weder Mangel sehn, noch Überfluss bemerken.
> [*Werke*, 1769, 1, 34]

Language is the organ of reason and should be its mirror,
as clear and "eternal" as possible: grammatically correct, free
of dialect or jargon (unless carefully glossed in footnotes!),
free of kennings and periphrasis, free of word play. Rejection
of metaphor is the last step, and except for occasional traces
of baroque metaphorical usage (especially noticeable in the
fourth book of the *Oden und Lieder*) Hagedorn takes this step.

Metaphor "disguises" truth. In this way language tends to be reduced to its purely denotative function. "Rien n'est beau que le vrai" was Boileau's maxim, and it is also Hagedorn's. To present eternal truths in language worthy of the subject is the task of poetry. This concept of poetry's function was also held in the Baroque. The difference lies in the changing concept of the most fitting *manner* of presentation, though the manner in turn is directly connected with the faculty to which poetry aims in each case to appeal. Through rhetorical embellishment the Baroque sought to move the *heart* to assent to the truth of Revelation; through argument, through precept and example (fables), the Enlightenment seeks to persuade the *mind* to accept the dictates of reason. To do so must inevitably lead to the acquisition of wisdom and virtue, which for the Enlightenment largely take the place of religion.

The *Fabeln und Erzählungen* are for the most part literature made out of literature. Hagedorn, as his work abundantly proves, is an adherent of the doctrine of selective borrowing, the leading theory of imitation in the eighteenth century.[4] This theory, ancient in origin, was an elaboration of the view that art can surpass nature by selecting and combining its most perfect parts, thus producing what Batteux called "la belle nature." The doctrine of selective borrowing held that the primary work of selection had already been done by the artists and poets of past ages and that the modern artist should therefore imitate *them*. By combining the virtues of his models the gifted imitator could create works of even higher quality; the present could stand on the shoulders of the past. In painting, Sir Joshua Reynolds, Anton Raphael Mengs, and Tiepolo were among those who adhered to this view; in poetry, it was the standpoint of Swift, Pope, Hagedorn, Uz, and many of the French writers from Du Bellay to Voltaire. Though opposed and even ridiculed by such men as Gainsborough, Chardin, and Hogarth, the theory was not seriously discredited before Edward Young's *Conjectures on Original Composition* (1759) and Blake's attacks on Reynolds' *Discourses*. Hagedorn is at pains to display rather than conceal his borrowings and conscientiously lists his sources in his notes, the philologist of his own work.

As a narrator, Hagedorn must rank far below Gellert. A closer look at his tales reveals many striking inconsistencies, both in those—comparatively few—that are original with him and in those based on other works according to the principle of selective borrowing. His best known poem, "Johann, der Seifensieder" (*Werke*, 1769, 2, 118), is an example of a work for which the poet lists a number of sources. It will, I believe, defy the keenest wit to make sense of the details of this poem, though the general message may come through clearly enough. The first stanza tells us that Johann sings constantly, "Vom Morgen bis zum Abend hin," but almost in the same breath it is also implied that he sings only at mealtimes and out of gratitude for his food: "Sein Tagwerk konnt ihm Nahrung bringen: Und wann er ass, so musst er singen . . . " The second stanza deals with Johann's reading: "Im Lesen war er anfangs schwach," but he learns to pray and this seems to have improved his reading ability, for we hear that then "er schlief, dem Nachbar gleich zu seyn, Oft singend, öftrer lesend, ein." About Johann's devotion to literature nothing else is said: it is a blind motif. The third stanza introduces the rich neighbor, "Ein Sprössling eigennutzger Ehe" and a gourmand. Hagedorn insists on his *gourmandise*, though like Johann's reading it really has nothing to do with the story. Neither, for that matter, does the fact that he is the offspring of a selfish marriage. The neighbor is characterized in a self-contradictory fashion: he is "steif und bürgerlich," yet he seems to lead a life of riot, always gluttonizing, keeping late hours, and forgetting to pay his debts ("Und seiner Wechsel oft vergass"), which is hardly straitlaced and bourgeois. In any event, because he goes to bed so late, he is annoyed by Johann's *aubade*. He calls him in and questions him closely about his income. Johann has no idea how much he makes, he is uninterested in money, work is his whole life and sole recreation—he even regrets the holidays. His declaration that he loves his work above all else "schien den Reichen zu erfreun." Why? The closest reader will not find the answer in the poem, I think. The rich neighbor then makes Johann a proposition:

> Hans, spricht er, du sollst glücklich seyn.
> Itzt bist du nur ein schlechter Prahler.
> Da hast du baare funfzig Thaler;
> Nur unterlasse den Gesang.
> Das Geld hat einen bessern Klang.

At this point comes the most puzzling development in the poem. Hans accepts the money and the condition under which it is offered. His character changes instantly and completely:

> Er dankt, und schleicht mit scheuchem Blicke,
> Mit mehr als diebscher Furcht zurücke.
> Er herzt den Beutel, den er hält,
> Er zählt, und wägt, und schwenkt das Geld . . .

In the twinkling of an eye our sturdy Johann has become a miser! There was not the slightest indication up to this point that he had such an inclination. Yet now he is suddenly a "karger Thor," who hoards his treasure, fears thieves, mistreats his pets.

The last two stanzas are devoted to Johann's insight into his folly: "Er lernt zuletzt, je mehr er spart, Wie oft sich Sorg und Reichtum paart." He returns the money and sings again. He also takes this occasion to give his neighbor a little sermon: "Fahrt fort," he tells him, "mich heimlich zu beneiden. Ich tausche nicht mit euren Freuden." Did the neighbor *envy* Hans? Hagedorn did not indicate it. And what about exchanging joys? The neighbor's joy, so far as we know, lies in gluttony, Johann's in making soap. Johann's words imply that the rich neighbor gave him the money because he wanted to make him (Johann) as unhappy as he was himself. But was the neighbor unhappy? Didn't he merely want his morning's sleep? The non sequiturs come so thick and fast that it seems hopeless to try to make sense of the details.

One might suspect—it would require more detailed investigation to prove it—that the incoherencies in "Johann" are at least partly due to an unsuccessful application of the principle of selective borrowing. Did the desire to incorporate appealing traits from Burkhard Waldis, La Fontaine, Blondeau, and Lesage get in the way of telling a psychologically unified tale? This was almost certainly the case with Hagedorn's version of "Philemon und Baucis," which is nevertheless considerably more successful than "Johann." But caution is indicated. A reading of "Mops und Hector" (2, 46), a tale of two dogs for which the poet gives no sources, turns up perhaps even more puzzling inconsistencies than either "Johann" or "Philemon und Baucis."

The sources of "Philemon und Baucis" (2, 169) are Ovid, Swift, Prior ("The Ladle"), and La Fontaine.[5] Hagedorn follows the main features of Ovid's tale, but quite in his own manner. The end of the poem offers a good example of his centonical procedure. The last thirteen lines tell of the magic power of the oak and the linden—into which the old couple has been transformed—on lovers who seek their shade. Here many a maid has become a woman to the subsequent consternation of her mother, who in her wrath would cut down the ancient trees, were they not protected by Jove. La Fontaine lets *married* couples visit the magic trees; they then remain in love with each other to the end of their lives:

> Pour peux que des époux séjournent sous leur ombre,
> Ils s'aiment jusqu'au bout, malgré l'effort des ans.

The motif of cutting down the trees derives from Swift, in whose Christianized version (the gods have become two saintly hermits) the elderly couple is "turn'd to yews," and Baucis is finally cut down by a parson "to mend his barn," whereupon Philemon withers and dies. Hagedorn combines the two motifs, neither of which is in Ovid, and not very happily. La Fontaine, following the spirit if not the letter of Ovid—those who hear the tale in the *Metamorphoses* are "deeply moved"—ends his poem with a pathetic touch. Hagedorn, after telling the story in a pathetic vein, ends it with a risqué joke. His uncertainty of touch is also apparent in his misplaced use of Swift's invention of letting the bed in the cottage be turned into a pew "der noch, nach alter Kraft, Die Hörer gähnen lehrt, und oft den Schlaf verschafft." In Swift, this touch is quite in place, since the gods are Christian hermits and the cottage becomes a chapel. In Hagedorn, where the house becomes a pagan temple, it is merely ridiculous. Hagedorn's wide acquaintance with the various treatments of the tale and his inability to resist an appealing or amusing turn fitting enough in another context make him spoil his own work. His uncertainty in these matters one can perhaps interpret as the uncertainty of his place and time. We must remember that in the genre of the sophisticated verse tale in German Hagedorn was an innovator. Gellert is already far beyond such gaucheries.

From the standpoint of the evolution of German poetry, especially of the lyric in a narrower sense, Hagedorn's *Oden und Lieder* (first edition 1742; augmented 1744 and 1752) are more important than the *Fabeln und Erzählungen*. In the handbooks Hagedorn is accounted as the father of the German rococo lyric, and not without justice, though he had certain predecessors and fitted into an incipient mode. In the "Vorbericht" to the *Oden und Lieder* (*Werke*, 1769, 3, v–xl) Hagedorn gives a thumbnail sketch of the history of the type of song he wishes to cultivate and places himself firmly within the tradition. Like his admired Opitzians, he too is striving to bring German poetry up to date and to give it an honorable place within a European context.

By studying Hagedorn's preface and the collection itself we can learn at first hand what an early practitioner of the rococo lyric himself understood by it. (The *term* rococo is later. It came into fashion in Germany in the 1830s as a pejorative designation for the life style of the *ancien régime*,[6] but the nineteenth-century usage of the term should not lead us to regard "rococo" as a chronological rather than a stylistic concept. Rococo is a certain kind of literary expression occurring within the age of the Enlightenment.) Hagedorn wants the song he cultivates "to possess not so much the sublime as the pleasing character of the ode, thus rendering it more charming and more social" (nicht so sehr den erhabenen, als den gefälligen Character der Ode zu besitzen, durch welchen dieselbe ihre Vorzüge reizender und gesellschaftlicher machet, p. v). "Pleasing" (gefällig), "charming" (reizend), "social" (gesellschaftlich) are the key terms. The emphasis is on sophistication and good form, on the public, not the private, mode. Not, however, on the public mode in its usual seventeenth-century acceptation as praise of generals, politicians, and other "heroes," nor yet in the sense of the inculcation of the truths of revealed religion, but public in the sense of social, of man's relation to man, a *humanum* up to now neglected in the literature of Germany. His ideal audience he conceives as the "grosse Welt," the beau monde, those "who are capable of understanding and interpreting the language of passion, of tenderness, of social jest and laughing satire in such a way that they are not confounded in their own tongue by the liberties to which they are accustomed in the lyrics of foreigners" (pp. xxxi f.). He is fully aware of his pathfinding role; he knows that he is attempting to add a new dimension to German poetry. It is the dimension of "Diesseitigkeit," the appreciation of the purely worldly. (There is no reference to the transcendent here, and they occur rarely elsewhere in Hagedorn.) But he has small hope that he will find an audience corresponding to his ideal. Such an audience existed in France and England, but hardly in eighteenth-century Germany, except for scattered pockets among the bourgeoisie. The courts read French and still mostly despised native talent. If such an audience was to come into being, it would have to be through his own efforts. Once more we see how prototypical is the example of Opitz.

The subject of such song, Hagedorn maintains (p. xxvi), may be anything under the sun. The point of view is what matters. In this type of "ode" the "free Britons" and the "lyric French" have long excelled (p. vi). The French, whose song he qualifies as "fein" and "natürlich," surpass all others presently producing such poetry (pp. vii f.). Among his German predecessors, Hagedorn mentions Opitz, Fleming, Gryphius (the younger), Pietsch, Besser, König, Mencke ("Philander von der Linde"), and the "feuerreichen Günther" (pp. xxx f.). These poets belong either to the "Vorbarock," i.e., they are belated practitioners of the Renaissance lyric, or to the classically inclined post-Baroque. (The poems of Günther that Hagedorn has in mind are probably his goliardic songs and love lyrics.) The poets of the Baroque proper do not appeal to him. He quotes with approval a long passage from the *Guardian* (pp. xx–xxv), in which Sappho, Anacreon, and Horace are held up as models and Donne and Cowley are violently attacked.

It is obvious that we are here confronted with a recrudescence of the *genus medium*, especially as it was employed by the long line of erotic poets from Anacreon, Horace, Tibullus, and Ovid, to Marot, Ronsard, Herrick, Prior, Gay, and the rest. The *genus medium* is limited on the one hand by the *genus grande*, which treats of acts affecting the public weal, of battles, deeds of valor, the founding of cities, etc., and on the other hand by the *genus humile*, which treats of the purely private, the coarse, the lowly, the subsocial, often in a scatological or pornographic fashion. It is also set apart from the Petrarchan mode, which since the late Middle Ages largely usurped the *genus grande* and treated of erotic themes in a highly serious, "romantic" manner.[7] Hagedorn, however—and in this he resembles his great model, Horace—does not intend to limit his employment of the *genus medium* to the treatment of erotic themes but to use it for all social relations insofar as these are neither official, i.e., concern the larger public weal, nor lowly and purely private. Their scene is that of sophisticated society, the "club" of "good-humored" men of which Shaftesbury speaks in his essay of 1709, "On the Freedom of Wit and Humour."

In their final form the *Oden und Lieder* are divided into five books, each of which stands under the aegis of a classical poet whose medallion appears at the head of the book in question. Book I (thirty-five pages in the edition of 1769) is under the protection of Horace, Hagedorn's ideal poet, Book II (thirty-nine pages) of Alkaios, Book III (thirty pages) of Anacreon, Book IV (twenty-five pages) of Sappho, Book V (fifty-nine pages) of Pindar. Renewal of song in the name of the ancients, the classical ideal, is what Hagedorn's book says in image as soon as we open it.

"An die Dichtkunst," the first poem of the first book, is a charming *captatio benevolentiae*. Immediately we feel a breath of purest rococo—playful, airy, ingratiating, ironical. Though the poet may have serious things to say, it would contravene rococo taste to say them solemnly. Avoidance of pathos does not mean lack of feeling. "An die Dichtkunst" is instinct with feeling, though poetry is here apostrophized as "Gespielinn meiner Nebenstunden" and the poems that follow are called "Kleinigkeiten: Sie wollen nicht unsterblich seyn." This "playmate" of the poet's leisure is at the same time the comfort of his inner life:

> O Dichtkunst, die das Leben lindert!
> Wie manchen Gram hast du vermindert,
> Wie manche Fröhlichkeit vermehrt!

Poetry is the voice of joy, "Freude," and "Freude" makes stern reason serene and humane: "Du erheiterst, holde Freude!/Die Vernunft" (3, 42). Stanzas two and three define levels of poetry and the poet's relation to them: the heroic, typified in Homer and Virgil, which he knows is denied him ("Die Fähigkeit von hohen Dingen/Den Ewigkeiten vorzusingen,/Verliehst du ihnen, und nicht mir"), and the *genus medium*, typified in Horace, in whose spirit he longs to live and write. But is even this more modest aim attainable? May it not prove his curse?

> Die Lust, den Alten nachzustreben,
> Ist mir im Zorn von dir gegeben,
> Wenn nicht mein Wunsch das Ziel erhält.

The end is resignation, and the brave words about "trifles" that lay no claim to immortality a *pis-aller*. Given my talents and the late times in which I live there is nothing left for me but the production of airy nothings. Here one clearly senses the burden under which the neoclassicist must labor. For who—in spite of the doctrine of "selective borrowing"—can aspire to equal the ancients? The poet of insight will be more modest, producing charming "Kleinigkeiten," though perhaps with a sigh of regret that he cannot produce something more.

But if one cannot *be* Horace, one can at least imitate him and translate him. Wasn't this the procedure adopted by the foremost poet of the age, the admirable Mr. Pope? It is also Hagedorn's. Of the next three poems in the first book, the first two are translations from Horace and the third an "imitation" in *vers irreguliers* of "Quantum distet ab Inacho" (*Odes* 3, 19), an ode in praise of sensual pleasures, humorous in tone and infectiously bacchantic. "Der Tag der Freude," the fifth poem of this book, attempts to transform the spirit of the third into rococo terms, but the result, compared with Horace, is more like a list of motifs on the theme of youthful joys, wine and roses, than a true poem. There is a peculiarly abstract air about it, and the Epicurean wisdom sounds more like grandfatherly advice:

> Umkränzt mit Rosen eure Scheitel,
> (Noch stehen euch die Rosen gut,)
> Und nennet kein Vergnügen eitel,
> Dem Wein und Liebe Vorschub thut.

Even Hagedorn's early work shows the characteristic abstractness of an "Altersstil." To a large degree, to be sure, it is also a "Zeitstil," that of neoclassicism. Epting, in his study of the poet's style, shows to what lengths Hagedorn goes to attain clarity of thought and fluency of rhythm. He employs parataxis almost exclusively, avoids tropes, favors transitive verbs and colorless copulas; his epithets tend to define rather than to ornament and are devoid of plasticity; his work swarms with abstract nouns. Naturally, such poetry displays "glatte," not "harte," "Fügung," i.e., we read on without pausing or lingering over a word or phrase—the part is strictly subordinated to the whole and all is absorbed in the rhythmic flow. All this, which is also typical of the neoclassical style in general, contributes to a homophonic style and creates an atmosphere of abstract clarity, however illogical the actual argument.

As a man of the world, urbane and ironical, Hagedorn likes to expose the gap between being and seeming or between true feeling and false. A number of pieces are built on

this binary principle, e.g., "Der Lauf der Welt," "Die ver-
liebte Verzweiflung," "Die alte und die neue Liebe,"
"Gränzen der Pflicht." Probably the most amusing poem in
a satiric vein is "Der ordentliche Hausstand" (3, 52), which
is quite worthy of a Prior or Gay and must inevitably remind the modern reader of Brecht's manner in the *Dreigro-
schenoper*. Here is the first stanza:

> Crispin geht stets berauscht zu Bette,
> Und ofters, wann der Tag schon graut.
> Sein Weib, die lächelnde Finette,
> Lebt mit dem Nachbar recht vertraut.
> Ihr ganzes Haus–und Wirthschaftswesen
> Ist ordentlich und auserlesen.

The insistence on *ratio* by no means detracts from the lyric
quality of these poems. Their very clarity of structure marks
them as typical of the rococo song. They were often set to
music, 234 times in fact, during the eighteenth century.
Görner was Hagedorn's chief early composer; five of his poems were also set by Telemann.[8]

But Hagedorn is not always an impersonal poet who
writes for a sophisticated ideal audience. One of the most
appealing pieces in the *Oden und Lieder* is the last poem of the
second book, "An den verlohrenen Schlaf," a prayer for sleep
as in the days of innocence and youth, which has a strong
personal note. Poems as expressive of deeper levels of consciousness as this one are rare in Hagedorn, but for that
reason all the more revealing. I quote the second stanza:

> Allein bedeckt vom himmlischen Gewölbe
> Schlief ich dann ein.
> Die stolze Thems, die Saal und Hamburgs Elbe
> Kann Zeugin seyn.
> Dort hab ich oft, in längstvergrünten Jahren,
> Mich hingelegt
> Und hoffnungsreich, in Sorgen unerfahren,
> Der freyen Ruh um ihren Strand gepflegt.

The rhythmical structure is mimetic, the long lines reflecting
the longing for sleep, the short ones easy fulfillment of this

longing, while the last two lines summarize and bring the stanza to a firm close. But these days are no more, and "wakeful Codrus" (Hagedorn), who "ever rhymes and ever translates," is condemned to continue without sleep, his prayer unanswered. He can no longer return to his roots and renew himself from within. He is the victim of his own polished routine. What this poem says in image "An die Dichtkunst" has already made fairly explicit. The neoclassical concept of poetry as the imitation of unsurpassed (and unsurpassable) models and as a public utterance militates against its function as self-fulfillment and self-expression. But the longing for self-expression is present: "Mein alter Freund, mein Schlaf, erscheine wieder! Wie wünsch ich dich!" Meanwhile, one composes "trifles" and "rhymes and translates."

No wonder then that Hagedorn adopts an apologetic tone in sending a copy of this collection to Bodmer (Guthke, p. 25): "I am sending you my Odes and Songs, which I have fabricated (verfertigt) as a pastime for myself and others. . . . They are trifles in the strict sense of the word, and I shall be more than satisfied if you (Ew. HochEdelgb.) only read the preface." This is not mere self-deprecation; it comes from the poet's heart, for, as he wrote to Bodmer the year before his death:

> To my mind a poet must have almost that perfection the Stoics attribute to their fabulous sage, and when I ponder this idea, I regret as unpoetic everything that I have allowed to fall from my pen and my thoughts and wishes wander into spheres that most of my German brothers in Apollo have not dared enter and into which neither years nor time nor ability will allow me to penetrate. (Guthke, pp. 104 f.)

In such a frame of mind, and it is no fleeting mood, it seems to him better "die Welt mit Kleinigkeiten zu verschonen." No one was more keenly aware of his limitations than Hagedorn himself. He felt his own time to be one of poetic poverty and his own work only a poor stopgap. And in this estimate he was fairly close to the truth.

Even so, within the limitations of the neoclassical aesthetic and above all within the limitations of the literary tradition as it was conceived in early eighteenth-century Germany, Hagedorn's accomplishment is not to be despised. He is no La Fontaine, no Pope, no Wieland, no Bellman. Nothing in his work equals the supreme productions of rococo poetry, the range, wit, depth, and virtuosity of the *Fables*, *The Rape of the Lock*, *Oberon*, *Fredmans epistlar*, but he does stand head and shoulders above his neoclassical German contemporaries, as the latter, who held him in highest esteem, were well aware.

The principal themes of rococo poetry, as Alfred Anger (*Literarisches Rokoko*, p. 54) has pointed out, are love, wine, nature, sociability (friendship), and the making of poetry. The level is that of the *genus medium*, the tone is jesting, though the jest may be serious, or at least half-serious. To a large degree and, insofar as it is erotic, probably entirely, this poetry represents a final flowering of that genre which Heinz Schlaffer has so brilliantly analyzed for us in his *Musa iocosa* (1971). The genre of jesting erotic poetry assumes special importance and undergoes a special development in the eighteenth century. From its ancient beginnings it had understood itself as holding up to society the image of a countersociety, a kind of erotic *pays de cocagne*, where the motto was "Erlaubt ist, was gefällt." It saw life from an empirical, Epicurean, anti-Platonic and (later) anti-Petrarchan standpoint. In modern times, i.e., after the advent of Christianity, and especially in the eighteenth century after the general acceptance by the aristocracy of bourgeois Christian standards of morality, it becomes poetry of poetry, that is to say, it becomes a poetic fiction with no real reference to actual conditions. It lives on itself *qua* genre. Nonetheless, it retains its value as criticism by presenting an image of a possible (even if utopian) countersociety. Its jesting tone is its passport. Society suffers it because it seems to take itself ironically and presents its concept of the world under the guise of wit.

Hagedorn, who knew his Shaftesbury, seeks to deepen

this mode by embodying in his work the concept that adjures us to "follow nature" (which is also reason) as a way of fulfilling the demands of social relationships. At the root of this doctrine lies Pelagianism. Hagedorn's clearest statement of this ideal is "An die heutigen Encratiten" (3, 141). The Encratites were, according to the poet's note, a second-century Christian sect that hated and feared all sensual pleasures and shunned human society. The "present-day Encratites" are the orthodox on the one hand and the pietists on the other, both of whom oversimplify and misconstrue the new life-style of the rococo. They do not understand the partnership of feeling and reason—the joy that makes reason serene—which is the basis of the new culture. In their own lives they exceed the bounds of nature.

> Was edle Seelen Wollust nennen,
> Vermischt mit schnöden Freuden nicht!
> Der echten Freude Wehrt zu kennen
> Ist gleichfalls unsers Daseyns Plficht.
> Ihr fallt oft tiefer, klimmt oft höher,
> Als die beglückende Natur:
> Ihr kennt vielleicht Epicuräer,
> Doch kennt ihr auch den Epicur?

The important thing to realize is that "noble souls" live life in figure, as elegant form:

> Sind nicht der wahren Freude Gränzen
> Geschmack und Wahl und Artigkeit?

One does not greedily "empty the cup of which the poet only sings."

This ethic is Shaftesburian to the core. The life of feeling and the senses is guided by reason, but reason aestheticized; in Shaftesburian terms, it is guided by "moral grace": "Geschmack und Wahl und Artigkeit." Just as an inner harmony rules in nature, "die beglückende Natur," which is "beglückend" precisely because it is harmonious, so in man and his relationships with others a unifying principle should prevail that binds all singularities into a harmonious whole.

Shaftesbury speaks of "interior numbers" or "inward form" as that principle which allows the achievement of "moral grace." This principle has in man the same task that God has in nature: to create a harmony. By "following nature" the microcosm (man) imitates the harmony of the macrocosm (nature). If the whole defense seems rather priggish, one must not forget that it undoubtedly reflects very real pressures to which this kind of poetry and its practitioners as well as the society they represented were subject.[9] And if not emptying the cup of which one sings is merely a topos taken over from the ancients—*crede mihi, distant mores a carmine nostri; vita verecunda est, Musa iocosa mea* (Ovid)—it is here still peculiarly apt.

The problem arises because a switch from one kind of poetry to another is taking place. Broadly speaking, the only kind of poetry that had previously been taken seriously was that which was oriented to revealed religion. Only it could lay claim to truth. Other poetry was for the most part decorative, encomiastic, or frankly jocose, and a drinking song was a drinking song. One recognized the conventions and knew where one stood. But here was a kind of verse that seemed to urge sensuality in the name of truth and morality. That it must be understood to speak in figure is the point of Hagedorn's sermon to the Encratites. He seems to have had little hope that he would be understood:

> Nie ist der Einfalt Urtheil schwächer,
> Als wanns auf Schriftverfasser geht.

Though separate, art and life are not unconnected: art reflects an ideal attitude toward life; it is life in figure. "An die heutigen Encratiten" is an attempt to find a standing place for this new function of poetry.

Love in the rococo understanding is not fundamentally different from wine. It too has the capacity to increase our humanity. It is neither purely sensual nor purely spiritual, but a symbiosis of both. What both love and wine signify for Hagedorn is well summed up in the first stanza of "Doris und der Wein":

O Anblick, der mich fröhlich macht!
Mein Weinstock reift und Doris lacht,
Und, mir zur Anmuth, wachsen beyde.
Ergetzt der Wein ein menschlich Herz,
So ist auch seltner Schönen Scherz
Der wahren Menschlichkeit ein Grund vollkommner
    Freude.

                        [3, 136]

"Scherz," for the rococo poet the most fitting rhyme with
"Herz," has overtones we may not catch. It is the term associated with easy social graces and erotic play as well as with
this very type of poetry, whose Muse is the "musa iocosa."
Love is jest for the rococo, not torrid, all-consuming, enslav-
ing passion, and like wine it helps us fulfill our "true humanity." Love is the sister of Joy, the "goddess of noble hearts."
Joy, "Freude," is for Hagedorn a kind of calm, enduring
rapture, akin to Shaftesbury's "enthusiasm." He addresses it
in one of his most familiar and most successful lyrics:

Muntre Schwester süsser Liebe!
Himmelskind!
Kraft der Seelen! Halbes Leben!
Ach! was kann das Glück uns geben,
Wenn man dich nicht auch gewinnt?
                  [3, 41]

Such are the things "noble souls call pleasure" and one must
concede that the poet was justified in warning the Encratites
not to confuse them with "mean joys."

Hagedorn's best nature poems are "Der May" (3, 146)
and "Der Morgen" (3, 164). "Der May" has the infectious
rhythm of a country dance and captures wonderfully the
sense of exhilaration that comes over us in the spring.
Rhythm is all; ideational content is reduced to a bare minimum; fleeting conventional images of spring—birds, sheep
and shepherd, zephyrs, flowers, gurgling streams, dancing
peasants—make up the content.

Der Nachtigall reizende Lieder
Ertönen und locken schon wieder

Die fröhlichen Stunden ins Jahr.
Nun singet die steigende Lerche,
Nun klappern die reisenden Störche,
Nun schwatzet der gauckelnde Staar.

There is no real developmental line. Image does not flow out
of image; the method of composition is purely additive. Had
Zesen written these charming verses, which would be easily
imaginable, he would have placed them among his "dance
poems," probably for bagpipe accompaniment.

"Der Morgen" is Hagedorn's best lyric. Meter and
strophic structure both correspond exactly to Goethe's (or to
Goethe-Lenz's) Sesenheim morningsong "Erwache, Frieder-
ike, Vertreib die Nacht." The alternation between the three-
beat and two-beat lines is mimetic (compare "An den verlohrenen Schlaf"), the former being expressive of the invitation
to join in the festival of nature, the latter of acceptance. An
occasional trace of baroque imagery is still present, as in the
kenning "Der Hügel weisse Bürde" for a flock of sheep, but
with typical explicitness this is "translated" in the next line as
"Der Schafe Zucht." As in "Der May" there is no development. Stanzas 2, 3, and 4 could come in any order, and only
the first and last two stanzas have to stand in the order given.
Each is a discrete unit, and no sentence is longer than half a
stanza. The effect is that of a series of short, separate impulses or rhythmic shocks, not of one continuous breath of
exaltation as in "Maifest" ("Wie herrlich leuchtet. . ."), which
is also composed on the principle of invitation and answer.
The last two stanzas (6 and 7) turn to an erotic theme. Stanza
6 is couched in typically rococo terms of shelter and cosy
isolation from the world:[10]

Lass uns die Thäler suchen,
　Geliebtes Kind,
Wo wir von Berg und Büschen
　Umschlossen sind!

The final stanza has at least a hint of the fervency of "Maifest" and, like Goethe's lyric, parallels the beloved and the
spring morning:

Erkenne dich im Bilde
  Von jener Flur!
Sey stets, wie diess Gefilde,
  Schön durch Natur;
Erwünschter als der Morgen,
  Hold wie sein Strahl;
So frey von Stolz und Sorgen
  Wie dieses Thal!

To be sure, this is still a long way from "So liebt die Lerche Gesang und Luft, . . . Wie ich dich liebe Mit warmen Blut." Hagedorn shows his Phyllis a picture of nature and says, "Be like this!" Goethe fuses self, nature, and "Mädchen" into one, as the expression of a love that is both heavenly and earthly. The rococo poet retains his distance—man and nature remain finally separate, reflect each other though they may.

His *Moralische Gedichte* (first edition, 1750; augmented, 1753) Hagedorn valued more highly than his fables, tales, and songs. Of these longish reflective poems the best is "Horaz" (1751), which contains 318 lines in *vers communs*, i.e., rhymed couplets in iambic pentameter, the measure favored by Pope. And in no respect is Hagedorn more akin to Pope—an unsuccessful paraphrase of whose "Universal Prayer" opens the collection—than in his attempt to form his life, or at least his poetic ethos, on the example and art of Horace. Hagedorn's *imitatio Horati* is earnest and fervent, and in this conversation with his poetic alter ego we probably come closer to knowing Hagedorn plain than in any other work. At the same time, it is the poem in which his neoclassicism reaches a high-water mark.

Just what "Horaz" is "about" is not immediately easy to state. It is about how to lead a fruitful and contented life. It is also about those specious antivalues we spend so much time and energy fending off. It is about the "science" of happiness,

about learning to know oneself, about the attainment of the
golden mean and the role of poets and poetry in society.
These are all Horatian themes, and to a large degree the
poem itself is a mosaic of passages from the Roman poet. It is
not, however, an "imitation" of Horace in the sense that "Der
Schwätzer" (*Werke* 1, 89) is, where Hagedorn transfers "Ibam
forte via Sacra" (*Satires* 1, 9), the famous account of the poet's
encounter with a bore, into local terms and contemporary
personalities. Rather it is a meditative identification with
Horace and his philosophy of life in the form of a conversation or *sermo*. Horace is for Hagedorn above all the poet-phi-
losopher who lived what he taught, the great moralist who
follows his own precepts. He addresses him with friendly but
respectful intimacy:

> Horaz, mein Freund, mein Lehrer, mein Begleiter,
> Wir gehn aufs Land. Die Tage sind schon heiter . . .

Hagedorn-Horace, alter egos, kindred spirits across the
ages—this is the guiding image of the poem.

Of the joys valued equally by Horace and Hagedorn,
none ranks higher than the cultivation of the private life of
the soul in country solitude. To be given back to one's self is
the highest boon we can attain and the goal of Horatian "philosophy." Despite first appearances, such a goal is not antiso-
cial, for out of the depths of self and self-knowledge comes
our best contribution to society. It gradually becomes evident
that discovery of self and the rewards of this discovery for
ourselves and our fellow man is the deeper theme of "Horaz"
and its structuring principle. The poem progresses from outward to inward, then outward again from the depths of inwardness. It is the recovery of the "lost sleep" of selfhood
that Hagedorn celebrates here.

We may divide the work into three main parts, the first
of 72 lines, the second of 194, the last of 52. The first section
establishes the situation, the anticipation of the pleasures of
rural retirement, so appealing to minds of the Horatian persuasion, who are sentimental in Schiller's sense. The motif of

holding the vulgar at arm's length (*odi profanum*) is introduced at once and sets the tone of exclusivity—only those endowed with "wit" can *feel*. "Spring and wit *together*" are the source of happiness for those of true sensibility:

> Des Daseyns Trost, das Recht vergnügt zu seyn,
> Der Kenner Glück macht Lenz und Witz gemein.
> Ja, auch der Witz! Die Einfalt kann nicht sehen;
> Ihr lachen nicht die Thäler und die Höhen.
>
> [lines 11–14]

Horace's Sabine farm is evoked with longing as the place where one can attain "Vergessenheit der Mühe" (*O rus, quando ego te aspiciam?*). Counterexamples in the manner of Pope's "Epistles" are interlarded: the miser who remains a slave to his fears even in rural haunts, the gourmand who goes to his country estate only to gorge himself, and so on. The end of this section then identifies, at least on the plane of values, the modern poet and the ancient:

> Du bist es werth, der Landlust Freund zu seyn.
> Horaz, mit dir hab ich den Trieb gemein.
> Uneingedenk der Stadt und ihrer Sorgen,
> Empfind ich hier die Freyheit und den Morgen.
> Wir bleiben hier, nun uns kein Schwätzer trennt,
> Und Harvesthud ist heute mein Tarent.
>
> [lines 67–72]

The long middle section is in praise of rural solitude and that calm which gives us back to ourselves, again with counterexamples of those incapable of appreciating such joys because they are sworn to the specious dignities of office and caught up in the competition for status, as desperate then as now. These are for Hagedorn as for Pope the "fools" (in Pope, usually "Fools!") we constantly encounter in their verse:

> Ein Thor eilt stets auf neue Wirbel los:
> Ein Weiser ist, auch in der Stille, gross.
> Ein Thor bedarf der Ämter und Geschäfte:
> Der Wand-Uhr gleich, giebt das Gewicht ihm Kräfte:

> Sonst kaum bemerkt, von eignen Trieben leer,
> Blieb er ein Thor; durch Würden wird er mehr.
>
> [lines 95–100]

The fool is the man who has not found his center. Perhaps he is also the man who has none.

In contrast, in lines 125–64 Hagedorn praises the life of the independent yeoman farmer, who lives entirely from what is *his*. The Horatian source is "Beatus ille" (*Epodes* 2). Horace himself is the model of such a man, and the life he depicts in "Hoc erat in votis" (*Satires* 2, 6) is the prototype of this middle section as a whole. The "simple" life depicted here must seem to us of the twentieth century almost one of luxury, but possession of things—vineyard, flocks, fish pond—may be primarily meant as a metaphor for possession of self.

Now follows a passage in which Hagedorn identifies himself with his master and model in the most inward way, sharing in his pride in humble origins, riding with him on muleback to Tarentum, eating with him his chick peas and greens, reclining at his board through the summer night to enjoy wine and good talk. An air of blessed contentment pervades this passage. The secret of such contentment is inward freedom and self-possession, which is the fruit of wisdom. Horace is free because he is wise:

> So giebt und nährt nur die Zufriedenheit
> Dein schönstes Glück, das täglich dich erfreut,
> Der Freyheit Frucht, die nur den Weisen rühret,
> Der herrschen kann, und würdig sich regieret.
> Was in der Welt ist von so hohem Wehrt,
> Als Freyheit ist, die jede Lust vermehret?
>
> [lines 233–38]

Horace is the opposite of all those poor slaves to wealth, greed, office, and appetite who constitute the foil against which he is seen. Because his values are just—so Hagedorn implies—the just gods could fulfill his profoundest desire: *Hoc erat in votis* . . . But Horace has always been happy, fundamentally, not merely since he acquired his Sabine farm, because he always lived from the center of his selfhood, though bound like all of us by time, circumstances, and society.

The way inward has now been shown; the last section is devoted to the way outward, that is, to the gift of self to one's fellow man. "Thou art content and teachest us contentment":

> Du bist vergnügt, und lehrest das Vergnügen,
> Wie Dichter thun, die Geiz und Gram besiegen:
> . . . .
> Der Welt zur Lust, zum Dienst und
>   Unterrichte,
> Sinnt er [der Dichter] auf nichts, als ewige
>   Gedichte.
>
> [lines 267 ff.]

The poet's task is the education of the young through inculcation of the harmony of language—a reflection on the psychological level of the poet's own inner harmony and on that of literary history of Hagedorn's neoclassical aesthetics: the young must learn "Im Ausdruck sich vom Pöbel zu entfernen." The poet's task is the ennoblement of the heart and mind, yes, even the elevation of the race to true humanity:

> Dann giebt er auch dem Herzen die Gestalt,
> Durch treuen Rath, durch freundliche Gewalt.
> Die Rauhigkeit der Sitten, die verwildern,
> Den Neid, den Zorn weiss seine Kunst zu mildern.
>
> [lines 285–88]

The poet is a sage whose example is for all times, his own and those to come. Art and life are intimately connected.

The round is now complete: by remaining true to the discovery of his inmost self the poet can lead others to a similar discovery through his art and thus raise the whole level of society. This ideal of the self-aware individual integrated into a harmonious whole through the medium of art is certainly closely akin to, if not identical with, the didactic ideal of German classicism and its equation of aesthetic and moral rebirth. With its implication of an almost unbelievably optimistic faith both in the nature of man and the power of suasion through the word, it is a worthy theme for the poet of the Enlightenment. We should note, however, that the exclusivity stressed at the beginning of the poem is never really abandoned, despite the assertion that

> Ein Dichter lehrt *das menschliche Geschlecht*
> Der Tugend Reiz und ihrer Thaten Recht.

The more specific examples of those who have been ennobled by the poetry of Horace are Petrarch (verses 297 f.) and the great Romans who were his patrons (verses 307 f.). The "Pöbel" is still kept at a distance. Does Hagedorn envision a society in which there will be no more "Pöbel"? The poem does not answer this question.

And what after all is the end of Horatian wisdom? Is it not something very close to Stoic resignation? Hagedorn's summary in lines 299–302 makes it sound so:

> Dein weiser Rath lehrt Vorurtheile hassen,
> Erhellt den Witz, und macht das Herz gelassen.
> Zufriedenheit besänftigt unsern Muth,
> Und sie allein nennt jede Fügung gut.

The distance between the Christian ethos of the Baroque and the refined Epicureanism of the Enlightenment can be measured in terms like these too. The peace that passeth understanding has become contentment with one's earthly lot.

Though the third book of the *Oden und Lieder* is dedicated to Anacreon, Hagedorn is no anacreontic poet in the narrower sense of the term, or at least he is so only very occasionally. On the contrary, he soon became disgusted with what he considered to be the shallow frivolity of his anacreontic contemporaries and was relieved when, in 1751, he thought he saw signs that this mode had run its course. Toward the end of his life he even forswore all poetry of wine and kisses out of repugnance for the wantonness and insipidity of those who produced endless verses in the name of Anacreon.[11] His few poems in this vein have a certain depth that sets them off from the production of a Gleim, the anacreontic poet par excellence. An example is "Der Traum" (3, 85), written in rhymeless iambic trimeter, a typical meter of this genre, and replete with half-bare bosoms, roses, myrtles, zephyrs, gently swaying treetops and rustling bushes, Amor, the isle of Cythera, etc.—in short, a representative catalogue of anacreontic motifs. But the theme, which is the connection between the dream of art and life, is not unserious. The fiction is that the poet falls asleep in a garden where "drey holde Schönen" are decking their half-glimpsed bosoms with flowers. Phantasus transports him to Cythera. The garden becomes the isle of Venus and the three maidens the three Graces with Amor in their train. This "voyage à Cythère" is profoundly satisfying—the syntax (as well as the vowelling, the alliteration, and the numerous melting liquids) reflects oneness of landscape, love, joy, and youthfulness:

> Wie manches Feld von Rosen,
> Wie mancher Busch von Myrthen
> War hier der Venus heilig!
> Der Göttin sanfter Freuden,
> Der Freuden voller Liebe,
> Der Liebe voller Jugend.

Amor challenges the sleeper—a second Paris—to say which of the three Graces shall be given preference, but at this moment the most beautiful of the three girls playing in the garden awakens him, and dream and waking, art and life, become one. If the dream of art was reality transfigured, waking reality is now transfigured by art. As in a declaredly moral poem like "Horaz," art and life interact.

When we turn to Johann Wilhelm Ludwig Gleim (1719–1803),[12] who exemplifies the anacreontic poets in a paradigmatic way, we seem to find a poet in whom lack of seriousness is raised to a principle. That this appearance is to some degree deceiving we shall see in the sequel. What must seem to us the general vapidity of Gleim's immense production, especially of his anacreontic verse, makes it difficult for a modern literary historian to judge him fairly. Yet he made a very considerable impression on his own time. He was admired by no less men than Lessing and Herder and emulated by others whose spiritual depth exceeded his own. Gleim is a pronouncedly formal talent, a Felix Krull of the lyric, who slips easily into one role after another and plays each with considerable virtuosity. There is, however, a connecting element among these roles, which are, as it were, different aspects or masks of the same character. Since the roles assumed were new, new that is for German poetry, which, we must not forget, was still trying to catch up with the rest of European literature, Gleim's work has genuine historical importance.

The first role assumed by Gleim was that of the anacreontic singer. We cannot unfold here the long and fairly complicated story of the influence of "Anacreon" and the Greek Anthology on European literature, a story that has recently been told in detail by Herbert Zeman[13] and treated as an aspect of the "musa iocosa" by Heinz Schlaffer. It must suffice to say that since the publication by Henri Estienne (Henricus Stephanus) in 1554 of sixty-four Greek lyrics (with Latin translations of thirty-one) supposedly by Anacreon of Teos but actually much later imitations in his manner—the so-called anacreonteia—there has hardly been a European literature without its quota of anacreontic writers. The vogue lasted well into the nineteenth century. The French were the first to transpose "Anacreon" into their own tongue, the poets of the Pléiade being the pathfinders, particularly Ronsard and Remy Belleau. The German humanists who followed this mode—Caspar Barth, Michael Haslob, Paul Fleming in his *Suavia*, and others—wrote in neo-Latin. The poets of the Baroque proper stood at something of a loss when confronted with "Anacreon." The baroque manner was not favorable to the *genus medium*, to which the mode properly belongs. Thus Zesen, though proud of being the first to write anacreontica in German and though keeping the meter and the thematic material of the originals, indulges in his usual vocalic playfulness to such an extent that his products are hard to recognize as belonging to the mode. Schirmer, following Zesen, also produced anacreontica. But it was not to their seventeenth-century predecessors that the anacreontic poets of the eighteenth century looked back when the mode burst into flower in the first half of the period. It was rather a new beginning based on Stephanus and guided by Madame Dacier's highly influential French prose translation and commentary (third edition, 1716).

A decisive impulse came from Gottsched, who in 1733 published a polished translation of six anacreontic odes in rhymeless three-beat iambics and four-beat trochees. It was Gottsched who established the anacreontic style in German. A good example of his art is:

ÜBER DIE ROSE

Lasst uns doch Cupidens Rosen
Mit des Bacchus Lust vermischen.
Lasst uns doch mit Rosenkränzen
Unsre muntre Scheitel krönen,
Und bey zartem Lachen trinken.
Rose! Königin der Blumen!
Rose! Liebling aller Götter,
Rose! die Cytherens Knabe,
Mit den Charitinnen tanzend,
Selbst auf schöner Stirne träget.
Kröne mich denn, lieber Bacchus!
So will ich dein Lob besingen,
Und mit einer schönen Dirne,
In den besten Rosenkränzen,
Deinen Festtag tanzend ehren.[14]

Wine, roses, erotic play, Aphrodite (Cythera), Bacchus, Cupid ("Cytherens Knabe"), the Graces ("Charitinnen"), song, dance, tender laughter, and ritualistic gestures (crowning with flowers) are all typical Anacreontic motifs, which, together with a dozen or so others (see Hagedorn's "Traum"), constitute the tirelessly reiterated stock in trade of this kind of verse. The aim is the celebration of grace, of life in figure, as an aesthetic attitude, as Hagedorn, who perhaps saw more deeply into the meaning of such "Tändeleien" than most of his fellow poets, tried to explain to the "Encratites." Like every genre, jesting erotic poetry is tied to and promulgates a certain philosophy of life or, as we would say today, life-style. The life-style this genre promulgates (I am following Heinz Schlaffer) jestingly contravenes accepted social conventions, but that does not mean that it is merely play—it implies serious social criticism. In its eighteenth-century reincarnation, it criticizes the deadly earnestness of the Enlightenment, hidebound pietistic morality, and the work ethic of the bourgeoisie and tries to show us another way of living. The anacreontic poets are a typical manifestation of eighteenth-century "paganism"; they are seriously concerned, though the conventions of the genre forbid seriousness of *tone*, with conveying a eudaemonistic, this-worldly view of life. "Freut euch des Lebens, weil noch das Lämpchen glüht" is spoken from the heart of the rococo. Such sincere eudaemonism would have been impossible in the Baroque, whose true values always lie beyond the earthly realm.

Alfred Anger, in trying to account for the sudden rise of anacreontic poetry in the 1740s, speaks of the emergence of a new sense of life, which in true premodern fashion casts about for models and predecessors it could imitate and reform in its own image.[15] This new sense of life was pagan, or strove to be. (We have seen Hagedorn taking Horace as his supreme guide with no hint of Christianity.) It was determined to see this world as a positive value and not to reject its pleasures for the sake of a heavenly reward. "Anacreon" fitted the needs of this new sense of life excellently. The rejection of the baroque stylistic ideal of *bene dicere, hoc est ornate dicere*, which had of course taken place earlier in accord with the aesthetics of neoclassicism, was also, Anger suggests, a contributing factor (*Forschungsbericht*, pp. 621 f.). The natural simplicity of style and content found, or presumably found, in "Anacreon" was a strong attraction.

The real, though not directly stated, problem was, as previously indicated in the discussion of Hagedorn, to find a

95

standing place for a poetry that reflected this new and yet ancient attitude toward life. The solution of the anacreontic poets was to produce a kind of poetry that did not have to be taken seriously on the literal level, but which nonetheless embodied fundamentally serious convictions. When attacked, they reverted to ancient topos about singing of wine and drinking water: who would be so stupid as to judge a poet's life by his work? The fictive "Doris" who writes the foreword to the reader in the second part of Gleim's *Versuch in scherzhaften Liedern* (1745) warns us:

> Schliesst niemals aus den Schriften der Dichter auf die Sitten derselben. Ihr werdet euch betriegen; denn sie schreiben nur, ihren Witz zu zeigen, und solten sie auch dadurch ihre Tugend in Verdacht setzen. Sie characterisiern sich nicht, wie sie sind, sondern wie es die Art der Gedichte erfordert. . . . (Anger, p. 71)

That is, it is all a matter of "decorum" and "Gattungszwang." The real question, however, is: Why did *these* poets choose a convention that demanded precisely *this* kind of decorum? Speaking, if he ever spoke thus, in his proper person, Gleim's answer is implied in "An Herrn***":

> Ich trink, ich lieb, ich lache,
> Indem sich Herrenhuter
> Zu Tode beten.
> Ich trink, ich lieb, ich lache,
> Ich singe frohe Lieder,
> Wann Priester schimpfen.
> > [Anger, p. 117]

Drinking, laughing, and loving are of course metaphors, but they are also expressive of an attitude that is more than a mere exercise in stylistics. It is at best a half-truth to say that rococo poetry represents the "aesthetic liberation of the poetical from the bonds of philosophy and morals."[16] Such liberation is not really possible; there is no such thing as poetry (or any other art) that does not imply, even advocate, a moral-philosophical attitude. That this new direction in poetry indicated a changed stance toward certain aspects of the Enlightenment—its unrelenting insistence on virtue and reason, for example—and even more a changed stance toward positive religion is undeniable, but the new stance had its own moral and philosophical implications.

The first part of the *Versuch in scherzhaften Liedern* was published anonymously in Berlin in 1744. A second part appeared in 1745. The first part bears the motto: "Nos haec nouimus esse nihil" (We realize these are nothings—Martial), the second Voltaire's often quoted lines:

> Ah! que j'aime ces vers badins,
> Ces riens naifs & pleins de grace.

A kind of continuation was published in Halberstadt in 1749, with Amsterdam as the fictitious place of publication. The poems in this third part are rhymed, except for one; those in the first two parts, except for thirteen, are unrhymed. Before bringing out original poems in Anacreon's manner, Gleim had tried his hand, in collaboration with his friend Uz, at translating Greek anacreontic verse.

Wherever we open the *Scherzhafte Lieder* the impression is the same: easy metrical patterns repeated time and again, a meager stock of motifs varied over and over, a coy air of erotic playfulness, an insistence on the enjoyment of the moment, and a denial of all problems: the ancient ethos of jesting erotic poetry and its "Weltentwurf" (Schlaffer). To work within these narrow limits required very considerable skill. The poet had to be able to lend his verse aural and rhythmical attractiveness to balance its vacuous content. The poverty of his themes drove him to strive for an enlivening *pointe* or sometimes even to develop a conceit.[17] Even so, the final effect on the present-day reader is inevitably the same as that on the dove of Venus who brings Gleim a message from a fellow poet:

> Ich sitz auf seiner Leyer
> Und horchend schlaf ich ein!
>   [Quoted after Pick, "Studien," p. 91]

97

What the collection is about is clearly stated in the opening programmatic poem "Anakreon," which sets tone and theme:

> Anakreon, mein Lehrer,
> Singt nur von Wein und Liebe;
> Er salbt den Bart mit Salben,
> Und singt von Wein und Liebe;
> 5   Er krönt sein Haupt mit Rosen,
> Und singt von Wein und Liebe;
> Er paaret sich im Garten,
> Und singt von Wein und Liebe;
> Er wird beim Trunk ein König,
> 10 Und singt von Wein und Liebe;
> Er spielt mit seinen Göttern,
> Er lacht mit seinen Freunden,
> Vertreibt sich Gram und Sorgen,
> Verschmäht den reichen Pöbel,
> 15 Verwirft das Lob der Helden,
> Und singt von Wein und Liebe;
> Soll denn sein treuer Schüler
> Von Hass und Wasser singen?
> [Anger, p. 5]

This is a very skillfully constructed poem, and its structure is typical of this collection. Numerous short clauses arranged paratactically give the impression of simplicity, but these are varied by light interior cola (pauses) in a way that forestalls monotonous singsong. For example:

> Er salbt den Bart : mit Salben,
> Und singt : von Wein und Liebe;

Or:

> Vertreibt sich : Gram und Sorgen,
> Verschmäht : den reichen Pöbel . . .

Rhymelessness, which still had the appeal of novelty in German, indicates the "ancient" quality, and the meter, though not strictly anacreontic (ĕgŏ nēgŏ Flōrŭs ēssĕ), is probably meant to serve the same end. Ritualistic gestures (anointing the beard, crowning with roses) or characterizing ones (sporting with the gods, laughing with friends) are paired with the formula that expresses the essence of anacreontic poetry: "Und singt von Wein und Liebe," which is thus given weight as the epitome of a whole attitude. A playfully parodistic *furor poeticus* is built up in lines 11–16, which vary the pattern of lines 1–10. It is emphasized by double and triple anaphora (two "er's" and three "ver-'s") before the refrain is allowed to enter again. (Gleim uses this little trick—imitated from the anakreonteia—often.) Finally, there is the *pointe* with which the poem ends, making all that precedes a pseudo-argument for the stance promulgated by the collection as a whole.

What is bracketed out of this kind of verse as well as what is included is clearly and accurately stated in "Der Wille":

>   Ich will nicht weinen,
>   Ich will nicht schelten,
>   Ich will nicht klagen,
>   Ich will nicht murren,
> 5   Ich will nicht trotzen,
>   Ich will nicht trauren.
>   Ich will nur küssen,
>   Ich will nur trinken,
>   Ich will nur tanzen,
> 10   Und bei dem Tanzen
>   Will ich nur lachen,
>   Und bei dem Trinken
>   Will ich nur scherzen,
>   Und bei dem Küssen
> 15   Will ich nur spielen;
>   Und diesen Willen
>   Hat auch mein Mädchen.
>   [Anger, p. 112]

Again it is the simple but sophisticated structural elegance that charms: six verses state what the poet does not want, three what he does. Beginning with verse 10, these three desiderata are combined in reverse order with three others. The original ones now become substantives, the new ones are expressed as verbs (as were the first three originally), but all are infinitives. At the same time the "Ich will" of the first nine lines is converted (by the natural exigencies of German grammar) into "Will ich." Verses 10–15 balance 1–6, each group expressing wishes, the first negative, the second positive. The poem closes with the usual *pointe*, a knowing smile of triumph over any who may disapprove of such anacreontic giddiness. The numerical relationships (6–3–6–2) are clear and pleasing, but not overly obvious. Nothing, we may feel, has been "said," but can we deny that an attitude has been elegantly conveyed?

One highly successful application of an anacreontic motif in a typical anacreontic situation poem is "Bacchus und Cithere":

> Soll ich trinken oder küssen?
> Hier winkt Bacchus, dort Cithere.
> Beide winken, beide lächeln.
> Bachus mit gesetzten Mienen,
> 5 Und Cithere mit verliebten.
> Bacchus zeigt mir seine Reben,
> Aber seht nur, dort im Schatten,
> Dort im Schatten, unter Reben,
> Liegt ein Mädchen lang gestrekket!
> 10 Seht, es schläft, es lächelt schlafend,
> Und es lächelte Cithere
> Nicht so reitzend, als sie winkte.
> O wie süss mag es nicht schlummern!
> O wie reitzend liegt das Mädchen!
> 15 Um den weissen regen Busen,
> Hangen schwarze reife Trauben,
> Und es glänzen um den Lokken,
> Um den Rabenschwarzen Lokken,
> Goldne Blumen in den Schatten.
> 20 Weingott, winke nur nicht länger;
> Denn ich muss erst, bei dem Mädchen,
> Unter deinen Trauben schlummern.
>
> [Anger, p. 100]

Structurally, as Wolfgang Kayser has pointed out, this poem relies for its effects largely on the handling of the caesuras according to the principles of parallelism, correspondence, and repetition.[18] The caesuras are strongly marked:

> Soll ich trinken | oder küssen?
> Hier winkt Bacchus, dort Cithere.
> Beide winken, beide lächeln.

In verses 4–5, whole lines forming breaks are used according to the same principles:

> "Bacchus mit gestzten Mienen,
> Und Cithere mit verliebten."

Further examples are found in lines 8, 13–14, and 17–18. The breaks of course reflect the theme of the poem: they are mimetic. The strong emphasis on the rhythmical element and a highly conscious feeling for the effects of the cola constitute, Kayser suggests, the gain that German verse derived from lack of rhyme, i.e., such measures made up for rhymelessness. It would need more investigation to say with certainty whether this is not an overstatement in regard to German verse as a whole—the principles of parallelism, correspondence, and repetition had naturally been widely used before in rhymed verse—but it is undoubtedly true that Gleim's masterly use of cola is one of his chief means of achieving highly poetic effects, and certainly rhymelessness is not felt here as a lack.

Though technically very skillful, even genial, poverty of content and a mania for self-imitation, both marks of his purely formal talent, make Gleim finally a bore. Not infrequently he is also lamentably lacking in taste. Heavy-handedness in airy form is especially disturbing, as in these verses:

AN DEN TOD

> Tod, kannst du dich auch verlieben?
> Warum holst du denn mein Mädchen?
> Kannst du nicht die Mutter holen?

Denn sie sieht dir doch noch ähnlich.
Frische rosenrote Wangen,
Die mein Wunsch so schön gefärbet,
Blühen nicht für blasse Knochen,
Blühen nicht für deine Lippen.
Tod, was willst du mit dem Mädchen?
Mit den Zähnen ohne Lippen
Kannst du es ia doch nicht küssen.

[Anger, p. 27]

Schlaffer (p. 97) cites this poem as an example of the "total eroticization of all life, indeed, even of death" characteristic of the genre, and the story is told by Gleim himself that, when he read "An den Tod" to Ewald von Kleist, who was convalescing from a dueling wound, the latter laughed so hard that his wound reopened.[19] A case of *de gustibus*, no doubt. In any event, others besides Gleim seem to have found such a gruesome *pointe* quite compatible with the tone of the *Scherzhafte Lieder*. This too was a jest. The genre subjugates all that it touches to its own laws.

It goes without saying that the *Scherzhafte Lieder* contain no love poetry with a hint of real passion or even lust—anything approaching what we find in Günther or Hofmanswaldau would contravene the anacreontic mode. Talk of kisses and swelling bosoms, a slightly sultry voyeurism, this is as far as one goes. Actual experience does not enter as such. That too, since it would involve one in time and through time in true human situations, lies outside the realm of jesting erotic poetry, which in fact introduced the convention of Arcadia to avoid this very problem.[20] All that is conveyed is an attitude, an Epicureanism that takes no thought of the morrow, has no past and only a formal present. The isle of Cythera lies outside of time.

The next role assumed by Gleim was that of the balladeer. Here too he broke new ground, becoming with his three "Romanzen" (1756) one of the founders of the German art ballad as with his *Scherzhafte Lieder* he had become the father of the anacreontic mode.[21] If anacreontic poetry stands outside of time, the ballad has time as its constitutive element. That Gleim was capable of handling both genres shows that his poetic limits were not as narrow as one might think.

Gleim's point of departure for his ballads was the so-called "Bänkelsang," a pop art form which typically treated a blood-curdling or sadly touching event in a sensational manner. It had developed from "Zeitungssingen" or singing out the news in crude verse for the semiliterate. (In the twentieth century Wedekind and Brecht still used Bänkelsang effectively.) In France the folk ballad had already been raised to a sophisticated level by François-Auguste Moncrif (died 1770), reader to the Queen and member of the Academy, and it is Moncrif's *romance* "Les constantes amours d'Alix et d'Alexis" that forms the direct model for Gleim's best-known ballad "Marianne" or, to give it its full and correct title:

> TRAURIGE UND BETRÜBTE FOLGEN DER SCHÄND-LICHEN EIFERSUCHT, wie auch Heilsamer Unterricht, dass Eltern, die ihre Kinder lieben, sie zu keiner Hey-rath zwingen, sondern ihnen ihren freyen Willen lassen sollen; enthalten, in der Geschichte Herrn Isaac Veltens, der sich am ll.ten Apprill 1756, zu Berlin eigenhändig umgebracht, nachdem er seine getreue Ehegattin Marianne und derselben unschuldigen Lieb-haber jämmerlich ermordet. (Stenzel, p. 51)

The moralizing introductory prose passage is typical, in fact almost *de rigueur*, for Bänkelsang. Moncrif had stressed that the *romance* demanded a touching theme and a naive style. It must not fall into the error of adopting an elevated odic tone. Preromanticism is in the air (Moncrif is the French Percy) and one is willing to learn from "das Volk." Naïveté is the connecting link between Gleim's anacreontic verse and the Romanzen; indeed, it is the unchanging element in all his work and the key to the understanding of his poetic endeavors.

Today, one is no doubt safe in saying, most of us can read Gleim's "Marianne" only in the spirit of camp. The question is, did Gleim also regard it in this light? Moncrif

103

wanted to revive an appreciation of popular poetry. This was not Gleim's aim. Rather, he seems to have delighted in the mask itself. A contemporary, Moses Mendelssohn, in reviewing the Romanzen, wrote: "Der Ton, welcher in diesen kleinen Gedichten herrschet, ist ein abentheuerliches Wunderbare, mit einer possierlichen Traurigkeit erzählt,"[22] and this, Kayser points out, seems to have been the response of most of Gleim's first readers: they regarded the Romanzen as parodies. It has also been the judgment of most later critics. It is not the judgment of Kayser himself, however, who insists (*Ballade*, pp. 68, 72) that "Marianne" is meant seriously. Müller-Seidel, on the other hand, is convinced that Gleim's stance is that of the comic poet wittily playing with the element of naïveté: "Das Naive wird damit zum Darstellungsmittel, aber die Darstellung ist nicht mehr naiv" (*Wege zum Gedicht* 2, 28). A brief look at the other two ballads in the collection ("Romanze" and "Ballade" were interchangeable terms in the eighteenth century) may influence the way we regard "Marianne," whether as conscious camp or as a seriously meant effort to move the emotions.

The first ballad in chronological order—composed in 1745–46, some ten years before "Marianne"—is "Der neue Jonas," called in the slightly revised later version "Wundervolle doch Wahrhafte Abentheuer Herrn Schout by Nachts [Konteradmiral], Cornelius van der Tyt, vornehmen Bürgers und Gastwirths im Wallfisch zu Hamburg, wie er solche seinen Gästen selbst erzählet. Aus seiner Holländischen Mundart in hochdeutsche Reime übersetzt" (Stenzel, p. 65). It is a comic ballad in an extravagantly fantastic vein sung in a tripping three-beat measure with a closing four-beat couplet. We need not rehearse the story here. Suffice it to say that it concerns the miraculous escape of a Dutch sailor and his Persian bride from Oriental captivity through the agency of a friendly whale which swallows them and finally casts them ashore at Amsterdam. The influence of Moncrif is not detectable in this poem, which Falk calls "die erste deutsche Kunstballade" ("Anfänge," p. 677). But there is another influence: in a letter to Uz on March 12, 1746, in which he enclosed a

copy of "Der neue Jonas," Gleim refers to it as a "Mordgeschichte." Since, as Falk points out, there is no murder in the
tale, Gleim can only be referring to the style of the
Bänkelsang or Moritat, familiar to all of us through Brecht. It
seems probable that Gleim was attracted to the form by the
freedom offered by the mask, the opportunity to indulge the
pure play of fantasy; again a kind of revolt against rationalistic restraint.

The second ballad in the collection is elaborately entitled
after the manner of the Bänkelsang "Damons und Ismenens
zärtliche und getreue Liebe, getrennet durch einen Zwey-
kampf, in welchem Herr Damon von seinem Nebenbuhler
am 20ten August 1755 auf Auerbachs Hofe zu Leipzig mit
einem grossen Streit-Degen durchs Herz gestochen wurde,
wovon er seinen Geist jämmerlich aufgeben müssen, zum
Trost der herzlich betrübten Ismene gesungen" (Stenzel, p.
61). The title is sufficient indication that we are dealing with
a sentimental ballad, and the opening stanza is confirmation
enough:

> Ach Damon, ach Ismene!
> Mein Herz ist weich!
> Ach welche heisse Thräne,
> Wein ich um euch!
> Von deiner Abentheuer,
> Du schöne Braut!
> Sing ich, in meine Leyer,
> Und weine laut!

But is it *seriously* sentimental? Is this not rather *"possierliche
Traurigkeit"*? The naive turn at the end, where the singer,
after having told of the cruel death of Damon and the bitter
remorse of his killer (who is haunted by the "winselndes
Gethöne" of Damon's ghost), invites Ismene to come out of
mourning and embrace *him*, the singer, is definitely humorous, that is, it makes fun of the singer himself and his ulterior
motives:

> Verzehrt von deinem Jammer,
> Gehüllt in Flor,

> Bleibst du auf deiner Cammer,
>   Ach komm hervor!
> Komm wieder an die Sonne
>   Wie gern bin ich:
> Dein Labsal, deine Wonne,
>   Komm küsse mich!

In "Der neue Jonas," then, fantasy for its own sake but indulged with tongue in cheek; in "Damon und Ismene," extravagant sentimentality toward which the poet himself (as distinct from the persona of his poem) assumes an air of detached amusement. Should we also read "Marianne" in this light? The wild coincidence that brings about the recognition of the lovers and, even more, the burlesque nature of the ending would seem to speak for categorizing the ballad as parody.

Marianne, whose heart is set on Leander, is tricked by her parents into marrying the much older and richer Herr Velten, for whom she has a distinct antipathy. Feeling is powerless before the court of parental authority:

> Du wilst ihn nicht? Ich muss nur lachen,
>   Sagt drauf Mama!
> Wir wollen dir den Willen machen,
>   Ich und Papa.

Once married, however, Marianne becomes a loyal and provident wife, though Leander remains the theme of all her thoughts even after five years. Hollow-cheeked and bearded, Leander is introduced into the house as an itinerant jewel merchant by the husband himself. He too is still consumed by grief for his lost love, whom he now recognizes, though she does not recognize him until he shows her her own picture:

> Sie macht es auf——allein erblasset,
>   Von Schrekk erfüllt,
> Fällt sie in Ohnmacht, denn sie fasset,
>   Ihr eigen Bild.

106

Leander is just grasping Marianne's hand in final leave-taking, when the husband—who had gone hunting!—suddenly returns. High bourgeois tragedy ensues:

> Stirb, sagt er, Räuber meiner Ehre,
>   Mit tausend Schmerz!
> Er tobt und stosst, mit Mord-Gewehre,
>   Durch Beyder Herz.
> Leander stirbt! Und Marianne
>   Spricht: GOtt Lob, ich
> Verdient es nicht. Sie spricht zum Manne:
>   Du jammerst mich!

This denouement is more than a little startling. With not a syllable have we been prepared for such jealous violence, for though the main title of the piece is "Traurige und betrübte Folgen der *Eifersucht*," Gleim has up to this point developed only the subtheme, "dass Eltern ihre Kinder zu keiner Heyrath zwingen sollen." The two themes gape apart unconnected. Are we to assume that Gleim did not realize this, or should we rather assume that he is consciously burlesquing the clumsy construction of a pop art form? The double murder is not the end of the "sad consequences of jealousy." The ghost of the loyal wife returns, like the ghost of Damon in "Damon und Ismene," to haunt the husband. It is more than he can bear:

> Ein klägliches Gewimmel irret
>   Um ihn herum.
> Ihn reut die That, er wird verwirret,
>   Und bringt sich um.

And what moral are we to draw from this "Mordgeschichte"? That parents should not cross the path of true love? No, that theme has now been jettisoned once and for all. Rather:

> Beym Hören dieser Mordgeschichte
>   Sieht jeder Mann
> Mit liebreich freundlichem Gesichte
>   Sein Weibchen an,

107

> Und denkt: Wenn ich es einst so fände,
>   So dächt ich dis:
> Sie geben sich ja nur die Hände,
>   Das ist gewiss!

Can we, after this, still believe (along with Kayser) that Gleim's intent was serious? Are we not missing the sly duplicity of his art if we do?

Gleim was not without a sickly sentimental strain, however, and indeed one so strong and so completely lacking in ironical overtones that it can almost lead the reader to doubt the justice of such an interpretation as that just suggested. The moral tale called "Der arme Mann: Sein Kind" from *Fabeln* (1756) is an example (Stenzel, p. 47). Nothing in Gellert can surpass it for luxuriating in pure bathos and for failure of taste. A poor man has cut a slice of bread from his last loaf for his little son. The boy, seeing his father's tears, tries to give back the bread. No, no, I'll cut another piece!

> Mit nassem Blikk,
> Sieht er auf seinen Sohn herab,
> Auf seinen Trost, und schneidet ab,
> Doch, wie erschrikkt er!
>   Plözzlich fällt
> Ein Haufen glänzend Silbergeld
> Aus seinem Brodt.

Naturally, the father hurries to fetch the baker to give back the money he must have inadvertently baked into the loaf. But the baker is as honest and magnanimous as the next man. He has received the loaf from a donor, who wishes to remain anonymous, with the express directions to sell it to a poor man who is sick and cannot earn a living:

> Drauf kommt ihr, und ich gab es euch!
> Seht, wie GOTT sorgt, nun seid ihr reich!

The poor man keeps the money, blessing the rich man who gave it (and, by implication, the system that attributes both social ills and their cure to the will of God). The final verses manage to wring still two more sobs from the material:

108

> Den segne GOTT! Ach lebt doch
> Sprach er: nun deine Mutter noch,
> Du liebes Kind!
>   Das Söhnchen spricht:
> Weint, Herzen-Vater, weint doch nicht.

There is no trace of ironical detachment here. For us, it is bathos pure and simple, but Gleim—so far as one may judge from the evidence presented—would seem to be taking it seriously. Or shall we say that he is again only adopting a mask, trying his hand at a modish heart-rending tale in the manner of Gellert? In the final analysis, Gleim seems to be a man without a center, a mercurial figure who constantly slips away from us. We can never say with certainty what is mask and what is Gleim. We can only say: Gleim in this mask.

In the *Preussische Kriegslieder von einem Grenadier* emotionality is sanctioned by the sentiment of patriotism. In contrast to the multifarious run-of-the-mill odes glorifying in an exalted tone the deeds of Frederick and his army in the Seven Years' War (E. v. Kleist's "Ode an die preussische Armee" also belongs to this category), Gleim's Grenadierlieder are genuinely popular in tone, so genuinely, in fact, that many were long persuaded that they were actually written by a common soldier.[23] Again it is the element of naïveté, the air of artlessness, that is the typical Gleimian ingredient of these songs as of his anacreontic verse and the Romanzen. To be sure, if we compare a folk song with Gleim's work, the difference is immediately apparent. Sauer quotes these lines from an anonymous ballad on the battle of Zorndorf:

> Ach, du grosse Kaiserin [Maria Theresia],
> Seynd das deine beste Trümpfe,
> Dass du solches Raubgesind
> Schickest her? Das ist zum Schimpfe
> Für dich selbst, und rechte Schand
> Ehrlichem Soldatenstand.
>   [*Kriegslieder*, p. ix]

Such honest cobbler's work bears little resemblance to Gleim's accomplished numbers. Gleim's most genial stroke was to take over the English ballad meter, which the Germans call the "Chevy-Chase-Strophe" (4/3/4/3) after the ballad of Percy and Douglas:

> The ladies cracked their fingers white,
>> The maidens tore their hair,
> All for the sake of their true loves,
>> For them they ne'er saw mair.

Klopstock had already used this meter in three poems, interestingly enough also in his only poem in praise of Frederick the Great.[24] Klopstock's poems are unrhymed. Gleim rhymes abab, thus violating the model in the other direction, but retains (as Klopstock had) the all-masculine endings, which strike the German ear, accustomed to many feminine endings, as particularly "virile." It is a meter of great buoyancy and tunefulness, originally meant for dancing. It calls for a singer.

Though closely associated with a number of military men, especially Ewald von Kleist, one of his chief sources of firsthand information on events in the field, Gleim was never himself in combat. The direct stimulus for the Grenadierlieder, however, came from Lessing, who in May 1757 addressed a prose dithyramb "An Herr Gleim," urging him to sing his King. (Lessing himself was a Saxon, though full of admiration for Frederick.) From the tone of Lessing's dithyramb it seems quite unlikely that he had anything in mind comparable to the Grenadierlieder with which Gleim responded to his challenge:

> Was hält dich noch? Singe ihn, deinen König! Deinen tapfern, doch menschlichen; deinen schlauen, doch edeldenkenden Friedrich!
> Singe ihn, an der Spitze seines Heers; an der Spitze ihm ähnlicher Helden; . . . Singe ihn, im Dampfe der Schlacht; . . . im Kranze des Siegs; tiefsinnig auf dem Schlachtfelde, mit tränendem Auge unter den Leichnamen seiner verewigten Gefährten.[25]

It was again Lessing who urged that the Grenadierlieder be collected, and it was he who contributed the enthusiastic foreword to the collection.

Goethe, in discussing the state of German literature around the middle of the eighteenth century in the seventh book of *Dichtung und Wahrheit*, maintains that any national poetry must necessarily become shallow unless it is based on "das Menschlich-Erste," i.e., on that which primarily concerns the nation as a political and ethnic unity, "the events of nations and their leaders, when both stand together as *one*." This vital content, Goethe points out, entered German literature only with Frederick the Great and the Seven Years' War. For the first time the Germans, at any rate those who sympathized with Prussia, felt themselves united in a common cause, a true nation. Through Frederick the nation-state had become a reality even in Germany. It is this that the Grenadierlieder celebrate, and they are thus Germany's first really successful national poetry. They are a true reflection, though an idealized one, of the first sense of German nationhood. It was inevitable that the modern poet in that classicistic age should be compared to an ancient one and Gleim, "the German Anacreon," now became "the German Tyrtaeus," the eighteenth-century counterpart of the martial singer of seventh-century Sparta.

These songs are only eleven in number. (A twelfth, "Der Grenadier an die Kriegsmuse nach dem Siege bey Zorndorf," which was published separately, is in unrhymed iambic pentameter.) Gleim's contemporaries were well aware of the special quality of the Grenadierlieder and immediately recognized that they represented a true *novum* in German letters. Gessner, though a Swiss, well expresses the constant refrain in a letter to the poet of March 14, 1759:

> Der Dichter ist bewundernswerth, der Genie genug ist, eine ganz neue Bahn zu betreten. . . . Das haben Sie in Ihren Siegesliedern gethan. Sie sind neu, ich weiss keinen, der vor Ihnen in diesem Ton gesungen hat. Wie eigen ist Ihnen die Kunst, mit bestem Anstand [with

perfect decorum] das grösseste Erhabene und das Naive
mit dem scherzhaften Tone abwechseln zu lassen! . . .
Sie müssen Wirkung thun bei der Armee. . . . (Sauer,
pp. xxii f.)

Lessing, in his foreword, plays the game of masks so dear to
Gleim's heart: "Der Verfasser [von diesen Liedern] ist ein
gemeiner Soldat." He too emphasizes the combination of sublimity and naïveté, adding that the language has an earthy,
somewhat archaic tinge characteristic of the speech of "alle
die niedrigen Stände, die wir *das Volk* nennen" and even goes
so far as to compare the poet with ancient Germanic bards
who accompanied warriors into battle: "true poets, fiery historians." Whatever, then, the reaction of the modern reader
may be to Gleim's battle songs, it is evident that his contemporaries saw in them a veritable national deed and a true
poetic reflection of the intoxicating sense of young national
pride.

Sublimity and naïveté—we may well take our cue from
Gessner and Lessing. The sublimity lies in the religiously
conceived patriotism, the naïveté in the manner of presentation. The ethic is of course militaristic-nationalistic: *dulce et
decorum est pro patria mori*, "Unsterblich macht der Helden
Tod/Der Tod fürs Vaterland!" Frederick is a half-divine
father figure, the Prussian army his ministering angels, while
the Austrians and their allies are cast in the role of fallen
angels with Maria Theresia as Queen of the Night. Nonetheless, the great, the famous generals of the day, including
Father Frederick himself, are not seen as superhuman and
inconceivably distant, as was still the accepted mode of the
time as in the Baroque. Instead they are humanized. This
was the startlingly new element for Gleim's contemporaries.
This naïve touch was made possible by the adoption of a
lowly persona, the grenadier. Ewald von Kleist, himself an
officer in Frederick's army, was shocked that his friend, in
the most memorable quatrain in the whole collection, should
depict the Prussian monarch resting on such an unkingly seat
as a drum, pondering tomorrow's battle:

Auf einer Trommel sass der Held,
  Und dachte seine Schlacht,
Der Himmel über sich zum Zelt,
  Und um sich her die Nacht.

The drum wouldn't do, Kleist wrote; the great Frederick in such a lowly position might give mean spirits "Neben-Ideen" (Sauer, pp. xvii f.). But though Frederick is for Gleim indeed a god, he is a god "voll menschlichen Gefühls":

Frey, wie ein Gott, von Furcht und Graus,
  Voll menschlichen Gefühls,
Steht er, und theilt die Rollen aus
  Des grossen Trauerspiels!
. . . .

So stand, als Gott der Herr erschuf,
  Das Heer der Sterne da;
Gehorsam stand es seinem Ruf
  In grosser Ordnung da!

Goethe, in the passage already referred to, writes that a king must be depicted in the midst of war and danger; there he will appear as a true prince for the very reason that he shares the fate of the lowliest. Such kings are much more interesting than the gods themselves, for these withdraw from the fate they impose upon mankind. It is exactly in such terms that Gleim depicts Frederick.

The Grenadierlieder vary in length from 12 to 252 lines. None is truly in the manner of a folk ballad—all reveal the hand and mind of a poet of classical education, well versed in the art of rhetoric. The tenth poem, for example, "Siegeslied nach der Schlacht bey Lissa den 5ten December 1757," begins with a single sentence five quatrains long, in which the first nineteen lines form the protasis, the twentieth the apodosis! Such a situation is unimaginable in a true folk ballad. Only the point of view is consonant with the persona in these songs, not the formal means of expression. That the reader may flavor the ethos of the Grenadierlieder I quote the third in its entirety (Sauer, p. 12). [*Tolpatsch* is a derogatory epithet for an infantryman, Hungarian in origin; *Panduren* were Hungarian troops in the service of Austria; Brühl was the prime minister of August III, King of Saxony.]

SCHLACHTGESANG

bey der Eröfnung des Feldzuges 1757.

Auf Brüder, Friedrich, unser Held,
　Der Feind von fauler Frist,
Ruft uns nun wieder in das Feld,
　Wo Ruhm zu hohlen ist.

Was soll, o Tolpatsch und Pandur,
　Was soll die träge Rast?
Auf! und erfahre, dass du nur
　Den Tod verspätet hast.

Aus deinem Schädel trinken wir
　Bald deinen süssen Wein,
Du Ungar! Unser Feldpanier
　Soll solche Flasche seyn.

Dein starkes Heer ist unser Spott,
　Ist unsrer Waffen Spiel;
Denn was kann wider unsern Gott,
　Theresia und Brühl?

Was helfen Waffen und Geschütz
　Im ungerechten Krieg?
Gott donnerte bei Lowositz,
　Und unser war der Sieg.

Und böt uns in der achten Schlacht
　Franzos und Russe Trutz,
So lachten wir doch ihrer Macht,
　Denn Gott ist unser Schutz.

Gleim wore still other masks, but these had little or no influence on the development of German poetry. Most interesting is perhaps his attempt to put into modern idiom the poems of the minnesingers, which were then being published by Bodmer from the Manesse Codex. That Gleim's paraphrases are unwitting travesties is hardly surprising. There was still no conception of the theory of courtly love that underlies these refined lyrics, nor had Middle High German yet been studied systematically. Gleim conceives Minnesang simply as a kind of medieval anacreontic poetry. What attracted him here was probably what had always attracted him: that which he took to be the naïveté of expression and outlook.

Gleim is bound to leave us with unanswered questions. The chief of these is: What does naïveté, i.e., naïveté as a conscious artistic device, mean within the context of the development of German literature in the eighteenth century? One might cautiously suggest that it represents an attempt to bring poetry closer to the people, to remove it from its humanistic-aristocratic exclusivity and make it available to the common man. This was undoubtedly the case with Gellert. But with Gleim the situation seems more problematical. Of the modes he cultivates, anacreontica and Bänkelsang already demand a naive viewpoint to fulfill the mode, and we can assume that one of their attractions for him was this very quality. And in the end it perhaps amounts to the same thing, whether one chooses a mode that demands a naive viewpoint or consciously adopts such a viewpoint in cultivating a mode that does not necessarily demand it. But Gleim plays with the element of naïveté with such virtuosity that, as we have seen, even a critic like Wolfgang Kayser could remain convinced, in the case of "Marianne," as were many of the poet's contemporaries in regard to the Grenadierlieder, that the naïveté is genuine, and not an ironical or playful or even serious artistic device. Gleim is as hard to pin down as old Proteus. Both playful and sincere, both ironical and serious, both humanistic and popular, he shimmers like watered silk and defies us to name his color.

Johann Peter Uz (1720–96), the son of an Ansbach (Mittelfranken) goldsmith, was a jurist by profession. He attended

115

the university in Halle, where he formed friendships with Gleim and J.N. Götz, and in Leipzig, where he attended Gellert's lectures. Though active in letters until past the middle of his life, Uz's main energies were devoted to the law; his poetry was an avocation, though a serious one. Despite the existence of a reliable critical edition of his poetry (*Sämtliche poetische Werke*, ed. August Sauer), Uz has received scant attention from literary historians. As an example of the possibilities of German poetry within the limits of neoclassicism he well deserves a monograph.[26] Though always mentioned in the same breath with Gleim, Uz is in fact much more nearly akin to Hagedorn, whom he greatly admired and whose Horatian ethos and stylistic ideal he strove to emulate.

At Gleim's insistence, Uz published in 1749 the first two books of his *Lyrische Gedichte*, twenty-nine poems in all (three others were added in subsequent editions); in 1755 a second edition appeared containing two further books with thirty-one additional poems; in 1768 another edition containing two more books was published, the sixth book consisting of religious poems, primarily hymns. Uz took infinite pains with his work, filing, revising, seeking advice, pondering arrangement. He was such a perfectionist that without Gleim's urging it is doubtful that he would have ever brought out a collected edition of his poetry.

Uz's literary sympathies and antipathies are clearly expressed in his poetic letter of 1755 "An Herrn Hofrath Christ" (Sauer, pp. 362 ff.), which is modeled directly on Voltaire's "Le temple du goût" (first version 1731). In these works, both Voltaire and Uz subscribe to the artistic ideals of the rococo, contemning the elaborate double-talk of the *précieux* on the one hand and the exalted enthusiasm of the new English school (Young, Thomson, et al.) on the other: "nos jeunes étourdis," as Voltaire calls them. In the temple of taste

> On sait fuir également
> Le précieux, le pédantisme,
> L'air emporté du syllogisme,
> Et l'air fou de l'emportement.

116

One could also call this a declaration of loyalty to the *genus medium* and the Horatian stylistic ideal. Those who cultivate "l'air fou de l'emportement" are, in essence, the sons of Milton (to whom the future belongs), and Uz regards such wild beauty with deep suspicion, especially when imitated by his own compatriots. The poets Uz has in mind are Bodmer and his protegé Wieland, Klopstock and the Klopstockians, who worshiped at the feet of Milton and who were to introduce—in fact, in some measure already had introduced—the kind of poetry that was to displace or at any rate to show up the severe limitations of the rococo.

Lost in the contemplation of the marble likenesses of Pindar and Horace, the visitor to Uz's temple of taste sees two groups of Germans enter by two different gates; one burns incense to the poets of Greece, Rome, and France, intoning their praises "in einem verständlichen Deutsch und unter dem Getöne des Reims," while the other, "sehr rauh," worships before the black marble statue of Milton, which stands across from the gleaming white image of Homer: "Sie sangen ihm zu Ehren uranische Lobgesänge voll Olymp und zu gleicher Zeit voll mizraimischer Finsterniss," says Uz, aiming a body blow at Bodmer and his followers, one of whose favorite epithets was "mizraimisch," i.e., Egyptian. There is, we should note, no dispraise of Milton himself—it is the apes of Milton, especially his German emulators, who are ridiculed. As he had written to Gleim some years before upon reading a translation of recent English writing by Klopstock's friend Ebert, Uz finds little nature and too much art in this kind of poetry: "art raises its shameless brow everywhere. . . . Even the commonest things are decked out in rhetorical splendor. . . . Nowhere is there a trace of the noble simplicity that always companions good taste in Greece, Rome and France. England herself wrote differently in the past century. . . ." Rochester, Prior, Addison, and Pope wrote and thought "nobly and boldly, but at the same time naturally." If the Germans persist in imitating writers like Young and Thomson, they will "ruin all our poetry again: we are not as far removed from the taste of Lohenstein as many think."[27]

Noble simplicity and naturalness, the neoclassical ideals, Uz defends out of fear that baroque excess, barely discredited, may resurge and wipe out the hard-earned gains of the last two decades. His attitude is typical of the situation of his generation: he was born too early not to fear Lohensteinism, too late to practice it with a clear conscience; too early to view it with historical equanimity, too late to grasp the fundamentally different drift of the new generation of poets, who, having already begun to write from "within," were safely out of the wake of the Baroque and its ideal of rhetorical decorativeness of set themes. He saw certain disquieting stylistic manifestations and trembled. He did not realize that, rather than being symptomatic of backsliding into recently overcome forms and an older poetic point of view, they sprang from a new attitude toward poetry and its function.

Criticism, the cicerone of the Temple of Taste, of course approves the visitor's love for the classics and the neoclassics ("Ich billige deine Wahl, welche von den herrschenden Vorurtheilen dieser Zeit nicht hingerissen worden") and points out to him the German poets here honored:

> Opitz steht voran: Sein Geist kennt keine Schranken:
> Natur ist, was er denkt, und was er schreibt,
> Gedanken.

Then come Fleming and (skipping three-quarters of a century and thus also the baroque classics) Canitz, Brockes, Haller (who stands next to Pope), Hagedorn (who receives special praise), Gellert, Johann Elias Schlegel (the dramatist and critic), Gleim, and Lessing (as an anacreontic writer). In short, Uz is a defender of what was, by the middle of the century, already the old-line, conservative party in German literature. It is true that he had been particularly sensitized to the split on the German Parnassus by young Wieland's virulent attack on the anacreontic poets in which he had been made to play the role of whipping boy. In 1752, under the tutelage of Bodmer and, it seems, at the latter's instigation, Wieland, who was then undergoing his "seraphic" period, penned a holier-than-thou diatribe against the anacreontic writers, returning to the attack again in the next year and once more in 1756. *One* Anacreon, Wieland maintained (and not without a show of reason), is enough. "Our purpose is to inculcate morality, to awaken a sense of religiosity and love in our readers, to offer them examples. . . . We despise from the bottom of our hearts the *bel-esprit* who is deprived of that inner beauty which is alone pleasing to the Creator. . . ." This is "l'air fou de l'emportement" of which Voltaire speaks, and it went much against Uz's grain. The epistle to Christ is his answer.

But the impression one might gain from Wieland's self-righteous polemic that Uz is a thoroughgoing anacreontic poet would be very wide of the mark. He regarded the anacreontic mode as only *one* of the possibilities of poetry of the day, and a quite minor one at that, though his first venture into verse was a translation of the Greek anakreonteia prepared in Halle together with J.N. Götz. This translation appeared in 1746 without Uz's foreknowledge and without his consent.[28] Already in the collection of 1749 there is a poem, "An Venus," against the shallow anacreontic poets, "die Affen . . . Gleims," whose verbose productions make their listeners yawn, because ground out mechanically and without enthusiasm. Uz's own poems in the anacreontic vein are few. When he essays this mode, he tends to transform it into the *galant* manner of the French masters of *vers legers*, the titillating, ironically turned eroticism of a Chaulieu or Voltaire, who had many imitators beyond the Rhine. In the first book of the *Lyrische Gedichte* there is a series of four poems (numbers 3–6), "An Chloen," in which the poet tries out the "new lyre" given him by Amor with the express admonition to abandon high Pindaric themes and follow in the steps of Anacreon, a typical topos of the jesting erotic genre:

> Auf! tritt in seine Spur;
> Da trit man Rosen nur:
> Und singe nur berauscht
> Und wo man Küsse tauscht.

This minicycle contains a mini love story: realization of being in love, Chloe's flirtation with the singer, and her anger, which silences his lyre. Delicately executed and full of self-irony, these poems are charming examples of rococo song. They are not, however, in spite of what Amor says, anacreontica. Neither is the best erotic poem in the entire collection, "Ein Traum" (number 7), with its gentle laughter at male eagerness for satisfaction.

Uz is by no means primarily a sportive erotic poet—rather, his characteristic tone is serious. Thus the main theme of the first book as a whole is finding a place for poetry. What kind of poetry is still possible for a late neoclassicist? This is the burning problem for Uz, and he returns to it a number of times in later books. ("Tempe" in the third book and "Die Dichtkunst" in the fourth are outstanding examples.) In the first book, the opening poem, "Lobgesang des Frühlings," the fifteenth, "Die Muse bey den Hirten," as well as the last poem, "Die lyrische Muse," deal specifically with this theme. "Die lyrische Muse" adumbrates two possibilities and rejects a third. Interestingly enough, none of these possibilities takes special cognizance of the anacreontic mode. The first possibility is philosophical poetry of a cosmological cast sung with "strenge Wut," that is, with controlled (intellectual) passion:

> Ich fliehe nun der Sterblichen Revier;
> Ich eil in unbeflogne Höhen.
> . . . .
> Ja bis dahin, wo mein entzücktes Ohr
> Der Sphären Harmonie verwirret,
> O Muse! fleug mir vor.
>
> [Sauer, p. 44]

This possibility Uz realizes only infrequently—the main instances are "Empfindungen an einem Frühlings-Morgen" and "Theodicee," both in the fourth book. The second possibility, related to the first through the idea of enthusiasm, is Dionysian poetry of self-release and return to a world lost through overcivilized convention. "Dir folg' ich nach," the poet tells his muse,

120

auch wann du trunken glühst,
Und in den ungebahnten Haynen
Mit Libers [Bacchus'] Priestern ziehst,
Wo keine Muse ging und andre Sterne scheinen.
[Sauer, p. 45]

In practice, such drunken song remains for Uz more an object
of longing than realization—he sings *about* it more than he
actually sings it. It is best realized in "Silenus" (book two)—a
cento from Virgil's sixth eclogue, Horace's *Odes* 2, 19, and the
story of Jove and Io in Ovid's *Metamorphoses*—and in "Horaz"
(book five), certainly one of his best poems, alive with veneration for the great Roman and his "alkäisch edlen Ton," his
spirit "Voll einer Raserey, Die keuscher Musen würdig sey"
(Sauer, p. 165).

The possibility that is rejected in "Die lyrische Muse" as
being out of tune with the times is praise of heroes. This
typical theme of the Renaissance and the Baroque no longer
presents an option for the poet of the Enlightenment, Uz
implies. (In this he stands in direct contrast to Gleim and
Kleist.) In a striking extended metaphor comparing the hero
glorified by poetry to the morning star ("Phosphor") Uz
speaks in the elegiac tones of Goethe's Tasso of the possibility
that he must forgo:

Die Zeit ist hin, da manchmal noch zum Dank
An eines klugen Helden Seiten
Die Muse Nektar trank,
Durch die er ewig lebt und glänzt durch alle Zeiten.

Wie Phosphor glänzt, der um den Morgenthau
Aus Thetis Armen sich entziehet
Und ans gestirnte Blau
Mit vollem Schimmer trit und vom Olympus siehet.

Ein Sternenheer, das letzte Chor der Nacht,
Traurt um ihn her in mattem Lichte.
Die Welt indess erwacht,
Und Nacht und Schatten fliehn vor seinem Angesichte.
[Sauer, pp. 45 f.]

121

The chief theme of the second book is the finding of self, the search for self-realization in a world of specious values, the great theme of Horace, Pope, Hagedorn. It is treated in "Der Weise auf dem Lande," "An das Glück," "Der May," "Einladung zum Vergnügen," and especially in "Die Wollust," the programmatic poem of this section. "Die Wollust" is Uz's muse, as, according to him, it is also that of Horace. "Wollust" is not lust, rather it is *voluptas*, delight of mind or body or both. As with Hagedorn, and indeed with the whole tradition here followed by Uz, the metaphor for the agent of release that allows us to enter the sphere of "Wollust" is "wine" or "Lyäus," the god of wine, whose name means "loosener." Through "Lyäus" we are enabled to participate in "eine Raserei, die *keuscher* Musen würdig sey."

True to the Enlightenment's habit of mind, which, in almost complete reversal of baroque values, considers worthy of song only that which is gay or contented or conducive to a wisdom that leads to contentment with our earthly lot, Uz's work contains no poetry of melancholy; this whole aspect of human existence is excluded on principle. It is unworthy of a world in which all is arranged for the best by a just and loving deity, a world in which, according to the theodicies, evil is only apparent, being at bottom an aspect of the good. Poetry should be an expression of joy, of an abiding optimism and unshakeably positive attitude toward all creation: sadness, mourning, a downcast mien, a sense of the desperateness of the human condition, these are finally an untruth or proof that one has not found life's true meaning. This is the central position from which Uz writes. True joy, however, is wisdom in union with "Wollust," or, as one might equally well say, true "Wollust" is an expression of wisdom:

> Die Wollust nicht, die auch der Pöbel kennet;
> Die viehisch ras't, nicht sich vernünftig freut;
> ....
> Nein! die vereint Natur und Weisheit preisen,
> Der Weisheit Kind und Königin der Weisen.
>
> [Sauer, pp. 74 f.]

The following lines from "Die Freude" (book three) suc-
cinctly express Uz's attitude, which is essentially also that of
Hagedorn:

> Lernt, wie sich finstrer Unverstand,
> Verhüllt in trauriges Gewand,
> Von wahrer Weisheit unterscheide,
> Die mit entwölkter Stirne glänzt,
> Und in der Wollust leichtem Kleide,
> Wie sie, im Schoose sanfter Freude,
> Auch oft mit Rosen sich bekränzt.
>
> [Sauer, p. 101]

The third book as a whole seeks to inculcate the "Lebens-
weisheit" of the Enlightenment, the "philosophy" of leading a
contented life. Uz's attempts at higher philosophical flights in
the fourth book, such as "Die Glückseligkeit," "Empfindungen an einem Frühlings-Morgen," and his best known
poem, "Theodicee," are outright confessions of faith in the
goodness and justness of creation, however difficult it may be
for man from his limited viewpoint to gain insight into the
divine reflected in the earthly. As poetry that appeals to modern sensibilities, these productions are probably farther from
us than anything in Uz's œuvre. We are no longer especially
impressed to learn that whatever is, is right and have it
proved to us by arguments diluted from Leibniz and Wolff.
There can be no doubt, however, that the poet himself set
considerable store by these works: the tone is earnest, the
attempt to persuade by close argument serious. Theodicies,
and such poems may all be loosely included under that rubric, are attempts to come to terms with actuality, to accept
the world as it is, and are thus very classicistic in tenor. They
commonly try to make acceptance possible by reducing the
tremendous mystery of creation to limits comprehensible to
human reason. What is "reasonable" must then be accepted.
It is self-evident that God, as the ultimate mystery, must
disappear in this process.[29] Uz is not troubled by this, nor
was the Enlightenment in general, for one did not feel that
one was making God superfluous by explaining His ways—

123

rather one was justifying Him. But justification of the deity in human terms is a *contradictio in adjecto* and has nothing to do with worship, which is an expression of perfect submission to that which is beyond all comprehension, and which is the only thing that keeps God alive. In the theodicies we see the beginning of His death. Haller's theodicizing as theodicizing is a resounding failure, but as poetry it is astoundingly successful. Uz's "Glückseligkeit" and "Theodicee" are creditable works of theodicizing, but failures as poetry.

Johann Nikolaus Götz (1721–81) was born in Worms, the son of a clergyman. From 1739 to 1742 he studied theology in Halle, where he formed friendships with Gleim and Uz. He earned his living first as a tutor and private secretary to persons of nobility, later as a court preacher in Forbach (Lorraine) and as a chaplain in the French cavalry regiment "Royal-Allemand." In 1761 he became "Consistorialrat" (an ecclesiastical office) in Winterburg (Zweibrücken), where he died. He was thoroughly familiar with French literature and was personally acquainted with Voltaire. Of the trio usually named in one breath—Gleim, Uz, and Götz—it is Götz who possesses the most pronounced lyric talent.

Götz was practically unknown as a poet during his lifetime. His almost pathological fear that he, a court preacher and Consistorialrat, might suddenly stand revealed as the author of erotic verse caused him to conceal his identity by publishing anonymously in various almanacs, "Taschenbücher," and anthologies. Karl Wilhelm Ramler, widely known in his day as an authority on metrics, composer of classicistic odes, and translator of the classics, especially Horace (he was called "the German Horace"), often acted as literary agent for Götz and finally as the executor of his literary remains. Ramler was a compulsive meddler with others' work: he "improved" everything that came into his hands. He faithfully preserved Götz's anonymity, however, so that during his lifetime the latter was commonly known as "Ramler's Anonymous." Herder and Karl Ludwig von Knebel, tutor to the ducal house of Weimar and himself a translator of the classics, admired Götz's work and were anxious to see it appear in an original, un-Ramlerized version. This did not come to pass, at least not until toward the end of the nineteenth century, when Carl Schüddekopf edited Götz's *Gedichte aus den Jahren 1745–1765*. Schüddekopf's edition, containing ninety-nine poems (eighty-six pages), is a selection, "eine bescheidene Sammlung," from the poet's work, mostly from the earlier period. It is upon this edition that we must largely rely in trying to form an image of the poet.

Götz's first collection of verse was a slim volume of only seven poems of a highly personal nature called *Versuch eines Wormsers in Gedichten* (1745). The tone is not infrequently reminiscent of Günther in a somewhat lower register. The opening poem, "Wünsche des Dichters," shows that the young poet is already well aware of the nature of his talent: the power to convey a certain inward fervency in a minor key and an artfully constructed line:

> O möcht ich, so wie ihr, geliebten Bienen, seyn!
> An innerm Geiste gros, obwohl von Cörper klein;
> . . . .
> Wie sehnlich wünscht mein Hertz, dass stets mein
> Reimgebäu,
> An Kunst und Ordnung reich, wie eure Cellen sey,
> Und mein gelinder Vers, wie euer Honig fliesse,
> So nahrhaft für den Geist, wie für die Sinnen süsse.

The leading themes of the *Versuch* are love of homeland and family and homoerotic love. There is no other way to read poems five through seven. "Warnung an einen schönen Knaben" is passionate pleading with ulterior motivation to avoid the snares of heterosexuality and its "Pfade voller Blut" and to follow "der ewigschönen Tugend." But "Tugend" here means that the beautiful youth addressed should preserve himself for the singer:

125

Die [Tugend] wird dich auch im Tode nicht verlassen;
Verlasse du sie nie.
Was wär ich, ach! wenn du mich wolltest hassen?
Was wärst du ohne sie?

Is this naïveté or the height of sophistication? "An seinen
Freund Damon" contains verses that sob with longing for the
departed (not deceased) friend; "Über seine Freundschaft mit
dem Thirsis" is an outright declaration of homoerotic love in
the measure of a church hymn:

Bekennen will ichs gerne,
  Ich bin nicht deiner werth,
Doch gäben mir die Sterne,
  (Was ich zwar nie begehrt)
Glantz, Schönheit, hohe Gaben,
  Was See, und Erdreich hat,
Sucht ich doch dich zu haben.
  Und dich nur früh und spath.
                    [p. 18]

It is true, of course, that the bounds of male friendship
were wider and the declaration of such emotional ties far
opener in the eighteenth century than in the nineteenth and
twentieth, but Götz's poems far exceed even these bounds in
this frankness of statement; above all, they reveal genuine
passion and are avowedly homosexual. It is noteworthy that
while his homerotic poems have a confessional ring, his het-
erosexual ones, with one exception, at least so far as one can
judge from Schüddekopf, are cast in the anacreontic mode or
conform to the pastoral convention. Successful as they may
be, they are not confessional poetry, but personalized treatments of set, conventional themes.

Though his own work is un-Klopstockian, Götz was an
ardent admirer of Klopstock and, somewhat surprisingly, also
of Bodmer and his biblical epic, *Noah*. In other words, his
literary sympathies lay with the new generation of poets,
though his own work belongs to the older generation. This
becomes clear in his "Prosaische Ode an den Marquis von

Montbary" of 1749 (Schüddekopf, pp. 45 ff.), a piece of advice to a young nobleman of literary ambitions who wishes to sing the deeds of the Maréchal de Saxe, the famous general who served under Marlborough and Prince Eugene. In elaborate language, full of mythological references, Götz strongly advises the marquis against such an undertaking, which will prove beyond his untried powers. Rather than treat heroic themes, he urges him to turn to the anacreontic mode. (His own translation of *Die Oden Anakreons in reimlosen Versen*, prepared with the help and advice of Uz, had appeared anonymously in 1746. In its revision of 1760 it was to become the standard eighteenth-century German version of these poems.) But the historically significant section of the "prosaic ode" is the final two paragraphs, in which the poet declares his unbounded admiration, even worship, of Bodmer and Klopstock, the first three cantos of whose *Messias* had appeared only the year before, in 1748:

> Gegrüset seyd mir, o kühnen Schwäne, an den Ufern erzogen, wo die Erde zunächst an den Himmel grenzt. Das Rad der Sonne stund verwundernd stille über dem Glücke eures Fluges. Alle andere sehen euch begierig nach, aber folgen können sie euch nicht. Seyd gegrüst, ersten Söhne dieses Weltalters, welche die Gottheit ihre Sprache völlig gelehrt hat. Eure Kronen hängen zu hoch für mich, und der Glanz, der euch umgibt, ist zu blendend für meinen irdischen Augapfel. Möchte ich, ein Schüler, euch nur von ferne nachfolgen können; möchte ich nur einen Bündel jener Lichtstralen auffangen können, die eure Seelen erleuchten; möchte ich nur ein Kränzgen von jenen Rosen gewunden, die ihr nicht würdigt, aufzulesen, meine Schläfe unwinden,

> O wie glucklich sties mir das Haupt an den
> Wagen Orions!
> (Schüddekopf, p. 49)

But if the crowns of Klopstock and Bodmer were beyond his reach and their splendor too blinding for his modest talent,

127

the power of tradition and the example of other contemporaries still kept Götz from renouncing poetry. If he contented himself with goals less noble than those set by Bodmer and Klopstock, he did at least attain them. And perhaps we may feel that *one* Klopstock (not to speak of one Bodmer) is even more sufficient than one Anacreon.

Götz's poems in the anacreontic vein are charming exercises; *études* is the right term for them, as for those of Gleim. Schüddekopf's selection contains ten examples, two of which were prefaced to the 1760 edition of the translation of Anacreon. The poet's wry humor—in contrast to Gleim's frequent tendency to heavy-handedness—and his skill in constructing ingenious dramatic fictions is well illustrated by "Hymen und die Truppen Amors":

> Hymen stand im Hinterhalte;
> Als ein Heer von Amouretten
> Seines Reiches Grenzen nahte!
> Wer da! rief er halberschrocken,
> Wer da!—oder soll ich schiesen?
> Holder Bruder, sprach ihr Führer,
> Fürchte nichts von Amors Truppen.
> Unser Endzweck ist nicht dieser,
> Deine Lande zu verheeren
> Oder in Besitz zu halten:
> Wir verlangen nur den Durchzug!
> [Schüddekopf, p. 77]

Here is a poem that is all imagery and nothing else. All the same, the feeling is inescapable that the imagery is making a statement. Götz was the first of the anacreontic poets to transform statement wholly into imagery.[30] One easily detects beneath the airy form an ironical attitude toward "the way things are" in the all-too-human institution of marriage, at least as marriage was conceived under the *ancien régime*. The ambiguity of the *pointe* contributes much to the wittiness of the poem: Will the troops of Amor, in passing through Hymen's domains, momentarily rekindle spent passion, or is marriage as an institution to serve as a screen for an extra-

marital affair? In either case, Hymen has nothing to fear, but
also in either case marriage must appear in an ironic light and
its hollowness stand revealed from the standpoint of Amor.

Among Götz's most appealing productions are those in
the apothegmatic style. Here, as in his cultivation of the
graceful, extravagant compliment, he shows his kinship with
the Baroque and his inner distance from the coming poetic
generation he so fervently professes to admire. The tone may
be ironic, humorous; or it may be pensive, tender. Whatever
it is, the touch is sure, the desired effect never-failing. The
following "Sinngedicht" is a good example:

> Den Fächer in der Hand, ging ich in meinen Garten,
>   Den jungen Zephir zu erwarten;
> Schnell spielt mein Unterrock, und hebt sich blähend
>   auf,
> Willkommen, o Favon, der Schäferinnen Diener!
> So dacht' ich — — Aber ach! es war in strengem Lauf
> Ein grober Nord: ein Capuciner.
>
> [Schüddekopf, p. 64]

Again a poem that completely converts its statement into
imagery. Three emotional states are conveyed in six lines.
The opening couplet reflects the firm confidence of this rococo lady, who seems to have stepped out of a painting by
Watteau—"den Fächer in der Hand"—in awaiting "Zephir,"
spring or a young lover. Lines 3 and 4 reproduce her excited
joy, but this joy is a misinterpretation—these lines do not
rhyme with each other. It is not the west wind—Favonius or
Zephyrus, the usher of spring and willing servant of shepherd-
esses, that is, of young women eager for love—who flutters
her petticoat, it is "ein grober Nord: ein Capuciner," a stern
moralist. The cross-rhymes humorously reflect the false interpretation, the confusion of the one with the other. The skill
and delicacy with which Götz here uses the rococo idiom is as
nearly perfect as we will find anywhere in the period, even in
other literatures.

The temptation to compile a miniature anthology-com-
mentary of Götz's poems is strong. That such a temptation is

easily resisted in the case of most of his contemporaries shows how vital remains the appeal of this most perfect of German rococo lyricists. The sureness of touch is astounding: suddenly we see what rococo poetry really intends. Götz is a minor poet, certainly, but within his limits he is almost flawless. In the revelation of those states of feeling that lie just beneath the surface of appearances and that we try to conceal from ourselves, he had few equals. Consider, for example, the following eight lines entitled "Fragment":

> *Aurora*, da sie früh aus ihrer Kammer geht,
> Trägt ein Gefäss, in dem manch blasse Lilge steht,
> In ihrer rechten Hand, geusst aus mit ihrer Linken,
> Den Krug, von Zähren voll, die Gras und Blumen
> trinken.
> Der West, der ihren Schlei'r, aus grauem Duft gewebt,
> Vorwitzig, über halb, von ihrer Stirne hebt,
> Zeigt ihr sonst lächlnd Aug', und rosenreiche Wangen,
> Uns mit Verzweiflung itzt, und Traurigkeit umfangen.
> [Schüddekopf, p. 72]

Dawn, usually conceived in positive, optimistic terms (ihr *sonst* lächelnd Aug'), is seen, when the western breeze blows aside her veil of grey mist, to be full of sadness and desperation. Are the tears in the jug in her left hand the tears of the goddess herself, or are they the tears of mankind? One is inclined to say that they are tears of insight into the human situation, though man is not specifically mentioned. Beneath the Apollonian veil of appearances lies the reality of Dionysian tragedy. The firm optimism that forms the basis of Uz's poetry does not obtain in any such categorical way for Götz. His verse is never far from *lacrimae rerum*.

Enraptured contemplation of the Apollonian veil itself is the theme of "On the Fountains of Paris—The Nymph of the Seine Speaks" (Schüddekopf, p. 73). Here man's transformation of the world into his own ideal image holds a mythological figure in raptured marvel and forces her to pay tribute to art. Again the "other" world stands for a human emotional state. The variation in length of lines reflects the pulsation of the fountains, the artful rhyme scheme the fluctuations of the fountains' "passionate tenderness," now tensed by separation, now pouring forth in abundant triple rhymes.

UEBER DIE SPRINGBRUNNEN ZU PARIS

(Die Nymphe der Seine redet.)

Beym Anblick deiner stolzen Wälle,
P a r i s, steh' ich gefesselt still;
Und kann nicht mehr von meiner Stelle,
Und weiss nicht mehr, wohin ich will.
Tausend Tempel, tausend Schlösser
Und jedes L u d w i g s werth, und jedes königlich
  Bezaubern mich.
    Verliebt in dich,
  Steigt mein rein'st Gewässer
  Durch geheime Thor'
  Ueber sich empor,
  Vor der Völker Ohr
Meiner Leidenschaft Zärtlichkeit zu mahlen,
Und aus ewigrinnenden Pokalen
  Dir Tribut zu zahlen.

We might call this an eighteenth-century "Dinggedicht" in the form of a "Rollengedicht." It stands in the same line that reaches its culmination in Rilke's "Spätherbst in Venedig." Götz's best known poem is "Die Mädcheninsel. Ein elegisches Gedicht" (1773), ninety-four lines in elegiac distichs. It has come down to us only in Ramler's redaction.[31] "Die Mädcheninsel" extends, or transforms, the anacreontic lyric into narrative form. The theme is the eroticization of all being, but the manner is almost completely devoid of erotic titillation. That the poem is allegorical is beyond question; but precisely how one is to interpret the allegory may not be. Shipwrecked on a desert island, the poet ("Athamas") prays to Venus, mother of "Wollust und Ruh," to populate the place with nubile maidens, "deinen Grazien gleich." Venus is envisioned as fulfilling this prayer, and the poet beholds himself as the master of a harem of harems, his throne the lap of his countless

131

enchanting female subjects. Loss of fatherland is more than outweighed by this delightful realm with its rosy-cheeked inhabitants and their ambrosial kisses. Athamas is the envy of Jove himself; Venus is drawn from Paphos by her silvery swans to keep him company and calls him her priest and friend. At his suggestion, she gives him Amor, his "brother," as his attendant, the Graces themselves in all their charming nakedness wait upon him, and peace dwells in his tent. He becomes as old as Tithonus, but unlike the lover of Aurora does not shrivel into a cicada but, when he finally dies, falls from the branch of life like a ripe peach. Amor embalms the body, places it on the altar of Venus, and holds a ceremonious funeral. Above the body one reads the inscription:

> Dies ist Athamas Rest des hundertjährigen Jünglings,
> Dessen Reden und Thun immer voll Grazie war.

The themes, attributes, and ideals of eighteenth-century German anacreontic poetry follow Athamas to his last resting place:

> Mit zerstreuetem Haar, in violettnem Gewande,
> Wie auf Anakreons Grab ehemals Griechenland sass,
> Folgen die sittsame Zucht, der Jokus, die Freundschaft,
>   die Musen,
> Und die Grazien all' ächzend dem Leichenzug nach.

From the tears shed by the Graces at this burial springs a race of young Cupids who marry the girls who had been the companions of Athamas; the inscription concludes (Athamas is speaking):

> Mädcheninsel, so wirst du bevölkert; so schwingt sich
>   mein Name
> Zu den Vätern der Welt, zu den Lykurgen hinauf!

And the allegory? My own inclination is to see "Die Mädcheninsel" as a trope for the poetic, i.e., purely formal, existence of the anacreontic poet. "Poems," Goethe once said, "are kisses we give the world, but from kisses we get no children." Athamas-Anacreon, despite his more than ample opportunities, begets no children either. In fact, there is no hint that his sex life ever goes beyond a kiss. He lives a poem—his life is a translation of anacreontic motifs into a miniature epic. The isle of Cythera, we remarked before, is beyond time. When time enters, that is, when death comes, tears are shed and life begins in earnest. Athamas's epitaph is an epitaph for the whole anacreontic mode, which, though it still continued to find followers, had passed its prime by the 1770s. It was time to bury Athamas.

CHAPTER THREE

THE CULT OF FEELING

Three Poets of Pietism

Luxuriation in feeling, even if disguised as an incentive to virtue, is by no means lacking, as we have seen, in some of the poets already discussed. We find it in Gleim, in Gellert, in Kleist. Kleist's "Frühling" we can classify as a genuine example of "Empfindsamkeit" or sentimentalism. The verse of Gleim and Gellert that plays on feeling, sometimes mawkishly, sometimes ironically, can perhaps be more convincingly seen as a confrontation of the rights of the emotions with a philosophical, moralistic, or literary point of view, the latter being the defining factors. The serious cultivation of feeling as a value in its own right appears with the strength of a "movement" in German secular poetry only around the middle of the century. The great exemplar is Klopstock.

If heretofore the head had taken precedence over the heart, the heart now takes precedence over the head. For the eighteenth century itself, however, this dichotomy was more apparent than real, at least in theory. The psychology of the day, especially that of the earlier decades of the century, regarded thought and feeling as ultimately one. For both Leibniz and Wolff the psyche is a monadic structure: the

134

senses, the imagination, memory, the reflective powers, the understanding, the will are all manifestations of a single power, the "soul."[1] In a sense, then, the poets of sentimentalism are only drawing the necessary conclusion from contemporary psychological doctrine when they emphasize the rights of feeling. Reason alone is seen as no longer enough: feeling enters as a fully equal partner, but not, it should be emphasized, as a rival.

The literary ancestry of sentimentalism is largely English. Edward Young, whose *Night Thoughts* (1745) began to attract lively attention in Germany in the 1750s, and whom Klopstock and his disciples regarded almost as a saint, is one of the chief progenitors.[2] The English moral weeklies, translated and widely imitated in Germany, Richardson's novels, Elizabeth Singer Rowe (Klopstock's "fromme Singer"), the author of *Friendship in Death . . . Letters from the Dead to the Living* (1728), were other strong influences, later reinforced by the immensely popular works of Lawrence Sterne.

The role of pietism in the rise of the cult of feeling is harder to estimate. The view that "Empfindsamkeit" is fundamentally secularized pietism has found wide acceptance. There is no doubt that pietism and the cult of feeling are intimately connected, but it seems unlikely that the latter would have attained such preeminence without the example of an admired literature that showed the way. Literature has a way of springing from literature, whether in emulation of a tradition or in revolt against it.

It is not strictly accurate to speak of a poetry of pietism. There are, however, at least three figures, all distinctly different from each other, but who, as much as they may contrast in detail, are yet akin inwardly and all of whom, though they might have rejected the name themselves, we can denominate as "pietistic" or at least as sympathetic with the central aim of pietism: the renewal of an immediate relationship with the divine, unconfined by intellectualistic doctrine. They are Gottfried Arnold, Gerhard Tersteegen, and Nikolaus Ludwig Reichsgraf von Zinzendorf, whose poetic works contribute a distinct note to the spiritual life of the era. One of them, Tersteegen, we may safely account one of the great lyricists of mysticism; Arnold was one of the most interesting religious thinkers of his day; and Zinzendorf was one of the great religious leaders of the age and the discoverer of possibilities of poetic expression (though not purely in the service of poetry) up to then unrecognized and indeed hardly recognized until our own times.

It cannot be our task here to attempt to trace the complicated and still-disputed history of the rise of pietism. This movement remained on the whole within the Lutheran church (though the Moravians, led by Zinzendorf, did not) and showed strong ecumenical tendencies, though accused by the orthodox of being schismatic. It is generally agreed that pietism sought to renew German Protestantism from within by proceeding from "two or three that are gathered together in my name," each of whom felt the conviction of Christ within (*Christus in nobis* as opposed to *extra nos*), and that it sought to cultivate a sense of nearness to the Savior in an intensely personal rather than ritualistic or churchly fashion.

In this way there arose a kind of church within the church, *ecclesiola in ecclesia*, frequently marked, it must be admitted, by self-righteous arrogance. The pietists referred to themselves as the "awakened" and the "reborn." The concept of rebirth is the central doctrine. One is reborn through Christ by utter identification of one's own life with His. This is also His rebirth in us. This gift of grace is what the pietists mean by "conversion." But since the danger of backsliding is ever present, the pietist is constantly observing his inner state to try to determine whether he is still in a state of grace. This emphasis on self-examination and self-analysis accompanies the transference of salvation from sacramental to personal rebirth. It did not remain without effect upon the means of expression. It showed itself in the manner of preaching, which sought to appeal directly to the feelings rather than to display rhetorical eloquence; it is evident in the autobiographical writings of men like Spener, Francke, and Jung-Stilling; it marks the verse produced by the three poets we wish to discuss.

136

The influence of pietism on the poetic language of the eighteenth century is best seen in contrast first to the language of the Baroque and second to the rationalistic, "flat" style of such poets as Canitz and Besser, who were in revolt against the ornate. The pietists were anti-art because they were for plain speaking that appealed to all hearts and could be understood by all minds. Their standpoint was that of Paul in 1 Corinthinians 14. "Divine truths," wrote Philipp Jacob Spener (1666–1704), the founder of pietism, "are of such illumination and power that presented even in their simplicity they penetrate of themselves into the soul and need not borrow from human eloquence."[3] This is precisely the reverse of the usual position of the poets of the Baroque, who were intent upon making revelation more impressive and penetrating by means of rhetorical elaboration. The contrast with the adherents of the flat style, i.e., the poets of the early Enlightenment, lies principally in the authority to which one appealed: the pietists to feeling, those of the Enlightenment to the understanding. To speak from heart to heart was the ideal of the pietists, and it was this ideal that was to prove revolutionary.

Gottfried Arnold (1666–1714),[4] the author of the widely read *Unparteiische Kirchen- und Ketzer-Historie von Anfang des Neuen Testaments bis auf das Jahr Christi 1688* (Frankfurt a.M., 1699),[5] and one of the most learned men of his time, was converted to pietism by Spener, after having studied at Wittenberg, the seat of Lutheran orthodoxy. He can probably most accurately be called a voluntaristic (as opposed to an intellectualistic) mystic. Pietism, as a religion of the heart that sought direct communication with the divine, was of course very open to mystical tendencies. Arnold's poetry, most of it written around the turn of the century, is the product of his most intensely mystical period. (Soon afterward he married and accepted a post as Lutheran pastor; his subsequent works are in prose.)

Arnold's poetry began to appear in 1698, in Frankfurt, under the title of *Göttliche Liebesfuncken / Aus dem Grossen Feuer Der Liebe Gottes in Christo JESU entsprungen. . . .* This volume

137

contains 169 poems and is preceded by a revealing foreword in which the author comments on the connection between stylistic levels and religious poetry.[6] The pietist's typical anti-art stance is immediately apparent in Arnold's "Vorrede" (Seeberg, *Auswahl*, pp. 261 ff.). Had it been possible, the poet claims, he would have limited the accessibility of his poems to those who would have looked upon them with "unpartheyischen Augen," but since they are to be generally disseminated he feels the need to place them in context and obviate "unfounded prejudice." He has no ambition, he states with a distinct touch of irony, "to increase the volume of German poetry" or earn the name of one skilled in the presently accepted "Poetischen Schreib-Art." Most of his poems, he avers, were written while he was deeply occupied with other matters; they were "gleichsam gebohren" and therefore display no "grosse Künste." "So wird [der Leser] auch viel weniger hochtrabende Worte / weit gesuchte verblümte Redens-Arten / oder sonsten viel affectirte Manieren drinnen finden" than is common among the "Gern-Poeten" (p. 262).

Arnold's concern is "die Sache selbst," even at the expense of "gemeine Kunst-Regeln." Misled by Horace's "Exegi monumentum aere perennius" (I have raised a monument more enduring than bronze), many a poet has thought to immortalize himself through his works, but God's word alone remains in eternity, all else is "nichtige Grillen." True poetry is divinely inspired—this is the central point of Arnold's doctrine: "Ich halte alles Dichten und Singen vor unnütze / das nicht auss dem Geist Gottes fleusset" (p. 262). Consequently a poet who relies on his own "Kunst und Hurtigkeit" is liable to produce "ärgerliche und unverantwortliche Sachen." A true Christian poet will listen to the voice within: he "speaks what he knows, and bears witness to what he has seen." Personal experience is the basis of poetry, but the only experience worth recording is the experience of the divine. Arnold closes his preliminary remarks with the constant refrain of all voluntaristic mystics, closely associating it with his kind of poetry: if one can succeed in emptying one's mind of all that is worldly ("die alte Unart ausschaffen"), then God will fill the vacuum with His own presence, and of this the poet must sing. Paraphrasing Matthew 12:34, Arnold asks: "Warum solte dann der Mund nicht übergehen / da das Herz biss oben an voll ist?" (p. 263).

The drift of Arnold's discourse is this: He begins by rejecting one kind of poetry held in general esteem, namely, that composed in the tradition of *ornatus*, and ends by pleading for a special kind of poetry, that which is divinely inspired and which, as it were, sings itself, is "gleichsam gebohren," semi-automatic. Such poetry can well afford to scorn "Kunst-Regeln" and "verblümte Redens-Arten," since its authority derives from an infinitely higher source.

Arnold is then above all by his own confession a poet of personal experience. It is therefore not surprising, since the hymn is a communal form exceeding the limits of the purely personal, that he should have have written only one that achieved popularity: "O Durchbrecher aller Bande" (Seeburg, p. 289). This hymn is nonetheless one of Arnold's best poems, a work of great rhythmical power and, like all his poetry, conducive to meditation:

> O Durchbrecher aller Bande,
> Der du immer bey uns bist,
> Bey dem Schaden, Spott und Schande
> Lauter Lust und Himmel ist:
> Übe ferner dein Gerichte
> Wider unsers Adams Sinn,
> Biss uns dein so treu Gesichte
> Führet aus dem Kercker hin.

The bonds from which the Christian prays to be released are not the bonds of earthly suffering, for the Cross is just what he must long for; he prays for release from passionate clinging to the earthly, "Adams Sinn," all that binds the will. Arnold's usual terms for these bonds are, as with other mystics (and many who merely adopt the mystical terminology), "Creatur" and "Natur." Strophe 4:

> Schau doch aber unsre Ketten,
> Da wir mit der Creatur

Seuffzen, ringen, schreyen, betten
Umb Erlösung von Natur . . .

If the breakthrough can be achieved, if the "Christ within" can "perfect us" by drawing us into His suffering, that is, if man's inevitable suffering can be made meaningful, we can be "brought back," restored to the image of God in which we were made ("Nach dem besten Bild gebildt"), which is what Arnold understands by salvation. Strophe 10:

Drum, so wahr du bist gestorben,
Must du uns auch machen rein,
Rein und frey und gantz vollkommen,
Nach dem besten Bild gebildt . . .

The final (eleventh) strophe expresses confidence that freedom will be achieved at last, though never on this plane. The final victory is supernal. Here we are ever in the flesh and "Wir verlangen keine Ruhe / Vor das Fleisch in Ewigkeit" (stanza 7). Such at least seems to me to be Arnold's meaning, though it is possible, one must admit, that he refers to the restoration of the prelapsarian man even on earth. If so, his doctrine is even more radical:

Liebe [,] zeuch uns in dein Sterben,
Lass uns mit gecreutzigt seyn,
Was dein Reich nicht kan ererben,*
Führ ins Paradies uns ein!
Doch wohlan! Du wirst nicht säumen,
Wo wir nur nicht lässig seyn,
Werden wir doch als wie träumen,†
Wann die Freyheit bricht herein.
[Strophe 11]

---

*I.e, Lass zugleich mit uns alles gekreuzigt sein, was dein Reich . . . Cf. Rom. 6:6, "We know that our old self was crucified with him so that the sinful body might be destroyed, and we might no longer be enslaved to sin." †Psalm 126:1: "When the Lord restored the fortunes of Zion, we were like those who dream." Luther's version uses the future tense: "Wenn der Herr die Gefangenen Zions erlösen wird, so werden wir sein wie die Träumenden."

Dörries points out that the concept of freedom is the fulcrum of Arnold's hymn. (*Geist und Geschichte*, pp. 190 f., footnote 63). Exploiting the paradox central to all Christian thought, Arnold tells us that victory can be achieved only by submission: by accepting the Cross we free ourselves from it. It becomes an easy yoke, as every homilist assures us. Assuming the Cross means accepting the struggle to free ourselves from sin, to which we are by nature condemned. The victory, however, cannot come by our efforts alone; grace is necessary, hence the hymn is a prayer for help to the "Durchbrecher aller Bande."

The diction of this hymn is almost entirely Biblical. The opening line is a reference to Micah 2:13: "Es wird ein Durchbrecher vor ihnen herauffahren; sie werden durchbrechen und zum Tor ausziehen. . . ." In other passages it is almost as though Paul himself were speaking. Figurative language in the sense of *ornatus* is almost wholly absent. Such turns as "Staub der Sünden," "des Vaters Hochzeit-Hauss," "Tod der Eitelkeit" are standard counters of the hymnology of the day; they are not meant to tease the mind with their "Scharfsinnigkeit" but to move the heart by their directness and familiarity. The tone is hortatory in consonance with the form of a prayer in which the poem is cast. One imperative— I count twenty-two direct commands—follows on the heels of another, reaching a climax in the sixth strophe:

> Herrscher herrsche/
> Sieger siege/
> König brauch dein Regiment/
> Führe deines Reiches Kriege/
> Mach der Scalverey ein End!

All commands are appeals to the will. What will is here appealed to, Christ's (or the Holy Ghost's) or our own? On the basis of Arnold's other writings it seems safe to assume that it is a will within us. Like all religious voluntarists, Arnold conceives of man as composed of two warring wills, and the will to will that will which leads to salvation constitutes the struggle of which his poetry is primarily the expression. But

141

here the interior struggle is exteriorized under a doctrinal guise and thus rendered public: we have a hymn. It has become the Christian's struggle, not only Arnold's.

The difficult inward struggle between the attractions of the world, in Arnold's case the attractions of scholarship, the life of reason that leads to fame, and those of pure wisdom, the contemplation of the divine, is treated in two narrative poems, "Liebes-Geschichte" and "Die seligste Vermählung" (Seeberg, pp. 270 ff.). Here we are wholly within the sphere of individual experience; the poet is "speaking of what he knows and bearing witness to what he has seen." The mode, however, is allegorical, or semi-allegorical: one of the wills is figured forth as Sophia, divine wisdom. Arnold's Sophia doctrine, to which he devoted an entire treatise, is not exactly simple. "All wisdom comes from the Lord, and remains with him forever," we read in the Wisdom of Sirach 1:1 (Goodspeed's translation); "Wisdom was created before them all" (1:4), i.e., before the heavens and earth; "The Lord himself created her . . . and poured her out upon all he made; upon all mankind, as he chose to bestow her; but he supplied her liberally to those who loved him" (1:9 f.); "She was created with the faithful in the womb" (1:14). Sophia is an integral part of all those who "fear the Lord," and "to fear the Lord is to be satisfied with wisdom, for she intoxicates them with her fruits" (1:16).

This doctrine Arnold, following Jacob Böhme, combines with the teaching of the androgynous Adam and the two falls of man. Adam was created perfect, combining within himself both masculine and feminine. But "Als Adam sich in seiner begierde von Gott ausgekehret, und ausser sich und seiner in ihm wohnenden heiligen jungfrau, der weisheit, etwas zu lieben suchte: verlohr er diese seine geheime braut" (Seeberg, p. 345). This was the first fall. Eve was created later as a poor substitute for Sophia. However, Sophia still dwells within close reach of us; we have only lost touch with her in turning "mit zweiffel und begierde" to the "Creaturen," to the earthly. "Vor allen dingen wisse und glaube, o mensch, dass diese edle Sophia nicht ferne von dir, sondern näher als du dir selbst bist, seyn wolle und könne, wo du sie nicht vertreibest" (Seeberg, p. 347).

Though we can no longer be united with her in "paradisische art," Sophia never ceases to try to win our heart and ear: "so unterläst sie doch nicht, aus hertzlicher liebe zu ihren alten thron-sitzen und wohnstätten [i.e., men's souls] auf Gottesbefehl sich bey einem jedem kinde Adams inwendig im hertzen zu melden" (Seeberg, p. 347). This she does in the hope of "bringing back" man to direct communion with God: Sophia offers us rebirth. Her call can come to us in various guises, according to our particular natures: she can come "as a virgin, as a bridegroom or also as a mother" (Seeberg, p. 344). In "Liebes-Geschichte" she comes as a virgin bride who first seeks to win the poet while still a youth. The price of her love is renunciation of the world, and while he is easily able to renounce riches and sensual pleasures, he cannot resist the temptation of fame to be gained "durch falsch berühmte Kunst." For a time he is under the delusion that he can serve two masters:

Halb könt ich mich der Welt, halb ihrer Lieb ergeben,
Damit ich dennoch blieb mit ihrem Thun bekannt.
So könt ich bleiben frey. . . .
[Seeberg, p. 271]

But:

Sophiam schmerzte diss: Ihr treu gesinnt Gemüthe
Liess doch nicht ändern sich durch meinen falschen
Sinn;
Biss dass ich meine Zeit sammt ihrer besten Blüthe
In eitler Wissenschaft vergebens brachte hin.

Sophia calls him again; compromise is impossible; he must give up "this whore" who can never bring him peace. She offers her lap for his weary head. He repents, accepts her love, and gives himself up as entirely to her as she to him. Their marriage is exceedingly fruitful:

Ihr sanftes Wesen macht mich ewiglich vergnügt;
. . . Und macht

143

dass unsre Eh viel 100. Kinder/kriegt,
Die vor dem Herrn stehn
und seine Weisheit preisen.

[p. 272]

"Die seligste Vermählung" (272 ff.) is a companion piece
to "Liebes-Geschichte." In the first, "God's bride" (one of the
names for Sophia; cf. Seeberg, p. 346) offers herself to man;
in the second, a soul which has experienced the blessedness of
union with the "pure spirit of Jesus" speaks to those souls
who have not, that is, Sophia here assumes the aspect of the
bridegroom. The course of conversion is similar in both poems: the soul lost in sin first refuses the bridegroom and
becomes even more obdurate. But Jesus refuses to be turned
away and the soul is gradually won over:

So offt ich ihn vertrieb,
So offte kam er wieder.

Until

Ich ward dem Liebsten gut,
Den ich zuvor verwarff.
. . . .
So ward ich auserkohren
Zu eines Königs Braut.

[p. 273]

The final section describes the union in erotic imagery.

When Arnold describes the process of conversion in
erotic language, he is firmly within the mystical tradition,
especially that of those poets who cultivated poetical allegory
that took its source from the Song of Songs. For Arnold,
Daniel Sudermann's *Hohe geistreiche Lehren / und Erzählungen:
Uber die führnehmbsten Sprüche dess Hohen Lieds Salomonis* . . .
(1622) represents a direct influence. According to August
Langen (*Deutsche Philologie im Aufriss*, 1, 1139), Sudermann is
one of the most important transmitters of the language of the
medieval mystics. Günther Müller states that Sudermann's

144

poetry is "rein privater Natur . . . , nicht für ein Publikum, nicht für die Gemeinde, sondern als Widerspiel seines Seelenlebens entstanden" (*Gesch. des dt. Lieds*, p. 37). Thus his spiritual kinship with Arnold is evident. Both employ allegorical interpretation as a medium for purely personal expresssion. The first part of Arnold's *Poetische Lob- und Liebes-Sprüche* is a direct adaptation of Sudermann's *Hohe geistreiche Lehren*, and while the two poems just discussed are not found in the *PLLS*, they are in much the same spirit.

However, Arnold's poetry is not usually cast in narrative form, which has a distancing effect, but is much more typically lyrically direct or else reflective in a peculiarly passionate way. A song from the *PLLS* begins:

> O rosen-mund, komm, küsse mich,
> Flöss deine lebens-säffte
> Unmittelbar und süssiglich
> In die verschmachten kräffte.
> [Seeberg, p. 327]

As an illustration of the reflective mood, also from *PLLS:*

> Verborgenes licht, geheimes leben,
> Der Göttlichen Vollkommenheit,
> Wer kennet deine reinigkeit?
> Wem hast du dich zu eigen geben?
> Ja niemand weiss von deinem Namen
> Noch merket deiner weissheit spur,
> Wiewol dein unbefleckter samen
> Liegt in der menschlichen natur.
> [Seeberg, p. 329]

Both these poems are of course addressed to Sophia.

In his reflective poetry, which is his most characteristic mode, Arnold is fond of bipartite strophic forms, in which the argument proceeds dialectically. The stanza just quoted is an example, though not all are so clearly structured, to be sure. Bipartite structure is put to excellent, if somewhat obvious, use in "Bitt-Lied um die vollendung," in which perfection is prayed for in the trochaic rhythm of the first half of the stanza, and the final triumph or surety of attainment of perfection is reflected in the dactylic rhythm of the second half:

> Hertzog unsrer seligkeiten,
> Zeuch uns in dein heiligthum,
> Da du uns die städt bereiten
> Und hier im triumph herum
> Als deine erkauffte sieg-prächtig willst führen:
> Lass unsere bitte dein hertze itzt rühren!
> Wir wollen dem Vater zum opffer da stehn
> Und in der gemeinschafft der leiden hingehn.
>
> [Seeberg, p. 308]

Arnold, like all pietists and most mystics, has little good to say for either nature around us or within us. Both are to be overcome for the sake of the true good. His eyes are always turned toward the supernal. In this respect he is thoroughly a poet of the seventeenth rather than the eighteenth century. It is the personally confessional nature of his utterance that points forward to the age that is dawning, and in this (like the pietists in general) he is a brother of Johann Christian Günther.

We cannot leave Arnold without mentioning three of his best-known poems: "So führst du doch recht selig, Herr, die Deinen," "Babels Grab-Lied," and "Als ich das nicht nahm wohl in acht," which reveal respectively his views of history and of organized religion, and the speculative aspect of his mysticism.

"So führst du doch . . ." (Seeberg, p. 284) is a meditation in thirteen eight-line stanzas on God's ways, which are not those of man. In contrast to the philosophy of the Enlightenment, which tries to reduce the divine to the level of human comprehension by making it rational, Arnold stresses the irrationality or superrationality and consequent incomprehensibility of God's ways. The danger for Arnold—and for all intellectuals—is the *superbia* of reason, which seeks to explain all, including the divine, by means of its "own light" *(lumen naturale)*. But human *"Klugheit,"* Arnold insists, is powerless to fathom "der tiefsten *Weisheit* Abgrund" (stanza 4)—God plays another game. His wisdom "plays with us" (stanza 6), and only if we are blessed by such wisdom can we in turn play with it—the price is renunciation of the claims of human reason. From the standpoint of reason the game God plays looks like this:

> Was unsre Klugheit will zusammen fügen,
> Das theilt dein Witz in Ost und Westen auss:
> Was mancher unter Joch und Last will biegen,
> Setzt deine Hand frey an der Sternen Hauss.
> Die Welt zerreist und du knüpffst in Krafft,
> Sie bricht, du baust; sie baut, du reissest ein.
> Ihr Glantz muss dir ein dunkler Schatten seyn,
> Dein Geist bei Todten Krafft und Leben schafft.
>
> [stanza 3]

What we must pray for is the ability to distinguish "Natur von Gnade," "das eigne Licht von deiner Heiterkeit" (stanza 10), God's serene nonchalance. This can be brought about only if we break "the will that loves itself" instead of God.

Dörries calls this poem "the finest expression of Arnold's concept of history" and speaks of the "joyous confidence" with which Arnold describes the defeat of the human will and human reason (*Geist und Geschichte*, p. 197). Evaluative judgments according to human standards are not applicable to God's ways in history: "Das Widerspiel legst du vor Augen dar / Von dem, was du in deinem Sinne hast" (stanza 9). Luther's doctrine of killing (the natural man) to make living (the spiritual man) and the concealment of God in history are also, Dörries points out, guiding concepts in Arnold (p. 198). Yet Dörries insists that reason has its place in Arnold's scheme of things: it has the first, if not the last, word: "die Gegenstellung . . . zur Vernunft . . . redet nicht etwa einem Irrationalismus das Wort, als sei die ratio durch Gefühl, Gemüt und andere Seelenkräfte ersetzt" (p. 199). The point is that reason has no *final* answer; its interpretation is necessarily provisional and partial. The problem for a man of Arnold's stamp, an erudite man strongly inclined to give reason

147

its dues and more, is that of submission. The last three strophes are a prayer to be granted the power not to conquer but to submit:

Will etwa die Vernunft dir widersprechen
Und schüttelt ihren Kopf zu deinem Weg;
So wolst du die Bevestung niederbrechen,
Dass ihre Höh sich nur bey Zeiten leg.

[stanza 11]

The Christian way to this end is to be drawn into the will of the Father through the Son, who (like Sophia, of whom He can appear as an aspect) is constantly announcing His presence within us:

So zieh mich denn hinein in deinen Willen
Und trag und heg und führ dein armes Kind.
Dein innres Zeugnuss soll den Zweiffel stillen,
Dein Geist die Furcht und Lüste überwind.
Du bist mein alles, denn dein Sohn ist mein,
Dein Geist regt sich gantz kräfftiglich in mir.
Ich brenne nun nach dir in Liebs-Begier,
Wie offt erquickt mich deiner Klarheit Schein?

[stanza 12]

"Babels Grab-Lied" (Seeberg, p. 276) is Arnold's only longer polemical poem (eighteen stanzas). Its motto is taken from Jeremiah 51:9: "We would have healed Babylon, but she is not healed: Forsake her and let each of us go into his own country. . . ." Babel is for Arnold the established church, particularly Lutheran orthodoxy, with its emphasis on dogma, its "Streittheologie," and its neglect of the needs of the inner man.[7] (For Luther, Babel was of course Rome.) Jacob Böhme had already penned these bitter words about Babel: "Der Heilige hat die Kirche in sich / da er inne höret und lehret: aber Babel hat einen Steinhauffen / da gehet sie hinein,"[8] and criticism against established religion was one of the principal polemical themes of the second half of the seventeenth century. The pietists were especially critical; their movement owed its origin in good part to a revolt against theological quarrels.

148

As in many other instances, Arnold, in "Babels Grab-Lied," adopts the strophic form of a well-known hymn, in this case Michael Kongehl's "Nur frisch hinein! / Es wird so tief nicht seyn" (cf. Friedrich, p. 17). This strophe Arnold makes speak with dreadful solemnity and scornful wrath. The two opening short lines (two and three beats) either state a portentous fact or voice a command: the three longer lines that follow (5–5–4 beat) develop the statement or command; the closing short line (two beats) brings the stanza to a firm close reflecting the inevitability of Babel's ultimate downfall, a certainty also imaged in the rhyme scheme (aabbaa) and in some instances in the identity or near identity of the first and last lines, as in stanza 7:

> So lasst sie gehn
> Und ihrem Richter stehn!
> O reisset Band und Pflaster ihr vom Leibe,
> Damit sie bloss und nackend stehen bleibe!
> Die Schande muss der gantze Himmel sehn.
> Drum lasst sie gehn!

The imagery derives almost wholly from Jeremiah, chapter 51. If, therefore, the poem is "wild," as Dörries calls it (p. 54), it is wild on firm authority. Stanzas 1–7 depict Babel as a sick whore who infects those who attempt to heal her: therefore it is better to abandon her to her fate. Stanzas 8–9 prophesy Babel's near demise; 10–13 call upon Zion to storm Babel and destroy her utterly; 14–17 are directed against the "Maul-Christen" who fulminate against Babel but still submit to her sway. Because they have not yet conquered the Babel within they cannot conquer the Babel without:

> Drum dämffet nicht
> Den Geist wenn er ausbricht
> In euch und andern, Babels Grund zu stöhren;
> Ihr sonderlich, die ihr wollt viel bekehren,
> *Seht dass nur erst in euch gantz Babel bricht,*
> Und heuchelt nicht.
>
> [stanza 15, emphasis added]

149

Stanzas 16–17 renew the call to action, while the final stanza (18) is a prophecy of final victory.

Arnold's high ideal of the church "nach dem Willen Gottes und dem Muster der ersten Christen" kept him from accepting a pastorate for a considerable time, though twice urged to do so by Spener. When he then, after much hesitation, accepted a call to Giessen as professor of history, it was in the hope that he could here better serve God and his fellow men. This hope was doomed to swift disappointment. Arnold soon resigned his position, full of disgust for the "hochtrabendes, ruhmsüchtiges Vernunft-Wesen des akademischen Lebens," as he says in his *Offenherziges Bekenntnis* (quoted by Dörries, p. 57). The universities also belong to Babel; in fact, they are her very source, for their ruling spirit is "die verkehrte Vernunft in ihren bösen Werken, die offenbare und gefährlichste Feindin Gottes und seines Sohnes" (ibid.). True knowledge, Arnold believed, must come through revelation, "Erleuchtung," and only by placing revelation above reason can we find truth. But Arnold also, as Dörries rightly maintains, found himself in secret sympathy with the rationalistic standpoint of the university: Babel infects the physician who would cure her. This was perhaps the deeper reason for his violent reaction and his decision to flee. "Babels Grab-Lied" thus reveals the same tension that we find throughout Arnold's poetry, the tension between "Vernunft" and "Erleuchtung," "Vernunft" being in Arnold's scheme an ally of the flesh ("Natur," "Creatur"), the other will that Sophia urges him to overcome. Arnold's life and poetry are of a piece.

Arnold uses the same strophic form (except for lengthening the fifth line to five beats) to quite different effect in "Der unbekannte Gott" ("Verborgenheit, wie ist dein Meer," Seeberg, p. 287). Here the ebb and flow of the short and long lines reflect an inward state, the pulsation of contemplation. The tone is calm yet fervent. The thematic material—God's concealment—is developed as follows: God's nature is "Verborgenheit," concealment; to be unknown is His way of being. Yet man is not wholly cut off from God: a trace of His glory is the share of His children, who do not include, however, all mankind but only the "awakened." These partake of the mystery even here and are comforted in the realm of time:

> Die Herrlichkeit,
> Die du hast allbereit
> Den Kindern deiner Lieb hie beygeleget,
> Ist sonderlich. Wer dies Geheimnuss hegt,
> Der träget auch zu der elendsten Zeit
> Die Herrlichkeit.
>
> [stanza 2]

It is from the pretended Christians, the hypocrites, the rationalists, and the lukewarm that God is completely concealed. These scorn the ways of the awakened and in so doing scorn God himself: "Und was nicht leidt ein Maul- und Heuchel-Christ / du selber bist" (stanza 3). (A touch of pietistic arrogance is undeniable here.) The "children of His love" God also "conceals," that is, makes their ways a mystery to the world, so that they reflect God's own concealment: "Darum versteckt / der Herr was er erweckt / Die Kinder gehn nur immer im Verborgen" (stanza 8). Their glory will be revealed at the end of time. In reality, God's children are concealed by the world itself, which, having lost touch with God, cannot fathom the ways of His children. Meanwhile, God maintains a secret commerce with His own:

> So wandelt Er
> Im Heiligthum einher
> Mit leisem Schritt. Der kan ihn nicht vernehmen,
> Wer sich zur Einfalt nicht gern will bequemen
> Wie Er sonst nichts zu thun pflegt ungefehr,
> So wandelt Er.
>
> [stanza 9]

Though sometimes regarded as a separatist, Arnold is here not advocating separatism. He is speaking of the church invisible. God's children may be, if not of any creed, then certainly of any Christian sect. Arnold is not trying to found a sect of his own; in fact, he is not a religious leader at all, though he is a deep religious thinker.

> Du selber bist der Brunn, der ihnen [den Erweckten] ist
> In ihrem Geist zum stäten Heyl entsprungen.
>
> [stanza 3]

Those who have a talent for inwardness, for conversation with the divine, one might say, are ipso facto members of the invisible church. Any creed is secondary. This is the standpoint of the genuine mystic.

"Als ich das nichts nahm wohl in acht" (Seeberg, p. 299), composed in the standard hymn stanza (here doubled), is meditative speculation, argument, and exhortation based on a personal mystical experience, namely, the complete revaluation of all values that follows upon the renunciation of creature will. The conceit on which the poem is based—and it is in this respect very "baroque"—rests on the ambivalent use of the word "nichts," which is used both in the sense of the opposite of "ichts" (something), i.e., the world of creation and the creature, and also in the ordinary sense of "not anything." That for the mystic "das nichts" is everything need hardly be pointed out. On this paradox Arnold rings his sometimes puzzling changes. The strophe with the most personal application to the poet himself is perhaps the eighth, which is addressed to the erudite, that is, to Arnold's own class and, by implication, to himself. It also exemplifies the height of the paradox:

> Gelehrte, kommt zum nichts heran,
> Sonst ist euer thun gewirre;
> Wer sich nicht find auff diese bahn,
> Bleibt ewig in der irre.
> Ohn nichts ist nichts was je geschieht,
> Im nichts muss ichts verschwinden,
> Im nichts auch wenn ichts recht gebricht,
> Ist ichts allein zu finden.

Stanza 15 tells of the difficulty of surrendering wholly to "das nichts"; it is the same struggle we have seen the poet experiencing in surrendering to the arguments of Sophia.

152

> Wie wenig sind, den nichts beliebt?
> Weil man so viel muss lassen:
> Denn wer dem nichts nur etwas gibt,
> Der muss sich selber hassen.
> Es find sich nichts [,] das nichts will seyn,
> Das nichts heist ichts auff erden;
> Es ist dem ichts die schwerste pein,
> Wenn es zu nicht soll werden.

But the rewards of surrender are inexpressibly great: in the divine nothing lies the all:

> Das nichts ist von so edler art,
> Es kan kein mund aussprechen.
> Wer sich mit nichts nur einmahl paart,
> Dem kan nichts mehr gebrechen.
>   [stanza 13]

The import of this poem is the same as that of all Arnold's poetry: if one wants to "taste God himself" (Gott selber schmacken, stanza 19) one must abandon the world utterly. It is written from the viewpoint of one already privileged to participate in the divine nothing and thus does not primarily emphasize—as do most mystical utterances—the *via purgativa*, but speaks, or attempts to speak, of the *unio* itself.

Gerhard Tersteegen (1697–1769)[9] states his credo in a letter from the year 1741 written to the Herrnhuter (Moravians), who had tried to win him over to their principles:

> My sentiments and my religion are these, that as one who is reconciled to God, through the blood of Christ, I suffer the spirit of Jesus, by means of mortification, affliction, and prayer, to lead me away from self, and all created good [allem Geschaffenen], in order that I may live safely to God in Christ Jesus; and cleaving by faith and love to him, I hope to become one spirit with him,

153

and to obtain eternal felicity through his mercy in
Christ alone.[10]

With all who have this same faith, whether of his "Erbreli-
gion" or not, Tersteegen feels himself united, and this includes the Herrnhuter, although he thinks they are creating
one more division in an already disunited religious world. Of
those who came to him for guidance he said, when asked of
what faith they were: "Ich frage nicht, von wannen sie kommen, sondern wohin sie wollen" (Nigg, *Auswahl*, p. 32). The
Herrnhuter, Tersteegen was convinced, made things too easy
for themselves by preaching conviction of forgiveness of sin
through "süsse Erfahrungen" instead of through union with
Christ's suffering. Justification was not that simple. This is
the theme of his "Warnungsschreiben wider die Leichtsinnigkeit" (Nigg, pp. 115 ff.). Self-denial, not self-indulgence, is
an outward sign of the awakened. The heart of Tersteegen's
warning is this:

> Man will leben, ehe man gestorben ist, und nur von
> Liebe, Freude, süssen Empfindungen und Versicherun-
> gen wissen, da man noch wohl kaum oder gar nicht
> erfahren hat, was wahre Herzensbusse und Bekehrung
> sei und das Fleisch samt seinen Lüsten und Begierden
> nicht einmal gekreuzigt, will geschweigen getötet ist.
> (Nigg, p. 127)

Tersteegen's faith, it might appear, is grimly ascetic. Yet
his poetry is of a sweetness and purity hardly equaled even
by that of Paul Gerhardt. It does not speak, as Arnold's does,
primarily of the struggle to attain inner peace but of peace
attained. As a mystic, which he is in every respect, Tersteegen cultivates an inward world that has abandoned all temptations of the "Creatur." Jesus says to the soul:

> Kind, schliess die Augen zu vor diesem ganzen Rund,
> Die Welt lass von der Welt und ihren Puppen handeln;
> Bleib du stets nah bei mir in deiner Seele Grund:
> So innig wollen wir hier miteinander wandeln.

Was geht die Welt dich an? Bald gehest du hinaus,
Dann sind wir stets beisamm'n in meines Vaters Haus.
[Nigg, p. 55]

The world and its "Puppen," its concern for wealth, esteem, erotic pleasure, and so on, Tersteegen could easily, even scornfully, dismiss. These were not true temptations for him, if we may believe his life, his letters, his poetry. His own particular cross was the demands of those who wanted him to lead them to the salvation it seemed he had so obviously attained himself. "Was mich betrifft," he writes in a letter to a "brother in Christ," "so gestehe ich, dass ich ganz anders leben würde, wenn ich die Wahl hätte. Ich muss reden, schreiben, mit Menschen umgehen und möchte gern nach meinem Wunsche beinahe immer schweigen, mich verbergen und nur an Gott denken" (Nigg, p. 197).[11] It is in his poetry that Tersteegen holds his peace, conceals himself, and thinks only of God. His poetry is above all a kind of speech that conjures up and celebrates silence. In it "die Stillen im Lande" find their most persuasive poetical voice.

Besides 111 longer poems (geistliche Lieder), Tersteegen wrote some 1,200 epigrams (Sprüche, Schlussreime) and pure lyrics. The former employ sixty-nine different meters, almost all of them, according to Nelle (p. 296), taken over from sixteenth- and seventeenth-century hymns; Tersteegen himself invented only eleven. The "Schlussreime" are strongly influenced by Johannes Scheffler, whom Tersteegen, like the pietists in general, much admired. Nelle compares the epigrammatic manner of the two poets, pointing out that Tersteegen has the tendency to expand and explicate where Scheffler leaves explication to reader (p. 280 f.). Scheffler, for example, writes:

Drei wünsch ich mir zu sein: erleucht wie Cherubim,
Geruhig wie ein Thron, entbrannt wie Seraphim.
[*Cherubinischer Wandersmann* 3,164]

Tersteegen's version explains the theological significance of the terms denoting angelic orders (incidentally also construing the Hebrew plurals as singulars):

155

> Wer Gott ganz reine liebt, gleicht einem Seraphim,
> Wer ihn im Geist beschaut, machts wie ein Cherubim,
> Wer Gott ruht, und auch Gott in sich lässt ruhn und
>   wohnen,
> Der ist nicht träg, er thut, was alle Himmelsthronen.

That Scheffler is a superior epigrammatist should be obvious enough, at least in the handling of the alexandrine. Tersteegen's epigram is watery compared to Scheffler's. But only about half of Tersteegen's epigrammatic poems are in alexandrines alone; those in other (or mixed) measures are much more characteristic of his true tone. The following example in mixed measures shows how supplely Tersteegen can make meter reflect message (Nigg, p. 63). The alexandrines (verses 1 and 3) not only convey the demand to prostrate the will, they also reflect rhythmically the prostrated will itself, while the short lines and quick rhymes reflect submission to the demand. Here we are wholly in the inward realm. The final couplet (in four-beat iambs) then refers us outward and interprets sententiously and homiletically. Two worlds, two rhythmic structures.

> So wie ein weisses Blatt ist unters Schreibers Hand,
> In solchem Stand
> Musst du dich bilderlos und ohne Widerstreben
> Nur übergeben:
> Durch Lassen, Warten und durchs Leiden
> Kann Gott aufs beste uns bereiten.

It is highly characteristic of Tersteegen that, although he frequently refers to suffering as a means of identification with the Savior and as an instrument through which we are brought to renounce the world, he does not dwell upon it. It is not his theme. His great theme is the attainment of gloriously fervent oneness with the divine. In order to achieve this state, Tersteegen constantly tells us, we must divest ourselves of all images, "Bilder"; we must become "ein weisses Blatt." It is the emptying of the will of which all mystics speak; into this emptiness God pours himself and converses with us inwardly. The measure of Tersteegen's success as a poet of mysticism lies in his ability to convey the sense of this union, and this ability is indeed astounding. Even in the communal form of his most popular hymn, "Gott ist gegenwärtig"— included in all hymnals in which Tersteegen is represented at all, Nelle informs us (p. 380)—the individual note receives the chief emphasis. In pietism it is not the body of believers that is of prime importance but the individual and his particular relation to the divine. But "Gott ist gegenwärtig," unlike most of Tersteegen's poems, is full of joyous enthusiasm as well as that silence which is more specifically characteristic of him. Believers or not, we cannot help feeling the exaltation of these rhythms, and it is probably this infectious quality that has assured its place among the great Protestant hymns. Nelle rightly says, "Bei aller Stille ist etwas wundersam Lebendiges in dem Liede" (p. 380). The hymn consists of eight eight-line stanzas structured on a bipartite principle (4 + 4), reflecting in a general way expansion and contraction or longing and fulfillment or anticipation of fulfillment. The same principle is likewise reflected within each stanza. I quote stanzas 1, 4, 5 and 6:

> Gott ist gegenwärtig! Lasset uns anbeten
> Und in Ehrfurcht vor ihn treten.
> Gott ist in der Mitte! alles in uns schweige
> Und sich innigst vor ihm beuge.
> Wer ihn kennt,
> Wer ihn nennt,
> Schlagt die Augen nieder,
> Kommt, ergebt euch wieder.
>
> Majestätisch Wesen! Möcht ich recht dich preisen
> Und im Geist dir Dienst erweisen!
> Möcht' ich, wie die Engel, immer vor dir stehen
> Und dich gegenwärtig sehen!
> Lass mich dir
> Für und für
> Trachten zu gefallen,
> Liebster Gott, in allen.

Luft, die alles füllet! Drin wir immer schweben;
Aller Dingen Grund und Leben!
Meer ohn Grund und Ende! Wunder aller Wunder!
Ich senk mich in dich hinunter:
Ich in dir,
Du in mir;
Lass mich ganz verschwinden,
Dich nur sehn und finden.

Du durchdringest alles, lass dein schönstes Lichte,
Herr, berühren mein Gesichte.
Wie die zarten Blumen willig sich entfalten
Und der Sonne stille halten,
Lass mich so,
Still und froh,
Deine Strahlen fassen
Und dich wirken lassen.

[Nigg, pp. 67 ff.]

The diction is at once simple and elevated, i.e., "sublime"; one is tempted to say Hölderlinian. But a comparison of this hymn with, say, Hölderlin's "hymn to the air" in *Hyperion* (I, Bk. 2, second letter) will show us how unworldly, even anti-worldly, Tersteegen is, despite his "Hölderlinian" metaphors for the noumenal. In Tersteegen all is dissolved in a formless all-pervasive flux. The sense of God's presence is conveyed intensely but unspecifically. Though he prays to "see and find" God on the earthly plane, he at the same time prays to be able to reject the very creation by means of which it is given man to attain such experience: "Mache mich einfältig, innig, abgeschieden, Sanfte und im stillen Frieden . . ." (stanza 7). "Abgeschieden" is here used in the technical mystical sense of separation from all created being. In other words, the experience longed for is the *unio mystica*, which is by definition union with the uncreated. That he must use metaphors involving created being to express this longing is a shortcoming of the human condition. Hölderlin, on the other hand, though he too is speaking of union with the divine, remains with the specific and allows the experience of the *unio* to shine through the creation he so lovingly depicts. Hyperion writes to Bellarmin:

> Es war so sichtbar, wie alles Lebendige mehr, denn tägliche Speise, begehrt, wie auch der Vogel sein Fest hat und das Tier.
>
> Es war entzückend anzusehn! Wie, wenn die Mutter schmeichelnd frägt, wo um sie her ihr Liebstes sei, und alle Kinder in den Schos ihr stürzen, und das Kleinste noch die Arme aus der Wiege streckt, so flog und sprang und strebt jedes Leben in die göttliche Luft hinaus, und Käfer und Schwalben und Tauben und Störche tummelten sich in frohlockender Verwirrung unter einander in den Tiefen und Höhn, und was die Erde festhielt, dem ward zum Fluge der Schritt, über die Gräben brauste das Ross und über die Zäune das Reh, und aus dem Meergrund kamen die Fische herauf und hüpften über die Fläche. Allen drang die mütterliche Luft ans Herz, und hob sie und zog sie zu sich. . . . O Schwester des Geistes, der feurigmächtig in uns waltet und lebt, heilige Luft! wie schön ists, dass du, wohin ich wandre, mich geleitest, Allgegenwärtige, Unsterbliche! . . . Ich war voll unbeschreiblichen Sehnens und Friedens. Eine fremde Macht beherrschte mich. Freundlicher Geist sagt ich bei mir selber, wohin rufest du mich? nach Elysium oder wohin?

Tersteegen's good is wholly transcendent; Hölderlin's, if not wholly this-worldly, is at the very least both transcendent and incarnate in the earthly. Union, "Ich in dir, Du in mir," can come to pass not only without renunciation of the *Creatur* but through the *Creatur* itself: "Es war entzückend *anzusehn!* . . . Ich war voll unbeschreiblichen Sehnens *und* Friedens." The astounding thing about Tersteegen is the degree to which he seems to convey the unconveyable almost without instruments of conveyance, almost without metaphor, without recourse to the visible. He achieves his magic mainly through rhythm and euphony, not through imagery and argument. He imparts his experience to us in movement and in sound. Thus the first four lines of each stanza are comparatively broken, excited and full of movement, expressive of intense desire, though they may not overtly speak of desire. At the same time, most of them show, as does the poem as a whole, a high incidence of nasals and liquids, which counteract the excitement of the syntax and anticipate the fervent stillness of the second part of the stanza which symbolizes the fulfillment. Stanza 5 (Luft, die alles füllet) is a good example.

Like Arnold, Tersteegen was well-versed in theology and anything but naive. One need only read his "Warnungsschreiben wider die Leichtsinnigkeit" and his "review" of the works of Frederick the Great to convince oneself of this. But unlike Arnold, he does not use poetry as a vehicle for argument or polemics. In his poetry he is concerned primarily with conversation with God, an experience which, since it is by nature inexpressible, is so to speak provided with a cone of silence in which it can take place. In "Der Stand der Beschaulichkeit," for example, Tersteegen tries to show us how "the friend of God" feels when he experiences that which is as close to being a return to the divine oneness as is given to man to experience in this life (Nigg, pp. 71 ff.). The poem, which consists of forty-four six-line stanzas, is in four parts. The first part speaks of the sense of awe and veneration at the awareness of the presence of the state of "Beschaulichkeit" itself and surprise that it is so near, namely, within the self. ("Beschaulichkeit" one can perhaps call intuitive awareness of God's immediacy.)

> Ein Etwas ist mir innig nah,
> Ein unbekanntes Gut ist da,
> Das meinen Geist erfüllet.
> Ich darf und wills nicht frei besehn,
> Ich bleib in Liebesehrfurcht stehn,
> Bestürzt und doch gestillet.
> . . . .
> Mein Geist, dies arm verirrte Kind
> Des Vaters Haus nun wieder find't

Nach langem, langem Fragen.
[Part I, stanzas 3, 8 (first half)]

Like Novalis, Tersteegen has discovered that "Nach innen geht der geheimnisvolle Weg":

Ich suchte draussen, hie und da,
Und wusste nicht, dass wir so nah
Im Geist beisammen waren.
[I, 10]

In contradistinction to Novalis, however, Tersteegen is interested almost wholly, if not entirely, in the *personal* experience, not in the salvation of creation through insight into the great design, i.e., by raising all creation to the level of spirit. Part II considers the purpose of the state of "Beschaulichkeit" from the divine point of view and speaks of the state of the soul after God has taken possession of it. The fundamental function of the soul is to provide a dwelling place for God:

Dass er [Gott] mit seiner Glorie-Glanz
Erfülle, zier und sel'ge ganz
Den Geist, und sich drin liebe.
[II, 2]

But this self-reflection of the deity in the human soul is not the salvation of creation; rather it is a personal glory that leads to indifference toward all else:

Wer diesen Adel kennte recht,
Dem wär die ganze Welt zu schlecht,
In Gott er sich erhübe.

Even on such a pure and humane man as Tersteegen, whom one can without hesitation call saintly, the hybris of mysticism (and of pietism in general) leaves its imprint. However, one should not overstress this aspect: Tersteegen is speaking of being in the world but not of it. It is the world's values to which he becomes indifferent, not his fellow men. What we have come to think of as the Kantian view of morality becomes meaningless in the state of grace that is the "Stand der

161

Beschaulichkeit": moral action demands no self-overcoming, but fellow man is not simply disregarded:

> Die Seel wird hier verändert sehr,
> Sie kennet sich kaum selber mehr,
> Sie ist als neu geboren:
> *Man übt die Tugend, eh' man's denkt,*
> Sie wird hier wesentlich geschenkt,
> Natur scheint gar verloren.
> [II, 8; emphasis added]

Part III attempts to describe the state of "Beschaulichkeit" from the viewpoint of the world, in terms of the rest of humanity. From this standpoint all values are reversed, pluses are minuses and vice versa. Arnold tells us the same thing in "Als ich das Nichts nahm wohl in acht," but there is a profound difference in tone between Arnold and Tersteegen. Arnold cannot belie his erudite nature, cannot even in a state of grace become childlike, but must turn and turn again his paradoxical conceit. Tersteegen *shows* what Arnold *tells:*

> Es ist ein wunderbarer Stand,
> Es fällt mir alles aus der Hand,
> Ich kann an gar nichts denken.
> Die Augen sinken sanfte zu,
> Mein Geist in höchst vergnügter Ruh
> Sich einwärts muss ersenken.
> [III, 1]

Tersteegen's quietism is especially marked in this section. The state of "Beschaulichkeit" is "divine idleness," incomprehensible to reason (III, 7). Reason (Tersteegen still uses "Vernunft" in the sense of "Verstand") can furnish us only with "Bilder," concepts, whereas union with God provides essence beyond all conceptualization:

> Vernunft will immer wirken viel,
> Was nutzt ihr magres Bilderspiel?
> Gott gibt allein das Wesen!
> [III, 8]

We are here of course back again to the insoluble problem of all mystical utterance: how to express the essence without resorting to reason's "magres Bilderspiel." Mystical poetry lives from this tension.

The fourth and last part speaks of the secret communion with God in the "Wüste." In pietism the term "Wüste" can have either a positive or a negative valence: it can refer to separation from the divine ("dryness") or to the exact opposite, union with the divine in the "ground" of the soul.[12] Tersteegen here uses it in the positive sense:

> Man lockt mich in die Wüste ein,
> Da Gott und ich nur sind allein
> Da Geist mit Geist umgehet.
>
> [IV, 1]

The "Wüste" is characterized above all by the absence of everything that constitutes the created world:

> O Einsamkeit, so weit, so weit
> Von Kreatur und Ort und Zeit!

In this "desert" (actually another word for "das Nichts") stands "das Liebste," the spirit of the divine ready to unite with the spirit in us. "God, as a spirit," Tersteegen writes in "On Inward Prayer," "is more especially near to our spirits, and to the most secret recesses of the heart. This spirit of ours does not belong to this world, nor to temporal objects; it was created for God alone, and therefore capable of enjoying true fellowship with him" (Jackson, *Life and Character*, pp. 277 f.). Nonetheless, this state of being is *in* the world, if not *of* it: "Ich hab auch unter Menschen Ruh" (IV, 2). It is as though the essential individual went about under a mantle of invisibility:

> Hier wird mich Welt noch Feind gewahr,
> Ich bin entwichen der Gefahr,
> Mein Freund hat mich verborgen.
>
> [IV, 4]

Tersteegen insists that this is no visionary state, it is a center of inward calm in the midst of worldly occupations:

"Ich bet daheim und auf der Strass', Beim Work und sonst ohn' Unterlass . . ." (IV, 3). In the "Wüste" he seeks no visions, no state of rapture, does not merely revel in "süssen Empfindungen":

> Ich such nicht dies noch jenes Licht,
> Ich hab kein bildliches Gesicht,
> Entzückung, hohe Gaben . . .
>
> [IV, 7]

The state of contemplation can be attained by all who are capable of "Einkehr," i.e., of sinking into themselves until they reach the true center of their being, which is a spirit and can commune with spirit:

> Schaut, müde Seelen, kommet her,
> Dies ist ein Tröpflein aus dem Meer
> Der ew'gen Gottheits-Fülle:
> Ihr werdet grössre Dinge sehn,
> Lasst alles nur um alles stehn,
> Kehrt ein und werdet stille.
>
> [IV, 11]

"Ihr werdet grössre Dinge sehn"—the state of contemplation is not, Tersteegen tells us in the last two stanzas, equivalent to essential union, "wesentlich vereinigt sein." This can come only when death has opened the gate to true life: "Die lange, dunkle Leidensnacht/Muss erst durchwandert werden." The "Stand der Beschaulichkeit" is indeed conversation with God, but in the midst of "Creatürlichkeit," it is not final and lasting union. Tersteegen does not reject the meaning of the world as a testing ground—this would be "Leichsinnigkeit"—though his poetry (unlike that, say, of Gryphius) does not place primary emphasis on it. The world may be for Tersteegen at bottom a "dream" in comparison to the reality to which we will one day awaken, but it is a dream that must be dreamt, though not believed in. This is the burden of "Ermunterungs-lied für die Pilger" with its (for us) Novalis-like tone:

> Was wir hier hör'n und sehen,
> Das hör'n und seh'n wir kaum.

Wir lassen's da und gehen
Es irret uns kein Traum.
. . . .
Wir wandeln eingekehret,
Veracht't und unbekannt.
Man siehet, kennt und höret
Uns kaum im fremden Land.
     [Nigg, p. 109; emphasis added]

(The "strange land" is of course the world of ordinary human intercourse.) The pietist "geht der Natur entgegen" (Nigg, p. 108). He dies to this world to be reborn to the promise of the other, which makes the present world a dream in the midst of which, if he is granted the state of "Beschaulichkeit," he holds converse with the eternal.

Tersteegen's best-known poem (in distinction to his hymns) is "Andacht bei nächtlichem Wachen." The longer one considers this poem, the more the certainty grows that it is one of the most nearly perfect lyrics in the German language. I quote the whole:

1. Nun schläfet man,
    Und wer nicht schlafen kann,
    Der bete mit mir an
    Den grossen Namen,
    Dem Tag und Nacht
    Wird von der Himmelswacht
    Preis, Lob und Ehr gebracht.
    O Jesu, Amen.

2. Weg Phantasie!
    Mein Herr und Gott ist hie.
    Du schläfst, mein Wächter, nie.
    Dir will ich wachen.
    Ich liebe dich,
    Ich geb zum Opfer mich
    Und lasse ewiglich
    Dich mit mir machen.

3. Es leuchte dir
   Der Himmelslichter Zier;
   Ich sei ein Sternlein, hier
   Und dort zu funkeln.
   Nun kehr ich ein:
   Herr, rede du allein
   Beim tiefsten Stillesein
   Zu mir im Dunkeln.

[Nigg, p. 102]

We are here on the borderline between allegorical and symbolical poetry. A particular situation seems to be conjured up: "*Nun* schläfet man," but this sleep is not merely the sleep of the weary on the particular night that Tersteegen wrote his poem: it is also, probably even above all, the sleep of the "unawakened." The sleepless are not merely insomniacs, they are the "awakened," those whose converse is with God.

The stanzaic structure (as is usually the case with Tersteegen) is bipartite, but the dichotomy is at the same time canceled by the *b* rhyme (aaa*b*ccc*b*) which joins the first half of the stanza to the second, indicating oneness in duplicity or union in separateness, the state of one sunk in prayer. The rhythm pulses in beats of 2–3–3–2–2–3–3–2, forming another dichotomy, but one structured on a different scheme from that of the rhyme. Here it is the two-beat rhythms in the first and last lines of each stanza and the two adjoining two-beat verses in the middle of the stanzas that reflect the "two in one" situation, first by enclosing the whole stanza and second by joining the two halves. After a calm beginning, the rhythm attains sudden intensity in the second stanza, an intensity that ebbs again into the calm of the opening lines only when the middle of the final stanza has been reached.

Paralleling not only the rhythmic line but also the stanza structure and the rhyme scheme is the voweling, also based on a bipartite principle. Stanza 1 is dominated by low vowels, especially the *a*'s in the rhyme words. The second stanza is dominated by high vowels, especially *ie* and *i*, but is connected to the first stanza (as the halves of each stanza with each other) by a rhyme with a low vowel (wachen–machen). The final stanza does not return, as one might perhaps expect it to do for the sake of symmetry, to the low voweling of the first; neither does it show even distribution of high and low vowels (which would be another way of achieving balance), but is structured like stanza 2 with a strong predominance of high vowels, only the *b* rhyme having low (funkeln–Dunkeln). In other words, the wakefulness now attained does not slip off again into the sleep of the unawakened symbolized by the low voweling in stanza 1.

"Nun kehr ich ein" in stanza 3 is wittily ambiguous, in fact, a kind of pun. On the nonmystical level it means "to turn in" (as at an inn) for rest, on the mystical level it means "to withdraw into the soul's center" (*introverto*), a highly wakeful state in which spirit holds converse with spirit. The constellation of low vowels embracing high in the last five lines of this stanza is especially eloquent. "Dunkel" ("Dunkelheit") is again a term with two opposite significations: it can refer to lack of divine illumination, distance from God, or, as here, to the silence in which the soul meets and reverently worships the divine majesty.[13] Within the frame of the divine darkness symbolized in the *-unkeln*-rhymes is the wakeful awareness of the conversation with God symbolized by the *ei* diphthong. It is, as Tersteegen puts it in "Der Stand der Beschaulichkeit," a "dunkle Klarheit":

> Ich bin gesammelt eh' ichs denk,
> Anbete, lieb und mich ersenk
> In Gottes dunkle Klarheit.
>   [Nigg, p. 79]

Wachen has now become true wakefulness: Es *funkelt* im Dunkeln.

A word of explanation about the term "Phantasie" ("Weg Phantasie!") is in place before we leave this poem. The usage of "Phantasie" approximates that of "Bild," "Bilder," which probably refers to the second commandment. The struggle to conceive God as purely spiritual is a constant one in Tersteegen and highly reminiscent of the famous passage at the beginning of the seventh book of the *Confessions* of St. Augustine:

> My heart passionately cried out against all my *phantoms*, and with this one blow I sought to beat away from the eye of my mind all that unclean troop which buzzed around it. And lo, being scarce put off, with the twinkling of an eye they gathered again thick about me . . . so that though not under the form of the human body, yet I was constrained to conceive Thee . . . as being in space. . . . (Pusey's translation; emphasis added)

The passionate effort to think about God without recourse to the categories of space and time can achieve success only in the mystic union, which is by definition spaceless and timeless and hence inexpressible. All the poet of mysticism can do is to bracket out a realm of silence in which God *speaks:* "Herr, rede du allein, Beim tiefsten Stillesein Zu mir im Dunkeln."

Tersteegen's work contains many poems of great pregnancy, all of them worthy of discussion. I will mention only one more, the fervent Christmas hymn, "Jauchzet ihr Himmel, frohlocket ihr englische Chören," containing eight four-line stanzas (as given in Nigg, p. 112; Nelle, no. 9, p. 34 has five-line stanzas). Stanzas 1–4 call upon heaven and earth to rejoice at the birth of the Savior; this section has a most infectious joyousness. In stanzas 5–8 there is a turn from *ihr* (you) to *ich:* Is the incomprehensible condescension of the divine in assuming human form also meant for *me?* "Hast du denn Höchster, auch meiner noch wollen gedenken?" (stanza 5). If this is the case, then it is incumbent upon me to give birth to the Christ within. The tone now becomes pensive and heavy with longing:

> Süsser Immanuel, werd auch geboren inwendig,
> Komm doch, mein Heiland, und lass mich nicht länger
>   elendig!
> Wohne in mir. Mach mich ganz eines mit dir,
> Und mich belebe beständig.
>
> [stanza 7]

168

Inward birth of the Savior is true conversion; it is what is meant by "becoming a child," putting away the proud claims of reason to live in perfect submission to that which passes understanding: "Gib mir auch bald, Jesu, die Kindergestalt, An dir alleine zu kleben" (stanza 8). ". . . whoever does not receive the kingdom of God like a child shall not enter it" (Luke 18:17).

This hymn is notable not only for its utterly convincing fervency but also for its lack of sentimentality. There is no cooing over the Babe. The Holy Infant remains a god, though a "Menschenfreund." Tersteegen is no "Schwärmer"; neither is he a sentimentalist. In spite of his intense inwardness, his religiosity has a sobriety that rejects all extravagance both in word and action. "Mystiker," he writes in "Kurzer Bericht über die Mystik," "sind keineswegs Enthusiasten zu schelten. . . . Gesichte, Offenbarungen, Einsprachen, Weissagungen und manche andere ausserordentliche Dinge können zwar einem Mystiker begegnen, gehören aber gar nicht zum Wesentlichen der Mystik" (Nigg, pp. 148 f.). When the mystic feels compelled to speak of his personal experience, and this is the matter of most of Tersteegen's poetry, he will do so soberly, expressing as clearly as possible what has happened to him. Our passage continues:

> Mystiker sind auch nicht Schwätzer von grosser Geistlichkeit, sie affektieren keine dunkle, hochtrabende, verblümte Redensarten, sondern sprechen das, was sie erfahren, so aus, wie sie es mit Worten, die der heilige Geist lehret, deutlich machen können. Sie reden wenig, sie tun und sie leiden vieles, sie verleugnen alles, sie beten ohne Unterlass, der geheime Umgang mit Gott in Christo ist ihr ganzes Geheimnis.

I have placed this quotation at the end of the discussion of Tersteegen rather than at the beginning in order to give the poet for once the chance to speak through his work rather than through a self-interpretation of it; it shows how closely akin Arnold and Tersteegen are, both in their attitude toward the nature of true poetry (it must be divinely inspired) and in

169

their attitude toward the linguistic means of its expression (rejection of *ornatus*, insistence upon simple, direct language). And yet, despite their agreement in theory, how radical is the difference in tone between these two poets of pietism! In Arnold we experience a constant struggle to surrender the will: his verse is speculative, argumentative, agitated, passionately turned against his constant inner foe, rationality; Tersteegen's sings of the joys of surrender in tones of poignant sweetness and purity: the struggle is over almost before it begins. It is perhaps not going too far to say that in Tersteegen we get a glimpse of how a saint is constituted inwardly. Intellectually, Arnold may be the more interesting of the two; Tersteegen is by far the greater lyricist.

Unlike Arnold and Tersteegen, Nikolaus Ludwig von Zinzendorf (1700–1760), the founder of the Moravian Brethren (Herrnhuter), can hardly be called a true mystic.[14] Despite his strong emphasis upon a personal connection with the Savior, there was for him "no Christianity without community," whereas the genuine mystic is fundamentally indifferent to the communal practice of religion. His experience, as we have seen, is unsharably private, and all his poetic expression can achieve is to give us a sense of the fervent aura of inwardness that accompanies it. Wolfdietrich Rasch maintains that Zinzendorf attempted to combine "Gemeine und Einsamkeit," the congregation of believers and individual isolation, by establishing communities and developing a special liturgy reflecting the particular cultic interests of the Herrnhuter (*Freundschaftskult und Freundschaftsdichtung*, pp. 58 ff.). This communal piety, however, was based on the religious experience of the individual members—it was not a matter of subscribing to a formulaic confession of faith. Thus, as Rasch paradoxically puts it, the Herrnhuter were a community of individuals whose community consisted in each having a particular relation with the Savior ("Spezialumgang mit dem Heiland"). What united them as a body—their private relation to the divine—separated them as individuals.

It was in the years between 1743 and 1750, after the foundation of Herrenhag in the Wetterau, that the poetry of the *Brüdergemeinde* attained its most characteristic form. This period, which the Moravians themselves called the "Sichtungszeit," or time of testing (literally "sifting" after Luke 22:31: "And the Lord said, Simon, Simon, Satan hath desired to have you, that he may sift [*sichten*] you as wheat"), was marked not only by religious excesses but also by great creativity. During these years the community energetically developed its theological concepts, its cultic forms (liturgy), and its educational system and founded new colonies and missions.

The poetry of the Sichtungszeit is a communal expression, for though we know that Zinzendorf himself is the author of somewhat more than half the pieces collected in the "Twelfth Supplement" (12. Anhang), which (along with the four "Zugaben") contains the verse of this period, he also instructed the brethren in song-writing and held competitions to determine which pieces should be included in the Moravian hymnal. Thus the 12. Anhang represents true communal poetry; it is the product of a homogeneous religious society, using the same vocabulary, themes, figures, and style throughout.

In a sense Zinzendorf may be said to be in revolt against both pietism and the Enlightenment. His emphasis on joyful communal piety sets him off from the former, his insistence on a personal religion of the heart from the latter. Though his utterances on language and poetry are purely ad hoc and not always self-consistent, a definite tendency is readily recognizable. As so often in the eighteenth century, we also find in Zinzendorf a longing for simplicity and naturalness:

> Denn es kan sich niemand vorstellen . . . was für einen wahren Geschmack und haut gout die wahre Simplicitaet in alles hinein bringt. Das geschieht oft durch das simpelste Wörtgen, wenn es gerade aus dem Herzen kommt, originaliter, ohne die geringste Schminke und Kunst und Correctur. . . ." (Reichel, p. 67)

171

Zinzendorf (I am following Reichel throughout) hoped to attain the strength and originality of Luther's language and that of the older hymns "mit völliger hintansetzung alles schmuks der rede" (Reichel, p. 67). His plea for simplicity is both a protest against baroque *ornatus* and against the erudite language of the theologians which remained largely incomprehensible to the layman, thus depriving him of the sacred word. To speak "naif und handgreiflich" was to speak the language of the people and also of the Bible.

It goes without saying that Zinzendorf stresses the role of feeling in linguistic usage: "Redet zum Herzen. Und das Herz, mit dem man redet, muss einen verstehen" (Reichel, p. 72). Bettermann thinks Zinzendorf must have been the first to insist upon feeling as a way of knowing (Gefühl als Erkenntnisprinzip) (p. 12): "Die Religion," Zinzendorf maintained, "kann ohne Vernunftschlüsse gefasst werden, sonst könnte niemand eine Religion haben, als der einen aufgeklärten Kopf hätte." And: ". . . Empfindung ist das Ursprüngliche und Bleibende, und darum das Echte und lebendige Wirkliche, die Begriffe das Abgeleitete und das Veränderliche, und darum das Künstliche und Unwirkliche" (quoted by Bettermann, p. 13). Zinzendorf, Bettermann says, is "a sensualist who applies sensualism to spiritual matters" (p. 16).

It would be a mistake, however, as Reichel points out, to think of Zinzendorf as a "Schwärmer," an "enthusiast," in the language of the eighteenth century (p. 74). This became clear during the Sichtungszeit itself when Zinzendorf, who was abroad at the time his followers in the Wetterau were indulging in their more extreme religious excesses, making themselves notorious throughout Germany and bringing the Herrnhuter into disrepute, took vigorous measures upon his return to put an end to the childish exultation of the brethren and even suppressed their hymnal as subject to misinterpretation by the unsympathetic. Like a schoolmaster entering a disorderly classroom, Zinzendorf himself thus brought the Sichtungszeit to a close. Feeling was for him no end in itself but an organ of knowledge.

Though it must be admitted that there is an occasional

strain of mysticism in Zinzendorf, such mysticism appears only sporadically and is not constitutive for his poetry. Though he hearkens to the "inner word," the concept of the *unio* seems hardly to play a part in his thinking. Still we must admit that in this regard Zinzendorf eludes clear classification. He is capable of saying, for example, "Wer auch sonst reden kan, der kan immer weniger reden, wenns auf die Hertzensmaterie kommt; . . . denn die Worte fehlen da; schmeckts und sehts" (Reichel, p. 79; "schmeckts und sehts" is a quotation from Psalm 34:8), which raises the old problem of mysticism and language.

Zinzendorf's aesthetics is a *Wirkungsästhetik;* his aim is to move the listener and thus awaken intuitive understanding. But it is by no means a matter of indifference *what* is understood. Zinzendorf is also interested in "die Sachen," the content of belief: "Unsre Sprache," he maintains, speaking of the language used by the Moravians, "drückt die Sachen fein naturell aus, und das macht eigentlich das Sublime in unsern Liedern" (Reichel, p. 97). But, as Reichel clearly sees, Zinzendorf really wanted to have it both ways: he wanted to arouse feeling and at that same time present merely the plain truth, "die Sachen" (p. 99).

When we turn to the poetry itself we are surprised to find that it seems to stand in flat contradiction to much of Zinzendorf's theory. We find ourselves confronted by a body of verse composed in what one can only call a code. We may be intrigued but we will hardly be moved by this poetry. Nor is it devoid of rhetorical devices, especially of extremely paradoxical and "dark" expressions, though Zinzendorf claims that it is "à la lettre so, es ist keine veblümte rede mehr, es ist die simple, einfältige, trokkene wahrheit."

Zinzendorf had the gift of composing extempore, inspired, as he believed, by the word of God. He listened to the voice and wrote down what it said "from dictation." All of his hymns are essentially extemporaneous, many of them totally so. "Denn das heist dichten, wenn das Herz denkt, und der Mund singt" (Reichel, p. 104). It was therefore natural for him to think that his poetry was a pure expression of

173

emotion (but also of "die Sachen"), devoid of all figurative language, "the simple truth." He did not realize that the heart does not necessarily "think" nonfiguratively. It too is the product of training and tradition. I quote in full a typical but by no means excessive or "dark" example of the poetry contained in the 12. Anhang (No. 1864):

1. Ausgeblutets theil der leichen!
   funkle mir ins angesicht;
   du, du bist der Gottheit zeichen,
   das der sünder härte bricht.
2. O du auserwähltes höhlgen!
   wie verwünsch ich mich hinein,
   dass mein kleines armes seelgen
   ewig möge in dir seyn,
3. Wie ein täubgen drinnen sitzen,
   auf Anachoreten-art,
   bis sich einst der strahl der ritzen
   und mich mit ihm offenbart.
4. Lamm, ach Lämmlein! ich vergehe
   über solchen wunder-blik,
   nims nich übel, denn ich stehe
   ganz verstummt bey solchem glük.
5. Herz und auge will mir rinnen
   über ieden dornenschrik.
   Schliesst euch zu, ihr blöden sinnen!
   ich vergess mich bey dem blik.
6. Wollt ihr ja noch resoniren,
   so gelobts der Pleura an,
   über nichts zu meditiren,
   als wie weit sie aufgethan.
7. Reine geister! euch gelüst es
   in den ritz hineinzuschaun:
   aber diese hohl (ihr wisst es)
   ist für sünder herz gehaun.
8. Diese Lammes-creatürlein,
   die betrübte sünderlein,
   haben macht, als wunderthierlein,
   in dem loch daheim zu seyn.

174

The poem is addressed to and is a contemplation of the pleural wound in the body of the crucified Christ. A great many of the hymns in this collection deal with the same theme, which is in itself only one aspect, though the central one, of the theme of the whole, the Passion of the Savior. Though not an extreme example, this poem shows most of the typical features of the pieces in the 12. Anhang, as pointed out by Reichel (pp. 30 ff.).

The Passion is here reduced to one particular motif, the pleural wound, the "ausgeblutets *theil*" and "*auserwähltes höhlgen.*" In stanzas 5–6, the worshiper even warns himself not to turn his attention elsewhere, i.e., to other wounds, but to concentrate exclusively on the gash in Christ's side. In this wound alone is salvation. Beyreuther writes:

> The source of all joys was supposed to be Jesus' sacrificial death. Because the language of the day tended more and more to abstractions and conceptualizations, Zinzendorf urged the Brethren to depict the Passion ever more realistically, more crassly, brutally, and concretely. Thus all came to be concentrated in Christ's "Blood and Wounds, Blood and Wounds" [the title of a famous Moravian hymn]. The lance wound given Christ in death attained as the "Seitenwunde," as a gaping hole, the status of a definite cult symbol for the Brethren of the Sichtungszeit. It was practically made independent and separated from the person of Christ. (pp. 17–18)

Sensualization and concretization (reification), another typical means of expression in this poetry, is also found in our example, though not to the extent encountered elsewhere. The pleural wound, "der Gottheit *zeichen,*" is fetishistically adored in a series of epithets appealing to the senses in the most direct fashion: it is called an "ausgeblutets theil der leichen [sg.]," an "auserwähltes höhlgen," a "ritz," "diese hohl," a "loch." The worshiper desires in the most literal way to creep into the wound and take up his dwelling there. The underlying doctrine is identification with the sufferings of the Savior,

175

but we are hardly made aware of the doctrinal aspect, so thoroughly are the senses taken captive and rational considerations excluded. Everything is spatialized, literalized. The method is very reminiscent of, if not actually derived from, Loyola's spiritual exercises and their "compositions."[15]

Excessive use of diminutives is one of the most patently perceptible features of the collection. Our example contains seven, not many for this body of verse. The critics of the Moravians decried the use of diminutives as a trivializing of the divine; Reichel, more in the spirit of the Brethren themselves, would see it as an expression of childlike piety (p. 39). Use of colloquial speech is another distinguishing mark of Moravian hymns. Our example is of course cast in the *genus humile;* use of colloquialisms is especially noticeable in stanza 4 ("nims nicht übel") and stanza 6 ("Wollt ihr ja noch resoniren [räsonieren]"). The use of foreign terms and loan words is likewise typical. Again, this example shows restraint: we find only "resoniren" and "meditiren." (Zinzendorf's prose as well as his verse swarms with foreign words, which he claimed he used for the sake of "more precise expression." He also claimed that his audience need not understand their exact meaning—they would feel the force of what was meant. He nonetheless glosses many of them.)[16]

As one of the basic compositional principles of this verse Reichel discovers the method of "assoziative Weiterführung" (pp. 34 f.). In this way he is able to explain many obscure expressions current with Brüdergemeinde as part of its code language. In the poem quoted, there is at least one striking example: "wundenthierlein" (stanza 8). If we read attentively, we soon see that the term is derived by "associative development" from "sünder-herz" (stanza 7) or even from "kleines, armes seelgen" (stanza 2). The associative process would then be: kleines, armes seelgen—täubgen—sünder-herz—Lammes-creatürlein—sünderlein—wundenthierlein. The "wound beastie" is the sinner's soul that takes refuge in Christ's wound like the dove (a soul symbol) in the rocks where it lives like an anchorite (stanza 3). This particular instance is clear enough and easy to fathom. But if, as is the case with a number of poems in the later parts of the 12. Anhang, a whole series of such code words, which have been arrived at through the process illustrated in *other* hymns, is used, then the matter becomes complicated indeed.

If one were asked to make a value judgment on the poem just discussed, one might find oneself in a somewhat embarrassing position. It certainly does what it sets out to do, and if we regard this as a criterion of excellence, we must mark up a plus. It is not without fervency, though it may not succeed in communicating it to us as outsiders, who are liable to be repelled by the object of devotion that arouses fervency. The imagery is highly concrete and, if one will, "plastic," but it is without atmosphere, at least for those who stand outside the charmed circle of the Moravian brotherhood. There is almost no developmental line; the poem merely takes fire again and again in each succeeding stanza from renewed contemplation of the wound, pulling itself up short when the attention shows signs of wandering beyond this one spot, as in stanza 5. The "room" of the poem is narrow indeed and does not contain great riches, except perhaps for the initiate. In short, it is a perfect example of cultic poetry, and for this reason lacks universality.

Zinzendorf himself was well aware of the exclusive nature of this kind of verse. He speaks of using diction comprehensible only to the initiate, those who have an "Inclination zur Sache." His term for this is "paradox reden": "Das heisst paradox reden, nemlich: man sagt die wahrheit, aber man spricht sie mit worten aus, dass andersdenkende gemüther den rechten eigentlichen sinn natürlicher weise nicht daraus nehmen" (Reichel, pp. 90 f.). In other words, Zinzendorf *strove* to make the language of the Brüdergemeinde incomprehensible to outsiders.

The Moravian hymnal contains a number of revisions of older hymns. Such revisions, Reichel points out, are a way of setting oneself off from the content of the original (pp. 35 f.). They are meant to show that the old hymn does not fulfill one's own ideal, which is then presented in the same form and at least partially with the same vocabulary but with contrasting content, in the manner of the "Kontrafaktur," a device still used by modern poets, e.g., Brecht ("Da schweigen die Vögelein nicht mehr / Über allen Wipfeln ist Unruh / In allen Gipfeln spürest du / Jetzt einen Hauch"). The best example is Zinzendorf's parody of Paul Gerhardt's "Nun ruhen alle Wälder," in which Gerhardt's text is largely retained but the meaning reversed. The parody also treats the obsessive theme of the pleural wound ("Höhlchen").

> Nun ruhen alle Wälder,
> Vieh, Menschen, Städt und Felder,
> es schläft die ganze Welt,
> ihr aber, meine Sinnen,
> auf, auf, ihr sollt beginnen,
> was eurem Schöpfer wohlgefällt.
>
> Wo bist du, Sonne, blieben?
> Die Nacht hat dich vertrieben,
> die Nacht, des Tages Feind,
> fahr hin; Ein ander Sonne,
> Mein Jesus, meine Wonne,
> gar hell in meinem Herzen scheint.

Zinzendorf's parody (No. 2338, stanzas 1–2):

> Jetzt schlaffen weder wälder,
> noch menschen, vieh, noch felder,
> es wacht die ganze welt:
> ihr aber, meine sinnen,
> mögt einen schlaff beginnen;
> im Höhlgen ist es schon bestellt.
>
> Wo sind die sterne blieben?
> hat sie der tag vertrieben,
> der blitz vom seitenschrein? [i.e., from the pleural
>   wound]
> O nein, das sternen-dunkel
> kommt her, von der carfunkel
> ins seitlein neingewischet seyn.

It would be hard to go further in the crass depiction of "Blut und Wunden" than the Herrnhuter. The total effect, however, is not so much realistic as surrealistic—where there is more realism that the mind can absorb, the effect veers toward the fantastic. The tone of this verse is one of joy, not sorrow, for in the blood and wounds lies man's salvation. One example out of hundreds of possible ones is No. 1963, sung to the tune of "Nun danket alle Gott":

1. Du blutger todes-schweiss,
   ders Lammes leib durchgangen,
   als ihm das antlitz weiss,
   die seele wie erhangen,
   das herz in einer press,
   das aug in thränen war,
   und die eisskalte näss
   ihm schwimmete am haar.

2. Schweiss, der am haupte glänzt,
   du tod-schweiss vor der stirne!
   schweiss, der die säh [Gesicht] umgränzt,
   und troknet das gehirne!
   du bange marterangst,
   die seinen geist erhitztst,
   und ihm den athem zwangst,
   und sein gebeine ritztst!

3. Fleuss eiland in den saal,
   dass es ums kirchlein trieffe,
   und bey dem abendmahl
   die Gott- und menschheits-tieffe,
   die in dem sacrament
   des leichnams und des bluts
   den kirchenleib erkennt,
   dis chor mach wunden-muths.

Windfuhr makes the telling observation that the pietists reverse the usual connotations of figurative and nonfigurative (*Bildlichkeit*, pp. 443 f.). For them the abstract is figurative, the figurative authentic. This looks forward to Hamann

("Rede, dass ich dich sehe!") and to Herder. In the hymn just quoted the description of the death sweat of the Savior may be construed as a figure conjuring up a reality. The reality is for the believer indubitable, but the question is, how make this reality present to the senses? How make the doctrine a living part of us? The pietist's way is through metaphorical language that refuses to admit its figurative nature but insists upon being taken as reality. Or is one to say that the prayer in the final stanza is to be taken literally? It seems unlikely that even a Zinzendorf would go so far as to maintain this.

"Die Gottheit will ich gläuben; die menschheit will ich sehn," Zinzendorf says in his "Imaginationslied" (No. 2085), words which imply "not only a theological but also a poetic principle," as Reichel justly remarks (p. 45). While the hymns of the Enlightenment emphasize Christ's moral sublimity, Zinzendorf, as a sensualist, emphasizes His lowliness and dwells on the homely circumstances of His life, His "condescension" to man. The senses, not moral law or the speculations of reason, are the source of religious belief. The following passages from the "Imaginationslied" will illustrate what is meant. The opening strophes state the reason for the "Lied."

1. Wenn ich Ihn essen kan, so ist mirs am gesündsten, und wenn mein lieber mann [Christ] sein öl lässt in mich dünsten; weil aber diese gnad in einem sacrament, das man nicht immer hat, dem leib wird zugewendt:

2. So muss ich mir nur schon beym wachen und beym schlafen imagination für meine seele schaffen, so süsse phantasie, die, wie sie sich formirt, in meinen sinnen hie wahr ist und werden wird.

7. Mich deucht, ich sehe Es [das "knäblein"] in vater Josephs hüttel, so handwerks-volk gemäss, bald in dem akker-kittel; bald gräbts nach einer wurz; bald schaffts so was fürs haus; bald nimts den zimmerschurz; bald mit der geissel naus.

14. Ich hör Ihn ins gespräch mit dem versucher kommen; mein Jesus ist gar träg, vom leibe abgekommen, das

> sprechen wird ihm schwer: wenn Satan auf ihn sticht,
> bet't er so sprüchel her, wie ers zusammen krigt.

Zinzendorf must seem to us a forerunner of Sturm und Drang with its advocacy of immediacy and naturalness, its concept of the original genius as an irrational creative force, but if we follow Reichel (pp. 103 f.), in reality his standpoint is basically different. He believes in inspiration and the intuitive production of poetry, but the only poetry so produced is religious poetry, a revelation of supranatural truth. The genius is for him a mediator rather than a creator, he is no "second maker under Jove." What the poet sings has a transpersonal bearing, it is not direct subjective expression, though it is an important step on the way to such expression. The same holds true of Arnold and Tersteegen: they sing of *their* experience only insofar as it is the experience of a power that transcends the personal. There is no glorification of the individual, there is only glorification of God.

I.J. Pyra

Immanuel Jacob Pyra (1715–44)[17] is always mentioned in the same breath with his friend Samuel Gotthold Lange (1711–81), who had the misfortune to gain notoriety as the butt of Lessing's criticism of his translation of Horace (*Vademecum für den Herrn S.G. Lange*, 1754). We are principally concerned with Pyra, however, who, as Lange himself was the first to recognize, had the greater talent.

Though strongly influenced by pietism of the puritanical Halle stamp, which rejected purely secular poetry, Pyra never wholly succumbed to pietistic antipoetical views. He translated Vergil, Lange Horace, and both imitated the ancients. What Pyra vehemently rejected, as Rasch points out, was the poetry of *delectare*, which inculcated pleasure for pleasure's sake (*Freundschaftskult*, pp. 158 ff.). If such poetry were to prevail, Pyra felt, "so wäre nichts verabscheuungswürdiger als die Poesie. . . . Das Vergnügen, das keinen wahren Nutzen hat, ist ein wahres Verderben."

In "Der Tempel der wahren Dichtkunst" (1737) Pyra pleads the case of sacred poetry. It was this work that was to induce Klopstock a decade later to drop secular themes and treat instead Christ's redemption of the world in his *Messias*. The "Tempel" is an allegory of 1,269 lines in unrhymed six-beat iambs (metrically alexandrines) modeled outwardly on Pope's "Temple of Fame" (1715).[18] Sauer regards it as Pyra's "bedeutendstes Werk" (p. xxv). As a poem in its own right it hardly qualifies for this rank, but as a document in the history of German poetry it undoubtedly does. The "Tempel" is an attempt to found a new concept of poetry: it is at once Pyra's aesthetics and his poetic credo. He wanted a poetry of new depth of feeling and dignity of expression whose ethos was thoroughly Christian, but whose manner was neither that of a sermon nor a hymn. In short, he advocates a kind of poetry that would secularize pietistic emotional attitudes and religious values. Milton, whose *Paradise Lost* Bodmer had translated into prose (1732), is a sublime exemplar in whose work Pyra's ideal had already been realized, and Miltonic echoes are found throughout the "Tempel" (cf. Sauer, pp. xxxiii ff.). Milton, however, is not the only, or even the supreme, exemplar. This honor is reserved for David the psalmist as the type of sacred poet who, like the eagle, establishes a connection between heaven and earth (I, 11–16).

The allegory is divided into five "Gesänge" or cantos. The mottos, from Vida (neo-Latin author of a religious epic, *Christias*, in six books, 1535) and Horace, underline the novelty and exclusivity of Pyra's undertaking and his poetic ideal: "Carmina nunc mutanda, novo nunc ore candendum" (let the melodies now be changed, a new voice shall sing). Vida calls upon the "casti vates," the virtuous poets, to leave the "polluted way" and sing a pure song of faith. And from Horace, in heavy type: "Odi profanum vulgus et arceo." The poem is addressed to Lange as the ideal auditor and aspirant to the title of sacred poet.

The first indication of novelty is the lack of rhyme. The singer prays the "Königin der wahren Poesie" to guide him so that his "Fesselfreyer Fuss" may not err "Auf dieser neuen Bahn" where "der gemeine Schmuck der leeren Reime fehlet" (I, 1 ff.). The story of the "Kampf um den Reim" is long, complicated, and confusing.[19] It must suffice to say here that Pyra, though he too employed rhyme even in his odes, was one of the chief defenders of rhymeless verse as a means of achieving sublimity.

Awake deep into the night, the poet induces self-rapture by singing the psalms of David. As though conjured up by these chants, Sacred Poetry shows herself to the singer in all her glory and majesty. She knows that he, the admirer of the ancients and the psalmist, seeks "die Bahn der wahren Dichtkunst" (I, 95 f.) and offers to show him her *new* temple, which no longer lies by Pindus (heathen) nor Mount Sion (desecrated by barbarians). Even in her first speech she warns the fervent emulator of the ancients against "den Tand verworfner Götzenfabeln" (I, 106). On the way to the realm of Sacred Poetry—the journey is seen as a kind of Pilgrim's Progress—singer and Muse come to a grove of firs (the tree from which the thyrsi of the Maenads are cut), the haunt of the "rabble of mad rhymesters," ruled over by False Poetry (I, 145ff.):

> Die in dem eitlen Schmuck unechter Steine prahlte,
> Das dünn gewebte Zeug des weiten Kleides schwoll
> In tausend Falten auf . . . .
> Doch war es lauter Schwulst und ein verstelltes Wesen.

Prominent here is a splendid opera house, on whose stage Voluptuousness struts lasciviously. In a passage parodying the late baroque style, False Poetry seeks to lure the singer into her domain (I, 162 ff.), but at a word from Sacred Poetry—"Weich, Lasterbrut!"—she vanishes with her train into thin air. As they come to the foot of a mountain, a frightful chasm full of vapors opens before the pair; the singer faints and finds himself upon awakening (in canto 2) in a "himmlischen Gefilde," the realm of True Poetry. The gulf between False and True Poetry cannot be passed by human effort; divine help must come to the rescue. This passage is imitated from Dante, Inferno III, 130–36, where the poet, guided by Vergil (i.e., human reason and ancient poetry) similarly passes the Acheron when Charon refuses to row him.

We are now in a lower region where the "virtuous poets" (as distinguished from the "sacred") dwell:

> Die, so die goldne Zeit und Unschuld wiederum
> In Wald und Wiesen sich bemühen einzuführen.
> [II, 89 f.]

In other words, this passage emblematizes the pastoral mode. The landscape is Arcadia. In a dark valley lie the caves of Pleasant and Frightening Dreams, whose nature is described in lengthy allegorical detail. The keeper of both is "leichte Phantasie," but *her* keeper is Reason, a "gestrenger Fürst," in so far as any dreams are allowed to play a role in True Poetry, though in False Poetry they swarm "unordentlich wie bey Besessnen" (II, 196).

True Poetry shows her protégé where "all that" happened of which the heathen poets sing, though she has now expelled "die schnöde Götzenbrut" from her dominions. It is the task of modern poets to people her realm "mit Tugendbildern" (II, 201–40). On the way up the mountain on whose summit lies the temple we come to the seat of the great poets of antiquity: Homer, Vergil, Horace, Tibullus, Theocritus, Euripides, Sophocles. This is Pyra's "*nobile castello*" which, like Dante's (Inferno IV), is the abode of the good and wise who were born before the second dispensation. Somewhat smugly True Poetry remarks:

> Es ist bedauernswerth, dass diese Dichter noch
> Auch in der blinden Nacht des Aberglauben irrten.
>
> [II, 273f.]

Noble, even unsurpassable, though their poetry may be, it is still "durch Götzendienst entweiht" (II, 267), and the poets are therefore excluded from the temple, even as the denizens of Dante's *nobile castello* must forever remain in Limbo. The standards by which poetry is judged are not purely artistic, Pyra is telling us clearly. A deep river separates these, the "greatest," from those poets equally great (they sing "according to the rules") but unfortunately erotic—Ovid, Catullus, Tibullus, Propertius, and Sappho.

At this point Lange suddenly appears, playing a lyre and dressed in a "holy gown." "The Highest's arm" has led him to His altar (has made him a pastor); now Sacred Poetry is to consecrate him as her priest. After a laborious ascent of the holy mountain the three reach the River of Oblivion into which all vanities must be cast before the close of the temple can be entered. The close itself is the earthly paradise, literally flowing with milk and honey. Again Pyra has taken a leaf from Dante, whose earthly paradise on the summit of the Mount of Purgatory is likewise enclosed by Lethe, the river of oblivion (Purgatorio XXVII). Hither angels descend to sing with the earthborn poets who stroll in the garden, just as the various virtues descend to Arcadia at the foot of the mountain to keep company with the pastoral poets.

The first two cantos of the "Temple" are by far the most engaging. In the three that follow, allegorical personifications crowd upon us so thick and fast that one would almost rather read a Brechtian "Lehrstück."

The third canto describes first the "Vorhof" of the temple, then the "Hof"; the fourth canto the four wings of the temple, then the main building itself; the fifth canto contains the address of True Poetry to the poets admitted to the temple and the investiture of Lange as her priest. Whoever wishes to enter the temple must pass through "der Künste und der Wissenschaften Wohnung," i.e., he must have an understanding of languages, philosophy, history (to which eighty-four lines are devoted), music, architecture, painting, sculpture, even weaving, sewing, and metalworking. Poetry, in other words, is seen as a craft among crafts and as a subject of study. At least it is strongly implied that no one can become a true poet who does not have an appreciation of technique and a deep fund of knowledge:

> Wer in der Poesie ein Meister denckt zu werden,
> Muss hier erst Schüler seyn, sonst bringt er es nicht hoch.
>
> [III, 175 f.]

Once more there is a parallel with Dante: one enters the *nobile castello* through seven gates, usually regarded as symbolizing the trivium and

THE CULT OF FEELING

quadrivium or seven liberal arts (Inferno IV, 110). Beside the great gate leading into the courtyard proper hang "die ewigen Gesetze, Die keines Dichters Lied mit Recht verletzen darf" (III, 179 f.). What these laws are we are not told, but they obviously warn against subjective license. In the courtyard spring four fountains indicative of the equalities Pyra (and his age) valued in poetry: Reinigkeit, Flüssigkeit, Lieblichkeit, and Nachdrücklichkeit. The first three, Schuppenhauer remarks, are literary virtues of the Enlightenment, but they, he claims, are not so important for Pyra as "Nachdrücklichkeit" or emphatic, persuasive expression (p. 184):

> Sie treibt die schwere Fluth bald schnell mit starckem Rauschen,
> Bald majestätisch fort.
>
> [III, 211 f.]

In the midst of a grove of dark cedars "hebet sich Der prächtig hohe Bau des Tempels zu den Sternen" (IV, 2 f.). Over its portal stands inscribed in gold "weicht, Eitle, weicht!" (IV, 7). But before we may enter, the four wings, which are devoted to Old and New Testament figures, must be described. From the steps of the temple one can see throughout creation, even into the hearts of nations and into the depths of hell, and, gazing upwards, one sees worlds uncounted. The lesson to be learned from this view is very "baroque"—the vanity of all created things:

> Hier sehn die Dichter oft in weiser Ruh hinab.
> Ihr hohes Aug entdeckt die Eitelkeit der Dinge.
> . . . .
> Und also lernen sie mit himmelhohem Geist
> Den Schein des irdischen nur immer mehr verachten.
>
> [IV, 76 ff.]

The kind of poetry Pyra is advocating here would overspring the earthly as completely as that of a Gryphius. On the great door one sees in chased work a scene allegorizing the power of song: David playing before Saul. Only Lange accompanies Sacred Poetry into the temple itself: "Ich blieb voll Scheu am Thore. Ihr aber gingt hinein" (IV, 141 f.). (The singer nonetheless knows precisely what is to be found inside and can report every word that is spoken!) Within dwell the various kinds of poetry: eclogue, elegy, ode, tragedy, epic, but *not* comedy. Sublimity is "one-eyed." In the middle of the hall stands the Throne of Poetry beside the Cross. The Muse now calls all the poets dwelling on the mountain before her throne.

It is instructive to note who appears, in so far as they are mentioned by name: Moses, David, Solomon, Luther ("der David unsrer Zeit"), Milton, Vida, Sannazaro (the poet not only of the *Arcadia* but also of an epic on the birth of the Virgin), Sedulius (fifth-century author of a poetical version of the history of the New Testament), Prudentius (chief poet of the early church), Marino (who appears as author of the "Massacre of the Innocents"; his "geile Zither" he has "Im Sterben noch betränt" [V, 40 f.]), "Sallust" (not the Roman historian but Guillaume de *Salluste*, Seigneur du Bartas, the sixteenth-century author of *La Sem-*

185

aine ou La Création, admired by Milton),[20] Opitz, Fleming, Gerhardt, Gryphius, Rist. Parnassus is a mountain with two peaks; Pyra's, however, has but one—he exhibits a lopsided, indeed exclusive, preference for singers of spiritual themes, for though Opitz and Fleming are admitted, it is because the former "bey der Krippen dich, du süsses Kind [the Christ Child], gepriesen," and the latter because he "vor dem in einem öden Ort . . . das Heyl der Welt beklagte" (V, 44 ff.).

True Poetry's address to the assembled vates (V, 56–136) emphasizes the poet as a "priest" with a holy message to convey. Simple piety, however, does not make a poet:

> Nein es ist nicht genug ein frommer Mann zu seyn,
> Es muss ein Dichter seyn, der sich ans Dichten wagt.
> . . . .
> Wacht nicht in eurer Brust ein himmlisch hoher Geist,
> Und hört man euren Mund nicht schön und prächtig tönen,
> Ja ist das Hertz nicht rein, und voll von Gottes Geist,
> So tragt ihr unvedient der frommen Dichter Namen.
>
> [V, 66 ff.]

The model of models for sacred poetry is the psalms of David (the poem here returns to its beginning), which are characterized by a "heilige, doch eigene Unordnung" (V, 78), i.e., they are "enthusiastic" odes. Divine inspiration is the sine qua non of such poetry, which is severely earnest, inimical to all wit. Its sole theme is praise of the divine in which it joins with all creation—which thus, despite its "vanity," is after all given worth:

> Es rauschen alle Blätter
> Des Waldes ihm [Gott] zum Ruhm, ...
> Die Sterne preisen ihn. Es jauchzen alle Himmel.
> Und ich und wer mir folgt, muss mit der Gottes Furcht
> Bey seinem Altar stets mit Ruhmgesängen wachen.
>
> [V, 91 f.]

Poets on earth imitate the angels in heaven, whose song is also sacred poetry. The Muse also has technical advice to give: she warns the tyro against trying high themes too soon (V, 117–20), she insists on gracefulness ("lieblich klingende gemessne Sätze") and *ornatus* ("wohlgewählte Blumen," V, 122 f.) and, like Opitz, she believes the poet has a right to plunder the ancients if he sanctifies, i.e., Christianizes, his booty:

> Ja ich erlaub es euch, entreisst mit kluger Hand
> Den Dichtern Griechenlands und Latiens ihr Gutes
> Doch eh ihr es dem Herrn auf seinem Altar legt;
> So heiligt erst den Raub; damit kein Götzenopfer
> Sein Heiligthum entweiht.
>
> [V, 128 ff.]

Her homily delivered, True Poetry consecrates Lange as her priest, while Pyra contemplates the life "in grüner Still" that, as he hopes, lies

186

before his friend as pater familias, holy singer, and minister of the Gospel. In this image of contentment he includes himself.

Looking back over Pyra's "Tempel" as a whole, one is struck by the *formal* adherence to the doctrines of neoclassicism while revolting against its *spirit*. Even the animus against rhyme was shared, or could be construed to be shared, by Gottsched, though his views on the use of rhyme were as self-contradictory as Pyra's practice was inconsistent. Nonetheless, insofar as the sacred Davidian ode is concerned—and this is what Pyra primarily has in mind—the "Tempel" comes out strongly against rhyme:

> Wer mit dem Geist, der erst ein Quodlibet gereimt,
> Auch Lieder dichten will, und, wenn ihm noch zum
> *Himmel*
> Ein Reim am Ende fehlt, den Tod zum *Schimmel* macht,
> Der spottest nur damit.
>
> [V, 82–85; emphasis added]

Reimzwang leads to degradation of content. Gottsched had used the same argument (cf. Schuppenhauer, pp. 134 ff.). Like the neoclassicists, Pyra is also scornful of bombast, the trademark of False Poetry (I, 145 ff.), though Sacred Poetry allows, even insists upon, *ornatus*, "wohlgewählte Blumen," as a necessary component of the *genus grande*. The emphasis is on "wohlgewählt"—the "flowers" of imagery must be in harmony with the subject matter, a classical and neoclassical precept. Pyra is against subjective license: reason must retain control over fantasy, as becomes evident in the passage on dreams (II, 130 ff.) as well as in the passage on the tablets of law that hang beside the gate into the main courtyard (III, 178 ff.). Like the neoclassicist, Pyra believes that one can enter the temple of True Poetry only through "der Künste Sitz, der Wissenschaften Wohnung" (III, 173): the poet must be *doctus*. His verse must also display the qualities of purity (Reinigkeit), ease of expression (Flüssigkeit), and charm (Lieblichkeit) (III, 197 ff.), all neoclassical poetic values. Even the ancients, as we have just seen, may be imitated, if the poet takes care to "sanctify" what he takes from them.

187

What then is new about Pyra's concept of poetry? Above all, the ethos and the subject matter. The former is strictly, even puritanically, Christian, the latter religious and, in Pyra's view, therefore sublime. Being sublime, it requires the grand manner. Pyra turns against what Paul Böckmann has called the "Formprinzip (or Formkultur) des Witzes" (*Formgeschichte der deutschen Dichtung* 1, 471 ff.), because, while operating with a concept of language oriented on mathematical unequivocalness, this principle allowed the poet elbow room for combinatory play of the intelligence and the imagination. "Scharfsinn," the ability to see connections among widely separated concepts, was the basis of "Witz" as well as the source, according to Böckmann, of "verblümte Redensarten," the invention of which required the ability to see similarities among dissimilarities. Pyra, though he urges the poet to employ "wohlgewählte Blumen," does not advocate a combinatory play of wit merely for the sake of intellectual entertainment. In entering the lists in the cause of sacred poetry that is neither purely didactic nor polemical—is not a poetry of wit, not based on personal mystical experience, not meant for use as a hymn, not cultic in its appeal but universal—Pyra was pleading for a kind of poetry that had not yet been fully realized in German, though the Baroque had made beginnings. One needed but look at the example of Milton to see this. Herein lies the historical importance of "Der Tempel der wahren Dichtkunst."

It is worth noting that Pyra did not derive his ideals from the Swiss theoreticians. Later, to be sure, he was to become their ardent supporter, but at the time of the composition of the "Tempel" he had not read them.[21] The aesthetician most closely akin to the ideals of both Pyra and Klopstock is John Dennis (died 1734), for whom the true source of the sublime was religion and who, like Pyra, felt that the weakness of the moderns lay in having departed from this wellspring of great poetry.[22] However, so far as I am aware there is no indication that either Klopstock or Pyra had heard of Dennis.

When we turn to the *Freundschaftliche Lieder* (first edition,

Zürich, 1745; second edition, Halle, 1749), we find Pyra's ideal only partially realized. The *Freundschaftliche Lieder* are a chance collection of poems celebrating the friendship between Pyra and Lange. They were written with no intent of publication and hence do not attempt to realize any stated aesthetic doctrine. Yet they exemplify as do no other poems before the midcentury the poetry of feeling as opposed to the poetry of wit and rationality. Lange, in his preface to the edition of 1749, calls them "Empfindungen des Hertzens, die wir [Pyra, Lange, and Lange's wife], ohne an die Kunst zu dencken, so auf zu setzen suchten, wie wir sie fühlten" (Sauer, p. 8). After Pyra's death in 1744, Lange had sent Bodmer in Zürich a sheaf of poems, which Bodmer had published without the consent, though apparently not against the will, of Lange for the delectation (as he put it in the preface to the first edition) of those who shared his (Bodmer's) tastes. The authors, Bodmer continues, "sind . . . natürliche Menschen, . . . welche die Grundsätze eines aufrichtigen *Hertzens* dem reichsten Putze des *Witzes* und allen gelerneten Moralitäten vorziehen" (Sauer, p. 5; emphasis added). Bodmer praises his find in extravagant terms, but not without insight into the true nature of this poetry. Some readers, Bodmer thinks, will find the feelings expressed in the *Fr. L.* "too un-German," the imagery "too Roman," the thoughts "too poetic"; and they will miss the rhyme. As for him and those sharing his tastes, this is compensated for by the "poetic rapture," the "apparent disorder," "the unheard-of expressions and the images that bring before one's eyes even the minutest circumstances." K.L. Schneider explains that Bodmer is here characterizing, in opposition to Gottsched, the new poetic ideal which derives in large measure from Milton and Addison ("Polemik gegen den Reim," p. 11). "Too Roman" refers to the tendency to imitate the manner of Horace; "too un-German" and "too poetic" were the usual scornful epithets employed by the Gottschedians for those who strove to attain Miltonic sublimity. "Poetic rapture" and "apparent disorder" (Schein der Unordnung) characterize the general linguistic attitude that obtains in the *Fr. L.*, the rapture of the high ode and its "beau désordre" (Boileau). In short, Bodmer finds here all that runs counter to the prosaic, the "klare Wassersuppe ohne Fett" palmed off as poetry by the adherents of Gottsched, as Pyra put it in his "Erweis."

Bodmer also took the liberty of substituting the pastoral names "Thirsis" and "Damon" for Pyra and Lange, which had stood in the original manuscript. R. Newald (*Vom Späthumanismus zur Empfindsamkeit*, p. 476) feels that in so doing Bodmer lays himself open to the charge of fearing to reproduce reality, i.e., he did not have the courage of his convictions. Bodmer himself speaks of rendering the matter more poetic by giving the Halle poets the names of Greek shepherds. That the *Fr. L.* exhibit strong traces of the pastoral mode is true enough. The poets sometimes call themselves shepherds, pagan deities or half-deities people the landscape at times, and there are sheep to be tended. But, as W. Rasch rightly remarks, these pastoral traits are secondary and hardly appear in the more central poems, or if they do, then not as "constitutive parts but as vestiges" of a tradition that had special appeal in this particular situation (*Freundschaftskult*, pp. 156 f.). Bourgeois realism, odically heightened or idyllically idealized, is the keynote of the collection rather than the atmosphere of the pastoral.

The experience celebrated in the *Fr. L.* is a holy intimacy of heart between two men in which Lange's wife "Doris" as well as Lange's infant son "Hilas" are included. This extended family, almost a *ménage à trois*—for Pyra (Thirsis) participates in Lange's (Damon's) marriage vicariously and with fervent identification—constitutes the whole human world of these poems. It is a world set off by intensity of feeling and devotion to high ideals from the uncomprehending world of the commonalty, the "Pöbel." The pattern of retreat into a secret realm where feeling may be cultivated in despite of the accepted standards of the establishment of the Enlightenment, a para-world with para-ideals that we find again and again in the German lyric of the eighteenth century, is especially evident in the *Fr. L.* In his enlightening study on the cult of friendship and its poetical expression W.

Rasch attempts to get at the psychological roots of the kind of friendship here glorified, a friendship that appeared "antic" and "quixotic" to those who could not or would not enter into its experience. Pietism, Rasch explains, in alienating religious truth from the church and making it a purely personal matter between the individual and his God, left religion without objective existence (pp. 48 f.). The friend, who strictly speaking should have been a "friend in Christ" only, could, with the general tendency of the age to evaluate the earthly positively, become a surrogate for the divine, and a circle of friends could become a kind of secular church. The friend, in the sentimental friendship of pietistic character, takes the place of God. He also fills the gap left in the life of every strict pietist by his renunciation of the world.

Lange's dedicatory poem to Georg Friedrich Meier,[23] professor of philosophy in Halle (Sauer, pp. 3 f.), develops the theme of the cenacle or invisible church of friendship founded in the name of love of divine virtue and wisdom, with Pyra as its *vates*. He whom poetry inspires can transcend the human condition; above all, he is endowed with "angelic power" to feel and practice friendship and is eager to teach others "die göttliche Kunst, durch Freundschaft glücklich zu werden." Lange stops just short of saying that eternal blessedness may be the fruit of friendship, but the whole tone of the dedication is that of secularized religion.

Life lived as poetry and poetry as the basis of friendship surpassing the bounds of ordinary human comprehension—this is a constant theme of the *Fr. L.* Günther Müller puts it this way: "das persönliche Leben und Erleben . . . rückt in die Sphäre des dichterischen Stoffes: man lebt so, dass aus diesem Leben ein Gedicht gemacht werden kann" (*Lied*, p. 168). Almost any poem in the collection will illustrate what is meant; for example, number 3, "Thirsis hört den Damon an Horatzens Seite singen," an ode in sixteen six-line stanzas imitating the Horatian manner when Horace is imitating Pindar. Having driven away the "hated swarm of rhymsters," i.e., the run-of-the-mill poets of the day, who disturb the "holy silence" of Pindus where he hopes to listen to the harmonies of

Horace as the emulator of Pindar, the singer (Pyra) invokes the great Roman. He appears and is greeted by chaste nymphs. But Horace is in no chaste mood: "Er schweifft umher mit Libers [Bacchus'] Priestern / In den schlaflosen tollen Nächten" and "singt, was nie ein Mund gesungen." Beside him sings a "deutscher Mund," none other of course than Lange, and his daring surpasses even that of Horace himself! Our singer begs Horace to teach him how one flies so "verwegen, klug, und frey, / Und doch bewundrungswürdig glücklich," for up to now all his efforts in this direction have proven vain. This is a nicely ironical use of the modesty formula, since what he is begging to be taught to do he is, one gathers, already doing, namely, composing an ode in the "Pindaric" manner. Horace tunes his lyre and sings two strophes on the theme of human dignity composed of snatches from his own works, thus providing a reflection of a reflection which contributes to the odic "beau désordre." The petitioner then wants to know how the Roman comes by his more than human knowledge of the ways of heroes and gods. To this there is no answer, but the implication is: through divine inspiration. The ode ends with an allocution to Horace and Lange:

> Steigt, steigt zugleich durch die bestirnte Luft
> Horatz und du, o deutscher Flaccus,
> Und setzt der Doris Bild bey Ariadnens Krantz.

Pyra himself will remain in the valleys and sacrifice lyrically to the constellation of Doris set in the heavens by the song of Horace-Lange.

The disposition of this poem is anything but simple. The fine disorder of the Pindaric ode is imitated so successfully that it confuses the reader almost as thoroughly as does Pindar himself. Yet it is only an apparent confusion—Pyra has his ecstasies well under control. The theme of life lived for and as poetry is convincingly evoked and is illustrated in the form itself. From the perspective of the outsider, i.e., of one not yet converted to this religion, there is possibly one false note, the thought of Lange's being the peer and rival of Horace. Yet is not this idea presented with a touch of amused irony? It seems hard to interpret the following allocution to Lange otherwise:

> Wohin, wohin, o Freund, o kühner Geist?
> Erstaunst du nicht vor diesen Klüften,
> Die rund um dich herum mit offnen Abgrund drohn?
> Erstaunst du nicht vor diesen Höhen?
> Wer Pindarn folgt, der stürzt und stürzt mit Spott;
> Wer aber darf dem Flaccus folgen?

Self-realization in the friend, which makes it possible for the tiny cenacle to stand against the world and all its values, is the basic configuration of the whole collection. Numbers 11, 12, and 13 are especially revealing in this regard. The titles alone tell the story: "Der Freundschaft Sieg über Gram und Neid" (No. 11), "Damons Zufriedenheit mit dem Himmel, der Dichtkunst, dem Thirsis und der Doris" (No. 12), "Des Thirsis Vereinigung mit Damon und Doris den Himmel zu besingen" (No. 13). Two typical stanzas from Number 12 read:

> Komm, banger Sorgen Feindin, edle Dichtkunst,
> Komm, du, den meisten unbekannte Tugend,
> Komm, du, von wenigen erfahrne Freundschaft,
>   Führ auch itzt den Kiel. (=Feder)
> Die kluge Nachwelt lobt einst meine Einsicht,
> Wenn sie, mein Thirsis, meine Liebe lieset,
> Mit der ich gegen meine Doris brenne,
>   Und dir eigen bin.

In Numbers 14 and 15, by Lange and Pyra, respectively, a vision of expulsion from the homeland is conjured up to intensify the sense of the church of true friendship standing against the world. Should Mars drive them from their home, Lange, Pyra, and Doris would take refuge in a pastoral setting and live as "in der güldnen Zeit der Dichter"; their songs would resound "von Gott und Unschuld" and angels would join in their singing:

> Hier würd uns keine Macht des Todes trennen,
> Er fände uns mit fest umschlungnen Armen,

193

> Derselbe Augenblick versetzt uns beyde
> In die Oberwelt.

> Mit Ehrfurcht würden dann die greisen Hirten
> Den Kindern unsers Grabes Hügel zeigen,
> Und sagen: dass man da, bey heitern Nächten,
> Oft Lieder höre!

Pyra answers in Number 15, spinning out Lange's vision in the first six stanzas, then awakening from this "lieblicher, jedoch schwerer Traum" in stanza 7, still apprehensive that the vision may yet come true. But no. He will find his loved ones at home:

> Mein theures Paar, ich werd, ich werd euch sehen;
> Ihr werdet mich mit eurem ofnen Arm
> Bald keuchend umfangen.

> Der Wanderstab steht wartend an der Pfoste [sic],
> Und mein Geräth liegt auf den Weg bereit.
> Erbittet mir zu meiner Reise nur
> Den fröhlichen Morgen.

Such homely, realistic turns in a poem that begins in a high odic tone are one of the delights of Pyra's verse. The fusion of the everyday with the elevated persuades us of the genuineness of the latter.

Number 18, "Des Thirsis Empfindungen, da er ihnen entgegen geht," in thirteen eight-line stanzas, is probably Pyra's most successful realization of "linguistic expression of individual emotion," which, as Rasch points out, is the aim of the most significant pieces in the *Fr. L.* (p. 169). These poems seldom set themselves the task of developing a single theme. Such motifs as the pastoral life, scorn of the world, "den Himmel besingen," going to meet one another, are subordinated to the central concern of revelation of individual feeling as reflected in the love for him who releases this feeling. In Number 18, for example, Pyra thus addresses his friend:

> Du durch die Huld des Vaters aller Liebe
> Für mich allein bestimmter Freund,

194

Sieh da das Bild des gantz entzückten Geistes,
Durchschau das ofne Heiligste
Des dir gewiedmeten Gemütes.
[stanza 1; emphasis added]

The striking feature is the sacralization of the rapture of friendship. The implication is that an emotion as all-consuming as this *must* be sacred. This is a thoroughly modern attitude: Wertherism *avant la lettre*. No wonder that those who still lived within the bounds of an older tradition that reserved such emotion, if it admitted it at all, for the relationship with the divine, found such excessive worship of an earthly object "antic" and "quixotic." That a narcissistic element is present here seems undeniable. The friends are two pools in which each sees his own emotional image.

In Number 18, the singer's emotional state is objectified in the image of the ascending lark, hovering, singing praise, calling to its mate: Pyra, poet-lark, going to meet his friends, looking out from the hilltop, returning home at evening, full of longing. The image is memorable and convincing. Its only fault, from the point of view of readers nurtured on Wordsworth, is overspecification of the symbolism (stanzas 8 f.):

Bald flittert sie [die Lerche] mit regen Schwingen,
Bald steigt sie schnell empor, bald ruht sie wiederum,
Und hänget hoch an unbewegten Federn;
Bald lehret sie hoch aus den blauen Lüften
    Die Welt das Lob des Ewigen;
Bald singet sie, die Gattin zu erfreuen;
    Und bald ruft sie ihr kirrend zu;
    Zuletzt sinckt sie stillschweigend nieder.

Die sah ich, wenn ich nach dir sah,
Und fand mit halbem Trost ein gleich betrübtes Bild.

The ode ends with a protestation of the purity of the singer's feelings for Lange's wife ("Wir lebten, wie Geschwister tun"—stanza 12) and the wish that the tiny community of kindred spirits may forever be all-in-all, untouched by profane society and its judgments:

Begraben in der Ruh der Liebe,
Von keinem hochgeehrt, von dir allein geschätzt,
Wollt ich bey euch mein Dach mit Zweigen decken,
Wenn GOtt mich nicht zu andern Diensten rufte,
    Und ich dir nicht zur lieben Last,
Mir selber zum Verdruss um deinetwillen würde.
    Die Armuth wär ein Überfluss,
    Ich hätte gnug. GOtt, dich, und Doris.

[stanza 13]

Arnold has his Sophia, with whom he lives and whom he loves in spirit in utter seclusion from the demands and cares of scholarship and ambition; Tersteegen "kehrt ein" and hears the divine voice speaking to him of the ineffable; Pyra longs to be buried in the peace of human love. For all, the world is a place from which to escape and their poetry a realm of virtuality, in which their dearest desire is realized.

Klopstock

With Friedrich Gottlieb Klopstock (1724–1803) German poetry frees itself of its leading strings and enters into its own.[24] "With his early odes," a modern critic, Emil Staiger, has said, "there begins, inexplicably, unexampled, the history of the modern German lyric" (*Wege zum Gedicht*, 1956, p. 106). Herder, in his *Nachruf* on Klopstock's death, lets the shade of the deceased poet address his countrymen in these words:

Als ich erschien, klimpertet Ihr auf einem hölzernen Hackbrett (dulcimer) von Alexandrinern, gereimten Jamben, Trochäen, allenfalls Daktylen, wohlmeinend, treufleissig und unermesslich; ich kam und liess aus meiner Region Euch neue Sylbenmasse hören. . . . Was kümmerte mich, wofür Ihr mein Messias haltet? Was er wirken sollte, hat er gewirkt und wird er wirken; nebst Luthers Bibelübersetzung bleibt er Euch das erste klassische Buch Eurer Sprache. Meine lyrischen Gedichte haben Eure Saitenspiele tausendfach belebt . . . ein reiches Psalterion, Apoll's Köcher voll musikalischer Pfeile. . . . (*Werke*, Suphan 24, 220 f.)

Herder here emphasizes Klopstock's technical achievements, which he sees as the chief means by which Klopstock liberated German poetry. And in this he is perfectly right. Klopstock is singularly unfruitful in all but technical wisdom, the *how* of poetic production. We hardly go to him any more for deeper insights into life, as we still go to Milton, Goethe, Wordsworth, or Emerson, and it is this that keeps him from assuming a place in the absolutely first rank of European poets.

Klopstock's poetry is not easy to describe. The guiding principle of his aesthetics is completely emotional: "Das Herz ganz zu rühren, ist überhaupt, in jeder Art der Beredsamkeit, das Höchste, was sich der Meister vorsetzen, und was der Hörer von ihm fordern kann," one reads in "Von der heiligen Poesie," the essay with which he introduces the first volume of the 1755 edition of the *Messias (Ausgew. Werke*, ed. Schleiden, 3d ed., p. 1009). Or, stated in the more abstract terms of the essay of 1759, "Gedanken über die Natur der Poesie":

> Das Wesen der Poesie besteht darin, dass sie, durch die Hülfe der Sprache, eine *gewisse Anzahl* von Gegenständen, die wir *kennen*, oder deren Dasein wir *vermuten*, von einer *Seite* zeigt, welche die *vornehmsten* Kräfte unsrer Seele [i.e. Verstand, Einbildungskraft, Willen] in einem so hohen Grade *beschäfigt*, dass eine auf die andre wirkt, und dadurch die *ganze* Seele in Bewegung setzt. (Schleiden, 3d ed., p. 992)

To "set the whole soul in motion" is always Klopstock's aim. It is not, however, that he rejects thinking or that he would appeal exclusively to the lower powers of the psyche, at least, that is not the way he himself conceived it. Rather, for him thinking and feeling are one. What one has not felt one also has not thought: thoughts are important to the degree that they are *felt*. G. Kaiser, in his stimulating Klopstock book, discusses the problem of "Gefühlsdenken" at length (pp. 86 ff.), showing that in this regard, as in a number of others, Klopstock's position is close to that of the liberal theologians of his day, the *Neologen* or neologists, who in Lessing's acrid words in the forty-ninth *Literaturbrief* "content themselves with a sweet quintessence extracted from Christianity and avoid all suspicion of freethinking by enthusiastically prattling (schwatzen) in general terms about religion *per se*." Lessing felt impelled to reprove what he regarded as an elevating of feeling over thinking. In an effusion in *Der Nordische Aufseher* entitled "Von der besten Art über Gott zu denken" Klopstock had characteristically maintained that the best way to think about God is to feel about him:

> Wenn die *ganze* Seele von dem, was sie denkt (und wen denkt sie?) so erfüllt ist, dass alle ihre übrige Kräfte von der Anstrengung ihres Denkens in eine solche Bewegung gebracht sind, dass sie zugleich zu *einem* Endzweck wirken; wenn alle Arten von Zweifeln und Unruhen über die unbegreiflichen Wege Gottes sich verlieren; wenn wir uns nicht enthalten können, unser Nachdenken durch irgend eine kurze Ausrufung der Anbetung zu unterbrechen . . .

then we are thinking about God in the best way. This kind of "thinking" Lessing pointed out (forty-ninth *Lit.brief*) was what other honest persons called feeling: "Seine dritte Art über Gott zu *denken* [Klopstock had distinguished three ways], ist ein Stand der *Empfindung;* mit welchem nichts als undeutliche Vorstellungen verbunden sind, die den Namen des *Denkens* nicht verdienen." We will probably agree with Lessing, as indeed did many of his contemporaries, but that will not help us too much in trying to understand Klopstock, for whom thinking and feeling remain one, and if either has the upper hand, it is feeling: unfelt thought is not thought at all. To make us *feel* thoughts is the chief aim of his poetry.

Though closer to the liberal theology of his day than to pietism, Klopstock was nonetheless accused (by the Gottschedians and even by Lessing) of pietistically tinged "Schwärmerei." The question of his relation to pietism is not simple. His birthplace, Quedlinburg, was a seat of pietism, but the Klopstock family was not pietistic; neither was Schulpforta, the Saxon royal academy he attended. In Denmark, Klopstock was intimate with pietistic circles, notably the Stolbergs, but the atmosphere of Hamburg was again more worldly and his wife Meta, though sincerely religious, was not a pietist. Klopstock's attitude toward Swedenborg, whom the pietists glorified, was ironic, not worshipful. We find nothing in his life that resembles a conversion, the personal conviction of rebirth so characteristic of the pietistic religious experience. Kaiser, in his detailed investigation of the question, concludes that pietism was for Klopstock a "Bildungserlebnis," not an "existenzielles Erlebnis" (p. 133). Like the pietists, Klopstock regarded himself as divinely chosen, but chosen as a *vates*, a sacred poet and prophet, rather than singled out for personal salvation. The pietistic conversion experience is secularized, turned toward literature that *treats of* religious experience rather than preoccupying itself with the purely personal relationship of the individual to his God. Klopstock's visions are given him—so he conceives it—for the benefit of all: the prototype is Moses descending from the mountain with the tablets of the Law.

After the publication of the first three cantos of his sacred epic in 1748, Klopstock wrote to Bodmer and told him what inspiration he had derived from his and Breitinger's critical writings. Though no poet, certainly no genuine poet, ever found his vocation merely by reading the critics, any more than critics become poets by reading poetry, the critical principles espoused by the Swiss do provide a kind of entering wedge into Klopstock's aesthetics and help to place him in his time. That Klopstock would have been so enthusiastic about the ideas of Bodmer and Breitinger seems most unlikely had he not, like them, been temperamentally inclined to the conviction that the primary purpose of poetry is to *move* the listener, to convince or at least bend to assent through arousal of the emotions, rather to persuade through argument or entertain through wit. But in the end these are unfathomable matters. Genius remains inexplicable.

The Swiss were thorough believers in the "herzrührende Schreibart" whose aim was the "Entzückung der Phantasie": the virtual (Klopstock calls it "das Fastwirkliche") should have utterly persuasive power. Bodmer finds many of his arguments in Addison's essays on *Paradise Lost* and in that group of essays called "The Pleasures of the Imagination," all of which were published in the *Spectator*.[25] J.P. Dubos's *Réflexions critiques sur la poésie et sur la peinture* (1719) and Dubos's key principle that "le premier but de la poésie et de la peinture est de nous toucher" was another source of inspiration for the Swiss. Given this basic aim, they set about illustrating how it could be achieved, and in fact *had* been achieved by Milton. *Poetry is not prose* and must be distinguished from it in every way. The opposite of the "herzrührende Schreibart" is the prosaic "kriechende Schreibart" (attributed to the Gottschedians) that would allow no construction in poetry that would not be allowed in prose. The poet, in contrast to the prose writer, will employ an elevated and noble style, with bold metaphors; he will consciously deviate from normal word order; he will express himself with emphasis and a brevity that compresses much meaning into little space. The poet must not merely tell, he must *show* and thus set "das Gemüthe in eben diejenige Bewegung . . . , als die würkliche Gegenwart und das Anschauen der Dinge erwecken würde." For this purpose, Bodmer continues, "ist die gemeine und gewohnte Art zu reden viel zu schwach: Sein [des Dichters] gantzer Ausdruck muss darum neu und wunderbar, d.i. viel sinnlicher, prächtiger, nachdrücklicher seyn."[26]

It was principles such as these that Klopstock's genius was capable of applying. Bodmer himself could do so only in modest measure, though he could see how Milton—and in some instances also Haller—had applied them. Pyra, a better poet than Bodmer, had also learned from Milton and had, to the degree that his talent permitted, been moderately successful in putting such principles to work. Klopstock learned from both Haller and Pyra. Schneider details the ways in which Klopstock sought to make use of the newly won poetic freedom (*Erneuerung*, chapters 3–5). The most significant can be subsumed under the rubric of "Verfremdung," the alienation of the language of poetry from that of prose in order to stress its poetic nature. Here belong the employment of obsolete or archaic words and forms such as *fleuch*, *kreuch* (for *flieg*, *kriech*); the changing of inflected forms by the addition or omission of a vowel; the use of the simplex for the compound (*fernen* for *entfernen*, *frischen* for *erfrischen*) as well as the formation of new words by the addition of prefixes and suffixes (*Vergehung*, *Erblickung*) and the invention of new plurals (*Verwesungen*, *Kühlungen*); the formation of new composites to achieve brevity and density of meaning, in which Klopstock rightly saw a peculiar advantage of German (*Flammenwort*, *fernherwehend*, *grabverlangend*); the transitive use of intransitive verbs, a Klopstockian trademark.

Deviation from prose order as well as the excessive exploitation of the natural tendency of German toward periodicity (by the insertion of dependent clauses, for example) can also contribute to the "Verfremdungseffekt." In regard to word order, Klopstock remarks in "Von der Sprache der Poesie," the poet differs most widely from the writer of prose: "und er muss es tun, wenn er sich anders . . . *poetisch-richtig* ausdrücken will. Das Abweichen ist ihm also nicht etwa bloss erlaubt, sondern Pflicht" (Schleiden, 3d ed., p. 1028). The principle followed is emotional: what touches us most should come first in the sentence. This leads to one of Klopstock's most characteristic techniques, that of arousing expectation or tension, which often makes his poetry daring (and difficult) beyond almost anything since Horace and most poetry since himself.

Highly typical for Klopstock is his extreme compression, which makes it impossible to read him superficially. Haller had also applied this principle to the point of mannerism, but Klopstock goes even further. It may be true, as Schneider (*Erneuerung*, p. 59) maintains, that Klopstock's brevity stands in the service of emotion rather than, as with Haller, concentration of thought, but the result is nonetheless that the reader must pause and deduce the meaning, just as he must keep all his wits about him if he is to follow Klopstock's syntax. Klopstock is the great master of "harte Fügung." Besides the elimination of prefixes and suffixes, the use of composites, etc., Klopstock is especially fond of participles, which can save a subordinate clause and give the impression of simultaneity. Metaphor, one of the main concerns of the Swiss critics, plays a subordinate role in Klopstock's work, especially in the odes, which achieve their effects above all through meter, syntax, and rhythm.

In the ode, Klopstock regarded Horace as the unsurpassed master: "Horaz hat den Hauptton der Ode, ich sage nicht des Hymnus, durch die seinigen, bis auf jede seiner feinsten Wendungen bestimmt," he writes in "Gedanken über die Natur der Poesie" (Schleiden, 3d ed., p. 992). "Man wird also den Wert einer Ode am besten ausmachen können, wenn man sich fragt: Würde Horaz diese Materie so ausgeführt haben?" As Hagedorn's central poetry harks back to Horace's epistles and satires, so does much of Klopstock's to his odes. But Klopstock is no "imitator" (in the eighteenth-century acceptation of the term) of the urbane Roman. He does not, as both Viëtor (*Ode*, p. 117) and Kaussmann (*Stil*, pp. 18 f.) stress, merely imitate the *writings* of Horace, he imitates their *spirit*, which may be what is meant by "Hauptton" in the passage just quoted. In Viëtor's opinion, however, it was the Psalms even more than Horace that were decisive for Klopstock's odic poetry, for they were the most sublime genre and the best suited for the outpouring of pure feeling (*Ode*, p. 117). Klopstock himself, it would seem, felt that the Psalms were rather the model for hymnic poetry, if a distinction may be allowed.

In any event, it was not from the Psalms but from Horace and Homer that Klopstock developed his metrics, and his innovations in this field were even more revolutionary than his cultivation of sublime themes. "Unleugbare Tatsache bleibt—das ist durch keine Kritik, mit der er im Leben und nach dem Tode reichlich bedacht wurde, zu ändern," writes A. Kelletat, "dass Klopstock durch seine Entscheidung für die antiken Masse unsre Dichtersprache fast von den Toten erweckt und mit bewegtestem Leben erfüllt hat" ("Zum Problem der antiken Metren im Deutschen," p. 51). The harvest from Klopstock's sowing was immeasurable, Kelletat continues, in the epic, the idyl, ode, hymn, epigram, in the poetry of Hölty and the "Hain," in the works of Goethe and Schiller, of Hölderlin, Platen, Mörike, and even later. Klopstock *is* the father of modern German poetry.

We do not know with certainty how ancient verse sounded: the osteology of ancient measures, the dashes and pothooks indicating length, is all we have.[27] The music that accompanied ancient strophes and which undoubtedly gave rise to various accommodations is also lost. The handbooks assure us that in ancient verse words gave up their natural (prose) accent in favor of musical stress, marked only by degree of tone. In transposing ancient measures into German the poets (what else can they do?) substitute as a rule of thumb a stressed syllable for what in classical metrics was designated as a "long" and an unstressed syllable for a "short." Quantitative criteria are abandoned in favor of natural word accent. Thus we say that "Kleine Blumen, kleine Blätter" is trochaic, "Erhalt uns Herr bei deinem Wort" iambic, and "Windet zum Kranze die goldenen Ähren" dactylic. The spondee presents certain difficulties, but spondaic effects can also be achieved. In a strict sense, then, ancient metrics are not possible in German; all one can do is to make an adaption that *reminds* one of classical meters.

The meter of meters in Greek and Latin is the hexameter, a predominantly dactylic measure in which trochees and spondees are also employed. The character of the individual hexameter is largely determined by the placement of the caesurae. There are twelve possible positions, the favorites being in the third and fourth feet. The caesura in the third foot is seldom lacking, falling almost, but not quite, in the middle of the line. Kelletat exemplifies some of the possibilities (p. 56):

1) Sage mir, Muse, die Taten | des vielgewanderten Mannes,
2) Welcher so viel geirrt | nach der heiligen Troja Zerstörung. (Voss)
3) Singe den Zorn, o Göttin, | des Peleiaden Achilleus. (Voss)
4) Waffen sing ich und Mann, | den Erstling, welchen vor Troja. (Schröder)
5) Sing, unsterbliche Seele, | der sündigen Menschheit Erlösung. (Klopstock)
6) Pfingsten, | das liebliche Fest, | war gekommen; | es grünten und blühten
7) Feld und Wald; | auf Hügeln und Höhn, | in Büschen und Hecken
8) Übten ein fröhliches Lied | die neuermunterten Vögel. (Goethe)

Obviously the hexameter is a verse of almost unlimited possibilities, and it was Klopstock's *Messias* that gave it a permanent place in German poetry.[28] The hexameter was the principal means of freeing German verse from the tyranny of rhymed iambs, the "hölzernen Hackbrett von Alexandrinern," as Herder puts it.

One of Klopstock's basic insights into the nature of German verse as compared with Greek and Latin is that the substitution of natural word stress for length is artificial, if we think of length in terms of ancient quantity. We do not hear quantities at all, we hear stresses. In the word "Donnergesang" ($-\cup\cup-$), for example, we do not note that $-$ is equivalent to $\cup\cup$, as is (theoretically at least) the case in ancient metrics. We hear four syllables, not six time equivalencies, the "calculated" duration according to the handbooks. In short, what we hear are "Wortfüsse" (which may include whole phrases), not artificially calculated metrical feet. Germanic stress and hence Germanic meter are dependent on meaning and word accent, on rises and dips, not on "longs" and "shorts," though Klopstock still uses the latter terms. He gives the following illustration in one of his essays on the German hexameter:

Schrĕcklĭch ĕrschōll dĕr gĕflügĕltĕ
Dōnnĕrgĕsāng ĭn dĕr Hēērschăr.

We do not hear the artificial feet "schrĕcklĭch ĕr-," "schōll dĕr gĕ-," etc., we hear the "word feet" "schrĕcklĭch ĕrschōll," "dĕr gĕflügĕltĕ," etc. It was this insight (at first, it seems, unconscious) that led the poet to the construction of "free rhythms" or free verse, in which the lines are controlled not by a set metrical scheme but by the word feet that follow (or create) the rise and fall of the emotions. Klopstock's free verse is widely regarded as his best and most characteristic.

Klopstock of course also transposed into German Horatian measures as well as inventing quite a number of measures of his own. He was a very fertile metrician. To fully appreciate his accomplishments (or to criticize them intelligently) one must himself be versed in classical metrics, something this writer cannot claim to be. However, since Klopstock indicates the metrical skeleton at the head of his odes and since he usually avoids "Tonbeugung" (conflict of metrical and natural accent), it is possible to read his verse correctly, but only because the poet gives us this guidance. Were our attention not called to the metrical scheme, and were the poems not printed accordingly, Klopstock's poems in classical (or pseudo-classical) meters could easily be construed as free verse; perhaps one must except the hexameters, but not always even them. An example is "Der Sieger" (1795), an ode in a measure invented by the poet, which is meant to be read according to the following metrical scheme (*Oden*, ed. Muncker-Pawel 2, 106):

$$-\cup\cup-, \ -\cup\cup-, \ \cup\cup-\cup$$
$$-\cup\cup-, \ \cup\cup-\cup(-), \ \cup\cup-\cup$$
$$-\cup-\cup\cup-, \ \cup-\cup$$
$$-\cup\cup-\cup-.$$

Kränzet mein Haupt, Lorber des Siegs: Mit des Manns
    Kraft
Hab' ich gekämpft. Die Verkennung, die Entedlung
Dessen, was sie erhöht die Menschen,

205

> Was sie zu Menschen macht!
>
> Zeigten sich mir; ach und der Gram, . . .

It is evident, I think, that these verses can only be read according to the meter indicated because they are so *printed*. If we read them naturally, according to the word feet or according to the brief pauses, which the poet indicates by commas, we might well distribute them as follows and end up with a poem in free verse:

> Kränzet mein Haupt, Lorber des Siegs!
> Mit des Manns Kraft
> Hab' ich gekämpft.
> Die Verkennung, die Entedlung dessen,
> Was sie erhöht die Menschen,
> Was sie zu Menschen macht!
> Zeigten sich mir.
>
> Ach und der Gram etc.

The point is that Klopstock's poetry naturally tends to fall into free verse. One of the reasons is that there is no rhyme scheme to guide us. But there is also no traditional rhythmical-metrical pattern that we all have in our ear, except perhaps in the case of hexameters and pentameters. Klopstock's imitation of classical meters "freed" German verse in more ways than one.[29] (We will take up this matter again later.)

The question of the relation of Klopstock's poetry to personal experience has concerned German critics to an unusual degree. This is largely due to the fact that they tend to see their poetry, especially lyric poetry, from the standpoint of Goethe's "Erlebnislyrik." "Es dürfte kein Ereignis von einiger Wichtigkeit im äusseren oder inneren Leben des Dichters geben," R. Hamel writes, "das er nicht durch eine Ode oder durch eine Andeutung in denselben dichterisch fixiert hätte" (DNL 47, xvi). Klopstock's poetry is indeed "Erlebnisdichtung" in the sense that he did not write about what did not personally move him. And he speaks in the most direct fashion of actual events and emotional situations he has himself experienced. In fact, he considers it absolutely necessary for the poet to have emotionally experienced what he presents: "Es ist eines der tollkühnsten Wagstücke, das ich kenne," says Klopstock's mouthpiece in the dialog "Von der Darstellung," "Leben, das man nicht mitfühlt, ausdrücken zu wollen" (Schleiden, 3d ed., p. 1034). What Klopstock does not do and what we have come to expect of "Erlebnisdichtung" is to symbolically universalize the particular experience. Rudolf Haller, in his *Geschichte der deutschen Lyrik*, remarks that Klopstock's love poems would not have been written if the poet had not actually been in love, but that it is not *love* that speaks through the "I" of these poems but the "I" expressing itself about its lovelorn state (p. 299). Goethe's "Warum gabst du uns die tiefen Blicke," on the other hand, to take a famous example of recognized "Erlebnislyrik," describes a highly individual situation and at the same time raises it to the plane of symbolic universality. The situation itself, rather than the "I" that experiences it, is given voice and form. Perhaps all this amounts to saying that Klopstock's poetry is presymbolical.[30]

G. Kaiser views Klopstock's relation to personal experience in a somewhat different light (p. 290). While Klopstock, Kaiser says, expresses his inner life with unheard-of directness, he regards the lyric "I" as representative of man, not merely himself. "Man" may be a somewhat too inclusive term, but it is certainly not going too far to say that Klopstock felt that he spoke for "die wenigen Edlen," those capable of nobility of feeling. Of these he was priest and cantor. The argument is circular of course, since if one is moved by Klopstock's poetry one is by definition a member of the elite.

Contrary to fairly widespread opinion, Klopstock's poetry is not without a developmental line both thematically and stylistically. K.A. Schleiden (*Der Deutschunterricht* 8, Heft 5, 31 f.) discerns four periods:

207

1. To 1754: cultivation of Horatian forms; dominant themes: the poet's office, friendship, love, occasional poems to the Danish ruling house.
2. To c. 1764 (1765 would be more accurate): introduction of free verse; predominantly religious themes.
3. To 1776: free verse and invented meters; turning to Teutonic themes ("Bardenlyrik"); odes on language, the progress of poetry, the fatherland.
4. To 1803: return to antiquity stylistically (Horatian measures frequent); reflective and political odes; the poet as one who warns and guides; language, poetics, immortality, the life of memory.

Such an outline can only be a rough approximation. Klopstock's themes have a way of announcing themselves in one or two odes, then subsiding, to be taken up again and developed vigorously. One of the most striking features of this outline is the weight it gives to the last period (Schleiden would like to call it Klopstock's "classical" period), which includes approximately one-third more poems than the three preceding periods combined: about 120 compared to about 94. This imbalance is largely due to two factors: the completion of the *Messias*, the burden Klopstock had been carrying since at least 1746, and the poet's burning interest in the French Revolution, which spurred him to intense poetic activity.

Klopstock himself in a contemplative ode of 1789 provides us with another organizing matrix (M-P [=Oden, ed. Muncker-Pawel] 2, 68). Here he casts a backward glance at his own production and interprets it from a psychological standpoint. I quote the whole poem.

DAS GEGENWÄRTIGE

1. Ehmals verlor mein fliegender Blick in des Lebens
   Künftiges sich, und ich schuf dann, was mir Wunsch war,
   Fast zu Wirklichkeit: seine Freuden
   Hatte das schöne Phantom!

208

2. Denn das Gesetz der Mässigung wurd' ihm gegeben,
   Wurde gethan mit der Strenge, die zu Hofnung
   Leitet: aber der Wunsch ist dann selbst
   Thor, wenn er Hofnung verdient.

3. Freue dich dess, das da ist! so sagt' ich mir öfter,
   Als dem Getäusch ich es zuliess zu gleissen:
   Sagt' es, thats! und erlebt' auch, was sich
   Über Gewünschtes erhob.

4. Jetzo verweilt der festere Blick in des Lebens
   Vorigem sich, und ich fühle, was dahinfloh,
   Fast, als hielt' ich's noch: süssre Freuden
   Gibt es mir, war nicht Phantom!

5. Freue dich dess, das da ist! so sag' ich mir dennoch
   Jetzt auch. Obwohl sich der Scheitel mit des Alters
   Blüthenhaare mir deckt; ich wandle
   Froh um das nähere Grab.

6. Aber ich werd' auch Leiden gewahr im Vergangnen,
   Wehmuth! es geht mit den Leichen der Geliebten
   Mir vorbey: wie vermöcht' ich dann mich
   Dessen, das da ist, zu freun!

This is a poem by an older man (Klopstock was sixty-five in 1789) and displays the resigned tone of age tinged by melancholy, in spite of the positive acceptance of all life has brought. Three different attitudes toward time are posited, all of them aspects of the present at particular periods of the poet's life. In stanzas 1–2, the future is embraced as the present and the actual present devalued for its sake; in stanza 3, the actual present is accepted and seen to be superior to all "Gewünschtes"; in stanzas 4–6, the past is embraced as the present, the past having become—in memory—"that which is there." Its remembrance brings both joy and sorrow: "ich wandle Froh um das nähere Grab" and "ich werd' auch Leiden gewahr." Stanza 4 corresponds antithetically to stanza 1; stanza 5 corresponds positively to stanza 3, both being admonitions to rejoice in the present. There is a caesura after the third stanza; here the past, which looked first to the future, then to the present, is separated from the actual present as experienced by a man of sixty-five, who looks back to the past and experiences it almost as the present, diminishing its phantom quality. The imagined experience of youth was "fastwirklich," i.e., it had the convincing virtuality of art, which lent it "das Gesetz der Mässigung," but in the end it is rejected in spite of its joys as foolish: "der Wunsch ist dann selbst Thor, wenn es Hofnung verdient." The sweeter joy of recollection is also "fastwirklich," but it too has its negative aspect, for memory brings back the thought of dead friends. It is notable that actual reality— one thinks of the odes to Cidli and such a poem as "Der Rheinwein"—plays a relatively minor role in the poet's review of his work. The ode was written, we may note, just as Klopstock was turning again to the present, the political actualities of the French Revolution, and thus excludes an important part of his production, in fact, about one-sixth of all his odes.

One of the most characteristic features of Klopstock's odes is the positing of some "overriding totality" (Betteridge) toward which emotion can be directed. This totality may be the ideal of friendship, love, freedom, the fatherland, poetry, the concept of immortality, and so on. From the standpoint of the linguistic expression, the poem itself, it does not make too much difference. From that standpoint the ideal is there in order to create a tension, a goal toward which expression can be aimed. The poem is the linguistic reflection of the effort to adumbrate the ideal. This explains why much of Klopstock's poetry, especially the earlier poetry, takes so little account of things as they actually are: it is constantly in the process of transcending reality in an attempt to show forth the ideal. However, it would be wrong to assume that this is always the case. Klopstock can also follow his own admonition and "take joy in that which is there." The odes to Cidli (Meta), to wine, to the sense of hearing, to exultant physical activity celebrate the here and now. In addition, there is the important body of poetry dealing with "das verlängerte Leben," or life relived in memory. While it may not have distorted our concept of his historical importance, the fact that Klopstock's best-known and most influential poems are almost entirely the earlier ones has skewed our view of his work as a whole.

But in his earlier odes, certainly, it is the projection of an ideal that provides the perch from which the poem takes flight. The earliest preserved ode, "Der Lehrling der Griechen" (1747), deals with the ideal poet and his rejection of all conventional recognition for the sake of a better fame to be granted by the *"future* tears" of those who can understand the heights to which he aspires. The involved syntax and plurality of references in this earliest ode (we have only the revised version) equal anything in Horace, whose second Asclepiadian meter (in reversed order) Klopstock here employs. The last fourteen lines will show what is meant (M-P 1, 4). The poet whose tastes have been formed by the immortal works of the ancients

> Ihn lässt gütiges Lob, oder Unsterblichkeit
> Dess, der Ehre vergeudet, kalt!
> Kalt der wartende Thor, der, des Bewunderns voll,
> Ihn grossäugichten Freunden zeigt,
> Und der lächelnde Blick einer nur schönen Frau,
> Der zu dunkel die Singer* ist.
> Thränen nach besserem Ruhm werden Unsterblichen,
> Jenen alten Unsterblichen,
> Deren dauernder Werth, wachsenden Strömen gleich,
> Jedes lange Jahrhundert füllt,
> Ihn gesellen, und ihn jenen Belohnungen,
> Die der Stolze nur träumte, weihn!
> Ihm ist, wenn ihm das Glück, was es so selten that,
> Eine denkende Freundin giebt,
> Jede Zähre von ihr, die ihr sein Lied entlockt,
> Künftiger Zähren Verkünderin!

The "denkende Freundin," we should note, proves her ability to "think," that is, to be moved by the sublimity of the poet's song, by her tears. The ode is also an attempt to indicate the ideal audience for the new kind of poetry Klopstock was in the process of writing, poetry appealing primarily to feeling, but intricate and severe in form.

*Singer, Elizabeth Singer Rowe (died 1737); see above, p. 135.

The famous ode "Auf meine Freunde" (1747), the revision of which (1767), called "Wingolf" ("temple of friendship"), transforms the Greek mythological references into Nordic, sings an ideal union of friends—they are Klopstock's Leipzig companions, the Bremer Beiträger—as the founders of a coming golden age of German literature. Again it is the note of exclusivity, the rejection of reality as it is that strikes one in this ode, together with the exaltation of these mostly second-rank *litterateurs* to almost mythic status. Pyra's and Lange's *Freundschaftliche Lieder* exhibit the same basic configuration, but there the ideal is not so all-inclusive; rather it is a personal realm of intimate coziness and shelter from the world that lends these poems their characteristic tone. Klopstock's goal is infinitely higher and more demanding, more arrogant, if one will, and intent upon changing the world to correspond to the ideal. Life lived according to a poetic ideal is the theme of the ode. Such a life is a fulfilled existence, a state in which friendship is poetic and poetry an expression of friendship. It establishes an overriding totality.

The opening stanzas are among the most persuasive that Klopstock wrote. I quote the first five stanzas of the two versions in parallel columns. Klopstock himself annotates the references to Nordic mythology, which were even more unfamiliar to the reader of his day than ours.

1. Wie Hebe,* kühn und
   jugendlich ungestüm,
   Wie mit dem goldenen
   Köcher Latonens Sohn,
   Unsterblich, sing ich
   meine Freunde
   Feyrend in mächtigen
   Dithyramben.
2. Wilst du zu Strophen
   werden, o Lied? oder
   Ununterwürfig, Pindars
   Gesängen gleich,

Wie Gna† im Fluge,
   jugendlich ungestüm,
   Und stolz, als reichten
   mir aus Iduna's Gold
   Die Götter, sing' ich
   meine Freunde
   Feyernd in kühnerem
   Bardenliede.
Willst du zu Strophen
   werden, o Haingesang?
   Willst du gesetzlos,
   Ossians Schwunge gleich,

Gleich Zeus erhabnem
    truncknem Sohne,
Frey aus des schaffenden
    Sel enttaumeln?
3. Die Wasser Hebrus
    wälzten sich adlerschnell
Mit Orpheus Leyer,
    welche die Hayne zwang
Dass sie ihr folgten,
    die die Felsen
Taumeln, und Himmelab
    wandeln lehrte;
4. So floss der Hebrus.
    Grosser Unsterblicher
Mit fortgerissen folgte
    dein fliehend Haupt
Blutig mit todter Stirn,
    die Leyer
Hoch im Getös ungestümer
    Wogen.
5. So floss der Fluss,
    des Oceans Sohn, daher:
So fliesst mein Lied
    auch, hoch und
    gedanckenvol.
Des spott ich, der es
    unbegeistert,
Richterisch und
    philosophisch höret.

Gleich Ullers Tanz auf
    Meerkrystalle,
Frey aus der Seele des
    Dichters schweben?
Die Wasser Hebrus wälzten
    mit Adlereil
Des Zelten Leyer, welche
    die Wälder zwang,
Dass sie ihr folgten,
    die den Felsen
Taumeln, und wandeln aus
    Wolken lehrte.
So floss der Hebrus.
    Schattenbesänftiger,
Mit fortgerissen folgte
    dein fliehend Haupt
Voll Bluts, mit todter
    Stirn, der Leyer
Hoch im Getöse gestürzter
    Wogen.
So floss der Waldstrom
    hin nach dem Ozean!
So fliesst mein Lied auch,
    stark, und
    gedankenvoll.
Dess spott' ich, der's
    mit Klüglingsblicken
Höret, und kalt von der
    Glosse triefet.

Hebe, goddess of youthfulness; *Latonens Sohn*, Apollo; *Dithyramben*, hymns to Bacchus; *Zeus . . . truncknem Sohne*, Bacchus; *Hebrus*, river in Thrace (the Maritsa), into which Orpheus's dismembered body was thrown when torn apart by the Maenads.

†*Gna*, messengeress of Freya, chief Nordic female deity; *Iduna*, goddess who kept the apples of immortality in a golden dish; *Haingesang*, bardic song; *Uller*, famous skater among the gods; *des Zelten*, Orpheus, a Thracian; K. considered the Thracians Celts and the Celts Germanic; *Schattenbesänftiger*, reference to Orpheus's descent to the underworld.

As a statement of Klopstock's attitude toward form and the nature of poetry these stanzas are particularly revealing. How shall I sing? Dithyrambically, i.e., enthusiastically and Dionysiacally, at all events. But shall my song be "gesetzlos," "ununterwürfig" (as Pindar's was thought to be), or shall it conform to a set metrical and strophic pattern? (The question is slightly disingenuous, since one strophe is already composed, and the one in which the question is asked follows the same pattern. In "Wingolf" the situation is a bit different, since here the poet seems to be *telling* his song to assume strophic form, not to roll "frey aus der Seele," whereas the "oder" of the first version leaves a real choice.) The magnificent comparison of the course of his song with that of the river Hebrus, with its swift flood carrying Orpheus's lyre followed by his bloody head, is one of the great passages in German poetry. The comparison was no doubt suggested, as Düntzer points out, by Horace, *Odes* 4, 2, and his comparison of Pindar's poetry with that of a rushing mountain stream (*Erläuterungen*, 2d ed., Heft 1, 90). (Horace, in the same ode, also characterizes Pindar's poetry as "ununterwürfig": *numerisque . . . lege solutis*, measures freed from rule.) The image of head and lyre being carried down the river are from Ovid, *Met.* 11, 50–53, a passage much admired by Klopstock. In a sense, then, this passage is an imitation of classical sources. Yet it is wholly and unmistakably Klopstock.

"So floss der Waldstrom hin nach dem Ozean! So fliesst mein Lied auch. . . ." What does this imply? Orpheus was not "lawless" but an imposer of order, as his taming of wild beasts indicates. Here his lyre, his essential being, imposes its order on nature, forcing the forests to follow it and causing the cliffs to sway and walk beside it as it is carried down the Hebrus. "So fliesst mein Lied auch. . . ." To those who are incapable of enthusiasm, who listen to his song with "Klüglingsblicken," it may appear wild and disordered, a tumultuous flood, but in its midst it bears the lawgiver's lyre that bends all to its rule.

The unifying fiction is that the singer, Klopstock, evokes his friends by the power of his song, causing them to appear before him and be united under the festive "wing of joy." As they appear one by one, each is characterized in a very personal manner but at the same time elevated to almost mythic stature. Among them are Ebert, known especially for his translations from the classics and the English and later for his bardic song, who appears "göttlich mit Reben umlaubt," a "Sohn der Olympier"; the gentle satirist Rabener, whose "holy image" Klopstock as officiating priest at this sacred ceremony sets beside that of Lucian and Swift; Giseke, the poet's most intimate friend and also a poet (though today unknown), is greeted with roses and asked to sing the funeral dirge for the singer of this song when he should die, whereupon he would become Giseke's guardian spirit; Cramer, preacher and poet (likewise today unread), is exalted as the author of patriotic poetry, which posterity would sing "hoch im Getöse Eiserner Kriege." And so it goes: these intimates of Klopstock, the Bremer Beiträger, were men of good will but mediocre parts, with the exception of Gellert, celebrated here as an inculcator of virtue, and Hagedorn, who is remembered *in absentia;* they are raised to the rank of demigods and seen in the vision that closes the ode as heralding a new era of German culture. The time is ripe, nature has now again formed souls worthy of a new golden age: "hat Seelen, *die sich fühlen,* Fliegen den Geniusflug, gebildet" (M-P 1, 31). In strophes as gripping as those with which Hölderlin, a son of Klopstock, a half-century later was also to close his "vaterländische Oden," the poet implores the new day to descend:

Komm, goldne Zeit, komm, die du die Sterblichen
Selten besuchest, komm, lass dich, Schöpferin,
Lass, bestes Kind der Ewigkeiten,
Dich über uns mit verklärten Flügeln!

Tief vol Gedancken, voller Entzückungen,
Geht die Natur dir, Gottes Nachahmerin,
Schaffend zur Seiten, grosse Geister,
Wenige Götter der Welt zu bilden.

Natur, dich hört ich durchs Unermessliche
Wandeln, so wie mit sphärischem Silberton

Gestirne, Dichtern nur vernommen,
Niedrigen Geistern unhörbar, wandeln.

Aus allen goldnen Altern begleiten dich,
Natur, die Dichter, Dichter des Alterthums,
Die grossen neuen Dichter; segnend
Sehen sie ihr heilig Geschlecht hervor gehn.

[verses 293–308]

It is hardly likely that Klopstock did not recognize medi-
ocrity when he saw it. He himself was the only truly great
genius among the Beiträger. But whether he did or not is not
the point. He *needed* such an ideal union of the poetically
minded as a refuge from commonplace bourgeois society, in
which, then as now, poetry played a minor role indeed. He
needed it not only as a refuge but also as a transcendental
mark for his linguistic expression and as a means of giving
such expression meaningful resonance. He needed it, so he
created it. The world, like language, he bends to his will, just
as the clouds and the cliffs must bend to the strains of Orpheus's lyre. He sings for "die wenigen Edlen," who are the
only ones admitted to this charmed circle. But they are to
serve as an example for future generations (cf. M-P 1, 26,
verses 239–44). With the coming of the golden age perhaps all
will be worthy of admittance and all society will live under
the sign of the spirit of poetry? This seems to be the force of
the eschatological vision with which the ode closes.

In one important respect "Wingolf," the Nordic version
of "Auf meine Freunde," is a better poem than the original,
despite the opinion of those critics who claim that almost any
revision involves a loss of freshness and immediacy. For there
is no doubt that in Germanizing his ode Klopstock provided a
native land for this idealized union of German poets. As
Wolfdietrich Rasch remarks, the "secret center" of the ode is
the German nation, and this community of kindred spirits
stands for the flower of the German-speaking peoples (as yet,
in fact, no true nation, but only a congeries of principalities
with individual loyalties), and by introducing Germanic mythology Klopstock gave his vision native roots (*Freundschafts-*

kult, p. 249). In any event, there is little doubt that this is the way he himself conceived it. In Rasch's words, "der Dichter der Freundschaft wird zum Dichter . . . des Nationalgefühls . . ." (p. 249). The revision falls in the period when the overarching ideal which Klopstock's poetry exalts was no longer friendship but fatherland. It would be possible to argue that the more universal nature of Greek myth, which belongs to all Western civilization, allows a purer development of the theme of friendship than when it is "contaminated" with patriotism. But it is also possible to see the patriotic element as reinforcing this theme.

The ode "An Ebert" (1748; M-P 1, 38) shows the perils inherent in dependency on friends. As Rasch (pp. 250 f.) convincingly argues, it is the reverse of "Auf meine Freunde." Here the poet imagines, instead of the assembly of his friends, their loss by death and the consequent destruction of his very existence. Without friends, life is meaningless. Again the friends appear one by one before the poet's inward eye, but always as leaving him forever. This "trüber Gedanke" plunges him "tief in die Melancholey."

> Um die Mitternachtszeit gieng das Bild vom Grabe der
>   Freunde
> Meine Seele vorbey.
> Um die Mitternachtszeit sah ich die Ewigkeit vor mir,
>   Und die unsterbliche Schaar.
>
> [verses 31–33]

The departed friends are mentioned by name and briefly characterized. The climax comes, as was to be anticipated, when it is imagined that Ebert also finally dies as well as the "künftige Geliebte." Now life is utterly desolate and devoid of meaning:

> Stirbt denn auch einer von uns, (Mich reisst mein
>   banger Gedanke
> Immer nachtvoller fort!)
> Stirbt denn auch einer von uns, und bleibt nur einer
>   noch übrig;
> Bin ich der einsame denn;

Hat mich alsdenn auch die schon geliebet, die künftig
    mich liebet,
Ruht auch ihr zartes Gebein;
Bin ich allein, allein auf der Welt, von allen noch übrig:
    Wirst du da, ewiger Geist,
Wirst du, Seele zur Freundschaft erschaffen, die leeren
    Tage
Sehen, und fühlend noch seyn?

                        [verses 59–68]

All that remains now is the thought of a cultic worship at the graves of his departed friends and of at last dying beside them. In this ode there is no mention of a reunion in the beyond. The closing lines are full of despair: "Finstrer Gedanke, lass ab! lass ab, in die Seele zu donnern! . . . Die verstummende Seele   Fasst dich, Gedanke, nicht mehr!"

The overriding totality represented by the ideal of friendship is here seen as undependable. It does not, however, disappear from Klopstock's poetry; rather it attains its apogee in "An Bodmer" and "Der Zürchersee" (both 1750), then ebbs away in the short odes devoted to the memory of the dead, "Weihtrank an die todten Freunde" (1751), "Die frühen Gräber" (1764), and "Die Sommernacht" (1766), which are like funeral monuments to the *Freundschaftsbund* celebrated in "Auf meine Freunde."

That friendship is the central theme of "Der Zürchersee" is not immediately apparent. Staiger, in his interpretation of this ode, compares Klopstock to "a spirit hovering over the waters, cautiously weighing the possibility of incarnation" (*Wege zum Gedicht*, p. 112). Should my poem take this form or that? What will be my theme? Klopstock's odes often remind one of what H. v. Kleist has to say in "Über die allmähliche Verfertigung der Gedanken beim Reden." He does not give us results, he gives us processes and makes us participate in them. This is the opposite of the method employed by poets of the Baroque and the Enlightenment, who typically begin with the known and then illustrate it, the Baroque poets through *ornatus*, those of the Enlightenment by argument and example.

"Der Zürchersee" contains nineteen four-line stanzas. The meter is the fourth Asclepiad, a form which Klopstock felt to be particularly suited to the ode which tends toward song. He uses it eight times.[31] We can discern the following disposition:

Stanzas 1–3: invocation to nature, to man as the interpreter of nature, and to joy as the Muse of the poem in progress.

Stanzas 4–8: narrative: nature, man, joy, and the epiphany of joy (Freude) in nature and man.

Stanzas 9–15: enthusiastically reflective: exemplification of the forms joy may take: in nature (springtime and love); in wine (philosophical friendship); in (poetic) fame.

Stanzas 16–19: enthusiastically reflective: friendship as the crown of joy: vision of a community of friends in an Elysian setting as the perfect realization of the three elements invoked in the beginning.

Like most of Klopstock's odes, "Der Zürchersee" conveys no particular wisdom. We can hardly maintain that we have been afforded any deeper insights into man, nature, joy. Rather, if we are of a temperament that can be affected by this kind of poetry at all, we are left with an afterglow and sense of heightened emotion, much as we might be upon hearing a piece of orchestral music. Schiller's remarks on Klopstock as a "musical poet" in *Über naive und sentimentalische Dichtung* are famous. By musical poetry Schiller means that kind of poetry which, like music, produces only a "certain emotional state" (einen bestimmten *Zustand des Gemüts*), without imitating any particular object, being in fact objectless (gegenstandslos). Though "Der Zürchersee" is by no means as disembodied as some of Klopstock's odes, it is not in sharp sense impressions that the poet is interested. Sense impressions receive only fleeting, stylized attention and are not conveyed in their particularity. They provide, as it were, brief resting points for the emotion before it takes flight again to higher spheres. The first strophe in this sense sets a program, and, in fact, not only for "Der Zürchersee," but for many of Klopstock's odes:

> Schön ist, Mutter Natur, deiner Erfindung Pracht
> Auf die Fluren verstreut, schöner ein froh Gesicht,
> Das den grossen Gedanken
> Deiner Schöpfung noch Einmal denkt.
>
> [M-P 1, 83]

The love poems of the early period have a markedly hypothetical air. They do not speak of the experience of love itself, the intimate personal intercourse between lovers, but only of an imagined ideal relationship. Love is here another all-embracing totality that provides the target for bolts of poetic expression. It is something to long for, rather than attain, valuable above all for its inspirational quality, not for itself. The Petrarchan tradition obtains. In the "Elegie" of 1748, composed for the wedding of a cousin, Klopstock does try his hand at a "tibullisches Lied," setting himself the task of praising the present moment, but here, as in "Die Braut," composed for the wedding of another relative in the next year, there is no existential connection between the poet and his theme, as the opening lines reveal clearly enough:

> Der du zum Tiefsinn und Ernst erhabner Gesänge
> gewöhnt bist,
> Und die einsame Bahn alter Unsterblichen gehst,
> Sing itzt, mein Geist, ein tibullisches Lied: Dich ladet
> die Liebe
> Deines Freundes, zum Scherz und zu Empfindungen
> ein . . .
>
> [M-P 1, 35]

The poet must keep urging his song to maintain contact with the here and now:

> Töne, mein Lied, wie liebende, sanft, mit gelinderer
> Stimme,
> Sey wie der Thau des erwachenden Tags, . . .
>
> [verses 9–10]

And with a touch of melancholy he is forced to admit that

> Ein beseelender Kuss, ist mehr, als hundert Gesänge
> Mit ihrer ganzen langen Unsterblichkeit werth.

220

Wer sein Leben durch liebt, nicht der, der in
    brauchbareren Stunden,
  Was er sich selber entzieht, Enkeln geniessbarer
    macht,
  Ist ein glücklicher Mann . . .

[verses 29–32]

The idea that a life of love is worth more than poetic fame is to
be sure a Renaissance topos (still current in Thomas Mann),
but it has here the ring of truth, for here there *is* a correspondence with Klopstock's existential situation. Love such as that
which is the theme of his wedding carmen is not the theme of
the poetry the early Klopstock writes in his own name. The
latter is rather typified by such a poem as "Die künftige Geliebte," also first called "Elegie" (1747), a vision of the woman
destined to love him, but even more the plaint of one who is in
love with love and finds no answering echo. "Die künftige
Geliebte" is one of the odes to "Fanny" (his cousin, Marie
Sophia Schmidt), to whom he sent it, and is in fact a plea for
her to return his love. As is usual in Klopstock, poetry and life
are inextricably fused. Schleiden calls this elegy a "Zeugnis
reiner Seelenliebe" (*K.s. Ausgew. Werke*, 3d ed., p. 1222). But
one is not so sure. First of all, what *is* "Seelenliebe"? Does it
mean falling in love with another's soul to the exclusion of all
corporeality? If this is the case, then lines such as the following
seem strangely out of place (I quote from the first version,
Schleiden, 3d ed., p. 22, verses 21–24):

Durch die Mitternacht hin klagt mein sanfttränendes
    Auge,
  Dass du, Göttliche, mir immer noch unsichtbar bist!
Durch die Mitternacht hin streckt sich mein zitternder
    Arm aus,
  Und umfasset ein Bild, das vielleicht ähnlich dir ist!

Verses 61–66 would also seem to bespeak healthy physicality:

Oder liebst du, wie ich? Erwacht mit unsterblicher
    Sehnsucht,
  Wie sie mein Herz mir empört, in dir die starke
    Natur?

221

> Was sagt dieser erseufzende Mund? Was sagt mir dies
> Auge,
> Das mit verlangendem Blick zärtlich gen Himmel hin
> sieht?
> Was entdeckt mir die brünstige Stellung, als wenn du
> unmarmtest,
> Als wenn du ans Herz eines Glückseligen sänkst?

Or is this "Seelenliebe" because all takes place in a vision and there is not a word of truth in it? If this is what is meant, then it is "Seelenliebe" with a vengeance. In any event, the closing lines, with their fine arched period and effective use of anaphora, speak of a love that almost surpasses even the power of the immortal soul to comprehend, a love which can exist only as an ideal and an establisher of poetic tension:

> Alles empfind ich von dir; kein halb nur begegnendes
> Lächeln;
> Kein unvollendetes Wort, welches in Seufzer verflog;
> Keine stille mich fliehende Träne, kein leises
> Verlangen,
> Kein Gedanke, der sich mir in der Ferne nur zeigt;
> Kein halbstammelnder Blick voll unaussprechlicher
> Reden,
> Wenn er den ewigen Bund süsser Umarmungen
> schwört;
> Auch der Tugenden keine, die du mir sittsam
> verbirgest,
> Eilet unausgeforscht mir und unempfunden vorbei!
> Ach, wie will ich dich, Göttliche, lieben! Das sagt uns
> kein Dichter,
> Selbst wir entzückt im Geschwätz trunkner
> Beredsamkeit nicht.
> Kaum dass noch die Unsterbliche selbst, die fühlende
> Seele,
> Ganz die volle Gewalt dieser Empfindungen fasst!

Hypothetical transcendence of the present to attain future fulfillment is also the theme of "An Fanny" and "Der Abschied" (both 1748). "An Fanny" is noted (or notorious) for the tremendous protasis (*wenn*-clause) that extends over the first five stanzas (twenty lines) before reaching its apodosis or result clause in stanza 6. Irmgard Böger has studied in detail this phenomenon, which she calls the "principle of greatest tension of feeling" in *Bewegung als formendes Gesetz*. Within the syntactic arch formed by the protasis time is prodigally consumed: the poet's own death and decay, his poetic accomplishments and ensuing fame, the death of Fanny herself, her noble life and her love for another are all foreseen as already past, whereupon the triumphant outburst releases the built-up tension: "Dann wird ein Tag seyn, den werd ich auferstehn! Dann wird ein Tag seyn, den wirst du auferstehn!" and the lovers separated in life are united in eternity. The present is radically devalued:

> Rinn unterdess, o Leben. Sie komt gewiss
> Die Stunde, die uns nach der Zypresse ruft!
> Ihr andern, seyd der schwermuthsvollen
> Liebe geweiht! und umwölkt und dunkel!
>
> [M-P 1, 64]

We should keep in mind, however, that Klopstock is not here offering a philosophy of life; he is no mystical despiser of the earthly. Rather he is exploiting a principle for creating poetry of high emotional tension. The never-ending introductory period, which, because of its intricate structure, must be read with care and concentration, is the work we have to do to receive the reward of the result clause: the tensing of the bow before the release of the arrow. The vision of eternal union that then follows is idyllic in tone and lacking in tension. No sentence extends over more than three lines. We continue to be rewarded for the syntactical labors we have accomplished. The final stanza, quoted above, expounds the view that must be taken if this vision is to be accepted as valid. It is the only nonironical closure possible.

The problem for the modern reader is undoubtedly one of emotional identification. We have come to expect poetry to be syntactically difficult, highly allusive, often resembling a puzzle that one must figure out pencil in hand, but we are

223

reluctant to give emotional assent to such self-commiseration as that expressed in these lines:

> Wenn ich einst todt bin, wenn mein Gebein zu Staub'
> Ist eingesunken, wenn du, mein Auge, nun
> Lang' über meines Lebens Schicksal,
> Brechend im Tode, nun ausgeweint hast, . . .

[M-P 1, 63]

There is no point in trying to persuade the modern reader that he *should* identify. The only standpoint for the critic-historian of literature is to try to show the poet's position in its peculiarity. Any other approach is a disservice to the poet. Many of Klopstock's contemporaries were also thrown off by what they felt to be his excessive emotionalism, especially his concern with the demands of his own heart, though many others were also conquered. But the main objection of the Aufklärer was to that facet of Klopstock's poetry that we are perhaps most ready to accept for the sake of the poetic qualities that may be its concomitant, namely, its obscurity. As Werner Küster points out, it violates the Cartesian principle equating truth with clarity (*illud omme esse verum quod valde clare et distincte percipio*) ("Das Problem der 'Dunkelheit' in Klopstocks Dichtung," p. 6). The popular philosophy of the Enlightenment admitted as true only that which could be made clear to common sense. But Klopstock's poetry seemed to be the opposite of common sense—it had to be understood in another way, though not in a completely irrational one. Actually, the fact there is not a great deal to understand in Klopstock's poetry may have constituted the real stumbling block for the advocates of clarity. They may have been looking for more profundity than was there. The organ for understanding his poetry is, as we have stressed before, the heart, not the head. Emotional identification equals understanding. This is *our* problem, while that of Klopstock's contemporaries was more grammatical and syntactical, though not exclusively so.[32]

With his marriage to Meta Moller, the Cidli of his odes, Klopstock's love poetry turns to the celebration of fulfillment in the present. The Cidli odes, especially the shorter ones, "Ihr Schlummer," "An Sie," "Furcht der Geliebten" (all 1752), and "Das Rosenband" (1753), have long been among Klopstock's most popular poems. Their popularity is due both to their accessibility and to their power to convey emotions sharable by all who subscribe to the conventions of romantic love. Rather than one of these better-known poems let us examine a less accessible one of the same period which combines a leading theme of the earlier odes, longing for the future, with gratitude for the present, the main theme of the odes to Cidli, though the present here seems only an imagined present, a vision:

GEGENWART DER ABWESENDEN (1752 or 1753)

1. Der Liebe Schmerzen, nicht der erwartenden
   Noch ungeliebten, die Schmerzen nicht,
   Denn ich liebe, so liebte
   Keiner! so werd ich geliebt!

2. Die sanfteren Schmerzen, welche zum Wiedersehn
   Hinblicken, welche zum Wiedersehn
   Tief aufathmen, doch lispelt
   Stammelnde Freude mit auf!

3. Die Schmerzen wollt ich singen. Ich hörte schon
   Des Abschieds Thränen am Rosenbusch
   Weinen! weinen der Thränen
   Stimme die Saiten herab!

4. Doch schnell verbot ich meinem zu leisen Ohr
   Zurück zu horchen! die Zähre schwieg,
   Und schon waren die Saiten
   Klage zu singen verstumt!

5. Denn ach, ich sah dich! trank die Vergessenheit
   Der süssen Täuschung mit feurigem
   Durste! Cidli, ich sahe
   Dich, du Geliebte! dich Selbst!

6. Wie standst du vor mir, Cidli, wie hing mein Herz
   An deinem Herzen, Geliebtere,

225

Als die Liebenden lieben!
O die ich suchet', und fand!
[M-P 1, 119]

The introductory period, whose protasis takes up the first two stanzas, defines the kind of pangs the poet had intended to make the theme of his song—not those of a lover in love with love but loveless that we know from "Die künftige Geliebte" (the reference is directly autobiographical), but the gentler pangs of one who looks forward to a reunion with the beloved: "*Die* Schmerzen wollt ich singen." The main clause is simply "Der Liebe Schmerzen . . . wollt ich singen," but Klopstock is nothing if not hypotactic. Instead of stating his purpose in a main clause and then specifying paratactically, he differentiates within the main clause itself by means of emphatic insertions that call attention to themselves and break the unity of the main sentence to such a degree that, upon reaching the conclusion, one is forced to go back and read the whole period again to be sure that one has understood. These insertions are like wedges driven into the main clause (nicht . . . , denn . . . , die . . . welche, welche . . . , doch . . .) and endow the period as a whole with inner tension. Especially the two intervening clauses ("Denn ich liebe . . ." and "doch lispelt . . .") that move in a contrary direction to the main clause, serve as arousers of tension. The syntactical tension reflects the thematic distinction between the pangs of the loveless lover and those of the loved lover looking forward to reunion. Stanza 3, after the apodosis, sets the mood—in one of Klopstock's most tenderly compelling images—for the poem on the pangs of hope-filled absence, the second theme which he has declared he means to treat: "Ich hörte schon des Abschieds Thränen . . . weinen"; departure, absence must precede reunion. But now the poem takes a sudden turn and the theme defined with such syntactical complexity is not developed after all: the poet forbids his ear to "hearken backward," and the tears that were weeping down the strings of his lyre cease to flow, i.e., the theme is dropped. Such arrests and changes of direction are frequent in Klopstock's odes. In "Der Gränzstein" (1782), an ode on the nature of poetry, he sees such sudden changes of direction as characteristic of the genre itself:

> Frey ist der Flug der Ode, sie kieset, wonach sie
> Lüstet, und singt's. . . .
>
> [M-P 2, 50, verses 65 f.]

But, as Ernst Kaussmann correctly maintains, as manifold as the transformations in Klopstock's odes may be, there are no real "leaps"—completely disconnected periods do not occur (*Stil*, p. 54). One grows out of the other associatively, though the new period may take a quite different direction from the preceding one. Than only unswerving center is finally the lyrical "I."

The two last stanzas are a vision—or are they? We must remember that the theme of the poem up to this point has been the determination of the theme itself, which is seen in terms of an *imagined* situation. What does it become after the sudden turn, and was the turn occasioned by the intervention of reality, that is, by the actual appearance of the beloved, or by the *imagination* of her appearance? ". . . schnell *verbot* ich meinem . . . Ohr zurück zu horchen!" This tells us that the poet decides to give his song a new direction, perhaps even to drop it altogether. Does it also make it necessary to take the final stanzas as a vision, an imagined situation, just as we must take the opening ones? It seems to me that it does. The bold image: "[ich] trank die Vergessenheit der süssen Täuschung" must be construed as showing willed forgetfulness of the imagined situation called up in stanza 3, the scene of parting. This scene is now replaced by another, also called up by the poetic will: the presence of the beloved, but her presence in absence, in the mind, "Gegenwart der Abwesenden." The ode as a whole could well be regarded as a treatment of the central doctrine of Klopstock's aesthetics, the reality of the "almost real" (das Fastwirkliche), which never ceases to stress that the poet must not describe but *present* (darstellen) in such a way as to make the auditor accept the virtuality as something hovering on the border between seem-

227

ing and being. The *locus classicus* in Klopstock's aesthetic writings is found in the dialog "Von der Darstellung":

> Von der Darstellung überhaupt sei dieses genung. Es gibt wirkliche Dinge, und Vorstellungen, die wir uns davon machen. Die Vorstellungen von gewissen Dingen können so lebhaft werden, dass diese uns gegenwärtig, und beinah die Dinge selbst zu sein scheinen. Diese Vorstellungen nenn ich *fastwirkliche Dinge*. Es gibt also wirkliche Dinge, fastwirkliche, und blosse Vorstellungen. . . .
>
> Der Zweck der Darstellung ist Täuschung. Zu dieser muss der Dichter den Zuhörer, soofte er kann, hinreissen, und nicht hinleiten. Wehe jenem, wenn er das letzte ohne Not tut.

As to what *kind* of "fastwirkliche Dinge" are most suitable for poetic presentation, we are left in no doubt:

> Der Gegenstand ist vornehmlich alsdann darstellbar, wenn er *erhaben* ist, und wenn er viel Handlung und Leidenschaft in sich begreift. (p. 1033, emphasis added)

"Handlung," action, in turn,

> besteht in der Anwendung der Willenskraft zur Erreichung eines Zwecks. Es ist ein falscher Begriff, den man von ihr macht, wenn man sie vornehmlich in der äusserlichen Tat setzt. Die Handlung fängt mit dem gefassten Entschluss an, und geht in verschiedenen Graden und Wendungen bis zu dem erreichten Zwecke fort. (Schleiden, pp. 1032–33)

This passage throws much light on the style of Klopstock's odes. We have seen in "Gegenwart der Abwesenden" how central to the course of the ode is the "application of will power for the attainment of an end." It almost seems as if the poem might have been composed to illustrate this very point, though it is in fact more likely that the theory was derived from the poetry than vice versa: "Der Liebe Schmerzen . . . *wollt* ich singen," "Doch schnell *verbot* ich." And the subject matter is, certainly in Klopstock's understanding at least, sublime, *erhaben*. "Geliebtere, Als die Liebenden lieben!" is a direct expression of the sublimity of the theme, but the whole is also sublime because, to put it rather cruelly, it treats of *Klopstock's* suffering and joy in a tone that leaves no doubt of the more than earthly importance of these emotions. This is the poet who in the ode "An Gott" (1748) dared, to the consternation of some and to the malicious amusement of others, demand that God grant him his beloved that he might love virtue more, praise the divine better, and sing more sublimely of the Redeemer. Thou art omnipresent and all-powerful, the argument runs, I am dust, yet not only dust, for I have an immortal soul: "Staub, und auch ewig!" Therefore I have a right in the name of my immortal part to demand fulfillment of earthly love: "gieb mir, die du mir gleich erschufst!" Such a conception of the importance of self must be either sublime or ridiculous, depending on how successful the poet is in making us achieve identification with his feeling. That for *him* it is sublime is beyond question.

Besides friendship, love, and the poet's office, we find also in the period up to 1754 poems adumbrating the ideal of the fatherland, particularly in connection with poetry, and five odes of an occasional nature on or to members of the Danish royal house, four concerning his patron Frederick V, and one on the death of Queen Louise. In a sense, these two groups of odes, those on the German fatherland and those on the rulers of his adopted country, complement each other. Denmark and Denmark's king serve as a foil against which Prussia and Prussia's king, Frederick the Great, are shown in a negative light, at least in regard to the furtherance of German poetry. Frederick's Francophilia and his denigration of German literature remained a thorn in Klopstock's side as long as Frederick lived. The telling blow fell early. The first three cantos of the *Messias* having been put into French and dedicated "Aux deux grands amis, Frédéric, roi de Prusse, et Arouet de Voltaire, auteur de la Henriade," Klopstock sought to have his work brought to the king's attention. It seems, however, that the king never saw it or at least never read it with any sympathy, while Voltaire could not resist a witticism: "Je connais bien le Messie, c'est le fils du Père éternel et le frère du Saint-Esprit, et je suis son très-humble serviteur; mais profane que je suis, je n'ose pas mettre la main à l'encensoir," the "encensoir" being of course Klopstock's epic. He couldn't accept it, he said, until he had something of comparable sublimity to offer in return, say a poem on the angel Gabriel and the Virgin. Two worlds, the world of reason, wit and skepticism, and the world of feeling and belief, stood in diametrical opposition. There could be no meeting of minds and hearts, as much as Klopstock needed a national hero as a center for his patriotic aspirations and as much as Frederick, had he not been an atheist, a Francophile, and a despiser of German poetry, was suited for this role.

Not that Klopstock, before the refusal of his epic, had not tried to swallow or ignore his objections to the Prussian monarch. The ode now known as "Heinrich der Vogler" was originally published in 1749 in the *Bremer Beiträge* as "Kriegslied zur Nachahmung des alten Liedes von der Chey-Chase-Jagd" and made specific reference to Frederick, who there appears as "der beste Mann Im ganzen Vaterland!" though the poet later pretended that he had never meant to refer to Frederick at all. "Heinrich der Vogler," the first German poem to adopt the Chevy Chase strophe (later used by Gleim in his *Grenadierlieder*), shows Klopstock on the lookout for a new overriding totality, the ideal fatherland. It was a theme he was to return to later, especially in the 1760s, and out of which sprang his "Bardenlyrik," in which Hermann, the conqueror of Varrus, figures as the great national hero, a better, because more tractable, Frederick. The jingoism of "Heinrich der Vogler," jangling as it must be for our nerves, is the measure of Klopstock's longing for the ideal, here given form as the ancient, if questionable, ideal denoted by *dulce et decorum est pro patria mori*:

Willkommen Tod fürs Vaterland!
Wenn nur unser sinkend Haupt

230

Schön Blut bedeckt, dann sterben wir
Mit Ruhm fürs Vaterland!

[M-P 1, 78]

But the matter nearest to Klopstock's heart is the bringing into being of a German poetry of European stature, a poetry that rivals that of the Greeks—always the supreme exemplars—and is equal or superior to that of other modern nations. Thus patriotism and poetry are inseparably connected. Odes of the first period dealing with this theme are "Fragen" and "Die beyden Musen" (both 1752); in the 1760s it then becomes dominant. To follow its development let us examine a later ode, "Kaiser Heinrich" (1764), a poem of seventy-six lines in Alcaic meter.

"Kaiser Heinrich" (Henry VI, son of Barbarossa, Holy Roman Emperor 1190–97), written a year after the conclusion of the Seven Years' War, which established the world fame of Frederick the Great and made Prussia a European power, contrasts those monarchs who protect and cherish poetry with those who do not. It celebrates poetic fame as undying and disparages political, martial, and regal fame as transitory. Only those princes who protected poetry are here given a place of honor. Frederick, who sits in the seat of the scorners (of German poetry), is of course relegated to swift oblivion. Stanzas 1–4 are a polemic against the Prussian king. With those who lie in elaborate marble tombs, forgotten by all but the genealogists, Frederick also will lie, despite his brilliant victories:

. . . Es schlummert ja
Mit ihnen der selbst, welche die blutigen
Siegswerthen Schlachten schlung, zufrieden,
Dass er um Galliens Pindus irrte.

[M-P 1, 161, stanza 3]

Erring about "Galliens Pindus" refers of course to Frederick's attempts to write French verse and his admiration for French literature. Stanza 4 continues:

Zur Wolke steigen, rauschen, ihm [Friedrich] ungehört,
Der deutschen Dichter Haine, Begeisterer,

231

Wehn nah am Himmel sie. Doch ihr* auch
Fremdling, erstieg er des Pindus Höh nicht.

Stanzas 5–11 celebrate reawakened German poetry (reawakened and largely written by Klopstock himself) as a return to truly German roots and hence as the tardy avenger of
those monarchs who once sought to further and protect native
poetry. Its inspiration is twofold, patriotic (*Eichenstamm*) and
religious (*Palme*):

> Schnell Fluss, und Strom schnell, stürzen am
>   Eichenstamm,
> In deinem Schatten, Palme, zwo Quellen fort.
> Ihr seht die reinen tiefen Quellen,
> Sehet der Dichtenden Grundanlagen.
>
> [stanza 5]

Drawn by this song, the shades of Charlemagne, Babarossa,
and Henry VI appear, and their services to native poetry are
judged. Charlemagne, despite his efforts to collect and preserve old heroic lays, which may even now still lie moldering
in dark monastery vaults, calling for rescue, is somewhat
harshly and illogically dismissed because of his forced conversion of the heathen: "Verschwind, o Schatten, Welcher uns
mordend zu Christen machte!" and because the writings he
collected have disappeared: "Denn Karl liess, ach umsonst,
der Barden Kriegshorn Tönen dem Auge" (i.e., had old
German poetry written down). Barbarossa, protector of
poets, is given a higher place: "Dein ist der Vorzeit edler
Gesang!" But supreme praise is reserved for Kaiser Heinrich,
enthusiastic friend of poetry and himself a minnesinger. In
him Klopstock sees both a statesman and a founder of a kingdom who participates in the inmost life of his people:

> Wenn jetzt du lebtest, edelster deines Volks,
> Und Kaiser! würdest du, bey der Deutschen Streit

---

*ihr refers proleptically to *des Pindus Höh,* here the German Parnassus in
contrast to the French Parnassus of stanza 3.

232

Mit Hämus [Griechenlands] Dichtern, und mit jenen
Am Kapitol [Rom], unerwecklich schlummern?

Du sängest selber, Heinrich: Mir dient, wer blinkt
Mit Pflugschar, oder Lanze; doch misst' ich eh
Die Kron', als Muse, dich! und euch, ihr
Ehren, die länger als Kronen schmücken!

[stanzas 18–19]

These final lines paraphrase one of the emperor's own minne-
songs as he would sing it if he lived today. In stanza 17 it is
quoted approximately as Kaiser Heinrich originally sang it:

Du sangest selbst, O Heinrich: Mir sind das Reich
Und untertan die Lande; doch misst' ich eh
Die Kron', als Sie! . . .

(Mir sind diu riche und diu lant undertan
swenn ich bi der minneclichen bin;
. . . e ich mich ir verzige, ich verzige mich e der krone.)

Heinrich, unlike Frederick the Great, would join in the cho-
rus of new German song, not sleep the sleep of the indifferent, whose reward will be oblivion in a marble tomb. The
ode thus returns to its beginning.

If we turn now to the occasional poems to Klopstock's
royal patron, Frederick V of Denmark, we see how the Danish king is held up as a model who contrasts in essential ways
with Frederick the Great. Were Frederick of Denmark a German king, the ideal fatherland would be nearer to realization
and, above all, German poetry would be granted the place of
honor it deserves. In the odes "Friedrich der Fünfte" (1750),
which appeared as the dedicatory poem prefacing the first
volume of the *Messias* in 1751, and in "Friedrich der Fünfte.
An Bernstorff und Moltke" (1751), the Danish monarch is
eulogized especially for his humanity, through which he emu-
lates divine goodness itself, for his scorn of martial glory, and
for his protection of poets and poetry:

233

> Und dann schauet sein Blick lächelnd auf die herab,
> Die der Muse sich weihn, welche, mit stiller Kraft
> Handelnd, edler die Seele macht!
>
> [M-P 1, 87, verses 30–33]

The ode of 1750 is preceded by a "Vorbericht" that makes the contrast between the two Fredericks fairly explicit. The King of Denmark, Klopstock points out, has given him, a German, the leisure to complete his sacred epic as he earlier protected and encouraged Johann Elias Schlegel, the German dramatist. When one reminds the more discerning members of the public, who are acquainted with the state of belles lettres in Germany, of these facts, it will not be difficult for them to draw their own conclusions: "so ist der Leser in den Stand gesetzt, noch vieles zu diesem kurzen Vorberichte hinzu zu denken" (M-P 1, 86, note).

Klopstock's attitude toward the Prussian king is complicated and contradictory. He is full of resentment because of Frederick's contempt for German literature and he bemoans his freethinking, but at the same time he admires him as a great general and ruler:

> . . . so offen ich sage,
> Dass dem Sieger bey Sorr [Frdr. the Gr.]
> Julianus [Julian the Apostate] zum Muster zu klein,
>   und, ein Christ zu werden!
> Würdig Friedrich ist.
> Aber das ist ein Gedanke voll Nacht: Er wird es nicht
>   werden!
>
> [M-P 1, 88, verses 9–13]

Klopstock may applaud the Danish King's rejection of martial glory, but he is still attracted, indeed, almost enthralled, by Frederick the Great's generalship and his "blutige siegswerthe Schlachten." We have already heard him singing the bliss of dying for the fatherland, a bliss much more readily available under Frederick of Prussia than Frederick of Denmark. Klopstock was by no means a pacifist. In this complex picture the thorn in the poet's side remains Frederick's heartless obtuseness toward the poets of his own country.

In dedicating any poem to a patron or ruling prince Klopstock always feared for his integrity as a man and a poet. This led him to write such anti-eulogistic poems as "Fürstenlob" (1775), composed in lieu of an ode of thanks to the margrave of Baden, and "Stintenburg" (1767), which tells why he cannot eulogize his friend and patron Count Bernstorff as the latter deserves. Both odes praise by resorting to the topos of inability to praise, but this topos is given a new turn. The genre of the euology, Klopstock felt, and not without reason, had been degraded to the point that no self-respecting poet could continue to use it. "Ehrenverschwender," who lavishly extol any person in a position of power, had made the mode suspect:

> Durch das Lob lüstender Schwelger, oder eingewebter
> Fliegen, Eroberer, Tyrannen ohne Schwert,
> . . . .
> Halbmenschen, die sich, in vollem dummen Ernst, für höher
> Wesen halten als uns. . . .
>
> ["Fürstenlob," M-P 2, 6]

The very violence of the language indicates the tortured nature of Klopstock's dilemma, which Thayer calls "the dilemma of praise" ("K.'s Occasional Poetry," p. 202). For Klopstock too was in a sense a court poet, being the recipient of royal patronage, no matter how much freedom his King might grant him and no matter how sincere the assurances of Bernstorff that he need not sing of the King if he did not care to. If he cannot avoid composing a *Lobgedicht,* and there were occasions when it would have seemed ungracious indeed not to have done so, he attempts to elevate it to an artistic level that will enable it to stand on its own merits, transcending the occasion that gave rise to it. And in this he is, on the whole, successful, though an "uneasy, apologetic self-concern" (Thayer) may at times be evident.

Of Klopstock's odes to high personages "Die Königin Luise" (1752), originally called "An den König," has perhaps the most immediate appeal. It is at once a funeral elegy on the

235

death of Denmark's beloved Queen (a daughter of George II of England) and a *Trostgedicht* for her royal husband, Frederick V, whence the original title. In at least one important respect "Die Königin Luise" is atypical of Klopstock: it is too simple. Seldom does he condescend to the reader as he does here. The meter is iambic, a measure he reserves almost exclusively for simple, direct expression and which he as a rule despises. The disposition of the ode is symbolic of its message:

> Stanzas 1–5: grief of the bereaved.
> Stanzas 6–14: death of the Queen and its meaning.
> Stanzas 15–21: the Queen in heaven, her thoughts turned toward earth.
> Stanzas 22–28: the transfigured Queen addresses her husband, still on earth.

Fourteen stanzas are devoted to grief and death, fourteen to comfort and eternal life. The basic configuration is the connection between the earthly and supernal spheres.

The ode moves from a grief so powerful it turns the bereaved to stone; it is as though the living were the dead:

> So steht mit starrem Blick, der Marmor auf dem Grabe,
> So schautest du ihr, Friedrich, nach!
>
> [M-P 1, 98, verses 9 f.]

It then proceeds through the lesson of the Queen's noble death, which closes with her translation to heaven. Here the ode itself also transcends, rising from this sphere to the beyond:

> Fleug, mein Gesang, den Flug unsterblicher Gesänge,
> Und singe nicht vom Staube mehr!
>
> [stanza 16]

But no sooner is the Queen in heaven than her thoughts turn back to earth—Klopstock spends no time depicting the joys of the blest contemplating the glory of the divine; for all his transcendence, his interest is fundamentally in this life, not the beyond, and that is true in other works than this ode.

The final section, which joins the two spheres, is concerned with the departed Queen's message to her husband. The deceased Queen, who has attained true life, shows her living husband, who in the beginning of the ode was seen as dead, how he too may become truly living. Nothing is said that pertains to conventional piety, nor is faith in the Redeemer mentioned, though the tone is Christian. The emphasis is on the fulfillment of life through being truly human: "Menschlichkeit," which Klopstock saw as Frederick's supreme virtue, can eternalize time, and the knowledge that it is practiced on earth can even increase the joy of those in heaven:

> Die Menschlichkeit, diess grösste Lob der Erde!
> ....
> Ich schwebe jeden Tag, den du, durch sie, verewigst,
> Dein ganzes Leben um dich her!
> Auch diess ist Lohn des früherrungnen Zieles,
> Zu sehen, was du thust.
>
> [stanzas 25 f.]

The two realms, the earthly and the heavenly, are dependent on and reflect each other.

The most affecting lines of the ode, and they are among the most affecting in all of Klopstock's poetry, are those describing the manner of the Queen's dying. They appear shortly after the ode has taken its first turn, announced in the determination to learn from the Queen's death, since her life can no longer teach us (stanza 6). In order that her death may teach us, the poet introduces a scene which posterity is to celebrate as the summation of a Christian death. It shall be "ein Fest der Weinenden," "ein Fest um Mitternacht! Voll heiliger tiefeingehüllter Schauer" (stanza 7). In other words, the poet institutes a kind of "gospel" which those who are gathered together in the Queen's name may remember and die by:

> Nicht diese Stunde nur, sie starb viel lange Tage!
> Und jeder war des Todes werth,
> Des lehrenden des ehrenvollen Todes,
> Den sie gestorben ist.

237

Die ernste Stunde kam, in Nebel eingehüllet,
Den sie bey Gräbern bildete.
Die Königin, nur sie, vernimt den Fusstritt
Der kommenden, nur sie

Hört, durch die Nacht herauf, der dunkeln Flügel
  Rauschen,
Den Todeston! da lächelt sie.
Sey ewig, mein Gesang, weil du es singest,
Dass sie gelächelt hat!

[stanzas 8–10]

That this "feast of the weeping" is not the last word is shown by the Queen's address to her husband, which concludes the ode. There is something that surpasses such luxuriation in feeling and that, we have seen, is "Menschlichkeit," human nobility expressed in action. As poetry, however, no part of the ode is as memorable as the stanzas just quoted.

It is worth asking why this should be so. The reason, it seems to me, is that here the poet has transformed with unusual success the *matter* of his ode into *substance*. He does this essentially through the creation of a semiallegorical scene with a distinct mythical aura with which we are able to identify imaginatively. Though it is said that only the Queen hears the approaching footstep of the "ernste Stunde," we hear it too. This method of achieving reader identification is common enough in Klopstock's work, but it is not always as persuasive as here. The reason is that he is usually reluctant to linger on the kind of physical detail that allows imaginative identification, but immediately transcends the physical for the spiritual, according to the principle of "thinking again" the thoughts of Nature enunciated in the first strophe of "Der Zürchersee." His most moving passages, however, are those in which we can grasp the spiritual *in* the physical. This is no doubt because we, as modern readers, expect the symbolical mode to obtain and are liable to be disappointed if it doesn't. But Klopstock, as we have already noted, is a presymbolical poet.

As we have already mentioned, for the ear, at least for

the ear of a modern European, there is often strikingly little difference between Klopstock's odes in classical or pseudo-classical (i.e., self-invented) meters and his odes in free verse (referred to in the critical literature as "freie Rhythmen"), despite the fact that the former are predetermined to the last syllable and the latter have no predetermined form whatever, but vary from verse to verse according to the demands of the content, i.e., strive for complete "Mitausdruck" of the content (the term is Klopstock's). Both forms are actually strictly controlled and the term "free" is misleading, but they are controlled by different principles. The fact that Klopstock places the metrical scheme before his odes shows that he does not trust the reader to find the correct scheme himself: ". . . kein Gemüt bewegt sich unwillkürlich nach alkäischen und asklepiadischen Systemen," Staiger remarks (*Wege zum Gedicht*, p. 108). If we only hear someone read

> Sie schläft. O giess ihr, Schlummer, geflügeltes
> Balsamisch Leben über ihr sanftes Herz!
> Aus Edens ungetrübter Quelle
> Schöpfe den lichten, krystallnen Tropfen!
>
> [M-P 1, 112]

it is highly unlikely that we will arrive at the metrical scheme of an Alcaic strophe:

$$\cup\_\cup\_\cup\,,\ \_\cup\cup\_\cup\cup\,,\ (2\times)$$
$$\cup\_\cup\_\cup\_\cup\_\cup$$
$$\_\cup\cup\_\cup\cup\_\cup\_\cup\,.$$

Indeed, it is doubtful that we will even be able to say with certainty how many verses the strophe contains. Heusler is quite right in exclaiming "dass die Gehörwirkung dieser gebundesten [the classical odes] und jener freiesten Gattung [the odes in free verse] gar nicht so weit auseinanderliegt!" (*Deutsche Versgeschichte*, pp. 289 f.). He may also be right in maintaining that Klopstock arrived at his free rhythms by "smashing" the strict odic form, with the result that "freier Rhythmus = zerschlagene Odenform" (p. 293). The best proof that the metrical scheme cannot be deduced from the text alone, even when one has the text before one's eyes, is given by "Der Tod" (1764), an ode in four strophes, each of which follows a different, though absolutely strict, scheme. In this case the poet did not furnish the metrical pattern, and the ode was generally reckoned to be in free rhythms.[33]

Though free verse has an indeterminate number of stressed and unstressed syllables, it always imposes upon the reader some kind of rhythmical reading, which may, however, vary from reader to reader and even from time to time with the same reader. For the first five syllables of the following line from the first version of "Die Frühlingsfeyer" Heusler (p. 283) deduces no less than six possible readings: "Und nun schweigen sie. Majestätischer." Ambiguity of this kind involves the reader in the process of composing the poem—he must, as it were, become co-poet. Odes in free rhythms replaced strict forms in Klopstock's work only between 1758 and 1760. During this period the original versions of the poems in free form were grouped in stanzas of varying length, but were then grouped in the collected edition of the odes (1771) in four-line strophes. The twenty-nine odes in free verse composed between 1764 and 1801, when Klopstock had again turned predominantly to strict meters (classical or invented), were written from the beginning in four-line stanzas.

The most famous of the odes in free verse—often called hymns—is "Die Frühlingsfeyer"(1759), originally entitled "Eine Ode über die ernsthaften Vergnügungen des Landlebens." Gerhard Kaiser has convincingly interpreted this ode as a theodicy, treating, like every theodicy, the problem of evil in a universe created by a God who is by definition absolutely good (*Wirkendes Wort* 8, 329 ff.). My remarks on the poem follow Kaiser's in general outline.

The title does not at first seem especially revealing. The storm, to which the last fifteen strophes are devoted, could occur in the summer as well as the spring, and there is no other direct indication of the season than the address to the "Frühlingswürmchen" (probably a rose beetle). The emphasis, however, is as much on "Feier" as "Frühling"—"the rites of spring" would be a fitting translation—and these rites, it develops, are consonant only with this season. We shall return to this point.

The ode can be blocked as follows:

Stanzas 1–5: the omnipotence of the Creator and the magnitude of His creation; man's place in the cosmos.

Stanzas 6–9: relation of the nonhuman creature to God.

Stanzas 10–12: transitional: renewed determination to praise the divine, whatever mysteries remain unresolved.

Stanzas 13–27: the storm.

The first five strophes define man's place in creation against the background of the inconceivable tremendousness of the cosmos. But praise of the whole, of the cosmos, the poet leaves to the angels, the "jubilant choirs of the sons of light," whose proper task it is. *His* role is to celebrate the divine as revealed on earth, the "Tropfen am Eimer" (the image derives from Isaiah 40:15). From the very beginning the poet (i.e., the lyrical persona) is determined to be moved to enthusiastic praise:

> Nur um den Tropfen am Eimer,
> Um die Erde nur, will ich schweben, und anbeten!
>
> [M-P 1, 133, stanza 2]

The tension, then, one would expect to derive from the testing of this determination: will anything be able to sway him from this purpose? Our expectations are indeed fulfilled, though perhaps not quite in the way we anticipated.

Vividly aware of the view of the universe as revealed by physics, Klopstock interprets this view in terms of the Biblical account of the creation, painting a Michelangelesque fresco of the coming into being of the cosmos:

> Da der Hand des Allmächtigen
> Die grösseren Erden entquollen!
> Die Ströme des Lichts rauschten, und Siebengestirne
>   wurden,
> Da entranntest du, Tropfen, der Hand des
>   Allmächtigen!
>
> [M-P 1, 134]

Our planet, the "drop on the bucket," is quantitatively as nothing compared to the greater planets, to say nothing of the cosmos as a whole. Whereas the "greater earths gushed forth" from the hand of the Almighty, our earth merely "escaped" (entrannte) from God's hand, as though by accident. Nonetheless it too is a part of the divine creation. So too are the uncounted myriads of inhabitants of this tiny speck: "Und wer bin ich?" (stanza 5). The question is asked in the name of all who inhabit or have inhabited the earth. The answer is the answer of unshakeable faith: "mehr wie die Erden, die quollen! Mehr, wie die Siebengestirne, die aus Strahlen zusammenströmten!" (stanza 5), because man is endowed with an immortal soul. Here the answer is only implied in the address to the "Frühlingswürmchen" in the next stanza, which is "vielleicht Ach nicht unsterblich!" In "Dem Allgegenwärtigen," where the same contrast between individual and cosmos occurs, the poet puts it thus:

> Hier steh ich Erde! was ist mein Leib,
> Gegen diese selbst den Engeln unzählbare Welten,
> Was sind diese selbst den Engeln unzählbare Welten,
> Gegen meine Seele!
>
> [M-P 1, 126]

The cosmos is God's creation, the personal revelation of the divine, who is seen as a paternal deity whom man, himself the vessel of a divine part, can address as "Thou." The counterweight of the cosmos is the soul, which God cannot let perish. Thus praise is possible and if possible necessary. By praising we demonstrate our faith in a meaningful creation. Klopstock, who underplays the role of original sin and who believes in universal salvation (cf. "Die Glückseligkeit Aller," M-P 1, 140), thus sees man as being in an essentially unassailable position. It would, however, give a distorted picture of Klopstock's religiosity if we disregarded his sometimes despairing utterances, such as the subsequently suppressed ending of "Dem Allgegenwärtigen" (1758), which treats the theme of the willingness of the spirit and the weakness of the flesh, and which finds its sole comfort in Christ's teaching and sacrifice. Even this comfort can at moments fail. In the first version the "I" finally sinks, like Peter when he attempts to walk upon the waters:

> Der für mich mit dem Tode rang!
> Den Gott für mich verliess!
> Der nicht erlag,
> Als ihn der Ewige verliess,
> Der ist in mir!
>
> Gedanke meines tiefsten Erstaunens,
> Ich bebe vor dir!
> Da die Winde gewaltiger wehten,
> Die höhere Wog' auf ihn strömte,
> Sank Kephas!
> Ich sinke!
> Hilf mir, mein HErr! und mein Gott!
> [M-P 1, 128, note]

We find the same imagery in "Die Welten" (1764), where the lyric persona founders in the "Ozean der Welten" like a ship in a storm, despite all the precautions taken by the pilot. Meaningless desolation has the final word:

> Lautheulend zuckt der Sturm!
> Singt Todtengesang!
> Der Pilot kennet ihn. Immer steigender hebst, Woge,
>   du dich!
> Ach die letzte, letzte bist du! Das Schif geht unter!
> Und den Todtengesang heult dumpf fort
> Auf dem grossen, immer offenem Grabe der Sturm!
> [M-P 1, 154]

Klopstock's faith is more endangered than we might surmise from a reading of "Die Frühlingsfeyer" alone. Here the world remains whole and saved. In fact, in spite of all the wind, thunder, and lightning, it does not seem even seriously threatened.

Nonetheless, the problem of evil in a creation stemming from an absolutely good creator is raised in the poem. The

243

two principal motifs after the introductory strophes are the "Frühlingswürmchen" and the storm. In both the central problem of every theodicy is implied: did God permit destruction? Is the insect perhaps not immortal? Will the storm destroy or bless? There is never any very serious doubt, however, that the storm brings blessing, not destruction. The unsettling uncertainty and threat of stanzas 16, 21, and 24, in which, as Kaiser puts it, "ein Tremendum bricht hier in Klopstocks harmonische Welt ein" (p. 333), are each immediately followed by a stanza of reassurance. Whether the insect has an immortal soul the poet must leave unresolved, but in a moment of stillness during the rising storm he lets it raise its head, as though participating in the manifestation of divine majesty, and his heartfelt question longs for a positive answer:

> Alles ist still vor dir, du Naher!
> Rings umher ist Alles still!
> Auch das Würmchen mit Golde bedeckt, merkt auf!
> Ist es vielleicht nicht seelenlos? ist es unsterblich?
>
> [stanza 19]

What we might call the kinetics of the poem does not exactly correspond to the thematic dispostion. In Klopstock, the kinetics is all. His intent, especially in the religious odes, is to carry us along with irresistible movement until we are outside ourselves with enthusiasm: "Bei dem Gesange [i.e., hymnlike songs of praise] kommen wir ausser uns. Sterben wollen wir, und nicht leben!" Therefore it is one of the hymnodist's chief duties "dass er schnell von einem grossen Gedanken zum andern forteile. Er fliegt von Gebirge zu Gebirge, und lässt die Täler . . . unberührt liegen" ("Einleitung zu den geistlichen Liedern," Schleiden, 3d ed., p. 1012). Moved by the sublimity of the thought or by the fervor of the feeling, our soul imitates the poem and realizes its own sublimity, its own capacity for enthusiasm. Klopstock calls this "thinking," but, as we have stressed, true thinking is for him inseparable from feeling: "Denn wenn unsre Seele entweder durch die Hoheit der Gedanken, oder durch das Feuer der

244

Empfindungen stark bewegt ist; so ist es ihrer Natur gemäss, so zu *denken.* Gewisse nähere Erklärungen, gewisse Ausbildungen will sie alsdann nicht. Sie eilt fort. Sie hatte das alles schon hinzugedacht" (ibid.; emphasis added).

There are four arcs of action ("peaks") in "Die Frühlingsfeyer," each representing a crisis and its resolution. In each a threat to the meaning of existence is presented and overcome. This we call the kinetic, in contrast to the thematic, disposition, though there is of course overlap. The ode opens fortissimo. Stanzas 1–5 constitute the first arc. Here the crisis is presented in terms of the infinity of the universe and the finiteness of man and resolved by pointing to man's infinity in his finitude: his soul. Stanzas 6–12 constitute the second arc and ask the question: is a part of animate creation destined to total destruction? This movement opens piano and rises at the end to a mood of resolute exaltation. Whether the insect is "only formed dust" or, like man, "dust, and yet eternal" will be resolved for the "I" only after death, but since this too is a manifestation of the divine will, the attitude of the "I" can only be one of praise. Submission to God's will, inscrutable as it may be, is the Christian answer to all unanswerable problems raised by nature. Such an answer is not defeat but triumph, for it saves the meaning, whatever that meaning may turn out to be, of all that is. Reverence is the only attitude possible for one who believes in a universe created by a paternal deity, and in strophes 1–5 we have just witnessed such a creation. Therefore:

> Mit tiefer Ehrfurcht schau ich die Schöpfung an,
> Denn du!
> Namenloser du!
> Schufest sie!

> [stanza 12]

The third kinetic arc or peak is constituted by stanzas 13–19, in which the storm rises, first as a gentle cooling breeze, then as sultry stillness, and finally as rolling clouds accompanied by high winds. The Eternal comes "visibly," as He came to Moses in the cloud on Sinai, and nature and man

245

"answer," bowing before Him ("And Moses made haste to bow his head toward the earth and worshipped." Exodus 34:8):[34]

> Nun schweben sie, rauschen sie, wirbeln die Winde!
> Wie beugt sich der Wald! wie hebt sich der Strom!
> . . . .
> Der Wald neigt sich, der Strom flieht, und ich
> Falle nicht auf mein Angesicht?
> Herr! Herr! Gott! barmherzig and gnädig!
> Du Naher! erbarme dich meiner!
>
> [stanzas 15 f.]

But immediately following this moment of highest intensity, the only passage indicating actual fear in the ode, there comes the reassurance: "Diese Nacht ist Segen der Erde. Vater, du zürnest nicht!" (stanza 17). The threatening *tremendum* is but a blessing in disguise. The certainty of God's mercy and goodness is not to be shaken. The movement ends as it began: piano, and in the breathless pause before the renewal of the storm, "das Würmchen . . . merkt auf," seeming to give a sign of its awareness of the divine. Such extreme use of the pathetic fallacy is not uncommon in Klopstock and is no doubt one of the traits most likely to alienate the modern reader, yet it is only an expression of his sense of "tat twam asi"—all life is one, for all comes from God.

Stanzas 20–27 constitute the final arc. All fear has now been overcome, there are no more cries of "erbarme dich meiner!" and the magnificent spectacle of darkness shot through with thunder and lightning can be experienced with joyful exultation. The poet achieves compelling rhythmic-aural effects. In strophe 21, for example, he begins with three tense dactylic verses–tense largely because of the initial stress (in verse 2 the opening dactyl is followed by two trochees)— and closes with an anapestic tripody in which the tension is released:

> Seht ihr den Zeugen des Nahen, den zuckenden Strahl?
> Hört ihr Jehova's Donner?

Hört ihr ihn, hört ihr ihn,
Den erschütterden Donner des Herrn?

The voweling is also expressive: the lightning flashes through a whole series of vowels (e–eu–a–u–a), while the thunder approaches with monotonous giant tread in the ö's and o's, changing key and rhythm in the final tension-releasing line in a long rolling reverberation.

The spectacular nature of the storm, the theatrical quality that keeps it from presenting a serious threat, is stressed, not blinked at, in the final arc of the poem. "We," in identification with the odic persona (who addresses us directly), are certain of salvation, and the rage of the storm only presses from us exclamations of awe and praise, not fear, of the divine author: "Angebetet, gepriesen   Sei dein herrlicher Name!" (stanza 22). The lightning strikes and the stricken forest smokes,

Aber nicht unsre Hütte!
Unser Vater gebot
Seinem Verderber,
Vor unsrer Hütte vorüberzugehen!
[stanza 25]

Like those of the Israelites in Egypt, our lintels and doorposts have been smeared with the blood of the Passover lamb, and the destroyer will not enter our dwelling.

It would be easy to cavil at Klopstock here. Is a spring storm a test of faith? Those who are conscious of Auschwitz, Hiroshima, and the fire-bombing of Dresden are ready to smile condescendingly. Does not Klopstock preserve his "heile Welt" too easily? But Klopstock was quite aware of comparable, if not man-made, cataclysms: the Lisbon earthquake, which shook the faith of theodicists almost as severely as the capital of Portugal, took place only four years before the composition of the "Die Frühlingsfeyer."

Though it is an important factor, the poet has more in mind than the *threat* of the storm, or the storm as a test of faith. The end of the ode, G. Kaiser shows, harks back to the opening (p. 335). The imagery tells the story: "Ströme des Lichts rauschten, und Siebengestirne wurden" (stanza 3); "Ein Strom des Lichts rauscht', und unsre Sonne wurde" (stanza 4); "Ein Wogensturz [des Lichts] . . . stürzte vom Felsen der Wolk' herab und gürtete den Orion" (stanza 4). These images anticipate the rushing uproar of the storm: "Und die Gewitterwinde? . . . Wie sie rauschen! wie sie mit lauter Woge den Wald durchströmen!" (stanza 23); "schon rauscht, schon rauscht Himmel, und Erde vom gnädigen Regen!" (stanza 26). The creation, like the spring storm, is seen as an atmospheric discharge of divine power—what happens at the close of the poem reflects the beginning, is a confirmation of the wonder of creation in a form man can experience. If the creation called the world into being, the storm restores it, purifies and fructifies it:

> Ach, schon rauscht, schon rauscht
> Himmel, und Erde vom gnädigen Regen!
> Nun ist, wie dürstete sie! die Erde erquickt,
> Und der Himmel der Segensfüll' entlastet!
> [stanza 28]

God appears in His mercy, not His anger. (The tension-release movement that informs the latter part of the ode derives principally from the contrast between the threatening aspect of the storm and the realization of the blessing it brings.) And now, in the final strophe, the rainbow of promise and peace between Man and Creator appears in the heavens just as it did after the Flood, of which this spring storm is, we now realize, a figure. Creation is renewed: the first creation was the birth, this the rebirth after the Flood, hence the rainbow. Kaiser formulates it well: "The Flood, as a renewal of creation, is a judgment, and the storm in the 'Frühlingsfeier' points both to the beginning of time and to its end, to the purification and re-instatement of the world in the Last Judgment and Resurrection" (p. 335). Against the background of such an understanding of the meaning of the storm—which must be a *spring* storm because of its significance as renewal—we can better comprehend the emotion with which the lyric persona experiences it. As a figure of the final epiphany of the divine on the Judgment Day fulfilling the promise of salvation, it has for the believer a force that must both arouse profound fear and give profound comfort. "Aber nicht unsre Hütte!" We are among the saved. In the final strophe the divine assures us that our interpretation is right: the promise of Genesis 9:11 ff. is renewed: "When I bring clouds over the earth and the bow is seen in the clouds, I will remember my covenant, . . ." Now, with a reminiscence of the "still, small voice" in 1 Kings 19:12,

> . . . komt Jehova nicht mehr im Wetter,
> In stillem, sanften Säuseln
> Komt Jehova,
> Und unter ihm neigt sich der Bogen des Friedens!

With the reference to the final judgment, Kaiser reminds us (p. 335), the motif of the "Frühlingswürmchen" also finds its place: will *all* creation be saved? This is the poet's hope, for he would like to praise the Creator "not only *in* nature but *with* nature."

Beginning with the year 1764 and continuing through 1767 Klopstock invented his own measures in confusing abundance. During this period he invented sixty different strophes plus three stichic measures, at least thirty-four of the former in a few weeks (February–March 1764) for the twentieth canto of the *Messias*. But after devoting almost three years to the invention of new forms, he drops them and returns to free verse, then in 1777 to classical measures.[35] Klopstock's self-invented measures afford us much insight into his poetics, though, unlike his free rhythms, they remained practically without influence on the future course of German poetry and, in fact, to a large extent even on his own later work.

The complicated problem of Klopstock's metrical theory we cannot treat here in detail. Even those who, like Schleiden and Hellmuth, have studied it in depth find it hard to arrive at final answers. Klopstock's basic view of poetical invention, that is, technical invention, is expressed in the following epigram:

Aufgelöster Zweifel

"Nachahmen soll ich nicht, und dennoch nennet
Dein lautes Lob mir immer Griechenland?"
Wenn Genius in deiner Seele brennet,
So ahm dem Griechen nach. Dar Griech' erfand.

[Schleiden, 3d ed., p. 180]

This is Klopstock's way of "freeing himself from the father," and he never departs from it, though of course it does not always manifest itself in the invention of pseudo-classical meters.

The factor of greatest consequence in the spawning of Klopstock's innovative measures is his discovery of word feet, i.e., cola or metrical phrases that demand to be taken together. These he contrasts with technical or artificial feet, as we earlier pointed out (pp. 204 f.). When he wrote his great free verse hymns of 1754–60, Klopstock still had no inkling of word feet, though it is obvious that these works are unconsciously composed according to that principle. For the self-invented strict measures, Hellmuth stresses, the opposite holds true: the concept of word feet obviously springs from the odes in free verse (p. 79). In other words, Klopstock realized what he had been doing. By the time of the first collected edition of the odes (1771), he had made a principle of constructing new strophic forms according to word feet—this is their most striking rhythmical characteristic. The cola are indicated in the metrical schemata by commas. Klopstock wants to make the rhythmical reality apparent—metrics and content correspond. These rhythmical figures are the building blocks of the new strophic forms and their employment, as Hellmuth shows in detail, is worked out according to a carefully considered scheme. A striking, though admittedly extreme, example is found in "Der Vorhof und der Tempel" (1765), analyzed by Hellmuth (pp. 170 ff.). This poem is one of the "cosmic" odes, of which "Die Gestirne," "Dem Unendlichem," and "Der Tod" (all 1764) are further examples. I quote the whole poem with Hellmuth's metrical analysis following.

250

DER VORHOF UND DER TEMPEL

1. Wer ermüdet hinauf zu der Heerschar der Gestirne,
   In die Höhen zu schaun, wo der Lichtfuss sich
   herabsenkt,
   Wo den Blitzglanz Fomahant und Antar, wo des Leun
   Herz
   Sich ergeusst, ins Gefild hin, wo die Ähr' und Winzerin
   strahlt!

2. Mit Graun füllt, und Ehrfurcht der Anblick, mit
   Entzückung
   Das Herz dess, der sich da freut, wo Freud ist, nicht
   allein ihn
   Ihr Phantom täuscht! Ich steh hier in dem Vorhof der
   Gottheit.
   Beflügelt von dem Tod' eilt mein Geist einst in den
   Tempel!

3. Mitternacht, höre du meinen Gesang, Morgenstern,
   Finde du preisend oft, dankend mich, Thränen im
   Blick,
   Bote des Tags! Wirst du darauf Abendstern, find' auch
   dann
   Über Gott, den erstaunt, welcher sein Heil nie begreift!
   [M-P 1, 175]

1. ∪∪—∪∪—, ∪∪— —, ∪∪— —, a+abb
   ∪∪—∪∪—, ∪∪— —, ∪∪— —, a+abb
   ∪∪— —, ∪∪—, ∪∪—, ∪∪— —, baab
   ∪∪—, ∪∪— —, ∪∪—, ∪∪—∪∪—. abaa+a
2. ∪— —, ∪— —, ∪— —, ∪∪— —, cccb
   ∪— —, ∪∪— —, ∪— —, ∪∪— —, cbcb
   ∪∪— —, ∪— —, ∪∪— —, ∪— —, bcbc
   ∪— —, ∪∪— —, ∪— —, ∪∪— —. cbcb
3. —∪—, —∪—, —∪∪—, —∪—, dded
   —∪—, —∪—, —∪—, —∪∪—, ddde
   —∪∪—, —∪∪—, —∪—, —∪—, eedd
   —∪—, —∪—, —∪∪—, —∪—. dded

The metrical structure, Hellmuth points out, displays almost mathematical precision. It is governed by the tension between freedom, shown in the constant change of meter, and the strict disposition of the feet in each strophe, as well as by the relation of these feet to the neighboring strophes. Each strophe is composed of two feet belonging to the same category: strophes 1 and 2 have "rising" meter (˘˘——, ˘——), strophe 3 "falling-rising" (—˘—, —˘˘—). The admissible word feet are either three- or four-syllable; each verse, except 1 and 4, has four feet. There is a certain agreement in the arrangement and numerical relationship of the feet in each group of four lines: two verses always have the same scheme (1,1 = 1,2; 2,2 = 2,4; 3,1 = 3,4). A further verse has the same feet but in a different order (1,3; 2,3; 3,2); still one other is distinguished from the other three by the relationship between three- and four-syllable feet (1,4; 2,1; 3,3). Of the six possible combinations of three- and four-syllable feet, Hellmuth shows, only one is not realized (pp. 172 f.).

This strictly calculated metrical scheme is meant to serve as "Mitausdruck" for a sense of strong exultation. In other words, its *function* is the same as Klopstock's free rhythms which follow no rule at all! In the latter, the meter changes from verse to verse, reflecting the content, and has "nichts Gedachtes," as Klopstock once expresses it (cf. Hellmuth, p. 174). An ode like "Der Vorhof und der Tempel," on the other hand, is *gedacht* to the last detail, yet both free verse and strictly calculated meter serve the same end: congruity between metrics and message. The same holds true for all of Klopstock's new strophic forms. This is no doubt the reason why a number of them were employed only once.

Klopstock's odic "Bardendichtung" belongs to the years 1764–67. It was long the fashion to speak of Klopstock's poetic use of Germanic mythology with condescension or to reject it as a well-meant failure.[36] But this attitude will not open the way to understanding. It goes without saying that Klopstock's notions of Germanic religion and ethnology, to say nothing of ethics and morality, will not stand the test of scholarly criticism, but neither will those of his sources. More important is the fact that the notion of a Germanic world and a Germanic world view afforded Klopstock a new overriding totality and inspired him to attempt to realize it in poetry. It fell in with his patriotism, which contains a large dose of resentment at boot-licking worship of the French, exemplified by Frederick the Great. Betteridge, it seems to me, is right in regarding Klopstock's patriotic poetry as fundamentally "hypostatizing a fantasy in order to give expression to his own needs" ("Mature Klopstock," p. 136). The sense of rejection by the fatherland, at least by his own king, who represented its greatest glory, caused him to seek a fatherland with which he could identify, a kindred community, even if one of his own making. This basic configuration is already apparent in the ode "Auf meine Freunde."

In 1756 a French translation by Mallet of the Younger Edda appeared. Stimulated by this—he also later became acquainted with the Elder Edda—Klopstock began to study old Germanic sources in scholarly and semischolarly works, e.g., Olaf Worms' *Monumenta Danica*. In 1760 Macpherson's *Fragments of Ancient Poetry collected in the Highlands of Scotland and translated from the Gaelic or Erse language* were published anonymously, and in 1762–63 the epics *Fingal* and *Temora* appeared. In Germany, where translations soon came out, these "Ossianic" poems, which were almost purely of Macpherson's own invention, were widely accepted as authentic. Celts were conflated with ancient Germanic peoples and, as we have noted, Orpheus himself was for Klopstock Germanic because a Celt, i.e., a Thracian. The success of "Ossian" was tremendous. It corresponded to the eighteenth-century notion of what the poetry of a primitive people *ought* to be like. "Poor moaning monotonous Macpherson," as Carlyle called him, was solemnly compared to Vergil and Homer. This work served as a powerful stimulus to Klopstock's "Bardendichtung." He also read Ulfilas and Otfried, discovered the Low Saxon *Heliand*, and went so far as to try his hand at writing hexameters in Gothic and Anglo-Saxon himself. He took his ancient Germans seriously, which meant, in his case, poetically and linguistically.

Klopstock's longing to penetrate to the heart of ancient German poetry in order to discover his own racial poetic origins was intense. But even he had to admit that his longing dimmed his view of the past:

> Ah es trübt, sinn' ich nach, was die Trümmer deckt,
> Mir den beweinenden Blick wünschender Schmerz!
>   [M-P 1, 195, verses 15 f.]

"Es hüllt Nacht die Telyn des Barden ein," but this does not keep Klopstock from trying to penetrate the darkness, from conjuring up a whole poetic landscape and community of ancient Germanic poets conceived according to his own ideals. These may at times be nearer the melancholy nebulosities of Macpherson than what we know from the Eddas, but as poetry they are of incomparably higher rank than "Ossian."

One of the most successful of Klopstock's bardic odes is "Thuiskon" (1764). Thuiskon is the mythical father of the Germans, the god Thuis (cf. "Tuesday"). The poem concerns his epiphany in the sacred grove of the bards, who are here, however, not ancient singers but the poets of modern Germany who sing in the spirit of their great ancestors. Klopstock is of course thinking primarily of himself and his own poetry. In "Stintenburg" (1767) he tells how Braga, the god of ancient Nordic song, instructs him in his art:

> Seines Gesanges erschallet noch;
> Mich lehret er älteren deutschen Ton,
> Wenn entwölkt wallet der Mond, und es sanft
> Um das Grab derer ertönt, welchen er sang.
>   [M-P 1, 198, verses 33–36]

The rhythmic character of "Thuiskon" is largely determined by paeonic word feet (paeon = one stressed syllable and three dips, called first, second, third, or fourth paeon according to position of stressed syllable). The correspondence between metrical and word feet is not quite perfect: there are eight minor exceptions. Hellmuth deduces the following scheme (p. 176):

⏑⏑‿⏑ | ⏑⏑‿⏑ | ⏑⏑‿⏑ | ⏑‿⏑‿,   aaab
⏑‿⏑⏑ | ⏑‿ ‿⏑ | ⏑‿⏑⏑ | ‿⏑‿,   cccd
‿⏑ | ⏑⏑‿⏑ | ⏑‿⏑‿,   eab
⏑⏑‿⏑ | ⏑⏑‿⏑ | ‿⏑⏑‿.   aaf

Klopstock first favored paeonic measures for his bardic poetry, associating them with a dithyrambic effect because their numerous dips contribute to the swiftness of the line.

THUISKON

1. Wenn die Strahlen vor der Dämrung nun entfliehn, und der Abendstern
   Die sanfteren, entwölkten, die erfrischenden Schimmer nun
   Nieder zu dem Haine der Barden senkt,
   Und melodisch in dem Hain die Quell' ihm ertönt;

2. So entsenket die Erscheinung des Thuiskon, wie Silber stäubt
   Von fallendem Gewässer, sich dem Himmel, und komt zu euch,
   Dichter, und zur Quelle. Die Eiche weht
   Ihm Gelispel. So erklang der Schwan Venusin,

3. Da verwandelt er dahin flog. Und Thuiskon vernimts, und schwebt
   In wehendem Geräusche des begrüssenden Hains, und horcht;
   Aber nun empfangen, mit lauterm Gruss,
   Mit der Sait' ihn und Gesang, die Enkel um ihn.

4. Melodieen, wie der Telyn in Walhalla, ertönen ihm
   Des wechselnden, des kühneren, des deutscheren Odenflugs,
   Welcher, wie der Adler zur Wolk' itzt steigt,
   Dann herunter zu der Eiche Wipfel sich senkt.
                                        [M-P 1, 171 f.]

An epiphany. Before the god himself appears, however, something else appears that prepares the way for his apparition and at the same time furnishes the term of comparison *for* his apparition, namely, the evening star, or rather, its gleam. The evening star sends as it were a messenger down to earth, and this messenger is greeted by the spring in the sacred grove (it is the spring Mimer, the Nordic Hippocrene): "Und melodisch in dem Hain die Quell' ihm ertönt." A voice of nature greets a natural phenomenon.

"*So* entsenket die Erscheinung des Thuiskon . . . sich dem Himmel . . . " The descent of the god is like the gleam sent down by the evening star, like the silvery spray of falling water. And again a greeting: "Die Eiche weht Ihm Gelispel." The sacred tree of the primitive Germans recognizes the Nordic god, the phenomenal greets the noumenal. This is the first intensification of the greeting motif.

The comparison of the murmuring of the oak with the song of the "Schwan Venusin, Da verwandelt er dahin flog" is a reference to Horace (*Odes* 2, 20), who prophesied that upon his death he would take his way singing through skies as a swan ("Venusin" because Horace came from Venusia). The classical and the Germanic worlds are for an instant fused into one. Even in his patriotic bardic poetry, with its emphasis on all that is Germanic, Klopstock is unwilling to renounce the classical heritage which is the true source of his art. Perhaps we can regard the comparison as a (subconscious?) confession of this fact, a confession that his bardic odes derive their strength not so much from the Eddas and Ossian as from the ancient classics. Are they not also, like the "Schwan Venusin," a transformation? Be this as it may, the god hearkens to the greeting:

> Und Thuiskon vernimt's und schwebt
> In wehendem Geräusche des begrüssenden Hains, und horcht;

The epiphany has taken place, the god has appeared to his worshipers. He "hovers" not so much in the air as in the atmosphere of greeting and recognition he receives.

But up to now it is only nature, even if slightly anthropomorphized nature, that has received the manifestation of the supernatural: first the spring resounded to the appearance of the light of the evening star, then the grove to that of the god. The final intensification of the motif must now enter and a *human* voice respond to the epiphany. And it does: The "grandsons" of Thuiskon, the "bards" of eighteenth-century Germany, welcome their holy ancestor with shouts of joy and song.

This song is the poem itself, the poem we are reading and whose development we are experiencing. It is the transformation into linguistic form of the murmuring of the spring and the wind in the grove. It is the "Melodieen . . . Des wechselnden, des kühneren, des deutscheren Odenflugs" that tell of this epiphany and greet the god. For the final strophe is nothing else than a description of the poem in which it occurs, a poem composed in newly invented meter, "kühn" and "wechselnd" and "deutsch." And this song rises and falls

> wie der Adler zur wolk' itzt steigt,
> Dann herunter zu der Eiche Wipfel sich senkt

like the second and third paeons in which it is principally composed: $\cup - \cup \cup$; $\cup \cup - \cup$.

Through this human song heaven and earth are united; the epiphany is continually repeated in the movement of the verse that celebrates it "Und Thuiskon vernimt's und *schwebt. . . .* " The hovering of the god is the hovering of the rhythm of the ode. The god who descends to earth is received as in Walhalla—the earth has become as heaven and this unity is reflected in the form of the poem. The heaven-earth dichotomy is mirrored in the dichotomous structure of the strophe: aaab, cccd; eab, aaf. But the same structure is also employed to overcome the dichotomy and to unite heaven and earth: the four-beat lines answer the five-beat lines. The longer lines are devoted to the supernal, the shorter ones to the earthly, which with threefold intensification answers and welcomes the supernal.

Hellmuth, in his enlightening discussion of Klopstock's paeonic odes, draws interesting parallels among "Thuiskon," "Die Sommernacht," "Unsre Sprache," and "Braga," all of which contain epiphanies (*Metrische Erfindung*, pp. 175 ff.). Since these odes show in a striking and easily perceptible fashion the application of Klopstock's doctrine of metrical "Mitausdruck," it is worthwhile to summarize Hellmuth's findings.

The closest parallel is with "Die Sommernacht" (1766), which one might call a kind of "negative epiphany." The theme is the same as that of "Die frühen Gräber" of three years earlier (1764): the sadness of night's beauty when crossed by thoughts of departed friends.

DIE SOMMERNACHT

1. Wenn der Schimmer von dem Monde nun herab
    In die Wälder sich ergiesst, und Gerüche
    Mit den Düften von der Linde
    In den Kühlungen wehn;

2. So umschatten mich Gedanken an das Grab
    Der Geliebten, und ich seh in dem Walde
    Nur es dämmern, und es weht mir
    Von der Blüthe nicht her.

3. Ich genoss einst, o ihr Todten, es mit euch!
    Wie umwehten uns der Duft und die Kühlung,
    Wie verschönt warst von dem Monde,
    Du o schöne Natur!

                              [M-P 1, 179]

Only two feet are employed, the third paeon ($\cup\cup-\cup$) and the anapest ($\cup\cup-$). The ode is built strictly on word feet, with the paeon as the main rhythmical determinant. Like "Die frühen Gräber" and "Thuiskon," the present poem is set at nightfall (or moonrise), for Klopstock the hour of consecration and inspiration, as we know from "Stunden der Weihe": "Euch Stunden grüss' ich, welche der Abendstern Still in der Dämrung mir zur Erfindung bringt, . . ." (1748; M-P 1, 46). "Thuiskon" begins:

Wenn die Strahlen von der Dämrung nun entfliehn . . .

and the first line of "Die Sommernacht" is exactly parallel:

Wenn der Schimmer von dem Monde nun herab. . . .

This similarity also holds for the syntactical structure of the whole first period, which in both odes extends over two stanzas. The first stanza consists of a temporal clause, the second introduces the main clause with *so*. In "Thuiskon" stanza 1 sets the scene for the epiphany, which then begins to take place in stanza 2 ("So entsenket die Erscheinung des Thuiskon . . . sich dem Himmel"). In "Die Sommernacht," on the other hand, where the second stanza has the same formal structure, the epiphany is refused, and we are left with a sense of nonfulfillment and loss:

So umschatten mich Gedanken an das Grab
Der Geliebten, . . .

In "Thuiskon" nature greets the apparition of the god: "Die Eiche weht Ihm Gelispel"; in "Die Sommernacht" nature remains unanswering: "und es weht mir Von der Blüthe *nicht* her." Only in the last stanza is a kind of epiphany granted— in memory—but it is full of melancholy for what is past.

Hellmuth remarks that in both poems Klopstock uses paeonic measure to intensify the "mood of the numinous," and that he also favors this meter in other poems of the same period in which epiphanies occur (p.192). He uses it in "Unsre Sprache" (1767), where the divinity of the German tongue appears to the poet, and in "Braga" (1766), where the god of poetry materializes out of the moonlit night.

Klopstock did not, however, continue to compose bardic odes in paeonic measures but switched to free verse. Hellmuth surmises that the former no longer seemed to him "bardic" enough (pp. 195 f.). Free verse was more dithyrambic. Macpherson's Ossianic compositions were almost certainly a contributing factor, as well as Klopstock's tendency at this time to distance himself from classical forms. The final

stanzas of the original version of "Unsre Sprache" (1767)—
composed in paeonic meter—stress the equality, if not the
superiority, of the native tradition versus the classical:

> Die Vergessenheit umhüllt', o Ossian, auch dich!
> Dich huben sie hervor, und du stehest nun da!
> Gleichest dich dem Griechen! trotzest ihm!
>
> [M-P 1, 201]

The first poem in free verse dealing with a bardic theme
is "Der Hügel und der Hain" (1767), a dramatic argument in
which ancient Germanic poetry—*der Hain*, personified in a
"bard"—struggles with classical poetry—*der Hügel*,
personified in a "poet"—for the loyalties of modern German
song, personified in a "Dichter." On patriotic rather than
poetic grounds, the "Dichter" finally decides to follow the
native tradition:

> Des Hügels Quell ertönt von Zeus,
> Von Wodan der Quell des Hains.
> Weck' ich aus dem alten Untergange Götter
> Zu Gemälden des fabelhaften Liedes auf;
>
> So haben die in Teutoniens Hain
> Edlere Züge für mich!
>
> [M-P 1, 205, verses 105–10]

The Greek lyric, "mit allen ihren goldenen Saiten," leaning
against the laurel, cannot tempt the singer so much as "die
inhaltsvolle Telyn," leaning against the sacred oak:

> Es weht
> Um ihre Saiten, und sie tönt von sich selbst: Vaterland!

In the lyric, the period from about 1776 to his death is
Klopstock's most productive, but by no means his most
influential. With only occasional exceptions, Klopstock's "Alterslyrik" has met with negative response in the critical literature from Muncker to Kaiser. The poet, it is claimed, at-

tempts to treat lyrically themes that resist such treatment, especially questions of prosody and linguistics; the fires of passion are burned out; preciosity and incredibly complicated sentence structure become ever more characteristic; the poet has outlived his day and begins to repeat himself; he ossifies; he has lost touch with the true source of his art, etc., etc.[37] A recent serious attempt to rescue the lyric production of Klopstock's last decades is the 1967 essay by Eberhard Wilhelm Schulz, "Klopstocks Alterslyrik."[38] Schulz's essay is, of course, only a beginning. Beginnings are in fact all we really have on Klopstock's work, particularly on his lyric.

Schulz sensibly calls attention to the fact that among Klopstock's more than 200 odes there are, in all periods, good ones and less good ones (p. 296). The proportion remains fairly constant. Since more odes were produced in the last period, the poet now having been relieved of the burden of the *Messias*, there should be more both of successes and failures. The emphasis of the critics, however, has been mostly on the latter.

There are some resounding failures, though it is doubtful that there would be complete agreement on which ones they are. Kaiser picks "Der Unterschied" (1771), which falls somewhat before the period under discussion, but which is characteristic of Klopstock's efforts to treat problems of prosody and aesthetics in odic form (*Klopstock*, pp. 321 ff.). Kaiser finds here "die innere Form der Ode verfehlt," and "die Sprachmelodie fast prosaisch" (pp. 323–24). Beneath the seemingly revolutionary form he finds the poet harking back to stylistic conventions (such as allegory) he had earlier rejected. It is indeed difficult to read this ode with sympathy after one has read Kaiser's analysis. My own emphasis will be on a few of the odes that seem to me particularly successful.

Two new themes appear in the poetry of this period. By far the most extensively treated is that of the French Revolution, with which forty-three odes are directly concerned and a number of others indirectly. The other new theme is that of "das verlängerte Leben" or life lived in memory, a typical theme of old age, and one to which some of Klopstock's most beautiful odes are devoted. In addition, we find didactic odes dealing with language and poetry (or other arts) as well as poems on the theme of poetry (or poets) and princes. Except for about eight odes, three of which must count among the poet's best, thre is little of a directly religious nature. If we are inclined to agree with Kaiser's dictum that "das religiöse Erleben der Welt ist die allein lebendige Quelle von Klopstocks Lyrik" (p. 320), we will be tempted to discount the quality of the poetry of his old age. But before we have examined the evidence, we should suspend judgment.

The odes dealing with the French Revolution cannot concern us at length, though Klopstock responded to the Revolution as did no other German poet of his day. He was a republican by temperament and conviction, though he was also capable of praising the blessing of enlightened despotism in his homages to Frederick V of Denmark, as in "Das neue Jahrhundert" (1760), composed in celebration of the centennial of the establishment of an hereditary absolute monarchy in Denmark, which replaced the old oligarchy with its elective kingship. Not only the "Demokrat," Klopstock sings (M-P 1, 148), knows what freedom is; an absolute monarch whose rule is guided by concern for the welfare of his people may know it too. This rather strained view of the nature of freedom was superseded in the odes on the French Revolution and even in several written before its outbreak. Betteridge discusses Klopstock's ideal of freedom at some length, seeing it in relation to his patriotic ideal as embodied especially in the bardic poetry ("Mature Klopstock," pp. 138 ff.). It is Betteridge's contention that "Klopstock's ideal of freedom was at no time anything else but the desire for cultural independence." Of such independence Hermann, the conqueror of Varrus, is the great symbolic figure, but the ideal also surfaces in the odes to the German language, in the writings on poetics, and in such works as *Die deutsche Gelehrtenrepublik* and the plan for a German Academy.

Nothing was nearer to Klopstock's heart than the founding of a German literature that would rank with or surpass that of other modern European nations, or even that of the ancients. This is the root of his patriotism. But, according to Betteridge, Klopstock was to discover that "the notions of 'patriotism' and 'freedom' were intrinsically irreconcilable" (p.145). When it came to the test of the French Revolution, Klopstock, certainly no admirer of French culture, sided wholeheartedly with freedom at the cost of the patriotic ideal. However vague and unrealistic his ideal of freedom may have been, he saw it always as freedom for the people and the right of self-determination. No revolutionary ever urged the people to throw off the yoke of tyranny in more convinced tones than Klopstock. The Jacobin Terror, as Betteridge points out, was not the decisive factor in turning Klopstock against the Revolution, though he was shocked, like all Europe, at the new tyranny of blood (p. 149). Rather, it is the violation of the promise of the new French republic not to wage wars of aggression that forms the ever-recurring theme of his odes from the middle of 1793 on. Casting himself in the role of the jilted lover, he mourns in "Mein Irrtum" (1793) (and in many other odes) in tones like these:

> Freyheit, Mutter des Heils, nanten sie dich
> Nicht selbst da noch, als nun Eroberungskrieg,
> Mit dem Bruche des gegebenen
> Edlen Wortes begann?

> Ach des goldenen Traums Wonn' ist dahin,
> Mich umschwebet nicht mehr sein Morgenglanz,
> Und ein Kummer, wie verschmähter
> Liebe, kümmert mein Herz.
>
> [M-P 2, 83]

Of the revolutionary odes the best are "Kennet euch selbst" (1789), in which the Germans are urged to follow the example of the French and rebel against tyranny; "Der Fürst und sein Kebsweib" (1789), a dialog in which the prince, gripped by fear of "the terrible spirit of freedom," finds all his usual pleasures repugnant and his will to act lamed; "Sie und nicht Wir" (1790), in which the enthusiasm for the Revolution is overshadowed by the thought that it is not the Germans but the French who have accomplished "des Jahrhunderts edelste That"—even the fact that Germany is the land of the Reformation is cold comfort; "An La Rochefoucaulds Schatten" (1793), an elegy on the murder of freedom by the Terror; "Mein Irrtum" (1793), mentioned above; "Freude und Leid" (1798), in which the poet finds comfort in the nobility of the impulse from which the Revolution sprang, for though its source is now poisoned, the ideal still lives in some breasts, and these are the victors with whom he will rejoice; "Wissbegierde" (1799), which poses the question whether God also speaks "durch die That . . . , Welche die Sterblichen thun . . . " or whether He is now silent: "Schweigt, jetzt, nicht leitend, Gott? und kannst du, Furchtbares Schweigen, nur du uns bessern?" (M-P 2, 146); "Die Unvergessliche" (1800), a moving ode on freedom murdered by this "Täuscher Bejochungskrieg." Of this ode I cannot resist quoting the last two stanzas with their magnificently excessive Klopstockian imagery:

> Hoch in die Wolken steigt die Zipress' empor;
> In meilenlange Thale des Trauerhains
> Sind hingesunken Völkerheere,
> Weinen nicht Thränen, wie sonst der Mensch weint:
>
> Blut strömt ihr Auge über der Freyheit Tod!
> Der todten Schatten finstert den Abendstern,
> Und wird, wenn nun zu seiner Heimat
> Er sich erhebt, den Orion finstern!
>
> [M-P 2, 154 f.]

With the ode "Losreissung" (September 1800) the poet determines to study war no more and to turn to nature and present human joys, but already in November 1800, in "Die Unschuldigen," he is forced to confess:

> Immer noch wilst du, bittrer Schmerz, mich trüben;
> Immer drohst du mir noch aus deiner Wolke,
> Kriegserinrung! . . .
>
> [MP 2, 160]

And even the "Mahl mit heitern Freunden" (Lord Nelson and
Lady Hamilton, as it happened) cannot drive away this memory. The depth of Klopstock's disappointment at the betrayal
of the ideal of freedom as he conceived it is the measure of the
sincerity of his devotion to it.

Klopstock's odes on language and poetics belong to the very
heart of his work. They do not first appear in the last decades
but form a constant, if not always overt, theme of his whole
œuvre. "Über manche seiner Gedichte, die er anders benannt
hat," writes Friedrich Georg Jünger, "liesse sich der Titel 'Die
Sprache' setzen" (Nachwort to Schleiden, 3d ed., p. 1366). The
theme of language and its use in poetry, which includes the
whole art of prosody, is closely connected in Klopstock with the
theme of fame. True fame, he never tires of reiterating, is
achieved not through martial deeds but through personal virtue and, most importantly, through raising great linguistic monuments. This is the main purport of his earliest ode, "Der Lehrling der Griechen," and on this article of faith he never turned
his back. It is still the theme of "Der Nachruhm" (1782):

> Glänzend ist, Krieger und Könige, was ihr thatet,
>   vielleicht auch
> Edel, o Wunder! so gar.
> Was es denn sey; es steiget gewiss zu dem Enkel
>   hinunter:
> Aber in welcher Gestalt?
> Etwa in der, die es hatte, da ihr es thatet? In jeder
>   Andern, in dieser nur nicht!
> . . . .
> Glücklicher fiel sein Loos dem Dichter. Was er uns
>   nachliess,
> Bleibet stets, was es war.
> Über ihn waltet sie nicht, die Geschichte,; da spielt die
>   Verwandlung
> Nicht, wie mit Thaten sie spielt.
>   [M-P 2, 39]

But Klopstock's thirst for fame is not entirely selfish. He sees
it in connection with fame for his native land. Kommerell has

good reason to say: "Sprache war ihm ja Vaterland, die Liebe zu ihm Liebe zur Sprache" (*Der Dichter als Führer*, p. 56).

In "Fragen" (1752), those poets who continue to imitate foreign models are scorned: "Soll Hermanns Sohn . . . in Ketten denen nachgehn, Welchen er, kühner, vorüber flöge?" (M-P 1, 106). In warlike enterprises, to be sure, the Germans can raise their head, but it is now imperative that they produce poetry equally worthy of undying fame. "Die beyden Musen" (1752) is an allegory on the rivalry—as Klopstock sees it—between German and English poetry, which are depicted as running a race for the crown of highest poetic achievement, particularly in religious poetry. Klopstock here has his own *Messias* in mind. In "Siona" (1764), an ode of great rhythmic power in praise of the sacred Muse, it is stated unequivocally that sacred poetry is superior to that inspired by Hippocrene:

> Es erhebt steigender sich Sions Lied,
> Wie des Quells, welcher des Hufs Stampfen entscholl.
> [M-P 1, 166]

The implication is that in this respect German poetry, and Klopstock means his own, can surpass that of the ancients. It glorifies the "Religion dessen, der ist! Seyn wird! und war!" which ancient poetry does not, and this, combined with its wide range of expressive power, makes it absolutely without equal:

> Hört ihr? Siona begint! schon rauscht
> Der heilige Hain von dem Harfenlaut!
> Des Krystals Quelle vernimts, horcht, und steht;
> Denn es wehn Lispel im Hain rings um sie her.
>
> Aber itzt stürzt sie die Well' herab
> Mit freudiger Eil! Denn Siona nimt
> Die Posaun', hält sie empor, lässt sie laut
> Im Gebirg' hallen! und ruft Donner ins Thal!
> [M-P 1, 167, verses 25–32]

Still, the challenge the German poet must ultimately face is that of "Griechengesang," the highest achievement of secular poetry. This is the theme of "Der Nachahmer" (1764), and like Young, Klopstock believes that the modern poet can become like the Greeks only by emulating their example, not by imitating their manner.

Some of the odes treat technical questions of prosody. "Sponda" (1764), for example, is an allegory on the lack of the spondee in German. The various *pedes* speak in their own praise, attempting to comfort the German poet—they can make up for the lack of the spondee—but he will not be comforted. At last he sends the pyrrhic ($\smile\smile$) as the nimblest foot into the sacred grove to look for the spondee, which surely had not been absent in the poetry of the old Germanic bards. The situation is not without a kind of "in" humor:

> Ach Sponda! rief der Dichter, und hiess
> In den Hain nach ihr Pyrrichios gehn.
> Flüchtig sprang, schlüpft' er dahin! Also wehn
> Blüthen im May Weste dahin.
>
> Denn, Sponda, du begleitest ihn auch
> Der Bardiete vaterländischen Reihn,
> Wenn der Fels treffend ihn mir tönt', und mich
> Nicht die Gestalt täuschte, die sang.
> [M-P 1, 170, verses 49–56]

W.H. Auden said: "Every poet has his dream reader: mine keeps a lookout for curious prosodic fauna like bacchics and choriambs."[39] So does Klopstock's.

In "Der Bach" (1766), another of the technical odes and one of the most difficult, Klopstock rather startlingly implies that through his self-invented meters his own poetry may even surpass that of the Greeks. If enough of the Greek lyric had been preserved to make a comparison possible, one would realize that his, Klopstock's, lyric has a "kühneren Schwung" and thus "mehr Wendung fürs Herz." In other words, the rhythmic quality of his poetry is superior. The following lines, an enigmatic explication of an esoteric doctrine, contain, according to Hellmuth "the quintessence of his theory of verse rhythm" (*Metrische Erfindung*, p. 11):

267

Inhalt, den volle Seel', im Erguss
Der Erfindung, und der innersten Kraft,
Sich entwirft, strömet; allein lebend muss,
Will es ihm nahn, tönen das Wort.

Wohllaut gefällt, Bewegung noch mehr;
Zur Gespielin kohr das Herz sie sich aus.
Diesem säumt, eilet sie nach; Bildern folgt,
Leiseres Tritts, ferne sie nur.

So säumet, und so eilt sie nicht nur:
Auch empfindungsvolle Wendung beseelt
Ihr den Tanz, Tragung, die spricht, ihr den Tanz,
All ihr Gelenk schwebt in Verhalt.

> [M-P 1, 183, verses 9–20]

If the content is to be effectively conveyed, the word *muss lebend tönen*, another formulation of the doctrine of "Mitausdruck." Two elements are involved: "Wohllaut" and "Bewegung," of which the second is the more important: "Wohllaut gefällt, Bewegung noch mehr; Zur Gespielin kohr das Herz sie sich aus." "Bewegung" or rhythm Klopstock regards as a function of the meter. But "Bewegung" itself is composed, according to Klopstock's theory, of two elements: "Zeitausdruck" and "Tonverhalt," the former having to do with the tempo ("säumet . . . eilet"), the latter with the relationship of stressed and unstressed syllables as expressive of feeling: "Auch empfindungsvolle Wendung beseelt Ihr den Tanz." The whole question is complicated, and Klopstock's theoretical explanations are by no means always clear and consistent. We cite the poem here only as an example of the kind of technical matters Klopstock was willing to try to treat in the ode.

"Unsre Sprache" (1767; 2nd version, 1775), an ode in praise of the German tongue, is cast, like "Siona" and "Thuiskon," in the form of an epiphany. In the first version the question of whether the new poetry (i.e., Klopstock's poetry) equals that of the Greeks is raised but left without a definite answer. In the final version this ending is deleted and another substituted in which no doubt is left that Klopstock's work is indeed immortal, i.e., the peer of ancient poetry. The chief theme of the ode, however, is praise of the powers of German as a vehicle for poetry. The goddess of the German tongue here manifests herself in two of Klopstock's most impressive strophes, remarkable for their striking use of rhythmical "Mitausdruck" to contrast "mächtiges" and "sanfteres Getön":

Wie sie herschwebt an des Quells Fall! Mächtiges
    Getön,
Wie Rauschen im Beginne des Walds ist ihr Schwung!
Draussen um die Felsen braust der Sturm!
Gern höret der Wandrer das Rauschen im Wald!

Wie sie schwebet an der Quelle! Sanfteres Getön,
Wie Wehen in dem tieferen Wald' ist ihr Schwung.
Draussen um die Felsen braust der Sturm!
Gern höret im Walde der Wandrer das Wehn.
                    [M-P 1, 200, verses 21–28]

We come at last to the period under closer discussion, the last period before Klopstock's death. Important poems dealing with language, poetry, and poetics in this period are "Verschiedene Zwecke" (1778), "An Freund und Feind" (1781), "Die Sprache" (1782), "Aesthetiker" (1782), "Die deutsche Sprache" (1783), "An Johann Heinrich Voss" (1783/84), "Die deutsche Bibel" (1784), "Die Rathgeberin" (1795), "Neuer Genuss" (1796), "Unsre Sprache an uns" (1796).

"Verschiedene Zwecke" (M-P 2, 17) deals with kinds of poetry and is directed against poetry as mere entertainment, the poetry of wit. Klopstock, we remember, sees "das Wesen der Poesie" in its power to engage "die *vornehmsten* Kräfte unsrer Seele" to such a degree that one affects the other and thus moves the *whole* soul (cf. "Gedanken über die Natur der Poesie," Schleiden, 3d ed., p. 992). This "der flatterhafte, gähnende Zeitvertreib" cannot do: "Gesondert sind die Freud' und der Zeitvertreib." Poetry that wants only to en-

269

tertain is in fact a "Gegen-Vergnügen," anti-art or non-art. Klopstock may have the anacreontic poets in mind, though by 1778 their day was in decline. He speaks specifically of "glatte Liederchen" and "Henriaden" (the date of Voltaire's *Henriade* is 1723; Klopstock had already excoriated it in the *Gelehrtenrepublik* in 1774), and paraphrastically (in stanza 4) of French neoclassical tragedy ("Leidenschaft in Bildergewand gemumt; Und jedes Knöspchen, Blümchen der Zierlichkeit"). All these—and one notes the animus against French culture—come not from the heart and do not speak to the heart. True poetry is then characterized in two magnificent strophes. The measure is Alcaic:

> Gleich einer lichten Wolke mit goldnem Saum,
> Erschwebt die Dichtkunst jene gewölbte Höh
> Der Heitre,* wo, wen sie emporhub,
> Reines Gefühl der Entzückung athmet.

> Auch wenn sie Nacht wird, flieht der Genuss doch nicht
> Vor ihren Donnern; feuriger lezt er sich!
> Drauf schwebt sie, schöner Bläue* nahe
> Nachbarin, über dem Regenbogen.
>
> [M-P 2, 17 f., verses 21–28]

The theme of "An Freund und Feind" (1781; M-P 2, 26), in free verse, is poetry and immortality. The poet here tells all who may approve or disapprove how he came to write the *Messias* and why he is convinced that he has thereby entered the ranks of the immortals. This ode deserves more detailed comment, not because it is one of the most nearly perfect, but for the light it throws on a striking aspect of Klopstock's personality: his insistent harping on the immortality of his own work, a trait which cannot be fully explained by references to Horace and Renaissance topoi.

The ode begins with reflections on mortality and immortality. A bizarre image depicts the wanderer, who feels the approach of old age (Klopstock was fifty-seven at the time),

---

**der Heitre, schöner Bläue*, gen. sg.; *wen* = der, den.

270

taking his way down life's path, his staff covered not only by the dust of the road but also by the ashes of "näherer Todter," which could mean "the more recent dead" or "dead ones who were nearer to me." But the "Aussicht drüben," beyond the limits of mortality, is serene, dustless, and eternally vernal: "O Pfad, wo Staub nicht und Asche bewölkt." Only one sad thought keeps the wanderer from rejoicing wholeheartedly in this prospect, that of separation from friends (though there must be friends in the beyond as well). Were it only possible to drain the bitter cup in one draught, instead of drop by drop! Again the imagery is puzzling, if not bizarre. It could be taken to mean that the "I" wants all his friends to die at once or it could be a wish for his own sudden death, in order not to have to experience the death of his friends one by one. In any event, it is a meditation on death that reaches no comforting conclusion, despite the "Aussicht drüben." In the fourth stanza (verse 15) the theme is apparently dismissed ("Weg vom Kelche [des Todes], Gesang!") and the main theme of the ode introduced: What can make mortal-immortal man happy?

> . . . . Tiefsinnig
> Hatt' ich geforscht,
> . . . . Was ihn mache,
> Der, zu leben! entstand, zu sterben!
> Glücklich den? Ich war es, und bins!
> [M-P 2, 26 f., verses 15–19]

One answer to this question is immortality. Immortality of the soul is not meant, for this is the birthright of all, but the immortality of fame. Stanzas 6–8 then return to an old theme, the false immortality of princes: "Sie [Unsterblichkeit] scheint der Könige Loos; allein sie werden in der Geschichte zu Mumien!" (verses 23 f.). The youth whom the poet here remembers thirsted for a better immortality, that of the poet, though his "Genius" warned him of the dangers of such an ambition:

> Voll Durstes war die heisse Seele des Jünglings
> Nach der Unsterblichkeit!

Ich wacht', und ich träumte
Von der kühnen Fahrt auf der Zukunft Ozean!

Dank dir noch Einmal, mein früher Geleiter, dass du
   mir,
Wie furchtbar es dort sey, mein Genius zeigtest.
Wie wies dein goldener Stab! Hochmastige,
   vollebesegelte Dichterwerke,
Und dennoch gesunkene schreckten mich!

[stanzas 9–10]

Stanzas 12–13 tell of the desperate search for an epic theme
(for Klopstock assumes, along with his century, that the sur-
est way to immortality is to become the peer of Homer,
Vergil, and Milton) and a hero whose deeds he might sing.
The figures of German history are rejected as unsuitable.
Then, in a sudden visionary revelation, the only possible hero
and the only possible theme come to him: Christ and His
Passion:

Welch Anschaun war es! Denn Ihn, den als Christ, ich
   liebte,
Sah ich mit Einem schnellen begeisterten Blick,
Als Dichter, und empfand: Es liebe mit Innigkeit
Auch der Dichter den Göttlichen!

[stanza 14]

Now all fear of failure is put aside and even the thirst for
immortality forgotten—the poet lives only for his work. The
concluding stanzas (17–19) speak of the foundations on which
the timelessness of his epic rests: the power of poetic language
and the sublime truth of the Christian religion. With them as
a basis, his work cannot perish, and with it its creator has
joined the ranks of the immortals. Happiness has been
attained:

Die Erhebung der Sprache,
Ihr gewählterer Schall,
Bewegterer, edlerer Gang,
Darstellung, die innerste Kraft der Dichtkunst;

Und sie, und sie, die Religion,
Heilig sie, und erhaben,
Furchtbar, und lieblich, und gross, und hehr,
Von Gott gesandt,

Haben mein Maal errichtet. Nun steht es da,
Und spottet der Zeit, und spottet
Ewig gewähnter Maale,
Welche schon jetzt dem Auge, das sieht, Trümmern
    sind.

It may now be possible, by surveying the ode from the prospect of its conclusion, to arrive at an interpretation of the puzzling opening strophes. The central problem of the poem is man's happiness and the solution to the problem immortality through poetic creation. The happiness of friendship is embittered by death; even the certainty of eternal bliss is, on an earthly plane, clouded by the death of loved ones. Enduring recompense for this inescapable human situation the poet finds in the conviction that his poem is immortal. From it he will never have to part, it is the firm rock of all his happiness. But it is the personal happiness of a poet, not of man per se. The question of *man's* happiness is left unanswered, though it seemed to be posed in stanza 5: "Was ihn mache, Der zu leben! entstand, zu sterben! Glücklich den?"

If we adduce other passages in Klopstock, we see that the process of composition itself—or the successful completion of a great work—is a foretaste of heavenly bliss, immortality now. In "An den Erlöser" (1773), a hymn of thanksgiving for the completion of the *Messias*, the poet confidently foretells that the welcome of the blessed in heaven will be, *mutatis mutandis*, like the inexpressible joy he feels at the successful conclusion of his life work:

Ich bin an dem Ziel, an dem Ziel! und fühle, wo ich
    bin,
Es in der ganzen Seele beben! So wird es (ich rede
Menschlich von göttlichen Dingen) uns einst, ihr
    Brüder dess,

> Der starb! und erstand! bey der Ankunft im Himmel
> seyn!
>
> [M-P 2, 2, verses 41–44]

The most compelling formulation of the ecstasy of poetic creation is the ode "Neuer Genuss," written in 1796. It belongs to those poems treating the theme of "das verlängerte Leben":

> Bild lebendiger Einsamkeit,
> Schwebe näher! Sie ist, die sie war,
> Da ich einst sie genoss, da ich voll Glut
> Dichtete, ordnete,
> Seelen gab dem Empfundenen,
> Ihnen tönenden Leib. . . .
>
> [M-P 2, 125]

Through the process of poetic creation the poet becomes like God, a second maker under Jove, and his bliss is of comparable intensity:

> Bild lebendiger Einsamkeit,
> . . . .
> Weile, Weile! In ihr durchdrang
> Frohes innig gefühlt den, der kühn
> In der Dichtenden Höhn schwebte, durchdrang
> Wonne den feyrenden!
>
> O der Wonne! . Ich hätte sie
> Da selbst, als sie mir ward, durch das Lied
> Nicht erreicht. Sie ergriff mächtiges Arms,
> Riss wie in Strömen fort!
>
> [M-P 2, 126, verses 25, 31–38]

Who will say that Klopstock did not attain happiness here on earth? It is a happiness even better than the prospect of eternal salvation, for on it the dust of the wanderer's path can never settle. This psychological situation, this superlative creative bliss, also throws light on Klopstock's sometimes disconcerting self-assertiveness, his way of pointing out his own poetic merits—in which by and large time has proved him right. His work *must* be immortal, it *must* be the supreme achievement of German poetry, for it is the one firm foundation on which his happiness rests. "Klopstock's preoccupation with immortality," Bernhard Blume has said, "is but the other side of his preoccupation with death."[40] "An Freund und Feind" offers a strong argument in support of this statement. Klopstock was perhaps not quite such a "durch und durch unproblematische, krisenfeste Natur" as he has been represented.[41] Had he been, would he have become a poet?

A central but difficult, because highly compressed and esoterically allusive, ode on language is "Die Sprache" (1782). Its analysis is imperative if we wish to enter more deeply into Klopstock's thought on his medium of expression. I quote the entire poem.

DIE SPRACHE

1. Des Gedankens Zwilling, das Wort scheint Hall nur,
   Der in die Luft hinfliesst: heiliges Band
   Des Sterblichen ist es, erhebt
   Die Vernunft ihm, und das Herz ihm!

2. Und er weiss es: denn er erfand, durch Zeichen
   Fest, wie den Fels hinzuzaubern den Hall!
   Da ruht er; doch kaum, dass der Blick
   Sich ihm senket, so erwacht er.

3. Es erreicht die Farbe dich nicht, des Marmors
   Feilbare Last, Göttin Sprache, dich nicht!
   Nur weniges bilden sie uns:
   Und es zeigt sich uns auf Einmal.

4. Dem Erfinder, welcher durch dich des Hörers
   Seele bewegt, that die Schöpfung sich auf!
   Wie Düften entschwebt, was er sagt,
   Mit dem Reize der Erwartung,

5. Mit der Menschenstimme Gewalt, mit ihrem
   Höheren Reiz, höchsten, wenn sie Gesang

Hinströmet, und inniger so
In die Seele sich ergiesset.

6. Doch, Erfinder, täusche dich nicht! Für dich nur
   Ist es gedacht, was zum Laute nicht wird,
   Für dich nur; wie tief auch, wie hell,
   Wie begeisternd du es dachtest.

7. Die Gespielen sind ihr zu lieb der Sprache;
   Trenne sie nicht! Enge Fessel, geringt
   An lemnischer Esse, vereint
   Ihr den Wohlklang, und den Verstanz.

8. Harmonie zu sondern, die so einstimmet,
   Meidet, wer weiss, welcher Zweck sie verband:
   Die Trennungen zwingen zu viel
   Des Gedachten zu verstummen.

9. Von dem Ausland, Deutsche, das Tanz des Liedes
   Klagend entbehrt, lernet ganz, was es ist,
   Dem viele von euch, wie Athen
   Ihm auch horchte, noch so taub sind.

10. Und es schwebt doch kühn, und gewiss Teutona
    Wendungen hin, die Hellänis so gar
    Nicht alle, mit stolzem Gefühl
    Des Gelingens, sich erköhre.

11. Den Gespielen lasset, und ihr der Göttin
    Blumen uns streun: Himmelschlüsseln dem Klang,
    Dem Tanz' Hyazinthen, und ihr
    Von den Rosen, die bemoost sind.

12. Sie entglühen lieblicher, als der Schwestern
    Blühendster Busch, duften süssern Geruch;
    Auch schmückt sie ihr mosig Gewand,
    Und durchräuchert ihr Gedüfte.

[M-P 2, 37 f.]

Klopstock's views on the nature of language show a distinct progression from the naively mechanistic to the highly sophisticated and organic, from the word as the picture or garment of the idea to the word as the discoverer or inventor of the idea, from, one might say, Cartesianism to something approaching Humboldtian linguistic theory.

In "Von der Sprache der Poesie" (1758) we read: "Wenn man den Gedanken hat; so wählt man das Wort, welches ihn ausdrückt" (Schleiden, p. 1019). Thought and expression are conceived as separate entities; we clothe our thoughts in words. This is still seventeeth-century thinking and the basis upon which the poetry of the Baroque rests. But as Schleiden points out, only a year later, in "Gedanken über die Natur der Poesie" (1759), Klopstock has already advanced beyond this view (*Dichtungstheorie*, p. 31). An expression that is perfectly consonant with the thought it expresses is "a shadow that moves with the tree." Nothing is commoner, Klopstock here maintains, than the confusion of thought and expression. "We say: that's the same thought, only differently expressed. And yet the thought is changed as soon as we change the expression" (Schleiden, 3d ed., pp. 994–95). Word and thought are no longer conceived as independent entities: one changes with the other. In 1779 Klopstock goes still a step farther. Now he views thought and language as functions of each other:

> Thought and language stand in an exact and firm connection with each other. According to their natures, they can give each other this or that direction. Language will do this oftener or less often according to the number and similarity of those concepts that have already received linguistic formulation. It can help us to phrase our thought more clearly and sometimes even act as co-discoverer (Miterfinderin) of thought. (Cited after Schleiden, *Dichtungstheorie*, p.31)

Here we can see that Klopstock is coming close to the view of the nature of language expressed in the apothegm by Karl Kraus: "Language is the divining-rod that discovers wells of thought." Late in life, expressly in the *Grammatische Gespräche* of 1794, but from other evidence even before this date, Klopstock takes precisely the opposite stand on the relation of

word and thought from that with which he began in 1758.
Now he can say that "if the right word is lacking, the right
thought is absent also . . . the thought rests on the word,
like the statue on its pediment; the statue will fall if its pediment cannot support it" (Schleiden, *Dicktungstheorie*, p. 32).
No thought is possible without language; language itself
thinks.[42]

"Die Sprache" obviously reflects a late stage in Klopstock's thought on the nature of language. The word is the
"twin of thought." Though it may seem a mere breath or
echo, "ein Hall nur," it is in reality a sacred bond among
mortals, forming the basis of society. Language elevates, develops, brings to awareness both intellect and feeling: *erhebt
die Vernunft und das Herz*. Knowing the incalculable value of
language man seeks to hold it fast through the written word:
"durch Zeichen, Fest, wie den Fels, hinzuzaubern den
Hall!" These magic ("hingezauberte") signs awaken to life as
soon as the eye lights on them.

Stanza 3 exalts poetry over sculpture and painting, the
art of time over the arts of space, succession over simultaneity. Stanza 4 speaks of the "Erfinder," Klopstock's honorific
term for the true poet in contrast to the mere "Nachahmer."
Through his identification with the nature of language, the
"Erfinder" can move the listener as he wills, for he is a god:
[*Ihm*] *that die Schöpfung sich auf*, i.e., he is at one with the word
through which man re-creates the creation, itself the embodied Word. The successive nature of language makes possible the "Reiz der Erwartung," the longing for fulfillment
based on the principle of expectation (denied to painting and
sculpture), which is for Klopstock one of poetry's chief
charms (cf. "Von der Wortfolge," 1779, Schleiden, 1030 f.).
This principle is one reason for his fondness for periodic
sentence structure and the inordinately long protasis, mannerisms which he greatly subdues in his later work, however,
as this ode itself shows.

The work of the "Erfinder" reaches its highest effectiveness when reproduced by the human voice, in declamation
and above all in song (stanza 5). Klopstock here probably has

in mind song in the manner of Bach's oratorios and perhaps especially the kind of delivery promulgated by Gluck, his favorite contemporary composer, who wrote in the foreword to his *Alkestis:* "It was my primary aim to confine music to its true task of serving poetry, in order to intensify the expression of feeling without interrupting the action" (cited after Freivogel, *K. der heilige Dichter,* p. 100). Klopstock himself declares that true music is declamation, nothing else than "completely fitting expression of the words" (Freivogel, p. 99). For Klopstock, words *are* music, and Freivogel is right in maintaining that "the decisive factor that entered the history of poetry with Klopstock's work was first and foremost the 'rebirth of the lyric from the spirit of music' " (p. 100).

The sixth strophe reflects the latest stage in the poet's thinking on the relation between thought and word: the former exists only in some solipsistic limbo unless given linguistic expression. He does not go so far, however, as to say that it is absolutely nonexistent. But, as in Stefan George's "Das Wort," if the Norn cannot find the word for the poet's "kleinod rein und zart," it must vanish and be lost forever to the poet's fellow men: "So lernt ich traurig den verzicht: Kein ding sei wo das wort gebricht."

A poem ostensibly on language has thus turned into a poem on poetry or language in its highest manifestation. Stanzas 7–10 deal with more technical aspects of poetry: Meter ("Verstanz") and the reflection of sense in sound ("Wohlklang"), which in good verse are fused in harmony: "geringt An lemnischer Esse," forged into ringed armor at Vulcan's forge. If one is emphasized at the expense of the other—this seems to be the force of stanza 8—the meaning will suffer: *zu viel des Gedachten verstummen.* One of Klopstock's epigrams, a dialog between "Silbenmass" (meter) and "Wohlklang," can help us understand what is meant:

DER DOPPELTE MITAUSDRUCK

Silbenmass, ich weiche dir nicht, behaupte mich, ziehe Dir mich vor! "Wohlklang, ich liebe das Streiten nicht. Besser

279

> Horchen wir jeder mit wachem Ohr dem Gesetz und
>   vereinen
> Fest uns. Wir sind alsdann die zweite Seele der
>   Sprache.
>
> [Schleiden, 3d ed., p. 186]

The "*erste* Seele der Sprache," by implication, is the meaning. Klopstock never advocated a pure autonomy of form; the content was for him always primary. The unversed reader of poetry (if one will pardon the pun) will not realize the finer points of versification in any case, Klopstock points out in one of his treatises on the hexameter (*Sämmtl. Werke*, 10, 152). He is not talking about those who are knowledgeable in metrical theory, he continues. They have accustomed themselves to notice technique and burst out in exclamations of admiration no matter what the content, if only the form is skillful. "And yet one should hold one's peace at verses that make a display of themselves and let the content take its course." If the meter doesn't suit the content, *it* loses and remains largely without effect.

Stanza 9 refers indirectly to Klopstock's own metrical innovations, of which he was justly very proud, and which, in his estimation, make German poetry (i.e., *his* poetry) superior to that of other modern national poetries. The ode "An Johann Heinrich Voss" (1784; M-P 2, 57) offers an illuminating parallel. Greek and Latin had "zween gute Geister . . . Wohlklang und Silbenmass" and these have preserved the poets of those tongues to our own day. Sound (Klang) modern poetry still has, but meter? No; for meter rhyme has been substituted, Vergil's and Homer's "Liedestanz" has given way to the alexandrine, the rhymed heroic couplet and madrigal verse:

> Die späteren Sprachen haben des Klangs noch wohl;
> Doch auch des Silbenmasses? Statt dessen ist
> In sie ein böser Geist, mit plumpem
> Wörtergepolter, der Reim, gefahren.
>
> [stanza 2]

This situation, the poet continues, he has himself remedied, and others have followed his lead. In spite of nagging criticism, "our poets" "Verliessen mich nicht, und sangen / Ohne den Lerm, und im Ton des Griechen." Thus German has been freed of the tyranny of iambics and rhyme:

> Dank euch noch Einmal, Dichter! Die Sprache war
> Durch unsern Iambus halb in die Acht erklärt,
> Im Bann der Leidenschaften Ausdruck,
> Welcher dahin mit dem Rithmus strömet.
>
> [stanza 5]

"Rithmus" here means "Metrum," the alternating verse typical of German poetry since Opitz; "der Leidschaften Ausdruck" is a Saxon genitive: the expression of emotion was in the grip of the meter, i.e., the possibility of manifold metrical "Mitausdruck" was severely reduced. This "Bann" was broken by the introduction of classical meters into German.

Now, since the reform (this is the purport of stanza 10), German poetry ("Teutona") is capable of producing metrical-rhythmical effects ("schwebt . . . Wendungen hin" is Klopstock's boldly effective expression of the situation) that even Greek poetry ("Hellänis") might not successfully achieve (erköhre, "might choose").

The two final stanzas propose in movingly fervent terms a floral offering of thanks to the goddess Language, to "Wohlklang" and to "Verstanz." The moss rose, an old-fashioned flower with an incenselike odor and Klopstock's prime favorite, is reserved for Language herself, while Sound receives cowslips (fortunately called "keys of heaven" in German) and Meter hyacinths.

Before leaving Klopstock's odes on language and poetics, we must note that, as revolutionary as his innovations were, Klopstock was not in sympathy with the uncontrolled subjectivism of the Sturm und Drang. *His* revolution demands a calculated control of his medium, not a direct outpouring of emotion itself, though this is the *effect* the calculated method is meant to achieve. Fundamentally, Klopstock remained throughout his life a "Lehrling der Griechen"—classical poetry was the standard by which poetic accomplishment must ultimately be measured. True, modern poetry might rival classical, and in subject matter it even surpassed it, for, as we learn in "An die Dichter meiner Zeit":

> Die Neuern sehen heller im Sittlichen,
> Als einst die Alten sahen. . . .
>
> [1800; M-P 2, 146 f.]

and those who have higher moral virtue behold a higher beauty (the insight of Goethe's Iphigenie):

> Die mehr der Stufen zu dem Unendlichen
> Aufstiegen, schauen höhere Schönheit. Er,
> Das Seyn, ward durch des Alterthumes
> Märchen entstellt, die von Göttern sangen.

But in spite of this reservation, classical poetry remains for Klopstock the ultimate measure, and it *is* a measure because subject to rule, though the rule may be hard to define. The anti-Sturm und Drang overtones are evident in the opening lines of "Die Rathgeberin":

> Regel des Dichtenden, oder hörst Rathgeberin lieber
> Du dich nennen? doch welcher der Name sey, den du
>   wählest;
> Bist du ernster, tiefsinniger, als im Taumel-
> Flug dich der Ungeweihte kent,
>
> Bist entscheidender! Wie verstumt' ich oft und wie
>   fühlt' ich
> Bleich mich werden, wenn empor ich sah zu der Höhe,
> Die mir zeigte dein goldener Stab! und mit welchem
>   Hinschaun
> Mass ich den einsamen, steilen Pfad!
>
> [1795; M-P 2, 112]

The "Rathgeberin," who is later (verse 32) called "die stolze Griechin," will never serve as a guide, never lift her golden staff, the aged poet advises the young, unless the spirit of the latter is capable of thought that can influence feeling; but this spirit must also be *master* of the emotion aroused and capable of pronouncing cool judgment:

282

> . . . wird euch nie
> Ihren goldenen Stab erheben; wenn euch nicht Geist
>   ward,
> Dem die Empfindung heisser glüht, wie ihn Bilder
>   entflammen,
> Und in dem, Beherscher der Flamm' und der Glut, das
>   Urteil
> *Unbezaubert* den Ausspruch thut; . . .
>   [M-P 2, 113, verses 24–28; emphasis added]

Much more than Storm and Stress this sounds like Hölderlin's "heilige Nüchternheit": "Da, wo die Nüchternheit dich verlässt, ist die Grenze deiner Begeisterung." To move the feelings and make us "beside ourselves" is the aim of Klopstock's poetry, but its aim is not to make the poet lose control of his faculty of judgment.

Life relived in memory is one of the most characteristic themes in the poetry of Klopstock's last period. From about 1776 on he seems to feel a need to assure himself of his past, to embrace life again in memory. This "Erinnerungslyrik" is the obverse of the "Zukunftslyrik" of his youth. Life thus relived, despite the tone of gentle resignation, is seen in a positive light. That Klopstock's poetry, like Rilke's, is meant fundamentally as praise is nowhere more apparent than in these poems. Acceptance of "dess, das da ist" is the keynote, whether it be "there" in actuality or memory. The prevailing atmosphere of most of the "Erinnerungsgedichte" is one of serenity. Though the note of fervency is never lacking, it is not the exacerbated fervency of the hymns of the early and middle periods.

"Das verlängerte Leben" (1796) is the programmatic poem dealing with the theme of life relived in memory:

> Ja du bist es, du komst, süsse Verneuerin,
>   Ach Erinrung der Zeit, die floh.

283

Inniger freust du mich oft, als die Erblickung mich,
Als mich Stimmen des Menschen freun.
Du erschafst mir kein Bild von dem Verschwundenen,
Scheinst zu wandeln in Wirkliches.

[M-P 2, 122]

E.W. Schulz remarks that memory, as here characterized, is similar to the creative power of poetry: it creates a "Fast-Wirkliches," it presents ("stellt dar"), quite in accord with Klopstock's chief requirement for true poetic creation, so that we must consent to its being ("K.s Alterslyrik," p. 303). Through its transforming power, memory lengthens life in later years by endowing the past with density of being and turning it at the same time into something that is like a work of art. And the work of art is more real than raw material because it is reality interpreted, endowed with meaning.

The work of art that memory creates is, as such, removed from the stream of time. But this is not the only function of memory, to escape time by causing time to stand still. It can also remind us that life's ineluctable direction is toward death. This trite but terrible thought, which the older Klopstock especially would like to forget, is the theme of "Die Erinnerung. An Ebert nach seinem Tode," his shortest ode in free verse and one of the most remarkable poems of his old age. It was composed in the autumn of 1795; Ebert, the friend of his youth, had died in March of that year:

Graun der Mitternacht schliesst mich nicht ein,
Ihr Verstummen nicht; auch ist, in dem Namen der
heiligen
Freyheit, jüngst kein Mord geschehn: dennoch ist mir
Ernst die ganze Seele.

Liebliches Wehn umsäuselt mich;
Wenig ist nur des Laubes, das fiel; noch blühn der
Blumen;
Dem Herbste gelingt Nachbildung des Sommers:
Aber meine ganze Seel' ist ernst!

Ach mich reisst die Erinnerung fort, ich kann nicht
widerstehn!

Muss hinschauen nach Grabstäten, muss bluten lassen
Die tiefe Wund', aussprechen der Wehmuth Wort:
Todte Freunde, seyd gegrüsst!

[M-P 2, 112]

The first two strophes are devoted to images emphasiz-
ing presence, nowness. The present is not mute, it answers
the lyric "I" and corresponds to its wishes and hopes: the
silence of midnight does *not* enclose it, no murder has lately
been committed in the name of freedom (a reference to the
French Revolution), the autumn is like summer—time seems
to stand still. All these images, however, are infected with
effort, with a struggle against their true direction. If "Graun
der Mitternacht" does not imprison the poet, still he cannot
help conjuring up its terror. If no murder has recently been
done in freedom's name, such murders have been done in the
past and may be done in the future. The whole first stanza
braces itself against terrible possibilities, which are then admitted in "dennoch ist mir ernst die ganze Seele." The second
stanza, modulating from man to nature, is built on the same
principle: "*Wenig* ist *nur* des Laubes, das fiel, *noch* blühen *der*
[some] Blumen"; "Dem Herbste *gelingt Nachbildung* des Sommers." Autumn's work is like the work of memory, if memory is an artist. But it is not truly reliable, cannot finally
comfort. With "Aber meine ganze Seel' ist ernst!" this whole
seeming is again set at nought. The final strophe then gives in
to memory's other direction, to a sense of the past that pre-
dicts a future without time: "ich kann nicht widerstehn! Muss
hinschauen nach Grabstäten. . . . " Time does *not* stand still,
it runs through us. The work of art is, if not a lie, yet not the
whole truth.
    Klopstock of course had the final comfort of religion,
and this gives his work its basically optimistic tone, though
the struggle to hold on to belief is more bitter than some of
his exegetes seem willing to admit. In the view of the Christian, to look toward the grave is to look toward life eternal.
This too may seem trite to the nonbeliever, or it may seem
simply childish self-deception. For the believer it provides

final meaning and allows him to live toward death with hope and joy. This is the theme of some of Klopstock's most beautiful poems of his old age, notably "Die Verwandelten" (1782), "An die nachkommenden Freunde" (1796), "Das Wiedersehn" (1797), and his last ode, "Die höheren Stufen" (1802). It is absurd, with these poems before us, to speak of "Erstarrung."

And there are others. For example "Mein Wissen" (1782), discussed below; "Die unbekannten Seelen" (1800), a cosmic ode on the all-animation of the universe; there are the odes on language which we have discussed and the poem on Luther's translation of the Bible ("Die deutsche Bibel," 1784), which we have not; at least a half-dozen superb odes on the French Revolution; the ode to Maria Theresia ("Ihr Tod," 1780); the odes to exultant physical activity and to wine, such as "Winterfreuden" (1797) and "Der Kapwein und der Johannesberger" (1795); and the sadly beautiful yet positive ode "Der Frohsinn" (1784). Klopstock's "Alterslyrik" alone would make a lesser poet immortal. For the most part this important body of poetry has been neglected by the critics, who seem hypnotized by the venerable dictum that Klopstock in his old age merely repeated himself, raising monuments to his faded glory, that he became odd and pigheaded, given to *outré* experiments that led nowhere, while the world looked in another direction. It may be quite true that the world *did* look in another direction, but this hardly seems a binding reason for the critic of literature to follow suit. In the poems of Klopstock's old age German literature possesses a treasure that has not yet been fully evaluated. Indeed, it has hardly even been estimated.

Nor can it be estimated here, for the discussion of Klopstock already exceeds bounds seemly for an introductory essay on the poetry of the Aufklärung. In closing I will glance at only two more of the late poems, "Mein Wissen" (1782) and "Das Wiedersehn" (1797). E.W. Schulz has emphasized that, while the lyric of Klopstock's early and middle periods is—as has long been recognized—characterized by its tendency to transcend reality and is consequently poor in images that have the saturated quality of the earthly, the poetry of his old age is much more friendly toward the world as we ordinarily experience it and thus richer in imagery drawn from the world about us. Though Klopstock's urge to transcend can be overemphasized—there are striking examples of his tarrying in the realm of the here and now, especially in those poems dealing with sports, with wine, with the senses—the *senus communis* is nonetheless largely justified. It is indubitable that the "Alterslyrik" shows a considerable change in this respect. Schulz cites the following lines, addressed to the poet's horse, as an example of the new tone (p. 305):

> Lass uns geniessen, du im Schatten, zu dem ich dich
>   lenke,
>   Frisches, kühlendes Gras,
> Von der weisslichen Blume durchwebt, und der
>   goldnen; auch hebt dort
>   Dein erkohrnes Gewürz,
> Heilende Wermuth ihr Haupt. Ich schau geniessend
>   den hellern,
>   Bläueren Himmel, des Sees
> Ebnen Kristall, und umschwebt von ziehenden Metten,
>   vergess' ich
>   Fast der Blüthe, die nun
> Fruchtet, und mit vielfarbiger Last, den biegsamen
>   Zweig krümt.
>   Also trink' ich reinere Luft,
> Und ein sanftes frohes Gefühl des Lebens berauscht
>   mich!
>   [M-P 2, 100, verses 15–25]

The lines pay tribute to the earthly not only in their serene relaxation, a quality of the poem's music, but also in their imagery.

Schulz speaks of increasing vividness ("zunehmende Anschaulichkeit") in the poetry of Klopstock's final period (p. 311). This vividness seems to be connected in Klopstock's later poetry with a tendency toward the symbolic mode. The

287

mode is never developed; it remains only a tendency, but nonetheless it is there. By leaving that which is in its "is-ness" and letting another "higher" meaning shine through, symbolic poetry achieves its effect. "Mein Wissen," one of the poems discussed by Schulz (pp. 315 ff.), works in this way. (The meter, of Klopstock's own invention, is choriambic: $-\cup\cup-$.)

1. Wenig ist nur des Wahren, das mir zu ergründen
   Glückte; doch ist mir es theuer, wie ein Kleinod,
   Durch vieljährigen Schweiss errungen,
   Oder erkämpfet mit Blut!

2. Ist mir ein Trunk im Kühlen geschöpft aus der Quelle;
   Einer, der alt von der Kelter, im Krystall blinkt;
   Frühlingssäuseln am Baum, der anblüht;
   Wehen des fallenden Stroms;

3. Liebliche Ruh, stäubt endlich der Fuss in des Weges
   Krümme nicht mehr: wie durchglühte von dem lichten
   Himmel sinkend der Strahl! wie fern lag
   Lange die thürmende Stadt!

4. Labt, wie ein Buch, worin es im Geist der verkanten
   Griechen sich regt, von sich selber, die Gestalten
   Nicht nachahmend, die auch ursprünglich,
   Lächelnd auf Ähnlichung sehn;

5. Heitert mich auf, wie lebender Tanz, den der Jüngling
   Schleunig begann, und sein Mädchen, da die Flöte
   Wo im Schatten erscholl, der Spieler
   Gern zu den liebenden kam:

6. Freundesgespräch, das ist es mir auch, wenn in Freud'
   und
   Leide das Herz nun dahinströmt! O geöfnet
   Wird es dann, wie vor Gott, dann rinnen
   Beiderley Thränen herab!

                                                    [M-P 2, 33]

A poem of this type is inconceivable in Klopstock's earlier work. It is an old man's poem. The tone, though fervent, is meditative, not enthusiastic. The theme is typical of the Enlightenment: What can we know, what can we say is true? The poet answers the question purely on the basis of personal experience, in a series of images that impart not apothegmatically formulated insights but wisdom derived from pregnant moments of life itself. Image is all. No further explanation is offered.

"Das Wahre," the poem tells us, is for the poet (ist *mir*) like a cooling drink of water or like old wine in a crystal glass, like the gentle rustle of new spring leaves (*anblüht*, "beginning to bloom"), like sweet rest at sundown after a long day's dusty foot journey. It refreshes like a book that breathes the inimitable spirit of the Greeks, it cheers like the dance of young lovers, is like a conversation among friends that reveals the depths of feeling, causing tears of both joy and and sadness to flow. "Das Wahre," Schulz summarizes, is *comparable* to all this, but at the same time all this *is* "das Wahre" (p. 316).

Stanza 4, cryptic and syntactically difficult, is a kind of comment on the poem itself and its method of presenting "das Wahre" through a series of images. That which is true is like a book (a poem) which lives by its own inner life, not because it is an imitation of something outside itself. Such a poem does not imitate "Gestalten" (nature), yet these *sehen lächelnd auf Ähnlichung*, i.e., nature smiles at the resemblance of that which is formed according to like principles. (I read the passage as though there were a comma after *die* in verse 15.) This is what the "verkanten Griechen" did.

The didactic ode in dialog entitled "Der Nachahmer und der Erfinder" (1796) can serve as a useful commentary. Here the "imitator" (of the Greeks) feels offended by the superior airs of the "inventor," whose work springs not from models but from his own inner sources. The imitator would not dare, he says, to depart from the "secure path" of proven models, and many are his joys if he succeeds in equaling them; greater still his rapture if he thinks he has surpassed them. This the inventor admits, but feels that the imitator is missing the point. When the latter asks him if he does not after all resemble him, the imitator, because he "imitates nature," the inventor replies:

> Gleichen? Ein rötherer Morgen gebar
> Deinen Freund. Nur selten ward die Natur von dem
> Griechen
> Nachgeahmet; er stellte sie dar.
>
> [M-P 2, p. 122]

Our point is that this is what "Mein Wissen" also attempts. "Das Wahre" cannot, at least not poetically, be intimated except through *Darstellung*, through images of things that have the feel of truth. (The ode "Sie" [1797; M-P 2, 140]— "sie" is *Freude*—works in the same way.)

The images in "Mein Wissen" refer to simple, age-old things, basic needs of the soul and the body. When we ponder the matter, however, we find something lacking; the knowledge shown forth in these images has little to do with larger human relationships. It seems a very private kind of knowledge, in spite of its universal character. The tone of the poem is idyllic, almost Gessner-like, an effect that is heightened by the lack of temporal tension so characteristic of much of Klopstock's poetry. Mankind's woe and striving is not a part of this knowledge; it is knowledge of private inner happiness, a pastoral motif: "Wie fern lag . . . die thürmende Stadt!" If we limited ourselves to this poem, we would have to class Klopstock among those who retreat from the world into a private idyll, which, as we have had more than one occasion to note, is a typical trait in the poetry of the age. That this would be a distortion of the facts is proved above all by Klopstock's intense identification with the ideals of the French Revolution and the odes he was to write on this theme only a few years later.

In his "Alterslyrik," we have said, Klopstock likes to tarry in this world. The tendency to immediately transcend the here and now ebbs noticeably. "Das Wiedersehen" (1797; M-P 2, 136), the last poem we intend to examine, might at first glance seem to call this statement into question, but a closer look will, I think, convince us that such is not the case.

DAS WIEDERSEHN

1. Der Weltraum fernt mich weit von dir,
   So fernt mich nicht die Zeit.
   Wer überlebt das siebzigste
   Schon hat, ist nah bey dir.

2. Lang sah ich, Meta, schon dein Grab,
   Und seine Linde wehn;
   Die Linde wehet einst auch mir,
   Streut ihre Blum' auch mir,

3. Nicht mir! Das ist mein Schatten nur,
   Worauf die Blüthe sinkt;
   So wie es nur dein Schatten war,
   Worauf sie oft schon sank.

4. Dann kenn' ich auch die höhre Welt,
   In der du lange warst;
   Dann sehn wir froh die Linde wehn,
   Die unsre Gräber kühlt.

5. Dann . . . Aber ach ich weiss es nicht,
   Was du schon lange weisst;
   Nur dass es, hell von Ahndungen,
   Mir um die Seele schwebt!

6. Mit wonnevollen Hofnungen
   Die Abendröthe komt:
   Mit frohem, tiefen Vorgefühl,
   Die Sonnen auferstehn!

This poem has been interpreted in detail by Alfred Kelletat ("Über ein Altersgedicht K.s"), and we are thus in the fortunate position of having the guidance of an outstanding scholar of eighteenth-century poetry and poetics in our perusal of it.

Meta, Klopstock's first wife, died in 1758, almost forty years before the writing of "Das Wiedersehn." The poem is a greeting from husband to wife; he still in this world, she long in the next. The tone of happy anticipation derives from the conviction of the soul's immortality and faith in its salvation. It is possible both as an idea and a poem only on the basis of

291

Christian belief and the mythology of an afterworld, a world which in Klopstock's imagination looks a great deal like the present one, if one may judge from such poems as "Die Verwandelten" (1782) and "Die höheren Stufen" (1802). Formally, "Das Wiedersehn" stands in contrast with almost all of Klopstock's lyrical production: here are no Alcaics, choriambs, Sapphics, Asclepiads, or self-invented measures, but a straightforward meter familiar to every English reader, and, by 1797, because it became the meter of Gleim's *Grenadierlieder*, to every German one. It is of course none other than the Chevy Chase strophe (4–3–4–3), which Klopstock had used only once before, in "Kriegslied" (1749), and was never to use again. There is, however, a tremendous difference in melody and rhythm between "Kriegslied" and the present poem. The first stanza of the former runs:

> Die Schlacht geht an! Der Feind ist da!
> Wohlan zum Sieg ins Feld!
> Es führet uns der beste Mann
> Im ganzen Vaterland!
> [M-P 1, 70]

Here, as Kelletat remarks, we have a marching tempo, urgently pressing onward, with heavily accented line endings, that seem to be trying to contain some great energy, whereas the rhythm of "Das Wiedersehn" is pensively earnest and subdued (p. 189). The effect is largely achieved through the slighter contrast between accented and unaccented syllables. (English readers will be forcibly reminded of Emily Dickinson.)

"Das Wiedersehn" is not without a few closer relatives among Klopstock's poems, Kelletat reminds us. "Das Rosenband" (1753), "An Done" (1762), and "Edone" (1767) are also simply structured songlike pieces in iambics. It is notable that they are all conversations with a beloved woman, not supplications or highflown "Ansingungen" (a point Kelletat does not mention). For such intimate intercourse the high odic form would be unsuitable.

292

Klopstock is never wordy, despite the length of many of his poems, but here the impression of laconic spareness is particularly marked. Within the limits of the simple form chosen Klopstock employs a number of rhetorical artifices that heighten the expressiveness without straining the form itself. These artifices are not of the kind we are accustomed to meet in the enthusiastic odes: the form will not permit them. There is no involved sentence structure, no periods of excessive length, no insertions of wedge clauses between subject and predicate, in fact, none of the typical Klopstockian mannerisms except the transitive use of an intransitive verb in the first two lines. The word order, with the exception of the embarrassingly awkward passage in verses 3–4 ("Wer überlebt das siebzigste Schon hat"—Kelletat calls it a "false" hyperbaton), is that of heightened prose.

The opening line immediately engages our imaginative powers: "Der Weltraum fernt mich weit von dir." Here is no rococo intimacy in a sheltered dell, but a setting of cosmic breadth. "Weit von dir" in verse 1 corresponds epiphorically to "nah bey dir" in verse 4 and in turn reflects the contrast between space and time which is the subject of the first stanza.

Stanzas 2–4 are dominated by the image of the swaying linden dropping its blossoms on the two graves, first Meta's, then his *and* Meta's. Again the pathos is heightened by a rhetorical device, here epanalepsis or repetition: Linde wehn: Linde wehet: Linde wehn; auch mir: auch mir: nicht mir; Schatten nur: Schatten nur; worauf . . . sinkt: worauf . . . sank; dann: dann. The thought is again contrastive and is of course based on the Christian paradox of death as the gate to true life, seeming and being. Union in the grave, greeted by the triumphant "auch mir, auch mir" in stanza 2, is at once taken back in stanza 3 by "Nicht mir!" to go on to a higher and truer union than that of "Schatten nur." Strict parallelism, indicating first conjunction, then separation, then higher conjunction, all presented with great economy of means (the image of the linden is retained throughout), lend the simple form dignity and seriousness.

293

With stanza 4 a new beginning is made. The bipartite structure reflects the theme of being and seeming, this world and the next. The image of the linden—now envisioned as seen by both husband and wife from the standpoint of the "höhere Welt"—connects the two halves, while the urgent anaphoric "dann's" mark the desire to transcend the here and now. But there is no transcendence. Or, perhaps more accurately, the urge to transcend is arrested:

> Dann . . . Aber ich weiss ja nicht,
> Was du schon lange weisst;

Instead of transcendence, *this* world is imbued with a sense of transparency which allows the other, higher world to shine through. It is "hell von Ahndungen," but it is still *this* world. Sunset is sunset, but it comes "mit wonnevollen Hofnungen" of the last sunset, death; sunrises are sunrises, but full of "frohem, tiefen Vorgefühl" of the resurrection.

We cannot say, however, that Klopstock is here operating in the symbolic mode. Rather, his procedure is essentially still that of the Baroque, of Gerhardt and Gryphius, not of Goethe. It is emblematic rather than symbolic. The emblematic mode *uses* nature as an interpretable sign pointing to something beyond itself; it is not valued for its own innate existence. The emblematic mode is therefore always welcome to the poet bent on transcendence. Nature, in Klopstock's poetry, is principally though not exclusively seen in an emblematic light. If true reality is not to be found on this plane, such a view of nature is inevitable for the believer in a universe created by a paternal deity. We stand here only in the "Vorhof der Gottheit," and nature is merely a "phantom" of that truth which will be granted us after death, as we have seen in "Der Vorhof und der Tempel" (cf. pp. 250 ff.). Yet counterexamples, some of which we have cited, may be found. They show that Klopstock is not always obsessed with a tendency to devalue this world and employ it merely for emblematic purposes.[43] On the whole, however, this tends to be the case. Kelletat reminds us that we need only glance at Goethe's late lyric, such as the "Dornburger Gedichte" of

1828, to become fully aware of the difference between a poet of transcendence and a poet of immanence (pp. 196 f.). For Goethe, this world, our cosmos, contains all that we long for if we will only accept it. Faust's admonition to himself is an admonition to all who would transcend (lines 11,445 f.): "Er stehe fest und sehe hier sich um; Dem Tüchtigen ist diese Welt nicht stumm." Neither was it "stumm" for Klopstock, but it spoke most audibly when it spoke not of itself but as a sign of the divine.

NOTES

Complete sources appear in the Selected Bibliography following the Notes.

FOREWORD

1. *Die protestantische Theologie im 19. Jahrhundert* (Zollikon/Zürich, 1947), pp. 16 ff. See also, among many other possible references, Hans M. Wolff's sketch of Luther's view of the right nature of the state in *Die Weltanschauung der dt. Aufklärung*, pp. 12 ff.
2. Toward the end of the century there was keen recognition of this situation, as we see in the revolt against statism of men such as Edmund Burke, Herder, Lavater, Schlosser, and Klopstock. Cf. Detlev W. Schumann, "Neuorientierung im 18. Jahrhundert."

CHAPTER ONE

1. Brockes, born in Hamburg as the only son of a wealthy merchant, received his early education through tutors. In 1700 he entered the University of Halle as student of law; among his teachers was the famous Thomasius, an early proponent of the Enlightenment and the first professor to lecture in German at a German university. After his *Bildungsreise* through Germany, Italy, Switzerland, France, and Holland (1702–4), he returned to Hamburg, where he set himself up as a gentleman of leisure whose express intention was to marry a rich woman. But it was an active leisure: as a pastime and to improve his knowledge of languages he began to translate from the French (Boileau) and the Italian (Marino's *La strage degl'innocenti* [Slaughter of the Innocents], published in 1715 as *Verdeutschter Betlehemitischer Kindermord*). This led to his trying his hand at original verse. In 1712 he published an oratorio on the Passion in the style

of the late baroque (*Der für die Sünden der Welt gemarterte und sterbende Jesus*), which achieved immediate success and was set to music by many composers, among them Telemann, Händel, and J.S. Bach (seven passages in the *Johannes-Passion*). In 1714 B. finally found a suitable wife, and they had twelve children. Elected in 1720 to the Hamburg City Council, a position of great honor, he was entrusted with diplomatic missions to a number of European courts (Hamburg was an independent state). He remained in the service of his native city until the end of his life. In 1721 the first volume of *Irdisches Vergnügen* appeared and was received with delight by both public and critics. Stimulated by his success, B. continued to add volume after volume to this work as long as he lived; the ninth appeared in 1747, shortly after his death. Composing this work was not, however, the only literary activity of his middle and later years. In 1740 he brought out a translation of Pope's *Essay on Man* and in 1745 a translation of James Thomson's *The Seasons*, discovering, like many of his contemporaries, a temperamental affinity with English literature, though too late in his career to be decisively influenced by it.

Long before Brockes' death the need for a selection from his prolix œuvre was felt and the demand met by M.A. Wilkens and the poet Friedrich von Hagedorn with an *Auszug der vornehmsten Gedichte aus dem . . . Irdischen Vergnügen in Gott* (Hamburg, 1738), which contains selections from the first five parts. This work is now available in facsimile with an afterword by Dietrich Bode. Reclam UB 2015 contains poems from Parts I, II, IV, VII, with an afterword by Adalbert Elschenbroich. Kürschner's *Deutsche National-Litteratur*, Bd. 39, ed. Ludwig Fulda, has a representative eighty-five page selection with an extensive introduction. *Deutsche Literatur in Entwicklungsreihen, Reihe Aufklärung*, Bd. 2, ed. Fritz Brüggemann, contains sixteen philosophical poems, all from Parts I and II (text abridged, spelling modernized, punctuation changed). A very important article is Hans M. Wolff, "Brockes' Religion." Further bibliographical information in the Bode facsimile (pp. 14* f.) to which should be added, however, Christof Junker, *Das Weltraumbild in der dt. Lyrik;* Eric A. Blackall, *The Emergence of German as a Literary Language* (see index for Brockes); Karl Richter, "Die kopernikanische Wende in der Lyrik"; Paul Böckmann, "Anfänge der Naturlyrik."

2. In Wolff, "Brockes' Religion," pp. 1124 ff. Strauss's essay is based on the last (ninth) volume of *Ird. Vergn.*, which perhaps accounts for his conclusion; the first books give a quite different picture. Elschenbroich, Reclams UB 2015, 90, is the last critic I have noted who still cites Strauss with approval.

3. Quoted after Böckmann, "Anfänge der Naturlyrik," p.116. The metaphor of Nature as God's book appears numerous times in Brockes, and is also apparent in the titles of such poems as "Die himmlische Schrift" and "Das Welt-Buch."

4. According to Junker, *Weltraumbild*, p. 45. Copernicus' *De Revolutionibus Orbis* was published in 1543 but removed from the Index only in 1757. Poets, at any rate German poets, were almost as slow as the Church in accepting the new doctrine, though Gryphius, for example, has an impressive ten-line poem entitled "Über Nicolai Copernici Bild."

5. Arthur O. Lovejoy, *The Great Chain of Being;* Marjorie Hope Nicolson,

NOTES TO CHAPTER ONE

The Breaking of the Circle; Hans Blumenberg, "Kopernikus im Selbstverständnis der Neuzeit," and *Die Kopernikanische Wende* (Frankfurt a/M., 1965); Karl Richter, "Die kopernikanische Wende" (see note 1) and *Literatur und Naturwissenschaft,* which contains an extensive bibliography.
6. Cf. "Über das Erhabene," *Sämtliche Werke* 5, 796 f.
7. Cf. Wolff, "Brockes' Religion," pp. 1130 f. Wolff maintains, and quite convincingly, that nominalism alone explains the concept of wonder, Brockes' chief theme.
8. Haller was born in Bern, October 1708, the son of a jurist. The family was nominally, but not actually, entitled to hold office in the effective governing body of the highly exclusive Bernese oligarchy. H.'s fanatic zeal for learning manifested itself at an early age. We hear of him as a lad of ten preparing Greek and Hebrew lexica and composing some 2,000 biographical sketches of famous men, feats that in the light of his later accomplishments do not seem entirely improbable. We know that he diligently sought to perfect himself in the composition of poetry, taking Lohenstein as his model. These early efforts he later consigned to the flames.

At the age of fifteen he entered the University of Tübingen to study medicine, but finding Tübingen too frivolous for his taste, moved to Leiden two years later, where he studied under the renowned Boerhaave, the greatest physician of his day. He was granted the doctoral degree in 1727, at nineteen years of age, for a dissertation on the salivary glands. He now traveled to London and Paris to improve his medical knowedge and surgical techniques.

In 1728 he returned to Switzerland and studied for a time in Basel under the famous mathematician Bernoulli. Through literary friends here he gained a more intimate acquaintance with English poetry of a philosophical cast. In the summer of 1728 he undertook an extensive expedition into the Alps to study the flora. The literary fruit of this journey was his best known poem, "Die Alpen," which soon made him famous. Returning to Bern in 1729 to practice medicine, he married in 1731 Mariane Wyss, and they had three children. His efforts to obtain some official position in the Bernese republic having met with no success, he reluctantly accepted in 1736 a professorship at the recently founded university of Göttingen, where he taught for seventeen years, contributing greatly to the fame of that institution as a center of science.

His beloved wife Mariane died shortly after her arrival in Göttingen, and Haller abandoned poetry. He was then twenty-eight years old. Though he continued to revise with minute care each successive edition of his collected poems, *Versuch Schweizerischer Gedichte,* which first apeared in 1732 and reached its eleventh edition in 1777, the rest of his life belonged chiefly to science. He was tirelessly active in the fields of botany, anatomy, surgery, practical medicine, and especially physiology, in which his eight-volume *Elements* is a landmark.

In 1753 H. left Göttingen to accept a modest post in the Bernese government. He spent the rest of his life in the republic. Toward the end of his life he habitually consumed opium to deaden the pain of chronic illness. Observing the effect of the drug upon himself, he wrote a treatise on the subject shortly before his death in 1777. Though physiologically impossible, the legend that his last words referred to the cessation of his heartbeat—"il bat, il bat, il bat—plus"—is psychologically consistent. Bern neglected its most illustrious son to the end. Of him it may be said as it was of Leibniz that "he was buried more like a robber than what he really was, the ornament of his country." The exact site of his grave is today unknown. His magnificent private library was sold to the Austrian government. But if his homeland seemed determined to forget him, the rest of Europe mourned the passing of its last truly universal scholar and Germany the death of one of the most honored poets of German tongue in the first half of the eighteenth century.

The standard edition of H.'s poetical works is *Albrecht von Hallers Gedichte*, ed. Ludwig Hirzel, which also contains the standard life (pp.ii-dxxxvi); likewise reliable is the edition by Harry Maync (Leipzig, 1923; Frauenfeld, 1923), to which is appended an essay on the poet. The selection by Adalbert Elschenbroich in Reclams UB 8963/64 contains a useful Epilogue. H.'s *Tagebuch seiner Beobachtugen*, ed. Johann Georg Heinzmann, is available in Athenäum Reprints (Frankfurt a/M., 1971); vol. 2, pp. 219–319, contains passages from H.'s diary. The literature on H. is reviewed by Christoph Siegrist in *A.v.H.* Besides these, my own presentation is particularly indebted to Blackall, *Emergence*, pp. 259 ff.; Eduard Stäuble, *A.v.H.: Über den Ursprung des Übels;* the following articles by Karl S. Guthke: "A.v.H.—der Arzt mit der 'poetischen Krankheit' "; "Zur Religionsphilosophie des jungen A.v.H."; "Der junge A.v.H. und die Bibel"; "Hallers Shakespeare-Bild"; and Werner Kohlschmidt, "Hallers Gedichte und die Tradition." The following studies have also been consulted: Margarete Hochdoerfer, *The Conflict between the Religious and the Scientific Views of Albrecht von Haller;* Karl Fehr, *Die Welt der Erfahrung und des Glaubens: eine Deutung des "Unvollkommenen Gedichts über die Ewigkeit"* (Frauenfeld, n.d. [1956]); Giorgio Tonelli, *Poesia e filosofia in A.v.H.;* Richard Toellner, *A.v.H.* Karl Richter, *Literatur und Naturwissenschaft,* appeared after the section on H. had been written. Subsequent study of this work has persuaded me that it would not have changed my view of H. substantially. The essay by K.S. Guthke, "Andacht im Künstlichen Paradies: A.H.s 'Morgen-Gedanken,' " in: *Deutsche Barocklyrik: Gedichtinterpretationen von Spee bis Haller,* ed. M. Bircher and A.M. Hass (Bern and Munich, 1973), pp. 327–47, also appeared too late to make use of here.

9. Cf. Guthke's article in *Neue Sammlung 5.* Richard Toellner, *Einheit im Denken,* has challenged this view; in fact, T. wrote his 228-page study to attempt to prove the contrary. The trouble with T.'s book is that, despite taking into consideration all the literature on H. (his bibliography lists 589 titles!), the author does not read poetry as poetry but as documentary evidence proving a preconceived thesis.

10. From a diary entry; quoted after Stäuble, *Ursprung,* pp. 48 f.

11. See Kohlschmidt, p. 215.

12. Quoted after Basil Willey, *The Eighteenth Century Background,* pp.63 f.

13. James Boswell, *The Life of Samuel Johnson,* ed. E. Fuller (New York, 1960), pp. 109, 149, 237.

14. Ibid., pp. 208 f.

15. See, e.g., verses 121–30; 131–40; 191–200; 271–80; 401–10.

NOTES TO CHAPTER ONE

16. Quoted after Guthke, "Hallers Shakespeare-Bild," p. 92.
17. Cf. Peter Gay, *The Enlightenment: An Interpretation* 1, 98 ff.
18. This is the reading of the first two editions: Haller then changed "der Glaube" to "der Priester."
19. Eduard Stäuble's analysis, "A.v.H.—der Dichter zwischen den Zeiten," leaves the important questions unanswered.
20. If we may take Karl Barth as our guide, it is Brockes, not Haller, who is in this respect a "representative man of the eighteenth century": "Allen repräsentativen Menschen des 18. Jahrhunderts ist eigen eine naive starke Überzeugung von der Überlegenheit ihres menschlichen Selbstbewusstseins gegenüber der Totalität dessen, was . . . irgendwie draussen ist. Sie wissen: ihr Erkennen, ihr Wollen und Fühlen wird dem da draussen in irgend einer Form sicher beikommen" *(Die protestanische Theologie im 19. Jahrhundert*, p. 54). It is just this unshakeable conviction that Haller lacks.
21. Kleist was born in March 1715 in Zeblin, Pomerania, of an ancient noble family distinguished for its military men. He entered the University of Königsberg as a student of law in 1731. Unable to find suitable employment after leaving the university, K. became an officer in the Danish army, but with the ascension to the throne of Frederick II in 1740 he was recalled from foreign service and made second lieutenant in an infantry regiment garrisoned in Potsdam. Here, while in hospital recuperating from a wound received in a duel, he formed an enduring friendship with the poet Ludwig Gleim and under his influence began to devote himself seriously to poetry. The spiritual bleakness of garrison life under the strict eye of Frederick weighed heavily upon him, and though it was looked upon as "almost a shame" for a Prussian officer to write verse, it was in Potsdam in the years 1746–49 that he composed "Der Frühling," the poem for which he lives in German literature. K. was a professional soldier, not a professional man of letters. Toward the end of his life he became fast friends with Lessing and is generally reputed to be the model for Major Tellheim in *Minna von Barnhelm*. The letters of his later years often reveal a longing for death, preferably on the battlefield. The gods granted him his wish. He died of wounds received while leading a charge at the battle of Kunersdorf (August 1759), one of the Frederick's most disastrous defeats. Lessing wrote to Gleim: "Meine Traurigkeit über diesen Fall ist eine sehr wilde Traurigkeit. . . . Er hatte drei, vier Wunden schon; warum ging er nicht? Es haben sich Generals mit wenigern und kleinern Wunden unschimpflich beiseite gemacht. Er hat sterben *wollen*. Vergeben Sie mir, wenn ich ihm zu viel thue!"
    The standard edition of Kleist's works, edited by August Sauer, is in three volumes; vols. 2 and 3 contain letters from and to the poet. The critical literature on Kleist is very scant.
22. Gellert was born in Hainichen (Saxony), the ninth child of an impecunious Lutheran pastor, and educated at the "Fürstenschule" St. Afra in Meissen and at the University of Leipzig, where he studied theology and philosophy, then French and English. Gottsched was one of his teachers and Gellert a contributor to one of Gottsched's periodicals (called *Belustigungen des Verstandes und Witzes)*, modeled on the extremely popular English moral weeklies. In 1745, when a group of young Gottschedians became alienated from the master and founded their own periodical under

the title of *Neue Beiträge zum Vergnügen des Verstandes und Witzes* (the famous *Bremer Beiträge*, so called because published in Bremen), Gellert was one of the important contributors. Gellert never entered the ministry, but became a professor at Leipzig. He was probably the most popular and influential teacher of his time. Goethe, who was one of his students, called him "Gewissensrat für ganz Deutschland." He taught what we would today call composition and also lectured to packed halls on such topics as "Why it is not good to have a foreknowledge of one's fate," "On the influences of belles lettres on our hearts and morals," "To what extent the rules of eloquence and poetry are of use," and "Advice of a father upon sending his son to the university." It is very indicative of Gellert's modest and rather timid nature that upon being offered a regular professorship in 1761 (he was at that time an "ausserordentlicher Professor," something like a permanent lecturer) with a far better salary, he refused both money and honor, saying that he might be able to fulfill the office to the satisfaction of others but not to his own. Though he corresponded with many women and was a great favorite with them, Gellert never married. He died at the age of fifty-four, mourned by the German nation as no poet before him and few since. He was by far the most widely read German author of his day, and his works were also translated into a number of European languages. Frederick the Great, who had a low opinion of contemporary German poetry and scholarship, offered him a handsome left-handed compliment: "Der Mann gefällt mir," he told his adjutant after a famous interview with the poet. "Hätten wir nur mehr von der Art.—Gottsched? Er hat mich ebenso abgestossen, wie Gellert mich angezogen hat. Gottsched ist ein aufgeblasener Frosh—und ein lederner Geselle dazu. Gellert hat meinen ganzen Beifall. C'est le plus raisonable de tous les savants allemands."

Besides the *Fabeln und Erzählungen*, his most famous work, Gellert wrote hymns, plays, a novel *(Das Leben der schwedischen Gräfin von G. . . .)*, a treatise on letter-writing, a Latin dissertation on the fable, and other works, besides carrying on a tremendous correspondence. The *Fabeln und Erzählungen* are available in a "historisch-kritische Ausbage," edited by Siegfried Scheibe, as well as in a reliable edition with an afterword by Herbert Klinckhardt, which also contains the *Geistliche Oden und Lieder* in their entirety. Kürschner's *Dt. Nat-Lit.*, 43/1, edited by Franz Muncker, with a thirty-four page introduction, contains all the *Fabeln und Erzählungen* and a selection from the *Geistliche Oden und Lieder*. The second half of the recent monograph by Carsten Schlingmann, *Gellert, eine literarhistorische Revision*, is useful and informative, though somewhat lacking in incisiveness. The study by Allesandro Pellegrini, "Die Krise der Aufklärung," is extremely well-informed but tiresomely verbose. Penetrating, if rather too pat, is the article by Wolfgang Martens, "Über Weltbild und Gattungstradition bei Gellert."

23. Gellert, *Sämmtliche Schriften*, 4, 78. Blackall, *Emergence*, p.205, also quotes this passage in his discussion of Gellert's prose. Gellert himself alludes to the passage from Pope ("nameless graces") in a footnote, p. 79.

24. Cf. Muncker, *Dt. Nat.-Lit.*, 43/1, 29. Richardson, over whose novels he wept copiously, Gellert called "Ehre des menschlichen Geschlechts und

Fürst der Romandichter!" According to Schlingmann, 140 f., it is not true, however, that G. translated *Pamela*, as is often stated; neither can the *Schwedische Gräfin* be regarded as an imitation of Richardson.

25. Beethoven composed six *Gellertlieder*, and Haydn likewise set six passages from his works. Carl Philipp Emanuel Bach provided musical settings for all fifty-four of the *Geistl. Oden u. Lieder.* Many other composers followed suit. According to Max Friedländer, *Das deutsche Lied im 18. Jahrhundert*, as cited by Schlingmann, p. 148, "keine einzige Lieder-Sammlung eines deutschen Dichters [ist] als Ganzes so oft in Musik gesetzt worden, wie die der Gellertschen Oden und Lieder."

CHAPTER TWO

1. Hagedorn, Haller's precise contemporary, was born in Hamburg in 1708. The family belonged to the old but lesser nobility. The poet's father, a highly cultivated man, was in the service of the Danish crown. Young H. grew up in an artistically lively atmosphere of books, music, and painting and was encouraged by his father in his early literary efforts. At eighteen, he entered the university of Jena as a student of law, but he seems to have neglected law for ancient and modern languages. In 1729 he published his first collection of verse, which like Haller's bore the word "Versuch" in the title and like that of a number of his contemporaries the word "Nebenstunden" in the subtitle. This immature production, which the poet was soon to regret, was called *Versuch einiger Gedichte, oder erlesene Probe poetischer Nebenstunden.*

The turning point in H.'s life came shortly afterward when he obtained the post of private secretary to the Danish ambassador to the Court of St. James and spent two years in London. These years were as decisive for H.'s development as Haller's English journey was for his. His ideal both of poetry and society remained for the rest of his life strongly under the influence of this experience. He came home "half an Englishman," as he said himself, and the London years, he later told the Swiss critic Bodmer, were the only ones he would ever wish to relive. England he always mentions in the same breath with "freedom." In 1733 H. became secretary to the "English Court," a British commercial enterprise in Hamburg. The post allowed him much leisure for reading, writing, and the cultivation of social pleasures, to which he was addicted. His wife contributed a further English quality to the atmosphere in which he lived, as she was the daughter of an English tailor living in Hamburg. He had married, however, more in the hope of coming into a tidy sum than out of Anglophilia. In this he was disappointed, and he was never free of financial worries. Much given to the joys of the table, he suffered in his later years from gout. He died of dropsy in 1754 at the age of forty-six, widely honored and sincerely mourned.

The most complete edition of H.'s works, which also contains letters and a biography of the poet, is by Johann Joachim Eschenburg, 5 vols., Hamburg, 1800. I have used *Des Herrn Friedrichs von Hagedorn Poetische Werke in drei Theilen*, Hamburg, bey Johann Carl Bohn, 1769. Kürschner's *Deutsche National-Litteratur*, vol. 45, ed. Franz Muncker,

NOTES TO CHAPTER TWO

Stuttgart, n.d. [1894], contains a useful introduction and a generous selection (136 pages) from all of H.'s work; Reclams UB 1321–23, ed. Alfred Anger, contains a representative selection, a good afterword, and a short bibliography. The most important monograph on H. is Karl Epting, *Der Stil in den lyrischen und didaktischen Gedichten F.v.H.s;* the publication by Karl S. Guthke, "F.v.H. un das literarische Leben," throws much light on what the editor calls "the literary seed-bed of the poet's work." Hagedorn is one of several important eighteenth-century German poets whose work still awaits thorough investigation.

2. Information gleaned from H.'s letters to Bodmer, Guthke, "F.v.H. und das literarische Leben."
3. My characterization of H.'s aesthetics follows in general that of Epting.
4. See Rudolf Wittkower, "Imitation, Eclecticism, and Genius," on which I am dependent for my information.
5. Hagedorn's treatment of the story has been investigated by Bertha Reed Coffman, *Modern Philology* 48 (1953): 186 ff.
6. See Alfred Anger, *Literarisches Rokoko,* pp. 1 f.
7. See Heinz Schlaffer, *Musa iocosa,* pp 10 ff. and 124 ff.
8. Cf. Gottfried Stix, *F.v.H.,* pp. 18 f.; Günther Muller, *Lied,* p. 167, finds in H. "das Ethos . . . des ausgeprägten rationalen Seelenliedes."
9. The best known and most reprehensible attack on the singers of wine and gallantry came somewhat later (1752) and stemmed from the youthful Christoph Martin Wieland—an irony of literary history, since Wieland was soon to become Germany's foremost rococo poet and to hang his head in shame at his earlier pietistic enthusiasms. Though Wieland's polemics were not directed specifically against H. (but rather against Gleim and Uz), they are indicative of the *kind* of criticism to which the ethos of the new rococo poetry was subject. Cf. *Sämtliche Werke von J.P. Uz,* ed. A. Sauer, pp. xxv ff.
10. The "darling place" or *locus amoenus,* where one is sheltered from the world and can lead a simple life of pure feeling and high thinking, is one of the primary "purely formal determining factors" of rococo literature according to Alfred Anger, "Landschaftsstil des Rokoko," pp. 151 ff. The topos is ancient; it would seem to have gained such a firm foothold in rococo writing through the introduction of "Arcadia" into the genre of jesting erotic poetry. Cf. Schlaffer, pp. 38 ff.
11. See Guthke, "F.v.H. und das literarische Leben," pp. 86 and 101.
12. Gleim was born in Ermsleben near Halberstadt in 1719, the son of a Prussian tax officer. After attending school in Wernigerode, he entered, almost penniless, the university of Halle in 1738 as a student of law. Here he met Johann Peter Uz and Johann Nikolaus Götz, both poets and both soon to become devotees of the anacreontic manner. These three, together with the somewhat older Immanuel Jakob Pyra and Samuel Gotthold Lange, are sometimes referred to as the "Halle poets" or "Hallische Schule." All studied under Alexander Gottlieb Baumgarten, the founder of the "science" of aesthetics, or under his disciple Georg Friedrich Meier, both of whom were partisans of the poetic theories of Bodmer and Breitinger. Halle was the center of German pietism, but both Gleim and Uz were strongly antipietistic, perhaps because they had been overindoctrinated. Gleim left Halle in 1740, and after holding positions as tutor

303

and as secretary to various Prussian princes and generals, had the good fortune to become, in 1749, secretary of the cathedral chapter in Halberstadt and some time later also canon of a religious foundation (Stift Walbeck near Magdeburg). With his living thus assured and with light duties, he was able to devote his leisure to the arts of poetry and friendship. Gleim knew personally almost all German men of letters of his day and corresponded with most of them. Many he also helped financially, harbored in his home, and conscientiously advised, always watching jealously over their loyalty. How strange it is to think that "Father Gleim," whose work is so dimmed by time that it takes a powerful effort of the imagination to understand how it could have ever been appreciated, welcomed into his home Heinrich von Kleist, a poet who seems to us as modern as though he had been born in the twentieth century!

Women played only a peripheral role in Gleim's emotional life. He never married, though he came perilously close to it once. Besides friendship—for men—and poetry, his great enthusiasm was Frederick the Great, whom he referred to as "der Einzige." He was the most loyal of Prussians. In 1785 he was finally granted an audience with the King and later managed to acquire the hat Frederick had worn on that memorable occasion to add to his large collection of pious mementoes. As an old man and half-blind, Gleim still dictated verses and made literary plans. He died in February 1803, a few weeks before Klopstock, whom he numbered among his dearly beloved. He was buried in his own garden, and urns inscribed with the names of his friends and the dates of their death were placed about his grave.

Gleim wrote out of an inner urge, compulsively. "Er hätte ebensowohl des Atemholens entbehrt als des Dichtens und Schenkens," Goethe writes in the tenth book of *Dichtung und Wahrheit*. Yet he was not, strictly speaking, a professional man of letters. Rather, he was a highly gifted dilettante who wrote for his friends' and his own amusement and perhaps edification. "Immer schrieb ich nur für einen Freund," he explained to a correspondent, and there is every reason to believe him. It was a way of giving himself, an extension of his cult of friendship. Most of his works were published at his own expense, and he generally gave them away or sold them for charitable purposes. He did not collect his writings, though he carefully revised some of them; the extensive three-volume edition by Wilhelm Körte (Halberstadt, 1811–13, supplementary vol., 1841) contains only about a third of G.'s total production. This edition is quite unreliable. There are critical editions of *Versuch in Scherzhaften Liedern und Lieder* (based on the first printings of 1744/45 and 1749), by Alfred Anger and of *Preussische Kriegslieder von einem Grenadier*, by August Sauer. Kürschner's *Dt. Nat.-Lit.*, Bd. 45, ed. Franz Muncker (Stuttgart, 1894), contains a representative selection (111 pages) from G.'s work; especially to be recommended for its excellent afterword and careful editing is the selection in Reclams UB 2138/39, ed. Jürgen Stenzel (Stuttgart, 1969). The *Briefwechsel zwischen Gleim und Uz*, ed. Carl Schüddekopf, contains extremely useful annotations.

13. *Die deutsche anakreotische Dichtung.*
14. *Gesammelte Schriften 5*, p. 206.
15. "Deutsche Rokoko-Dichtung," pp. 618 f.

16. Alfred Anger, *Literarisches Rokoko*, p.36. This view seems to be widely held.
17. Pointed out by Jürgen Stenzel, Reclams UB 2138/39, 161.
18. *Geschichte des deutschen Verses*, pp.46 f.
19. See *Ewald von Kleist's Werke*, ed. A. Sauer, 1. Theil, pp.xx f.
20. Cf. Schlaffer, pp. 39 ff.
21. On Gleim's place in the history of the German art ballad, see Wolfgang Kayser, *Geschichte der deutschen Ballade;* Walter Müller-Seidel in *Wege zum Gedicht II*, pp.17 ff.; Walter Falk, "Die Anfänge der deutschen Kunstballade."
22. Quoted after Kayser, *Ballade*, p. 73.
23. Cf. *Kriegslieder*, ed. Sauer, p.vi.
24. The Germans first became acquainted with this strophe through a translation of the *Spectator* (No.70) by Gottsched's wife. Addison there lauds the ballad of Chevy Chase, quoting the appreciations of Ben Jonson and Sir Philip Sidney. A few others had used the form before Gleim. He was in turn emulated by Chr. F. Weisse, Gerstenberg, and Lavater.
25. Quoted after Erich Schmidt, *Lessing*, 2d ed. (Berlin, 1899), p. 324.
26. The dissertation by Helena Rosa Zeltner, *Johann Peter Uz*, written under the direction of E. Staiger, is unfortunately far from filling this desideratum.
27. *Briefwechsel zwischen Gleim und Uz*, p.24 (letter of 26 June 1751).
28. Cf. Johann Nikolaus Götz, *Die Gedichte Anakreons*, pp.29* ff.
29. On this question see Karl S. Guthke, *Die Mythologie der entgötterten Welt*, chapter II, "Der Alptraum der Vernunft," pp. 51 ff.
30. Cf. Zeman, p. 213.
31. In *Dt. Nat.-Lit.*, 135/1, 269 ff.

CHAPTER THREE

1. See Gerhard Kaiser, *Klopstock, Religion und Dichtung*, pp. 94 ff., for a discussion of this problem, which we will return to in connection with Klopstock.
2. Cf. Lawrence Mardsen Price, *English Literature in Germany*, pp. 113 ff.
3. Cited after Manfred Windfuhr, *Die barocke Bildlichkeit*, p. 440.
4. A selection from Arnold's work is available in *Gottfried Arnold in Auswahl*, ed. Erich Seeberg, 501 pp., 74 pp. of poems (referred to as "Seeberg"). Besides the editor's introduction to this volume, I have consulted the following secondary literature on A.: Hermann Dörries, *Geist und Geschichte bei G.A.;* Traugott Stählin, *G.A.s geistliche Dichtung;* Roger Friedrich, *Studien zur Lyrik G.A.s.* The literature dealing directly with A.'s poetry is very limited.
5. By "unparteiisch" A. means "open-minded." His work is not a defense of heretics but an attack on heretic-makers.
6. A second edition appeared in 1701, together with an *Anderer Theil der Göttlichen Liebes-Funcken*. As the second part of *Das Geheimnis der Göttlichen Sophia oder Weisheit* (Leipzig, 1700) (in prose) there appeared *Poetische Lob- und Liebes-Sprüche* (PLL) and *Neue Göttliche Liebes-Funcken*, both of which contain a goodly percentage of adaptations of poems by other hands.

NOTES TO CHAPTER THREE

Finally, in 1704 in Frankfurt there appeared *Gottfried Arnolds Neuer Kern wahrer Geistes-Gebete*. Affixed to this book of prayers is a "Kern recht-geistlicher Lieder," a hymnal containing 30 entries by Arnold, the other 187 being by other hymnists. (Bibliographical information after Stählin, pp. 119 ff., who gives complete titles of works here cited in abbreviated form.)

7. Cf. Stählin, pp. 63 ff.; Friedrich, pp. 117 ff.

8. Cf. Friedrich, p. 38.

9. Gerhard Tersteegen (accent on second syllable) was born November 25, 1697, in the tiny principality of Mörs on the Lower Rhine, a Reformed protestant enclave, and died in 1769 at Mühlheim an der Ruhr. He was the eighth child of a well-to-do tradesman of religious mind. Gerhard, though he early showed a strong predilection for learning, was apprenticed at the age of fifteen to a merchant in Mühlheim. Here he came under the influence of the "awakened" and received his first deeper religious impressions. Though not inimical to the church, he withdrew from public worship and refused to take the eucharist along with known sinners. A severe attack of colic while alone in the woods made him think he was about to die; he begged God to give him time to prepare himself for death, whereupon his pains disappeared. T. forthwith promised himself wholly to the Lord, gave up his merchant calling because it interfered with his meditations, and became a ribbon-maker, leading a lonely, retired, and extremely ascetic life. All he could spare he gave to the poor. This way of living made him "so vergnügt wie kein König." But a five-year period of "dryness" set in, and relief did not come until 1724. Upon this occasion he formally signed his life over to Jesus in a testament written in his own blood. His life now began to turn more outward: he took charge of the education of his nieces and nephews, accepted the presence of a companion in his room, ceased to chastise himself so severely. Now he also began to write, strongly under the influence of the French mystics (Poiret, Labadie, Bernières Louvigny, Mme. Guyon), some of whose works, as well as that of his famous countryman, Thomas à Kempis, he translated. In 1727 the first collection of his poetry, *Geistliches Blumengärtlein inniger Seelen*, appeared. It was to see seven editions within T.'s lifetime. 1733, 1735, and 1753, the three volumes of his *Auserlesene Lebensbeschreibungen heiliger Seelen* were published, depicting the lives of quietistic men and women of various religious orders, mostly from the time of the Counter-reformation. Though pronouncedly ecumenical, T. was not tempted to become a Catholic; rather he regarded the pious men and women, the story of whose lives he related, as Protestants within the Catholic church. The *Auserlesene Lebensbeschreibungen* are a kind of pendant to G. Arnold's *Unparteiische Kirchen- und Ketzer-Historie*. T. greatly admired Arnold, along with the French Reformed mystic Pierre Poiret (1646–1719), his spiritual father.

T. was an extremely popular preacher, much too popular for his own liking. In 1728, he felt obligated to give up his ribbon-making and devote himself entirely to spiritual ministrations. Rich friends forced as much money on him as he would accept; what he did not use for his modest needs, he gave to the poor. His influence was widespread, though he never attempted to found any kind of separate church. He had followers in Holland (which he often visited), on the Middle Rhine, in the Palatinate, in Nuremberg, in Frisia, Denmark, Sweden, even in Pennsylvania. For ten years (1740–50) T.'s "Übungen," as he called his own peculiar way of conducting divine service, were officially forbidden on the Lower Rhine. But when he began to preach again, more people than ever streamed to hear him. His homilies were collected under the title of *Geistliche Brosamen* (1769–73).

A man of independent mind, T. was cool toward the Herrnhuter, though Zinzendorf himself made an effort to win him over. His independence is also shown in his review of the works of Frederick the Great, in which he exclaims: "O ihr Gern-Philosophen de Sanssouci, werdet doch erst Philosophen de grand souci oder ihr betrüget euch jämmerlich!" To this the Prussian monarch is said to have remarked: "Können das die Stillen im Lande?"

There is no critical edition of Tersteegen's works. Wilhelm Nelle, *G. Tersteegens Geistliche Lieder*, contains sixty-eight pages of "Hymnologische Nachweisungen zu den Liedern nebst Charakteristik der bedeutenderen." Unfortunately, Nelle modernizes spelling, punctuation, and to some degree vocabulary. *G.T. Eine Auswahl aus seinen Schriften*, ed. Walter Nigg, contains both poetry and prose, as well as a sampling of T.'s letters. I have also used *Life and Character of G.T.*, trans. Samuel Jackson. The *Realencyclopädie für prot. Theologie u. Kirche*, 3d ed. (Leipzig, 1904) has seven and a half pages on T. At least four dissertations deal with T.: Heinrich Forsthoff, *Die Mystik in T.s Liedern* (Diss. Bonn, 1919); Rudolf Zwetz, *Die dichterische Persönlichkeit G.T.s* (Diss. Jena; Halle, 1915); Gertrud Wolters, *G.T.s geistliche Lyrik* (Diss. Marburg, 1929); Cornelis Pieter van Andel, *Gerhard Tersteegen* (Proefschrift Utrecht; Wageningen, 1961) which contains an extensive bibliography. Of these I have consulted only Wolters and Andel. The article by Waldtraut Ingeborg Sauer-Geppert, "Zur Mystik in den Liedern G.T.s," treats only those twelve hymns included in the *Evangel. Kirchengesangbuch* (1951). Albrecht Goes, *Freude am Gedicht* (Frankfurt a/M., 1952), contains an interpretation of "Andacht bei nächtlichem Wachen."

10. *Life and Character of G.T.*, trans. S. Jackson, p. 40. Cf. Nigg, *Auswahl*, pp. 31, f.

11. Schleiermacher, himself educated by the Herrnhuter and intimately acquainted with their mystical cast of thought, writes in the second of the *Reden über Religion:* "Die religiösen Gefühle lähmen ihrer Natur nach die Tatkraft des Menschen und laden ihn ein zum stillen, hingegebenen Genuss; daher auch die religiösesten Menschen, denen es an anderen Antrieben zum Handeln fehlte und die nichts waren als religiös, die Welt verliessen und sich ganz der müssigen Beschauung ergaben."

12. Cf. August Langen, *Der Wortschatz des dt. Pietismus*, pp.171 f.

13. The following passage from "Abendgedanken einer gottseligen Seele" (Nelle, No. 32, p. 77) makes the second usage clear:

> Da nun der Leib sein Tageswerk vollendet,
> Mein Geist sich auch zu seinem Werke wendet,
> Zu beten an, zu lieben inniglich,
> Im stillen Grund, mein Gott, zu schauen dich.

Die Dunkelheit ist da und alles schweiget,
Mein Geist vor dir, O Majestät, sich beuget;
Ins Heiligtum, ins Dunkle, kehr ich ein,
Herr, rede du, lass mich ganz stille sein.

This passage is one more exemplification of the experience given perfect formulation in "Andacht bei nächtlichem Wachen."

14. "Nikolaus Ludwig, Graf und Herr von Zinzendorf, Pottendorf u.f. geboren 1700, ging im Jahr 1760 als ein Erobrer aus der Welt, desgleichen es wenige, und im verflossenen Jahrhundert keinen wie ihn gegeben. Er konnte sich rühmen, dass er 'in Herrnhut und Herrenhag, Herrendick und Pilgerruh, Ebersdorf, Jena, Amsterdam, Rotterdam, London, Oxford, Berlin, in Grönland, St. Cruz, St. Thomas, St. Jean, Barbesien, Palästina, Surinam, Savannah in Georgien, Carolina, Pensylvanien, Guinea, Lievland, Estland, Litauen, Russland, am weissen Meer, in Lappland, Norwegen, in der Schweiz, auf der Insel Man, in Aethiopien, Persien, bei den Boten der Heiden zu Land und See' Gemeinen oder Anhänger habe. . . . "

These words of Herder, famous in the literature on Zinzendorf, indicate something of the tremendous restless energy of this remarkable man, whose life one despairs of summarizing in a thumbnail sketch. As a Reichsgraf (Imperial Count), Z., whose family was of Austrian origin, belonged to the highest nobility. His father, who died shortly after Nikolaus Ludwig's birth, was Privy Councilor and Minister at the court of Saxony. The child was raised by his maternal grandmother, a talented and learned woman of deep religiosity, who corresponded (in Latin) with Leibniz, with whose ecumenical ideals she was in strong sympathy. "I have my principles from her," Z. said. At the age of ten, the boy was entered in the Pädagogium Regium in Halle to be educated for six years under the tutelage, direct and indirect, of August Hermann Francke, whose "Stiftungen" (Institutes) had made Halle a center of pietism. He was then sent to Wittenberg, the seat of strict Lutheran orthodoxy, to wean him, as his uncle and guardian put it, from his "pietistic grimaces." Here he was enrolled as a student of law, prohibited from attending lectures on theology, a stricture he was able to circumvent by private intercourse with the Wittenberg theologians and by reading Luther's works on his own. His ecumenical turn of mind evidenced itself here in his attempts to reconcile the inimical faculties of Wittenberg and Halle. There followed a journey to Paris by way of Holland. In Paris, Z. moved in the highest court circles, where he was something of a curiosity due to his unshakeable religious principles. Here, at the age of nineteen, he formed an intimate friendship with Cardinal de Noailles, archbishop of Paris and the most powerful prelate in France, who was approaching seventy. Upon returning to Germany, he married a Countess von Reuss and entered the service of the Saxon state under August the Strong. In Dresden, he made himself obnoxious and notorious by his criticism of the loose morals of the court, the formalistic nature of the established church, and the social evils of the day.

The founding of the community of Herrnhut, which was to spread Z.'s name to the ends of the earth, was accidental. Cryptoprotestants had a difficult time under the Habsburgs, who vigorously supported the Counterreformation, and refugee villages sprang up on the borders of the Habsburg Empire, especially of Bohemia, which had a strong Protestant tradition. Z. had, rather absentmindedly it seems, granted permission to a small group of Moravian refugees to settle on his estates in the Oberlausitz southeast of Dresden. When he later discovered how thoroughly at home they had made themselves, he energetically took the matter in hand and organized a religious community according to his own ideas. This was the beginning of Herrnhut, to which religious dissidents were to come not only from Bohemia but from all parts of Germany, seeking a place to live according to their own lights. The guiding principles of the community were tolerance, equality, freedom, self-dependence, and self-government. No one, including Catholics, was required to change his religion; serfs were freed, women placed on an equal footing with men. The Herrnhuter were united to each other and to Z. by brotherly love and a communal life. "Ein jeder Einwhohner in Herrnhut soll arbeiten und sein eigen Brot essen. Wenn er aber alt, krank und unvermögend ist, soll ihn die Gemeine ernähren." Inhumane behavior and dissoluteness were severely punished, but Z. was no ascetic: the members of the community were expected to lead a normal life. Marriages were largely intracommunal. The first settlers in Herrnhut were mainly workmen and artisans; later, persons of nobility were attracted, and a countess might be found living in the next room to a milkmaid.

Z. imbued the Herrnhuter with his own "Streiteridee," the will to transform belief into action. This showed itself above all in widespread missionary activity. Z. himself journeyed constantly, not only over most of Europe but also to the New World (the West Indies and Pennsylvania). In 1736 Z. was forced to leave Saxony on charges, not unfounded, that he was luring the inhabitants of neighboring Habsburg territories across the border. He left, taking part of his community with him, and founded a new colony in the Wetterau, east of Frankfurt am Main.

Theologically, Z. remained within the Lutheran church and was even at pains to have his orthodoxy officially recognized by submitting to an examination by a pastoral college. He enjoyed the protection of Friedrich Wilhelm I, King of Prussia, and became his private spiritual adviser.

After spending over five years in London (1749–55), where he attracted many followers, especially among the nobility, and strongly influenced John Wesley, the founder of Methodism, Z. returned to Germany, dying in Herrnhut in 1760. His leading modern biographer, Erich Beyreuther, from whose work the foregoing has been extracted, calls Z. "ein Genie des Herzens," "unbürgerlich und genial," one of the great "unprejudiced" who were willing to experiment with Christianity in an effort to find the way to men's hearts. Z.'s personal ethos finds characteristic expression in the following lines:

Ich war ein Zinzendorf, die sind nicht lebenswert,
Wenn sie ihr Leben nicht zu rechten Sachen brauchen:
Drum hat die Sorge mich beinahe ganz verzehrt,
Zu früh, und ohne Nutz der Erden, auszuhauchen.
Nun hiess ich gar ein Christ, verdoppeltes Gesetz!

NOTES TO CHAPTER THREE

Die Christen dürfen nicht verbrennen ohne leuchten.
Der Glaube, der nichts tut, ist ein verdammt Geschwätz.

Z.'s published writings comprise 20,000 pages. His poetry is found in the *Ergänzungsbände zu den Hauptschriften*, Bd. 2, which contains Z.'s *Teutsche Gedichte neue Auflage* (Barby, 1766) and the *XII. Anhang* (zum Gesangbuch der Evangelischen Brüdergemeinen), Ausgabe 1745 (Nos. 1863–2156), together with *Zugaben* I–IV, Ausgabe 1746–48, to this hymnal (Nos. 2157–2313). Besides G. Meyer's introduction to the poetry in this volume, I have used: Hans-Günther Huober, *Z.s Kirchenlieddichtung;* Wilhelm Bettermann, *Theologie und Sprache bei Z.;* Erich Beyreuther, *N.L.v.Z.;* Jörn Reichel, *Dichtungstheorie und Sprache bei Z.* Both Beyreuther and Reichel contain extensive bibliographies. My own discussion is heavily indebted to Reichel, without whose study I would not have ventured beyond barely mentioning Zinzendorf as a poet.

15. Cf. R.M. Browning, *German Baroque Poetry*, p.49.
16. Cf. Reichel, pp. 84 ff.
17. Immanuel Jacob Pyra was born on July 25, 1715, in Cottbus (Lausitz), the son of a Prussian official. His father, a lawyer, lost his position, leaving the family in very straitened circumstances. P.'s first love in literature seems to have been Lohenstein; in the gymnasium he became acquainted with the classics (his great love was Vergil) and turned from Lohenstein to Benjamin Neukirch. In 1734 he entered Halle, the seat of pietism, as a student of theology; he attended lectures by Joachim Lange, an opponent of Christian Wolff and the father of Samuel Gotthold Lange, who was to become his bosom friend. His chief interest still remained literature and the development of his own literary talent. Though bitterly poor, he was willing to go hungry in order to be able to send his parents part of his small stipend. His friend S.G. Lange, who was four years his senior, had founded a literary society in which Opitz, Haller, and Günther were regarded as models and Gottsched's *Critische Dichtkunst* as the Bible. Taking Gottsched (who had advocated rhymeless verse, especially in the epic) as his model, Pyra began a translation of the *Aeneid* in an eight-beat unrhymed meter and sent it to the "Literaturpapst" in Leipzig for criticism. Gottsched, as it turned out, had a good deal to criticize. This was the beginning of Pyra's antagonism toward Gottsched and his school and led in 1742/43 to his "Erweis, dass die Gottschedianische Sekte den Geschmack verderbe." Bodmer, on the other hand, praised Pyra as "einer der ersten Zeugen der Wahrheit, der aufstand." Lange became pastor in Laublingen near Halle, where Pyra joined him after leaving the university. In 1742 he was finally able to obtain a teaching post in Berlin, where he died at the height of his powers two years later, in July 1744.
      The fame of Pyra and Lange rests on *Thirsis und Damons Freundschaftliche Lieder*, 1st ed. 1745, ed. Bodmer; 2d, augmented ed. 1749, ed. S.G. Lange, available in *Deutsche Litteraturdenkmale des 18. und 19. Jarhrhunderts*, no. 22, ed. August Sauer (cited as Sauer), which also contains a "Neuer Anhang einiger Gedichte des seligen Immanuel Jacob Pyra," in which is included "Der Tempel der wahren Dichtkunst" (1737). The secondary literature on Pyra is not extensive: Gustav Waniek, *Immanuel Pyra und sein*

Einfluss, appears to be the only monograph devoted entirely to Pyra. Valuable discussion is found in Karl Viëtor, *Geschichte der deutschen Ode*, pp. 98 ff.; Günther Müller, *Geschichte des deutschen Lieds*, pp.168 ff.; Wolfdietrich Rasch, *Freundschaftskult und Freundschaftsdichtung*, pp. 152 ff.; Karl Ludwig Schneider, "Die Polemik gegen den Reim"; Claus Schuppenhauer, *Der Kampf um den Reim* (see index for page references). The article by William P. Hanson, "Lange, Pyra and 'ankreontische Tändeleien'," *German Life & Letters* 18 (1964/65): 81–90, is of little value.

18. See Christoph Siegrist, *Das Lehrgedicht der Aufklärung*, pp. 44 f. for a discussion of temple poems in the German Enlightenment.

19. Claus Schuppenhauer has unfolded the story in great detail.

20. Schuppenhauer, p. 182, is thus mistaken in saying "kein Franzose [wurde] in den 'Tempel der wahren Dichtkunst' aufgenommen." Who "der Francke, dessen Kiel Susannens Keuschheit pries" (V, 50) may be I have not been able to determine. One thinks of Paul Rebhuhn, but he was an Austrian active in Silesia.

21. Cf. Waniek, p. 38; Sauer, pp. xxx f.; Schuppenhauer, p. 175.

22. Cf. Marjorie Hope Nicolson, *Mountain Gloom and Mountain Glory*, pp. 281 ff.

23. Meier was a student of A.G. Baumgarten, the "founder" of aesthetics, at least insofar as he coined the term and sought to formulate a coherent theory that would place the study of the beautiful on the footing of an independent discipline. Meier, whose work apeared *before* Baumgarten's (in 1748–50), was not such a genial mind. Unlike Baumgarten, he still had a utilitarian view of art and was unable to keep aesthetics separate from ethics. See Armand Nivelle, *Kunst- und Dichtungstheorien zwischen Aufklärung und Klassik*, chapters I and II.

24. Friedrich Gottlieb Klopstock was born on July 2, 1724, in Quedlinburg, a small city on the edge of the Harz founded by Henry the Fowler around 930. He was the oldest of seventeen children. His father, a deeply religious man of independent temper, was a lawyer; his mother, whose life was spent in childbearing, was the daughter of a well-to-do merchant. Klopstock thus came from the upper burgher class. He was a healthy, active child, more interested in sports than studies. When his father decided to try his hand at gentleman farming, the family moved to the country, where K. spent two and a half golden years of his childhood. After the failure of this venture—which initiated the decline of the family fortune—the Klopstocks returned to Quedlinburg and young Friedrich entered the Gymnasium. His interest in his studies remained slight until (though Quedlinburg belonged to Prussia) he was fortunate enough to obtain a scholarship to Schulpforta, near Naumburg on the Saale, a Saxon royal academy for the education of privileged youth. A third of the scholars came from the nobility. (Schulpforta later sheltered another famous Friedrich: Friedrich Nietzsche.) The instruction at Schulpforta, which K. entered at the age of fifteen, was strictly Christian-humanistic; the life led by the pupils was modeled on that of Christian monasticism (the Fürstenschule was housed in a former convent) and exclusively masculine. The main emphasis was placed on ancient languages and the study of the Bible. The pupils were required to compose about 2,000 original Latin and Greek verses each year, an exercise that was later to

stand the poet in good stead. The language of instruction was Latin. It was not until around his seventeenth year that K. became aware that he might have a talent for poetry himself. His valedictory address (in Latin) delivered to his fellow students and his teachers upon leaving the academy in 1745, at the age of twenty-two, has become a famous document in German literary history. K. took as his topic the various treatments of epic poetry through the ages, ending with a veiled reference to himself as the future author of a great German epic poem. The *Messias*, which was to be his life work, had already taken shape in his mind. While at Schulpforta he had discovered the critical writings of Bodmer and Breitinger and had read the former's prose translation of *Paradise Lost* (he did not learn English until much later). The new view of poetry he found in the writings of the Swiss critics (they were largely inspired by the English, especially Shaftesbury and Addison) came to him as a revelation—imagination here once more came into its own and the ancient concept of the *poeta vates*, the poet as prophet and mouthpiece of the supernal, was renewed and vindicated. And K. felt himself to be just that: a *poeta vates*, a *heiliger Dichter*. The valedictory address shows that K. knew, besides Homer and Vergil, Tasso, Marino, and Milton, and that he had been fired by Pyra's *Tempel der wahren Dichtkuust*, but that, like his age in general (Pyra is an exception), he was ignorant of Dante. Milton is seen as the acme of Christian epic poetry.

In the autumn of 1745 K. entered the university of Jena as a student of theology, but remained only one semester before moving on to Leipzig, where his cousin Johann Christoph Schmidt was studying law. Leipzig was Gottsched's "feste Burg" and K. was already a follower of the Swiss, who were in the process of reducing this fortress to dust. His own work was to make the quarrel between Leipzig and Zürich nugatory. In Leipzig K. came in touch with an enthusiastic group of young *littérateurs*, the so-called Bremer Beiträger, who had split off from Gottsched and undertaken the publication of their own organ, which bore the typically eighteenth-century name of *Neue Beyträge zum Vergnügen des Verstandes und Witzes*, called, because published in Bremen, the *Bremer Beyträge* (1744–48). It was in the *B.B.* that the first three cantos of the *Messias* were published in 1748, an event that marks a distinct turning point in German poetry. Meanwhile K. was also producing his first odes and had fallen stubbornly in love with his first cousin, Maria Sophia Schmidt (the Fanny of his odes), the sister of his Leipzig roommate, and she was just as stubbornly refusing to succumb to his solicitations, while at the same time playing roguish rococo games with her languishing lover. Having run out of funds, K. took a position as private tutor to the sons of a rich uncle in Langensalza, the town where his vainly beloved also lived. Propinquity did not further his suit, though he was now, after the publication of the first three cantos of his epic, already almost famous and a declared "sacred poet." In fact, he was already the prisoner of his too-early fame, typed as a seraph while still very interested in most unseraphic pursuits, especially flirtations with any available girls, though his love for "Fanny" remained the theme of his exalted erotic odes.

The question of what to do in order to live while continuing his sacred task, the writing of the *Messias*, was gradually becoming acute.

Klopstock was a "Nur-Dichter," a man with one calling and that an irrevocable one. He felt, and what is much stranger, many agreed with him, that the world owed him a living so that he might reveal to the world the supernal message that had been entrusted to him. Bodmer, who had greeted the *Messias* with unbounded enthusiasm, seeing in K. the fulfillment of all his deepest aspirations for a new German poetry, and naively raising the poet himself to the ranks of the angels, invited K. to spend an indefinite period with him in Zürich and even advanced him 300 thaler to defray the expenses of the journey, a sum to be paid back, he implied, at the end of time.

Other offers also began to come in: teaching positions in Braunschweig and Berlin with the prospect of light duties, even an offer from Albrecht von Haller as a tutor to his son. But most promising, as K. was not slow to realize, was the prospect of a pension from Frederick V, King of Denmark, held out to him at the instigation of the King's Minister of Foreign Affairs, Johann Hartwig Ernst von Bernstorff, a Hanoverian nobleman who had read the famous three cantos in Paris.

Before this arrangement could be completed, however, K. made the trip to Zürich to visit Bodmer in July 1750. The outcome was tragicomic. Bodmer, whom it is hard to think of as anything but a rather pig-headed and naive old fool, in spite of his great services to German philology and criticism, expected K. to behave like an angel and found that he behaved like a normal young man with a strong interest in socializing, particularly with the girls. A rupture became inevitable. It was a case of plain jealousy: the pupil outshone the master most embarrassingly and refused, in addition, to play any other role than that of the lionized young poet full of self-assurance. And lionized he was. Zürich lay at his feet, the literary Zürich, that is, and the Zürich of feeling. It was the kind of worship K. had become accustomed to in the north, where he was already a legend among the "Empfindsamen," and his love for Fanny was discussed and mooned over as though he were a prince royal. Something of the atmosphere of those heady days we can recapture in the ode "Der Zürcher See" and in the famous letter of 4 August 1750 to Ewald von Kleist from Dr. Joh. Kaspar Hirzel, one of the members of the party on that most renowned of literary outings, the boat ride on the Lake of Zürich. While Bodmer continued to pout and even to dun K. for the 300 thaler, things began to take such a serious turn that the poet, in order not to see his cause discredited, made a sincere effort at reconciliation. Things were then patched up after a fashion. The whole affair must strike us as another example of K.'s martyrdom to his fame: because of his poem he could not afford to be himself; the persona conjured up by his poetry was in conflict with his true personality, and the latter had to be sacrificed to the former. This does not mean that K., in his poetry, was insincere; it means rather that his life had more sides than one saw in his poetry.

In Denmark, where K. was now awaited, there was some impatience. The poet finally left Zürich on St. Valentine's Day 1751, and returned to Quedlinburg, proceeding from there to Hamburg, where he intended to visit Hagedorn. It so happened that Hagedorn was not immediately available, and K. used the interval to call on one of his ardent admirers, Meta (Margaretha) Moller, who had been recommended to him by his close friend Giseke. This visit had far-reaching consequences: Meta, whose letters show her to have been a woman of education, character, and great charm, became the poet's wife in June 1754, after the consent of the bride's family had finally been gained. In the meantime, K. had taken up residence in Denmark. The generous stipend awarded by Frederick V (it later amounted to 800 thaler per annum) had no strings attached except that the poet should reside in Denmark and continue to write the *Messias*. (Extended visits to Germany seem to have been granted without a murmur.) K's relations with the royal house, which was one of the most pious and, though governing absolutely, one of the most liberal in Europe, were relatively democratic. Bernstorff, with whom K. at first lived, was a powerful figure at court and K.'s intimate friend. Altogether, the poet spent—with interruptions—almost twenty years in Denmark.

The marriage with Meta, which by her testimony and his was truly idyllic, lasted only four years; Meta died in childbed November 1758. Her unborn infant son was buried with her. The first years in Denmark were also marked by the death of that Kingdom's beloved Queen Louise, a daughter of George II of England. K. mourned the occasion in an ode startlingly entitled simply "An Den König," later retitled "Die Königin Luise." In 1755 the Copenhagen edition of the first ten cantos of the *Messias* appeared, and in 1756 K.'s first drama (if one can call it a drama), "Der Tod Adams," appeared. In 1762–64, K. visited Germany. It was during this time that he suddenly fell in love with a wealthy girl, Luise Sidonie Diedrich ("Done"). His hopes of marrying her seem to have been squelched by her father.

Upon returning to Denmark in 1764, K. actively entered into the life of the circle of German intellectuals residing in the northern Kingdom. Their influence on the cultural life of their adopted land was for a time decisive. Among them were Heinrich Wilhelm von Gerstenberg, lyricist, dramatist, critic, and founder of the so-called Bardendichtung; K.'s old friend of Leipzig days, Joh. Andreas Cramer, preacher to the court (appointed upon K.'s recommendation) and editor of a moral weekly, *Der nordische Aufseher*, to which K. was a frequent contributor; the fervent pietist Count Christian Günther zu Stolberg, privy councillor to the Queen Mother, whose sons Christian and Friedrich became poets and founding members of the "Göttinger Hain." K. often repaired to the house of the Stolbergs and became almost a second father to the sons. Characteristic for this circle was a lack of class distinction between burgher and noble. This was largely due to the influence of pietism, at that time very strong in Denmark, and its refusal to regard man in any light other than his relationship to God, before whom all are equal. We have already obvserved this attitude among the Herrnhuter. The years from July 1764 to June 1767, spent in Denmark, were devoted above all to "Bardendichtung" and the glorification of the fatherland. Connected with his patriotic enthusiasms is K.'s elaborate plan for the founding of a German Academy of Arts and Sciences under the protection of Emperor Joseph II in Vienna. Neither the Emperor nor his minister Kaunitz seems to have considered the plan very seriously and K. was, after high hopes, bitterly disappointed. This was also the period of still another love, albeit sight unseen, this time for Cäcilie Ambrosius, the daughter of a wealthy

Flensburg merchant, to whom K. addressed many letters. The affair remained secret and was revealed only long after the poet's death when a number of the letters were published. In 1766 Frederick V died and was succeeded by his much weaker son Christian VII, who in 1770 was manipulated to dismiss Bernstorff. K. followed his patron to Hamburg, which now became his permanent residence.

The first momentous event of the Hamburg years was the publication in 1771 of a carefully revised edition of the *Oden*, which had been appearing for years in periodicals or had been circulating in manuscript form among admirers. The collection bore the simple dedication "An Bernstorff"; there was no indication of author and indeed none was needed: all Germany knew who he was. In the next year Bernstorff, who had been recalled to Copenhagen, died. In 1773 the final cantos of the *Messias* appeared: K. had successfully completed his life's work.

Margrave Karl Friedrich of Baden, one of Germany's most enlightened and most German-minded princes, invited K. to Karlsruhe in 1774 with the rank and salary of *Hofrat*. The poet, uneasy about the fate of his Danish pension, was glad to accept. On the way to Karlsruhe, he paid a visit to his boundlessly enthusiastic disciples in Göttingen, the members of the "Hain," and stopped in Frankfurt to visit Goethe, who was already famous as the author of *Götz* and *Werther*. Goethe complained that K. seemed disinclined to talk about literary matters, preferring to discourse on skating and horseback riding, two of his favorite sports. The margrave received him with every courtesy, though the courtiers were shocked at his independent air and democratic manners. In Baden, K. finally had an opportunity to meet personally with the composer Gluck (en route from Paris to Vienna), of whose works he had long been passionately fond and with whom he had corresponded. Gluck set a number of K.'s odes to music. But the intrigue-ridden atmosphere of the Baden court was distasteful to K., and after a few months he took French leave. Even this impolite gesture the margrave did not hold against him; his pension was not discontinued, and prince and poet remained friends until K.'s death.

Upon returning to Hamburg K. moved into the house of Johanna Elisabeth Winthem, a niece of Meta's, whose husband's fortunes were at a low ebb. Tongues wagged, but K. and "Windeme" paid slight attention. Upon the death of Johanna Elisabeth's husband the pair married (1791).

K. took a consuming interest in the French Revolution. His high hopes for the realization of its stated ideals had a rejuvenating effect on the aging poet. He entered into correspondence with the Duke de la Rochefoucauld and composed an ode to him; he was made an honorary citizen of the French Republic by the National Assembly. But K. was a moderate, a Girondist, not a Jacobin, and when the Terror came and especially when the French broke their word never to wage wars of aggression, K. turned away like a jilted lover. It was a hard blow. His odes on the Revolution, for and against, which are basically odes to freedom, constitute a large part of his later poetry.

K. outlived his immediate influence and his popularity, but not his fame. His last years are like a monument raised to himself: he continued to compose odes and produce essays and began to make extremely successful translations from Greek and Latin prose and poetry. One of his best odes was written in 1802, the year before his death. He was still full of projects. The "Ausgabe letzter Hand" of his works began to appear in 1798, though it was not finally completed until 1817. He died March 14, 1803, and was buried in Ottensen near Hamburg above the Elbe beside his beloved Meta: "Saat von Gott gesäet, dem Tage der Garben zu reifen." His funeral was a state occasion—never before had a German poet been buried with such honors. The first volume in the first critical edition of K.'s complete works appeared only in 1975. The standard edition of the odes is (at least for the time being) *Friedrich Gottlieb Klopstocks Oden*, ed. Franz Muncker and Jaro Pawel (cited as M-P); Kürschner's *Dt. Nat.-Lit.*, Bd. 47, contains a selection of 107 odes with highly useful annotations as well as 140 epigrams; *F.G. Klopstock, Werke in einem Band*, ed. Karl August Schleiden, contains 78 odes, 42 epigrams; the 3d ed., called *F.G. Klopstock, Ausgewählte Werke*, contains 112 odes, 57 epigrams; *F.G. Klopstock, Oden*, ed. Karl Ludwig Schneider, contains 57 poems with notes and Epilogue; I have also used *Klopstocks sämmtliche Werke*, 10 vols. (Göschen: Leipzig, 1854–55). The standard biography remains Franz Muncker, *F.G. Klopstock*; Kürschner's *Dt. Nat.-Lit.*, Bd. 46, also contains a life of the poet (136 pp.) by R. Hamel; *Briefe von und an K.*, ed. J.M. Lappenberg, contains 227 letters with annotations. Of the older critical literature I have found invaluable Heinrich Dünzter's *Erläuterungen zu den deutschen Klassikern*, which contains six fascicles on K.'s odes.

More recent critical literature includes: Karl Viëtor, *Geschichte der deutschen Ode*; Max Kommerell, *Der Dichter als Führer*; Ernst Kaussmann, *Der Stil der Oden Klopstocks*; Gerhard Fricke, "Klopstock," in *Studien und Interpretationen*; Wolfdietrich Rasch, *Freundschaftskult und Freundschaftsdichtung*, pp. 240–63; Irmgard Böger, *Bewegung als formendes Gesetz in K.s Oden*; Karl Kindt, *Klopstock*; Paul Böckmann, *Formgeschichte*; Karl August Schleiden, *K.s Dichtungstheorie*; Max Freivogel, *K. der heilige Dichter*; Werner Küster, "Das Problem der 'Dunkelheit' von K.s Dichtung"; K.A. Schleiden, "Friedrich Gottlieb Klopstock, der Begründer der neueren deutschen Dichtung"; Eric Blackall, *The Emergence of German as a Literary Language*, pp. 314–50; Jean Murat, *K.: Les thèmes principaux*; Karl Ludwig Schneider, *K. und die Erneuerung der dt. Dichtersprache*; Gerhard Kaiser, *Klopstock, Religion und Dichtung* (with extensive bibliography); Dieter Lohmeier, *Herder und Klopstock*; Hans-Heinrich Hellmuth, *Metrische Erfindung*.

Valuable articles treating special aspects of Klopstock's work include: Emil Staiger, "Der Zürcher See"; Alfred Kelletat, "Über ein Altersgedicht Klopstocks"; Gerhard Kaiser, "Klopstocks 'Frühlingsfeier' "; Elida M. Szarota, "Die Wandlungen der Klopstockschen Lyrik"; Harold T. Betteridge, "Young Klopstock" and "Mature Klopstock"; Bernhard Blume, "Orpheus and Messiah"; Hans Jaeger, "Verstummen und Schweigen in der Dichtung Klopstocks"; Alfred Kelletat, "Zum Problem der antiken Metren"; Eberhard Wilhelm Schulz, "Klopstocks Alterslyrik"; Terence K. Thayer, "Klopstock's Occasional Poetry."

25. Those on *P.L.* are in Nos. 267, 273, 285, 291, 297, 303, 309, 315, 327, 333, 339, 345, 351, 357, 363, 369; those on the pleasures of the imagina-

tion are Nos. 411–21. The *Spectator* was published daily from 1 March 1711, to 6 December 1712.

26. Cited after K.L. Schneider, *K. und die Erneuerung*, p.21; I am here following Schneider, pp. 18 ff.

27. I am here following Kelletat, "Problem," pp. 53 ff.

28. W. Bennett, *German Verse in Classical Metres*, p.43, reminds us that there was "occasional usage" of the meter before 1730, "when Gottsched seriously supported the rhymeless hexameter in his *Critische Dichtkunst*" and that he, rather than Klopstock, "rightly deserves to be called the 'father of the German hexameter'." However, Bennett also admits that it was "with the appearance of the first cantos of Klopstock's *Messias* in 1748, based on Gottsched's example, that the hexameter became the real heroic verse for German and ousted the Alexandrine" (p. 45).

29. Even in the case of Klopstock's hexameters the tendency toward free verse is marked. The poet himself transformed "Das Wort des Deutschen" (M-P 2, 80), originally composed in hexameters, into a hymn in free verse.

30. "In der Odendichtung Klopstocks," writes G. Fricke, "vermählt sich zum ersten Mal das Erlebnis mit der Dichtung," but, he adds, "Klopstock vermag noch nicht [!], wie später Goethe, das Persönliche und Konkrete des eigenen Erlebens als solches ganz zu bewahren und es *zugleich* zum durchsichtigen gültigen Symbol menschlichen Daseinserfahrung und Daseinsbewältigung überhaupt umzugestalten" (*Studien*, pp. 18–19).

31. Cf. H. Düntzer, *Erläuterungen*, 1. Heft (1874), p. 17.

32. Cf. Küster, p. 92: "Eine Dichtung verstehen hiess nun nicht mehr einen Sachverhalt begreifen, den der Dichter in poetischer Umschreibung rational fixiert . . . hatte. Das Verstehen gründete vielmehr in einem seelischen Akt, der den Leser für sich den gleichen seelischen Zustand wiederherstellen liess, in dem der Dichter die Gegen-Stände sich anverwandelt hatte." The most effective way in which the anti-Klopstockians could criticize the poet was to "translate" his work "into German." Thus he became clear and of course not so deep after all! Küster discusses these "translations," pp. 44 ff., and gives examples in his "Anhang," pp. 143 ff.

33. Cf. Hellmuth, pp. 166 ff. The schemata for "Der Tod" were discovered in the middle of this century among the literary remains of Heinr. Christian Boie, a member of the "Hain." See Hellmuth, pp. 62 f.

34. God in the storm is a frequent Old Testament motif; one of the most impressive instances is 2 Samuel 22: 8–17.

35. Cf. Hellmuth, pp. 15 ff. In this section I shall be guiding myself on Hellmuth's investigations.

36. Viëtor's judgment in *Gesch. der dt. Ode* is typical: "Was ihm [K.] seinem Volke näher verbinden sollte, hat ihn nur noch mehr isoliert. Zu den metrischen Schrullen [!], den sprachlichen Absonderlichkeiten kam noch die jedem Ungelehrten dunkle Welt der pseudogermanischen Götter und Helden" (p. 126). Muncker, in *Klopstock*, is perhaps even harsher: "Es war ein böser Irrtum, zu welchem den Dichter sein übertriebener Patriotismus verleitete, ein entschiedener Missgriff des Künstlers und ein wirres Missverständnis des gelehrten Forschers" (p.375).

37. Cf. Muncker, pp. 501 ff., esp. p. 503; Viëtor, p. 121; G. Kaiser, *Klopstock*, pp. 319 ff.; Rudolf Haller, p.313.

38. Schulz refers, p. 295, n. 3, to the excellent analysis by Alfred Kelletat of "Das Wiedersehn" (*Euphorion* 45) as being "soweit ich sehe, nach langer Zeit der erste entschiedene Versuch, eine der späten Oden Klopstocks in Sympathie mit dem Gegenstand zu lesen und analysieren." Though Kelletat's analysis is confined to one poem, it throws light on Klopstock's "Alterslyrik" as a whole.
39. Cited after Paul Fussell, Jr., *Poetic Meter*, p.3
40. "Orpheus and Messiah," p. 218.
41. Karl Kindt, *Klopstock*, p. 653.
42. The development of Klopstock's thinking on the nature of language is not infrequently puzzlingly self-contradictory. Thus even in the essay of 1758, "Von der Sprache der Poesie," in which he posits the separation of word and thought, he says of the German language, in speaking of its ability to adopt "etwas von dem Tone anderer Sprachen," that in so doing it may give more than it takes, for: "Sie [die deutsche Sprache] ist, wie die Nation, die sie spricht, *Sie denkt selbst*, und bringt die Gedanken andrer sur Reife" (Schleiden, 3d ed., p. 1026; emphasis added).
43. In none of the poems from which the following passages, adduced at random, are taken is nature used emblematically:

> Sein Licht hat er in Düfte gehüllt,
> Wie erhellt des Winters werdener Tag
> Sanft den See! Glänzender Reif, Sternengleich,
> Streute die Nacht über ihn aus!
> ["Der Eislauf," 1764, M-P 1, 173]

> Insel der froheren Einsamkeit
> Geliebte Gespielin des Widerhals
> Und des Sees, welcher itzt breit, dann, versteckt
> Wie ein Strom, rauscht an des Walds Hügeln umher,
> Selber von Hügeln voll,
> Auf denen im Rohr die Moräne weilt, . . .
> ["Stintenburg," 1767, M-P 1, 197]

> Voller Gefühl des Jünglings, weil' ich Tage
> Auf dem Ross', und dem Stahl' [Schlittschuh], ich seh des Lenzes
> Grüne Bäume froh dann, und froh des Winters
> Dürre beblühet.
> ["Der Frohsinn," 1784, M-P 2, 59]

SELECTED BIBLIOGRAPHY

ADDISON, JOSEPH. *The Works of* . . . *Joseph Addison*, ed. Richard Hurd. 6 vols. Vol.4, London, 1811.
ALLISON, HENRY E. *Lessing and the Enlightenment*. Ann Arbor, Mich., 1966.
ANDEL, CORNELIS PIETER VAN. *Gerhard Tersteegen*. Wageningen, 1961.
ANGER, ALFRED. "Deutsche Rokoko-Dichtung. Ein Forschungsbericht." *Deutsche Vierteljahrsschrift* 36 (1962): 430–79; 614–48.
——— ed. *Dichtung des Rokoko nach Motiven geordnet*. Tübingen, 1969.
———. "Landschaftsstil des Rokoko." *Euphorion* 51 (1957); 151–91.
———. *Literarisches Rokoko*. Stuttgart, 1962.
ARNOLD, GOTTFRIED. *Gottfried Arnold in Auswahl*, ed. Erich Seeberg. Munich, 1934.
BARFIELD, OWEN. *Poetic Diction: A Study in Meaning*. New York and Toronto, 1964 (1st ed. 1938).
BARTH, KARL. *Die protestantische Theologie im 19. Jahrhundert*. Zürich, 1947.
BENNETT, W. *German Verse in Classical Metres*. The Hague, 1963. (Anglica germanica 6)
BERGER, KURT. *Barock und Aufklärung im geistlichen Lied*. Marburg, 1951.
BETTERIDGE, HAROLD T. "Young Klopstock: A psycho-literary study." *Orbis Litterarum* 15 (1960): 3–35; "Mature Klopstock." *Orbis Litterarum* 17 (1962):129–53.
BETTERMANN, WILHELM. *Theologie und Sprache bei Zinzendorf*. Gotha, 1935
BEYER, MARIANNE, ed. *Empfindsamkeit, Sturm und Drang*. Leipzig, 1936. (Dt. Lit. in Entw.reihen, Reihe Deutsche Selbstzeugnisse 9)
BEYER-FRÖHLICH, MARIANNE, ed. *Pietismus und Rationalismus*. Leipzig, 1933. (Dt. Lit. in Entw.reihen, Reihe Deutsche Selbstzeugnisse 7)
BEYREUTHER, ERICH. *Nikolaus Ludwig von Zinzendof in Selbstzeugnissen und Bilddokumenten*. Reinbek, 1965.

319

BIBLIOGRAPHY

BINDER, WOLFGANG. "Grundformen der Säkularisation in den Werken Goethes, Schillers und Hölderlins." *Zeitschrift für dt. Philologie* 83 (1964): 42–69.

BLACKALL, ERIC. *The Emergence of German as a Literary Language.* Cambridge (England), 1959.

BLUME, BERNHARD. "Orpheus and Messiah: The Mythology of Immortality in Klopstock's Poetry." *German Quarterly* 34 (1961): 218–24.

BLUMENBERG, HANS. "Kopernikus im Selbstverständnis der Neuzeit." *Abhandlungen der Akademie der Wissenschaften und der Literatur, Mainz. Geistes- und Sozialwissenschftliche Klasse no. 5* (1964): 339–68.

———. *Die kopernikanische Wende.* Frankfurt a/M., 1965.

BÖCKMANN, PAUL. *Formgeschichte der deutschen Dichtung.* Hamburg, 1949.

———. "Die Anfänge der Naturlyrik bei Brockes, Haller und Günther." *Literatur und Geistesgeschichte. Festgabe für H. O. Burger,* ed. R. Grimm and C. Wiedemann. Berlin, 1968, pp. 110–26.

BODMER, JOHANN JACOB. *Critische Abhandlung von dem Wunderbaren in der Poesie.* Faksimiledruck nach der Ausgabe von 1740 mit einem Nachwort von Wolfgang Bender. Stuttgart, 1966. (Deutsche Neudrucke, Reihe Texte des 18. Jahrhunderts)

BÖGER, IRMGARD. *Bewegung als formendes Gesetz in Klopstocks Oden.* Berlin, 1939. (Germanische Studien 207)

BREITINGER, JOHANN JACOB. *Critische Dichtkunst.* 2 vols. Faksimiledruck nach der Ausgabe von 1740 mit einem Nachwort von Wolfgang Bender. Stuttgart, 1966. (Deutsche Neudrucke, Reihe Texte des 18 Jahrhunderts)

———. *Critische Abhandlung von der Natur, den Absichten und dem Gebrauche der Gleichnisse.* Faksimiledruck nach der Ausgabe von 1740 mit einem Nachwort von Manfred Windfuhr, Stuttgart, 1967. (Deutsche Neudrucke, Reihe Texte des 18. Jahrhunderts)

BROCKES, BARTHOLD HEINRICH. *Auszug der vornehmsten Gedichte aus dem irdischen Vergnügen in Gott.* Faksimiledruck nach der Ausgabe von 1738 mit einem Nachwort von Dietrich Bode, Stuttgart, 1965. (Deutsche Neudrucke, Reihe Texte des 18. Jahrhunderts)

———. *Irdisches Vergnügen in Gott. Gedichte.* Auswahl und Nachwort von Adalbert Elschenbroich. Stuttgart, 1966. (Reclams UB 2015)

BROWN, ANDREW F. *Gotthold Ephraim Lessing.* New York, 1971. (Twayne World Authors Series 113)

BROWNING, ROBERT M. *German Baroque Poetry, 1618–1723.* University Park, Pa., 1971.

BRÜGGEMANN, FRITZ, ed. *Aus der Frühzeit der deutschen Aufklärung. Christian Thomasius und Christian Weise.* Weimar and Leipzig, 1928. (Dt. Lit. in Entw.reihen,, Reihe Aufkl. 1)

———. *Das Weltbild der deutschen Aufklärung. Philosophische Grundlagen und literarische Auswirkung: Leibniz–Wolff–Gottsched–Brockes–Haller.* Leipzig, 1930. (Dt. Lit. in Entw. reihen, Reihe Aufkl. 2)

————. *Gottscheds Lebens- und Kunstreform in den zwanziger und dreissiger Jahren.* *Gottsched, Breitinger, die Gottschedin, die Neuberin.* Leipzig, 1935. (Dt. Lit. in Entw.reihen, Reihe Aufkl. 3)

BRÜGGEMANN, FRITZ AND HELMUT PAUSTIAN, eds. *Die bürgerliche Gemeinschaftskultur der vierziger Jahre.* *Erster Teil: Lyrik und Roman.* Leipzig, 1933. (Dt. Lit. in Entw.reihen, Reihe Aufkl. 5)

————. *Der Anbruch der Gefühlskultur in den fünfziger Jahren.* Leipzig, 1935. (Dt. Lit. in Entw.reihen, Reihe Aufkl. 7)

BURGER, HEINZ OTTO. "Deutsche Aufklärung im Widerspiel zu Barock und 'Neubarock.' " *Formkräfte der deutschen Dichtung vom Barock bis zur Gegenwart.* Göttingen, 1963, pp. 56–80.

CARR, HERBERT WILDON. *Leibniz.* Boston, 1929.

CASSIRER, ERNST. "Shaftesbury und die Renaissance des Platonismus in England." *Vorträge der Bibliothek Warburg, 1930/31.* Leipzig and Berlin, 1932, pp. 136–55.

————. *The Platonic Renaissance in England,* trans. J.P. Pettegrove. Edinburgh, 1953.

————. *The Philosophy of the Enlightenment,* trans. F.C.A. Koelln and J.A. Pettegrove. Boston, 1955.

CLOSS, AUGUST. *The Genius of the German Lyric,* 2d ed. London, 1962.

DÖRRIES, HERMANN. *Geist und Geschichte bei Gottfried Arnold,* Göttingen, 1963. (Abhandlungen der Akademie der Wissenschaften in Göttingen, philologisch-historische Klasse, dritte Folge, Nr. 51)

DÜNTZER, HEINRICH. *Erläuterungen zu den deutschen Klassikern,* 5. Abteilung: *Erläuterungen zu Klopstocks Werken,* Hefte 1–6, 2d ed. Leipzig, 1874, 1878.

EPTING, KARL. *Der Stil in den lyrischen und didaktischen Gedichten Friedrich von Hagedorns.* Stuttgart, 1929.

FALK, WALTER. "Die Anfänge der deutschen Kunstballade." *Deutsche Vierteljahrsschrift* 44 (1970): 670–86.

FREIVOGEL, MAX. *Klopstock der heilige Dichter.* Bern, 1954. (Basler Studien zur deutschen Sprache und Literatur 15)

FRICKE, GERHARD. *Studien und Interpretationen.* Frankfurt a/M., 1956, pp. 7–24.

FRIEDRICH, ROGER. *Studien zur Lyrik Gottfried Arnolds.* Diss. Zürich, 1969.

FUSSELL, PAUL, JR. *Poetic Meter and Poetic Form.* New York, 1965.

GAEDE, FRIEDRICH. *Humanismus, Barock, Aufklärung. Geschichte der deutschen Literatur vom 16. bis zum 18. Jahrhundert.* Bern and Munich, 1971.

GAY, PETER. *The Enlightenment: An Interpretation,* vol. I: *The Rise of Modern Paganism.* New York, 1966.

GELLERT, CHRISTIAN FÜRCHTEGOTT. *Sämtliche Fabeln und Erzählungen, geistliche Oden und Lieder.* Vollständige Ausgabe nach dem Text der Ausgaben letzter Hand. Mit einem Nachwort von Herbert Klinkhardt. Munich, 1965.

————. *Fabeln und Erzählungen.* Historisch-kritische Ausgabe bearbeitet von

BIBLIOGRAPHY

Siegfried Scheibe. Tübingen, 1966. (Neudrucke deutscher Literaturwerke, Neue Folge 17)

———. *Bremer Beiträger, 1. Teil: Gellerts Fabeln und Geistliche Dichtungen*, ed. Franz Muncker. Berlin and Stuttgart, n.d. (*Dt. Nat.-Lit.* 43/1)

GLEIM, JOHANN WILHELM LUDWIG. *Versuch in Scherzhaften Liedern und Lieder*, ed. Alfred Anger. Tübingen, 1964.

———. *Preussische Kriegslieder von einem Grenadier*, ed. August Sauer. Heilbronn, 1882. (Deutsche Litteraturdenkmale des 18. Jahrhunderts in Neudrucken 4)

———. *Gedichte*, ed. Jürgen Stenzel. Stuttgart, 1969. (Reclams UB 2138/39)

GLEIM, JOH. WILH. LUDWIG and UZ, JOH. PETER. *Briefwechsel zwischen Gleim und Uz*, ed. Carl Schüddekopf. Tübingen, 1899. (Blbliothek des Litterarichen Vereins in Stuttgart 218)

GOTTSCHED, JOHANN CHRISTOPH. *Versuch einer Critischen Dichtkunst für die Deutschen*, 2. und verbesserte Aufl. Leipzig, 1737.

———. *Gesammelte Schriften*, vol. 5. Berlin, n.d. (Ausgabe der Gottsched-Gesellschaft)

———. *Schriften zur Literatur*, ed. Horst Steinmetz. Stuttgart, 1972. (Reclams UB 9361/65)

GÖTZ, JOHANN NIKOLAUS. *Die Gedichte Anakreons und der Sappho Oden*, Faksimiledruck nach der Ausgabe von 1760 mit einem Nachwort von Herbert Zeman. Stuttgart, 1970. (Deutsche Neudrucke, Reihe Texte des 18. Jahrhunderts)

———. *Gedichte aus den Jahren 1745–1765 in ursprünglicher Gestalt*, ed. Carl Schüddekopf. Stuttgart, 1893. (Deutsche Litteraturdenkmale des 18. und 19. Jahrhunderts 42)

———. *Lyriker und Epiker der klassischen Periode*, 1. Teil, ed. Max Wendheim. Stuttgart, n.d., pp. 266–73. (*Dt. Nat.-Lit.* 135/1)

GUTHKE, KARL S. "Albrecht von Haller—der Arzt mid der 'poetischen Krankheit'?" *Neue Sammlung*, 5. Jahrgang (1965): 555–60.

———. "Friedrich von Hagedorn und das literarische Leben seiner Zeit im Lichte unveröffentlichter Briefe an Johann Jakob Bodmer." *Jahrbuch des Freien Deutschen Hochstifts* 1966, pp. 1–108.

———. "Zur Relionsphilosophie des jungen Albrecht von Haller." *Colloquia Germanica* 2 (1967): 142–55.

———. "Der junge Albrecht von Haller und die Bibel." *Jahrbuch des Freien Deutschen Hochstifts* 1968, pp. 1–21.

———. "Hallers Shakespeare-Bild." *Seminar* 6 (1970): 91–110.

———. *Die Mythologie der entgötterten Welt.* Göttingen, 1971.

HAGEDORN, FRIEDRICH VON. *Des Herrn Friedrichs von Hagedorn Poetische Werke in drei Theilen.* Hamburg, bey Johann Carl Bohn, 1769.

———. *Anakreontiker und preussisch-patriotische Lyriker: Hagedorn, Gleim, Uz, Kleist, Ramler, Karschin*, ed. Franz Muncker. Stuttgart, n.d. [1894]. (*Dt. Nat.-Lit.* 45)

——. *Friedrich von Hagedorn, Gedichte*, ed. Alfred Anger. Stuttgart, 1968. (Reclams UB 1321/23)

HALLER, ALBRECHT VON. *Albrecht von Hallers Gedichte*, ed. Dr. Ludwig Hirzel. Frauenfeld, 1882. (Bibliothek älterer Schriftwerke der deutschen Schweiz, 3. Bd.)

——. *Die Alpen und andere Gedichte*, Auswahl und Nachwort von Adalbert Elschenbroich. Stuttgart, 1965. (Reclams UB 8963/64)

——. *Tagebuch seiner Beobachtungen über Schriftsteller und über sich selbst*, ed. Johann Georg Heinzmann. 2 vols. Frankfurt a/M., 1971 (1st ed., Bern, 1787).

HALLER, RUDOLF. *Geschichte der deutschen Lyrik vom Ausgang des Mittelalters bis zu Goethes Tod*. Bern and Munich, 1967.

HECKEL, HANS. "Zu Begriff und Wesen des literarischen Rokoko in Deutschland." *Festschrift Theodor Siebs*, Breslau, 1933, pp. 213–50. (Germanistische Abhandlungen 67)

HELLMUTH, HANS-HEINRICH. *Metrische Erfindung und metrische Theorie bei Klopstock*. Munich, 1973. (Studien und Quellen zur Versgeschichte 4)

HEUSLER, ANDREAS. *Deutsche Versgeschichte*, 3. Bd., Teil IV und V: *Der frühneudeutsche Vers, der neudeutsche Vers*. Berlin and Leipzig, 1929. (Grundriss der germanischen Philologie 8/3)

HOCHDOERFER, MARGARETE. *The Conflict between the Religious and the Scientific Views of Albrecht von Haller*. Lincoln, Nebraska, 1952. (University of Nebraska Studies in Language, Literature, and Criticism 12)

HUOBER, HANS-GÜNTHER. *Zinzendorfs Kirchenlieddichtung. Untersuchung über das Verhältnis von Erlebnis und Sprachform*. Berlin, 1934. (Germanische Studien 150)

JAEGER, HANS. "Verstummen und Schweigen in der Dichtung Klopstocks." *Wirkendes Wort* 12 (1962): 281–88.

JANTZ, HAROLD. "Brockes' Poetic Apprenticeship." *MLN* 77 (1962): 439–42.

JUNKER, CHRISTOPH. *Das Weltraumbild in der deutschen Lyrik von Opitz bis Klopstock*. Berlin, 1932. (Germanische Studien 111)

KAISER, GERHARD. "Klopstocks 'Frühlingsfeier.'" *Wirkendes Wort* 9 (1957/58): 329–35.

——. *Klopstock, Religion und Dichtung*. Gütersloh, 1963.

KAUSSMANN, ERNST. *Der Stil der Oden Klopstocks*. Diss. Leipzig, 1931.

KAYSER, WOLFGANG. "Die Grundlagen der deutschen Fabeldichtung des 16. und 18. Jahrhunderts." *Archiv für das Studium der neueren Sprachen* 160 (1931): 19–33.

——. *Geschichte der deutschen Ballade*. Berlin, 1936.

——. *Geschichte des deutschen Verses. Zehn Vorlesungen für Hörer aller Fakultäten*. Bern and Munich, 1960.

KELLETAT, ALFRED. "Über ein Altersgedicht Klopstocks." *Euphorion* 45 (1950): 186–97.

——. "Zum Problem der antiken Metren im Deutschen." *Der Deutschunterricht* 16 (1964): 50–85.

BIBLIOGRAPHY

KINDT, KARL. *Klopstock.* Berlin-Spandau, 1941.

KLEIST, EWALD CHRISTIAN VON. *Ewald von Kleist's Werke.* 3 vols., ed. August Sauer. Berlin, 1884 f. Reprinted Bern, 1968.

KLOPSTOCK, FRIEDRICH GOTTLIEB. *Klopstocks sämmtliche Werke.* 10 vols., Göschen: Leipzig, 1854-55.

———. *Klopstocks Werke,* 3. Teil, ed. Richard Hamel. Berlin and Stuttgart, n.d. [1883]. (*Dt. Nat.-Lit.* 47)

———. *Friedrich Gottlieb Klopstocks Oden,* ed. Franz Muncker and Jaro Pawel. 2 vols. Stuttgart, 1889.

———. *Friedrich Gottlieb Klopstock: Oden,* ed. Karl Ludwig Schneider. Stuttgart, 1966. (Reclams UB 1391/92)

———. *Friedrich Gottlieb Klopstock. Werke in einem Band,* ed. Karl August Schleiden, Nachwort by Friedrich Georg Jünger. Munich, 1954.

———. *Friedrich Gottlieb Klopstock. Ausgewählte Werke,* ed. Karl August Schleiden, Nachwort by Friedrich Georg Jünger. 3. Auflage. Munich, 1969.

———. *Briefe von und an Klopstock,* ed. J.M. Lappenberg. Bern, 1970. 1st ed. Braunschweig, 1867.

KOHLSCHMIDT, WERNER. "Hallers Gedichte und die Tradition." *Dichter, Tradition und Zeitgeist.* Bern and Munich, 1965, pp. 206–21.

KOMMERELL, MAX. *Der Dichter als Führer in der deutschen Klassik.* Frankfurt a/M., n.d. [1929?], pp. 9–60.

KÖSTER, ALBERT. *Die deutsche Literatur der Aufklärungszeit.* Heidelberg, 1925.

KÜSTER, WERNER. "Das Problem der 'Dunkelheit' von Klopstocks Dichtung." Diss. Cologne, 1955. (microfilm)

LANGEN, AUGUST. "Deutsche Sprachgeschichte vom Barock bis zur Gegenwart." *Deutsche Philologie im Aufriss,* Bd. I. Berlin, 1952, pp.1077–1522.

———. *Der Wortschatz des deutschen Pietismus.* Tübingen, 1954.

———. "Zum Problem der sprachlichen Säkularisation der deutschen Dichtung des 18. und 19. Jahrhunderts," *Zeitschrift für dt. Philologie* 83 (1964): 24–42.

LEIBFRIED, ERWIN. *Fabel.* Stuttgart, 1967.

LOHMEIER, DIETER. *Herder und Klopstock.* Bad Homburg, Berlin, Zürich, 1968. (Ars poetica, Studien, Bd. 4)

LOVEJOY, ARTHUR O. *The Great Chain of Being. A Study in the History of an Idea.* Cambridge, Mass., 1936.

LOWINSKY, EDWARD E. "Taste, Style, and Ideology in Eighteenth Century Music." *Aspects of the Eighteenth Century,* ed. Earl R. Wasserman. Baltimore, 1965, pp. 163–205.

MACLEAN, NORMAN. "From Action to Image: Theories of the Lyric in the Eighteenth Century." *Critics and Criticism, Ancient and Modern,* ed. R.S. Crane. Chicago, 1952, pp. 408–60.

MAINLAND, WILLIAM F. "Brockes and the Limitations of Imitation." *Reality and Creative Vision in German Lyrical Poetry.* London, 1963, pp. 101–16.

MARKWARDT, BRUNO. *Geschichte der deutschen Poetik,* Bd. II: *Aufklärung, Ro-*

koko, *Sturm und Drang*. Berlin, 1956. (Grundriss der germanischen Philologie 13/2)

MARTENS, WOLFGANG. "Über Weltbild und Gattungstradition bei Gellert." *Festschrift für Detlev W. Schumann*, ed. Albert R. Schmitt. Munich, 1970, pp. 74–82.

MARTINI, FRITZ. "Von der Aufklärung zum Sturm und Drang, 1700–1775." *Annalen der dt. Literatur*, ed. H.O. Burger. Stuttgart, 1952, pp. 405–63.

MEYER, HERMAN. "Hütte and Palast in der Dichtung des 18. Jahrhunderts." *Formenwandel. Festchrift zum 65. Geburtstag von Paul Böckmann*. Hamburg, 1964, pp. 138–55.

MILTON, JOHN. *The Complete English Poetry of John Milton*, ed. John T. Shawcross. Garden City, N.Y., 1963.

MÜLLER, GÜNTHER. *Geschichte des deutschen Lieds*. Munich, 1925. Reprinted, Bad Homburg, 1959.

MÜLLER-SEIDEL, WALTER. "Die deutsche Ballade. Umrisse ihrer Geschichte." *Wege zum Gedicht* II, ed. R. Hirschenauer and A. Weber. Munich and Zürich, 1963, pp. 17–83.

MUNCKER, FRANZ. *Friedrich Gottlieb Klopstock. Geschichte seines Lebens und seiner Schriften*. Stuttgart, 1888. 2d ed. Berlin, 1900.

MURAT, JEAN. *Klopstock, Les thèmes principaux de son oeuvre*. Paris, 1959.

NEWALD, RICHARD. *Die deutsche Literatur vom Späthusmanismus zur Empfindsamkeit, 1570–1750*. Munich, 1951. (de Boor and Newald, Geschichte der deutschen Literatur von den Anfängen bis zur Gegenwart 5)

———. *Von Klopstock bis zu Goethes Tod*, 1. Teil: *Ende der Aufklärung und Vorbereitung der Klassik*. Munich, 1957. (de Boor and Newald, Geschichte der deutschen Literarur von den Anfängen bis Gegenwart 6/1)

NICOLSON, MARJORIE HOPE. *Mountain Gloom and Mountain Glory: The Development of the Aesthetics of the Infinite*. Ithaca, N.Y., 1959.

NIVELLE, ARMAND. *Kunst- und Dichtungstheorien zwischen Aufklärung und Klassik*. Berlin, 1960.

PELLEGRINI, ALLESANDRO. "Die Krise der Aufklärung. Das dichterische Werk von C.F. Gellert und die Gesellschaft seiner Zeit." *Literaturwissenschaftliches Jahrbuch im Auftrag der Görres-Gesellschaft*," Neue Folge 7 (1966): 37–96.

PFEIFFER, JOHANNES. *Wege zur Dichtung. Eine Einführung in die Kunst des Lesens*. Hamburg, 1953, p. 61–66.

———. *Dichtkunst und Kirchenlied. Über das geistliche Lied im Zeitalter der Säkularisation*. Hamburg, 1961.

PFUND, HARRY W. *Studien zu Wort und Stil bei Brockes*. New York, 1935.

PICK, ALBERT. "Studien zu den deutschen Anakreontikern des XVIII. Jahrhunderts." *Studien zur vergleichenden Literaturgeschichte* 7 (1907): 45–109; 9 (1909): 22–64.

POPE, ALEXANDER. *The Poems of Alexander Pope*, ed. John Butt. New Haven, 1963.

PRICE, LAWRENCE MARDSEN. *English Literature in Germany*. Berkeley, 1953. (University of California Publications in Modern Philology, vol. 37)

BIBLIOGRAPHY

PYRA, IMMANUEL JACOB and SAMUEL GOTTHOLD LANGE. *Thirsis und Damons Freundschaftliche Lieder*, ed. August Sauer. Heilbronn, 1885. (Deutsche Litteraturdenkmale des 18. und 19. Jahrhunderts 22)

RASCH, WOLFDIETRICH. *Freundschaftskult und Freundschaftsdichtung des 18. Jahrhunderts.* Halle, 1936.

REICHEL, JÖRN. *Dichtungstheorie und Sprache bei Zinzendorf. Der Anhang zum Herrnhuter Gesangbuch.* Bad Homburg, Berlin, Zürich, 1969. (Ars poetica 10)

RICHTER, KARL. "Die koperikanische Wende in der Lyrik von Brockes bis Klopstock." *Jahrbuch der deutschen Schillergesellschaft,* 1968, pp. 132–69.

————. *Literatur und Naturwissenschaft. Eine Studie zur Lyrik der Aufklärung.* Munich, 1972. (Theorie und Geschichte der Literatur und der schönen Künste, Bd. 19)

ROBERTSON, J.G. *Studies in the Genesis of Romantic Theory in the Eighteenth Century.* Cambridge (England), 1923.

SAUER-GEPPERT, WALDTRAUT INGEBORG. "Zur Mystik in den Liedern Gerhard Tersteegens." *Festschrift für H. Kunisch.* Berlin, 1961.

SCHERPE, KLAUS R. *Gattungspoetik im 18. Jahrhundert. Historische Entwicklung von Gottsched bis Herder.* Stuttgart, 1968.

SCHLAFFER, HEINZ. *Musa iocosa: Gattungspoetik und Gattungsgeschichte der erotischen Dichtung in Deutschland.* Stuttgart, 1971.

SCHLEIDEN, KARL AUGUST. *Klopstocks Dichtungstheorie als Beitrag zur Geschichte der deutschen Poetik.* Saarbrücken, 1954.

————. "Friedrich Gottlieb Klopstock, der Begründer der neueren deutschen Dichtung." *Der Deutschunterricht* 1956, Jahrgang 8, Heft 5: 23–48.

SCHLINGMANN, CARSTEN. *Gellert, Eine literarhistorische Revision.* Bad Homburg, Berlin, Zürich, 1967. (Frankfurter Beiträge zur Germanistik 3)

SCHMIDT, MARTIN. "Evangelische Kirchengeschichte in Deutschland." *Deutsche Philologie im Aufriss,* Bd. III. Berlin, 1957, pp. 1569–1684.

SCHNEIDER, FERDINAND JOSEF. *Die deutsche Dichtung der Aufklärungszeit.* 2d, revised ed. Stuttgart, 1948.

SCHNEIDER, KARL LUDWIG. *Klopstock und die Erneuerung der deutschen Dichter-Sprache im 18. Jahrhundert.* Heidelberg, 1960.

————. "Die Polemik gegen den Reim im 18. Jahrhundert." *Der Deutschunterricht* 16/6 (1970): 5–16.

SCHÖNE, ALBRECHT. *Säkularisation als sprachbildende Kraft. Studien zur Dichtung deutscher Pfarrersöhne.* Göttingen, 1958. (Palaestra 226)

SCHULZ, EBERHARD WILHELM. "Klopstocks Alterlyrik." *Euphorion* 61 (1967): 295–317.

SCHUMANN, DETLEV W. "Neuorientierung im 18. Jahrhundert: ein Vortrag." *MLQ* 9 (1948): 54 ff.

SCHUPPENHAUER, CLAUS. *Der Kampf um den Reim in der deutschen Literatur des 18. Jahrhunderts.* Bonn, 1970.

BIBLIOGRAPHY

SHAFTESBURY (Anthony Ashley Cooper, third Earl). *Characteristics of Men, Manners, Opinions, Times* . . . 2 vols., ed. John M. Robertson. London, 1900.

SIEGRIST, CHRISTOPH. *Albrecht von Haller.* Stuttgart, 1967.

————. *Das Lehrgedicht der Aufklärung.* Stuttgart, 1974.

SILZ, WALTER. "On Rereading Klopstock." *PMLA* 67 (1952): 744–68.

SØRENSEN, BENGT A. "Das deutsche Rokoko und die Verserzählung im 18. Jahrhundert." *Euphorion* 48 (1954): 125–52.

SPERBER, HANS. "Der Einfluss des Pietismus auf die Sprache des 18. Jahrhunderts." *Deutsche Vierteljahrsschrift* 8 (1930): 497–515.

STÄHLIN, TRAUGOTT. *Gottfried Arnolds geistliche Dichtung. Glaube und Mystik.* Göttingen, 1966. (Veröffentlichungen der Evangelischen Gesellschaft für Liturgieforschung, Heft 15)

STAIGER, EMIL. "Der Zürcher See." *Wege zum Gedicht,* ed. R. Hirschenauer and Albrecht Weber. Munich and Zürich, 1956, pp. 104–18.

STAMM, ISRAEL S. "Some Aspects of the Religious Problem in Haller." *Germanic Review* 25 (1950): 5–12.

STÄUBLE, EDUARD. *Albrecht von Haller, "Über den Ursprung des Übels."* Zürich, 1953. (Zürcher Beiträge zur deutschen Literatur- und Geistesgeschichte 3)

————. "Albrecht von Haller—der Dichter zwischen den Zeiten: Versuch einer stilistichen und geistesgeschichtlichen Interpretation seines 'Unvollkommenen Gedichts über die Ewigkeit.' " *Der Deutschunterrricht* 8/5 (1956): 5–23.

STIX, GOTTFRIED. *Friedrich von Hagedorn. Menschenbild und Dichtungsauffassung.* Rome, 1961.

SZAROTA, ELIDA M. "Die Wandlungen der Klopstockschen Lyrik aufgewiesen an der *Wingolf*-Ode." *Etudes Germaniques* 1959, pp. 106–27.

TERSTEEGEN, GERHARD. *Gerhard Tersteegens Geistliche Lieder. Mit einer Lebensbeshreibung des Dichters und seiner Dichtung,* ed. Wilhelm Nelle, Gütersloh, 1897.

————. *Gerhard Tersteegen. Eine Auswahl aus seinen Schriften,* ed. Walter Nigg. Basel, 1948.

————. *Life and Character of Gerhard Tersteegen, with selections from his letters and writings,* trans. Samuel Jackson. 2d ed. London, 1834.

THAYER, TERENCE K. "Klopstock's Occasional Poetry." *Lessing Yearbook* II (1970): 181–212.

————. "Klopstock and the Literary Afterlife." *Literarturwissenschaftliches Jahrbuch der Görres-Gesellschaft,* N.F. 14 (1973): 183–208.

THOMSON, JAMES. *The Poetical Works of James Thomson.* Boston, n.d. (Riverside Edition)

TOELLNER, RICHARD. *Albrecht von Haller. Über die Einheit im Denken des letzten Universalgelehrten.* Wiesbaden, 1971. (Sudhoffs Archiv. Zeitschrift für Wissenschaftsgeschichte, Beihefte, Heft 10)

BIBLIOGRAPHY

TONELLI, GIORGIO. *Poesia e filosofia in Albrecht von Haller*. Turin, 1961.

UZ, JOHANN PETER. *Sämtliche poestische Werke*, ed. August Sauer. Stuttgart, 1890. (Dt. Litteraturdankmale des 18. und 19. Jahrhunderts 33)

VIËTOR, KARL. *Geschichte der deutschen Ode*. Darmstadt, 1961. 1st ed., Munich, 1923.

WANIEK, GUSTAV. *Immanuel Pyra und sein Einfluss auf die deutsche Literatur des 18. Jahrhunderts*. Leipzig, 1882.

WASSERMAN, EARL R. "The Inherent Values of Eighteenth Century Personification." *PMLA* 65 (1950): 435–63.

WIEGAND, JULIUS. *Geschichte der deutschen Dichtung nach Gedanken, Stoffen und Formen, in Längs- und Querschnitten*, 2d expanded ed., Cologne, 1922.

WILLEY, BASIL. *The Eighteenth Century Background*. New York, 1941.

WINDFUHR, MANFRED. *Die barocke Bildlichkeit und ihre Kritiker*. Stuttgart, 1966.

WITTKOWER, RUDOLF. "Imitation, Eclecticism, and Genius." *Aspects of the Eighteenth Century*, ed. Earl R. Wasserman. Baltimore, 1965, pp. 143–61.

WOLFF, HANS M. *Die Weltanschauung der deutschen Aufklärung in geschichtlicher Entwicklung*. Munich, 1949.

———. "Brockes' Religion." *PMLA* 62 (1947): 1124–52.

WOLTERS, GERTRUD. *Gerhard Tersteegens geistliche Lyrik*. Diss. Marburg, 1929.

YOUNG, EDWARD. *The Poetical Works of Edward Young*. Boston, n.d. (Riverside Edition)

ZELTNER, HELENA RESA. *Johann Peter Uz: Von der "Lyrischen Muse" zur "Dichtkunst."* Diss. Zürich, 1973.

ZEMAN, HERBERT. *Die deutsche anakreontische Dichtung. Ein Versuch zur Erfassung ihrer ästhetischen und literarhistorischen Erscheinungsformen im 18. Jahrhundert*. Stuttgart, 1972.

ZINZENDORF, NIKOLAUS LUDWIG VON. *Ergänzungsbände zu den Hauptschriften*, Bd. II: *Teutsche Gedichte, XII. Anhang und Zugaben I-IV zum Herrnhuter Gesangbuch*, ed. Erich Beyreuther and Gerhard Meyer. Hildesheim, 1964.

ADDENDUM: The *Klopstock-Bibliographie*, compiled by Gerhard Burkhardt and Heinz Nicolai, Berlin, New York, 1975, appeared after the completion of the manuscript for this book.

INDEX

The Index lists mainly names. Topics and titles are listed only when of particular importance and when they might not otherwise be easily found.

INDEX

Bayle's Dictionary, 54
Beethoven, 63, 302
Belleau, Remy, 93
Bellman, Carl Michael, 81
Bennett, W., 317
Bernoulli, Christophe, 298
Bernstorff, Johann Hartwig Ernst
von, 235, 313, 314, 315
Besser, Johann von, 75, 137
Betteridge, Harold T., 210, 253,
262, 263, 316
Bettermann, Wilhelm, 172, 310
Beyreuther, Erich, 175, 309
Blackall, Eric A., 7, 297, 299, 301,
316
Blake, William, 70
Blume, Bernhard, 275, 316
Blumenberg, Hans, 9, 298
Böckmann, Paul, 188, 297, 316
Bode, Dietrich, 297
Bodmer, Johann Jacob, 18, 68, 69,
80, 115, 117, 118, 126 ff., 182,
188, 189 f., 199 f., 302, 303,
310, 312, 313
Boerhaave, Hermann, 298
Böger, Irmgard, 223, 316
Böhme, Jacob, 142, 148
Bohn, Johann Carl, 302
Boie, Heinrich Christian, 317
Boileau, 69, 70, 190, 296
Boswell, James, 299
Brecht, Bertolt, 79, 103, 105, 178,
184
Breitinger, Johann Jacob, 18, 68,
69, 188, 199 f., 303, 312
Bremer Beiträger, 212, 215 f., 312
Brockes, Berthold Heinrich, 3–17,
39, 45, 51, 63, 118, 296 f.
Browning, Robert M., 310
Brüggemann, Fritz, 297
Brühl, Graf Heinrich von, 114
Burke, Edmund, 296
Butler, Samuel, 25

Canitz, Friedrich Rudolf, 25, 118,
137
Carlyle, Thomas, 253
Catullus, 184
Celts, 253
Chardin, Jean Baptiste, 70

Charlemagne, 232
Chaulieu, Guillaume Amfrye de,
119
Chevy-Chase-Strophe, 110, 230,
292, 305
Christ, Hofrat, 116, 119
Cidli. *See* Meta
Coffman, Bertha Reed, 303
Copernican view of universe, 9 f.
Copernicus, 297, 298
Cowley, Abraham, 76
Cramer, Johann Andreas, 215, 314

Dacier, Madame, 94
Dante, 183, 184, 312
David (psalmist), 182, 183, 185,
186, 187, 202
Dennis, John, 188
Diedrich, Luise Sidonie ("Done"),
314
Divine wisdom (Sophia), 142 ff.,
148, 150, 152, 196
Done. *See* Diedrich, Luise Sidonie
Donne, John, 76
Dörries, Hermann, 141, 147, 150,
305
Du Bartas (Sallust), 185 f.
Du Bellay, Joachim, 70
Dubos, Jean Baptiste, 200
Düntzer, Heinrich, 214, 316, 317
Dürer, Albrecht, 14

Ebert, Johann Arnold, 117, 215,
217, 284
Edda, 253
Elsenbroich, Adalbert, 297, 298,
299
Emblematic structure, 7 f., 25, 51,
294, 318
Emerson, Ralph Waldo, 196
Encratites, 82, 83, 95
Ennui, 20, 35, 36, 40
Epictetus, 29 f.
Epicurus (Epicurean), 81, 91
Epting, Karl, 78, 303
Erlebnisdichtung, Klopstock's, 206 f.
Eschenburg, Johann Joachim, 302
Estienne, Henri (Henricus Stepha-
nus), 93, 94
Eternity, concept of, 35 ff., 285 f.

Euripides, 184

Falk, Walter, 104, 305
Fanny. *See* Schmidt, Marie Sophie
Father, The (moral weekly), 55
Fehr, Karl, 299
Fleming, Paul, 75, 118, 186
Forsthoff, Heinrich, 307
Francke, August Hermann, 136, 308
Frederick V, of Denmark, 229, 233
f., 235 ff., 262, 313, 314, 315
Frederick the Great, of Prussia, ix,
47, 109, 110, 111 ff., 229 ff.,
233, 234, 253, 300, 301, 304,
307
Free verse, 239 f., 259 f., 270
Freivogel, Max, 279, 316
French Revolution, 208, 210, 261,
262–65, 285, 286, 290, 315
Freude, 77, 82, 84, 123, 269 f.
Fricke, Gerhard, 316, 317
Friedländer, Max, 302
Friedrich, Roger, 305, 306
Friedrich Wilhelm I, King of Prussia, 309
Fulda, Ludwig, 297
Fussel, Paul, Jr., 318

Gainsborough, Thomas, 70
Garve, Christian, 57
Gay, John, 76, 79
Gay, Peter, 300
Gefühldenken, 48, 197 f., 244 f.
Gellert, Christian Fürchtegott, xi,
3, 52–67, 71, 74, 109, 118,
134, 215, 300 f.
Fabeln und Erzählungen, 52–61
Geistliche Oden und Lieder, 62–67
George, Stefan, 279
Gerhardt, Paul, 62, 154, 178, 186,
294
Gerstenberg, Heinrich Wilhelm
von, 305, 314
Gessner, Salomon, 46, 111, 112,
290
Giseke (friend of Klopstock), 49,
215, 314
Gleim, Johann Wilhelm Ludwig,
91, 92–115, 116, 118, 119, 121,
126, 134, 230, 292, 300, 303 f.

*Preussische Kriegslieder von einem
Grenadier,* 109–14
Romanzen, 102–9
Versuch in scherzhaften Liedern, 96–
102
Gluck, Christoph Willibald, 279,
315
Goes, Albrecht, 307
Goethe, Johann Wolfgang von, 18,
47, 57, 85, 86, 111, 121, 132,
197, 203, 206, 207, 282, 294 f.,
301, 304, 315, 317
Görner, Johann Valentin, 79
Gotthelf, Jeremias, 22
Göttinger Hain, 203, 314, 317
Gottsched, Johann Christoph, and
Gottschedians, 1 f., 68 f., 94,
187, 189, 200, 300, 301, 305,
310, 312, 317
Götz, Johann Nikolaus, 116, 119,
124–33, 303, 305
*Gedichte aus den Jahren 1745–1765
in ursprünglicher Gestalt,* 128–31
"Das Mädcheninsel," 131 ff.
"Prosaische Ode an den Marquis
von Montbary," 126 ff.
Versuch eines Wormsers in Gedichten,
125 f.
Greiffenberg, Catharina Regina
von, 3, 4
Gryphius, Andreas, 27, 185, 186,
294, 297
Gryphius, Christian, 75
Günther, Johann Christian, 33, 73
f., 102, 125, 146, 310
Guthke, Karl S., 18, 299, 300, 303,
305
Guyon, Madame, 306

Hagedorn, Friedrich von, 3, 25, 26,
68–92, 94, 95, 116, 118, 122,
202, 215, 297, 302 f., 313
Fabeln und Erzählungen, 70–74
Moralische Gedichte, 86–91
Oden und Lieder, 74–86, 91 f.
Haller, Albrecht von, 3, 9, 17–44,
45, 46, 47, 48, 49, 62, 63, 68,
118, 124, 200 f., 298 f., 300,
302, 310, 313
"Die Alpen," 18 ff.

INDEX

336

SWORDS and SCALES

KENNIKAT PRESS

NATIONAL UNIVERSITY PUBLICATIONS

SERIES IN AMERICAN STUDIES

General Editor

JAMES P. SHENTON

Professor of History, Columbia University

WILLIAM T. GENEROUS, JR.

SWORDS and SCALES

The Development of the
Uniform Code of Military Justice

National University Publications
KENNIKAT PRESS
Port Washington, N. Y.   London   1973

Library of Congress Catalog Card No: 72-91173
ISBN: 0-8046-9039-1

Manufactured in the United States of America

Published by
Kennikat Press, Inc.
Port Washington, N.Y./London

For reformers, everywhere

Acknowledgments

Anyone who has ever completed a piece of work like this knows that it depended on the help of a great many people. Those who gave a few hours of their time to be interviewed, and others who replied to questions by mail, are cited in the bibliography. Some bought me lunch, many gave me ideas, all were quick to respond to my requests.

Literally from coast to coast, archivists and librarians were eager to help. Those at Treasure Island stretched their security rules to let me work late nights, long after everyone else went home. The staff at the Eisenhower Library broke out their files on a moment's notice. Mrs. Judy Fair and her associates at the Stanford Government Documents Center were indispensably helpful. There were many others; in every case, they were courteous and thoughtful.

A number of individuals also helped. In the military, Navy Lieutenant Homer Moyer and Army Captain Myron Sugarman became my friends as well as "liaison officers." Colonels John Wasson of the Air Force and Robert Miller of the Army each did me a special favor, besides providing general assistance. Civilians like Felix Larkin and Frederick Wiener donated large chunks of their extremely expensive time to dwell on matters I thought important. Because of my excitement at Richard Wels' permitting me the unfettered use of all his pertinent papers and memorabilia, I repeatedly rejected his offers of hospitality; but he overlooked my rudeness. And Daniel Carney of the Court of Military Appeals gave me an interview, some data, and one very important legal service.

The trouble with all these debts (and those mentioned only

scratch the surface) is that the following text frequently criticizes those to whom I owe the most. Generally, however, I expect these men will condone my candor; there are few small minds among them.

Closer to home, Carl N. Degler was a dynamo in assisting, correcting, and steering me through a project about which he had very little original concern. I hope he is more interested now. George H. Knoles and Terence Emmons also put themselves at my disposal with surprising and gratifying alacrity.

Financial support for the project came from three sources. A Stanford University Fellowship and GI Bill benefits provided the necessary means for general expenses throughout the four years of my graduate school career. And the Mabel McLeod Lewis Fund made available a very generous grant specifically for the travel and research associated with this work

I should also mention that the Stanford University History Department office staff—Lorraine Sinclair and the other ladies—cheered me on when I needed it. The skill of Mrs. Beverly Oudijk at the typewriter relieved me of that bothersome detail. And finally, my wife Diane put up with widowhood for many weeks so I could go away researching and shielded me from workaday worries for longer weeks so I could stay home writing.

Without these people, what follows would not have been written.

William T. Generous, Jr.

Wallingford, Connecticut
August, 1972

Contents

SWORDS and SCALES

1 Ansell, the Articles, and the AGN

Public attention during the last few years has focused on the court-martial system employed by the United States Armed Forces to a degree unknown since the period immediately following World War II. Incidents such as the massacre at My Lai and the so-called mutiny at the San Francisco Presidio have brought home to the American people certain issues heretofore the exclusive province of military lawyers and a handful of scholars who specialized in the arcane field of "military justice." Now nearly everyone is interested, and hardly a week passes that some national magazine or prominent newspaper does not have a feature article about a specific court-martial trial or the system in general.

But in the earlier period, from the last year or so of World War II to about 1950, no less attention was paid to the military's methods of handling its criminals. Studies were made; a variety of learned and not so learned writings were published; and much as today, several legislative proposals were introduced in the Congress to eliminate real or imagined wrongs.

Studying both of the eras of turmoil, it is tempting to make simplified contrasts. All too many observers have seen the struggle as one which pitted enlightened civilian reformers, bent on bringing the blessings of civilian judicial practices to the military, against arch-reactionaries in the service, fabricated from the Prussian mold and determined to preserve the autocratic power of commanders.[1] A more penetrating inquiry reveals how erroneous such a contrived dichotomy is. Those alleged to be villains are frequently high-principled, and the putative heroes are more than occasionally found with unclean hands themselves.

It is customarily asserted, for example, that the reforms in military justice that followed World War II resulted from massive pressure put on the armed forces by people and groups who had experienced or perhaps suffered from injustice at the hands of military inquisitors.[2] Doubtless numerous unpleasant events occurred,[3] but available evidence indicates that the popular agitation generated by them could not alone have caused the subsequent changes in military law. The same is true of more recent court-martial reforms; they, too, seem to take place in an atmosphere remarkably free from outside influence.

One purpose of this study, then, is to illustrate, as regards this small segment of the American military establishment, just how reforms are achieved. Who are the men who have the power to make changes? What attitudes inform their actions?

In addition, there are virtually uncountable instances of reforms initiated from within the services themselves. As we shall see, the military has frequently criticized its own court-martial methods, sought solutions to the problems it found, and then altered the system in an apparently enlightened way. It is significant that during the two decades between the end of World War II and the onset of the Vietnam War, the American public and political-world as a whole either forgot or ignored the problems of military justice. But a few men both in and out of the service made it their business, and their accomplishments and failures strongly influenced what was possible when public interest reawakened in the late 1960s.

Finally, one should not lose sight of the fact that an attempt to graft onto courts-martial certain concepts borrowed directly from civilian law might raise its own set of problems. There are limits on the extent to which the essentially autocratic armed forces are able to adopt notions regarded as precious by a democratic society. And there are limits on the extent to which civilian society will accept whatever such adaptations the services attempt, however much in good faith the military may be acting. The tension between *discipline* — regarded as indispensable in a military force — and *justice* — similarly respected in the civilian community — may help to determine where those boundaries lie.

To understand the reforms alluded to above, some historical context is necessary. Up until the beginning of the Korean War, the

United States had always operated two distinct court-martial systems, the Army's and the Navy's. The Army Articles of War, borrowed almost in entirety from the British during the Revolutionary War, were occasionally revised and updated during the Nineteenth Century. But none of those changes was in the nature of reform, so that the Army fought World War I with essentially the same court-martial rules under which it had fought for independence.[4]

During World War I, however, several unusual things occurred. When Major General Enoch H. Crowder, the Army's Judge Advocate General (JAG)—the title held by the service's highest ranking lawyer —was temporarily assigned the additional duties of Provost Marshal General and administrator of the Selective Service System, the Acting JAG in his place was Samuel T. Ansell, who proved himself a man of vision and force, if not tact. A graduate of West Point and the University of North Carolina Law School, Ansell had been a protégé of Crowder's ever since the latter brought him into the Army's legal department in 1909.[5]

During his tenure as Acting JAG, Ansell suffered from a number of frustrations. Although he was in fact the chief of the military justice system, he was forced to labor in the shadow of Crowder's renown. The resulting anonymity may have stabbed at his ego. More substantively, he was repeatedly shocked by the sentences handed down by Army courts-martial, and his utter powerlessness to do anything to correct them. The Fort Sam Houston "mutiny" of 1917 particularly galled him. There, Negro troops, angered by their treatment at the hands of the Army and the local Texas community, protested violently, were subdued, and court-martialled. Although the resulting trials themselves are reported to have been scrupulously fair, the review then required by the 1916 Articles of War was handled in such a way as to arouse General Ansell. AW 48 provided that in time of war the local commander could execute sentences without approval by the Office of the JAG, but the commander at Fort Sam Houston stretched even that liberal rule. At the end of each court session, the record of the trial was sent to his staff judge advocate, who reviewed the proceedings for legal errors. Since none was found on this day-to-day basis, the commander was in a position to carry out the sentences almost immediately after the verdict was in. Thus, thirteen of the black soldiers were executed before any higher authority was even officially apprised of the trial.[6]

Ansell was outraged. When a few months later another unreasonable exercise of court-martial power occurred at Fort Bliss, Texas, he moved into action. This time the victims were still alive, so the legal question was not moot. Ansell argued before the Secretary of War that those portions of the law which preceded the 1916 Articles and which had not been specifically repealed by them were still operable. This would have the effect of granting Ansell the right of JAG review and revision of all general court-martial sentences as had been provided in the 1874 Articles. But, at this point, General Crowder asserted himself, arguing in favor of the action of the commander in question and the 1916 Articles and against Ansell.[7]

The personal aspects of this clash should not be overlooked. Crowder was generally considered the author of the 1916 Articles, and his defense of them was to be expected. As for Ansell, he was motivated at least as much by the ambition to take over Crowder's job as by the substance of the controversy. In November 1917, for example, he had surreptitiously persuaded the Acting Chief of Staff to sign an order appointing him permanent Judge Advocate General. When Secretary of War Newton D. Baker learned of this, he revoked the order. Thereafter the Secretary was increasingly suspicious of Ansell, and when the question of JAG review arose, he decided in favor of Crowder.[8]

But Ansell was not a man easily shoved aside. To begin with, he had won a major concession. By General Order 7 of 1918, the War Department administratively provided for mandatory JAG review in cases involving death sentences or dismissal of officers. This was too late to help the Fort Sam Houston troops, and too little to affect the Fort Bliss case, but it was a step. In another change, Ansell himself established in the Office of JAG a quasi-judicial body, the "board of review," to provide a sounding board for the parties involved and to assist the JAG in making his decisions in cases reviewed by him under the new general order. But Ansell's personal career in the Army was doomed. To take advantage of his scholarship, and yet to deprive him of administrative power, he was detailed shortly after the Armistice to help revise the Articles of War. This was a tactical error on the part of those who thought they could silence him by putting him away where he could play harmlessly with his new ideas. Ansell tackled his new assignment with gusto and by early 1919 had drafted a thorough overhaul of the Articles. In March of that year he lost his temporary rank of Brigadier General and resigned from the Army, but the publicity attending his controversy with Crowder and his subsequent banishment earned him the alliance of some important people. Notable among them was Senator George Chamberlain, of Oregon, the ranking minority member of the Senate Military Affairs Committee, who now became Ansell's chief supporter.[9]

Ansell's code reflected an utterly different philosophy from that prevailing in the military up to that time. William Winthrop, an Army Judge Advocate General in the post-Civil War period, had published a second revised and enlarged edition of his treatise on military justice just before the turn of the century. This work was regarded as scripture in its field. Winthrop's theory on courts-martial was the constitutionally sound and judicially authorized one that military trials were not part of the judicial branch of the government. That being the case, he wrote:

It follows that courts-martial must pertain to the executive department; and they are in fact simply *instrumentalities of the executive power,* provided by Congress for the President as Commander-in-Chief, to aid him in properly commanding the army and navy and enforcing discipline therein . . .

From that, Winthrop deduced that such constitutional guarantees as the right to counsel, the right to confrontation, and the prohibition against self-incrimination, among others, applied to courts-martial only if and to the extent that Congress by statute conferred them on the military tribunals. That this was a generally agreed upon position is indicated by the difficulty the Ansell articles experienced.[10]

In the Spring of 1919, Senator Chamberlain introduced Ansell's articles in Congress.[11] During the hearings that followed, Edmund M. Morgan, then a professor of law at Yale, who was to play a larger role in a later, more successful revision of the military law codes, testified that the Articles of War as they then existed were deficient in a half-dozen major areas. First, charges could be made almost capriciously. Neither an oath to accompany their filing nor a formal pretrial investigation to test their validity was required. Second, the commander who convened the court could pick its members to suit his own purposes, thus frequently presenting the accused with a stacked deck from the beginning. Third, there were no ironclad guarantees of court-martial impartiality. Since the court was simply an instrumentality of the executive, as Winthrop put it, the commanding officer could and often did intervene at his pleasure to see that things progressed the way he, the local "executive," wanted them to. Fourth, a lawyer being a rarity and there being no provision whatever for a judge figure, the officers of the courts—president and both prosecutor and defense counsel (if the accused were lucky enough to have one!)—were almost always line officers. The results, Morgan said, were uniformly amateurish and inexpert. Fifth, when the trial was over, the proceedings, verdict, and sentence were reviewed by the very commander who levied the charges, convened the court, and appointed its members and officers. Moreover, he was further authorized on review to revise the sentence upward if he were so disposed and to return to the trial court for reconsideration any finding, including an acquittal, with which he disagreed. And finally among Morgan's list of shortcomings, and what got Ansell involved in the first place, the review provisions were inadequate and unjust.[12]

Much of the sting was taken out of Morgan's testimony by his admissions that the Army had recently begun on its own initiative to correct a number of potentially unjust features of the old articles. For example, Morgan conceded that investigation of the facts was already required before a case could go to a court-martial, in accordance with an administratively promulgated change to the *Manual for Courts-Martial*. One of Morgan's complaints was that fully one-third of all the acquittals during the war had been "revised" to guilty during reconsideration sessions at the direction of the convening authority. But even here, he was obliged to acknowledge that the recently published General Order 88 of 1918 ended that practice by prohibiting revisions that were unfavorable to the accused. Finally, he recognized the gains Ansell's personal efforts had won within the War Department, admitting that he approved of General Orders 7 and 84, which set up the review procedure, and that his only wish was that they be made statutory.[13]

The bill introduced by Chamberlain, as Morgan later described it, would cure the defects he saw by: (1) requiring that charges be made under oath and be thoroughly investigated before being brought to trial; (2) establishing a "court judge advocate" who would perform the duties of trial judge; (3) providing that the court members would be selected by the court judge advocate from a panel of officers and men supplied to him by the convening authority; (4) requiring a sufficient number of enlisted court members in the case of an enlisted defendant so that, if voting *en bloc*, they could veto any finding or sentence; (5) abolishing the reviewing power of the commanding officer except for clemency authority; (6) perhaps most importantly, establishing a court of military appeals, three judges with life tenure, who would review every case involving certain specified major punishments.[14]

At the heart of these proposals was a radically new concept of military law, one which would divorce the court-martial from the commanding officer and move into the vacuum thus created lawyers, civilianlike rules of procedure and evidence, and a complex system of appellate review to filter out whatever remnants of past attitudes still remained. That this was advanced in scope and content is proven by subsequent history. And its failure to win general approval provides us with the first illustration of the difficulty of achieving military justice reforms.

Ansell himself, the far-sighted reformer, demonstrated little personal restraint or tact. Perhaps that is a characteristic of visionaries in general, but it must have hurt the chances of his articles. In a letter to Major General Leonard Wood, a professional soldier, who, as a crony of Theodore Roosevelt in the prewar days and a potential presidential candidate of the renascent Republican Party, was not a person to be attacked without risk, Ansell wrote:

> Never again can or will we fight a great war with an Army of American citizens subject to a system of discipline that was designed for the Government of the professional military serf of another age. . . . It will come, as such changes have ever come, in the face of the efforts of narrow professionalists to hinder and prevent it.[15]

Noble sentiments, to be sure, but in their indirect attack on Wood himself, somewhat lacking in prudence. Ansell also wrote an intemperate article for a law review which he hurried to have published during the hearings on his articles. There he indiscriminately condemned the entire system and all those who participated in it as "lawless"; charged that the system was in the first place a "witless" borrowing from the British; and claimed that court-martial results were anything but "judgments," but were in fact "un-American" in their despotism. This indicated the frustration of the man, and probably did his cause more harm than good.[16]

Ansell, Morgan, and Chamberlain were trying to conquer an establishment that they thought was reactionary and monolithic in its attitudes regarding military justice. But the existence of those reforms to which Morgan had to bow in his testimony demonstrated that there were men within the service who were willing to try to correct whatever injustices existed. Sweeping attacks on the entire system and all the men in it were unfair then, and probably even counterproductive.

What finally emerged from all of this was not the Ansell code, but the 1920 Articles of War. Although limited in scope when compared to the Chamberlain Bill, this statute was the first revision of the Army's law since Revolutionary days to make substantive changes in court-martial law, additional proof that there existed reform-minded men in the service. The new AW 70 greatly changed pretrial procedure by requiring sworn charges, a "thorough and impartial" investigation, and expert legal advice for the commanding officer before he convened a court. Other articles established procedural reforms in the court itself. Most notable was the creation of a "law member" by AW 8 and AW 31. He was a voting member of the court, but was assigned some of the duties of a trial judge, such as ruling on admissibility of evidence and instructing the court on its responsibilities and on the applicable law in a given case. Defense counsel were for the first time made mandatory by AW 11 and AW 12 for all but the lowest form of court-martial. Ansell's review system was given statutory sanction by AW 50½, and AW 40 did the same for the ban on upward revision of sentences and reconsideration of findings.[17]

Some of these measures were unsatisfactory to Ansell and his supporters. The recommendations of neither the AW 70 pretrial investigator nor the commander's own legal advisor were made binding on the convening authority. Court members were to be those "best qualified by reason of age, training, experience, and judicial temperament," but enlisted men were not eligible to sit on the courts. Even the law member, a mere shadow of Ansell's court judge advocate, was not required to be a lawyer and could be overruled on most matters by a majority of the other members. And finally, the Secretary of War and the President of the United States were not bound by decisions of the Board of Review.

Such then, were the forces that fashioned the Articles of War under which the Army fought World War II. The commander remained the most powerful man in the entire system and could, if he chose, exert great influence over the results of courts-martial. As a whole, the trial machinery was simple, requiring a bare minimum of legal knowledge and expertise. Soldiers were supposed to fight wars, not lawsuits, and the simpler the trial, the less effort and time was required to train people to conduct one properly. The review procedure readily lent itself to quick confirmation of verdicts, another attribute thought crucial to military justice. If courts-martial were devices by which discipline was enforced, offenders had to be brought to their just desserts speedily so that their barracksmates would not fail to see the penalty that bad conduct necessarily carried with it.

Nothing so dramatic as the events surrounding the Chamberlain Bill happened in the Navy after World War I. In fact, the Articles for the Government of the Navy (AGN) as they stood in 1950 were essentially unchanged from 1862.[18]

Like the Articles of War, the AGN were borrowed wholesale from the British. The Articles for the Government of the Royal Navy of 1649, as modified in 1749, formed the basis of the American naval regulations of 1775. When the U.S. Navy itself was permitted to disband after 1783, the 1775 rules went with it. But with the reconstitution of the fleet during the quasi-war with France in 1798 came the enactment of "Rules and Regulations of 1799." These were slightly revised in 1800, and a few new wrinkles were added thereafter, but these rules stood virtually intact until the 1862 codification, which primarily reflected the fact that the United States had become transcontinental and its Navy worldwide.[19]

The Navy court-martial system was very much the same as the Army's. The power of the commanding officer to initiate charges, convene courts, appoint members and officers, and conduct a review of the proceedings was the same.[20] Similarly, although there was no writer on naval law who compared to Winthrop, the basic understanding was that the sailor surrendered his claim to constitutional rights upon enlistment. In fact, the Supreme Court case which established the basic law about the jurisdiction and methodology of courts-martial, *Dynes v. Hoover*, grew out of a habeas corpus action brought by a sailor seeking relief from a Navy court-martial conviction.[21]

Like the Army's, the Navy system included three different types of courts-martial. Each was identified by its power to punish and number of members. The lowest, called the "deck" court in the Navy and the "summary" in the Army, was limited to one or two months confinement. In both services, this court consisted of one officer, who acted as judge, jury, prosecutor, and defense counsel. The next higher court, the Army's "special" and the Navy's "summary," was composed of three or more officers. A prosecutor assigned to these courts had both the duty of advising them on points of law and certain other administrative tasks such as keeping and verifying the record of trial. The Army special court could award punishment up to six months confinement. Although the Navy summary court was limited to handing down two months confinement, it could give a convicted sailor a bad conduct discharge, something the Army has always been loath to do at the inferior court level. The highest court in both systems was called a "general" court-martial. General courts had the power to try any person subject to military or naval law for any offense punishable by law, and to adjudge any legally permissible sentence, including the death penalty. They were composed of not less than five officers; the Navy set a maximum of thirteen, but in the Army there could be "any number."[22]

General Ansell might have found the Navy's ultimate review system more acceptable than the Army's. For convictions of a general court-martial, the Navy provided that the Judge Advocate General review the record of trial for legal errors and that the Bureau of Naval Personnel review it "for comment and recommendation as to disciplinary features."[23] But this apparently thorough system did not guarantee due process to the accused. The Navy never placed a high premium on lawyers in uniform, and the JAG review was most often done by nonlawyers. In fact, Edmund Morgan reported that the Navy's World War I JAG, George R. Clark, boasted that there was not a single lawyer on his staff.[24]

Intermediate stages of the Navy review system seem to have been about the same as those of the Army. The convening authority had almost plenary powers over findings and sentences, except that he was not authorized to commute sentences.[25]

Another similarity between the two codes was the nature of the punitive articles. These were truly military laws, dealing with matters such as mutiny, misuse of military property, disrespect and disobedience, countersigns, false muster, and other esoteric items. "Civilian-type" offenses, such as murder, rape, robbery, arson, and other felonies, were grouped together almost inconspicuously, indicating the minor roles they were assigned in the military statutes. Both systems, moreover, provided that courts-martial were not to try cases involving capital crimes of a "civilian" nature in peacetime in the United States.[26]

Despite the essentially similar nature of the two codes, the Navy law was untouched by the agitation that produced the Chamberlain Bill, which calls for some reflection. The reforms embodied in the 1920 Articles of War are sometimes attributed to the pressure of public opinion following the first exposure in the Twentieth Century of large numbers of Americans to military justice and its flaws. But the fact that the Navy, which experienced a similar expansion during 1917-1918, was not the target of legal reformers makes this analysis suspect. It is possible that the Navy's system was less unjust than the Army's. But the foregoing description of the two codes makes that unconvincing. It might also be that the sailors, primarily volunteers, had a higher tolerance for injustice than their drafted brothers in the

Army. But there is no way to prove or disprove such a contention. The Navy, of course, had no upstart reformer like the Army's Ansell. The Navy Judge Advocate General recommended in 1919 that his service adopt the law member concept for general courts and also recommended a Judge Advocate General's Corps for the Navy.[27] This would have the goal of enhancing service lawyer prestige, thus boosting recruitment and helping to overcome the shortage of men to which Morgan had pointed. But these suggestions seem to be the work of, on the one hand, a man alert to developments in the sister service, and on the other, one who could propose a solution to the needs of his own unit. His failure to persevere in these matters clearly stamps him as a man not cut out of the Ansell pattern.[28]

A more subtle explanation for the relative peace enjoyed by the Navy system is given by a lifetime student of these questions. Frederick Bernays Wiener, Reserve colonel, judge advocate, scholar and lawyer, thinks the reason is that the Navy did much less to rearrange the social patterns and customs of its population than the Army did. During peacetime, both services made officers out of gentlemen and enlisted men out of lower class recruits. During the mobilization, the Navy continued that practice by commissioning mostly college graduates. But the Army selected its officers on the basis of merit. The result, according to Wiener, was that in the Navy those who were the likely victims of perceived court-martial abuse were the same who had been abused in civilian life. In the Army, on the other hand, the scions of high society who were forced by circumstances to serve in the enlisted ranks complained at every real or fancied maltreatment. The overall consequence was great agitation for changes in military law, but much less, almost none, in the sea service.[29]

Following the 1919 burst of activity, however, both the Army and Navy settled back into a comfortable peacetime routine much like the one that had existed before 1917. Their court-martial systems were largely forgotten by the American population as a whole. The reforms of 1919 would prove to be limited and not very effective, as Morgan and Ansell had predicted. But a pattern of change had been established that would continue with different results after the next great war.

2 World War II:

A Time to Study

During World War II, the United States expanded its armed forces to a maximum strength of something over twelve million men and women. In a sophisticated and complex study published shortly after the war, two social scientists analyzed one facet of that inflated wartime military society. Because induction standards were low, they argued, criminals and potential criminals were not automatically excluded from enlisting. Moreover, the military population was heavily skewed towards males between the ages of seventeen and forty, the largest crime-producing segment of the society at large. Arraying these facts against the 1940 census and other known data pertaining to civilian society, the scientists argued that the World War II Armed Forces included about 30 percent of the nation's potential criminals.[1]

It was not surprising, therefore, that court-martial business during the war was brisk. There were about eighty thousand general court-martial convictions during the war, an average of nearly sixty convictions by the highest form of military court, somewhere in the world, every day of the war. There were about two million convictions handed down by American courts-martial of all types during the hostilities.[2]

The most obvious result of all this activity was that a great number of Americans, most of them servicemen only reluctantly, had been brought into contact for the first time with military justice. Among them were not only the youthful offenders themselves, but also a large number of civilian lawyers who served as legal specialists or judge advocates. For example, Ernest W. Gibson, who become Vermont's postwar governor, complained angrily about a South Pacific area commander he had known who demanded convictions regardless of guilt or innocence and about the cruelty imposed on GI's in stockades in some places in that theater of operations. Another prominent critic was Franklin Riter, who as a brigadier general was the chairman of the European Theater board of review that confirmed the death sentence of Private Eddie Slovik. After the war, Riter, a well-known Salt Lake City lawyer, used his position of importance in the American Legion as a platform for his attempts to obtain military justice reforms. Still another important figure was Robert E. Quinn, a wartime naval legal officer, who in the 1930s had been Governor of Rhode island and number two man behind Theodore F. Green in his state's Democratic Party. That smoothly run machine would wield heavy influence in the postwar years, some of it directed toward court-martial affairs, as we shall see. Many others could be added; some of them will appear in these pages later.[3]

Some of these men found military justice not to their liking. Sentences often seemed harsh and inconsistent. Court-martial personnel were so often grossly inexperienced that results were frequently a shame and a sham. Nearly all of the citizen-soldier lawyers had personal knowledge of what they considered improper command influence over trials.[4]

Official concern echoed this popular displeasure. It was apparent to most high officials within the military departments that the court-martial system, which had worked well enough for the small, compact, prewar Navy and Army, displayed major weaknesses under the stress of wartime expansion. During the interwar years, the services had been composed almost entirely of Regulars, both officers and men. Because of the small numbers, there could be a leisurely and thorough orientation for enlistees, allowing them to become familiar with their rights and obligations. Similarly, officers in the peacetime military were highly trained professionals, who considered it one of their primary duties to be able to conduct a skilful court-martial, whether as court member, prosecutor, defense counsel, or even law member. But these conditions were destroyed in the fast-paced mobilization that came with the war, and the result was creaking and groaning in the framework of the ancient system.

The Navy and War Departments themselves had an interest in correcting defects in the machinery, because disciplinary problems were a serious source of manpower drain. In the first place, a major share of the offenses committed by servicemen were unauthorized absences of one form or another. Another form of manpower loss occurred when a man was convicted by court-martial. Sentences including confinement or punitive discharges also cost the military badly needed men. Moreover, the services as institutions were acutely aware of the role morale plays in the efficiency of a combat unit and were therefore quick to investigate anything that might be responsible for the lowering of that precious commodity.[5]

With these things in mind, the secretaries of the departments commissioned a series of study groups during and immediately following the war. These included, in the Navy, the two Ballantine committees, 1943 and 1946; the Taussig study in 1944; the McGuire committee of 1945; the Keeffe General Court-Martial Sentence Review Board, 1946; and Father White's study of prisoners, 1946.[6] Similar bodies worked on Army problems: the Roberts board on clemency, 1945-47, the Vanderbilt committee and the Doolittle board, both 1946.[7]

None of the reports was comforting. The criticism was intended to be helpful, and obvious efforts were made to find good points in the old ways. For example, the Vanderbilt report claimed that

the Army system of justice in general and as written on the books is a good one; that it is excellent in theory and designed to secure swift and sure justice, and that the innocent are almost never convicted and the guilty seldom acquitted.

But this optimistic beginning was contradicted by the criticism within. In its summary, the committee reported that it could find serious faults in seven major areas; (1) there was a regrettable lack of attention to, emphasis on, and planning regarding military justice matters in the Army as a whole; (2) there were not enough qualified men in the Army to serve as court members and officials; (3) commanding officers frequently dominated the courts in the rendition of their judgments; (4) defense counsel were inadequate, either because they lacked experience or knowledge or because they failed to exercise the properly vigorous defense attitudes; (5) sentences were frequently severe, and "sometimes fantastically so"; (6) there was sometimes discrimination between officers and enlisted men, both in bringing charges and in handing down convictions and sentences; (7) the pretrial investigations under AW 70 were frequently inefficient or inadequate.[8]

As harsh as this report was, the War Department's initial response was to take corrective action. In fact, two of the Vanderbilt complaints had already been anticipated. The committee's finding that sentences were "fantastically" severe, if true, meant that some Army men languished overlong in stockades and prisons. Aside from the injustice of the situation, this represented an unnecessary loss of Army manpower and possibly an avoidable adverse morale factor. But the Army had begun work in this area of criticism before the publication of the Vanderbilt report. Several months before Vanderbilt began his hearings, the Roberts board was busily at work remitting or reducing about 85 percent of the 27,500 general court-martial convictions it reviewed. Another Vanderbilt charge, that there had been discrimination in the system between treatment afforded officers and that given enlisted men, was studied by the Doolittle board, also commissioned earlier than the Vanderbilt committee. Doolittle delved into the entire range of officer-enlisted relationships and reported back, among other things, that the court-martial system was thought by enlisted soldiers to be rife with "inequities and injustices" to them, thus corroborating the Vanderbilt findings.[9]

The Navy authorized similar investigations, two of them while the war was still in progress, the 1943 Ballantine report, and the Taussig study. The first Ballantine committee was directed to find solutions to the then overwhelming logjam in the Navy courts. It concluded that the basic cause of the problem was the centralization of convening authority in Washington and recommended the establishment of more or less permanent courts in the various Naval District headquarters and the streamlining of certain AGN procedures. These suggestions were implemented, and they worked. But Ballantine went further and, decrying the lack of a judge in Navy courts, proposed the adoption of the Army's law member concept, a notion that was rejected.[10]

The Taussig study on naval discipline was devoted in large part to developing a profile of the typical naval offender, analyzing why he went wrong and what could be done to rehabilitate him. Taussig also found fault with the Navy's review system, asserting that it took so long to confirm verdicts that many convicted sailors completed their sentences before the case was closed, a complaint future military men would register repeatedly.[11]

Professor Keeffe's General Court-Martial Sentence Review Board (GCMSRB) and the 1946 Ballantine report dug more deeply into the AGN than either of the wartime studies. Ballantine was heavily influenced by contemporary Army practice. He recommended extending the confinement power of a Navy summary court to six months, thus making it equal to the Army's special court. He also urged the establishment of boards of review like the Army's, and he repeated his 1943 call for a trial judge figure, this time going beyond the law member concept and recommending a "judge advocate," who would rule and advise on points of law.[12]

The Keeffe board studied 2115 cases and in "almost half" of them found "flagrant miscarriages of justice." The board originally had authority only to make recommendations to the Secretary of the Navy regarding sentences. But at the insistence of its chairman, who as we shall see was rarely content with less than his idea of perfection, Secretary Forrestal expanded its purview to include the entire naval court-martial machinery. Thus armed, the Keeffe board examined and criticized AGN courts-martial and proposed reforms to overcome what it thought were the system's defects. Among those suggestions were the establishment of a board of review, chaired by a civilian, to assist the Secretary in the exercise of his plenary powers; the elimination of convening authority review and the power of the court-martial to set sentences; and the creation of a trial judge advocate, who would be a nonvoting member of the court and would be "trained in the law" in order to advise the court on legal points.[13]

The composition of these study groups is significant. The members came from a variety of backgrounds and represented a broad diversity of views within the legal profession. This reflected the complexity of the problem of reforming military justice. The 1946 Ballantine committee, for example, was composed of Mr. Ballantine, (himself a prominent New York attorney and former Undersecretary of the Treasury), plus a United States District Court judge, a professor from Columbia Law School, three Navy admirals, a Coast Guard captain, a Marine general, and two junior naval officers. These last two, Lieutenant Commander Richard L. Tedrow and Lieutenant John J. Finn, submitted an extensive minority report which attacked the "pre-war half-time legal system" by which the Navy continued to do business during the war. The young officers' target here was the traditional Navy way of attempting to conduct its legal affairs on an *ad hoc* basis, a custom which, as we shall see, endured long after the end of World War II.[14]

At least as significant as this lack of complete unanimity on the committee was the general agreement among the majority, a mix of high-ranking military lawyers and prominent civilian legal authorities. Similar harmony prevailed on the other Navy boards. Neither the

Keeffe nor the McGuire bodies produced dissenting views. The GCMSRB, like the others, included both civilians and military, although here the military men outnumbered the civilians to a greater degree than anywhere else. The McGuire committee was a three-man group—two federal judges, Matthew McGuire and Alexander Holtzoff, who would later sit on the Army's Vanderbilt board, and a Marine Corps lawyer, James Snedeker.[15]

While the membership of these groups did not fit in neat molds, the intention of the Secretary of the Navy in appointing them was clear enough. Forrestal took these panels seriously and in many cases adopted their suggestions. To get the most out of them, he tried to harvest the ideas of both civilian and military legal scholars. Only in such mixed groups would the twin bases of military law be fully considered. Civilian systems of law aim to produce justice, but it was the opinion of nearly all concerned that military ones must seek, as Keeffe put it, "the exact relationship and balance between 'discipline' and 'justice.' " Determining just where that balance lay would be at the root of a series of debates over the next twenty years.[16]

War Secretary Patterson took a different tack in appointing the Vanderbilt board. Because he invited the American Bar Association to select the committee, its membership was entirely civilian. Because of that, this body serves as a control group against which some basic concepts might be tested. If it is true that the reforms in military justice of the last fifty years do spring from sources outside the services, it might be expected that an all-civilian panel would bring in recommendations more radical than groups heavily laced with military officers. But that did not occur; the results of all the studies were quite similar in scope and content.[17] In fact, some of the military men on the various boards made contributions that were highly innovative. For example, Tedrow and Finn focused on a problem which bewildered the Navy for the ensuing two decades: how much of a sailor does a Navy lawyer have to be? Their solution, a minority dissent at the time, was the one ultimately adopted, but not until 1968! Tedrow and Finn were both Navy lawyers; not Regulars, to be sure, but Reservists on active duty in the Navy's legal department. Men in this status would continue to join the services for the next quarter-century at least, and if Tedrow and Finn were typical, their presence would tend to prevent any hardening of the cerebral arteries within the legal corps.[18] Moreover, Colonel Snedeker, the one military member of the McGuire committee, who unlike Tedrow and Finn was a Regular, was the actual author of the panel's draft of new Articles for the Government of the Navy, which would be influential over the next few years.

Nor was the Army without its share of officer-lawyers who sought to correct the system from within. One notable example was Colonel Eugene F. Smith, who wrote directly and vigorously to the Army Judge Advocate General in 1945 to advise against the use of a misleading press release that was being circulated to whitewash the court-martial system, then receiving a great deal of unfavorable publicity.[19]

All of this is to suggest only that military justice is a highly complex institution, and that like other complicated structures, it can be reformed only by the work of many people, representing many viewpoints and occupying many strategically located positions. Easy contrasts between civilians and soldiers do not provide useful analyses of the problems involved, a fact that will become increasingly clear.

The movement towards enlightened change was sometimes tortuous. For example, neither the Keeffe nor the Vanderbilt committeemen thought that removing the commander from the court-martial would thwart discipline. In fact, they made nearly identical recommendations. As Keeffe reported,

In most cases [discipline and justice] are perhaps perfectly reconcilable. In a few, perhaps, they are not. In the latter, certainly a good case can be made for the proposition that once a case has been referred to trial, it ceases to be a mere disciplinary matter, and that from then on, the processes of law should be paramount.

The Vanderbilt committee urged a similar solution to the problem. Let the commander control the prosecution, the report said, and let the JAG department manage all other aspects of the trial, including the appointments and the review of findings and sentence.[20] This idea would be repeated many times in the future by reformers.

Many men in the services disagreed with the conclusions or recommendations of the boards. As might be expected, a good deal of the opposition was *sub rosa* and documentation is not available. But some men who occupied key positions in those days still have bitter memories concerning the studies. Ira H. Nunn, now a retired rear admiral, who was then serving as the head of the Navy's legislative liaison team, thought that the AGN was cast in an unfavorable   light by the very willingness of its supporters to cooperate with the groups who were studying it. For example, he said, commanders were asked by the Ballantine and Keeffe boards to supply cases where justice might possibly have gone awry. Navy men complied with this request and provided the investigators with "hard cases," involving difficult legal points. When the findings were published, the men in the Fleet were shocked to find that these "hard cases" had been considered by the boards as *typical*. Admiral Nunn, recalling the old law school aphorism that "hard cases make bad law," was thereafter distrustful of the work of such bodies and remains skeptical of the legislation that ultimately resulted. This was an appraisal apparently shared by many naval lawyers who had less sea and command experience than Nunn, a Navy Cross winner for his heroism in combat at the Battle of Leyte Gulf.[21]

3 The Elston Act:
A Halfway House

As it should be in a society whose political system is intended to respond to public opinion, the dissatisfaction with the court-martial systems expressed by the various study groups was matched by the general public's antipathy towards the methods and results of military justice. Even as the official reports were making their way around Washington, other people were also discussing, and sometimes vehemently so, injustices that they had heard about or suffered.

Congressional utterances often reflected the popular views. Senator Wayne Morse, of Oregon, and Representative Mendel Rivers, of South Carolina, reckoned in the Vietnam era as almost opposites in most things dealing with the military, were once of like mind on the court-martial issue, when in separate statements they charged that the United States had a "rotten court-martial system" and that "military courts were guilty of the grossest types of miscarriage of justice."[1] Other Congressmen, some of whom had served during the recent war and developed their own opinions about military justice, responded with genuine passion to alleged injustices done to their constituents. Michigan Representative Gerald Ford, for example, was nearly incoherent with anger as he described the hardships suffered by a resident of his district because of some arbitrary Air Force action. Representative Leon Gavin, of Pennsylvania, was similarly incensed by the "Gestapo" methods of MP's who had clubbed into unconsciousness a young GI whom they were guarding.[2]

A few years after the war, some people were still so agitated by their experiences that, with only the flimsiest of provocations, they let their opinions be heard. A Pawcatuck, Connecticut, lawyer read in the *New York Herald Tribune* about a committee set up in the Defense Department to draft new court-martial legislation and wrote to urge on the chairman some ideas regarding counsel before the military courts. He was apparently not the victim of court-martial injustice but had merely seen or heard reports of it. That he should be so moved three years after discharge is indicative of his depth of feelings and a hint that many others probably felt much the same way.[3]

The Vanderbilt committee had helped to publicize the inquiry being conducted by the services. Composed of lawyers whose homes suggested that they were selected with geographic distribution in mind, the committee's public hearings were held in several cities outside Washington. The impact that this roadshow had on Congress was enough to gain mention for it in a later House report.[4]

Activity on Capitol Hill was not limited to protest and rhetoric. To those most eager for reform, the pace might have seemed intolerably slow, but in its own fashion, Congress began to move. A subcommittee of the House Military Affairs Committee under Congressman Carl T. Durham, of North Carolina, investigated the matter in 1946, at about the time the Vanderbilt hearings were beginning to capture attention. Durham's work resulted in a comprehensive report, issued near the end of the 1946 session, which discussed court-martial justice in critical terms familiar to those who had studied the reports of the military boards and committees. In the early days of the next session, Mr. Durham introduced a bill which reflected the conclusions of his subcommittee.[5]

Nothing much came of the Durham Bill, for about the same time it was introduced, another subcommittee, chaired by Charles H. Elston, of Ohio, undertook even broader hearings on military justice. This subcommittee, a subsidiary of the newly created Armed Services Committee, had before it both the Durham report and the so-called "Navy bill," which had grown out of Colonel Snedeker's work on the McGuire committee. For a number of reasons—the spotlight of public and Congressional interest on the Army system, Durham's spadework, and some high-level reluctance in the Navy Department —the Elston panel put aside the Navy bill for the moment and went to work on the Articles of War.[6]

Veterans' groups and bar associations now began to clamor for genuine reforms. The American Legion, its membership swelled by huge numbers of World War II ex-GI's, was one of the early protesters against the "outmoded system of Military Justice" that then existed. Another veterans' organization was composed of former military lawyers: the Judge Advocates Association, founded at the instigation of the Army's Judge Advocate General shortly after V-J Day. The JAG probably intended this group to be a bridge from the Army to the civilian bar. But, following the leadership of former Colonel Charles M. Dickson, the association proved to be considerably independent. Dickson was an indefatigable letter writer. Largely through his efforts, the association was persuaded to support the creation of an "Armed Forces Supreme Court," an old Ansell idea that was only a few years away from fruition.[7]

Bar associations, too, became active in advocating changes. In and around New York City, for example, there were a number of lawyers, all ex-servicemen and members of the various city, county, and state bar organizations, who devoted almost full-time effort to obtain meaningful court-martial reform legislation. These men, several of whom will appear in later pages, maintained close harmony among themselves and developed important contacts in Washington. Although they gave their attention to a number of the features of the current Articles of War and AGN, their main goal was to divorce the commander from the court-martial system.[8]

Agitation for military justice legislation was not limited to organized pressure groups. A few people wrote to President Truman to protest incidents of alleged injustice. Some others even undertook to prepare legislative drafts which they believed would solve the problems.[9]

In this charged climate, the Elston subcommittee conducted lengthy hearings. The result, H.R. 2575, was reported to the floor of the House in July 1947 and passed the following January. The bill included several innovations. It attempted to correct the Doolittle allegations of discrimination by providing that, at the option of the accused, at least one-third of the court members in a trial of an enlisted man must be enlisted themselves. This was a compromise between the Durham Bill, which had proposed two-thirds enlisted membership in such a case, and War Department insistence that enlisted members be permitted only with the concurrence of the convening authority.[10] Other antidiscrimination measures held officers subject to more severe penalties awarded by their commander as nonjudicial punishment and for the first time made them triable by special court-martial.[11]

The new bill provided for greatly increased participation by lawyers at all stages and in all roles. For the first time, counsel was available for an accused during the pretrial investigation. The law member of a general court-martial would now be required by statute to be both a member of a federal or state bar and certified by the JAG as specially qualified for his duties. AW 11 provided that the legal qualifications of the defense counsel must be at least equal to those of the prosecutor and that both should be lawyers certified by the JAG, unless military exigencies dictated otherwise.

Minor changes were made in the punitive articles. The new AW 93 made all types of wrongful taking, such as embezzlement, robbery, and wrongful appropriation, chargeable as larceny, thus ridding the code of potential confusion. The ancient provision that conviction of an officer for cowardice had to be publicized in his hometown was blessedly omitted. But the geographic requirement that courts-martial had no jurisdiction over capital murder and rape cases committed in the United States during peacetime was retained.

As for the review phase of the system, the original bill cleared by the subcommittee gave the Judge Advocate General wide clemency powers over sentences. But the full committee eliminated that section, leaving things as they had been after the enactment of the 1920 Articles: the JAG could refer cases to boards of review but had little substantive power himself.

Despite the action of the committee to cut the power of the JAG, a major change in appellate review was effected. Those procedures that General Ansell had won in 1919 were continued, and an entirely new review tribunal was created to cap the appellate hierarchy. This was the Judicial Council, which in some meager respects resembled Ansell's "court of military appeals." A board composed of three generals, the council would be a permanent agency in the Office of the Judge Advocate General. It would review cases involving sentences of life imprisonment and dismissal of officers or cadets and whatever other ones were submitted to it by the JAG. This latter category would usually include cases where the JAG disagreed with a board of review decision. The council, like the boards, would be authorized to "weigh evidence, judge the credibility of witnesses, and determine controverted questions of fact." Moreover, the decisions made by any of the appellate bodies would be "binding upon all departments, courts, agencies, and officers of the United States."[12]

The Judicial Council was warmly embraced by many high officers of the Army. Those who sought preemptive measures to head off more radical reforms probably thought this was the answer to their prayers. Others were happy to remove court-martial decisions from the political arena, where they had frequently been overturned in the past.[13] As Colonel Wiener put it: "No longer will the White House be the ultimate agency of appeal for parents of misbehaved lieutenants found drunk, or in the wrong bedroom, or caught passing rubber checks." Moreover, what possible harm could come out of a body whose members could be hired and fired by the Judge Advocate General?[14]

And yet, less than two years after the Elston Bill hearings, Mendel Rivers had occasion to recall the Army's vigorous opposition to the bill.[15] Much of it had to do with the creation of the Army JAG Corps. According to one section of the bill, Army lawyers would thereafter be promoted separately from other officers. General Thomas H. Green, then the Judge Advocate General, fought long and hard for this idea, in the belief that if it were enacted, his lawyers would no longer stand last on the promotion lists in comparison to the line officers with whom they had always had to compete.[16]

The idea of a JAG Corps was popular among reformers in the civilian community, too. The New York State Bar Association's Committee on Military Justice, for example, called the JAG Corps an even more fundamental reform than all the procedural innovations contained in other parts of the bill. Other articles would require defense counsel, prosecutor, law member, and members of the boards of review and the Judicial Council to be JAG Corps officers. Still others guaranteed staff judge advocates the right to consult directly with their commanders and with judge advocates at higher and lower echelons. Considered in conjunction with these provisions, the creation of a separate promotion list for military lawyers seemed to ensure freedom from fear of retaliation for them personally and to make truly independent action by courts-martial and appellate tribunals more probable.[17]

Many line officers in the Army, however, resented the proposed divorce of lawyers from the rest of the officer cadre. Some thought it representative of a false division in the service, as if line officers and lawyer officers did not have the same goals. At the opposite pole, others believed that the promise of greater opportunity in the lawyer corps would be inimicable to intraservice harmony. General Dwight D. Eisenhower, at that time the Army Chief of Staff, was of this opinion. Despite this high-level resistance, however, the House approved the JAG Corps proposal, although the Elston subcommittee felt it had to assuage Army apprehension by explicitly stating that the mission of the Army and its JAG Corps were identical: the winning of wars.[18]

As a mark of how well it came up to the hopes of civilian reformers of the day, the Elston Bill can be compared to the recommendations of the Special Committee on Military Justice of the American Bar Association. Among other, rather esoteric procedural suggestions, the ABA urged that the new legislation include a prohibition against improper command influence over court decisions. The bill implemented this suggestion in AW 88, although it did not define just what was meant by "unlawful" command influence and failed to provide a specific penalty for a violation. The ABA also wanted a statutory mandate that the law member and both counsel be lawyers; that there be a separate JAG Corps promotion list; that enlisted court members be authorized; and that the power to convene courts be taken from the commander, although he might retain his review and clemency authority.[19] We have seen that all but the last of these recommendations were included in the Elston Bill.

The power to convene courts-martial is a kind of nonnegotiable item as far as the services are concerned. Most career officers, for one reason or another, could endure and even support the bulk of the Elston Bill. For example, the requirement that defense counsel at a general court be a lawyer would guarantee that an accused be apprised of his rights, the law he was accused of violating, and the most potentially successful tactic he could employ to defend himself. In the eyes of the commander this was as fair as any man could expect. The effect of such good treatment would be apparent to the rest of the unit, and morale would profit by it. If a conviction resulted from a trial where the accused had been represented by skilled counsel, the convening authority could be sure that the man was actually guilty. And not the least consideration, having a lawyer for counsel would mean that some platoon leader or battery commander could keep busy at his primary duties and not be tied up in a court-martial for several days.

On the other hand, the line officer would be rare indeed who would go along with the ABA proposal that the Judge Advocate General or his local representative should have the authority to convene courts-martial. There were at least two reasons for this almost unanimous view. First, a court-martial was still regarded as a means by which discipline was furthered, and discipline was the cement that held a unit together. No commander would conceive of surrendering to some lawyer the power to decide whether a court-martial best suited the interests of his outfit's discipline. Second, in time of war, such a provision could do severe damage to the combat efficiency of a military team. It could reasonably be asked, for example, how great an impediment would it have been had Patton's army had to supply company commanders and tank battalion officers for courts-martial during its race across France in 1944. Only a line officer in command could determine in situations like that who could most easily be spared for such collateral duty. No rear echelon lawyer was so qualified, line officers insisted.

Reformers, however, argued that the commander did not have the legal qualifications to convene a court or that the combination of command and convening authority made the latter inferior to the former. But they would get no satisfaction on this point. The Elston subcommittee recognized the validity of the command position, and the resulting bill left convening authority virtually intact.

Having completed work on the Articles of War, Elston turned in July 1947 to the Navy bill. But just as serious work on S. 1338 was due to begin, it became apparent that the Army bill was not going to do very well in the Senate. General Eisenhower had enlisted Secretary of the Army Robert Patterson to support his opposition to the JAG Corps idea. The staff of the Senate Armed Services Committee was also persuaded to accept Eisenhower's position, and as a result, the bill ground to a halt.[20]

The chairman of the Committee, Senator Chan Gurney, of South Dakota, had his own reasons for rejecting the bill. While the Elston subcommittee in the House was hard at work on the new Articles of War, Gurney had been just as deeply involved in the proceedings that resulted in service unification in July 1947. Having finally completed action on that measure, Gurney was not favorably disposed towards the Elston Bill which, as legislation relating to the Army only, was a step away from unification.[21]

Meanwhile, plans were being made within the newly created Department of Defense to take over the legislative programs of all the services. Felix Larkin, who as second man on the Keeffe board had come to the attention of then Secretary of the Navy James Forrestal, was one of the earliest recruits hired by Forrestal when he became Secretary of Defense. Larkin's first major assignment was to supervise the legislation then being sent to Congress by the Army, the Navy, and the new Air Force, and to consolidate it into a unified Defense Department package. Since unification was the touchstone by which Larkin and Forrestal evaluated things, and since Senator Gurney fervently hoped that he had seen the end of fragmented, single-service legislation, the support that carried the Elston Bill through the House disappeared when it reached the Senate.[22]

Chances of its passage therefore remained bleak for many months. In the summer of 1948, however, Senator James P. Kem, of Missouri, engineered a parliamentary coup. As the Senate was about to complete final action on the peacetime draft, Kem moved to attach to it the Elston Bill as passed by the House. He later maintained that "[i] t was my position that if Congress had time to reinstate the Selective Service system, it had time to pass legislation to revise the Articles of War." His point was a telling one, and it convinced the Senate, which thereupon passed without hearings the new Articles as Title II of the Selective Service Act.[23]

Kem may rightly be given credit for his part in the enactment of the Elston Act. But generally overlooked is the role played by yet another veterans' organization, the Reserve Officers Association (ROA). Shortly before the Selective Service Bill came up for a vote, the ROA congressional lobby called on Kem to argue on behalf of the Elston Bill, then languishing in committee. The Senator, an active member of the American Legion, and perhaps of the ROA too, was sympathetic, and took the action that led to passage.[24]

Kem's position on conscription is an early statement of an argument advanced with increasing frequency during the Cold War: if the United States must have a military establishment manned largely by drafted civilians or those who volunteer only to avoid the draft, then Americans should ensure that these reluctant GI's are governed by rules which resemble the ones they knew as civilians and protect them to the same extent. This was the fulfillment of Samuel Ansell's rather testy prediction to General Wood in 1919.[25] The marriage in 1948 of the draft and this military justice code dramatized that the old idea that a serviceman surrendered his rights upon enlistment was at last beginning to weaken, if it were not already dead.

Supporters of the Navy bill, which had been put aside by Elston when the Army bill ran into trouble in the Senate, hoped for similar action to rescue Snedeker's articles.[26] They were disappointed when no such miracle occurred. In several ways the Navy bill was even more interesting than its luckier Army counterpart.

S. 1338 was still, very clearly, a naval law code. The language was more modern, but the subject matter dealt with problems a ship's commanding officer was likely to meet. Such items as striking the flag and hazarding a vessel, for example, were part of the punitive articles. But some of the procedural changes included in the new proposals were quite revolutionary. The Navy had not had the benefit of an Ansell, it should be remembered, whose influence helped to bring the Articles of War out of the dark ages. Nor had there been a reform like the Army's 1920 revision, which now served to make the Elston Act seem only mildly innovative.

Like the Elston Act, the Navy bill retained the traditional role of the commander as convening authority. But the Navy bill would have cut the commander's review powers. Here is another example of how far some in-service reformers were willing to go. The old system gave the commander the power of revision and reconsideration during his review of courts-martial findings. But the 1947 bill would not only remove from him that potentially unjust authority, it would deprive him of any review power at all. He would be permitted to exercise clemency in regard to sentences, but no more.

Under the new AGN, the convening authority would appoint a prosecutor and a defense counsel, with qualifications described by statute. For a general court, both would have to be certified by the Judge Advocate General. For summary courts, the defense counsel would "be a person qualified to perform his duties." In either case, the accused would be permitted to engage civilian or military counsel different from the appointed officer, if he chose. In the summary court situation, the notion that the defense counsel must have legal credentials at least equal to the prosecutor's was included, as in the Elston Act.

The Navy bill provided for a trial judge, to be called "the judge advocate." This officer would be appointed by the convening authority, but he would have to be selected from among those men certified by the Judge Advocate General as qualified for the post, and he would be subject only to the JAG for supervision. He would be liable to challenge for cause, the court itself deciding the issue, but would thereafter rule on all interlocutory questions and would instruct the court before it retired to deliberate. This measure differed so greatly from the Army's law member concept that a small interservice war broke out when attempts were made to unify the two systems two years later.

The new bill would overhaul the Navy's review procedures. Whereas under the old system, review provisions were scattered among statutes and regulations, now all relevant measures would be gathered in the AGN. The JAG himself would have plenary powers over all results of courts-martial, in a provision similar to that struck out of the Elston Bill by the full House Committee. This was another idea not consummated finally until the 1960s. The same article envisaged a clemency panel, a sort of permanent Keeffe board, which would have the power to remit, mitigate, or commute sentences. And finally, the bill planned a "Board of Appeals" as the capstone on the new appellate system. Unlike the Army's Judicial Council, these men, some of whom would probably be civilians, would be authorized to hear cases on petition from convicted sailors, as well as those received from the Judge Advocate General. The bill did not make clear whether the Board of Appeals would be limited to review for questions of law or whether it could go into factual and evidentiary matters as well. But its location in the office of the Secretary of the Navy gave it another promise of probable independence as compared to the Judicial Council, which was situated in the office of the JAG.

It cannot be said which service was "ahead" in the modernization of courts-martial at this point. Each proposal had elements of strength. What is striking is that both, starting with systems that were not much different in essentials in the first place, had by 1948 seemed to move even closer to each other in details.

More fundamental, however, is the fact that the precise combination of methods and resources that would lead to a general reconstitution of military justice had not yet been found. Despite all the public agitation, the departmental studies, and the congressional interest, neither the Army nor the Navy bills did well. The Elston Bill was made law only by an eleventh-hour stroke of parliamentary sleight-of-hand on the part of a single Senator. The Navy bill failed to get past the first step.

Unification, of course, was in the air. We have already seen that many officials favored holding off on both bills to await the action of the newly created Department of Defense. Unification would have its postwar impact on military justice reforms, but for the moment it only delayed things.[27]

It caused some confusion, too. No one was quite sure whether the Elston Act applied to the Air Force. President Truman signed the new articles into law on June 24, 1948; they were to become effective on February 1, 1949. But on June 25, 1948, the President signed the Air Force Military Justice Act, which extended the Articles of War to the newly created air service. This statute, which took effect immediately, spoke of "laws now in effect." But the laws then "in effect" were the 1920 Articles of War, not the Elston Act.

It was as if no one had read the two bills before Truman signed them; not the last time that the left hand of military justice did not seem to know what the right was doing. At a conference in 1951, an Air Force general admitted that, because of the Kem coup, the Elston Act had been a surprise to those who had worked on the drafting and passage of the June 25th law. The latter legislation, he continued, had never intended the 1948 Articles to be included in the phrase "now in effect."[28]

A major point of contention was the Air Force JAG Corps. The Judge Advocates Association cheered its establishment, accomplished they thought by the combination of the June 24th and 25th laws. As a matter of fact, the Air Force in 1970 had still not created a JAG Corps. Because of the loophole created by the conflicting statutes, the Air Force found itself in a position to pick and choose those parts of the Elston Act it liked. It is well known, for example, that General Reginald C. Harmon, the first Judge Advocate General of the Air Force, was opposed to the JAG Corps concept. The Air Force, he said, was like a large banquet where, if something should run out, those guests who sit at a table with twenty-five others are much more likely to get remedial service than are the four people who sit at a card table out on the back porch. Similarly, if a promotion slow-down were to occur five or so years after the war, Harmon continued, Air Force lawyers would be better off to be in with large numbers of line officers than off by themselves on a promotion list that might not seem important to Congress when it got around to corrective action. This argument was so effective, Harmon recalled, that when he pressed it on General Green, who had fought so hard for the Army JAG Corps, Green changed his mind. As a result, the Army did not put its separate promotion list into operation.[29]

There were other reasons why the Air Force legal department considered the Elston Act inapplicable. The law provided that the JAG be a permanent major general. But the first regulations published by the personnel department of the new service described him as having temporary rank only. This seemed proof that authority higher than the legal department did not intend to follow the letter of the Elston Act, either. The Air Force did, however, adopt the Articles of War contained in the 1948 legislation, even to the extent of establishing a Judicial Council. And finally, in 1950, a federal appeals court ruled that the Elston Act did apply to the Air Force, despite the wording of the June 25 act.[30]

By the end of the regular session of Congress in 1948, then, military justice had reached a halfway house. The Army had a new, relatively modern system on the books, but it was not thought satisfactory by large numbers of reformers. The Navy was still operating under a court-martial system that, in essence, was three hundred years old. The best that could be said of the Air Force justice machinery was that it was a question mark. Given the existence of a new unified Department of Defense, and the general agreement among most parties, private and public, that World War II had exposed serious flaws in court-martial law, this situation was not likely to last.

4 The Uniform Code:

Mr. Inside, Mr. Outside,
and a Good Blocking Back

Less than a month after President Harry Truman signed the Elston Bill into law, the Department of Defense began laying the foundation for its repeal. That the Congress, within a year after unifying the Armed Forces, should have passed a law reforming courts-martial in only one of the services (or *perhaps* two!), contradicted the fundamental concepts on which unification was based, and Forrestal and his staff set out to change it.[1]

The first step was the establishment of still another committee. But unlike the many earlier bodies designed only to study the old court-martial systems, this one was directed to bring back a legislative proposal for a wholly new law. According to Secretary Forrestal's mandate, the new committee was to: (1) integrate the systems of the three services into a Uniform Code of Military Justice; (2) make the new code a modern one, "with a view to protecting the rights of those subject to the code and increasing public confidence in military justice, without impairing the performance of military functions"; and (3) improve the arrangement and draftsmanship of the military justice statutes. This was to prove a formidable task.[2]

One of the reasons for its success was James Forrestal himself. He was a man who, having delegated the authority and responsibility for a certain job to a trusted subordinate, would thereafter support the work done and would generally accept the results turned in. The members of the committee on a UCMJ could therefore be confident that their work would not be rejected by the same man who commissioned it, an ignominy suffered by parts of the Vanderbilt report, for example. Forrestal also had considerable political credit in Congress. This fact was recognized by the New York civilian reformers as early as January 1948 when one of them urged him to throw his weight behind the Elston Bill, then stalled in the Senate committee. Some of this influence probably derived from Forrestal's respected persuasiveness, but much of it was due to the complete honesty he maintained in all his relations with the men on Capitol Hill.[3]

Another major reason for the success of the new group was the stature of the man named to head it, Edmund M. Morgan. Morgan, who had been at the Harvard Law School since leaving Yale in 1925, was at the very pinnacle of esteem in the profession of legal scholarship. The author of several well-known and widely used textbooks dealing with general legal principles and the specialized field of evidence, as well as a legal study of the Sacco and Vanzetti case, he was also apparently one of the best-liked teachers on the Harvard staff. Students and acquaintances who revered him were innumerable, and some of them would be in positions to help him in his new job.

There are no contemporary records to document the precise reasons for the selection of Morgan for the UCMJ Committee. Apparently Secretary Forrestal, who made the official appointment, did not know Morgan at the time either personally or by reputation. But the General Counsel of the Defense Department, Marx Leva, did; it was he who recommended Morgan to Forrestal. Leva had been a student of Morgan at Harvard in the late 1930s. He and John Ohly, another Defense Department lawyer who had also been Morgan's student at Harvard, knew very well of their professor's World War I activities on behalf of General Ansell. Since Forrestal was of the opinion that "given the then existing climate in the field of military justice, what was needed was a 'stormy petrel,'" Leva and Ohly thought that Morgan was just what the Defense chief was looking for. They described their former mentor and his background to Forrestal, who apparently liked what he heard and invited the Harvard professor to head the committee.[4]

This raises an interesting question. Since the officials who selected Morgan knew of his support for the 1919 radical ideas of Ansell, it seems fair to assume that they may have hoped that the UCMJ Committee would be heavily influenced by his ideas and that its results would approximate what Ansell had failed to accomplish after the first war. General Ansell was still alive, practicing law in

Washington, D.C. during the time when Morgan's committee was thrashing out the new code. The professor obviously continued to hold the old general in high esteem, even to the extent of keeping him informed of the progress he was making on the project.[5]

Ansell's own reputation, as one might expect of such a contro-versial man, was somewhat mixed. On the one hand, the American Broadcasting Company thought enough of him to invite him to serve as moderator on its regular weekly feature, "On Trial," in February 1949, just as the new code was being submitted to Congress. But, on the other hand, many men in the Army still bitterly remembered Ansell as an ungrateful upstart who had tried to undercut his chief and mentor, General Crowder.[6]

One might expect some of this contempt to touch Morgan, a former disciple of Ansell, thus making his function on the UCMJ Committee nearly impossible, at least to the extent that he would require the cooperation of the military. This does not seem to have occurred. The Air Force and Navy were not concerned, of course. What difficulties arose by Army instigation were substantive and not personal. No doubt the complex organization of the committee, which we will look at in a moment, served to cushion some of the expected shock waves. Time may have dulled the former hostility. And yet, Morgan made no secret of his intellectual debt to Ansell. In an article originally written in 1953, Morgan compared the provisions of his own handiwork to those included in Ansell's code. In most cases he thought the UCMJ had fallen short of the goals of S. 64. And he left no doubt that he thought the 1950 Code was the lineal descendant of the abortive Chamberlain Bill.[7]

In simple laymen's terms, military justice traditionally has existed in the form of a written statutory code, while civilian common law is based to a great degree on interpretations of relevant precedent. The code system is less flexible than common law, which can be adapted by the interpreting courts to fit contemporary needs and ideas. These characteristics generally make liberal reformers look upon a code with disapproval, seeing in it the likelihood of reaction-ary legalism. But the appointment of Edmund Morgan to chair the UCMJ Committee suggests another possibility. A codal system of law might, under very limited circumstances, lend itself more readily to reform than the common law can. Reform by common law must depend on the slow pace of courtroom work, an incomplete reporting system on which to base precedent, and the confusion that results from the necessarily conflicting opinions of various men. To change a codal system, all that is needed is will. Or, in this case, if the Office of the Secretary of Defense decided that it wanted a uniform code of military justice conceptually based on the ideas of Samuel Ansell, what better way to accomplish it than by appointing Ansell's chief supporter to write it?

But, before one can decide whether the UCMJ was bent to the shape of Samuel Ansell's notions by Edmund Morgan, one should first ask whether that was even possible. There is strong evidence for the negative. The UCMJ Committee was really three bodies in one. At the top was the so-called "Morgan Committee," composed of Morgan; Messrs. Gordon Gray and Eugene M. Zuckert, the Assistant Secretaries of the Army and Air Force, respectively; W. John Kenney, the Undersecretary of the Navy; and Felix E. Larkin, the Assistant General Counsel of the Department of Defense. The second body was the "Working Group," chaired by Larkin, and including field grade officers from all three services. The third panel, called the "Research Group," was in fact Larkin's own personal office staff.[8]

The methods employed by this trinity of committees bear some study. The process began when a member of the Research Group took a certain Article of War and compiled its history, including those statutes and cases which related to it, and a capsule description of what the article sought to accomplish. Then he found the corresponding Article for the Government of the Navy, if one existed, and did the same for it. The next step was to collect all the comments and recommendations that had been made by the various study groups and any post-World War II legislative proposals that had been made concerning the topic covered by the article in question. This task was enormous. The Articles of War and the Navy Articles were laid out in completely dissimilar fashions. The services had different ideas about any number of aspects of military justice. Each of the study groups had made unique suggestions: the McGuire board recommended the abolition of the lowest court-martial, while the Vanderbilt committee wanted convening authority vested in the Judge Advocate General. The items which had to be compiled were countless, and each was as subtle or complex as the next, but each had to be listed and filed in some usable way.[9]

The result of this tedious search was the "Comparative Studies Notebook," a huge bound volume of reproduced typescripts, which served as the primary workbook for both the Working Group and the Morgan Committee.[10]

On the basis of all the material gathered by the Research Group, the Working Group was able to agree at its very first meeting on a tentative index for the new Uniform Code. At subsequent meetings the Working Group, still using the "Comparative Studies Notebook" as the basis for discussion, labored over the precise wording for each of the new articles, seeking to cover all the points thought important by each of the services within one code that would be applicable to all three. This, too, was extremely difficult work.

When the highest body, the Morgan Committee, gathered for its weekly meeting, it considered, debated, and sometimes changed the draft prepared for it by the Working Group. These discussions were also based on the material in the "Comparative Studies Notebook," and the work here was as laborious and tedious as at the lower levels. The final step in the process was a report, containing the minutes of the meetings held by the Morgan Committee and the Working Group, which was forwarded to Secretary Forrestal.

This review of the membership and method of the three branches of the UCMJ Committee makes it clear that Felix Larkin, who represented Secretary Forrestal and who was the only person to sit on all three panels, was the key man in the organization. Larkin arranged the meetings, kept the minutes, submitted the reports, and shepherded memos here and there. But he was no mere clerk. It was his own staff that did the research and wrote the memos that make up the "Comparative Studies Notebook." It was Larkin who presided over the meetings of the Working Group and who reported its results to the Morgan Committee. And it was Larkin who represented the authority of Secretary Forrestal at every stage of the work.

Judging from the things they have written about each other, Larkin and Morgan comprised a mutual admiration society. Larkin wrote of Morgan:

As Chairman of the Committee his erudition, and his amazing fund of legal knowledge, was smoothly and quickly translated into the most practical solutions. The reasons for his national reputation for scholarship and teaching excellence became quickly evident.[11]

On the other hand, Morgan repaid the compliment, calling Larkin

a man of real ability. . . . [who] has been and still is in charge of legislation for the Secretary. This has covered some one hundred and fifty bills. . . . and this, as you may imagine, involves the delicate work of resolving controversies. . . . I have been much impressed by his foresight and his extraordinary capacity for planning a job, organizing the work, and pushing it to a conclusion.[12]

There is nothing to suggest that these two men did not have an almost perfect meeting of the minds on most issues faced during the drafting of the UCMJ.[13] From Morgan's point of view, this was fortunate, since Larkin could probably have diverted the work away from what Morgan hoped to make it. On the other hand, the obvious awe with which Larkin regarded the professor confuses even further the question of whether Morgan did, or even could, dominate the UCMJ Committee. The debate about the civilian appellate court provides a good illustration of this problem.

On October 11, 1948, Morgan proposed to the Committee that a "Judicial Council" composed of three civilians be constituted in the Office of the Secretary of Defense. The Council, according to Morgan, would have the power to review on points of law three types of cases: (1) those involving sentences of death, or any court-martial conviction of a general; (2) those forwarded to the Council by the Judge Advocate General of any service; and (3) those received on petition of an accused, if the Council found reasonable grounds. The similarity of Morgan's "Judicial Council" to Ansell's 1919 "court of military appeals" is striking, leaving no doubt that this particular idea of Morgan's derived directly from Ansell's articles. It is equally clear that the idea was first introduced to the UCMJ Committee, not "from the bottom up," by way of Larkin's staff work, but at the very top by Morgan himself. And finally, when the Army representative, Gordon Gray, vigorously opposed the entire concept, Secretary Forrestal ruled in favor of the position taken by Morgan. Morgan's dominance of the process, at least on this one issue, could not be clearer. Whatever mystery might linger can be over only those questions where the documentation is not so obvious.[14]

By 1970, Felix Larkin thought that Morgan's influence over the work of the Committee was severely limited by the circumstances and methods of operation employed by the various panels. Larkin believed that the Research and Working Groups were free from all outside constraints, including Edmund Morgan's intellect. He conceded that Morgan could affect the work done at the uppermost level but insisted that that represented at most only a small fraction of the entire project.[15]

But there is evidence to suggest that Larkin himself may have been the medium by which Morgan's ideas filtered down through the lower levels. In 1970, he thought that he had come on his own to believe in the idea of a civilian court at the top of the court-martial system. But it is clear that the Judicial Council was entirely the result of Morgan's proposal, argument, and influence. On other issues which the existing records reveal less completely, Morgan might have been similarly able to shape the work of the UCMJ Committee, even at its lower levels, through Felix Larkin. Perhaps it is only the communion of philosophy that he shared with Morgan that has made Larkin believe that all the ideas came from the work of his staff.

If there was such a complete blending of mentality between Larkin and Morgan, it was not matched in the work of the rest of the group. Although unification was an accomplished fact in statute and government organizational manuals, it was not so in spirit. Each representative came to the Committee meetings convinced that in certain respects the system then in use in his own service should be adopted by the others.[16]

The sharpness of future debates was foretold at the September 17th meeting. Although the Committee had been at work a month, the project only then had advanced to the point where agreements could be reached. One of the first things decided at that meeting was that review of courts-martial should be conducted within the service of the accused.[17] This flew in the face of unification and the reasons for the inception of the Uniform Code itself. There were a few concessions to the concept of unification; for example, one Article gave commanders the power to convene courts for all persons in their units who were subject to the code, regardless of their service connection. But this was the exception, aimed primarily at those cases involving joint task forces. Interservice rivalry was more normal.

The Committee worked through the winter, trying to meet a deadline set for it by Senator Gurney, who wanted a uniform code ready for presentation at the opening of the 1949 Congressional session.[18] By early January, while Congress was organizing, the Committee was nearly finished; but there remained four points on which no agreement could be reached.

The question of the Judicial Council, with Morgan, Kenney, and Zuckert lined up against Gray, was one issue, as we have seen. A second was whether to permit enlisted court members. On this, John Kenney, arguing in favor of Navy tradition which had always had courts composed entirely of officers, stood alone. Morgan again echoed Ansell, and the Army and the Air Force were in favor of one-third enlisted membership, if an enlisted defendant so requested.[19]

A third issue was over the "law officer." The Army had had a "law member" on general courts since 1920, and the only fault the

Pentagon would admit existed in that system was that the law member did not have to be a lawyer. But since that deficiency had been corrected by the Elston Act, the Army strenuously argued for its retention, and the Air Force generally concurred. On the other hand, the Navy bill in 1947 had provided for a trial "judge advocate," and Kenney argued for something like that. This was very similar to Ansell's "court judge advocate," and Morgan, as might be expected, joined the Navy representative in urging the adoption of the "law officer" concept. A law officer would be more like a judge than the law member; he would be separate from the court, thus establishing a bipartite form of court-martial, much like the judge-jury system in civilian criminal courts.[20]

The final point of disagreement was the right of servicemen to elect trial by court-martial in lieu of nonjudicial punishment. This issue is discussed in detail in Chapter XII. For the time being, it suffices to say that because of the complexity of the issue, the problem was resolved by permitting each service to establish its own regulations to govern nonjudicial punishment, another affront to unification.

The first three arguments were not so quickly settled. Tribute is due here to an important contribution of Felix Larkin, which made possible their resolution. When Larkin was the executive secretary of the Keeffe Board in 1946, he had learned first-hand about the frustrations faced by some of the studies conducted in the Navy and War Departments after World War II. As he himself wrote in 1965,

The usual result is that after a committee has worked hard and long on a difficult subject and has rendered its report, the report is sent for comment to the appropriate governmental departments that are involved. The comments and criticisms and subsequent analysis either delay the implementation of the report for an interminable period or the report is quietly filed away never to be seen again.

Once back in Washington in the newly created Department of Defense, Larkin was assigned to the UCMJ project because of his experience in military justice. On accepting the job, however, he insisted on a guarantee from Forrestal that would prevent the "studied-to-death" fate that befell the other reports. Forrestal agreed to the demand and put the following ground-rules into effect when the UCMJ Committee was convened: (1) the services would be permitted very high-ranking representation on the Morgan Committee and comprehensive membership on the Working Group, *but* (2) once the military representatives on these two panels agreed with a certain drafted provision, there would be no further study or comment by the departments, *and* (3) if the representatives could not agree on certain issues, then Forrestal himself would hear their arguments and decide and his ruling would be final. These rules were followed scrupulously, and what was decided at the meetings of the Morgan Committee went into the bill finally sent to Congress.[21]

The three remaining insoluble points were brought to Forrestal. On January 7, 1949, he called in the entire five-man Morgan Committee, heard their arguments, and promised them a decision soon. A month later, having ascertained which divisions still existed, Forrestal announced his decisions. In each case, he approved the position taken by Morgan. Incorporated into the UCMJ, then, were provisions for a civilian Judicial Council, a law officer at general courts-martial, and eligibility of enlisted personnel to sit on courts as members.[22]

This completed Defense Department action on the UCMJ proposal. Larkin's demands now paid off; the very day after Forrestal's final decisions, February 8, 1949, the UCMJ was introduced in the House by Carl Vinson, of Georgia, and by Millard Tydings, of Maryland, in the Senate.[23]

At this point the House and Senate versions were identical. The bill included some one hundred forty articles, organized in a logical fashion that paid tribute to the work of Felix Larkin and his staff. The code had eleven divisions. The first section of a half dozen articles included jurisdictional items and definitions of terms. The second dealt with apprehension and restraint. Part three was one very long article on nonjudicial punishment. Parts four and five described the powers and composition of the various courts-martial. Parts six through nine dealt with pretrial and trial procedure, sentences, and review. Part ten included the nearly sixty punitive articles. Part eleven, "Miscellaneous Provisions," included, among other matters, courts of inquiry and redress of wrongs.[24]

The targets of the UCMJ were the same ones that had drawn the attention of S. 64 and the Elston Act. Foremost was "command control." The committee report that accompanied the UCMJ to the floor of the House claimed that several restrictions had been placed on command:

The bill provides that the convening authority may not refer charges for trial until they are examined for legal sufficiency by the staff judge advocate or legal officer; authorizes the staff judge advocate or legal officer to communicate directly with the Judge Advocate General; requires all counsel at a general court-martial to be lawyers or law graduates, and, in addition, to be certified as qualified by the Judge Advocate General; provides a law officer who must be a lawyer whose ruling on interlocutory questions of law will be final and binding on the court;

and a number of other things. In fact, however, the only things listed by the House report that differed substantially from the Elston Act were the law officer, the civilian court, and the guarantee of appellate counsel.[25]

The duties of the law officer were not spelled out in the code. Article 26 prohibited his retirement with the court to deliberate except in the presence of the accused or to assist in putting findings into proper form.[26] But nowhere in the code did it state positively what he was to do. That was left for the *Manual for Courts-Martial* which was promised by Article 36, the enabling act for Presidential prescription of rules of procedure and evidence. Still, the intent of Congress on the law officer was clear. When Senator Kem, the hero of the Elston Act, tried to resurrect the law member idea on the Senate floor, Estes Kefauver, of Tennessee, the manager of the UCMJ bill, cut him short. The law officer concept "is merely getting a little closer to the civilian approach," Kefauver told him: "It approaches the judge idea." Senator Leverett Saltonstall, of Massachusetts, added that the law member idea was like permitting a lawyer to sit on juries, a practice rightfully prohibited in most jurisdictions, Saltonstall explained, because a lawyer with his superior knowledge of the law could easily sway the rest of the jurors during closed sessions.[27]

When the *Manual* appeared, these ideas were in concrete form. It would be the responsibility of the law officer to insure a fair and orderly trial. He would rule on interlocutory questions and could be overruled only on motions for a directed acquittal or on questions of insanity. This gave him the power to determine the admissibility of evidence, an important protection for the accused. The law officer would also instruct the court in open session before it retired to deliberate, and if supplementary instructions were requested, these too would be given in the presence of the accused and his counsel.[28]

The provision for appellate defense counsel was detailed in the code itself. Whenever a case went to the civilian court for review, or whenever the Judge Advocate General decided that the government's case before any review body should be presented by counsel, he was required also to provide services of counsel to the accused. Moreover, if requested by the defendant, counsel had to be provided in any case on review. There was nothing vague, therefore, about an accused's right to appellate counsel.

In fact, if any of General Ansell's battles can be said to have been won by the enactment of the UCMJ, it was the one for effective review procedures. Cases of a minor nature would be reviewed in the Office of the JAG. If he should find either the verdict or the sentence unsupported either in law or in fact, he could send it to a board of review. On the other hand, if the case included certain specified major sentences, it would automatically go to a board of review, where it could be reviewed for fact or for law.[29]

Less perfect gains were made regarding the civilian appellate tribunal. Reformers won the opening round when the body had its name changed in the House hearings from "Judicial Council," which the Congressmen thought sounded too much like a "city council," to "Court of Military Appeals," the very term used by Ansell in his Articles. After the name change, however, the court went through some alterations at the hands of Congress that made it less than what had been intended by the 1919 proposal. Perhaps as the price of Navy support for the idea, the Morgan Committee had given to each of the service Secretaries the right to appoint one of the three judges. This provision survived all subsequent controversy within the Defense Department but was deleted following a protest from an unexpected quarter. The Bureau of the Budget must be canvassed for all executive department legislative proposals, and on this one, that agency gave its enthusiastic endorsement, with one exception. Budget thought that the appointment of the members of the Judicial Council, as it was then called, should belong to the President, not the service Secretaries. The draft was changed accordingly and sent to Congress with that provision included. Senatorial confirmation of the appointments to the court was added almost whimsically by the House subcommittee.[30]

The House and Senate did not agree on the question of tenure for the judges of the new court. In the original H.R. 2498, no mention was made of the term these men would serve. This was an intentional omission, so the issue could be resolved in Congress. The House subcommittee thought it important to take the court out of the political arena and to give the judges life tenure. Over in the Senate, however, this provision was immediately rejected by the sub-committee. Senators Kefauver and Saltonstall feared that short terms would be necessary to keep the court from becoming a lifetime refuge for political hacks. Another factor was the well-known opposition of Senator Richard Russell, of Georgia, the second ranking majority member of the full Armed Services Committee, to life tenure for any judge on any court. The Senate version, therefore, cut the terms down to eight years, with varied initial terms. A conference committee compromised the two positions by settling on a term of fifteen years, staggered at the beginning.[31]

A few other minor changes were made in the Court of Military Appeals. At one point, for example, there was some argument over pension and retirement benefits for the men who would serve. This, and other alterations in Morgan's civilian appellate tribunal, must not be considered trivial. Each of them was a skirmish in the war to make it a real court. Reformers were determined to give the Court of Military Appeals all the prestige and influence of other federal courts. When the law was finally enacted, they had fallen short of their goal in only one respect: tenure. But the failure of Congress to provide life terms for the judges of the Court of Military Appeals was a problem which would haunt the court for several years, as we shall see.[32]

These few measures, like the law officer and the new civilian court, were all that the House could point to as bars to future command control. This was not because the Congress had not heard other proposals. In fact, a large number of men, some of them representing popular organizations, appeared before the subcommittees to argue in favor of more radical changes. Three of the most eloquent were George Spiegelberg, of the American Bar Association; Frederick V. P. Bryan, of the New York City Bar Association; and Arthur E. Farmer, of the War Veterans Bar Association.

Spiegelberg testified that about one-third of the high-ranking Army officers interviewed by the Vanderbilt committee actually boasted about having influenced the results of courts-martial to see that the trials came out "right," as they saw it. Spiegelberg thought that this habit of thinking was too deeply ingrained to eradicate merely by legislative exhortation and proposed instead the removal of convening power from the commander. Let the commander refer the case to trial by court-martial, but some other officer should actually convene the court. The commander would then submit a list of officers eligible to sit on the court, and this other officer would select from it a list of nominees to be further culled at the time of trial.[33]

Bryan testified that by placing lawyers at key positions in trial and review sessions, the UCMJ aimed at the wrong target. The commander's illegal influence was not wielded over counsel, he said, but over court members by explicit or implicit threats concerning promotions, efficiency reports, assignments, or by other powers commanders possessed to make life either pleasant or miserable for junior officers in their commands. Bryan's recommendation was like Spiegelberg's: remove convening and appointing powers from the commander and vest them instead in the Judge Advocate General's office. To dramatize his point, Bryan asked Congressman Brooks whether he would like to defend a criminal case before a jury that had been selected at the sheriff's office or by the district attorney.[34]

The third witness, Farmer, cited a poll taken by the Judge Advocates Association. More than seven out of eight replies advocated separation of the appointing and reviewing functions currently exercised by the commander. Farmer conceded that the goal of the Army was to win wars, but he expressed doubt that command control over courts-martial contributed in any way to victory. In fact, he continued, the Vanderbilt study seemed to prove that troop morale was more closely linked to justice than to discipline.[35]

But Farmer had no precise solution to the problem he had raised and admitted that legislation separate from the UCMJ might be the only way to accomplish what he thought necessary. This concession goes to the heart of the problem of military justice reform. The simple fact was that civilian reformers like Spiegelberg, Bryan, and Farmer were in no position to influence the legislation in any significant way. Their arguments were given short shrift by the managers of the bill and other influential men in Congress. Congressman Vinson, for example, said that while JAG convening authority was perhaps desirable, it was impractical because it would "unduly restrict those who are responsible for the conduct of our military operations." Mr. Elston went further by pointing out that since under Spiegelberg's plan the commander would still select the panel, the step where the JAG appointments would take place would only be an additional delay. In his opening remarks to the House subcommittee, Secretary Forrestal asserted that the goal of the UCMJ was a balance between "maximum military performance and maximum justice." The authors of the code had maintained that mix while negotiating the treacherous route through the executive branch simply by limiting how much effective comment groups and persons other than themselves could make. In the Pentagon, this action had saved the bill from those who were in favor of "military performance" at the expense of "justice."[36]

On Capitol Hill, where there was agitation for both sides of

Forrestal's equation, the bill succeeded for the same reasons. The congressional military committees had been living with the problem of military justice, and all the complaints of constituents that went with it, for several years. To them, the UCMJ seemed a suitable means by which to rid themselves of these burdens and at the same time do substantial justice to American GI's. The controversial suggestions of civilian reformers could be listened to, therefore, but not permitted to delay or alter things.

The bar association men seemed to recognize from the beginning the essential impotence of their position. Even before the House hearings began, Spiegelberg decided that, despite the inadequate protections against command control, it would be best to emphasize the improvements embodied in H.R. 2498 and to work for future reforms in the area of command control. Spiegelberg had high hopes that the judges of the Court of Military Appeals would be "good" men and therefore allies of the civilian reformers. Other bar association leaders testified before the subcommittees and wrote letters to potentially sympathetic congressmen and to newspapers arguing their case. But in the end, they accepted what Congress wrought. In a letter to Senator Wayne Morse, Arthur Farmer summed up the dilemma he and his colleagues faced, when he wrote,

there is one course which will be far worse than the enactment of the Uniform Code without the amendments to eliminate command control, and that is a deadlock in the Senate Committee which might result in no legislation whatever. . . .

These men, Spiegelberg, Bryan, Farmer, Wels, and their allies, were reformers, not revolutionaries. In losing the battle, they tried to salvage their ability to fight again another day by keeping open their bridges to those men who were at the seat of power on the chance that later they might have the opportunity to exert some influence. But that was the best they could do.[37]

A similar fate befell conservative spokesmen, the most dynamic of whom was Frederick Bernays Wiener. A graduate of Brown University and the Harvard Law School, Wiener served as a colonel on active duty in the Army's legal department during World War II. He became an articulate defender of the 1920 Articles of War, and according to his testimony, liked the Elston Act even better. Wiener left the Congressmen a series of epigrammatic ideas. On ultimate goals, he told them that

[t]he object of civilian society is to make people live together in peace and in

reasonable happiness. The object of the armed forces is to win wars, not just fight them [but] win them, because they do not pay off on place in a war.[38]

The maxim was impressive enough to be repeated almost verbatim in the House by Mr. Elston during the floor debate on the bill. Wiener also warned the subcommittee, "You cannot maintain discipline by administering justice." Expressing his distaste for the fact that the UCMJ would take courts-martial out of the hands of line officers and put them into those of lawyers, he attributed to William T. Sherman, himself a member of the bar for a time before undertaking the more famous career of laying waste to vast areas of the Confederacy, the following idea:

[i]t will be a grave error if by negligence we permit the military law to becone [*sic*] emasculated by allowing lawyers to inject into it the principles derived from their practice in the civil courts, which belong to a totally different system of jurisprudence.[39]

Wiener buttressed his antilawyer argument by assuring the Congressmen that they would have "to appropriate an awful lot of money to supply the lawyers that will be necessary to run the simple cases, desertions, and the small larcenies, and the disobedience cases, if this goes through." Wiener predicted that the Court of Military Appeals would run aground on at least two shoals: first, courts of such limited jurisdiction had always been staffed by poorly qualified men; and second, civilians sitting on the proposed bench would be unable to comprehend the subtleties of sophisticated military cases.[40]

Wiener was most vehement in his opposition to the law officer idea. Echoing the position taken by Gordon Gray during the UCMJ Committee days, he referred to the law member when he argued that the UCMJ would take "the one trained person off the court." Pointing out that neither Morgan nor Larkin had ever been on a court-martial, he charged that their assumptions about command control over the law member were founded on thin air.[41]

The tag line of Wiener's statement in the House was perhaps the high point of his lengthy testimony. He argued that

if you trust [the line officer] to command, if you trust him with only the lives and destinies of these millions of citizens under his command . . . you can certainly trust him with the appointment of a court.

Chairman Brooks expressed his argeement with that argument, and when Wiener was finished a few minutes later, Brooks' farewell to him seemed more cordial than protocol required.[42]

It might be argued that the force of Wiener's closing remarks prevailed over the suggestions of Spiegelberg and the others who had preceded him. Certainly Brooks' warmth seems to reinforce that hypothesis. But little of what Wiener argued for was incorporated into the bill. An incident that took place during the Senate hearings may illustrate why. The point being discussed was whether judges on the Court of Military Appeals should be statutorily required to have had some military experience. Wiener delivered his customarily cogent and persuasive argument, liberally sprinkled with supporting data and historical documentation, asserting that military experience was an absolute must for these men who would have final and binding powers over courts-martial. His physical bearing was apparently quite impressive to those who saw him. One reporter even described him as resembling "the popular conception of a Prussian officer." When he finished, it was obvious that Wiener had swayed some of the subcommittee members, perhaps as much by his physique as by his argument. But later, when the same question was directed to Edmund Morgan, the diminutive professor quietly pointed out to Saltonstall that Wiener, a prominent civilian lawyer with military experience, was a perfect candidate for the court which he himself had described. Morgan then asked Saltonstall if that was the type of man he wanted on the court. The subcommittee was apparently taken aback by this query, considering all the other comments on military "justice" Wiener had made, and promptly went "off the record." When they returned to verbatim transcript, it was decided that military experience would not be a prerequisite for appointment to the court.[43]

This was only the most dramatic example of the way Morgan and the other authors kept interlopers from changing their handiwork. Like the more radical reformers he opposed, Wiener was outside the small circle of men who had the power to change things, and his eloquence and force, while imposing at the moment of delivery, were without effect in the long run.

The Congressmen who shepherded the bill along the often rocky road on Capitol Hill were jealous guardians of their charge, too. One of the most important debates over the bill in the Senate occurred as a result of the attempts by the Senate Judiciary Committee to acquire jurisdiction over it. Senator Morse urged that the bill be referred to Judiciary, in accordance with a request from Senator Pat McCarran, of Nevada, the chairman. Morse argued that keeping the bill in channels that dealt only with military affairs would maintain the differences that existed between civilian and military trial systems. But Saltonstall, the number two man on the Armed Services Subcommittee, rebutted, calling the proposed referral an "inexcusable" delay after so much study and debate. Saltonstall's position was carried by a vote of 43-33, and whatever contributions Judiciary might have made, or destruction it might have caused, were not allowed to materialize. This should come as no surprise; within the inner sanctum of the UCMJ's authors, no one wanted the code to be exactly like civilian law. They were seeking a balance, along the lines laid out by Secretary Forrestal.[44]

Another attempt to sidetrack the code was made by Senator Kem, who introduced an eleventh-hour proposal that would have made the Elston Act applicable to the Navy. Although there was considerable support at the Pentagon for such a measure, it too was rejected.[45]

This is not to say that there were no alterations in the bill as a result of the public hearings. For example, as drafted, Article 66(e) would have permitted the Judge Advocate General, if he received a board of review decision with which he disagreed, to send the case to a different board for reconsideration. Bryan and many others opposed this point on the grounds that it would give the JAG virtually dictatorial powers over the review system. Their arguments were so vigorous, unanimous, and undeniably correct, that the paragraph was deleted from the bill as reported to the House. But this was a rare occurrence.[46]

The fact was, the UCMJ Committee had heard most of the arguments already. Morgan and Larkin had each had his own personal experience criticizing military justice, one as an Ansell supporter, the other as a Keeffe associate. They had also heard the military's point of view, in their work on the UCMJ itself. And they had studied and researched until there was very little on the subject they had not heard.[47] Perhaps more than any other men in American history, Morgan and Larkin had the opportunity to overhaul the court-martial system. They chose instead to balance it.

Professor Morgan was very familiar with the panel selection idea suggested by the bar association men. It was, after all, one of Ansell's ideas. And he and Felix Larkin had conferred closely with Spiegelberg and the others on the matter during the days when the UCMJ Committee was at work on the draft of the new code. But the best Morgan could say for the idea now was that it "might help." As Morgan saw it, the ultimate solution if illegal command influence continued in spite of the UCMJ would be to have a court-martial system convened under, composed of, and reviewed by civilians. But he believed that that was "impractical." Since his primary goal was to draft a system that would work, he dismissed this idea.[48]

In Morgan's eyes, then, the UCMJ conferred on military commanders a probationary status, whereby they might prove whether they were willing to accept the notion of real justice in their court-martial procedures. Felix Larkin had a more positive, though hardly rosy, view of the code's potential. Larkin conceded the validity of the claim that only the commander could decide which of his unit's personnel could be spared for court-martial duty. He also recognized that those in the service who held out for commander convening, appointing, and reviewing authority were still in an unbreachably strong position. He therefore elected not to challenge either the correctness or the strength of the military view on this question. Rather, he resolved to focus his energies on the enactment of measures that would prevent abuses of command authority. On this point, as on so many others, Morgan and Larkin were of a single mind.[49]

Congress ended up making many changes to the proposal that came from the Morgan Committee, but the compromise between command and justice was left intact. The commander would appoint counsel, law officer, and court members, and he would be the first reviewer. But the presence of a lawyer at the pretrial investigation, an idea carried over from the Elston Act, was intended to guarantee that a man would not be tried on spurious charges, perhaps filed by a vindictive commander. The law officer would ensure that the trial itself was conducted according to law and not the general's whim. Lawyers at the trial and in the review system would use every possible defense argument that could be squeezed out of the fact situation. And perhaps most importantly, the all-civilian Court of Military Appeals would reverse every case where there was evidence of command tampering.

Although "command influence" was by far the major issue to which the UCMJ Committee and Congress addressed themselves, it was not the only one. An important innovation in the new code was the enumeration of "civilian" offenses. Both the AGN and the Articles of War had been content to list common law crimes only briefly, and by their ordinary names, without any definition of the elements of the crimes, a gap which the accompanying *Manual for Courts-Martial* was expected to fill. Like so many other aspects of the old systems, this was amateurish and unencumbered by the niceties and protections of law.

To clarify this situation was one of the main goals of Larkin's Research Group. The rest of the UCMJ Committee concurred, and the result was a section of fourteen articles detailing offenses not peculiar to military life. Each was defined in terms of its elements, including the intent of the offender, and degree of seriousness.

While the bill was in Congress, a number of other changes were made. The House, in fact, made so many alterations in the Morgan draft that it was thought necessary to use a different legislative proposal number, H.R. 4080. Most of these changes were in phraseology, with the few exceptions which we have studied. One important difference between H.R. 2498 and H.R. 4080 not mentioned before was in Article 3(a). As originally drafted, this provided for trial by court-martial of Reserve personnel who had committed serious crimes while they were on active duty. As we shall see in a later chapter, however, Congress was so influenced by two contemporary federal court decisions that it extended the jurisdiction conferred by this article to cover ex-GI's who had become civilians, with historic consequences.[50]

Perhaps no one has better captured the essence of the Uniform Code than the Court of Military Appeals did ten years later:

> Members of the legal profession within the military establishment are made primarily responsible for the elimination of the abuses formerly affecting military justice, and are relied upon for the establishment of a court-martial system truly judicial in viewpoint, and administered in accordance with established American concepts of jurisprudence, under the guidance of a civilian tribunal serving as the Court of last resort.[51]

This was no mean accomplishment. Edmund Morgan reported that the code was the result of the study of the law and practices of the services, complaints against the old system, replies to those complaints made by the military, suggestions by professionals for reform, and a few ideas borrowed from foreign nations. This appraisal has all the earmarks of the scholarly view one would expect from the professor. Felix Larkin, ever the technician, saw the adoption of the code as the result of "a confluence of a tremendous war, great public interest, the circumstances of unification, and glaring deficiencies in what had existed before."[52] These recipes for court-martial reform are not complete, however, without adding to them men like Forrestal the mover, Morgan the intellectual, and Larkin the administrator, who among them recognized the great opportunity, accumulated the needed resources, and had the know-how to push the job to completion. Without them, future attempts to reform court-martial law would be very different, both in technique and in results.

5 The Manual:

Scripture Becomes Universal

Harry Truman's signature on the UCMJ Bill did not complete the system envisaged by the new code. The editor of the Navy's legal journal called the new law only a "skeleton whose framework will be filled in by a law manual."[1] This was a common attitude, for the services had for years relied actually less on the statutes containing their court-martial systems than on the manuals derived from them.

The Army publication was called *Manual for Courts-Martial, Unites States Army.* A new edition was customarily printed whenever there was a change of some consequence in the Articles of War. Thus there was an *MCM 1916*, another one in 1921, and another in 1949. There were some exceptions to this rule, as in the case of the 1928 *Manual*, an abridgement of the 1921 volume, which accompanied the World War II Army all around the globe.[2] After the Elston Act, the Air Force published its own *Manual*, which, although bound in blue to distinguish it from the Army's crimson, was identical in content except for the substitution of the words "Air Force" wherever "Army" appeared. The Navy analog had had a number of names, but all three editions after 1917 were known as *Naval Courts and Boards.*[3]

These manuals had overwhelming importance in the pre-UCMJ days. There were few lawyers in the military, and most court-martial work was done by line officers. There had to be a guide for these amateurs, a need that was filled by a manual which contained within its covers everything an officer assigned to a court would have to know. The role and duties of prosecutor, defense counsel, law member or court member, the rules of procedure and evidence, and the guidelines for findings and sentences could all be found in the *Manual.*

There was, however, more than just a need; there was also professional pride. Officers whose chosen career was the Army or the Navy considered it part of their duty to learn about the court-martial system and to be familiar with the provisions of the *MCM* or *NC&B.* A 1929 writer, for example, noted that "a working knowledge of the Manual is . . . accomplished with typical Army thoroughness, by means of garrison schools conducted by older and experienced officers."[4] The same was true of the Navy.

Since 1916, the President of the United States had been responsible for the promulgation of rules governing Army court-martial procedure. Corresponding naval law authorized the Secretary of the Navy to prescribe the rules, although Presidential approval was required prior to publication. Until the passage of the Elston Act, the Army rules had to be laid before Congress annually. Congress never took advantage of this measure, however, and the unused provision was omitted in the 1948 Act. There was never any such law regarding the *NC&B.*[5]

As might be expected, the Uniform Code scrapped the variations. Some consideration was given to the idea of vesting the Secretary of Defense with the authority for the *Manual.* Since he was a civilian official above the three services, such a provision would have been consistent with the overall wave of unification then sweeping through military affairs. But precedent for Presidential authority had already been accumulated, and for that reason, it was decided to follow the Army's practice.[6] Article 36 of the UCMJ, therefore, gave to the President the power to. "prescribe rules . . . [of] procedure, including modes of proof, in cases before courts-martial." In doing so, the statute continued, he "shall, so far as he deems practicable, apply the principles of law and the rules of evidence generally recognized in the trial of criminal cases in the United States district courts." Whatever rules were prescribed under this mandate had to be reported to Congress, on a one-time basis when promulgated.

In writing about the 1916 Articles, Samuel Ansell sneered at the protection allegedly built in by giving *MCM* authorship to the President. The idea was that these rules would no longer cater to the military. But Ansell rejected that notion as naive by arguing that

the actual draftsmen would be "ultra-military men" in the Army.[7]
Ansell, as we have noted, had a tendency to overstate, but in this
case, he seems to have been precise: military men did write the 1951
Manual.

On February 21, 1950, a little over a year after the UCMJ bill was
sent to Congress, Felix Larkin called a meeting with the three Judge
Advocate Generals.[8] This conference decided to prepare a joint
manual to accompany the bill, which by this time seemed virtually
assured of passage in Congress. This decision was a step towards
service unity of no mean significance itself. Because the Army had
had the recent experience of preparing a new manual in response to
the Elston Act, little over a year earlier, it seemed natural to call on
the same team to prepare this one. The head of that group was
Colonel William P. Connally, the Assistant JAG for Military Justice,
but the workhorse on the 1951 project was Colonel Charles L.
Decker, the "Chief of the Division." Although the other services sent
representatives to this team, there was little doubt that it would be
an Army affair and that the result would follow the Army's old
format and content.

The work was divided into thirty projects. When completed, the
staffwork on these tasks included the relevant sections from the
MCM 1949, *NC&B*, and the Coast Guard *MCM*; the legal authority
and legislative history of the pertinent topic; a draft proposal for the
new *MCM*; and a memo supporting the draft. The finished projects
were forwarded through Connally to a board composed of representatives from each of the services.[9] As approved, the drafts proceeded
from the board to each of the Judge Advocate Generals himself,
where further study was conducted. The documents finally were sent
to the Department Secretaries for their approval. Meanwhile, Colonel
Decker was assigned to get the approval of agencies, such as the
Bureau of the Budget and the Justice Department, which lay outside
the Defense Department.

There are no available minutes of meetings comparable to those on
the UCMJ to tell us about controversy among the services over the
MCM. But, despite the several layers of approval required for this
work, something Felix Larkin strove mightily to avoid in the UCMJ
project, there was probably little disagreement of any consequence.
As we have seen, the UCMJ was not very different, quantitatively
speaking, from the 1948 Articles. The *MCM* that derived from the
new law was not, therefore, very different from the earlier one.
Where differences did exist, the battles had already been fought.

Consequently, for the Army and the Air Force the new *Manual* was an exercise in familiarity. The opposite was true in the case of the Navy; the UCMJ was a vast departure from the almost timeless AGN, and the 1951 *MCM* was as different from the *NC&B*. But the very width of the chasm helped to still criticism in the sea services, in the beginning at least. Naval officers were numbed by the sheer novelty of the new code and gave themselves up in resignation to the inauguration of a whole new court-martial world.[10]

The speed with which the project was completed indicates general unanimity among the parties involved. The idea was agreed upon only in late February 1950. Yet the entire draft was completed by September 15 of that year. Thus, the planning and writing of a 665-page manual of complex legal procedures, based on a law not yet in effect, and designed to be used by disparate military services, was accomplished in a little less than seven months. This could not have been done were there major opposition.

Departmental review of the draft was completed during the fall of 1950. Finally, on the second anniversary of the date the Uniform Code was introduced in Congress, President Truman, following Article 36, published the new *Manual* in an Executive Order.[11] The book thereupon went into publication, and strenuous efforts were made to get it to units in the field and at sea in time to be useful in preparing for the effective date of the new law.

From beginning to end, the operation was so smooth that the civilian reformers once again found themselves cut out. Richard Wels had earlier delivered a scathing denunciation of *Naval Courts and Boards*, calling it "badly organized" and "incomprehensible." But he did not get involved in the writing of the new *Manual*. Likewise, Arthur Farmer had warned his colleagues that they should pay closer attention to the 1951 edition than they had to the 1949 *Manual*, which, he charged, had done much "to nullify the spirit of the Elston Act." But this advice was wasted either on deaf ears or ineffective hands; the bar associations played no role in the drafting of the new court-martial rules.[12]

Here then was a rather mild and uneventful beginning for a manual that within the next decade would come under severe criticism. For the time being, Colonel Connally and his team were quite proud of their work. As for the rest of the military legal departments, they now thought they had all the tools they would need. Thus equipped, they set about learning to operate the new system.

6 The "Computer" Picks a New Court

The enactment of the code and the writing of the *Manual* did not complete the machinery for the new system. There were, of course, thousands of details to be settled before courts-martial could be run according to the new law. And there was one more creation of major proportions: the Court of Military Appeals.

Professional courtroom personnel like to tell stories about the jockeying for position that customarily takes place whenever a vacancy in the federal bench occurs. In such situations, political IOU's are called, men find out about their actual standing in the party, and somehow the list of absolutely unrefusable candidates gets cut down to the one finally nominated. Since appointment to it would not be for life, the Court of Military Appeals fell somewhat short of other federal courts in the job security it provided. But the rush nevertheless was on.

Some men did not want the job. Felix Larkin was told by Secretary Forrestal that he could have one of the seats if he wanted it. But Larkin thought the $17,500 salary too low and declined. Edmund Morgan was also considered, in spite of his 72 years of age. More than 3,000 persons either applied or were suggested for the positions to President Truman. Over one hundred of these were seriously considered by the Administration.[1]

The bar associations, as we noted earlier, pinned high hopes on the Court of Military Appeals as a possible future ally in the war against command control. They did all they could to influence the appointments. In fact, in a plan reminiscent of the Vanderbilt committee's selection, they thought they had Defense Secretary Marshall's promise that the American Bar Association would be invited to submit a list of nominees from which the judges would be chosen.[2]

But that was not the way it worked out. George Spiegelberg enlisted the help of former War Secretary Patterson, after predicting that Marshall would have a major role in determining the final selections. Patterson approached Marshall on behalf of the bar associations and thought he came away with the Defense chief's promise to consult with the civilian reformers on the matter before any final decisions were made. But in the political reality of Washington, appointments such as those of CoMA judges did not depend on any one man or one line of approach. Whatever transpired between Marshall and Patterson, the general was in no position to give a *carte blanche* to anyone. He and the reformers were both frustrated, and the latters' complaints about foul play accomplished nothing.[3]

This is not to say that President Truman followed the selection process closely. Truman's interest in military justice was, at the most, marginal. He was criticized by a member of the White House staff for having made no endorsement of the Uniform Code save "one modest" comment uttered long before the bill was even drafted. Truman made no mention of the code in his memoirs. Contributing to his lack of interest at the time of the CoMA appointments were the early crises of the Korean War and the controversy with General MacArthur, both of which occurred between the enactment of the UCMJ and its effective date. The result was that although he could have made the appointments to the court any time after the first of March, 1951, Truman did not get around to the nominations until May 21, 1951, only a few days before the new code became effective.[4]

The project that resulted in these tardy appointments was originally researched within the Department of Defense. On February 16, Marshall sent a list of the eight candidates he considered finalists to the White House. On that list were the names of Morgan, Congressman Brooks, and Felix Larkin's longtime associate, Robert S. Pasley. But the Marshall list was apparently defective, because the work continued in the White House as if the Secretary had made no recommendations at all. Marshall nominated Brooks as Chief Judge, but Brooks received only scant notice among the President's advisors. More important in the minds of the men close to Truman were political tests. In March, for example, when Utah Congresswoman

Reva Beck Bosone heard that Franklin Riter was being considered for a CoMA post, she phoned the White House to advise that the retired general was a "vitriolic and venomous hater of the President, the Administration, [and] practically all Democrats." Representative Bosone, thus alerted to the possibility of a Utah appointment, then asked for an opportunity to speak to the President on behalf of her own candidate. Obviously, the politicians around the capital had their eyes on the 1952 elections, a consideration that may never have crossed George Marshall's apolitical mind.[5]

When the selections finally were announced, they looked as if they were the products of a computer programmed to cover as many constituencies as possible. Named to the fifteen-year term as Chief Judge was Robert E. Quinn. Associate judges named were George W. Latimer and Paul W. Brosman, to ten-year and five-year terms, respectively.

Quinn was a veteran Democratic Party warrior. Along with Theodore F. Green, he led the insurgence of the young Democrats in 1925 that had broken the stranglehold long held by the Republicans in Rhode Island's state legislature. In 1932, when Green rode a landslide into the governor's office, Quinn was elected along with him as lieutenant governor. Then in 1936, when Green went to the U.S. Senate, Quinn was elected to succeed him as governor. Thereafter he was appointed to a state court, a position he resigned in 1942 to join the Navy's legal department. At the end of the war, he returned to Rhode Island, where he resumed his political activity and maintained contact with the Navy through participation in the Naval Reserve.

Latimer, on the other hand, was a registered Republican. Born, raised, and educated in Utah, he had extensive experience in the interwar National Guard, in which he served as an artillery officer, spurning legal work even though he was a practicing attorney in his civilian life. During World War II, he served as the chief of staff of the Fortieth Infantry Division during that unit's Pacific campaigns. Although elected to the Utah Supreme Court in 1947, he interrupted that career at least twice to serve "short tours of duty with Army Field Forces, Fort Monroe, Va., 1948-49."

Brosman, unlike his brother judges-designate, seems not to have been involved in political office-seeking at all, although he was a registered Democrat. Born in Illinois, he received most of his education in the Midwest, and then embarked upon a career of teaching law. In 1942, he was commissioned in the Army legal corps and thereafter served as the Chief of Military Justice for the Army Air Force. The war interrupted his career at Tulane, where he had risen to become Dean of the Law School. Even after the war, the Air Force made demands on his time, as we shall see.

The law required that no more than two of the three judges could be from the same political party. To that extent, then, a certain distribution was statutory. But the appointments Truman made went a great deal further than was required by law. The three men were, first, an Easterner with Navy legal experience, who had been a professional politician; second, a Western attorney and judge, who had served in the combat arms of the Army; and finally a Midwesterner transplanted to the South, who possessed great intellectual and scholarly credentials and considerable Air Force experience. As if to complete the picture, Quinn was a Catholic, Latimer a Mormon, and Brosman an Episcopalian Mason. There was no "Jewish" seat, as the Supreme Court had come to include, and it was too early in American history for a Negro or a woman appointee, but, with those exceptions, President Truman came very close to touching all his political bases, with only three appointments.[6]

Most of the men who have been close to the court during its two decades of operation can recite a sort of litany about what political strings were pulled for each of the successful candidates. Judge Latimer, for example, campaigned strenuously for the job. His is one of the thickest files accumulated by the Truman staff during its search. Besides Congresswoman Bosone, he was supported by Senator Arthur V. Watkins of Utah, and the Chief Judge of the Utah Supreme Court, James H. Wolfe. But Latimer's most important booster was Harry Vaughan, Mr. Truman's military advisor, with whom Latimer had once served during his Army days.[7]

Chief Judge Quinn did not actively seek the position. His name was first brought up in connection with the new military court in a conversation between Senator Green and the President in August 1950. Later, Green and newly-elected Senator John O. Pastore of Rhode Island both called on Truman to reinforce the suggestion. Green's persistence was due to more than a desire to do an old friend a favor. Quinn had been in on parts of the studies which resulted in the Ballantine and McGuire reports, and was not, therefore, ignorant of the problems of court-martial justice. Moreover, finding Quinn a satisfying job was a political necessity if the tightly organized Rhode Island machine were to avoid possible infighting in the years to come. Quinn could make trouble for any of the Democratic incumbents if he were so inclined, and that included both Pastore and Green. Another person working in Quinn's behalf was J. Howard McGrath, the United States Attorney General. No judge is appointed to any federal bench without the approval of the Attorney General, according to the unwritten law of Washington protocol. McGrath, another Rhode Island Democrat, and Quinn were old allies dating back to the fiery days in Providence before the war.[8]

Paul Brosman's appointment to the Court was heavily endorsed by the Judge Advocate General of the Air Force. General Harmon and Brosman were both alumni of the University of Illinois Law School and had been introduced by a mutual acquaintance in 1949, when Harmon was looking for a recruiting assistant in the Air Force legal department. Brosman did such an excellent job for Harmon that when positions on the new court became available, Harmon strongly recommended him. But Brosman should never have been appointed. The law required that the court be appointed "from civilian life," a qualification Brosman, who was still in the Air Force for the Korean emergency, could not meet. Nevertheless, after a madcap affair, involving a request for the owner of a men's store to open late at night so the new judge could exchange his uniform for a suit, and a "special processing" of his request for relief from active duty, Brosman was duly nominated more or less legally. In the press releases, however, he was carefully referred to as the Dean of the Tulane Law School; no mention of his more recent Air Force service was made.[9]

The political support and influence rendered on behalf of these three may have been matched in many of the other 3,000 candidacies. But Quinn, Latimer, and Brosman had in addition just the right blend of geographic distribution and military background. Geography was important to Truman, as it ever is in politics, where men always look ahead to the next election. As for military experience, although it was not required by the law, thousands of men with suitable credentials had been in the service during the war, and it would have been difficult to pick a judge who was not a veteran. That being the case, it was prudent, given the nature of Pentagon politics, to choose men who were from each of the three services.

These credentials made for easy sailing in the Senate. Armed Services Committee Chairman Russell told reporters that the nominees were so outstanding that the Senators "took the unusual step of voting unanimous approval, with the appointees present in the committee room."[10]

By themselves, the UCMJ and the *Manual for Courts-Martial* would have established a military justice system not very different from the traditions just repealed. The code would probably have been relegated to some archive, while the *Manual* would have become the same well-worn Bible of the court-martial its predecessors had been. The substantive law which would have resulted would have been somewhat rigid, varying perhaps from region to region, or from service to service, but not growing with time. Some of the more radical reformers had been apprehensive of this likelihood. Although Felix Larkin and the other unificationists in the Defense Department viewed the Court of Military Appeals primarily as a tribunal that would ensure standardization of court-martial findings and sentences throughout all the services, many other reformers who were more interested in civilianizing court-martial law hoped that it would become a court of interpretive capacity with the potential to bring flexibility and growth into the military courts.

Such expectations explain why these men were so dissatisfied with the appointments that were made. In Quinn, they saw a former governor who, in an intraparty war over a race-track, had once taken upon himself nearly dictatorial powers in suppressing the process of law.[11] In Latimer, they saw an old crony of President Truman's military fix-it man. And in Brosman, a man with otherwise excellent qualifications, they saw the practically illegal appointment of an active duty Air Force officer. To them, the future—if it depended on men of the *law* like these—must have seemed as empty of promise as the recent past had been full of frustration.

It remained to be seen how the thing would work in practice.

7 ...At First Sight

As might be expected of a law whose legislative history was so stormy, the UCMJ was greeted with some widespread disapproval. Even as he signed it, President Truman anticipated future problems. Although he praised the new code as an "example of real unification," Truman thought that in its failure to curb command control over courts-martial the new system had left itself open to renewed attacks.[1]

The President was right. Criticism of military justice was not even diminished by the appearance of the Uniform Code. Professor Arthur John Keeffe, whose study of courts-martial began with his 1946 General Court-Martial Sentence Review Board, continued his blistering attack, focusing it now on the code. Keeffe tried to change the UCMJ while it was still under consideration by Congress. Like other reformers at that time, however, he was outside the mainstream of influence, and his critique went unheeded, if not unnoticed. After passage of the new law, Keeffe delivered another, this time rather emotional blast at the code, which again did little more than demonstrate his frustration.[2]

Those who worked for or with Professor Keeffe knew him as a chronic critic. Not unlike Samuel Ansell, Keeffe's own impatience and sensationalism often worked to defeat him. When the GCMSRB went beyond its original mandate to review World War II sentences, the idea to write a general critique of the Navy's court-martial system had been Keeffe's own, and an admirable one it was. Along with the several other studies, it was a direct antecedent of the Uniform Code.

And yet, in its finished form, it was not Keeffe's work but Robert Pasley's. Keeffe preferred to release findings, data, and conclusions to the press, hoping to maintain the public's interest in military justice, which he seemed to fear would wane without an occasional jolt. But Pasley and Felix Larkin restrained the professor and turned the "Synopsis" into the dignified and forceful document it became.[3]

Still, Keeffe's criticism continued. In a 1949 article, he saw eight points where the UCMJ came up short.[4] First, it was not "uniform" at all, since the three services were permitted in a number of places to maintain their autonomy. There was a variety of nonjudicial punishment methods, and even more importantly, each Judge Advocate General had his own review apparatus, permitted by Articles 66 and 69, by which he could steer the administration of justice in his own service along paths that might be quite different from the others. Second, Keeffe attacked the provision that allowed revival of court-martial jurisdiction after discharge in the case of major felonies. Third, he saw two items in the new system that could lead to double jeopardy. The first was the omission of any statement clarifying those situations where military and state jurisdiction overlapped. The other was that a GI could be given nonjudicial punishment and subsequently tried by court-martial for the same offense.

His fourth criticism was levelled against the special court-martial. The Elston Act had given the Army permission to use the Navy's century-old Bad Conduct Discharge (BCD). A variety of military spokesmen, including a Secretary of the Army, a Commissioner of the Court of Military Appeals, and a long line of Navy and Marine officers, maintained that the BCD was not so serious a punishment as the Dishonorable Discharge (DD). The DD had been adjudged by general courts of both services apparently since the beginning in 1775. But in 1855, the Navy asked for permission to award a "lesser" punitive discharge at a lesser court-martial. The Navy's position was that, because most of its ships were small, they lacked the requisite personnel to staff a general court. But despite this, the Navy claimed, all ships needed a means to rid themselves of chronic offenders. Congress accepted this argument, and what was then known as the Navy summary court was granted authority to hand down a BCD.[5]

But Keeffe was not swayed by the justifications military men gave. He saw the BCD as a lifetime punishment and was appalled that the UCMJ permitted its utilization by the three-man special court, which did not include a law officer and whose counsel were not required to be *bona fide* lawyers.

Keeffe's fifth charge was against the Article 32 pretrial investigation. As written, the law provided that if noncompliance with Article 32 were found by appellate agencies, they could merely reverse convictions and remand for retrial. Keeffe wanted noncompliance to be a jurisdictional error which would result in automatic dismissal of charges.

His sixth point was that CoMA review was discriminatory. Article 67 provided for mandatory review by the court of death sentences and those convictions involving generals and Navy flag officers, or of those cases certified to the court by a Judge Advocate General. If any other accused demanded CoMA review, he would have to petition the court, which would hear the case only if it found good cause. Keeffe called this unequal justice.

Next, Keeffe argued that a "Chief Defense Counsel" should be appointed. Counsel for defense, as envisaged by the UCMJ, would most probably be a lawyer from the office of the staff judge advocate. The SJA was responsible in each case, under Article 34, for providing the commander with legal advice before trials could be ordered. Keeffe thought it absurd that the counsel for the defendant should be subordinate in his everyday duties to the officer who was essentially the government's lawyer. He urged the elimination of this possible area of abuse, by the creation of a world-wide Chief Defense Counsel, independent of all commanders, who would supervise a pool of lawyers whose sole job would be to represent all defendants in court-martial trials.

Finally, Keeffe attacked Article 76, which stated that court-martial proceedings and review would be "binding upon all departments, courts, agencies, and officers of the United States." This was included only to codify rulings handed down by civilian courts ever since 1857 and was essentially identical to provisions in earlier Articles of War. But Keeffe charged that it was designed to prohibit collateral attack of court-martial decisions in the federal courts on issues such as habeas corpus, and back pay litigation.[6]

Keeffe renewed these complaints in his less systematic, more flamboyant *Reader's Digest* article. He had long claimed that one of the very worst failures of the court-martial system was the lack of a civilian "Advisory Council." The time for study groups was over, he proclaimed, and the joint annual reports required of CoMA and the JAG's by Article 67 (g) of the code would be useless because of their authorship. It now seems clear that what he envisaged was a permanent Keeffe board, perhaps with himself as chairman, to be granted watchdog and possible corrective powers over the courts-martial of all the services.[7]

Some of Keeffe's dissatisfactions may have arisen from frustrated personal ambitions and a lack of patience.[8] But his opposition to the new code was right on the mark. Things which he called short-comings would be targets of reformers again and again over the next twenty years. Under the influence of Felix Larkin, the UCMJ Committee had based much of its discussion on observations originally made by the Keeffe board. A history of the UCMJ in operation could likewise be written following the failures the professor saw in the new law.

But grievances against the new code were aired in other quarters, too. There was, as we have seen, strong Congressional sentiment in favor of maintaining the Elston Articles and extending them to cover the Navy. Others agreed. In a poll conducted by the Judge Advocates Association, a five-to-one margin favored a uniform code, but one which would follow the Elston Act in most characteristics. Even after the enactment of the UCMJ, many officers charged with the responsibility for the operation of courts-martial felt that a mistake had been made in the scrapping of the 1948 act. This latter group included the Judge Advocate Generals of the Army and the Air Force. General Green was quoted shortly after the completion of the House hearings on the UCMJ that the Elston Act should be retained long enough "to prove its worth."[9] But more outspoken was Air Force General Reginald C. Harmon.

Harmon was the first Judge Advocate General of the new service. Appointed in 1947, he served in the post for over twelve years, until he reached the mandatory retirement age in 1960. His was not a typical career officer pattern; he had in fact rejected a Regular Army commission on two occasions in the 1920s, when there seemed no reason to pursue a military future. But he did maintain Reserve status, and after passing the Illinois bar, transferred into the Army Reserve legal department. Like so many others, he was called to active duty in World War II, and, because his civilian legal practice entailed corporate and contract law, was assigned to the Army Air Corps industrial expansion program. Remaining in the service after the war "for a couple of years only," to help in reconversion, he found himself selected from fairly far down the list when the new organization picked its Judge Advocate General.

Harmon's field was not criminal law. His civilian firm had rejected criminal cases, and as an Air Corps lawyer, he was involved in courts-martial only incidentally. But by 1951, he was in the unique position of having been JAG under three different systems: the 1920 and 1948 Articles, and the UCMJ.

Any man who serves in a position of leadership for a dozen years is bound to leave a permanent imprint on that organization. So it was with Harmon. We have seen that his opposition to an Air Force JAG Corps prevailed in the 1940s and continued to be the policy of the service into the 1970s. He often expressed his preference for the Elston Act over the UCMJ. In 1954, he asserted that justice was only more expensive under the code, not any better. A few years later, he expanded the point, saying that the code, with all its complicated and time-consuming procedures, would not be able to handle the work that would arise if the United States ever had to mobilize as it had in World War II.[10]

Many Air Force lawyers shared the general's views. For example, the presiding officer at a 1951 conference of Air Force judge advocates, Brigadier General Herbert M. Kidner, told the assembled lawyers that they were going to take a look at "some of the more pleasant things about the new code," clearly implying that there were many less pleasant things. One of the major items of discussion was the new law officer concept. Several speakers remarked that the men appointed to the newly created position would probably have trouble with predeliberation instructions, which were now required to be given in open court. Here it was heavily implied that having a law member, who could give his instructions in private as the legal questions arose, was simpler and more effective than the new system. But Brigadier General Albert M. Kuhfeld, while conceding the difficulty of the new situation, warned the audience that trying to skirt the new law would not be acceptable. Kuhfeld singled out for prohibition the idea of appointing to a court some lawyer who would act as a *sub rosa* law member. This was explicitly contrary to the spirit of the code, Kuhfeld said, and would not be countenanced.[11]

General Kuhfeld's comments are typical of an enduring official Air Force attitude. This, the newest of the services, often seemed more willing than its older sisters to accept what was thrust upon it and to go beyond what was merely required, anticipating problems and seeking new solutions. This is not to say there were no forward-looking men in the other services. But, in the early days of the UCMJ, there was not the same institutional eagerness in the Army and the Navy to accept the new ways of doing things as there was in the Air Force.

Take Colonel Charles L. Decker, for example. Soon after he completed his assignment as executive officer of the team that wrote the *MCM*, Decker was detailed to supervise the establishment of the Judge Advocate General's School at Charlottesville, Virginia. The school, to which every career Army lawyer must eventually go to study, also serves as a kind of think-tank for legal problems which arise in the Army. Many of the ablest minds in the JAG Corps work and teach there, and when the Pentagon has a question about the law, it usually seeks an opinion from the staff. Decker, the first commandant of the school, was a man of importance and great influence, despite his relatively junior rank. Yet he was and remains an outspoken opponent of the adversary system of law. Without prompting, he recites that "84 percent of the civilized world" lives under an inquisition system of criminal justice, a method he believes more likely to find truth than the Anglo-Saxon courtroom debate. A man such as this could hardly be expected to find much to favor in the UCMJ, which, with its lawyers and intricate appellate review system, represented a move away from the old inquisitorial Articles of War. As Decker moved up in the JAG hierarchy, he gained greater opportunities to influence the service's official policy on matters of such basic philosophy, as we shall see.[12]

The first great test of the new code and the Army's attitude toward it came in the Korean War. The Army was badly surprised by Korea in matters of combat readiness. Likewise, although specific blame cannot be fixed with certainty, there was great confusion when the new court-martial system was implemented. Publication of the new *Manual* fell badly behind schedule, and the recruitment of lawyers in numbers thought sufficient for the demands of the UCMJ went slowly. Because of these and other malfunctions, and despite the thirteen months lead time provided between the enactment of the law and the effective date of the system, the Army considered asking for more time to put the code into effect.[13]

When word of this filtered down to Colonel George Hickman, the Staff Judge Advocate in General MacArthur's Far East Command headquarters, he opposed the idea. Hickman recommended that, whatever the difficulties, it would be better to start the new code on schedule, thereby testing it under wartime conditions, than to defer its operation until some perhaps never-to-come more suitable day in the future.[14] Hickman's unit was in combat, a status not enjoyed by any other major Army command, and that gave his recommendation a certain influence. Shortly after receiving his message, the Army Department recanted and made no further move to delay the inauguration of the UCMJ.

In the Navy, steps had been taken to make the transition into the new system as smooth as possible. Although some soldiers thought the jump from Elston Act to Uniform Code a major one, it was nothing compared to the repeal of an 1862 system forced on the Navy. In a message to all subordinate activities, the Chief of Naval Operations (CNO) summarized the code in terms of the differences naval personnel would find in it. The names of the courts were new, he told them; there was now a judge-figure, the law officer; enlisted men would sit on courts-martial; and special courts had more powers than the old Navy summary. A close reading of this message makes clear that CNO thought the most revolutionary parts of the new code were the procedures. Some of the ones he listed were the Article 32 pretrial investigation and the requirement that lawyers be assigned as counsel and law officers. The admiral anticipated that there would be grave problems in setting up the new system, but he urged all naval commanders to begin then to adapt their disciplinary actions as much as possible to the new law.[15]

The obvious intention of CNO to comply with the code was matched in spirit by the editor of the Navy's *JAG Journal,* who wrote, rather frankly, that the UCMJ reflected congressional intention to establish "additional safeguards against the exercise of undue control, by convening authorities" over courts-martial.[16]

But many naval officers further away from the center were less receptive to the changes. Many old salts felt that the AGN, despite its age, was a perfectly suitable vehicle for the administration of justice within the peculiar Navy environment. These men believed that the bulk of the criticism directed at World War II court-martial excesses did not include naval courts but was meant only for the Army, whose sentencing policy and frequent executions had drawn down public wrath on military justice in general. The Navy, in short, had been unfairly blamed, and the resulting new legislation, as it pertained to the sea services, was unwise and unnecessary.[17]

By 1952, the Navy JAG was Admiral Nunn, whose previously mentioned reverence for the AGN continued after the enactment of the UCMJ. A former destroyer commander himself, Nunn believed that most aspects of the Navy's attitude toward military justice were explained by the fact that men aboard ships live in small communities more like families than anything else and that an effective discipline system must reflect the paternal and fraternal relationships that result. Nunn's disapproval of the code stemmed fundamentally from its curtailment of the powers formerly exercised by the ship's captain at "mast." Cutting this authority forced the commander to look to courts-martial to find punishments he believed equal to the offense. But the road there was blocked by the UCMJ's intricate legal obstacles that a ship's captain had neither the training nor the time to work his way through.

If the Navy's Judge Advocate General reckoned the code in this fashion, what about the people in the Fleet? One of the most revealing glimpses into the minds of the administrators of the new code was provided by the answers to a poll taken among Navy units in the Far East in 1952. The shock felt by the operating forces upon first exposure to the UCMJ is seen in the opening paragraph of the report:

1. Personal reactions in the fleet concerning the Uniform Code of Military Justice when it became effective one year ago were decidedly negative. In six months time the feeling abated to the extent that in the main the Code itself was considered sound and workable but that the Manual for Courts-Martial needed drastic revision. The current opinion is that, generally, the concepts of the Manual are also basically sound and workable.

The pollsters reached thirty-three conclusions. Some supported Admiral Nunn's positions that mast powers were inadequate and that paperwork was greater under the Code. Others argued that stiffer punishment powers be given to courts-martial. The *Manual*, "sound" in concept, was described as "too confusing and technical for laymen," although some of this was mitigated by the explanatory articles that appeared from time to time in the *JAG Journal.*[18]

Comments much like these had been heard before and would be heard again; they need no further study here. What is most significant about them is found in those opening sentences. In the sixteen months since it went into effect, the code had evolved from a totally foreign and reprehensible beast to something that was "basically sound" and could therefore be lived with. The message was clear: what was really wrong with the UCMJ was that it was new. Even Admiral Nunn came around to this position. Addressing a conference of Navy lawyers at the end of his second year in office, Nunn advised his audience that the code was here to stay and that "[w]e may as well resolve our differences with it." Seventeen years later, he agreed that there were "some very good things" about the new system, including the Court of Military Appeals.[19]

Nunn never became a total convert to the Uniform Code. His belief that it upset traditional and effective Navy "family ways" was unshakable. He remained convinced, as did Generals Harmon and Decker, that the system would not work in time of total mobilization, when a commander's energy and resources must be directed toward fighting the battles, not the lawsuits.[20] But there is a difference among the men that is worth pointing out. Ira Nunn and Charles Decker were fighting men before they were lawyers. Each was a graduate of his service's academy, and each served "in the line" before going before the bar. Each was sent to law school at government expense, Decker to Georgetown and Nunn to Harvard, while on active duty. And each patterned his legal career on the premise that its ultimate goal was victory in war. The legal departments of the Army and the Navy were filled with men of similar background and outlook. Steeped in a tradition of West Point, Annapolis, and William Winthrop, they could scarcely be expected to embrace a new code that contained many of the elements of Samuel Ansell's articles.

General Harmon in the Air Force, on the other hand, was a different sort entirely. He had repeatedly rejected military life and a military career as a young man. When he did enter the service it was more as a technocrat than as a combat soldier. Even after the war, he remained primarily a "contracts man" rather than a military justice specialist. And he imposed on the Air Force legal department innovative and flexible ways of seeing and doing things. Compared with Decker and Nunn, his "tradition quotient" was about zero. Thus, his opposition to the new system was merely an intellectual exercise, not a matter of soul-shattering importance. Consequently, when the battle was lost, it was much easier for him and for his lawyers to accept the Uniform Code, than it was for men like Nunn and Decker.

Perhaps an entirely new generation of military lawyers, trained away from the interwar traditions, might bring similar acceptance of the code in the other services. Time would tell.

8 The Court's Business:

It Means Business

The first few years of any institution are usually those during which custom and habits are set. The Court of Military Appeals was no exception. A number of important issues before the new court were made clear by the force of circumstances and the clash of personalities and philosophies.

The deletion from the UCMJ of the provision for life tenure of CoMA judges left the court with a kind of institutional neurosis from which it long suffered. Congressmen who favored life tenure did so for the reason that judges secure in their jobs are supposedly free from external influences. Some opponents of the idea argued that only second-rate judges would be attracted to a military court, thus burdening the entire system for the lifetime of the incompetents appointed. Neither of these fears has materialized. The court has been blessed with men of integrity and competence; there is no evidence whatever that any of them has ever tried to encourage his own reappointment by following a certain line in an opinion. But while the individual judges have been of such high quality, the court as a whole has wrestled with a need for institutional identity. This is shown by a series of incidents; each alone seems unimportant, but taken together they form a recognizable pattern.

The first event was the search for housing. The author of an unofficial "Ten-Year Chronology" of the court, published in 1961, mentioned on the first page the physical location of the court's building and about midway through the article devoted nearly a full page to describing how the court acquired the facilities. Visitors to the court are given a six-page pamphlet which outlines the goals and methods, personnel, and history of CoMA. This pamphlet, too, closes with several paragraphs on the physical plant and how it came to be acquired. Such a heavy emphasis on buildings takes on some significance when one talks to the Clerk of the Court.[1]

Alfred C. Proulx has been clerk of CoMA since its inception. His close personal relationship with Chief Judge Quinn, a long-time neighbor in Rhode Island's Pawtuxet Valley, and his broad legal, government, and military background explain his appointment and competence. Amiable and gregarious, Proulx obviously loves his job and the Washington environment in which he works. During an interview, he talked at great length about some rather clever manipulating he engaged in to help secure the present site for his court.

Briefly, what happened was that in 1952 the staff of the Court of Military Appeals learned of the imminent relocation of the U.S. Court of Appeals from its space at 5th and E Streets, NW. Judge Quinn thereupon exercised his influence at the White House and the Justice Department to elbow aside the agency for whom the building had originally been earmarked, and gained possession of it for his own court.[2]

There was, of course, a real requirement for space, and the military court did well to acquire the quarters it did. But perhaps even more essential than the physical need was the psychological one. The statute provided that the Court of Militry Appeals would "be located for administrative purposes in the Department of Defense." Although their first meeting in June 1951 was in the Pentagon, three weeks later the judges moved out to occupy temporary housing until a permanent site could be obtained. The court was determined never to be actually located at the Pentagon. CoMA was very much attuned to the importance of images, and one of the first to be considered was its own. Facilities located in Washington near the other courthouses and away from the military would help.[3]

Similar ideas dictated the setting of a calendar. The late appointment and confirmation of the court meant that courts-martial had been conducted under the UCMJ even before CoMA was actually established. But Judge Quinn refused to be pressured by that fact. His new court needed time to organize, to appoint clerical and legal staffs, and to do all the other chores such a beginning required. For those reasons, the first hearings could not be conducted until the Fall of 1951. This enforced delay gave the court an opportunity to enhance its prestige as well. The Supreme Court of the United States and most other federal courts begin their annual business in the first week of October and generally take the summer off. Judge Quinn decided to follow suit, in order to give his staff time to get organized but at the same time to put his court on a calendar similar to that in use by other courts. This was a measure designed to have a salutory effect on CoMA's standing within the judicial community.[4]

The next item was the matter of reports of court decisions. Since one of the primary aims of CoMA was to set standards that would apply in courts-martial of all the services, it was necessary that some method be established by which lawyers in the field could be apprised of the court's business. The obvious answer was a modern system of published reports. Except for Supreme Court decisions, which are published in a separate set of volumes, the opinions of federal courts are "reported" on a selected basis in two series: *The Federal Reporter* and *The Federal Supplement*. West Publishing Company, which produces these sets, told Proulx that selected CoMA decisions could be printed in *The Federal Reporter*. But since this would not satisfy the need to communicate all decisional law to the Armed Forces, Proulx turned the offer down.[5]

A few years earlier, at the inception of the Elston Act, the newly created Air Force had faced a similar problem. When he first went on active duty in 1940, Reginald Harmon had found the old Army board of review reports to be essentially unusable. In order to trace a line of decisions relating to a given point of law, one had to read the entire collection, each case in each volume. This was impossible, of course, and so the opinions were not used. Harmon felt trapped by the lack of usable precedents when he sat from time to time as law member on a court-martial. Mentioning this to the local staff judge advocate, an old veteran of the Regular Army, Harmon was given a typical traditionalist response. The colonel told him, "The Army has gotten along with them for so many years, we can make it another few." That should have ended it, except that Harmon later became the Air Force Judge Advocate General. As JAG, he was determined that Air Force cases would be reported from the beginning in a way which would make them usable to future lawyers. He convinced Lawyers Co-operative, a Rochester, New York, firm, to take on the job, and the Air Force soon had a modern reporting system.[6]

When the UCMJ was enacted, the other services voted to adopt this system. Their decision was not reached because Harmon's reporting was the best, but because it was the only one of any value at all. The Army's system was thirty-some volumes of chaos, and the Navy's, which had been derided by the McGuire committee report, was even worse.[7] As a result of the unification of reports, Lawyers Co-op began publishing *Court-Martial Reports* in 1952. These volumes include selected board of review opinions, segregated by service, and all of the CoMA decisions. But the Court of Military Appeals still maintained that its reports had to be published separately. After failing in the negotiations with West, Proulx turned to Lawyers Co-op, too. A deal was made, and the arrangement has continued for twenty years.[8]

The historically significant thing about all this was that CoMA held out for its own separate but complete reporting. The publication of selected opinions in *The Federal Reporter* would not satisfy the mandate that CoMA had to standardize military law. But publication of opinions in the *Court-Martial Reports* would thwart the court's need for independence from the military.

Another early administrrative detail undertaken by the new court was the promulgation of rules of procedure. Here, the cumulative judicial experience of the men involved became evident. The judges were appointed on June 22, 1951, but regulations governing the procedures to be used before the court were published less than three weeks later. These rules covered such things as the duties of the clerk of the court, requirements for filing, and procedures for oral arguments. The regulations have been changed a few times since the original ones, but the basic contents of the 1951 version still stand.[9]

The apparent ease with which the new tribunal swung into operation is startling in view of the fact that no one quite knew what its workload would be. Admiral Russell, the Navy JAG in 1949, estimated that the court would see only about the same number of cases that he became personally involved with under the AGN. This amounted to about five percent of all Navy trials, or about 25 to 30 cases a month. An Army spokesman, however, guessed that some 85 percent of its cases would go to the new court. Since the Navy and the Army were at opposite sides of the question of whether a civilian court was desirable, the variance in their predictions was probably at least partially intended to persuade. In any case, Congress based its report mainly on guesswork provided during the hearings and supposed that there would be two thousand to three thousand cases docketed at CoMA each year.[10]

As it turned out, this Congressional estimate was not far off.

During the first five years of the court's existence, an annual average of about two thousand cases, including those from all three statutory sources, was maintained.[11] After the Korean War, when the number of men in uniform dwindled, so did CoMA business, and for the next few years the average was about a thousand five hundred. In the decade of the 1960s, for reasons to be explored later, the court docketed only about a thousand cases a year from all sources. Although the load turned out to be less burdensome than anticipated, it was nevertheless heavy, as indicated in Figure 1, which compares the work of a CoMA judge and that performed by his counterpart on a United States District Court of Appeals.[12] The military court's heavy workload once led Mississippi's Senator John Stennis to ask Judge Quinn, "How in the world could you handle that many cases a month, Judge?"[13]

FIGURE 1. COURT OF MILITARY APPEALS WORK LOAD
COMPARED WITH OTHER FEDERAL APPELLATE COURTS

| Year | CoMA | | U.S. Courts of |
	Total Cases Docketed	Load Per Judge	Appeals (average of all circuits) Load per Judge
1953	2180	726	50
1957	1636	545	54
1960	970	323	57
1964	957	319	69
1966	730	243	74

One thing that helped to lighten the load was an in-house commissioner system. The word "Commissioner" as used by CoMA had no statutory or regulatory definition. It was merely court terminology applied to the team of lawyers who assist the judges during the review process.

The commissioners prepare preliminary studies of the cases docketed and direct the judges' attention to the pertinent law and precedents which bear on the issue. With this advice in hand, any one of the judges might decide that a certain case merits review. The others, by tradition, have always agreed, whereupon the case is then set down for oral argument.[14]

The accused is not usually present when his case is heard, but he is represented either at no cost by military appellate counsel or by a civilian lawyer of his choice and at his own expense. Each side is granted thirty minutes to argue its case, and the appellant usually saves a few minutes of his time to rebut the appellee's argument. A system of colored lights mounted on the speaker's podium warns the counsel about his elapsed time, and the Chief Judge has on occasion cut off those who exceeded their time limit. The judges interrupt from time to time to ask what seem unsettling and sharply honed questions.

There are usually three or four cases heard on a day the court is in session. When the oral arguments are completed, the judges retire to a conference room where they discuss the points among themselves and reach a tentative decision. On a day when there is unaminity, the Chief Judge gives himself the task of writing the opinion in the first case and makes the other assignments in order of seniority. Adjustments in this pattern are made to try to even out the work load when there are split opinions. When the opinions are written, they are circulated to the other judges, who then make comments or suggestions for amending the original draft. The judges are still free to change their views at this point. The two *Gibson* cases of the October 1953 term illustrate how this works. In both, the original conference room decision was subsequently changed several times. One of the cases, known by the CoMA staff as "Gibson evidence," involved at least four proposed principal opinions. A tentative decision was made in conference and an opinion written to support it, only to elicit dissents from the other two judges. One of them was then assigned to write the new majority's opinion, but when he finished, it also got two dissents. This continued until finally Quinn and Brosman agreed on one result. But all three finally published long opinions, Latimer's in dissent.[15]

Unlike the Supreme Court, CoMA does not read its decisions from the bench. Once the final opinions are written, they are printed by Lawyers Co-op and released to the public. This is done once a week, at noon on Friday. A messenger is sent to CoMA from each of the three JAG's to pick up whatever cases pertaining to that service may be released that day. In this way, the government and the accused, through his assigned military appellate counsel, are each informed at the same time.[16]

Some of the court's early problems of identity and organization were partly offset by an obvious pioneering spirit shared by the judges. Brosman, for example, once described CoMA as "freer than any in the land—save again the Supreme Court, to find its law where it will, to seek, new-fledged and sole, for *principle*, unhampered by the limiting crop of the years." These were sentiments uttered, although less lexiphanically, by the other judges, too.[17]

But the harmony was not destined to last long. The major controversy on the Quinn-Latimer-Brosman court was over the application of the "harmless error" statute. Articles 59(a) of the code stipulated that convictions should not be reversed on appeal for procedural error unless it "materially prejudices the substantial rights of the accused." The essence, if not the precise doctrine, of harmless error is deeply rooted in the traditional view of courts-martial; a military court was recognized as a function of amateur lawyers and was governed by rules written especially for them. If the result of such an affair was punishment of the guilty and release of the innocent, why should there be concern about whether some arcane rules of procedure were followed exactly? Given this attitude and the general lack of professional expertise by these amateurs, however well-trained the services tried to make them, errors were likely to be frequent, and a harmless error rule was a necessity. A similar federal statute was first enacted just before the 1920 Articles of War, and the Army incorporated it in somewhat more detail in those articles. The Navy, too, adopted such a rule for the first time in the 1923 edition of *Naval Courts and Boards*. When the Uniform Code also embraced the provision, the services applauded, for the reason that it would permit them some reasonable latitude in following the new and more intricate procedural requirements of the UCMJ.[18]

In one of its first opinions, *U.S. v. Lucas*, the Court of Military Appeals had to contend with the issue of harmless error. At the trial, the defendant had pleaded guilty to charges brought against him. The president of the special court-martial warned him that his plea would not be accepted unless he acknowledged that he understood its effect. Lucas answered that he knew that his pleas "admitted every act or omission charged and every element of that offense." Upon receiving this reply, the president announced that the specifications stood proven by the plea, and, without instructing the court or even polling the other members as to findings of guilt or innocence, proceeded to the sentencing phase of the trial. On appeal, the board of review reversed, on the grounds that both the code and the *Manual* prohibited deletions of key parts of a trial, such as voting on a verdict. But CoMA reinstated the conviction in a unanimous decision.[19] Judge Latimer wrote for the court that there are trial proceedings which can be waived by an accused and if he pleads guilty to an offense after being fully and fairly informed of the consequences of the plea we can see no prejudice because formalities were not strictly followed.

So far, so good; *Lucas* upheld Article 59(a) in precisely the terms by which it had always been understood by the military. But an almost imperceptible alteration in the *Lucas* concept began later the same term, in *U.S. v. Clay*. Ironically, this was also written by Judge Latimer. Here Latimer introduced the concept of "military due process," which provoked a minor but heated controversy among students of military law. The facts in *Clay* were rather different from *Lucas*. Arraigned before a special court, the accused pleaded guilty to one charge brought against him, but not guilty to another. The president of the court in this case did conduct the voting procedure that had been omitted in *Lucas*, but he failed beforehand to instruct the court on the elements of the offense, the presumption of innocence, the idea of reasonable doubt, and the concept of the government's burden of proof, all of which were required by Article 51(c). Clay was found guilty on both charges, and despite defense counsel's objection to the failure to instruct, the court let the conviction stand. Intermediate reviewers upheld the judgment on the grounds that the error was harmless. That would have settled the matter except that the Judge Advocate General of the Navy was not satisfied and certified the case to CoMA.[20]

When the court published its opinion, Judge Latimer listed certain rights granted to military defendants which were not "bottomed on" the Constitution, but on "laws as enacted by Congress." Although their source was different, the military rights did "parallel" those accorded civilian defendants. One of them was the right "to have the court instructed." The fact that the president in this case had not instructed at all, Latimer wrote, forced CoMA to hold that "the error materially prejudiced the substantial rights of the accused." As Latimer saw it, the major difference between *Lucas* and *Clay* was that Lucas had by his guilty plea waived all of his procedural rights. But Clay's not guilty plea had not, and Latimer ruled that "the court cannot waive them for him."

"Military due process" was merely another way of approaching the issue of harmless error. Judge Latimer was in effect warning the services that if those rights granted GI's by Congress which parallel the Constitutional rights enjoyed by civilians were violated by sloppy procedure at courts-martial, CoMA would not consider such infringements harmless and would reverse the convictions that followed.

The decision in *Clay,* as in *Lucas,* was unanimous. Up to this point, the Court of Military Appeals was of a single mind on the question of harmless error. But a wide gulf soon began to yawn. In *U.S. v. Lee,* Judge Brosman first expressed himself on the issue. The accused was convicted by a Navy special court-martial of larceny after it heard "overwhelming" evidence of his guilt. What bothered Brosman was the fact that the prosecutor in the case had also been the accuser and then had conducted an investigation into the alleged offenses before charges were filed. Brosman confessed that in the instant case there was "no suggestion whatever of specific prejudice" against the defendant. But he warned that the facts suggested that someday there might be a situation where the error would consist not of "a violation of constitutional or legislative provisions," but rather of "an overt departure from some 'creative and indwelling principle'—some critical and basic norm."[21]

What Brosman had done in this dictum was to enunciate for the first time the doctrine of "general prejudice." As he saw it, it was not essentially different from Latimer's "military due process." Only five days after the *Lee* decision, CoMA handed down *U. S. v. Berry,* in which the vaguely anticipated "departure from [a] creative and indwelling principle" first materialized. The offenses in this Army general court case were committed before the UCMJ went into effect and were therefore governed by the Elston Act and the 1949 *Manual.* The issue that Brosman focused on was the usurpation of the duties of the law member by the president of the court. Finding this to have happened on several occasions during the trial, Brosman refused even to look for specific prejudice to the rights of the accused. Instead, he said that the clear mandate of Congress in AW 8 of the 1948 Articles was to make the law member "closely analogous to the judge" in a civilian criminal case. Congress' intent was equally clear: the law member was supposed to present another obstacle to the exercise of illicit command influence through the president of the court. Thus, one of the "creative and indwelling principles" that Brosman thought CoMA must protect, namely, "[t]he complete independence of the law member and his unshackled freedom from direction of any sort or nature," had been violated. Judge Quinn agreed with this view, but Latimer, while concurring in the result, rejected emphatically the principle used. Latimer argued that had the law member exercised his statutory powers, one of the charges brought against Berry might have been dropped and the sentence would have been reduced accordingly. That was specific material prejudice, he held, and grounds enough for a reversal.[22]

A few months after *Berry*, the court considered the first of the so-called "jury-intrusion" cases, *U.S. v. Keith*. At issue here was an instance where the law officer and court reporter were called in to give advice to the members of the court during their deliberations, without the accused and his counsel. The opinion was written by Quinn, whose attention focused on the differences between the UCMJ law officer and Elston Act law member instead of on their similarities as Brosman had done in *Berry*. Without going to the correctness of the advice given or whether there was specific damage done to the accused's interests, the two judges voted to reverse.[23]

Judge Latimer was not present for the *Keith* decision, nor was he for the later and almost identical *McConnell* case. Hospitalization took him off the court for a few weeks during the Summer of 1952. But he was ready for a showdown in *U.S. v. Woods and Duffer* during the next term. This was another jury-intrusion case. The precedent set in *Keith* and *McConnell* made the decision in *Woods and Duffer* a foregone conclusion: Quinn and Brosman voted to reverse on the grounds of "general prejudice." The principal opinion by the Chief Judge took up only a few sentences more than a column of type. But Brosman, in a nine-page concurring opinion, and Latimer, in an eight-page dissent, tore into the issue of general prejudice and each other.[24]

Latimer argued that because the UCMJ was so new and unfamiliar, CoMA should be more charitable in its criticism of procedural errors than it might be later, after operational experience had been gained. He listed a series of cases in which there had been procedural error but where CoMA had declined to reverse. One of them, of course, was *Lucas*. Latimer also asserted that in his eagerness to protect some undefined "indwelling principle," Brosman violated the clearly expressed wish of Congress in its prescription that convictions should not be overturned unless there is error which materially prejudices the rights of the accused. "Surely," Latimer protested, "a guilty person should not be rewarded with a new trial because we desire to reprimand a law officer for an infraction of the Code when the accused is the beneficiary of the error."[25] Latimer also belittled Brosman's "general prejudice" because it was too vague to provide guide-lines for court-martial officials in the field.

Brosman's concurring opinion was no more than a rebuttal to Latimer's position. He began by confessing the difficulty of dealing effectively with "a position the origins of which sound almost wholly in psychology, rather than in logic, in history, in analysis or in function." Such an admission would almost certainly have lost him a college debating match. But he went on to say that general prejudice was not "novel in juristic thinking." The name he had given it may have caused some consternation, he admitted, but "general prejudice" was the same familiar concept elsewhere known as "prejudice per se," "presumed prejudice," and "prejudice as a matter of law." The former Tulane dean then focused on *Clay* and asserted that Latimer had been referring to the same thing when he wrote that *"we cannot say one of the historic cornerstones of our system of civil jurisprudence is merely a formality of military procedure."* Latimer did not look for specific prejudice in that case, Brosman claimed, and "I think he was absolutely right."

Brosman continued to argue *tu quoque* on Latimer's charge that general prejudice was unworkably vague. In *Berry*, Brosman reminded readers,

Judge Latimer ... specifically rejected the necessity for a search for specific prejudice, but agreed to reversal because he found "no difficulty in arriving at the conclusion that accused was not accorded a *fair trial*, and that to me is *prejudice*."

Brosman seemed to chuckle, and wrote, "Now *there* is a specific and 'identifiable' standard for the ages!"

Finally, Brosman took issue with Latimer's belief that charity was more appropriate in review of errors until experience had been gained. Brosman held to the opposite view that "the surest and shortest route" to establishing the idea of a bipartite court-martial lay in "drawing violations up short through utilization of the principle of general prejudice."[26]

The heat and mutual derision generated in this decision are the first symptoms of a growing isolation in which Judge Latimer would find himself. The full manifestations of it were still in the future and could not yet be clearly seen. Nor could it be said for certain who won the debate in *Woods and Duffer*. It was a fact that "general prejudice," accepted by a two-to-one majority of the court, was the law. But in only a year's time, it began to be severely qualified by CoMA decisions. In *U.S. v. Gibson*, Brosman himself held that defendants in general prejudice cases could not always expect CoMA to reverse their convictions. Further erosion of the principle occurred as the court moved to fulfill the promise made by the Chief Judge, who had written in *Keith* that once the tradition of non-participation [by the law officer in deliberations] is well-established in the service, it may be possible to assess the occasional lapses in terms of specific prejudice.

In *U.S. v. Albee* the Court did this for the first time, when it was decided that prejudice occurred in intrusion cases only if the law officer gave the court legal information in the absence of the accused, thus preventing his rebuttal or objection.[2 7]

There were other small steps away from the *Woods and Duffer* hard line, but the death knell was sounded in *U.S. v. McCluskey*. Here Judge Brosman came full circle and announced that

It is never necessary, however, to inquire into the desirability of a reliance on the notion of general prejudice where there is a "finding of a probability of specific prejudice against the accused."

This, of course, was precisely the view taken by Latimer in *Keith*.[2 8]

What to make of this turnabout poses a problem. It took only about as long for the court to retreat from general prejudice as it had for it to develop the idea in the first place; a couple of years in each instance. Judge Latimer, who was never shaken from his opposition to the idea, thought its rise and fall were the products of two circumstances. First, he said, general prejudice was Brosman's way of reversing a conviction that disturbed his sense of fair play despite the fact that he could find no specific reason to quash it. Second, the relative swiftness of the shift towards and then away from it is easy to understand, said Latimer, because a three-man court has a kind of inherent instability built into it. When one man changes his mind, the whole tenor of the court is altered, and all that went before is nullified.[29]

There is merit to Latimer's analysis. But there was more to general prejudice than that. The promise in *Keith*—that a day would come when the general prejudice line would no longer be necessary—is proof that the outcome was a conscious thing and not simply the result of fortuitous events. General prejudice was intended to teach the military men who were operating courts-martial under the UCMJ two things: first, that the provisions of the code were meant to be scrupulously followed; and second, that the mandates of the Court of Military Appeals were to be taken seriously.[30]

Given the history of American military justice it could have been no other way. The essence of the general prejudice concept was that if the issue at review of a certain trial was one in which Congress had been particularly interested during the drafting of the law, then violation of Congressional intent dictated immediate reversal without search for specific items of damage done to the accused. Jury intrusion was one of these. The court here was only doing what the American public bade it do. During and after World War II, grievous abuses in military justice came into the public arena. Whether these excesses were real or fancied is no matter; masses of Americans believed in them. The Court of Military Appeals held that Congress desired to end even the appearance of jury-tampering by commanders, or any other sort of so-called command influence. Judge Brosman's doctrine of "general prejudice" was its way of acting on that belief.

9 Early Attempts at Reform:

The Admiral Almost Pulls a Coup

Preoccupied as they were with the question of harmless error, the judges of the Court of Military Appeals did not, in the first few years, provide much of the evolutionary interpretation some early reformers had hoped for. The Brosman-Latimer debate can be seen as one manifestation of the court's searching for its own powers; testing here, trying there, and generally casting about to see just what it was capable of doing.[1] Once custom and tradition were established, CoMA might then get into more sophisticated decisional law.

But there was another way the new court could help refresh the vitality of the UCMJ. As provided by the code itself, the court and the three service JAG's plus the Coast Guard General Counsel were to meet annually to prepare a "survey of the operation" of the new system. They were directed to submit a report of their findings and a summary of their work during the past year to the Department Secretaries and the House and Senate Armed Services Committees. The members of the group established by this mandate referred to themselves collectively as the "Code Committee."

Because the code went into effect on May 31, 1951, the first full year's report was scheduled to be submitted on the same date a year later. But May 31 is not a good time of year to make reports to Congress. By that time, the lawmakers have been sitting continuously for almost five months and are thinking more about ending the session than about how to wring legislation out of newly received reports. In 1952, moreover, some Congressmen were impatient to see how the new system was working out. CoMA partially accommodated them by printing its own "Interim Report" on March 1 of that year. In this six-page pamphlet, the court presented statistics about its work and work load but made only a few comments on the system as a whole. These included some of the controversies which had been part of the UCMJ debate a few years earlier: expansion of the review apparatus during wartime; a separate JAG Corps for the Navy and the Air Force; and possible changes in the convening authority's appointive powers.

When the first annual report of the entire Code Committee appeared in May 1952, it established a format that was followed in all later years. The work was broken into sections: first, the joint report which included those items common to CoMA and all the services and which made recommendations that were unanimously favored by the court and the military. This was followed by the other individualized sections: first the court's report, then separate comments and suggestions made by each of the service JAG's and by the General Counsel of the Treasury Department (later the Transportation Department) on behalf of the Coast Guard.

According to the 1952 *Report*, more questions were tabled during Code Committee meetings than were resolved. In fact, only three recommendations were made. One was that the Code Committee be permitted to submit subsequent reports on December 31 of each year. This would make it available at the opening of the Congressional session and therefore more likely to collect legislative attention and support for its ideas. The only substantive proposal made was that the special court-martial be deprived of its bad-conduct discharge power. The third recommendation was that Congress take no legislative action on any other issues then being discussed by the Code Committee.

This last proposal suggests that the Code Committee thought that Congress would be so eager to make needed statutory changes in military law that it was necessary to warn the lawmakers not to do anything until the issues had been thrashed out in the Code Committee. In retrospect, the admonition was laughable, for it was more than ten years before any important legislation regarding court-martial law would pass Congress. Such a misapprehension of basic political facts of life illustrates how incorrectly most people close to the postwar reforms interpreted them. Perhaps they thought that popular and Congressional interest in military justice would remain at a fever pitch and all that was needed was a mere suggestion from them to get speedy legislative action. A more accurate appraisal would have concluded that the success of the UCMJ, and the Elston Act too, for that matter, was due to the nearly miraculous combination of skill, circumstance, luck, and inept or ineffective opposition.

If Code Committee misunderstanding helps focus on the past, the recommendation concerning BCD's given by special courts provides insights into the future. Although this was a joint proposal when originally made, Navy endorsement was almost immediately withdrawn.[2] As we have noted, the Bad Conduct Discharge was a Navy device, dating back to the mid-Nineteenth Century, and the Navy continued to believe in the need for a punitive discharge at the inferior court level.

The other services were not so enthusiastic. The Uniform Code, which made the BCD applicable to all, required that a verbatim record of trials resulting in such a sentence be kept, in order to facilitate the automatic review which was mandatory in cases involving punitive discharges. Like so many other parts of the code, this provision was taken directly from the Elston Articles. Under those rules, the Army had appointed reporters only for special courts where it was anticipated that a BCD might result. This had its dangers, of course; when a reporter showed up for a trial by special court, the court members were likely to think that the convening authority wanted a BCD, a deduction that might influence their decision.[3]

On the other hand, providing a reporter at all special courts, even those with no reasonable chance of a BCD sentence, was wasteful and inefficient. For these reasons, the Army soon decided to do away with special court reporters altogether. The wording of the implementing regulation indicated that authority to appoint reporters, and therefore to award a BCD at the lower court, could be obtained from the Secretary of the Army or the Judge Advocate General. The main thrust of this new rule, then, was not to abolish inferior court punitive discharges but to save manpower. Subsequently, great sentiment arose in Army legal circles that the awarding of such a severe punishment as a BCD without the protections built into the general court-martial was unjust and indefensible. But the original aim was mere efficiency. This is one of the earliest examples where practical military considerations led to essentially enlightened results. But it would not be the last.[4]

The Air Force's perception of the problem was similar to the Army's. One of the generals at the Bolling AFB conference in April

1951 said that he would not want "to have a finger pointed at us that we only have a reporter present when a bad conduct discharge is expected." The speaker advised the lawyers in the audience that they would have to provide reporters until further notice but that he expected a regulation to be issued shortly to "amplify" the situation. The Air Force finally decided on a policy different from those of the other services. Instead of effectively abolishing the lower court's punitive discharge power as the Army had done, or permitting BCD's to be handed down by amateurs as the Navy was doing, the Air Force ordered that the defense counsel and the prosecutor at special courts-martial both must be qualified lawyers. It was hoped that this would make egregious injustices in the matter unlikely. Here again is an example of the Air Force's practice of going even further than the law required; it would be 1966 before the services were forced to provide lawyers at the lower courts.[5]

The Navy favored neither the Army nor the Air Force method. Approximately 15 percent of Navy special courts resulted in bad-conduct discharges and the sea service vigorously defended the practice. The Air Force procedure was impossible at sea, because the majority of naval vessels had no lawyers or a place to put them. As for shore commands, the Navy's tradition of getting along with a very small number of lawyers left the service with insufficient numbers to provide two for each of several thousand special courts convened each year.[6]

The fact the Congress failed to act on the Code Committee's recommendation regarding the BCD was more probably caused by lawmaker apathy than by the merits of opposing views. Congress did nothing about the recommendation that the annual reports be submitted at year's end, either. Faced with this inaction, the Code Committee put its own recommendation in the latter case into effect without specific Congressional approval.

The 1953 Report, then, covered more than a year and a half, from June 1, 1952, through December 31, 1953. It was in this volume that the issues of post-UCMJ reform were first fully enunciated. Two separate studies were included in the report. The first was the work of a body of "outstanding civilian attorneys," chaired by Whitney North Seymour, which was engaged by the Court of Military Appeals in January 1953. CoMA charged the Seymour committee with "studying and making recommendations concerning ways and means to, and the desirability of, amending the provisions of the Code and to more fairly and expeditiously administer military justice."[7]

Although the members of the Seymour committee in the aggregate possessed a vast amount of military justice experience, they used as a basic document a report submitted to them by the three service JAG's and the Coast Guard General Counsel. The report Seymour submitted in turn reflected the military's recommendations in most respects, although there were important differences. For example, one suggestion made by the military men was that the law officer should be permitted to help the general court-martial put both findings and sentences into the proper form. The UCMJ allowed such assistance in regard to findings, but in view of concurrent CoMA decisions on jury intrusions, the Seymour committee rejected the suggestion that would permit the law officer to help during the sentencing phase, too.[8]

The Seymour committee submitted its report to CoMA on December 21, 1953; the court adopted it as its official position in the 1953 Code Committee pamphlet. Then the full Code Committee considered the proposals and made what were proclaimed to be unanimous recommendations for legislative action to reform the Uniform Code.

But the establishment of the Seymour committee was a major organizational anomaly, which permitted the military men some flexibility in action.

FIGURE 2. THE ANOMALY OF THE SEYMOUR COMMITTEE

JAG's	→	Seymour committee	→	CoMA	→	Code Committee (CoMA & JAG's)	→	Congress

In Figure 2 the irregularity in the position of the JAG's can be seen most clearly. On the one hand, they had reported to the Seymour committee. But on the other, as members of the Code Committee, they could vote on the Seymour report after it was submitted by CoMA. This double-filter operation curiously reflected the role of the court-martial convening authority who refers a case to court-martial and then reviews the results. But it suggests much more. CoMA probably intended the Seymour group to act as a third-party buffer in its dispute with the service representatives. But the anomaly also gave the military a reason for independent action.

The suggestions made by the JAG's in their own separate report had been the result of considerable forethought and study. The Navy was particularly active during those days. We have already noted the Pacific Fleet survey conducted during the Korean War. A similar source of feedback came from a seminar conducted at Norfolk by an Atlantic Fleet commander. His findings stressed in particular the need to have greater nonjudicial powers vested in ship commanders, both to maintain discipline and to prevent permanently branding a youthful offender with a court-martial conviction.[9]

A much broader Navy inquiry was conducted by a committee headed by Rear Admiral Robert J. White, the priest-lawyer former dean of the Catholic University Law School. This group concluded that there was too much unnecessary paperwork in the UCMJ procedures, such as the verbatim records which were required even in general courts-martial which resulted in acquittals. The White committee also recommended less complicated review measures for guilty plea cases, and less adversarylike action in the pretrial investigation. In his final report, Father White bemoaned the overcrowded conditions in most Navy brigs and offered some recommendations to correct them. He concluded that the best solution to many of the Navy's problems in these areas was to increase nonjudicial punishment powers.[10]

After the arduous labor that went into these studies, the Navy Judge Advocate General, Ira Nunn, was displeased that his recommendations had to go through the Seymour committee and the Court of Military Appeals before they would reach Congress via the Code Committee report. This organizational obstacle course, he thought, both required and permitted him to send the original proposals to Congress more directly.[11]

As it was, the Code Committee in 1953 reached unanimity on seventeen suggestions for reform. Many of them sought to simplify and streamline review procedures by giving the Judge Advocate General more power or by eliminating some steps in the cases involving guilty pleas. Others urged an increase in nonjudicial punishment, the inclusion of a bad-check law in the UCMJ, and some changes in the time limits on review and retrial applications. More innovative were the suggestions for trial by law officer only—the so-called "single officer courts"—at both the general and the special court-martial levels. Many of these ideas surfaced time and again over the next decade and a half.[12]

Although the seventeen proposals were well accepted in the community which remained interested in military justice, the services themselves almost immediately began to go their own ways.[13] As

early as June 1954, Admiral Nunn proposed additional changes in
the code. Most of these were minor alterations to the Code
Committee recommendations concerning nonjudicial punishment,
but they were nevertheless clear proof that the apparent unanimity
of the 1953 report was flimsy and might not survive in the future.[14]

The 1954 Code Committee Report showed further erosion in the
year-old agreements. The seventeen proposals were again offered in
the joint report, but in its own section, each service criticized the
UCMJ to a degree not encompassed by the joint recommendations.
The Army charged that the code would never survive in time of full
mobilization because of the slow pace of the review procedures and
the fact that all cases had to be referred to Washington, where
logjams could be expected. The Navy and the Air Force made the
same charge. Although General Harmon repeated some of his
customary complaints about the code, the Air Force position was
one of wait-and-see, at least for one more year. Apparently Harmon
anticipated some legislative relief from the next Congress.

The Navy was not so patient. Admiral Nunn's list of additional
proposals had grown in size and scope. In the 1954 report, he
submitted several startling recommendations for legislative action.
Among other things, these included a reversion to the law member
concept, the deletion of the requirement that the Article 32 pretrial
investigation be "thorough and impartial," and an overhaul of the
article which prohibited self-incrimination. The Army JAG in his
report specifically endorsed each of these measures, as well as the
proposal to establish a Judicial Appeals Board. This board would
consist of three officers who would rule on the validity of petitions
submitted to the Court of Military Appeals. If any one of the three
gave his approval to the petition, it would go to CoMA for review.
But if all three rejected it, the high court would never see the case.

To the members of the court, these ideas seemed reactionary. The
judges opposed the proposals

because of a belief that either the need for them has not been demonstrated or
they turn back the wheels of progress and destroy some of the substantial rights
granted by Congress to members of the Armed Forces.

There was no Congressional action on either the Nunn amendments
or the seventeen suggestions of the Code Committee during the 1954
session. This was probably because of the highly visible mutual
antagonism that existed between the two plans; the lawmakers could
not be expected to interest themselves in measures so lacking in basic
political support.[15]

In the Spring of 1955, Admiral Nunn began to drum up the interest of the press, utilizing some of the contacts he had made during his years as the legislative liaison officer for the Navy during the 1940s. The respected *New York Times* military analyst, Hanson Baldwin, gave Nunn's ideas some publicity in two articles which the bar association men regarded as tantamount to a declaration of war. Baldwin stressed what the admiral regarded as wastes in expenditures, manpower, paperwork, and combat efficiency, all due to the misdirected changes in military and naval law brought on by the UCMJ. Similar sentiments were prominently expressed in other newspapers. Shortly thereafter, perhaps because of the pressure from the fourth estate, bills embracing some of Nunn's ideas were introduced in both the House and the Senate.[16]

It is important to note that these bills were Defense Department proposals, not Code Committee ones. Nothing could make this more evident than the vigorous opposition to the House version, H.R. 6583, thrown up by the Court of Military Appeals. The judges did not fully recognize the differences between H.R. 6583 and their own offerings until sometime after the bills were drafted. In the joint Code Committee report for 1955, for example, they had acquiesced in the statement that the seventeen proposals were incorporated in S. 2133 and H.R. 6583. That was true; but so were several other items. The bills were sent to Congress by the Acting Secretary of the Navy, Thomas S. Gates, and a close reading of their contents shows that their ancestry was the 1953 "Report of the JAG's," not the Code Committee's seventeen points. Nor could there be much doubt that their midwife was Ira Nunn.[17]

Apparently Judges Quinn and Latimer came to recognize this by the time of the hearings. Many of Nunn's controversial proposals were omitted from the new bill, but a few remained. The main debate centered on the "Certificate of Good Cause," which, although rejected in the 1953 discussions, was resurrected in the 1955 bills. Under the latest version of this idea, the Court of Military Appeals would not be permitted to hear cases on petition by the accused unless his defense counsel or appellate counsel certified in good faith that there were good legal grounds for such a review. Admiral Nunn, who was the Defense Department manager of the bills, testified that this would get rid of much inordinate delay in the review system by eliminating frivolous appeals and would in any case be no different from a similar requirement for cases heard by the U.S. Supreme Court. But Judge Quinn argued that such a law would return review control to the military. Most of the men who would be eligible to submit these certificates were military officers and therefore subject to retaliation by commanders who might be irritated by appeals to CoMA. The whole idea, the Chief Judge asserted, "is so hostile to the spirit and intent of the code that I most earnestly oppose its adoption." Quinn objected to certain other parts of the bill as well, but it is clear that he considered the threat to the single nonmilitary agency in the entire court-martial system a jolt to the cornerstone on which the code was built.[18]

Judge Latimer appeared in the 1953 military reports as a kind of hero. In one of the earliest examples of an increasing respect service lawyers and commanders would profess towards the Utah jurist over the next several years, the JAG's had urged that Article 31, the self-incrimination prohibition, be changed to conform to one of Latimer's dissenting opinions. The flattery was not returned, however, at the 1956 hearings. There, the judge delivered a scathing attack on H.R. 6583, which, he claimed, "sought to disturb the present balance between justice and discipline." As for requiring certification of petitions to CoMA, Latimer said that although the work load was often heavy, if it ever got too burdensome, the judges themselves could make adjustments to keep the traffic flowing. But if CoMA were prevented by the proposed process from ever seeing the record, then it would have no chance to find errors, and a valuable protection for individuals would be lost.[19]

The judges were joined in their opposition to part of H.R. 6583 by a few prominent pressure groups. The American Legion, particularly, fought the expansion of nonjudicial powers and urged the retention of the review system as it was. Another opponent of the bill (surprisingly so, perhaps, in view of the official Navy position) was the *Navy Times* editor, John Slinkman, who attacked Nunn's arguments directly, finding them almost devoid of merit on any of the issues discussed. But it was probably the stand of CoMA that killed the 1956 bills. Not too many years had passed since Congress heard the testimony of Edmund Morgan and Frederick Wiener, and not too many Congressional memories had forgotten the conclusions reached then. The Court of Military Appeals had been considered the one absolutely indispensable part of the code's court-martial system. To reject its counsel now during the very first controversy would be to discard some of the most fundamental ideas that lay behind the code, and most Congressmen were not ready to take that step.[20]

H.R. 6583, and its competition, the seventeen Code Committee proposals, were not the only attempts to change the UCMJ in the early 1950s. In 1952, Congressman Louis G. Clemente, of New York, introduced a bill which would have provided the Court of Military Appeals with the authority to rule on all questions of fact.[21] This would have restored to the court the power it had enjoyed in Edmund Morgan's draft. But the idea was not supported by any of the Code Committee members, and nothing came of it.

Another attempt at reform was undertaken by Professor Joseph M. Snee, like Father White a lawyer-priest interested in military justice. Snee's program was used as the basis for discussion by a panel of members of the District of Columbia Bar Association, who had hoped to influence the Congressional work then being done to H.R. 6583. The plan was radical in essence, although it resembled the old UCMJ in form.[22] Snee proposed to remove military law from the specter of command control by abolishing courts-martial altogether. He would replace them with "U.S. Military Justice Courts," to be organized on a circuit basis. What were formerly known as "court members" would now be "juries," selected from a panel provided by the commander. The Court of Military Appeals would be increased to five judges, and would be given the power to prescribe rules of procedure and modes of proof, heretofore a province of the President in his role as author of the *Manual for Courts-Martial.* Some of Snee's ideas, which went well beyond what is given here, were admirable. But like many others before him and since, he was outside the channels where things could actually be done.

The one piece of legislation relating to the code that Congress did pass during these years was almost a joke and helps to amplify the difficulties faced by the various would-be reformers. The new law added to Articles 2(11) and 2(12), which dealt with the jurisdictional limits of the code, the word "Guam" and a comma after "Puerto Rico."[23] So ended the first five years of attempts to reform the UCMJ by legislation. But about this time, some real action was beginning in the Court of Military Appeals.

10 The Court of Military Appeals:

Ferguson's Revolution

The Court of Military Appeals was shocked in December 1955 by the sudden death of Judge Brosman. Appointed by President Truman to the junior seat on the bench, Brosman's term was due to expire in May 1956. His failure to live that long probably saved him some embarrassment, because he would not likely have been reappointed.

The available evidence indicates that like Truman before him, Dwight D. Eisenhower had only scant interest in military justice affairs once he became President. Shortly after the inauguration, Chief Judge Quinn invited the President to make a brief visit to a reception being given by the Court of Military Appeals, but the reply was a rather brusquely telephoned "Sorry." With all of his other obligations, Eisenhower can hardly be blamed for this one rejection. But in June 1954, one of the White House staff members noted with barely disguised disapproval that the President in seventeen months in office had still not met Quinn, implying that such a slight was odd. There is no evidence that the two men ever did meet, although they were in Washington together for the eight years of the Eisenhower tenure.[1]

But, if, as this suggests, Ike himself was not interested in military justice matters, other members of his entourage were. Bernard Shanley of the White House staff, for example, sought out the views of Judge Arthur Vanderbilt on one of the early bills proposing life tenure for CoMA judges. The Eisenhower Administration was noted for its highly structured staff-work methods. On most routine issues, the President himself was the last person to be apprised of a given situation. It is no surprise then that on questions of military justice, matters were anticipated, initiated, and handled at relatively low levels.[2]

This seems to have been the way things were in Brosman's case. Papers in the Eisenhower White House files indicate that the Administration staff had begun a search for a suitable Republican to replace the CoMA judge in the late Fall of 1955.[3] After his death, on the recommendation of the Justice Department which confirmed "the worth of Judge Brosman's work," it was decided that grief should be the official posture assumed by the Administration.[4] But the speedy appointment of a successor was no fluke; the groundwork had been laid while Brosman was alive.

There was a scramble for Brosman's seat on the CoMA, as is customary whenever there is a federal court vacancy. *Navy Times* reported that the two "leading candidates" were Robert W. Smart, the chief counsel for the House Armed Services Committee, and Richard Tedrow, chief commissioner at CoMA. But this assertion reflected the wishful thinking of the editor of the *Times*, who was actively promoting Tedrow's candidacy at the White House. Knowing men today doubt that either Tedrow or Smart ever had a chance.[5]

Speculation over the identity of the new judge centered around men who had experience in military justice. This explains the mention of Tedrow and Smart. But Eisenhower's nominee came to the court completely untouched by any exposure to courts-martial. He was Homer Ferguson of Michigan, former Republican U.S. Senator, Detroit trial judge, and, at the time of his appointment, the United States Ambassador to the Philippines. Nominated on January 13, 1956, and confirmed on February 17, Ferguson took his seat on April 9, to complete the last month of Brosman's term and a fifteen-year term of his own.[6]

The selection of Ferguson was odd in many ways. The new judge's lack of military experience was perplexing. Although the statute specified that CoMA judges were to be "appointed from civilian life," Truman had compromised by naming three Reserve officers, one from each service, for reasons previously mentioned. It seems ironic that Eisenhower, the five-star general in the White House, should have leaned the other way and named a man who had never had any connection whatever with the military. Ferguson was a man of proven tenacity and moral fearlessness. As the Wayne County single-man grand jury, a unique provision of Michigan law, Ferguson once indicted a number of powerful Detroit political figures in a giant graft scandal. During World War II, he served on the Truman Committee, a trouble-shooting body which oversaw the relations between governmental agencies and business corporations during the wartime industrial expansion. Later in his Senate career, Ferguson disagreed with the official explanations given by several Administration departments for the disaster at Pearl Harbor. Along with one other member of the select Congressional committee to investigate the raid, he refused to go along with the majority opinion and wrote a blistering attack on what he suspected was a whitewash. This skepticism, which has made Ferguson the most controversial of the CoMA judges, may have been just what the Administration was looking for.[7]

In 1952, Chief Judge Quinn had written that it was an asset for CoMA judges to have had military experience because they would then "know, through personal experience, the military problems incidental to the conduct of courts-martial." That Ferguson lacked that experience was seen by many as a weakness in his credentials. But the judge himself replied that such apprehension about his qualifications for an appointment to the highest military tribunal in the land betrayed a misunderstanding of CoMA. The court is required to rule on the law in court-martial cases, Ferguson rightly observed. It was important, in his view, that the judges know the law, but they need not know the military. These were views that the court as a whole had subscribed to in 1954 before Ferguson joined, by noting that prior to the UCMJ, "the guidelines for determining guilt or innocence could be known only to one thoroughly acquainted with the decisions of military tribunals." The authors of the UCMJ, however, sought to provide clearer standards within the punitive articles. These new definitions could presumably be understood better by men with legal rather than military experience.[8]

President Eisenhower, then, in appointing Ferguson followed the original Congressional intent even more closely than Truman had. And Ferguson, who believed himself the first judge appointed in accordance with the proper spirit of the code, brought to the court a definite civilianizing impact. Although this may have been what was desired by the court's founders, it nevertheless turned military justice on its ear. During Ferguson's career, the court applied the Constitution of the United States to trials by court-martial for the first time; followed the mandates of the nearly contemporaneous Warren Supreme Court very closely; and systematically rejected certain customs of military justice which had long been hallowed by inclusion in the *Manual for Courts-Martial*.

Because he was perceived as the primary agent in this revolution, Ferguson incurred the wrath of many military lawyers. He was an extremely unpopular man at the Pentagon, where a series of Judge Advocate Generals, and no doubt many of their subordinates as well, believed that he was the model on whom the incompetent "Louis Sears, American Ambassador to Sarkhan," in the novel *The Ugly American*, was based. There are certain superficial similarities between Ferguson and Sears, but at least as many differences, too. Nevertheless, the slander persisted, and was told frequently by military lawyers who had no love for the Michigan jurist.[9]

Ferguson in the flesh was not the boob his antagonists liked to believe him, but he was indeed a scourge of traditionalist military justice. A good example of this is his interpretation of the question of constitutional applicability.

As we have noted, it was long held that the Bill of Rights was not pertinent to military courts. Certain cases decided at various levels of the federal court hierarchy during and shortly after World War II confused this issue somewhat.[10] But when the Court of Military Appeals uttered its first opinion on the matter in *U.S. v. Clay*, it chose to "bottom" the rights of a military defendant not on the Constitution but on statutes, as we have seen.

Shortly after Ferguson joined the court, the issue narrowed, focusing on the constitutionality of written depositions supposedly taken in accordance with Article 49 of the code. Earlier, in *U.S. v. Sutton*, Latimer and Brosman had upheld the admissibility of a prosecution deposition even though the accused had not been present when it was taken. The rationale behind this decision was that military courts encountered certain unusual difficulties in procuring testimony not faced by civilian tribunals, such as transfers, combat casualties, or the need for testimony from foreign nationals. Judge Quinn dissented in *Sutton*, arguing that such a practice violated the accused's right to confront witnesses against him, a guarantee of the Sixth Amendment. The Chief Judge even went so far as to imply strongly that because Article 49 seemed to contradict the Constitution, he might rule it invalid.[11]

The same question was raised shortly after Ferguson's appointment, probably to test his opinion on the matter. In *U.S. v. Parrish*, Ferguson voted with Latimer to affirm a conviction based in large measure on a deposition taken from an intermittent psychotic during one of his lucid periods, when neither accused nor his counsel were present. Ferguson said he voted that way out of respect for the doctrine of *stare decisis*. But almost four years later he changed his mind and joined Quinn, who had dissented again in *Parrish*, in overturning the deposition practice long popular in the services.[12]

The 1960 case was *U.S. v. Jacoby*. Ferguson wrote the principal opinion, freely confessing that it represented a shift from an earlier, mistaken view. On the constitutional question, he wrote that the safeguards of the "Bill of Rights, except those which are expressly or by necessary implication inapplicable, are available to members of our armed forces." Since the right to confront hostile witnesses fits neither exception, Ferguson and Quinn ruled that no prosecution deposition should be admitted into evidence unless the accused, accompanied by his regularly appointed counsel or other counsel of his choice, had been present when it was taken and given the opportunity to cross-examine. Judge Latimer dissented, holding that by this action the court had absurdly decided to invalidate part of the act which had created it. It was Latimer's position that *Jacoby* had the effect of overruling Article 49. But the majority saw it otherwise; an opinion which seems justifiable. Article 49 is one of the longest in the code, but nothing from the *Jacoby* decision seems to negate any of it. *Jacoby* aims rather at the *Manual for Courts-Martial* provisions that amplified the article.[13]

The main issue here was the constitutional one. A number of contemporaneous federal court decisions held that constitutional guarantees had to be considered whenever civilian courts tested military justice.[14] Perhaps in response, CoMA in *Jacoby* said squarely that the Bill of Rights is applicable in courts-martial, except in a few rare instances. But critics of the decision overlooked the lofty constitutional issue and rested their gaze on what the decision did to the written deposition, a long- and well-respected feature of courts-martial. As a naval scholar later wrote, *Jacoby* "killed" the practice.[15]

Military men were not myopic in their view of *Jacoby*, however. As many of them perceived it, the second half of the 1950s saw all too many ancient and useful court-martial procedures thrown out by the Court of Military Appeals, and they blamed Judge Ferguson.[16]

Even the Army admitted, however, that overrulings of *MCM* provisions did not start with Ferguson's arrival on the court. A prominent early example occurred in *U.S. v. Wappler*, where the court ruled that the *Manual* paragraph permitting courts-martial to award sentences including bread and water rations was contrary to the Uniform Code, which mentioned bread and water only as a nonjudicial punishment. This decision followed *U.S. v. Lucas*, where the court held that the code and the *Manual* were of equal status, so long as the latter is within the bounds granted it and does not conflict with the code or other well-founded legislation. The same principle was reaffirmed only a few months before Ferguson joined the court, in *U.S. v. Villasenor*. But, in *Wappler*, there had been such a conflict and the court held that the code was superior.[17]

Both the *Lucas* and the *Villasenor* opinions expressed reservations about the *Manual*. In fact, the court had found several weaknesses in its provisions. Judge Latimer, the author of the *Villasenor* decision, told an Army conference in 1954 that law officers do not satisfy their obligation to instruct the court merely by reading passages from the *MCM*. And in one of its earliest cases, *U.S. v. Simmons*, the court even went so far as to recommend that a portion of the *Manual* be revised.[18]

Despite these assaults on the *MCM* during the first few years of the new system, the tempo did pick up noticeably after Ferguson's appointment. But even more significant to the historian and upsetting to the military than the *rate* of invalidations were the specific *issues* involved in cases where they occurred. Many of the procedures and concepts overthrown at Ferguson's instigation were considered by the military to have been sanctioned, if not actually sanctified, by long usage.

It is not possible to pinpoint the exact moment when the Ferguson revolution in military justice began, but *U.S. v. Boswell* might serve as well as any other arbitrarily selected case. The opinion by itself was not very startling. In fact, it was written by Quinn. Ferguson concurred, while Latimer dissented. The majority criticized the practice whereby court members took the *Manual for Courts-Martial* into closed sessions. The *MCM* was no different from other legal texts, Quinn advised, and should therefore not be used indiscriminately by amateurs who were likely to misunderstand it. Underlying this was the argument that the law officer should be the sole source of legal instructions for a court-martial, a point which the court had long insisted upon, and that the *Manual* should not compete with his preeminence in this field.[19]

Boswell laid down no new rules, but if traditionalists could therefore hope to ignore its warning, their respite was brief. Four months later, in *U.S. v. Rinehart*, the court, in another two-to-one decision, ordered an outright ban on the use of the *Manual* in secret court sessions. The change from *Boswell* to *Rinehart* illustrates some differences between Quinn and Ferguson. In many earlier cases, the Chief Judge had found fault with the reliance of the trial courts on legal authorities other than the law officer. For example, in the sensational *U.S. v. Deain,* which involved a permanent court-martial headed by a semiretired admiral who bullied the other members into agreement with him, Quinn found that the admiral's reliance on certain provisions of the *MCM* amounted to "an antecedent conviction which a court member brings with him to the trial.[20]

But as unfavorably as he regarded such jury-intrusion by legal writings, Quinn had shown no disposition to lay a blanket prohibition on their use. Ferguson, on the other hand, took a *Boswell*-like fact situation in *Rinehart*, and lowered the boom. Reminding readers of *Boswell*, he argued that "court members may not understand the *Manual's* passages," and went on to assert flatly that

We cannot sanction a practice which permits court members to rummage through a treatise on military law, such as the Manual, indiscriminately rejecting and applying a myriad of principles – judicial and otherwise – contained therein.

Judge Latimer, who had dissented in *Boswell* too, counterattacked. He decried the civilian analogy drawn by the majority, asserting that the military was different because officers serving on courts-martial "must be both judges and jurors." Besides, he pointed out, the court is often in a position where it must overrule the law officer and therefore should have a source of law independent of him.[21] Latimer's primary reliance was on tradition. The *Manual* was familiar to most professional officers, he argued, and they had developed confidence in its use over many years.

Latimer's arguments were to no avail. *Rinehart* stood, the *Manual* was not to be used by court-members, and Latimer's isolation had begun.[22]

Another major pillar of court-martial practice was struck down in *U.S. v. Cothern,* an absence case decided the same day as *Boswell*. During the trial, the law officer instructed the court that from evidence of a "much prolonged absence," it could be properly inferred that the defendant had intended to stay away permanently and could therefore be convicted of desertion, a much more serious offense than mere unauthorized absence. In reversing, Ferguson wrote that because the accused had introduced evidence that he did not intend to stay away permanently, the prosecution had the burden to prove the intent positively and not merely by inference. Not content with establishing his point only under the particular circumstances of this case, however, Ferguson went on to invalidate the entire paragraph from the *MCM* on which the law officer had based his instructions.[23]

Latimer, although concurring in the result, again disagreed with Ferguson's reasoning. He argued that the majority went too far in striking down "absolutely and without necessity or justification a rule which is founded on good sense and logic and has long enjoyed approval in military forums." There is no more concise statement of Latimer's objections to the line of cases involving the *Manual*.

A few months after *Cothern*, Judge Ferguson attacked another long-standing military practice in *U.S. v. Nowling*. Here, the defendant was charged with deceitful possession of an unauthorized liberty card. An Air Force policeman who had reason to suspect that Nowling was not allowed to be on liberty asked to see his pass. Because the one produced did not match Nowling's identity card, the AP took him into custody and court-martial proceedings were initiated. When the subsequent conviction finally reached the Court of Military Appeals, Ferguson wrote for the now customary two-to-one majority that asking a suspect to perform an act that would incriminate him was a violation of Article 31 of the code. The AP, Ferguson asserted, had grounds to suspect Nowling, and should therefore have warned him of his rights before asking to see the incriminating pass.[24]

Latimer dissented, basing his argument on the havoc the *Nowling* rule would cause among service police trying to carry out the necessary function of separating men who are AWOL from those who are on authorized liberty. Ferguson's ruling had been directed only at those incidents where there was suspicion of wrong-doing, Latimer conceded, but the results could be chaotic. The old procedure, under the old rules, was much better, he thought.

Later that term, the Ferguson-Quinn majority assaulted the very essence of the military structure in *U.S. v. Curtin*, ruling that there were times when a GI was not even bound to obey routine orders! Here, the majority reversed a disobedience conviction on the grounds that the order in question could not be considered a "general order." Disobedience of a "general order" can be proven by the introduction of evidence which establishes so-called "constructive knowledge." That is, a man can be presumed to know about an order issued by a high-ranking officer that is broadly recognized and widely disseminated. But disobedience of less lofty orders requires proof of "actual knowledge," that is, that the defendant actually knew the contents of the order in question. The majority held that in this case, the law officer had mistaken the one for the other and that the man was convicted erroneously.[25]

Latimer's dissent on this point adduced a number of legal treatises and exalted the *Manual* provision on which the law officer had relied. He also rejected the civilian court decision on which Ferguson had based his principal opinion as irrelevant and inappropriate.[26] Again, Latimer's position was traditionalistic and ineffective.

Only a few weeks after *Curtin*, Quinn and Ferguson struck again at the *Manual* in *U.S. v. Varnadore* and *U.S. v. Holt*. The issue in these nearly identical cases was the validity of the *MCM* provision which directed that a court-martial sentence of confinement for more than six months automatically included a punitive discharge. In an earlier decision, *U.S. v. Brasher,* the court had upheld this practice. But in *Holt-Varnadore*, the majority voted to overrule *Brasher* and strike down the offensive paragraph. In doing so, they argued that no sentence could be considered automatic, since that would deprive the trial court of independence of action. Latimer, as might be expected, dissented, this time on twin grounds. First, he argued, this decision overturned several prior ones, including *Brasher*, which were based on good law. Second, it violated the *Lucas* rule that omission of a certain provision by the legislature in writing the code did not require similar silence on the part of the executive in promulgating the *Manual*.[27]

Perhaps the new majority's most vigorous attack on a *Manual* procedure came in *U.S. v. Cecil* and *U.S. v. May*. Both these cases involved suspended punitive discharges. A number of suspension techniques were used by the military in punitive discharge cases. Some of them were intended to provide the convicted GI a chance to redeem himself while in confinement. In 1956, for example, the Army undertook a program of encouraging all convening authorities to suspend punitive discharges in every case, unless it was clear that the accused was incorrigibly unfit for service. The Pentagon conscientiously followed up on this policy, even to the extent of issuing critical letters to those commanders who failed to comply. But other suspension procedures were intended merely to prevent the inadvertent punitive discharge of a man before his review was completed, an event which would be embarrassing should the conviction be reversed by appellate courts. The Court of Military Appeals in *Cecil-May* struck at the *Manual* provision that these suspensions could be vacated administratively, that is, without a hearing where the accused could demonstrate that he had observed the terms of his probation. Such a procedure, the court ruled, contradicted Article 72 of the code, which ordered that there could be only one kind of suspended sentence, the probationary one. Moreover, probation could be ended only upon proof of further misconduct, the court continued. Latimer again dissented, arguing that suspensions should not be construed so narrowly. Earlier court decisions, he said, had upheld the variety of procedures, and *Cecil-May* would only undo them, for no good reason.[28]

There were other issues which split the Court of Military Appeals during the period 1957 through 1961; some of them will be discussed later. But the war over the *Manual* is an accurate touchstone for evaluating the Quinn-Latimer-Ferguson Court. A few generalities apply. Latimer stood on custom and tradition. A former line officer himself, he placed great value on the *Manual*, mostly because of the assistance it provided court-martial members and officials. Accordingly, he based his opinion on what personnel in the field would probably find most workable. Throughout this period, he grew increasingly to be the darling of the services.

Ferguson, on the other hand, brought a different viewpoint to the court. Utterly devoid of personal experience in the use of the *Manual*, and unimpressed therefore by the scriptural status it enjoyed among military men, he cast a critical eye on it whenever it appeared to contravene the law—that is, the code. Ironically, in taking this position, Ferguson, who is often thought the most "civilianized" of the CoMA judges, had an important ally in William Winthrop, the Army's greatest judge advocate. Ferguson saw the same difference between the code and the *Manual* that Winthrop described in pointing out that passing from the Articles of War to Army regulations was going from statute to executive order. Winthrop left no doubt that regulations may not encroach on legislation, although he conceded that the distinction was often difficult. In a 1960 case, Ferguson joined in the view that making that distinction was the responsibility solely of the Court of Military Appeals.[29]

That opinion was actually written by Chief Judge Quinn, who went along with Ferguson in virtually all the cases dealing with the *Manual*, perhaps for a variety of reasons. Unlike Latimer, who had been an Army line officer both in the Reserve and on active wartime duty, Quinn was a lawyer first and showed less concern for what was easy for the field officer than his colleague did. As Chief Judge, he sought to elevate the court in the eyes of other jurists and was therefore more open to concepts that were current in other courts. In this light, the *Manual* was anachronistic, and modernization of court-martial law was his goal. Finally, the fact that CoMA was a three-man court had an influence on Quinn's voting. Given the positions of Ferguson and Latimer, Quinn would have to be the "swing man." He might not like either pole very much, but would have to choose one or the other. For example, having taken in *Boswell* his stand on the use of the *Manual* in closed sessions, what could he have done when Ferguson assumed an uncompromising stance in *Rinehart*? To side with Latimer against Ferguson's immoderation would overrule the *Boswell* holding. Quinn probably saw in Latimer's opinions a dangerous tendency to drift back to the ideas of the pre-UCMJ days. Even though Ferguson's rulings might be more radical than what Quinn would reach by himself, voting for them was by far the less unpleasant alternative.[30] We will have further occasion to investigate this phenomenon after the court personnel change that occurred in 1961.

Judge Ferguson sensed Quinn's ambivalence. His comment in the *Rinehart* opinion seems to have been designed to sway the Chief Judge towards his own views:

We are fully aware that the change in the system of military law occasioned by this decision represents a substantial departure from prior service practices. However, we cannot but feel that such change was imperatively needed if the system of military law is to assume and maintain the high and respected place that it deserved in the jurisprudence of our free society.[31]

If Judge Brosman's "general prejudice" doctrine was designed to bring military justice out of the primitive days of the Articles of War and the AGN, Judge Ferguson's war on the *Manual* had even grander ambitions: the parity of the UCMJ with other systems of law in use in American courts.

11 In-Service Reforms

It would be a mistake to think that the Court of Military Appeals was the scene of all the action in military justice during the 1950s. Despite the number of important CoMA decisions during the period, primary responsibility for the administration of the law continued to rest on service lawyers, from the Judge Advocate General down to the lowest ranking trial counsel.

The author of an article published in 1929 argued that, although there were few lawyers in the military, the men who filled important court-martial posts were well-trained and expert at their duties.[1] This may have been possible under the 1920 Articles, when no single position had to be filled by a lawyer. Even the Elston Act required only one lawyer, the law member, and he only at general courts-martial. The 1948 act did urge the appointment of *bona fide* lawyers as prosecutors and defense counsel, but only "if available."

The Uniform Code represented a major change in this situation. After 1951, general courts of all the services needed three certified lawyers, a fact which required a severalfold increase in the number of judge advocates on active duty. The problem was recognized early, and procurement of military lawyers became the first concern of all the JAG's for several years.[2]

Part of the manpower shortage was caused by the fact that not all judge advocates could be assigned to court-martial work. This was one of the arguments the Air Force used against the establishment of a JAG Corps. Aviators, staff officers, and lawyers were all members of the various teams involved in procurement, project management, and operational planning. The official Air Force position was that distinguishing the lawyers by a separate promotion list would hurt the morale and efficiency of these teams.[3]

The Navy had a similar reliance on equipment and machinery, but the resulting diversity required of its legal men triggered a major intraservice controversy. Because the law did not require that the Navy JAG have any legal training, the first lawyer to hold the post, Walter B. Woodson, took office only in 1938. Even so, his experience had been mostly naval, not legal, and Undersecretary Forrestal found him unable to provide the procurement advice the wartime Navy needed.[4]

Forrestal rectified this situation by creating the position of "General Counsel of the Navy Department," which he filled with a civilian lawyer who could help him with contracts and procurement. Later, in 1946, the JAG was further circumscribed when matters dealing with copyrights and patents were taken from him and assigned to the Chief of Naval Research. As a result of these limitations, uniformed personnel in the Navy's legal department became concentrated in court-martial affairs. In 1954, however, Admiral Nunn led a fight against the general counsel concept, arguing that the JAG was the only legal advisor authorized by law, and soon all the lost powers were returned. But that meant that large numbers of uniformed lawyers had to be diverted to projects other than military justice. Coming as this did on the heels of the Uniform Code with its increased demands for lawyers, it caused a major personnel shortage.[5]

Even the Army, traditionally the least hardware-oriented of the services, devoted a large share of its legal manpower to these other fields. In his 1952 annual report, the Army JAG estimated a need for approximately 1200 JAG Corps lawyers, almost 40 percent of whom would work outside of court-martial law. Despite this, the same general reported less than a year later that his personnel demands were "quite modest," and that therefore the Army had been able to be selective in its lawyer recruitment. This surprising statement was contradicted by the annual reports of all the services over the next few years.[6]

Air Force reports for 1957, 1958, and 1960 give some interesting comparative figures. At the beginning of 1957, there were 1201 lawyers on active duty; at the end of that year, despite a strenuous recruiting program, there were 1202, a net gain of only one. In 1958, the same efforts produced the same results: there were 1203 Air

Force JA's by December 31 of that year. In 1960, there was another increase of one man. The Army maintained this forlorn habit in 1961 by reporting the addition of 30 Regular Army JA's, but a loss of 29, another net gain of one.[7]

Nor were sheer numbers the only problem: distribution of lawyers throughout the various ranks was badly askew. The Army reported in 1958 that only twenty of the 392 lieutenants in the JAG Corps were Regulars, signifying that the overwhelming majority of the young lawyers on whom the service lavished its recruiting efforts came into the Army for only a two- or three-year term, retained their Reserve status while on active duty, and got out as soon as possible to return to a supposedly superior civilian career. The Deputy JAG of the Air Force reported in 1957 that whereas only 10 percent of the Air Force lawyers should be first lieutenants, in fact more than half of them were. The Navy, trying to make do with only 40 percent of the number of qualified men the other services found inadequate, complained in 1958 that three-fourths of its law specialists in the rank of commander had already been passed over twice for promotion and could therefore be separated at any time.[8]

Attempted solutions to this manpower problem were varied. Charles Decker had one idea. As Assistant JAG from 1957 through 1960, he noted the excessive number of Reservist junior officers in the corps and concluded that one solution to the problem was to recruit lawyers from among those officers already committed to a military career. This idea developed naturally from Decker's own experience; he was a 1931 graduate of West Point and had served in infantry regiments as a line officer before the Army sent him to Georgetown Law School. Most of the other high-ranking JAG Corps officers of his era had had similar careers. In Decker's eyes, these men had proven that a military lawyer could be loyal to his twin professions. Moreover, Decker held firmly to the proposition that "the most essential experience an Army man can have is as an enlisted man or a commissioned officer in the line."[9]

But there were no funds to support such a program in the Cold War. The Army's modest prewar legal requirements had been satisfied by sending a few officers a year off to law schools. But in the postwar period, the Army needed several hundred a year. Unable to get the necessary support for his idea in the late 1950s, Decker instituted a partial substitute for it in the 1960s. By this time he was the Judge Advocate General and on his own authority put into effect the "Excess Leave Program," which permitted selected Regular officers to pursue a legal education at their own expense and without military pay and allowances. This system was not the best, but thirty to thirty-five Regular Army lawyers would be created by it annually, once it matured.[10]

Decker's ideas about line experience were widely shared by World War II vintage naval officers. In the Navy, the concept was amplified by the nature of the ship-shore rotations and the existence of small combatant vessels. There was scant space in these ships for a lawyer who could do nothing but practice law. On the other hand, the system did not allow the Navy the luxury of full-time lawyers who stayed ashore. For every one of these land-locked barristers, there was one fewer job which could be filled by a man who had completed a tour of sea duty.

The Navy's way out of this dilemma during the interwar years was very much like the Army's. Naval Academy graduates went to sea to gain basic shipboard experience. After a few years, when they first became eligible for shore duty, a number of them were sent to civilian law schools. Such a man would be able to serve in line billets as a deck, engineering, or ordnance officer during his sea duty periods and in legal offices during his shore rotation. While attached to a ship's company, he would also be available to help out with whatever legal problems might arise.

Unfortunately, this system was shattered, along with so many other traditions, by the explosive expansion of World War II. In the emergency, line experience was found more valuable than legal prowess. Ira Nunn, for example, a Harvard Law graduate, served as a destroyer skipper and squadron commander in various Pacific theaters. In between campaigns, he sometimes performed legal tasks, but throughout the war he was assigned to one or another command jobs. The bulk of the legal work done by the Navy during hostilities, including most of the court-martial caseload, was handled by Reservists called in only for the duration.[11]

The oddity of this situation—that those who during the peace were trained in court-martial work abandoned it when the shooting started—was noted by the 1946 Ballantine committee, which suggested two alternatives: a JAG corps or a "law specialist" program. The Navy chose the latter and put it into effect by administrative action in 1947. Although law specialists were considered line officers, wore line insignia, and competed for line promotions, everyone knew they were fit only for legal jobs. The Navy became trapped in its own mythology here. Even during the

UCMJ deliberations, spokesmen continued to argue for the old system of "lawyers among seamen and seamen among lawyers." Colonel Curry, the marine who represented the Navy Department on both the UCMJ Committee and the *MCM* drafting team, argued that if Congressmen could return to legal practice with only a little "brushing up" after years in government, surely naval and marine lawyers could do the same after periods of sea duty. This reasoning led the Navy to maintain the fiction of line status for its lawyers even while it established a quasi-JAG corps in the law specialist program.[12]

By the weight of numbers and the effect of attrition the law specialists soon began to make their presence felt in the Navy's legal department. They were frequently supported by the same battery of ex-service lawyers who had worked for the reforms in the late 1940s. When Admiral Nunn was proposed as Navy JAG in 1952, a number of the bar association reformers clamored against his nomination. Nunn had not bothered to take and pass a bar examination until 1949, fifteen years after winning his law degree. Because of this, he had not accumulated the eight years experience in practicing law that the UCMJ required of a Judge Advocate General. Bar association pressure forced Congress to acknowledge this fact, although Nunn's appointment was ultimately confirmed, due in large measure to the support given him by House Armed Services Committee Chairman Carl Vinson. But the lawyer groups won from Congress a promise that, when possible, legal specialists would be given priority in future nominations.[13]

A law specialist, Chester Ward, succeeded Nunn as JAG in 1956, and thereafter the post was invariably held by one of the new breed of Navy lawyers.[14] Psychological factors now went to work. Before Ward's appointment, JAG had merely been another post to be held by a high-ranking naval officer as he worked his way up the promotional ladder. After 1956, however, it became the highest achievement a naval lawyer could aspire to. Moreover, because by holding the job he would have fulfilled his ultimate career ambition, the JAG would have less reason than heretofore to be obsequious when dealing with line admirals around him.

With this victory won, law specialists began to criticize the remaining vestiges of their halfway status. The JAG corps idea came into favor among them during the late 1950s, when many officers argued that the lack of prestige suffered by law specialists contributed to the manpower problem. Admiral Ward's successor, W.C. Mott, was the first JAG to go on record in favor of the corps, and in

1961 legislation was proposed by the Navy to create it.[15]

The traditions which intruded so heavily in Army and Navy legal affairs were never as important in the Air Force. This was partly because of the influence of General Harmon, whose background was not typical of the Regular Army and Regular Navy men who were his contemporaries. The very newness of the air service also added to the lack of restrictive customs. There was, however, a minor controversy in the early 1950s that seemed to parallel the Army and Navy debate over line experience for lawyers, when all Air Force legal personnel were withdrawn from flying status. But the issue then was not whether lawyers had to be pilots to understand their duties, but rather whether it was fair to deprive them of the additional pay earned by flyers. Harmon himself fought the new ban, but the best he could do was to gain for the men affected the right to choose a legal career or a flying one. Some ninety-eight lawyers were lost as a result of this option, putting another crimp in the manpower situation.[16]

Despite the frequent claims of lawyer shortages, existing human resources were not used to the maximum extent posssible. Apparently there were many lawyers in the Army's enlisted ranks. On at least two occasions in the mid-1950s, the JAG's School encouraged local Army JA's to send these men to legal training centers where they could be channeled into JAG activities. Much later, both the Coast Guard and the Navy showed signs of similar mismanagement. The Coast Guard, for example, admitted in 1966 that the majority of its lawyers were actually in nonlegal jobs. Finally, in 1969, a high-ranking naval officer wrote that almost nine out of every ten of the highly skilled enlisted court reporters in the Navy were assigned to jobs where their talents were not used. Many of the perceived personnel shortages might have been alleviated if responsible officials had paid closer attention to utilizing resources that were actually on hand.[17]

Although this emphasis on JAG personnel issues smacks of empire-building, important reasons lay behind it. The Uniform Code brought "lawyerization" to military justice. But the lawyers so heavily burdened by the UCMJ could not hope to function in the highly stratified military structure unless they were able to command some prestige of their own. A JAG corps and a vigorous recruiting program, particularly one aimed at Regular officers, would help. So could a lively "alumni" organization, like the Judge Advocates Association. Lists of JAA officers always included all the JAG's;

General Harmon once referred to the association as the "stockholders." Just as other veterans' groups did for their in-service counterparts, the JAA provided a civilian forum for the JAG's and a political lobby for many of their ideas. And like other activities aimed at enhancing the "clout" of the service legal departments, its ultimate goal was to help the military lawyer do his job more effectively.[18]

Despite the problems of manpower allocation, the service JAG's compiled an impressive list of achievements during the 1950s. In fact, in the absense of any statutory changes of consequence, the first decade of the UCMJ might be viewed as a period of regulatory reform. It must be underscored that military lawyers were the administrators of court-martial law, not its theorists. Their reform endeavors were generally pointed at greater efficiency. Even so, the beneficiary of many of their projects was the soldier, sailor, or airman whom the law protected.

One of the complaints levelled at the UCMJ review system, for example, was its failure to provide specific authority for branch offices of the boards of review. In 1949 and 1950, Army men in particular had vivid memories of their World War II experiences, when the branch boards literally saved the system by obviating the time and trouble that would have followed if cases had to be sent to Washington for final review. The Navy never established branches in the pre-UCMJ days, but with the increase in business the new system brought, a need for them was soon felt. In November 1955, the Navy instituted a West Coast office of JAG, including two boards of review.[19]

In another innovation, the Navy established the "Dockside Court," a program by which small ships lacking the personnel, skill, and experience to conduct courts-martial could utilize better equipped and trained shore-based facilities and personnel near by. The ship's captain would still be the convening authority, and his crew might supply some of the court members, but the high-skill roles, such as counsel, recorder, and perhaps court president, could be borrowed from the local legal staff. Not dissimilar were the "JAG Task Forces," one on the East Coast, one on the West, which were set up in February 1958 to help clear up the backlog of court-martial cases faced by several undermanned Navy shore commands.[20]

The prime motivation behind these steps was the desire to make things easier for the Fleet units which had to operate under the code. Included, however, was the intent to purge the system of errors in procedure that led to reversed convictions. These are not unworthy goals. Efficient and correct process, given a well-constructed body of law, can do little else than protect the individual who finds himself face to face with the awesome prosecuting power of the state or service.

A good example of this was the outcome of the Navy's 1957 "Operation Tapecut," which was frankly designed to "speed up" the administration of military justice. The Navy announced at the end of one year of "Tapecut" that the total number of men in Navy and Marine brigs had been cut by 30 percent as a result of the project. Even more dramatic was the 42 percent drop in the number of men confined before trial.[21] If one bears in mind the reason for the constitutional guarantee of a "speedy trial"—the prevention of arbitrary pretrial imprisonment—"Operation Tapecut" clearly worked to the benefit of individual sailors and marines.

The focus on Navy innovations brings us to a peculiarity in Navy legal outlook. The Navy's military justice posture is an "*ad hoc*" thing. The other services have permanently assigned, specifically trained military police. The Navy has a shore patrol, composed of men only temporarily appointed, who return to their regular duties when their tours as policemen are ended. The Navy's reliance on commander's nonjudicial punishment, which is essentially a means of informally trying and punishing military offenders, is deeper and of much longer historical standing than that of the other services. The attractiveness of the special court-martial, an *ad hoc* tribunal if there ever was one, fits into this pattern. So does the naming of nonlawyers to the post of Judge Advocate General. Deeply ingrained in the Navy way of doing things is the notion that criminal and judicial matters can be handled free from legal formalities. The Navy thinks of itself as a family; since families do not ordinarily have to send out for lawyers and judges to help resolve their problems, neither should the Navy.

There is some of this attitude in all the services, as we shall see in Chapter XIII; but the reluctance of naval officers to relinquish their traditional, highly paternalistic legal system, even after the enactment of the very formalized UCMJ, has frequently driven them to seek means to overcome the contradictions inherent in such an ambiguous situation. As a result, the Navy has relied on commissions and study groups to a greater degree than the other services and, paradoxically, seemed more willing to adopt the recommendations that these boards make.[22] But tampering with the basic paternalism and informality that the Navy believes is the correct approach to military justice and discipline was not acceptable.

This is not to say that the other services contributed no new ideas; the Army and the Air Force by the late 1950s were frequently looking into the future, or at least trying to improve on the present. We have already seen one example of this: the Air Force's policy of supplying trained lawyers as defense counsel at special courts, where the law did not require it. The Army, too, made enlightened contributions; two in particular merit study: the negotiated pretrial agreement and the independent judiciary.

The negotiated plea is usually thought of as a borrowing from civilian practice, but it may actually have originated in Army experience. Charles Decker recalled the numerous complaints levelled against Army justice in the years immediately preceding World War II to the effect that many innocent men, despairing of their chances for a fair trial, pleaded guilty in order to get light sentences. To prevent such abuses and to halt the criticism, Army JAG announced that all defendants would henceforth plead innocent, thus forcing the prosecution to prove its case. But the extra work proved staggering, as Decker remembered, and a way out was sought. In the Fall of 1953, as commandant of the JAG's school, Decker suggested that an accused might arrange with the convening authority to plead guilty to all or part of the charges in return for the commander's promise to affirm on review no more than a certain punishment. This idea, although never formalized in an Army directive, quickly caught on in the Army courts. The Army JAG in 1957 reported that about 60 percent of all defendants at general courts-martial were pleading guilty, whereas prior to 1953, only about ten percent had done so. The difference, he wrote, was a direct result of the negotiated plea system.[23]

In 1958, the Navy adopted the idea. Two differences between the services were that the Navy's program was formally promulgated by the Secretary and that the Navy's policy applied to special courts, too. The Coast Guard copied the Navy program in 1964. But the Air Force rejected the entire notion of negotiated pleas. General Harmon testified to a Senate subcommittee that the contracting parties were not equals, and the risk that the commander might bring pressure on the defendant was too great. As of 1970, the Air Force still had not adopted the policy, although there was continuing discussion regarding its values and disadvantages.[24]

Pretrial agreements soon came to the attention of the Court of

Military Appeals. In *U.S. v. Hamill*, where the accused claimed to have misunderstood the terms of the negotiations, a unanimous court ordered a rehearing or remission of the sentence. A week later, in *U.S. v. Allen*, Judge Quinn warned the services that the existence of a pretrial agreement must not permit the trial to degenerate into an "empty ritual." In *U.S. v. Walker*, Quinn went on to say that the continuation of lethargic performances by counsel and court members whenever they suspected that a pretrial agreement had been made would force the court to examine the legality of the concept of negotiated pleas itself. In a 1960 case, *U.S. v. Watkins*, Judge Latimer praised the law officer who, before accepting a guilty plea, closely examined the defendant on the nature of his counsel's advice, on the substance of his own intent, and on his understanding of the terms of the contract. This line of questioning followed Rule 11 of the Federal Rules of Criminal Procedure. Judge Quinn concurred in the result in *Watkins*, but citing his own objections in *Walker*, charged that the negotiated plea program was "not as salutory as [Latimer's] opinion made it out to be."[25]

But if Judge Quinn were skeptical of the new policy, Judge Ferguson was thoroughly opposed to it. In his dissent in *Watkins*, he condemned the entire program on the grounds that justice, which he considered sacred, became the object of barter in these deals. More practically, he argued that the defendant may suffer because the agreements tend to encourage carelessness in the defense counsel, who may therefore fail to discover a good defense open to him. Ferguson's opposition was also based partly on his own personal experience; such contracts are not allowed in Michigan.

But Ferguson was unable to get the other judges to agree with him that negotiations should be banned, and the practice has continued. The services have accepted the court's criticism in principle, and defense counsel are frequently urged to be careful in weighing the possible advantages of the deal against the certainty of conviction. In fact, Decker's first notice of the idea in 1953 warned that negotiations must not be permitted to restrict the defendant's right to defend himself in the sentencing phase before the trial court.[26]

If the negotiated plea idea met with a mixed response, the other major Army reform, the independent judiciary, was greeted with nearly unanimous approval. The basic idea here was the creation of a corps of men whose only duty would be to sit as law officers on general courts-martial. Before the change, law officers had merely been judge advocates with special qualifications. When not engaged in trial work, their primary jobs had been any of the variety of tasks performed by military lawyers. The court-martial results turned in by these part-time judges were, as might be expected, inconsistent.[27]

In June 1957, therefore, a study was made of the feasibility of appointing men to permanent duty as law officers. A pilot program inaugurated in January 1958 proved the system would work, and in November 1958, the "Field Judiciary Division" in the Office of JAG was created. Eight judicial areas, roughly coinciding with the eight Army areas, were established. Within them were nineteen judicial circuits manned by about thirty permanently assigned judges. The law officers, although still appointed to specific trials by the convening authority involved, were responsible only to the Judge Advocate General, who rated them only on the basis of their procedural performances.[28]

Once again, the Navy saw a good thing in this Army innovation. The concept was perfectly compatible with the Navy's notions of legal task forces and dockside courts. In December 1960, then, a pilot program was begun in certain commands around Washington and Norfolk; the results were favorable, and a year later, the Navy incorporated all of its law officers into an independent branch.[29]

Like the negotiated plea, the independent judiciary was rejected by the Air Force. It was announced that the small number of Air Force general courts-martial did not justify setting aside such a large number of lawyers to serve only as law officers. Again, the reason for this particular policy may be traced directly to General Harmon. The Air Force JAG strongly believed that artificially created institutions, such as a so-called independent judiciary, were not necessary to guarantee the impartiality of a court-martial. There could be no chance, Harmon argued, of an Air Force law officer's doing less than a good job, with or without a new judiciary organization.[30]

Judge Ferguson's well-known antipathy to many of the legal procedures employed by the services makes his reaction to the new judiciary plans of the Army and Navy particularly interesting. In 1966, he submitted a statement to a Senate subcommittee extolling the concept, calling it "one of the most significant developments of the last 10 years in military justice."[31]

Ferguson was joined in his praise of the new idea by an uncommon ally, Frederick Wiener. The reasons that led these men, who were generally opposed on most matters of military justice, to approve of a given program, tells us something fundamental about the question of reforms in military justice.

From Ferguson's viewpoint, the new idea promised a further guarantee against command control. Under the old system, men who would be assigned as law officers came from the office of the staff judge advocate, who was himself responsible to the convening authority. This made possible the worst sort of illicit influence over trials by court-martial. The new concept would free the law officer from any chance of such control. The new judges were also able to continue their study in the free time they had between cases, thus keeping up with the latest decisions which would affect their future trials.[32]

Wiener's acceptance was based more on efficiency. Because of the expertise full-time law officers would accumulate, trials would be more properly conducted. Commanders would applaud this improvement, because it would result in fewer reversals and less work for the commander and his staff in retrials and paperwork. In the first year and a half of the new program, reversals for law officer error were cut to less than 50 percent of the previous rate, Wiener reported. During the time saved, the commander could go about his primary concern, with a consequent gain for everyone from taxpayer to soldier in the field. Moreover, morale would be enhanced as GI's grew in the confidence that if they ever should go before a general court-martial, their cases would be heard fairly. And the service itself would reap the benefits of increased good behavior as potential offenders became discouraged from going astray by the certainty of quick punishment.[33]

The lesson here is clear. The best chance of success for future reforms would be for those ideas that on the one hand promoted more perfect procedure and justice in the theoretical sense, and on the other ensured less bothersome detail for the commander. The formula was simple, but, as we shall see, its implementation would prove difficult.

A number of other activities undertaken by the services during this period helped to improve the cast of military justice. The legal periodicals, for example, became both professional and scholarly, and were important both in informing judge advocates in the field about late decisions and programs and in sparking healthy debate among the service lawyers about the substance and method of military law. The Army and Navy conducted schools where lawyers could learn or sharpen skills particularly appropriate to problems found in the military. Ironically, an Air Force training center of the same type was discontinued in January 1955; it was considered uneconomical to waste so much of a newly graduated lawyer's active duty time in yet another school, when he could allegedly learn as much from on-the-job training.[34]

Many things were accomplished administratively. A 1961 directive from the Navy Department ordered an end to all pretrial confinement unless it was absolutely necessary. Admiral Ward once suggested a way to skirt the problems created by the requirement that all general court trials have a complete verbatim record. Set up priorities, he said; type up all the convictions with major sentences that will require review; when caught up on them, do the convictions that require only JAG confirmation; and only if you get caught up there, do the acquittals.[35]

The same power of fiat was used in other ways. General Albert M. Kuhfeld, who succeeded Harmon as Air Force JAG, once testified that courtroom injustices not made clear in the record of trial were brought directly and unofficially to his attention, because defense lawyers around the world knew that he wanted to hear about such things. Another important power was the authority to certify cases for Court of Military Appeals review. General Harmon, despite his general skepticism about the code, was quick to send his "hard" cases to CoMA, a characteristic for which he is still remembered and praised by the legal personnel at the court.[36]

This chapter would be incomplete without mention of the ambitious rehabilitation programs undertaken by the services. The Air Force led the way when officials became dissatisfied by the treatment accorded airmen at the Army disciplinary barracks. As a result, the 3320th Retraining Group was established at Amarillo AFB, Texas, in September 1951. The approach taken by this unit was remarkably enlightened, especially in comparison to the general run of contemporary civilian methods. The "retrainee" is confronted by no guards, no bars, and no other visible restrictions on his liberty. The basic goal is to develop within the man the will to correct his own delinquency. In fact, the first test of his motivation comes when he is given a plane ticket to take him from the site of his prior confinement to the 3320th; he travels in uniform and alone. Men convicted of both "civilian" and "military" type offenses are handled by the retraining group, and great emphasis is placed on psychological and social therapy. When he completes the program—usually in about four months—the airman is offered the opportunity to re-enlist for a period long enough—generally two years—to earn an honorable discharge. More than three-fourths of the retrainees are salvaged.[37]

The Army has more recently begun a rehabilitation effort of its own, with different problems and methods, and an uncertain chance of success. The Army Correctional Training Facility (CTF) is like a traditional prison, heavily guarded and locked, and its inmates are clearly prisoners. More than 90 percent of them are convicted absentees. According to an insightful study done in 1958 by a young sociologist, this type of "military offender" enjoys the least chance of successful rehabilitation, since he suffers from "role conflict." That is, his absenteeism is symptomatic of a deeply rooted rejection of his role as a soldier, which is not easily cured by customary correctional methods. Ironically, then, the murderer, rapist, and even thief—generally considered the bane of a military unit—are more suitable for military rehabilitation than the AWOL or disobedient GI with "role conflict." Nevertheless, since the Army was composed for the most part of unwilling soldiers in the first place, it had to try to do something with the most unwilling, those who run away.[38]

The very size of CTF is staggering; while the Air Force handles about 200 retrainees a year, the Army took in over 15,000 in its first two years of operation. Army methods follow traditional military training. Although there are some psychological and sociological services built into the curriculum, for the most part it resembles basic training with heavy emphasis on personal and unit pride in order to develop esprit in these essentially demoralized men. This is the antithesis of the Air Force program, where it is believed that the usual "lines of authority [must] take a back seat in order that treatment goals be achieved," and where there is even a form of self-government for the retrainees.[39]

The Army facility opened at Fort Riley, Kansas, in April 1968, and it is still too early to judge its performance. Yet, like the 3320th, CTF is marked by a willingness to experiment and innovate in the hope of turning young misfits into useful citizens, whether that be inside or outside the service.[40] In a day when other federal and state institutions are "correctional" in name only, these programs are to the credit of their founders—the frequently maligned military policemen and lawyers.[41]

The foregoing only begins to illustrate the intriguing mix of perceptions, philosophies, and activities that make up the military's administration of the UCMJ. Operational motives have frequently led to brilliant reforms. But the variety of attitudes within the services is also noteworthy in itself. There is no evidence of monolithic thinking in any of these issues; inter- and intraservice disagreement is at least as common as harmony. Towards the end of the 1950s, many of these tensions came to a head.

12 The Code's Administrators Turn to Administrative Dodges

As the first decade of the Uniform Code drew to a close, many men within the service continued to view it as seriously defective in many respects. In order to overcome these liabilities, some proposed legislative overhaul, others simply disregarded the more onerous parts of the law, and most began increasingly to rely on non- and extra-judicial means of handling service delinquency problems.

The idiosyncrasies which most glaringly survived the alleged uniformity imposed by the UCMJ were those regarding nonjudicial punishment practices. Although everyone in the military agreed that there was a need for NJP, the details of implementation were so varied, even after 1951, that an observer might not identify the Article 15 process in one service with that of another.

The differences were grounded in tradition. Commanders' arbitrary punishment power antedated any legal authorization for it. For example, statutory grant for the Army's "summary punishment" was given only in the enactment of the 1916 Articles of War, although Army commanders had long before meted out punishment for disciplinary offenses. The Navy "captain's mast" appeared in the earliest codification of the federal law, but specific legislation was never considered necessary for a ship's commander to punish his crew. As late as 1963, the Navy JAG told his lawyers that laws were not the source of NJP, but that the authority was "inherent in the disciplinary powers of the CO."[1]

The debate within the Defense Department and the Congressional committees in 1949 and 1950 revealed how dissimilarly the systems had evolved. Felix Larkin's staff listed four differences between the Army's AW 104 and the Navy's AGN 24. Unlike the sailor, a soldier could refuse nonjudicial punishment, electing instead trial by summary court. The soldier could also appeal NJP to his commander's next superior officer; the sailor could not. The army commander who originally imposed the penalty could at any later date remit, mitigate, or suspend it, a power not possessed by his Navy counterpart. And finally, if a soldier were subsequently convicted by court-martial for an offense which had already earned him NJP, the trial court could consider that a fact in mitigation during the sentencing phase, another provision that was not part of the Navy system.[2]

The differences are explained by the fundamental approaches taken by the two services. In the Navy, the NJP officer was almost always the commander of a ship. The Navy reposed special faith in its ships' captains and gave them the power to discipline their crews in order to carry out assigned missions. By the time he was appointed to command, an officer had usually accumulated great experience and had been observed and rated by so many senior officers that his character and judicial temperament were thoroughly known. In the Army, on the other hand, NJP was exercised by company commanders. These officers were very junior to the usual Navy ship's captain and had correspondingly less experience. The Navy commander was also authorized to convene both deck and summary courts-martial, while the Army company commander had no convening authority whatever, and was required to refer cases to his superiors for court-martial.

Given these differences, the right of election by a sailor from NJP would have been absurd. The commanding officer in such a case would have to convene a court consisting of one of his subordinate officers, who would then have to pass on the legitimacy of his captain's judgment. In the Army, the right of election meant that a soldier who disputed the justice of an AW 104 finding handed down by his inexperienced company commander could have the case studied by a senior officer and perhaps heard by a court-martial composed of officers from other units. The other three differences in NJP procedures are explained by the reverence fit for a minor god traditionally bestowed on Navy commanders. It would be demeaning for a captain if his decisions were reviewed or mitigated, whether by his superior or by himself.

Not only were there two basic attitudes regarding nonjudicial punishment, there were also two different ways of conducting the procedure. Navy captain's mast resembled a trial. The commander called witnesses, heard evidence, and interviewed the accused at a formal hearing set aside for the purpose. When satisfied that he knew the facts, he handed down a finding and awarded a punishment. In the Army, on the other hand, the commander consulted such sources as he thought pertinent, but in his office or command post, out of the presence of the accused.[3]

There is irony in the differing methods. Although the Army treated NJP like an administrative task, it permitted appeal from this utterly nonjudicial affair to a court-martial, which had the power to hand down a federal conviction. But one of the reasons the Navy refused to grant the right of election was that it considered mast a disciplinary matter, not a criminal one, and therefore not suitable for a trial by court-martial. These peculiarities did not lend themselves to logical analysis, but they formed the basis of some heady disputes.[4]

From the beginning, naval spokesmen asserted that the unique quality of shipboard life demanded special consideration in the NJP article of the Uniform Code. The Navy argued for the power to confine a man at mast, on the grounds that restriction or loss of privileges were ineffectual punishment for a sailor who was already restricted to his ship in the normal course of his duties. This demand prevailed, and the UCMJ in original draft included authority for a CO to confine a member of his command for up to seven days. The same line won inclusion of a provision for "confinement on bread and water or diminished rations" for up to five days. The Navy also argued for authority to award forfeiture of pay at mast. The original AGN had no such provision, but the Navy felt so strongly about it that it was part of the proposed 1947 Navy bill, S. 1338. Again the Morgan Committee adopted the Navy position.[5]

The UCMJ Committee conceded that shipboard life required special considerations. But the Army and the Air Force representatives promised that they would not use the punishments for which the Navy so strenuously argued. Felix Larkin tried to persuade Congress that the solution to these quirks was to provide in the law all the punishments desired and "then let each Department determine which ones ... are necessary for their own disciplinary purposes." The House subcommittee thought that leaving the law so vague was unwise. While the Congressmen agreed with the concession made to shipboard peculiarities, they decided to limit the special punishments only to those persons actually assigned to a ship for duty. The subcommittee also deleted the provision for forfeiture of pay, on the grounds that to dock the already low pay of a married GI would penalize his innocent family.[6]

As finally enacted and signed into law, Article 15 authorized two types of commanding officer's nonjudicial punishment. The first applied to officers, the second to enlisted men. Officer offenders could be restricted to certain limits or could have their privileges withheld, each for a period up to two weeks. An officer could also be punished by forfeiture of one-half his pay for one month and could be reprimanded either orally or in writing. Enlisted men could also be restricted and lose their privileges for two weeks and could be reprimanded. Additionally, enlisted men could be assigned extra duties of two hours a day for two weeks and could be reduced in rank. And finally, as we have seen, if "attached to or embarked in a vessel," an enlisted man could be confined for up to seven consecutive days or confined on bread and water for a shorter period. Combinations of these punishments were prohibited, with the single exception that a reprimand could be given in addition to any of the others.[7]

The article also included a provision for the Secretary of a Department to "place limitations" on the powers authorized by the code. This was to permit the services to maintain, by regulation, whatever idiosyncrasies they chose, a peculiar admission on the part of the drafters that precise uniformity was, after all, impossible.[8]

As might be expected, the Air Force followed the Army lead in most Article 15 matters, and the Marine Corps copied the Navy. But the Coast Guard, which was included under the code although a member of the Defense Department only in wartime, presented some peculiar problems. A number of small cutters were commanded by senior Coast Guard petty officers, known generically as "officers-in-charge." A subparagraph of the new article, then, provided that the Secretary of a Department, including Treasury, might grant by regulation the nonjudicial powers to officers-in-charge.[9]

Department Secretaries were also authorized to publish regulations governing the right of election and other administrative details, another confession of the inability of the drafters to reach agreement on divisive service methods. Granting these concessions to the Secretaries was the reason the question of NJP, originally one of the four insoluble issues laid before Forrestal by the Morgan Committee, was dropped from the final list.[10]

The code incorporated the Army's old NJP review procedure. A

GI awarded punishment could appeal to his commander's superior, and that officer, as well as the commander himself, could suspend, set aside, or remit the sentence, in whole or in part. The question of whether NJP was a bar to trial by court-martial also followed Army usage; it was not, but it might be introduced as mitigating evidence by the defense.

Along with many other parts of the code which we have examined, Article 15 was greeted with less than enthusiastic welcome. Many reformers outside the service found fault with it. Arthur Farmer objected to the bread and water provision, calling it a "barbarous relic of earlier days." A vigorous argument by John P. Oliver, the lobbyist for the Reserve Officers' Association, claimed that the powers granted commanders under Article 15 were excessive. Most Army veterans agreed; the Uniform Code gave a CO far greater NJP powers than the old AW 104 had permitted. Arthur John Keeffe levelled his customarily pithy attack by claiming that only "the intrepid or the insane" would ever utilize the appeal machinery of Article 15(d).[11]

The opposition to the new system that ultimately proved loudest and most effective, however, came from within the services. The Navy led the attack. Father White's 1953 report asserted that his committee was convinced that the weakness of Article 15 had a "detrimental effect" on naval discipline. A spokesman at a 1955 conference correctly observed that the NJP powers of all Navy commanders were weaker than they had been under the AGN, although he conceded that in the case of a ship's captain, the differences were slight. The Navy's position was that in foreign ports and waters virtually none of the punishments allowed were useful to a ship's commander.[12]

The only provision considered adequate was the one which permitted reduction in grade. And yet, a demotion amounted to a long-term forfeiture of pay, among other things. But this flew in the face of the Brooks subcommittee's opinion that docking a GI's pay was unfair to his family.

The other services ultimately agreed with the Navy on the question of Article 15 inadequacy. The change in the Army and Air Force started as early as 1954, when Eugene M. Caffey, the Army JAG, wrote that the UCMJ, with its accent on formal trial procedures, had deprived commanders of the ability to maintain effective discipline in their units. He urged that petty offenses—the bulk of the Army's justice workload—be handled summarily by nonjudicial punishment, without resort to court-martial and its attendant smear on the soldier's record. The Air Force JAG, in his report the same year, agreed substantially with these views. From early 1949, when Felix Larkin could predict with certainty that the Army and Air Force would not use the power to confine, to the end of 1954, both services had come full circle and arrived at a point of almost total agreement with the Navy on the question of nonjudicial punishment.[13]

Father White's study showed that Caffey's fears about the use of court-martial in cases that involved only minor infractions were valid. In some 63 percent of the Navy cases investigated by the White board, courts-martial had handed down penalties only slightly stiffer than those authorized by Article 15. The implication was that if the CO had possessed these added powers, he might have exercised them, thus saving young sailors a court-martial conviction.[14]

Despite the growing unanimity of the services on the fundamentals of nonjudicial punishment, it was not easy to find the same spirit of agreement in seeking solutions. In his 1954 report, Admiral Nunn recommended increased NJP powers across the board and even greater increases for commanders who were also general court-martial convening authorities. But in that same report, General Harmon, who agreed that Article 15 was weak, proposed a much less extensive augmentation. H.R. 6583 reflected this lack of agreement; it included only relatively simple, presumably noncontroversial alterations. Generally, the maximum limits on all punishments would be extended to one month from two weeks; confinement powers would be conferred on all commanders, not just ship captains; and forfeits of one-half of one month's pay for enlisted men would be authorized.[15]

We have already seen the fate of H.R. 6583. The lack of harmony among those entrusted by Congress with the administration of military justice would have doomed the Article 15 provisions even had they stood apart from the rest of the bill. Before significant legislative changes in the code could be obtained, the services would have to clear their own disagreements and secure the endorsement of the Court of Military Appeals.

But, in the meantime, the notion that the use of Article 15 punishments was a way to avoid what General Caffey called the UCMJ's "heavy accent on formalities" seems to have spread out into other areas. The most significant, and perhaps unjust, of these overflows was the administrative discharge. Simply stated, this was the means by which military personnel could be separated from the service for alleged inaptitude, unsatisfactory performance, or chronic poor behavior. There was statutory authority for the practice, so the services were within their rights in using it.[16] No realistic argument could be made that a man who demonstrated his unsuitability for military duties enjoyed some kind of right to remain in the service; the Armed Forces were public functions, in which all taxpayers shared costs and expectations. Citizens should get their money's worth, and misfits did not give it to them. The problem lay in the regard the general public had for the type of discharge an ex-GI took with him into civilian life.

There were five kinds of discharge. Two of them, the bad conduct and the dishonorable, were called "punitive" and could be given only by order of a court-martial. The other three, honorable, general, and undesirable, were the "administrative discharges" which concern us here. According to figures produced in 1962, more than 92 percent of all GI's separated in a given year received honorable discharges. The recipients were thus given proof of good behavior and proficient performance of duty. Oddly, some of these men may have been convicted by court-martial during their careers, for the implementing directive did not exclude former military convicts from an honorable discharge. A man granted an honorable discharge was eligible for all benefits conferred by the Veterans Administration and other state and federal agencies.[17]

The benefits for a holder of a general discharge were the same, but because of the reasons for his separation, this veteran may have found himself ostracized to one degree or another in civilian life. The governing instruction rather cryptically noted that a general discharge was given to a man whose "military record is not sufficiently meritorious to warrant an Honorable Discharge." The standards established by that guide-line were meaningless, and the rest of the directive included nothing else more helpful. It was left up to the man's commanding officer to decide, rather arbitrarily it would seem, whether to give him an honorable or a general discharge. Either one could be issued for expiration of enlistment, convenience of the government, hardship or dependency, minority, disability, unsuitability, security violations, or resignation. It was in the area of "unsuitability" where most problems arose. Depending on no more than his commander's appraisal of the situation, a man might be given either an honorable or a general discharge for inaptitude, character and behavior disorders, apathy, enuresis, alcoholism, or homosexual tendencies. But these reasons were not far different from those by which the GI could earn the third type of administrative discharge, the undesirable.[18]

A UD placed a veteran in exactly the same position as a holder of a BCD as far as VA benefits were concerned. Worse, however, was the stigma. Air Force General Kuhfeld once admitted that the loss of reputation suffered by a UD holder was probably as great as that incurred by a BCD. A Court of Military Appeals judge later guessed that the stigma might be worse. These were just personal opinions, and it is difficult to compare degrees of shame. But a Senate subcommittee poll taken in 1966 revealed that civilians did not distinguish at all among any of the less-than-honorable discharges and considered all veterans so discharged as morally defective.[19]

The undesirable discharge, then, was a kind of life-long penalty, equated by Veterans Administration regulations to the BCD. The latter, however, could not be awarded except after a fair trial, conducted under rigorous procedural rules, and subject to possible review by the Court of Military Appeals. Until the mid-1960s, the undesirable discharge could be given at the whim of the military commander without regard for procedure and without review before execution. Moreover, most of the prerequisites for an undesirable discharge were matters which could be charged under the Articles of the UCMJ. Thus, the same convening authority had the option of referring the matter to trial or simply separating the alleged offender administratively.[20]

Military men have frequently made a connection between non-judicial punishment and the administrative techniques. In 1953, a note appearing in the Army's JAG school paper mentioned that, although a quirk in the regulations implementing Article 15 forbade demoting a man from paygrade E-2 to E-1 by NJP, the same effect could be accomplished administratively, by reducing the man to the rank of recruit for "inefficiency." In the 1955 edition of Decker's warmly received book, he told the NJP officer, "If you decide the offender is guilty, you must decide whether administrative corrective action . . . or . . . punishment is in order."[21]

Decker was representative of the many Army officers who adopted nonjudicial methods where the UCMJ thwarted them. But the connection between summary punishment, court-martial law, and administrative power was not limited to him, nor even to persons in the military. Admiral Colclough, the Navy JAG during the last years of the AGN, thought that naval justice had two "broad subdivisions": the "application of military law" and "corrective measures short of trial." Admiral Nunn believed that an administrative discharge was only like firing a man and that the services must have the power to do that.[22]

This attitude is not limited to line officers. Admiral Ward, the first law specialist to become JAG, entitled a subsection of an article published in 1960, "The Short Cut for Hopeless Cases," and argued that the one way to lessen brig overpopulation was to use the "short-cut" of the administrative discharge. One Army lawyer who on another occasion gloated over an apparently unjust civilian law while gleefully extolling those points of the UCMJ he thought superior, also favored administrative discharges in certain cases. Even as late as 1970, General William Westmoreland, the Army Chief of Staff, spoke of the need for "some method to remove an offender" who could not be rehabilitated.[23]

Some civilians, too, frequently adopted the administrative discharge in their plans. Father Snee, in his otherwise radical proposal for an overhaul of the code, specifically condoned administrative elimination of offenders. Father White urged even greater use of the practice to save the taxpayer money that would otherwise be spent on trying and imprisoning chronic violators of the law. And finally, a blue ribbon panel of civilians selected to investigate the Army's prison system in the wake of the Presidio "mutiny" in 1968 endorsed the initiation of "new screening methods aimed at eliminating at the point of intake a larger proportion of men unsuitable for service."[24]

With such widespread approval of this method of circumventing the code, it was surprising that it took so long for the UCMJ watchdogs to catch on. In a 1956 exchange with Congressman Brooks, who thought the services might be using administrative methods as a dodge, Chief Judge Quinn seemed unfamiliar with the practice. Civilian reformers were likewise ignorant of the issues. Sidney A. Wolff of the New York Bar Association once wrote that the undesirable discharge was purely an administrative matter and made it clear that he was not interested in the subject. Arthur John Keeffe and Richard Wels were surprised when the abuses finally came to the public's attention.[25]

This is not to say there had been no interest in the subject. Only a few months after the UCMJ went into effect, legislation was introduced that would have brought administrative discharges under the scrutiny of the Court of Military Appeals. Nothing became of this proposal, a fate which befell a series of bills designed to give the administratively discharged veteran a way to eradicate the stain from his reputation. Congress, like most other groups with the one exception of the American Legion, seemed uninterested in the matter. When the darkness was finally overcome, the torch bearers turned out to be not allegedly "enlightened" civilian reformers, but a rather crusty southern senator and an Air Force major general.[26]

The first bomb was dropped by General Harmon at the 1958 annual meeting of the Judge Advocates Association in Los Angeles. Harmon, no uncritical supporter of the UCMJ, as we have seen, had grown skeptical of the glowing accounts customarily given by CoMA judges and service JAG's at these banquet speeches. His report started off routinely when he pointed out that the Air Force had a lower court-martial rate than the other services. But, he continued— and one can imagine the response of his audience to what followed—this was not to the credit of anyone in the Air Force legal department, because "many commanders are using the legally authorized administrative discharge procedures instead of trial by court-martial to take care of and get rid of offenders."[27]

This speech made the administrative separation a topic of increasing discussion. Professor Keeffe wrote to urge the New York bar groups to investigate the issue. The Coast Guard boasted in its next annual report that its drop in court-martial cases was not matched by a corresponding increase in undesirable discharges. The Court of Military Appeals, heretofore officially blind to the problem, began to comment on it, frequently using Harmon's own language.[28]

But the difficulties posed by the administrative discharge easily matched the obstacles faced by the post-World War II court-martial reformers. Sheer inertia was the highest hurdle. One of the leaders of the fight in Congress was Senator Sam Ervin, Jr., of North Carolina, a southern conservative who would enhance in the process his reputation for strict construction of constitutional rights. But his work on the problems of military justice and injustice would last more than a decade and would meet with only limited success.

As the end of the first decade of the Uniform Code approached. the most enduring consequence of the new system grew clear. The bewilderment experienced by the Navy in the early days of the UCMJ as naval officers tried to grasp the foreign system thrust on them had spread by 1958 to all the services. Military men, overwhelmed by what they regarded as unreasonable complexities in court-martial law and practices, looked for simpler ways to handle their delinquency problems. The administrative discharge was one readily available solution for extreme cases. For lesser offenses, they sought expanded Article 15 powers, a quest that consumed great time and effort over the next five years.

13 The Powell Report:

The Army Counterattacks

The loss of the legislative battle over H.R. 6583 in 1956 by no means slowed attempts to correct the UCMJ's flaws by changing the law itself. In fact, during the ensuing few years, the frequency of legislative attempts became even greater, precipitating some peculiar and heated clashes and finally resulting in limited reform action.

The sometimes antagonistic members of the Code Committee had learned a few lessons from their first half-decade together. No longer did they operate on the assumption that mere suggestions from them would produce immediate legislation. In 1956, for example, they actually prepared their proposals in the form of the bill. Subsequent reports included detailed analyses, introductions, and finally, in 1959, a style of printing identical to that used by Congress itself. These steps were intended to save time and effort on Capitol Hill, thus increasing the chances of passage.

If the Code Committee as a whole was increasingly impatient with Congressional inaction, its military members were even more so. But JAG criticism began in the late 1950s to focus on the Court of Military Appeals as a culprit in the system. The 1957 Navy report, for example, mentioned a number of CoMA decisions which naval officers thought revolutionary. Army reports were much harsher. Beginning in 1957, General Hickman listed a series of "innovations" in military justice to which he objected. All of them stemmed from decisions handed down by the Court of Military Appeals which Hickman claimed placed "an increased burden and responsibility on the service lawyer." The Army's complaints amounted to the beginning of a counterattack on the influence then being wielded by Judge Ferguson, for most of the opinions cited in Hickman's list came from the new judge's pen.[1]

The Army JAG summarized what he thought of the situation and what he proposed to do about it when he wrote that because of the "sharp departures from previous military legal practices" occasioned by the Ferguson revolution, "proposed remedial legislation is under study." This idea represented a shift from the basic strategic concept of H.R. 6583. Then, service tactics recognized the need for CoMA approval of the bill, and the legislative package offered at that time had even disguised the one major deviation from Code Committee unanimity, the "Certificate of Good Cause." But Hickman threw down the gauntlet in 1958 and 1959; his main target was the court and he made no attempt to hide that fact. The promise of "remedial" legislation implied that at least the Army would try to go it alone.[2]

The Air Force had similar ideas. General Harmon's discovery of the administrative discharge abuses led him to give up his patient waiting for corrections to be made in the code by Congress. He had long been critical of what he found to be unnecessary delays in the code's system and its reverence of form over substance. Now that he had evidence that that complexity led to injustices to young airmen, he resolved to act.[3]

What resulted was an Air Force proposal that would have effected radical changes in the Uniform Code, had it been adopted. There were two major changes envisaged and a half-dozen or so minor ones as well. The first fundamental reform would be twofold: first, the abolition of the inferior courts-martial, both summary and special, leaving only a tribunal resembling the UCMJ's general court; and second, a major increase in nonjudicial punishment powers for a commanding officer. The proposed Article 15 divided eligible commanders into three groups, depending on the rank of the commander involved and whether he had a judge advocate on his staff.[4]

Harmon proposed equally startling changes in courts-martial. They would be permanently established bodies, serving fixed geographic areas. Commanders would be deprived of convening or reviewing power and would be limited to supervision of the prosecution. Juries would be selected from panels of available officers and men by a unique method of eliminating names until only the requisite number was left. Law officers would be elevated in stature and authority;

they would appoint the pretrial investigators and defense counsel; their rulings on interlocutory questions would be final; and after convictions, they would set sentences, and even suspend them, if they chose.

Harmon's plan would eliminate the commander from the court-martial machinery but compensate him with greatly increased nonjudicial powers. The idea was that if an offender were salvageable the commander could handle the case by NJP with a minimum of fuss but with powers of punishment sufficient to sting the offender into self-correction. On the other hand, if the man were a candidate for elimination, the commander could refer his case to trial by court-martial and be done with it. Both these approaches to problems of misbehavior involved a minimum of formality, which Harmon hoped would make them at least competitive with the unjust administrative separation procedure. As for the accused, he would face severe nonjudicial punishments only at the hands of very senior commanders where, it could be hoped, those powers would be moderated by the mature wisdom of the experienced officer. On the other hand, if he were tried by court-martial, the trial would be free from possible commander intervention, and the accused would be sure to receive a fair hearing from the experts assigned to his case. If convicted, he would be sentenced by a professional judge whose experience would dictate what a suitable penalty was.

These ideas closely resembled those proposed by men like George Spiegelberg and Arthur Farmer, who had vigorously argued during the 1940s and beyond for the removal of the commander from the court-martial process. Here, in 1958, the same position was taken by the legal department of the Air Force. But the measure was never submitted to Congress. Harmon realized that without some semblance of service harmony on a package so frankly innovative as this, it had little chance of Congressional success. And the Army and the Navy let him know they would not support it.

The Navy's argument was predictable. The Air Force bill would be of no benefit to the sea service, Admiral Ward wrote Harmon. Most Navy courts were at the inferior level, and were convened by officers junior to the rank—colonel or Navy captain—where there would be increased Article 15 powers. Thus the envisioned barter of increased NJP for the abolition of the two lower courts was simply inoperative in the Navy. Ward listed a few more objections, but his conclusion indicated the main thrust of the Navy position: "the Navy must have a type of court-martial which can be convened aboard ship."[5] That meant one without law officer and lawyers. Harmon's plan had no such provision, so the Navy voted nay.

The Army's position was more detailed but just as direct. On December 17, 1958 Hickman appointed a committee of lawyers from the various divisions of the JAG Office to study the Air Force bill. One of them was directed to obtain the views of the Commandant of the JAG's School, Colonel John G. O'Brien. Despite his claim that the press of business and the deadline given permitted only a cursory study of the proposal, O'Brien's reply was twenty-seven pages long. Analysis like this is one of the fringe benefits which accrue to the Army for its maintenance of a full-time bank of legal scholars at the school.[6]

Substantively, O'Brien found much value in Harmon's idea. He particularly praised the fact that it would end any possibility of command influence over courts, the perennial complaint made against military law. But O'Brien thought that the two sides of Harmon's swap had serious flaws. First, he found that the proposed Article 15 powers were "far too severe" to bestow on any one officer. Second, he argued that a system with only a single type of court-martial would be liable to grave stress if too many offenders elected trial instead of NJP. If this should occur, predicted O'Brien, the commander would face the Hobson's choice of either setting in motion the "full panoply" of general court-martial procedures or dropping the charges altogether.

The fact that a man in O'Brien's lofty position could express the views he did, presumably after consulting with the faculty of the school, indicated that there were officers within the JAG Corps whose views did not follow the traditional Army line. They were sensitive to the problem of command control and were reluctant to give too great powers to commanders for arbitrary use, no matter what their rank or experience. Conversely, they shied away from any plan which might overwhelm the capacity of the military courts; the result would only be speeded up process with the increased likelihood of injustice.

The recommendations of the Pentagon committee appointed by Hickman were much closer to traditional views. This body, like the Navy JAG, found that the increased NJP did not compensate for the loss of the lower courts. It predicted that the proposed system would be a burden to a variety of officials. More paperwork would be generated by the need for verbatim reports for all trials by courts-martial; and more lawyers, already a scarce commodity, would be needed since all courts would require a law officer and two lawyer counsel.[7]

In sum, both General Hickman and Admiral Ward advised Harmon that his plan did not satisfy the needs of their respective services. Each urged him instead to throw his weight behind the Defense Department's "omnibus bill," the name now given to the seventeeen Code Committee suggestions for reform. Submitted to Congress on various occasions since the demise of H.R. 6583, the package was now known as H.R. 3387. Essentially, it was identical to its 1956 predecessor, without the controversial "Certificate of Good Cause" provision. Unlike the earlier bill, it did not have the spotlight to itself. There were some minor bills on the Hill, like the one introduced by Judge Quinn's old friend, Senator Green, of Rhode Island, that would have changed the name of CoMA to "The Supreme Court of Military Appeals." But a more serious competitor was H.R. 3455, the American Legion bill.[8]

Because the Legion is composed of ex-servicemen, one of its primary aims is to make conditions within the service as attractive as possible for succeeding generations of Americans and to see that those who are serving get a fair deal. As applied to military justice, this outlook frequently led the Legion to make proposals which the services found unpalatable. An example of this is the 1956 Legion publication of a study of the Uniform Code and a number of recommendations for its improvement.

The report listed a number of "Fundamental Concepts." The first could have been written by the most traditionalist general or admiral: ". . . The purpose of an Army . . . is to fight battles. . . . Discipline, fairly and equitably enforced, is necessary to produce a fighting force." But the second argued for a balance which the services have had difficulty in establishing: "Discipline and justice do not necessarily conflict. . . . Justice can be and should be the means of creating and enforcing an effective discipline."

The other "fundamental concepts" flowed from these two. The Legion recognized that the character of the military had changed; there were younger officers and more draftees than there had been in the interwar service. But, because of this, courts-martial had to be made free from the possibility of "despotic power." The court-martial system should be made more efficient, of course, but the primary goal was to ensure the independence of the courts themselves.[9]

When the Legion bill, H.R. 3455, was introduced, it contained provisions that were the most radical military justice proposals ever seen on Capitol Hill. Civil authorities and courts were to have primary jurisdiction over felonies committed by GI's in the United States in peacetime. The Court of Military Appeals would set rules of procedure for courts-martial and would rule on controverted issues of fact in cases before it for review. A law officer would preside over all courts, including special and summary courts-martial, and would rule on all issues, including challenges of court members. The entire JAG departments of all the services, including lawyers and boards of review, would be removed from the military Departments and placed under the Secretary of Defense. And finally, there would be an amendment to the U.S. Code that would set five years confinement and a $5000 fine as penalties for the offense of attempting to influence a court-martial.

The American Legion bill gained very little support in Congress. But during 1959 and 1960, it stirred up a hornet's nest of reaction. Its main target was the old presumed evil of command control, and its basic theory was that every possible avenue for such influence should be closed. In this regard, it went even further than General Harmon's plan, and it sparked the same sort of response. Admiral Ward's successor as Navy JAG, William C. Mott, called the bill "drastic" and unnecessary since instances of command influence were only occasional and were "invariably corrected" when detected. The official Army view agreed. Command influence was not rampant in the Army, and the Legion's proposals, based therefore on a faulty premise, "would be disastrous to good order and discipline."[10]

These military views were not surprising. But opposition to the bill came from an unexpected quarter when the New York City Bar Association, long a champion of proposals to eradicate the commander's court-martial power, rejected what it called the Legion's "basic dissatisfaction with the administration of the present system of military justice." The bar association, as always, was a liberal force, not a radical one; it sought reforms not revolution. The same spirit which prompted Arthur Farmer and Richard Wels in 1951 to accept the UCMJ, with all its shortcomings, was still alive. The association found no great favor with H.R. 3387, either, seeing it as no more than an efficiency measure; essentially the bar reformers seemed to want to go slow.[11]

While all of this Congressional skirmishing was going on, a major development was occurring within the Army. In the late summer of 1959, the Army JAG, General Hickman, went to work on his promise that the Army would take independent steps in the matter of legislative action. Strongly supported, if not in fact prompted, by his assistant for military justice, Charles Decker, Hickman decided that with the end of the UCMJ's first decade approaching it would be useful to gather the impressions and suggestions of the operators of the code: those line officers who had to use it. The two men approached Army Secretary Wilber M. Brucker about their idea, and he gave them enthusiastic encouragement. A list of recommended members was thereupon submitted to Brucker, who endorsed it in October 1959, thus establishing the "Committee on the Uniform Code of Military Justice, Good Order and Discipline in the Army." This body is referred to as the "Powell committee," after its chairman, Lieutenant General Herbert B. Powell.[12]

The nine men who made up the committee all held important, high-echelon posts. Only two of them, Hickman and Decker, were lawyers; the others represented a broad spectrum of the combat arms, technical commands, and staff and logistics supporting branches of the Army. Perhaps the member who became best known in later years was William C. Westmoreland, in 1959 the commanding general of the 101st Airborne Division. Westmoreland was selected for the committee because during an assignment on the General Staff he had impressed Hickman and Decker as a man of perception and intelligence who was capable of assisting in the often tedious legal work that lay ahead. Similar attributes were sought in the other members.[13]

The gathering of such powerful men made it unlikely that anyone would dominate the committee. Despite the resulting possibility of democracy, the group seems not to have been plagued by controversy. Harold Parker, then a lieutenant colonel serving as "recorder" for the committee, remembered being surprised at the extent of unanimity among these strong-willed generals. He recalled no disagreements, although some things were greeted with less enthusiasm than others.[14]

Those who participated in the work of the Powell committee described it later as an attempt to make the code better able to handle its mission in the future than it had been able to do in the past. The work took about three months, and the report was submitted to the Secretary on January 18, 1960. The document itself comprised some 287 pages of studies, analyses, and recommendations, plus a sixty-nine page legislative proposal and explanation.

The plan envisaged simplification of procedure, reduction in review time, enhancement of commander punishment powers, and legislative reversal of a number of decisions rendered by the Court of Military Appeals. It is surprising in view of the Army's speedy rejection of General Harmon's proposal a year earlier to note the similarities between that package and Powell's. One suspects that had Army commanders been asked about the Harmon bill, they would have approved where Army lawyers disapproved. Both Harmon and Powell included the same implicit bargain: an increase in NJP power in return for the scrapping of the summary and special courts. There was a graduation of commanders in both packages, although where Harmon had three groups, Powell had only two: all commanders and commanders authorized by the 1951 Code to convene general courts-martial. Under the Powell proposals, all commanders, not just those aboard ship, would have the power to impose physical restraint on a man for up to seven days. Senior commanders would have the additional authority to award a man ninety days loss of freedom. This was not confinement, however; it was called "correctional custody," a term borrowed from the Canadian Army. In the American style, correctional custody would permit the soldier to remain with his unit during the normal work or training day. When his regular duties were completed he would report to a detention center where he might be given extra duty or participate in some guidance sessions. This was to be a "stern"facility; the Canadians had found that a "lounge type"of stockade was ineffective. The man was, however, to be provided some time to reflect on the cost of his offenses, preferably while his buddies were drinking a beer or going to town. In short, the punishment would not deprive the unit of badly needed manpower, but it would be restrictive enough to impress the subject GI, thereby helping him back to the straight path.[15]

There were other parts of the proposed Article 15 that differed from the original code. For example, the time limits on such things as restriction, extra duty, and loss of privileges were all increased from two weeks to thirty days for junior commanders and ninety days for senior ones. Punishments, except in a few specified instances, could be combined. And some of the powers held by a senior commander could be delegated by him to subordinate officers in his command.

Members of the committee remember their work aimed primarily at eliminating the injustices of the lower courts-martial while at the same time permitting commanders in the field enough power to maintain the discipline they thought they needed. But at least as obvious were the attempts to cope with the Court of Military Appeals. Each of the sections of the report decried a number of decisions proclaimed to be adverse to the efficient administration of military justice. One of these issues was the question of self-incrimination.

The Uniform Code's Article 31 was so far in advance of comparable civilian protections in 1951 that as late as 1966 it could still be held up by the Supreme Court of the United States as a model of enlightenment.[16] In some ways, in fact, the article went further than the Fifth Amendment, as it was then interpreted. Beginning in 1951, no military person, whether he was a suspect or not, could be forced to give any self-incriminating statement. Nor could he be compelled to give degrading evidence if it were not material to the issue at hand. Furthermore, no interrogation of an accused or suspect could be undertaken without first advising him of the nature of the accusation, his right to remain silent, and the fact that anything he did decide to say could be used against him in case of trial by court-martial. And finally, whatever evidence might be taken in violation of these prohibitions would be inadmissible before a court-martial. Civilian law did not provide any of these protections in a systematic way until the 1960s.

The article went through several fascinating series of cases, until nearly every word had been interpreted and reinterpreted. The Court of Military Appeals dealt with Article 31 issues in search and seizure, corroboration of confessions, and entrapment. It labored long over defining the word "statement" and differentiating it from "evidence." Some of the earlier cases were conflicting and confusing, but as the court settled into the Quinn-Ferguson alliance a fundamental idea peeked through. Article 31, the court's majority believed, had to be more protective than civilian analogs because of the unique military compulsion to obey orders. A civilian taken into custody does not feel the same inherent obligation to follow the directions of a policeman as does, say, a private being interrogated by a sergeant. Without Article 31, the military senior might order the junior to tell him about the alleged offense. If the junior replied truthfully, he might incriminate himself; if he refused or was evasive, he could be charged with failure to obey an order. The drafters of the code and the majority members of the court sought to avoid that situation.[17]

Briefly mentioning two specific decisions will suffice to make the point. *U.S. v. Jordan* was one of Ferguson's early Article 31 cases. There, in a concurring opinion, he exalted the rights of the individual over whatever right the services might claim to have effective law enforcement machinery. More important in Article 31 cases, he wrote, was that the individual must be protected. Judge Latimer dissented here on the grounds that such an interpretation was an unnecessary bar to law enforcement.[18]

Even broader than *Jordan* in its sweep was *U.S. v. Minnifield*. Here the court adopted a standard for the self-incrimination issue that is still more protective of the suspect than the federal rules. *Minnifield* involved the coercion of a handwriting sample from a suspect in a forgery case. The CoMA majority, with Ferguson writing the principal opinion, ruled that a man's handwriting was a statement in the meaning of Article 31; a person could not be forced to surrender such a sample if it might incriminate him. By extension, this decision has been taken to mean that no person subject to the code can be forced to do anything that might incriminate himself, an interpretation which the Quinn-Ferguson tandem upheld as long as they remained together on the court.[19]

The Powell committee was shocked by these decisions. Its report specifically cited only one Article 31 case, *U.S. v. Nowling*, discussed earlier, involving the self-incrimination of an AWOL airman who was asked to produce his liberty pass without first being warned that he was suspected of wrongdoing.[20] But the committee condemned the entire line of Article 31 decisions for their invalidation of "rules expressed by the President in the Manual for Courts-Martial," which were "consistent with the usual legal construction of the scope of the right." The result was, the committee argued, that detection and prosecution of offenses was unnecessarily impeded.

These ideas followed the dissents of Judge Latimer, by this time a hero of great magnitude in the eyes of the Army. The committee referred to three cases in which Latimer had dissented, and proposed new legislation that would adopt his losing positions.[21]

The Powell Article 31 would do three things. First, physical evidence would not be inadmissible for the sole reason that it was obtained without the proper warning. For example, if a suspect were to tell an investigator where a murder weapon was hidden without first being advised of his rights, the gun itself could be used against him even if the statement could not. According to the *Minnifield* doctrine, the gun would be tainted evidence because of the Article

31 violation. Second, the article would refer only to oral and written statements.Specifically excluded from its coverage would be physical acts, documents, and other so-called "statements" which "do not require the active and conscious use of the mental faculties of the accused." This too ran counter to *Minnifield*. And finally, even in the case of those closely circumscribed oral and written statements, the Powell bill would force appellate courts to consider the overall merits of the case and would prohibit peremptory reversals on the sole grounds of no warning.

It is perhaps true, as Hickman and Decker insisted, that these measures would not have made a dead letter out of Article 31. But it seems equally probable that the Court of Military Appeals, if forced to work within such a law, would have considered again what it threatened once in *Jacoby*: the invalidation of a section of its creator statute. The court threw up the code as a check on the *Manual*; it enhanced the law officer as an antidote to command influence; and it was determined to uphold Article 31 as a protection for the accused individual who came face to face with all of the power and resources of the federal government. If Ferguson and Quinn could help him, a defendant would never unwillingly be the best evidence the United States could produce.

The Powell committee did not limit itself to indirect attacks on the court. Reminding readers that the size of CoMA had been established in 1950 only because "[no] one had any experience with this kind of jurisdiction," the committee asserted that time had proven the three-man court to be too fickle, an oblique complaint about Ferguson. The committee recommended that CoMA membership be increased to five judges and that two of them be appointed for four-year terms from among the retired commissioned officers of the armed services. The most likely result of this plan would have been the appointment of retiring Judge Advocate Generals to the two military seats on CoMA. Traditionalists hoped to gain thereby a stranglehold on the court. The appointment to the new seats of, say, Generals Hickman and Harmon, who both retired in 1960, would not only alter the composition but reverse the prevailing philosophy of the court. On many issues, Quinn and Ferguson would find themselves outvoted by a Latimer-plus-two majority. And even as the civilian membership changed over the years, if the two ex-JAG's voted *en bloc*, they would need to convince only one of the other three judges in order to carry any case.

The depth of the split caused by the Powell controversy is

indicated by the fact that in the twenty years of the Code Committee reports, only in 1960 was there no joint section. Moreover, each of the individual reports was separately paged, instead of the cover-to-cover pagination usually employed. This is a minor point, perhaps, but it illustrates the chasm the debate created.

The Powell ideas were contrary in many particulars to the original intent of the code's drafters. As we have seen, Morgan and Larkin and their Congressional supporters compromised on the issue of command involvement in the court-martial system only because of the check that would be provided by the all-civilian review tribunal. The court defended itself on this point in 1960 in the same *Annual Report* which contained the Powell report.

There, in its rebuttal of the Army's ideas, the court wondered about the "extent of the unanimity heretofore reached." Apparently the judges had awakened to the contradictions between those proposals made independently by the JAG's and the ones they made in concert with CoMA, as in the case of H.R. 6583. The court then related its own achievements, noting its consistent demand for competent performance by counsel for both sides, its support of the law officer, and its constant vigilance on the question of command influence. To trump Army claims that the "instability" of military law had caused a degeneration of discipline and morale, the court quoted recent statements made by the Army Chief of Staff and the Chairman of the Joint Chiefs to the effect that morale and discipline were at an all-time high in the Army because of the code. The court concluded that it was "appalled" by the Powell report.

And yet, the judges made gestures probably intended to bridge the gap that had been opened. They pointed with approval to the Army's abolition of special court-martial BCD's and to the field judiciary program, urging that both improvements be enacted into law. Like the Powell committee, the court recommended the elimination of the summary (but not the special) courts and the transfer of their powers to the officers then authorized to convene them. These statements suggest that the 1960 acrimony derived from the Army's attack on the court itself rather than from the substance of the other recommendations for change.[22]

Powell ran into opposition from the other services, too. The Navy thought so little of the report that Admiral Mott refused to spend the money to have it distributed along with the rest of the 1960 Code Committee document. Most Navy commands, then, never saw the Powell work. But Mott was careful not to assert his disapproval too strongly. The harshest criticism he could bring himself to deliver in a law review article was that the Powell ideas may have been examples of "idealism over practicability," although the goals of "fairness, decentralization, simplicity, and stability," were quite worthy. As usual, the real reason why the Navy would not support the plan was that the Navy could not do without the special court-martial.[23]

The Air Force gave Powell even less consideration. The men in blue apparently ignored it completely in public; no published statement about the report by a high Air Force official can be found. This may have been retaliation for the Army's rejection of Harmon's plan a year earlier.

Faced with the lack of outside support, the Powell report was doomed to failure. But it was not all wrong. Its drafters could see in 1959 that the increasing demands placed on court-martial justice by the high standards of the Court of Military Appeals had brought them to a fork in the road. Non-lawyer line officers were no longer able to conduct special courts-martial whose convictions would endure. As for the summary courts, the convening authority himself could better handle cases usually brought before these lowest tribunals, if given added NJP powers. The alternative solutions available were, first, to abolish the troublesome inferior courts and let the lawyers have complete control over all trials, while the commander handled all minor problems; or, second, to apply the strictures of the general court-martial—lawyers, law officers, recorders, etc.—to the lower courts. No one in the services in 1959 or 1960 was prepared to follow the latter route, so both Harmon's and Powell's plans recommended the former. As it turned out, failure then made inevitable the adoption of the second alternative nearly a decade later.

The 1960s ushered in a number of important changes in the Uniform Code. Many of these were proposals springing from many sources, such as the American Legion bill, the New York City Bar Association, or the Code Committee. But a number descended directly from the Powell report. The most immediate of these was the 1963 overhaul of nonjudicial punishment.

14 The First Reform:

Article 15 Increases

Having publicly committed itself on paper in 1960 to a specific philosophy of military justice and having described in detail the machinery by which certain goals might be achieved, the Army was able for the next several years to fall back on Powell whenever that was thought necessary or desirable.

The first opportunity to do so occurred even before the deeply split 1960 *Annual Report* was published. Apparently desiring to bury the hatchets of the previous few years, all three services sent representatives to a high level conference of JAG officials on January 4, 1961 in the office of the Navy Chief of Military Justice. The purpose of the gathering, as reported by the Army delegate, was to discover points of agreement among the three JAG's on the various programs that had been proposed during the previous two years and to overcome some of the unreasonable rivalry that had, for example, led to the Army's rejection of the 1958 Air Force proposal and the Air Force "pocket veto" of the Powell report.[1]

Some soundings were taken at the meeting. The Navy submitted a poll revealing that of nineteen senior Marine Corps commanders questioned, nine favored the omnibus bill, seven supported the Powell bill, and three urged some kind of compromise. The split among the marines reflected the larger controversy among the services in general. Each representative at the meeting enumerated what he considered the most vital priorities. The Navy and Air Force men headed their lists with reform of Article 15, as proposed in the omnibus bill. The Army, too, put nonjudicial punishment first but urged that reform follow the ideas of the Powell report and warned that the Army would not retreat from that position. If the Navy and the Air Force clung to their views as well, agreement would be possible only on noncontroversial points such as depositions and redefinition of AWOL offenses.

Cooler heads suggested that since Article 15 was the primary item on every agenda, efforts should be made to resolve the differences between Powell and omnibus on that point. Everyone agreed that NJP powers should be increased, and the amount of increase could probably be worked out at a generally acceptable level. But the omnibus bill did not envisage an abolition of the inferior courts in return for this enhancement of commander's powers. Therein lay the apparently insoluble issue. The day was saved, however, by the chance appearance of Admiral Mott, the Navy Judge Advocate General. After listening to the arguments for a few moments, he let it be known that although the Navy would vigorously defend the retention of the special court-martial, there was nothing sacrosanct about the summary. Given the proper increases in the commander's powers, there would be no need for the lowest court, which had always been something of a freak aboard ship, anyway. This concession represented a major breakthrough; the conference thereupon decided that Mott's proposal could serve as the basis for a suitable compromise.

While this meeting was being held, the Secretary of Defense was being advised that the next military justice proposal submitted to Congress should be a simple one. One of the problems with the omnibus bill had been its very comprehensiveness. Congressmen uneducated in the intricacies of court-martial law were usually overwhelmed by a complex and lengthy bill aimed at amending the UCMJ. Unlike the original code, the omnibus bill was not coherent but contained such gibberish as

(3) Section 815 is amended—
(A) by striking out in subsection (a)(1)(C) the words "one month's pay" and inserting the words "his pay per month for a period of not more than two months" in place thereof;

and

(8) Section 841(b) is amended by inserting after the words "law officer," the words "and an officer appointed as a single-officer special court-martial."

Without a solid working knowledge of the UCMJ itself, this language would mean little to a busy Congressman, who would have to read a paragraph or two of the accompanying literature or perhaps the code itself in order to understand it. Multiplying this by the twenty-five or thirty such proposed amendments gives one an idea of the dimensions of the work this bill would promise a Congressman. Sandwiched between items more important to his constituency or pet pressure group, the bill was not likely to win much of his attention. Nor was there a skilful and energetic team such as the 1949 Defense-Congressional alliance to prod him and help him until the bill was enacted.

The people in JAG had finally become aware of this problem. In January 1961, they and the Defense Department simultaneously concluded to press for the enactment of the three or four most important features of the omnibus bill. As a result, the Air Force was assigned the task of preparing a legislative proposal to abolish the summary court, increase NJP powers, and permit one-man (law officer only) special and general courts-martial.[2]

The notion that Congress was too busy to work on a major revision of the code was successfully urged on the judges of the Court of Military Appeals as well. A change in court personnel in 1961 meant that all three judges were now former legislators, familiar with the capacities and limitations of law-making bodies.[3] When the Code Committee *Annual Report* for 1961 was sent to Congress, then, instead of the indigestible omnibus bill, it proposed three small sections, labeled respectively, bills "A," "B," and "C."

So successful was the new tactic that two of the three bills were signed into law within a year, an impressive scoring record after the shutout of the previous decade. In fact, bill "C," a bad-check law, was enacted in October 1961 before it could be officially endorsed by the Code Committee report.[4]

But the main interest continued to be focused on bills "A" and "B." "A" was Article 15 reform; it incorporated a number of ideas that had been discussed during the preceding several years. If enacted, it would permit the combination of punishments, thus giving the commander much greater flexibility and power than he had enjoyed under the original code. The new bill described commanders in two groups, *viz.*, all commanders and commanders possessing general court-martial convening authority, with a corresponding difference in NJP powers. In this regard, the new bill followed the Powell committee report more closely than the Air Force proposal. Like Powell, it contained a provision whereby the senior commanders could delegate their NJP authority. There was, of course, a general increase in all powers of punishment. Forfeiture of enlisted men's pay and correctional custody, neither part of the original code, were included in the bill. Most other types of punishment could be awarded for periods up to thirty days, an increase over the two weeks formerly allowed. Review procedures in the case of an offender who felt wronged were left essentially intact. But the powers to execute, suspend, mitigate or remit, formerly exercised only by the reviewing authority, were granted to the officer imposing the punishment, too.[5]

Bill "A," originally introduced as H.R. 7656, sailed through Congress with a minimum of controversy, although it did collect a few amendments. For example, the concept of "detention" of pay—whereby an offender's pay would be docked for up to a year but ultimately returned to him—was made a part of the final act. This was intended as a form of "enforced savings" by which the commander could help the man in his unit who consistently threw away his payroll in misguided ventures and generally got himself in trouble doing it. The influence of those who saw Article 15 as a manifestation of command paternalism could not be clearer. Another modification was made at the insistence of Senator Ervin, who addressed himself to what he thought was a senseless discrimination between a marine rifleman and an Army rifleman in the field. Because the marine was a member of the naval service, he had no right to elect a court-martial in lieu of nonjudicial punishment. That right was granted the soldier by Army Regulations, but Ervin thought it should be statutory and applicable to all services. Under his influence, the Senate subcommittee amended the bill to extend the right of election to all enlisted men except those actually embarked in ships.[6]

A final significant change made to bill "A" in Congress was to distinguish further among commanders. The House committee amended the bill so that commanders in the lowest three commissioned grades gained nothing at all over the original Article 15. The increases proposed by the Code Committee were to be enjoyed only by majors or lieutenant commanders and above.

With these alterations, the bill was approved by Congress in August 1962 and signed into law by President Kennedy in September. By its own language, it became effective on February 1, 1963.[7]

But the other half of the bargain did less well. Bill "B," the abolition of the summary court-martial, was not even considered by the 87th Congress nor by any Congress thereafter. In fact, shortly after the passage of the Article 15 reforms, the section in bill "B" dealing with the summary courts was deleted, and the proposal was carried thereafter solely as a measure to provide for one-officer special and general courts. No mention is made of the abortive idea in later Code Committee reports. It now seems clear that those men in the Pentagon who had previously offered the summary court as a kind of sacrifice to pay for the desired increases in nonjudicial punishment no longer saw any need to give up that power after bill "A" became law. As late as June 1962, the provision was included in drafts of bill "B" then under study within the Army Department. But not long after bill "A" was enacted, Army planners began lining out the abolition paragraph from their worksheets.[8]

Thus the true intentions of the self-proclaimed in-service reformers came to light. Army arguments that Article 15 increases should be included in the same package with elimination of the lower courts had been long and loud. In fact, a virtual ultimatum along those lines had been delivered to the other services at the January 1961 meeting. Army representatives at subsequent interservice conferences continued to press for the *quid pro quo*, arguing that "passage of one without the other would be ineffective." The notion that NJP increases would lead to fewer court-martial convictions with their indelible marks on a man's record was one reason why the Pentagon was able to get civilian reformers to go along with bill "A." But as things turned out, the Army was evidently more enthusiastic for the *quo* than for the *quid*. From the beginning, bill "B" was not so vigorously pushed as its companion measure, and it was quietly subverted after bill "A" was signed into law. The chairman of the Powell committee himself, once Article 15 reforms were passed, forgot the former importance his group had given the abolition of the lower courts. General Powell exulted to the Army Chief of Staff that the new rules "paralleled" what his committee had recommended in 1960 and that that was the most important of their proposals. Nowhere in this letter did Powell mention the inferior courts-martial.[9]

This is not to say, however, that the promises were unfulfilled. Although the summary court remained on the books, its use was greatly diminished after 1963 as commanders began to exercise their new powers. The Army's Chief of Military Justice testified that he anticipated a 75-percent cut in the number of summary courts following the enactment of the new Article 15 bill, a figure not too far off from what actually happened. Figure 3 compares the number of all courts convened by Army commanders in calendar 1962 with the same figures for 1964.

FIGURE 3. ARTICLE 15 ARMY COURTS-MARTIAL CONVENED
BEFORE AND AFTER 1963

	1962	1964	Decrease	Rate of Decrease
General courts	1,876	1,865	11	.06%
Special courts	26,607	24,327	2,280	8.5
Summary courts	43,542	16,926	28,616	65.5

The reduction in general and special courts may be regarded as either negligible or due to extraneous factors. But the great drop in the summary courts is rightly attributed to the new Article 15. The same data for the Air Force show very similar results; there was a drop of 62 percent in Air Force summary courts from 1962 to 1964. The Navy experience was about the same: summary courts decreased 67 percent after the enactment of the new law.[10]

There were some surprises during the next year or so when the JAG offices began to analyze the effects of the new law. A 1963 Navy report showed that in the first six months of the new NJP law, appeals were rare and that elections to courts-martial, even where permitted in the Navy, were even less frequent. As for punishments, the Navy analyst noted that most commanders made extensive use of the new power to combine the authorized penalties but that very few availed themselves of the new correctional custody or detention of pay. Finally, the Navy noted that reductions in grade, which forced a man to take "the long road back," and were therefore discouraged, were still very common. The spokesman thought that this was because the junior commanders who had not shared in the 1963 expansion of powers were using demotions to compensate for their otherwise meager mast power.[11]

Statistics released by the Air Force indicated a different pattern; in that service some 60.9 percent of the Article 15 cases ended in demotions. There were many "long roads back" in the Air Force. The next most frequent punishment was the newly authorized forfeiture of pay; a little over half of the offenders were docked cash in 1964, and about 60 percent were so punished in 1967. As in the Navy, detention of pay was almost never used, although correctional custody was more frequent; it was awarded in about 15 percent of the cases.[12]

The Army record was different, too. Taking the quarter ending March 31, 1964 as typical, we find that forfeiture, restriction, and extra duties were awarded in almost exactly the same number of cases. It is likely that the three were combined by most commanders, who might have reasoned that if the man were to be restricted, he might as well be assigned extra work; and furthermore, while he was restricted, it would do no good for him to have a lot of money he would not be able to spend, because that would only breed gambling and other ills. Reduction in grade was only half as frequently handed down as the three most popular punishments. Detention was very rare and correctional custody almost never imposed.[13]

Some of the differences can be explained by the varying conditions and customs of the services. For example, correctional custody is obvious more adaptable to an Air Force base where the necessary facilities could be easily constructed than to a small combatant vessel where space is precious. Similarly, the Air Force promotes its enlisted men locally; in the Navy, on the other hand, promotions depend on the results of Navy-wide examinations. Therefore, an Air Force commander might be less cautious about awarding reductions in grade than his Navy counterpart, since he himself could create the replacement that the demotion would require.

In view of the Powell report's extensive study of correctional custody, the Army's reluctance to use the new feature requires a different explanation. A close reading of the report leaves one with the impression that correctional custody was less a unanimous desire of the committee than the private idea of General Decker. Most commanders wanted some form of confinement power for use at Article 15 proceedings. But the chronic legislative failure during the previous ten years had shown that Congress was not likely to give them an unrestricted authority to imprison. Decker, whose faith in nonjudicial punishement extends even into the civilian world, discovered the quasi-therapeutic custody system used in Canada and grafted it onto a proposed Article 15 reform, hoping that this would be more palatable on Capitol Hill than simple confinement. He succeeded, of course; but Army commanders never understood the system. As late as 1970, Parker, the former administrative aide on the Powell committee, confessed that the Army was still unable to indoctrinate its commanders in the proper use of the new concept. The idea was too subtle for busy field commands to grasp. Putting a man in the stockade is one thing, but assigning him some kind of semiconfinement, where he comes and goes, sees clinical analysts, and is given time to "meditate," is more complex, and for that reason, less likely to be used.[14]

Another peculiarity is that detention of pay has never been a popular punishment among commanders. No one anticipated that the temporary deprivation of a man's pay could be applied to all cases. It was intended mainly for the man who had trouble managing his own funds. And yet, although that is a plausible explanation for its infrequent use, the suspicion remains that all the pre-1963 talk about returning the commander to his proper role as father-figure was less than genuine. Detention was the most paternalistic of all the new penalties, but it is almost never used.

The main goal of the new Article 15 was improved discipline. Whether that was accomplished is impossible to say; there are no yardsticks by which to measure an improvement in discipline. Certainly the performance of American troops in the first years of the Vietnam War would indicate that discipline was good, but to what degree that can be attributed to the 1963 act cannot be determined. And yet, most commanders thought there was an increase in discipline.[15] This may have been due to a lessening of frustration on the part of these CO's. Armed with their new powers they were probably more active personally in disciplinary matters than ever before, and that may have enhanced their own morale. A content and confident commanding officer is the *sine qua non* of good unit discipline, and in this way perhaps a direct link between the Article 15 reforms and improved Armed Forces discipline can be established.

The 1963 legislation was a result of nearly the same combination of forces that had produced the UCMJ in 1950. The services were generally united in their support of the measure. Unlike their go-it-alone attitudes in the 1950s, they had gained the endorsement of the Court of Military Appeals and the various civilian bar and veterans' groups, too. But, without the special kind of support given the original UCMJ by Forrestal, Morgan, and Larkin, it was impossible in the early 1960s to obtain omnibus legislation. The tactic employed, then, was to offer measures to Congress piecemeal. This resulted in some peculiar occurrences—the scrapping of the paragraphs that would have eliminated the summary court, most notably—but it did achieve some success. After a full decade of fruitlessly petitioning Congress for amendments to the code, this was enough. Some lessons were learned, and the methods found successful in the first years of the new decade would be called upon again at the end of it.

15 The Court in the 1960s:

An Expansion of Power

For better or worse, the Court of Military Appeals was politicized by the provisions written into the UCMJ that not more than two of the judges could be from the same party. We have seen the jeopardy that Judge Brosman faced at the hands of the Republican administration of 1955 before his death. Similarly, Judge Latimer must have read the epitaph of his own career in the narrow victory Democrat John F. Kennedy scored in 1960. With one other Republican, Ferguson, on the bench, Latimer had little chance of reappointment when his term expired in May 1961. Nevertheless, he did his utmost to save his seat, asking nearly everyone of importance in the military justice arena to approve his candidacy to succeed himself. Most complied, so that by the time Latimer was finished, he had a dossier perhaps as thick as the one he originally compiled in 1951.[1]

But such considerations do not usually govern final decisions in the world of Washington politics. It is tempting to assert that Latimer was let go because his traditionalist judgments were not agreeable to the more liberal New Frontiersmen. The 1960 *Annual Report* containing the Powell controversy was printed between Kennedy's election and inauguration. In it, Latimer contributed to the state of divisiveness by withholding for the first time his "outright" support of the court's position. Although it was explained that "his objections are to some of the proposed modifications," it seems clear that the Judge agreed generally with at least the goals of the Powell committee, if not all of the details. He was, after all, a kind of star of the report, and the Army's court-packing scheme counted on his retention to give them a 3-2 majority. It would be a logical consistency to suppose that this unyielding devotion to the customs of military law made Latimer a pariah in the eyes of the Harvard liberals in the White House.

But this was not the case. Like Truman and Eisenhower before him, President Kennedy's interest in military justice was nil. In the spring of 1961, besides the normal enormous burdens of his new job, Kennedy had to deal with the Bay of Pigs operation and its consequences and plan for the Vienna meeting with Nikita Khrushchev. Things were so hectic for the Administration, in fact, that Latimer's term was allowed to expire with no mention of a designated successor. Latimer stayed on at CoMA, a rather sorrowful figure who could not even clean out his desk on the chance that he might still be renominated. At last, a full month after it became legally vacant, Kennedy announced from Paris that Latimer's seat would be filled by Congressman Paul J. Kilday of Texas.[2]

Kilday decided to retain his Congressional seat during the rest of the session then sitting, for the sake of his constituents. After confirmation by the Senate, he joined the court at the beginning of the October 1961 term. The records concerning his appointment are not yet available, but it appears that Kilday was sponsored for the position by no less than Vice-President Lyndon Johnson and Speaker of the House Sam Rayburn. He had long been a Texas Democratic Party crony of those two gentlemen; significantly, he had supported Johnson in his incredibly close Senate victory in 1948, when every vote counted. For his own part, Kilday was a member of the House Armed Services Committee or its predecessor for his entire career in Congress, some twenty-three years. Compared to the utter lack of experience brought to the court by Judge Ferguson, this was an impressive credential. With political backing from Rayburn and Johnson, there is little doubt as to why Kilday got the job; why he wanted it is not known. Perhaps he was tired of running for office every two years. At the time of his appointment, Kilday was sixty-one years old; a fifteen-year term, he may have contemplated, would bring him to the end of his useful government days.[3]

With the change in personnel in 1961, the court returned more nearly to the precise balance that marked the original three nominees. Gone was the mixed service representation, of course; neither Ferguson nor Kilday had ever served in the Armed Forces. But, as in the 1951 court, there was an Easterner, a Westerner, and a Southerner; two Democrats and a Republican.

The accession of Kilday in 1961 brought about a startling change in the way the members of the court divided in decisions. To a much greater degree than larger courts, a three-man tribunal is a fickle thing; it tends to polarize, one judge going one way, another a different way, and the third acting as a "swing man." This phenomenon is illustrated by Figure 4. It is clear from the data that Brosman was the swing vote on the original court, Quinn on the second, and Kilday on the third.[4]

FIGURE 4. DISSENTING OPINIONS BY THE JUDGES OF THE COURT OF MILITARY APPEALS

A. Court I (Oct. 1951-Dec. 21. 1955)
Total Decisions: 920 (approx.)

Judge	*Dissenting Opinions*
Quinn	50
Latimer	63
Brosman	28

B. Court II (April 9, 1956-May 1, 1961)
Total Decisions: 760 (approx.)

Judge	*Dissenting Opinions*
Quinn	38
Latimer	254
Ferguson	142

C. Court III (Oct. 1, 1961-Oct. 12, 1968)
Total Decisions: 880 (approx.)

Judge	*Dissenting Opinions*
Quinn	135
Ferguson	102
Kilday	3

The figures bear out our substantive analysis of the first two benches. Latimer was slightly out of step with the prevailing opinions during the 1951-1956 periods, an isolation that grew after Ferguson joined the court. But the third table is astounding. It is difficult to believe that any man could make judicial decisions on a three-man bench for seven years and only three times find himself alone in his views. Perhaps Kilday's Congressional experience taught him the art of conciliation to an advanced degree; perhaps he made it a practice to take no position of his own, content merely to select the view of whichever of his brothers most suited him. The quality of his opinions would seem to belie this latter hypothesis. In *U.S. v. Culp*, for example, Kilday traced in great detail the development of the right to counsel at common law and in military custom. His opinion was a masterpiece of legal history, presented in a fashion that would do any scholar of the law proud. Although *Culp* is perhaps the best known of Kilday's opinions, it is by no means atypical.[5]

More significant for students of the court than Kilday's record, however, was the Chief Judge's performance. In the major decisions of the second court, Quinn most frequently sided with Ferguson. We have already supposed that Quinn may have found himself between the scylla of Ferguson's innovations and the charybdis of Latimer's conservatism during the late 1950s. After 1961, with Latimer gone, Quinn was no longer bound to the unpleasant alliance with Ferguson. For the first time in over five years, he could state his position when opposed to Ferguson, confident that there was no reactionary on the court whose decisions might drive military justice back to days of rocks and shoals.

As a whole, the court of the 1960s concerned itself with a number of important issues, some of which will be discussed in later chapters. Several key decisions amounted to reconsiderations of old questions, and the results suggested that the court was "mellowing." For example, in *U.S. v. Wimberley*, CoMA declared the end of the state of war that had existed between the court and the *Manual for Courts-Martial*. A unanimous court in this case specifically stated that Presidential rules not contrary to the Constitution or the UCMJ would not be invalidated by the Court of Military Appeals. In substance, this was no different from *Cecil* and *May*, but its great significance was that it was couched in affirmative language whereas those two had announced prohibitions. This spirit continued. The *Rinehart* mandate that outside legal sources, particularly the *Manual*, were banned from use by court members was modified in *U.S. v. Lewandowski*. Judge Kilday wrote in that opinion that the use of the *Manual* by that particular court was no violation of the *Rinehart* doctrine because there was "no perusal" since the prosecutor had already set out for the court the section in question. A unanimous court agreed.[6]

Freed from the pressure of Latimer's views, Judge Quinn joined Kilday in a number of decisions that seemed pro-prosecution. In *U.S. v. Smith*, for example, they brushed off Ferguson's dissenting opinion that exorbitant delay had injured the defendant. In *U.S. v.*

Erb, the same majority explained away as harmless a half-dozen errors, any one of which might have demanded reversal under Judge Brosman's "general prejudice" doctrine. There was even one case where Quinn and Kilday found "no fair risk" of harmful error in a case involving jury intrusion by a law officer.[7]

Although Quinn seems to have changed significantly, CoMA as a whole did not do a complete conservative turnabout. Reading only the pages of the *Army Times* newspaper chain, one might think the court was in the business of releasing criminals. In the very beginning of Kilday's term, these papers openly hoped that the court would act more harmoniously than it had during the days of the Ferguson-Latimer battles. When the first three decisions of the new Court were unanimous, *Navy Times* headlined: "THREE JUDGES AGREE!" But in 1966 and 1967, the papers began to find frequent fault with certain reversals, most of which were the work of Ferguson and Kilday, Quinn dissenting. The criticism was seldom direct; but the tone of the reporting was unmistakably disapproving. *Navy Times* deplored the reversal of a disobedience conviction in February 1967, and later that year *Army Times* unhappily reported the reversal of a Fort Dix verdict on an Article 31 technicality. In March 1967, *Air Force Times* reported that the court was "bitterly warring" as the majority overruled the murder conviction in *U.S. v. O'Such*. The same paper later asserted that CoMA had reversed more than two-thirds of the convictions it considered during 1967, an increase of 23 percent over the previous year. The clear implication was that the huge jump in reversals was inexplicable and should therefore be the cause for some alarm.[8]

Perhaps more than any other single case, it was *U.S. v. Breen* in 1966 that created newspaper hostility against the Ferguson-Kilday majority. In that case, by a margin of 2-1, the court held that a conviction for unlawful entry into a man's shipboard locker was void because the charge sheet did not correctly allege an offense. The format used by the prosecution, Kilday and Ferguson decided, was proper only in the case of unlawful entry into a structure, such as a warehouse or a tent. The majority did concede that "rummaging through the personal gear of another member of the service undoubtedly might" be an offense under the code, but only if the charge were properly drawn up.[9]

Chief Judge Quinn was stunned; in dissent he wrote:

I know of no place in the military establishment that is more widely used . . . than the locker assigned [a GI]. It is, in a very real sense, part of the enlisted man's *home*. . . . "Generally a military person's place of abode is the *place where he bunks and keeps his few private possessions!*"[10]

Of course, Quinn had one advantage over his brothers: he had been in the service and knew better than they the importance his one place of privacy had to the soldier or sailor. Without such experience, the others could fall back only on the strictest interpretation of the *Manual* provision. Judge Ferguson claimed that to be a CoMA judge, one need not know the military but only the law. In *Breen*, at least, knowing the law was not enough. Even considering the case at the level of theoretical law, as John Slinkman of the *Navy Times* rightly pointed out, the court allowed the defendant in *Breen* what it would not permit a commanding officer to do, *viz.*, conduct a search of private possessions without "probable cause."[11]

Because of their growing disillusionment, the papers campaigned for Judge Quinn's reappointment. His original fifteen-year term was due to expire in May 1966, and there was the usual interest in whether a new man would be named. One factor was Quinn's age; in April of that year, he became seventy-two years old. But there was no political test at stake this time. A veteran Democrat who had maintained his contacts in the state and national party, Quinn was never in any real danger of being replaced involuntarily. Accordingly, the Chief Judge, having decided to stay on the court, was nominated to succeed himself by President Johnson on April 28.[12]

To this *Navy Times* proclaimed "QUINN AGAIN (THANK GOD!)." Slinkman wrote his approval, praising the Chief Judge for not attempting to write law from the bench, "as so many federal judges [do] these days." As far as *Navy Times* was concerned, another "Ferguson" would have been a disaster: "Two Kildays with a Quinn, yes. Two Kildays with a Ferguson, no," was the way Slinkman somewhat implausibly put it.[13]

Politics adjourned, the court returned to work. Perhaps the most important issue to come before CoMA during Judge Kilday's term was the question of court power in the area of "extraordinary relief." Generally speaking, this refers to an action taken by a court in going beyond the narrow limits of its statutory or constitutional limits. The two most common forms are writs of habeas corpus and writs of coram nobis. In the former, the petitioner alleges that he is illegally detained. If the court determines that wrongful imprisonment has occurred, it may order the victim released, without even considering the question of his guilt or innocence. In a coram nobis action, the petitioner argues that there has been a procedural error of such magnitude or nature that the tribunal which erred has thereby lost jurisdiction, rendering all subsequent proceedings null. The remedies for this vary, but usually the case is remanded to the highest level of litigation where no error occurred, and the process begins again.

The drafters of the code considered the need for these measures within their new system. Apparently they were reluctant to grant the powers to the military courts directly, perhaps because of the unresolved issue of whether legislative courts could properly exercise the extraordinary writs. Felix Larkin testified about this matter before the House subcommittee, explaining that it was the UCMJ Committee's intention that Article 73, "Petition for a New Trial," be considered to include the writ of coram nobis. Because the article did provide for a new trial on grounds of "fraud on the court," the Congressmen were satisfied with this reasoning.[14]

But only three years after CoMA began hearing arguments, it had to consider in *U.S. v. Ferguson* what amounted to a petition for coram nobis. At issue was whether alleged command influence over a court-martial was a jurisdictional error. Judge Latimer, who wrote the principal opinion, said it was not, so the question of coram nobis was moot. Quinn agreed but asserted that the court at least had the power to investigate the matter. Judge Brosman also agreed with the result but in dictum expressed the opinion that the court was included within the provisions of the All-Writs Act of 1948, the statutory ratification of the common law powers of courts to "issue all writs necessary or appropriate."[15]

Ducking the issue did not make it go away. In *U.S. v. Tavares*, it arose again, but again the court hedged. Ferguson wrote the principal opinion here, but both he and Latimer, who wrote a separate opinion, found other grounds to dispose of the coram nobis question. In a 1961 case, *In re Taylor*, the court rejected the petition of a judge advocate disbarred from Air Force practice, on the grounds that it was not a court of original jurisdiction, another hedge. In the early 1960s, a number of cases, straightforwardly denominated by the litigants as coram nobis petitions, were brought before the court, but all were denied without hearing or opinion.[16]

When the court finally acted, it was only under outside pressure. The petitioner in *U.S. v. Frischholz* originally sought CoMA review of his conviction in 1960. The petition was denied, apparently because the court found no merit in his assignment of error. Frischholz then applied to the U.S. District Court for relief. There he was told that he had not exhausted the remedies available to him within the military system. The federal court directed him to seek his writ at the Court of Military Appeals. Spurred by this mandate, CoMA accepted Frischholz' petition for writ of coram nobis, the first such argument it had ever agreed to hear. But, on the merits, CoMA rejected the application and refused to grant the writ.[17]

Beginning with volume 17 of the CoMA reports, a new administrative technique indicated which way things were going. The court, anticipating a large number of extraordinary relief cases, began to categorize such actions separately. *Gale v. U.S.*, for example, was listed in the table of contents as "Misc. Dock. No. 67-2," instead of by its docket number as *Frischholz*—"No. 14,270"—had been. And in its *Annual Report*, besides listing the number of cases heard by mandate, certificate, and petition, the court began to list "Miscellaneous," a tabulation of the extraordinary cases, in recognition of the "increasing number of varied pleadings" that were now coming before it.[18]

Still, the court had not yet granted relief in any of the cases. In *Gale* it repeated the claim, first made in *Frischholz,* that, "In an appropriate case, this Court clearly possesses the power to grant relief to an accused prior to the completion of court-martial proceedings against him." But it denied Gale's petition. Two months later, in the celebrated case of Captain Howard Levy, the Green Beret doctor who refused to help train troops for what he considered an "illegal war," the court again ruled that while it possessed all-writs power it had no reason in the instant case to exercise it to provide the relief Levy sought.[19]

The court granted its first writ in *U.S. v. Jackson*, a 1967 case very similar to the earlier *Tavares.* The court ruled that the question of defendant's mental capacity had not been properly handled by the trial court and issued the writ of coram nobis, ordering the Army JAG to refer the case to another general court-martial where the issue could be disposed of. In a 1968 coram nobis case of note, *U.S. v. Bevilacqua and Braun*, decided by the two-man court after Kilday's death, CoMA again refused to issue the writ, but the judges gave notice that their purview included alleged errors occurring in special courts-martial, even where the sentence was too light to merit CoMA review under the terms of Articles 66 and 67.[20]

The business of extraordinary writs has grown, following a kind of law of supply and demand. In 1966, there were only two cases listed under "Miscellaneous." In 1967, the number grew to twenty-four.

There were twenty-two in 1968, but then, as if defendants and counsel finally caught on, in 1969 there were seventy-nine such petitions. Part of this spurt was the result of the Supreme Court decision in *Noyd v. Bond,* which gave specific sanction to CoMA's adoption of all-writs powers. In the first nine months of 1970, there were sixty-two miscellaneous petitions docketed at the court, indicating that the practice will probably continue to expand.[21]

The significance of the extraordinary relief power is twofold. In the narrowest sense, it means that GI's can now receive within the military court system all the procedural rights, privileges, and benefits they could enjoy in the federal courts. *Noyd v. Bond* asserted that unless a military petitioner exhausted the now considerable remedies available to him before the Court of Military Appeals, there could be no airing of his case in the civilian courts. In the broader sense, the adoption of this power, added to some of the other advances in military justice soon to be described, has made virtually a new federal district out of the military jurisdiction. There are differences in law and procedure, but for most practical purposes, by the Summer of 1969, the law covering the population governed by the Uniform Code was analogous to that employed in the other federal court districts. The supreme irony here is that although the Supreme Court tacitly ratified this situation by its *Noyd v. Bond* decision on June 16, 1969, it had already rejected much of it in *O'Callahan v. Parker*, two weeks earlier. We will look into this in Chapter XVII.[22]

A "fourth" Court of Military Appeals was formed following Judge Kilday's death on October 12, 1968. This came at a time when the election campaigns were beginning to peak and the pressures on President Johnson deriving from war, peace, and domestic problems were at their greatest. Based on the experience of earlier administrations, one might expect the court to limp along with two members for a long time. But two things prevented that. First of all, Kilday and Johnson were old friends, and the President could hardly fail to notice the judge's passing as Eisenhower had apparently done when Brosman died. Johnson thereupon made a recess appointment of William H. Darden of Georgia to fill the unexpired term. In 1968 Darden was only forty-five years old but had been the chief of staff of the Senate Armed Services Committee for fifteen years, the second factor that eliminated the usual delay. Darden's boss on the committee was Richard Russell, whose power in the Senate was legendary. It is a mark of that eminence that the appointment of

Darden to the Court of Military Appeals was the only Johnson lame-duck nomination to be confirmed by the Senate.[23]

But this court did not sit together long enough to establish any recognizable pattern. Quinn and Ferguson remained largely un-changed, it seemed, and Darden was not noticeably more "liberal" than Ferguson, nor as "conservative" as Latimer, thus making him fit rather easily into the seat formerly occupied by Kilday.[24] But even more recently, the CoMA torch has been passed to a young man. Judge Ferguson retired in 1971, and after an abortive attempt to name a Southerner with a racist record to the bench, the Nixon Administration swung the other way and appointed Robert M. Duncan, a Negro justice on the Ohio Supreme Court, to the empty seat. Duncan began serving in November 1971. President Nixon in June of that year, moreover, had elevated Judge Darden to the position of Chief Judge, thus leaving the venerable Mr. Quinn, the one survivor of the original court, merely an associate.[25]

16 The Federal Courts and Military Justice:

To Intervene or Not?

The influence of civilian courts over court-martial law has become considerable only in the very recent past, an ironic turn of events. During the primitive days before World War II the courts scrupulously avoided courts-martial except under the most narrow circumstances. But since that time, although military law has become more sophisticated and protective, the federal courts have become less inclined to permit military courts to operate without supervision.

The first important case in which the Supreme Court considered the issue was *Dynes v. Hoover* in 1857. The *Dynes* doctrine was two-pronged. The court held that a court-martial verdict was beyond the power of the federal courts to review or revise unless it could be shown, first, that the military court "had not jurisdiction over the *subject matter or charge*;" or second, "having jurisdiction over the subject matter, it has failed to observe the rules prescribed by the statute for its exercise."[1]

As a result of this decision, all forms of military tribunals were able to operate utterly without regard for the trends in civilian judicial circles and generally without fear of interference from the civil courts. A peculiar thing about this doctrine was that many writers who interpreted *Dynes* omitted the second half of the test, that courts-martial must follow their own prescribed procedure. William Winthrop was the most important of these, but even as late as 1962, Chief Justice Earl Warren made the same error. These men asserted that following the *Dynes v. Hoover* ruling, if a court-martial had jurisdiction over the person and the offense, no other question

165

could be asked by civilian courts.² It took many cases and much tortuous interpretation over the next hundred years before the forgotten part of *Dynes* was ever effectively enforced.

Part of the reason was the eminence of William Winthrop. Even as late as 1953, scholars such as Edmund Morgan were compelled to begin any explication of their ideas by dealing with Winthrop. But, besides Winthrop, a major reason the "failure to follow rules" test was forgotten was the nature of subsequent Supreme Court decisions themselves.³

Dynes v. Hoover probably came as no surprise to contemporary court-watchers. In an 1840 case, *Decatur v. Paulding*, the High Court had branded as "mischief" any interference by the judicial branch in the "performance of ordinary duties of the executive departments." Since courts-martial were regarded as legitimate functions of one of the executive branch departments, it would readily follow in 1857 that no inquiry into them by the courts would be appropriate.⁴

In the years after *Dynes* the concept of noninvolvement was confirmed in a number of cases. *Abelman v. Booth* in 1858 and *Tarble's Case* in 1871 had the effect of permanently forcing the state courts out of the court-martial business. Two well-known actions deriving from the Civil War helped to limit federal court power, as well. The first, *Ex parte Vallandigham*, was a wartime case involving a leading Copperhead who had been tried by military commission. Vallandigham appealed the resulting conviction directly to the Supreme Court, which rejected his application on the grounds that it had no jurisdiction over the proceedings of a military court. This denied to all future court-martial defendants the *certiorari* route to the High Court. But after the war, when the court presumably had regathered its courage following the embarrassments of the *Dred Scott* debacle and Chief Justice Roger Taney's humiliation by President Lincoln, the *Vallandigham* doctrine was severely modified. In *Ex parte Milligan*, the court ruled that the military courts and commissions could not try civilians who had no connection with the service, if local civilian courts were open and operating. A writ of habeas corpus was granted Milligan on the grounds that his detention was illegal.⁵

A few more important definitional cases were decided toward the end of the century. In *Ex parte Nielsen*, an 1889 decision, the court partly retrieved the forgotten half of *Dynes v. Hoover*, when it ruled that the jurisdictional test included whether the court-martial had handed down a sentence in excess of its legal power. The following year, however, in *In re Grimley*, it reaffirmed that other procedural errors of a court-martial were not subject to its scrutiny. The cumulative effect was that, since 1857 the court, perhaps itself under the mighty influence of Winthrop's recently published treatise, had retreated from *Dynes*. All that was left were the jurisdictional and sentence tests, a fact confirmed by two decisions around the turn of the century, *Swaim v. U.S.*, and *Grafton v. U.S.*[6]

It is well to note at this point, especially in light of subsequent history, that during the Nineteenth Century the military claimed for itself only the most limited jurisdiction. According to Colonel Winthrop, a man was not subject to the Articles of War unless he had received pay for service in the armed forces. He argued that AW 63, which subjected "retainers to the camp, and all persons serving with the armies of the United States . . . to orders," was a wartime measure only.[7]

The Nineteenth Century situation, then, was marked by restraint on both sides. The laws governing the armed services closely circumscribed the extent of court-martial jurisdiction. Within those narrow limits, the Supreme Court granted immunity from its purview. As noted earlier, the military codes were primarily aimed at controlling those offenses which were specifically military in nature. The federal courts could, with wisdom and rectitude, claim to lack expertise in such matters. On the other side, neither the Army nor the Navy showed any great desire to become involved in serious felony litigation. For example, the AGN gave Navy courts jurisdiction over murder only if the site of the crime were outside the United States. This rule applied in wartime as well as in peace. The Articles of War, right up to 1951, had a similar provision covering both murder and rape, although the ban was lifted in time of war.

In the early 1900s, there were a number of Supreme Court decisions bearing on the question of civilian court interference. The basic doctrine, however, remained intact. In *Reaves v. Ainsworth*, a 1911 case dealing with a dispute over a promotion, the court wrote: "To those in the military or naval service of the United States the military law is due process." This position may have been valid and supportable in the years before World War I, when the Army was tiny, intimate, and composed entirely of Regulars, but it was less applicable in the greatly expanded Army of World War I, composed mostly of civilians in uniform only temporarily. This was at the heart of the argument advanced by Samuel Ansell and Edmund Morgan in 1919. As we have seen, the Ansell ideas were rejected. The services went back to their splendid isolation during the interwar years, trying those over whom they had the power, with no fear whatever of outside interference.[8]

In 1938, however, the Supreme Court handed down a decision in *Johnson v. Zerbst* which provided the first crack in the wall. This case had nothing to do with the military directly, but its implications were felt in later decisions that did. In *Johnson*, the court expanded its definition of "jurisdiction" by holding that if at any point during litigation the defendant was deprived of some basic constitutional right, jurisdiction was lost by the court which perpetrated the denial. In short, a man's trial had to be fair by constitutional standards, and if it were not, jurisdiction would not lie.[9] Here, eighty years later, the Supreme Court began to find its way back to the lost half of *Dynes v. Hoover.*

Coming on the eve of World War II with its massive infusion of civilians into the military, the *Johnson* doctrine served as a handy springboard for ambitious lawyers and desperate defendants who sought to reverse court-martial findings. And yet, in a number of wartime cases dealing specifically with military tribunals, the Supreme Court continued to follow the customary line. In *Billings v. Truesdell*, a court-martial conviction was thrown out on the narrow grounds that a draftee who refused to take the oath of induction was not subject to military law. In the case of the Nazi agents landed from submarines along the Atlantic coast, *Ex parte Quirin*, the high court again washed its hands of any responsibility to review evidence or procedural errors in military trials, a position it reasserted in *In re Yamashita*, a Japanese war criminal case. Even in what appear now to be instances of injustice, *Hirabayashi v. U.S.* and *Korematsu v. U.S.*, litigation brought by the victims of the forced relocation of Japanese-Americans from the West Coast was defeated when the court refused to intervene in the exercise of executive branch and military power. None of these cases involved courts-martial, and all were decided somewhat reluctantly. But they nevertheless indicated the diffidence of the Supreme Court in military affairs.[10]

The first military exploitation of the *Johnson* opening came in 1943 in *Schita v. King*. Schita was a Zulu soldier of fortune who, as a U.S. Army provost sergeant, shot two men under his guard, was convicted of murder, and sentenced to life imprisonment. So ingrained was the Winthrop interpretation of *Dynes v. Hoover* by this time that when Schita brought suit in a habeas corpus action the government counsel did not even bother to refute the Zulu's claims that he had been deprived of due process. The Court of Appeals hearing the case was less apathetic and, because of Schita's uncontested allegations of procedural errors, ruled in his favor, issued the writ, and remanded the case for a new trial. Schita's conviction was subsequently upheld, but a major point, originally made in 1857 but lost in the intervening years, had been reintroduced: if courts-martial violated their own procedural rules, they were subject to federal court scrutiny. *Dynes v. Hoover* had been restored, at least in this one court.[11]

Perhaps under the influence of the inquiry into court-martial matters then being conducted by many other agencies of the government, other federal courts began to march to the same beat. In *U.S. ex rel. Innes v. Hiatt*, a district court of appeals, while conceding that the Constitution itself did not apply to servicemen, ruled that the Fifth Amendment guaranteed at least that "military procedure will be applied to them in a fundamentally fair way." And in *Hicks v. Hiatt*, a federal court in the same district found that by not conducting a "thorough and impartial" pretrial investigation, by admitting hearsay evidence, and by committing other violations of the Articles of War, a court-martial convened to try a rape case in England had not applied military procedure in a "fundamentally fair way."[12]

But without guidance from the Supreme Court, the performance of the inferior federal courts lacked consistency. In *Hunter v. Wade*, a court in a different circuit returned to the ideas of William Winthrop by ruling that the "scope of the inquiry is limited to questions of jurisdiction." Only the Supreme Court could resolve the conflicts.[13]

Meanwhile a new approach to the problem of rectifying unjust court-martial verdicts was being tried out. In the wake of World War II, many men dissatisfied with their treatment at the hands of military courts sought relief in the form of judgments for back pay. The outstanding example of this was *U.S. v. Shapiro*. Shapiro was an Army second lieutenant appointed defense counsel for a 1943 court-martial trial. In order to demonstrate the flaws in the prosecution's case, he substituted for the defendant an impostor, who was identified in court as the criminal by every one of the witnesses to the alleged crime. Although the case was lost in spite of his gambit, the Army authorities took a dim view of Shapiro's tactics. Only two days after the ruse was discovered, he was charged, arraigned, tried, and convicted of "conduct of a nature to bring discredit upon the military service," all within a five-hour period.

Moreover, the officer he preferred as defense counsel was named prosecutor, leaving Shapiro only two nonlawyers to defend him. Needless to say, he was dismissed from the Army and shortly thereafter drafted as a private.

When the war was over, Shapiro brought suit in the U.S. Court of Claims, petitioning for a back-pay judgment. That court observed that a "more flagrant case of military despotism would be hard to imagine" and ruled that both the court-martial and the dismissal were void. Shapiro was awarded an amount of money equal to second lieutenant's pay from the time of his dismissal to the time of his ultimate discharge from enlisted status, less what he had been paid as a private.[14]

The back-pay solution became fairly common after this. But as a collateral attack, it was less than completely satisfactory for those GI's who sought to have their records expunged of what they believed to be unjust court-martial convictions. What was still missing was Supreme Court guidance.[15]

As the courts began to free themselves from the tacit agreement struck with the military during the Winthrop era, the restraint on the other side was also beginning to erode. Most of the post-World War II study groups singled out as a major flaw in the contemporary systems the inadequacy of their jurisdiction provisions. For example, nowhere in the AGN was there explicit mention of those classes of persons subject to Navy courts. To uncover the relevant rules, the Navy JAG admitted, one had to search through *Naval Courts and Boards*, a number of statutes, and several court decisions. Jurisdiction as to place was also a problem under the AGN; although the Keeffe board urged new legislation to remove all statutory limits on geography, the McGuire committee recommended retaining the provision that forbade naval trials for murder committed in the United States.[16]

In directing their attention to such problems, the UCMJ drafters went too far. Article 2 of the new code listed specifically all those classes of persons subject to its provisions. In addition to men and women on active duty, reservists, and retired personnel either receiving pay or hospitalization, the code claimed jurisdiction over several extraservice classes of people. Prisoners of war were included for the first time, in accordance with the recently ratified Geneva Convention, which demanded that POW's be disciplined by the same rules used in the detaining power's own armed forces. More controversial were the provisions which extended court-martial authority to a variety of civilians. In a wartime situation, all persons serving with or accompanying the forces "in the field" would be subject to the code. Felix Larkin testified that "in the field" meant both overseas and at home and applied to employees, war correspondents, Red Cross workers, and the like. Another section extended jurisdiction to all persons serving with or accompanying the armed forces, whether in peace or war, any place outside the continental United States and the major American territories where American courts were unlikely to be in operation. Thus far the Uniform Code expressed no jurisdictional claims not already included in the Elston Act. The new article was merely a consolidation of the older one, a few other statutes and some relevant court rulings. Congress recognized this; there the only important discussion on Article 2 concerned retired personnel and the unintended inclusion by Article 2(11) of the native populations of Guam and the Pacific Trust Territories.[17]

But two highly publicized federal court decisions impelled the Congressmen into less familiar areas. The first of these was the case of the Hessian crown jewels. WAC Captain Kathleen Nash Durant, having completed a tour of duty in Europe, was granted terminal leave on her arrival in the United States and ordered home to await discharge. Only six days before she would no longer have been subject to trial by court-martial, it was discovered that she had stolen the crown jewels of the former German state of Hesse. She was ordered back to active duty to stand trial, was convicted, and sentenced to five years in prison. Although she was temporarily successful in obtaining habeas corpus relief, the conviction was ultimately confirmed on appeal.[18]

The second case involved Navy petty officer Harold E. Hirshberg, a prisoner of the Japanese in the Philippines during most of the war who, while in captivity, committed certain crimes against his fellow POW's. Hirshberg's offenses were not discovered until after he had re-enlisted following his release from the Japanese. A court-martial convicted him on the prison-camp charges, but Hirshberg brought a habeas corpus action to the Supreme Court, where he was freed because of the inadequacy of the AGN jurisdictional rules. In court, the Navy conceded that had Hirshberg not re-enlisted, he could not have been tried by court-martial. But the fact that he was "in the Navy" at the time of the offense and again at the time of the trial was enough to justify jurisdiction, government counsel argued. The court was curt: "Jurisdiction to punish rarely, if ever, rests upon such illogical and fortuitous contingencies."[19]

Both *Durant* and *Hirshberg* were well-known to the drafters of the code and the Congressmen who considered it. Mrs. Durant had almost escaped punishment for a crime of potentially serious international dimensions. And Hirshberg had escaped paying the penalty for his disloyalty. The Congressmen were determined to avoid such miscarriages in the future. Mr. Elston was particularly pointed on this question and pressed for a revision of Article 3(a) as a remedy. This article originally provided that reservists, even if no longer subject to the code, could be returned to court-martial jurisdiction if they were found to have committed major felonies while in a subject status. That provision was based on an old Navy law, but it would not be enough to try future Hirshbergs or Durants. After some discussion of those cases by the House subcommittee, Larkin promised to prepare something to cover the loopholes. The result was a revolutionary expansion of court-martial jurisdiction: any person who, while he was subject to the code, committed a crime serious enough to merit five years confinement or more, did not escape liability to trial by court-martial solely by virtue of discharge from the service.[20]

Despite his willingness to draft what the Congressmen wanted, Larkin warned them that the new law might not be constitutional, since the offenders envisaged by it would not be "in the land and naval forces." Most military officials were equally skeptical. The old Army law included a provision that persons accused of frauds against the government did not escape trial by court-martial simply by being discharged. When this was first proposed as a part of the UCMJ in 1948, the Navy JAG, Admiral Russell, strenuously opposed: "I can not- buy, and neither will Congress, court martial jurisdiction over civilians in time of peace, no matter where they are." Russell's prediction about Congress proved wrong, as we have seen. But his opposite number in the Army, General Green, opposed Article 3(a) even after it was passed in the new form by the House. When it was signed into law, the Army continued to treat the new provision like a hot potato. The committee assigned to write the new *Manual for Courts-Martial* warned in its report that since Article 3(a) might cause a "serious impact on the civilian population" it should be invoked only with the approval of the highest authorities in the Pentagon.[21]

As it turned out, the military lawyers foresaw the future more accurately than the lawmakers. One may wonder why the Congress refused to provide for federal court jurisdiction in cases like *Hirshberg* and *Durant*, a solution that was suggested a number of times. A major reason was the belief of the drafters of the UCMJ that the federal courts, particularly the Supreme Court, would continue their traditional hands-off policy. This idea was not expressed anywhere by a Congressman, but Congressional assumption that court-martial law would remain isolated is suggested strongly by the enactment of Article 76 of the code.[22.]

This was an essentially identical adaptation of an earlier Army law, which provided that the findings and sentences of courts-martial as approved, reviewed, and affirmed in accordance with the code would be "final and conclusive" and "binding on all departments, courts, agencies, and officers of the United States."[23] There was virtually no Congressional discussion on this point, indicating that the lawmakers expected no change in federal court relations with military justice.

Prevailing contemporary opinion agreed that the courts would preserve their traditional diffidence. Daniel Walker thought that the existence of the Court of Military Appeals would lessen the need for civilian collateral review. The Supreme Court itself contributed to this belief by handing down, in the same year the UCMJ was enacted, its decision in *Hiatt v. Brown*, reaffirming the traditional narrow scope of federal court review. This decision reversed two lower court rulings which had followed the *Johnson* doctrine by inquiring into the procedure of a court-martial and the resulting fairness of the trial. But the Supreme Court held that such a view exceeded the jurisdictional test and was therefore null.[24]

Despite the inferior court's inability to sway the High Bench's opinions on this matter, the Supreme Court did begin to move, albeit slowly. In *Gusik v. Schilder*, the court ruled that the "final and conclusive" provision applied only within the military court system and that the federal courts would not feel themselves barred thereby from conducting their customary jurisdictional inquiries into court-martial actions. To rule any other way, the court declared, would be to imply that Congress had intended a major "break with history" without directing special attention to it. On the same day, in *Whelchel v. McDonald*, Justice William O. Douglas opened the door to expanded federal court review. The issue here was whether the court-martial had properly disposed of an insanity issue. The Supreme Court denied the petition for habeas corpus, ruling that it was beyond the reach of the civil courts to review alleged court-martial errors in the evaluation of evidence. But in dictum,

Douglas wrote that the court ruled this way because the defendant had been granted full opportunity to present his argument, thus satisfying the rules of military law. This was double-edged; if a later case should arise where the military rules were not fulfilled, the court might step in.[25]

That opportunity came in *Burns v. Wilson*. This 1953 case is a great landmark along the road of Supreme Court relations with military tribunals. But the reluctance of the Vinson Court to embroil itself in military trials is shown by the breakdown of the vote. The split was 4-1-1-1-2, and if that is not confusing enough, the most important doctrine that emerged was held by the plurality and the two dissenters and rejected by the concurring judges. The four —Vinson, Reed, Clark, and Burton—held that GI's were guaranteed due process by the framers of the federal Constitution, who had entrusted the balance between rights and discipline to Congress. The civil courts were incompetent to do this, they ruled, but they did claim for themselves "the limited function . . . to determine whether the military [courts] have given fair consideration to each of [the defendant's] claims." A "manifest refusal" on the part of a court-martial to give such consideration could result in the granting of a writ of habeas corpus. The plurality decided that there had been no such refusal in the *Burns* trial, and, joined by Justices Jackson and Minton, who concurred in the result for different and separate reasons, voted not to issue the writ. Justice Frankfurter reserved his opinion, begging for more time, although he did state he thought the jurisdiction-only test was too narrow. The dissenters, Douglas and Black, agreed that where military courts followed their own rules, a "rehash of the same facts by a federal court would not advance the cause of justice." But where the court-martial disregarded its rules, then a federal court should "entertain the petition for habeas corpus."[26]

Thus was the Supreme Court dragged, kicking and screaming, by its inferior courts and a determined minority of its members, into the era of the Uniform Code of Military Justice. To this point, the majority was still willing to accept the rule of "fundamentally fair" trials. The "manifest refusal" test was only a halfway house. In the next few years, however, encroachments by the UCMJ and changes in court personnel forced the High Court to come squarely to grips with military justice.

There were a number of CoMA cases dealing with jurisdiction during the first few years of that court's existence. But in those days, the court had not yet begun to consider its invalidation powers, and so it restricted itself to interpretation and differentiation.[27]

As in so many other areas, it was the Warren Supreme Court that finally approached the problem directly. The first confrontation was over Article 3(a). One almost suspects that the case, *U.S. ex rel. Toth v. Quarles*, was handpicked for the event, the issues were so sharp and clear. While serving as security guards in Korea, Robert W. Toth and a fellow airman cold-bloodedly killed a Korean whom they found on their post. The accomplice, Thomas L. Kinder, was tried and convicted by court-martial, but by the time the crime was discovered, Toth had been honorably discharged and returned to civilian life.[28]

Article 3(a) was designed to cover just such an eventuality, so Air Policemen were sent to apprehend Toth to return him to Korea for court-martial. As the drafters of the *Manual* had prophesied, there was an uproar in the civilian community, in the person of Toth's sister. She filed for writ of habeas corpus in the federal district court, contesting the constitutionality of the controversial article. The court issued the writ on the grounds that the arresting officers had failed to follow the Federal Rules for Criminal Procedure in not taking Toth before a federal commissioner. The Air Force appealed this ruling and the Court of Appeals in the District of Columbia reversed the decision of the lower court, remanding Toth to Air Force custody. The appeals court based its ruling on the ground that Article 3(a) was valid because a man is customarily subject to trial in the jurisdiction where the offense was committed.[29]

But Toth's sister went to the Supreme Court. There had been two changes in the personnel of the high Court since *Burns v. Wilson*; Earl Warren was now the Chief Justice and John Harlan occupied Robert Jackson's seat. But these new faces do not completely explain the Tóth decision. Justice Clark, one of the plurality in *Burns*, now voted for invalidation and was joined by the two new men, the two dissenters from *Burns*, and Frankfurter. Together they formed a 6-3 majority which ruled Article 3(a) was unconstitutional.

As we now know, the Warren Court often sought some higher standard than the cold printed law. Here in *Toth*, however, the court restricted itself to the traditional jurisdictional test. There was nothing revolutionary in that; what was new was the concept of jurisdiction that it used. In all the cases heretofore, the court had asked only if the case were one that had arisen in "the land and naval forces," as provided in the Fifth Amendment. Before the enactment of the Uniform Code and the establishment of a large peacetime standing army, there had been no reason for any other test. Now, however, millions of Americans were entering and leaving the services at a rate and in a volume unimagined by the Founding Fathers or even the veterans of the pre-Pearl Harbor days. The new UCMJ provided for court-martial jurisdiction over varieties of people who in the past had been in such small numbers as to be insignificant: dependents, employees, retired officers, reservists. And, in Article 3(a), the code authorized court-martial trials for some people who had been completely separated from the service. Under these conditions a new test—the status of the accused, rather than the facts of the offense—was applied in Toth's case; he was found lacking the requisite status and was freed.

There were a number of consequences of this decision. Not the least was the majority's view of military justice. The reason civilians were not to be tried by court-martial, they argued,was that although military law might be good enough for servicemen, it was not good enough for civilians. This argument would be heard again. Another result was the gap in jurisdiction the decision left. Toth could not be forced to stand trial anywhere in the world for the crime he was alleged to have committed. The nightmare predicted by Congressman Elston had come to pass; future Hirshbergs and Durants would go free despite their crimes. This is a continuing problem.[30]

A final important effect was the reaction of the Court of Military Appeals. In at least three important cases following the *Toth* decision, CoMA had the opportunity to deal with the new doctrine. The first case was *U.S. v. Gallagher*, which was almost a replica of *Hirshberg v. Cooke*. Here the defendant was a Korean War ex-POW who was tried for camp crimes after his re-enlistment. CoMA distinguished *Toth* here, because Gallagher, like Hirshberg, had resumed his status as a GI, whereas Toth had ended his. Gallagher later went into the federal courts, which in effect sustained CoMA's ruling. The issues in *U.S. v. Martin* were similar. A 2-1 majority found that Martin's discharge, because it had been solely for the purpose of re-enlistment, did not terminate his amenability to trial for offenses committed during the earlier enlistment. Then in *U.S. v. Wheeler*, the defendant re-enlisted in order to be tried by court-martial (probably to avoid extradition) for crimes committed in Germany. In this case, CoMA was unanimous; Article 3(a) was valid and applicable, and the conviction was affirmed. Wheeler also had his day in the federal courts, but like Gallagher, lost out there, too.[31]

In its interpretation of *Toth v. Quarles*, the Court of Military Appeals, which never has invalidated a part of the statute that created it despite some threats to do just that, recognized that it was only an instrument of the UCMJ. Even after the Supreme Court apparently smashed Article 3(a), the military court continued to find uses for it. This is not unusual; the Supreme Court did not say 3(a) was invalid in all cases, and CoMA was free to find distinguishing aspects in cases before it. But, in view of its later response to *O'Callahan v. Parker* in 1969, a case we shall look at momentarily, it is noteworthy that in Article 3(a) issues, CoMA chose to defend the original Congressional intent and by so doing, refused to expand the *Toth* doctrine.

An interested spectator to the *Toth* decision was Frederick Wiener. Wiener had been retained by the father of Dorothy Kreuger Smith, who was accused of killing her Army colonel husband while they were living in Japan. Tried by court-martial under Article 2(11) of the UCMJ, she was convicted and the findings were affirmed by the entire appellate hierarchy all the way up through the Court of Military Appeals. Within the military system, the jurisdictional question—whether it was constitutional to try a civilian wife by court-martial—was more or less taken for granted. Of seventeen issues dealt with during CoMA review, only one involved jurisdiction. The case was generally considered a landmark on insanity issues, and Judge Brosman's observation on the "Durham rule" is one of the few Court of Military Appeals opinions ever cited by civilian federal courts. Over Quinn's dissent on the insanity question the Smith conviction was affirmed, 2-1.[32]

At this point, however, Wiener was inspired by the *Toth* decision to shift his emphasis to the jurisdictional issue. If the test were status, as *Toth* indicated, his client was no more subject to court-martial than the ex-airman had been. Accordingly, he filed suit, on behalf of Mrs. Smith's father, in a federal district court, seeking writ of habeas corpus. The government expedited the case by petitioning for a Supreme Court hearing. In granting the request, the High Court consolidated the case with a similar one involving the murder of a GI in England by his wife. The opinions, *Kinsella v. Krueger* and *Reid v. Covert*, were handed down on June 11, 1956 and, following tradition, the court decided not to intervene.[33]

Justice Clark, who wrote the principal opinion for a five-man majority, maintained that the Congressional power to create courts other than those specified in Article III of the Constitution was well established. Given that power, Clark continued, Congress did a laudable job in drawing up the Uniform Code. The underlying notion here was that if Americans accompanying the troops overseas had to be tried for alleged crimes committed on foreign soil, they would enjoy greater protections under the UCMJ than in the foreign courts.

The dissenters, Warren, Black, and Douglas, wrote no opinions for these cases, promising to submit them at the next term. But the most important vote, from a historical point of view, was Justice Frankfurter's. As in *Burns v. Wilson*, Frankfurter had not had enough time to make up his mind. The majority was relying on an obsolete precedent, he wrote, which had no relevance to the issues at hand. Because of that, he reserved his opinion.

On his way out of the courtroom that day, Wiener was accosted by a friend who excitedly told him that he should regard Frankfurter's vote not as indecision but as a mandate to petition for rehearing. Wiener took the hint, and the court agreed to rehear arguments. This was a rare thing; it had been seven years since the last rehearing had been granted, another strong suggestion that the court's interest in military justice was on the increase.[34]

The great importance of the battle rejoined was obvious to all concerned. In its grant, the court invited parties to discuss specific issues of broad significance. Among them were: (1) the practical necessities that justify court-martial authority over civilians; (2) possible alternatives to such jurisdiction; (3) historical evidence on the question; (4) the constitutional issues involved; (5) differences between courts-martial for dependents and those for other civilians, if there were any; (6) differences between petty crimes and major offenses, if pertinent. Clearly, this would be no minor decision.[35]

When it was handed down on June 10, 1957, the court reversed its earlier ruling.[36] Critically important for the shift were the retirement of Justices Minton and Reed and Justice Harlan's change of view. One of the new justices, Charles E. Whittaker, declined to take part. But William J. Brennan, the other newcomer, voted with the former dissenters, thus constituting a majority to reverse. Frankfurter now found time to make up his mind and voted with the new majority; and Harlan, a member of the former majority, joined, too. Harlan's view was that because the case involved a capital offense, Article 2(11) could not be constitutionally applied. Frankfurter was even more careful to limit the scope; he insisted that the decision was to be applied only to dependents in peacetime capital cases and should not be extended in any way from that. The dissenters, Clark and Burton, followed the line they had taken in the earlier decision.

But Justice Black, writing the principal opinion, was extremely critical of military law. The Constitution, he argued rather sardonically, permitted Congress to regulate the land and naval forces, not all other persons who "might have some relationship" to them. Even Winthrop, he reminded the parties, had admitted that no statute could be framed to force a civilian to submit to court-martial. Military trials had always been subject to the outside influence of commanders, he charged. And although some improvements had been made, there was still no trial by jury, no independent judiciary, no indictment by grand jury, and no certainty that the protections of the Bill of Rights applied to courts-martial.

Black's critique of military justice was not incorrect. *Reid v. Covert* was decided before the establishment of the Army's field judiciary program and before the Court of Military Appeals decided in *Jacoby* that the Constitution did apply to military trials. The reforms of the 1960s, discussed in the next chapter, may have derived in part from Black's criticism of the UCMJ in *Reid v. Covert*, although the connection cannot be clearly demonstrated. Still, it remained to be seen how little those reforms would influence the Supreme Court.

For the time being, despite Justice Frankfurter's careful definitions, the fate of the other elements of court-martial jurisdiction over civilians was obvious. After a string of cases decided on January 8, 1960, no civilian of any sort could be tried by court-martial anywhere for any crime. Unlike the legacy of *Toth*, the Supreme Court in its decisions on Article 2(11), left nothing to be interpreted by other courts.[37]

Reid v. Covert came at at time of great activity in the career of the Warren Court. Only a week earlier, in the controversial *Jencks* case, the court had prohibited an FBI practice of secrecy that unfairly restricted defendants in federal cases. A week after *Reid v. Covert*, the court had what one newsmagazine termed a "field day," when it issued opinions that limited the power of legislative committees, both at the federal and state levels, to conduct investigations and subpoena witnesses; announced a landmark decision in freedom of speech; and limited the government's power to dismiss civilian employees. Taken together, this three-week burst amounted to a major assault on the power of the state against those individuals whom it summoned to defend themselves.[38]

And yet, in the sphere of military justice alone, the court had merely returned things to the balance of the Nineteenth Century. As in *Dynes v. Hoover*, the court looked at jurisdiction over the person and the subject matter as the main test in military cases. But as in the forgotten half of the century-old ruling, the High Bench was alert to gross unfairness even where jurisdiction normally would lie. Military jurisdiction was forced back into the Nineteenth Century, too. After 1957, only people who were receiving pay for military service were subject to trial by court-martial. What could be more logical? The renewed compromise, however, would last only a decade.

In the meantime, there were other jurisdictional issues to deal with. In a 1955 administrative action the Departments of Defense and Justice agreed on guide-lines to be followed by the investigative forces of the two agencies. At about the same time a major imbroglio was raging over the Status of Forces Agreements negotiated by the State Department with the NATO states and Japan. These pacts were widely misinterpreted. Their intent and effect was to preserve for the United States primary jurisdiction over GI's and accompanying American civilians for on-duty offenses committed in foreign countries. But a number of prominent American chauvinists chose to emphasize the negative, claiming that the treaties surrendered Americans to foreign powers and arguing that the courts of no other country on earth were good enough to try United States citizens, no matter what the circumstances. Senator John W. Bricker, of Ohio, for example, claimed that the "American GI was sacrificed on the altar of international cooperation." The treaties have been the subject of passionately critical articles, ameliorative legislative proposals, and one important Supreme Court decision. In the latter, *Wilson v. Girard*, handed down only a month after the second *Reid v. Covert*, the court upheld the legality of the SOF agreement with Japan, thus in effect turning Girard over to the Japanese. The combination of those two decisions raised more controversy. To many, the Supreme Court was unpatriotically forcing some Americans like Girard to submit to trial by foreigners, while denying trial by Americans to others, like Mrs. Smith and Mrs. Covert. The strife continues; high-level officials feel required to issue occasional reports concerning the number and condition of GI's in foreign jails. They are, respectively, few and excellent.[39]

The impact of the federal courts on military justice was not limited to the jurisdiction question alone. The establishment of the Court of Military Appeals created within the court-martial system a funnel for all applicable federal decisions and rulings. CoMA proved to be highly selective in this regard, however. It is a source of continuing pride for military apologists that in some areas the military rules are more protective than those prevailing in civilian courts.[40] Most of the credit for this can be given to the Court of Military Appeals for its discriminating application of federal court decisions. For example, the controlling civilian case in the question of bodily fluids taken from a suspect by force or coercion and then used against him as evidence, *Breithaupt v. Abrams*, permits the practice under a wide range of circumstances. But as we have seen, CoMA roundly condemns it. There are a great number of such comparisons that can be made, which do not merit much space in an historical text.[41]

The *Miranda* decision does deserve space, however, for at least two important reasons.. The first is that it provided a wonderful contrast among the attitudes of the three services. The second is that it leaves a baffling question about the Supreme Court.

Miranda v. Arizona is already one of the most famous decisions ever handed down by the High Court. Basically, it continues a line of right-to-counsel decisions that started ten years earlier. Throughout this period, the court expanded the right of a felony suspect to lawyer counsel until, by 1966, the obligation was firmly laid on the state to prove that the defendant had been permitted and even provided counsel at every stage in the proceeding, from the first moments of his arrest, unless he affirmatively waived the right. Specifically, *Miranda* established these rules: if in custody, a suspect must be warned that (1) he may remain silent; (2) if he elects not to remain silent whatever he says may be used against him; (3) he may have counsel even during the interrogation stages; (4) if he is indigent, the state will appoint a lawyer to assist him. If that were not enough, the court warned all future law enforcement agencies that should the suspect indicate that he wishes to remain silent, the interrogation must cease.[42]

The first two parts of the *Miranda* rules were not new to the military. In fact, Chief Justice Warren in his principal opinion favorably referred to Article 31 warnings that had been mandatory in the services since 1951. But several parts of the new order, if applicable to the military, would require changes in military practice. The problem was: did *Miranda* apply? The decision had mentioned the possibility of a "fully effective equivalent"; perhaps Article 31 and certain traditional military rights to counsel which were also approved in the Warren opinion would suffice. The responses of the services to this possibility were predictable.

The Army, in effect, took the path of least resistance and decided to comply with *Miranda* pending clarification. The Navy, however, probably viewing the *Miranda* mandate as the genesis of new and exorbitant requirements for lawyers, elected to fight. In a message sent to all commands, the Secretary of the Navy, on the recommendation of the Judge Advocate General, directed naval lawyers that they should follow the old guide-lines and disregard *Miranda*. The Navy had good reason to hope for a favorable resolution of the issue. Besides the language of the decision itself, with its outright approval of some military procedures and implication that others would be accepted, there was Chief Justice Warren's studious and generally benevolent 1962 critique of the UCMJ in an address at New York University Law School which had condoned variations from civilian practice if, "because of the peculiarities of the military service," they were "best suited to the administration of military justice." But the Navy JAG must have overlooked the next clause of Warren's text, which promised that the same test "may bring about a departure from a prior service rule." In effect, such a "departure" is what occurred.[43]

The Air Force chose the most direct, and as it turned out, the wisest path. Like their Army counterparts, Air Force personnel were directed to comply with *Miranda* pending clarification of the applicability issue. But in addition, the Air Force JAG certified to the Court of Military Appeals the case of an airman where *Miranda* issues were sharp and clear. This was *U.S. v. Tempia*, which had been tried the day after *Miranda's* effective date, but not following the new rules. The Navy sent a representative to act as *amicus curiae*, arguing against applicability. Ultimately, however, the court, in a 2-1 decision, reversed Tempia's conviction, holding that *Miranda* did apply to military proceedings.[44]

The second important aspect of *Miranda* had already been mentioned: Warren's laudatory comments on military justice. As if in rebuttal to the harsh criticism of the Uniform Code made by the Supreme Court in the *Reid v. Covert* and *Toth v. Quarles* cases, Judge Quinn in his *Tempia* dissent cited the great improvements that had occurred under the Court of Military Appeals. Quinn was on firm ground; there had been significant changes since 1957, most notably the movement toward an independent judiciary and circuit court system in the Army and Navy. While Warren did not address himself in *Miranda* or in his NYU speech to these developments,

Quinn might have taken the Chief Justice's praise, added in those reforms that had actually occurred and others which were then making their way through Congress, and concluded that the Supreme Court would be more favorably disposed towards the military justice system in the future.

But if this scenario really were the way Quinn foresaw things, he was woefully wrong. In a 1969 decision, *O'Callahan v. Parker*, the Supreme Court delivered a blockbuster. The plaintiff in this case was an Army sergeant when he broke into a girl's hotel room in Waikiki and attempted to rape her. Tried and convicted by court-martial, he was sentenced to ten years in prison. From his cell he sought habeas corpus in the lower courts but was repeatedly rejected without hearing. When the case reached the eight-man Supreme Court, however, the writ was granted. The majority, in an opinion written by Justice Douglas, ignored the "status" test set in the *Toth* and *Covert* cases. Instead the court ruled that in order for court-martial jurisdiction to lie, an offense must be "service-connected."[4][5]

Justice Douglas here gave a literal reading to the Fifth Amendment phrase "cases arising in the land and naval forces." That terminology, he proclaimed, referred not to the offender alone, as was thought after *Covert*. The fact that the offender was in the land and naval forces was no longer enough; the offense must be, too.

Unfortunately, Douglas was not so literal in giving guide-lines that might be followed. The decision did not even indicate whether it was to be effective retroactively or not. The court illustrated what "service-connected" meant mostly by negatives. At the time of the crime, O'Callahan was not in a duty status; the crime was not connected to his military duties; it was not wartime; the crime was committed within United States territory where the local courts were open and operating; and finally, there was no question of flouting military authority.[46]

Douglas argued that GI's who faced courts-martial got second-rate justice. He observed that this might be acceptable in cases where only military men were competent to judge innocence or guilt, as in disobedience issues, for example. But the court must restrict military jurisdiction as much as possible, he declared, lest it "deprive every member of the armed services of the benefits of an indictment by a grand jury and a trial by a jury of his peers."

It was peculiar that Chief Justice Warren, after his praise for the UCMJ in *Miranda*, went along with this sweeping condemnation of military justice. Justice Brennan's acquiescence was also baffling since he would join Warren and the *O'Callahan* dissenters only two weeks later in *Noyd v. Bond*, the decision that condoned the all-writs power of CoMA. These inexplicable shifts in opinion were a source of irritation to Judge Quinn and many of the staff at the Court of Military Appeals.

As we have seen, CoMA chose to interpret the 1955 *Toth* decision narrowly. But following *O'Callahan*, a broad-sweeping ruling to begin with, the military court seemed actually to expand the impact of the High Court's decision. In one case, for example, a Ferguson-Darden majority found that the offense was not service-connected even though the victims of manslaughter and assault were military dependents who had received extensive hospital treatment at taxpayer and service expense. The majority ruled that the crimes were committed off-base, on liberty, and that the state courts nearby were in operation. Therefore, they held, *O'Callahan* applied and jurisdiction did not lie.[47]

To summarize: it can be seen that the federal courts over the last twenty years have intervened increasingly in the work of the military courts. The original impetus for the greater involvement was the expanded jurisdiction claimed for courts-martial by the drafters of the Uniform Code, coupled with the large numbers of persons brought under that jurisdiction during the Cold War; this combination upset the tacit agreement struck by the courts and the military during the Nineteenth Century. But once having forced the UCMJ back into the old mold by a series of decisions from 1955 to 1960, the Supreme Court itself extended its power beyond the ancient compromise.

The court argued that this was done only to protect servicemen. If one read *Reid v. Covert* and *O'Callahan v. Parker* in quick succession, he might think that there had been no improvement in military justice during the intervening dozen years. In fact, however, great changes had occurred, and the seeds of even more fundamental reforms had been sown, as we shall see. Moreover, one wonders whether the advances themselves did not make the intervention possible. In the Nineteenth Century no federal judge was likely to understand the arcane procedure and substance of military justice. As the system grew closer to civilian law, civilian judges become more adept at "reading" the military techniques. Some of them, like Douglas and Black, saw only those areas where courts-martial were still different and complained.

Actually, Justice Douglas and his colleagues had not kept abreast of developments. Even before *O'Callahan* was argued, the Military Justice Act of 1968, which corrected some of the weaknesses cited in the opinion, had been signed into law. In the American political system, when the courts are hyperactive, it usually indicates a general malaise in the other branches of government. As regards military justice, the failure of the various reform attempts during the 1950s and the resulting *Toth* and *Covert* decisions confirm this theory. But the 1960s were fruitful years for those who sought improvements in court-martial law, and *O'Callahan* did not fit the generalization. The already enacted Military Justice Act was to become effective only sixty days after the critical decision was issued.

17 Senator Ervin and the Military Justice Act of 1968

The new legislative campaign to overhaul the Uniform Code that began in 1961 did not end with the 1963 changes in Article 15. For the next five years, ideas first advanced long before began to gain momentum, until finally in 1968 a major reform was enacted by the Ninetieth Congress. The road was not uniformly smooth, and the signposts along the way were not always easy to read. But there was substantial coherence to the movement. What resulted, above all, was the enhancement of the prestige and power enjoyed by the military lawyer, producing in turn a significant improvement in certain heretofore unsatisfactory aspects of the code.

Tactics employed in this campaign were combinations of those proven successful in the past. Again and again, it was demonstrated that nothing could be wrung from Congress unless all the services plus the Court of Military Appeals agreed on the point in question. And sometimes that was not enough.

During the 1960s, an important figure joined the military justice reformers: Senator Sam J. Ervin, Jr., Democrat from North Carolina, who by happy coincidence was a member of both the Judiciary and the Armed Services Committees. Ervin had considerable political influence, primarily as a result of his own personal integrity and background. A Harvard Law graduate, he served in a variety of judicial positions in his home state before he became a United States Senator in 1954. This broad experience, coupled with his even temperament, led Majority Leader Lyndon Johnson to appoint Ervin to his first important Senate position: membership on the select committee that investigated and ultimately condemned Senator Joseph McCarthy in 1954. Thereafter Ervin's stature grew as a result of his vigorous defense of constitutional rights. An enlightened strict constructionist, he more recently gained publicity for his stands on the Fortas nomination, the controversial District of Columbia crime bill, and the Army's alleged surveillance of civilians. His forthright positions on these difficult issues gained him respect not only on both sides of the Senate aisle but also on both sides of the ideological split in American politics. Within the military justice sphere itself, he was also well regarded. At the Pentagon, his Army record endeared him to those men for whom such things are important. A World War I veteran, Ervin was twice wounded, highly decorated, and an active member of several organizations of ex-servicemen. The Court of Military Appeals honored him in 1963 by making him the 10,000th member of that court's bar, in a suitable ceremony. With all these credentials, Ervin was a valuable acquisition in the movement to reform the Uniform Code.[1] But the Senator had a great deal to learn about how these changes could be accomplished.

Ervin first became interested in military justice because of his concern with some of the jurisdictional questions discussed in the previous chapter. In 1957, the Judiciary Subcommittee on Constitutional Rights, of which he was chairman, sent an observer to attend the Japanese trial of William Girard. Enticed into the field by that experience, Ervin and his subcommittee expanded their purview in the next few years to include virtually all aspects of GI justice.[2]

The first major step was a wide-ranging round of hearings conducted in February and March, 1962, on the "Constitutional Rights of Military Personnel." These hearings were held by a subdivision of the same Judiciary Committee which, when headed by Senator McCarran in 1949 and 1950, had been unable to acquire the UCMJ for consideration. McCarran was an obstructionist in the eyes of the Senate managers of the code bill, but Ervin's reputation was such that both traditionalists and reformers expected fair and equitable treatment from him.

Through the 1962 hearings, the Senator's fairness and balance manifested themselves repeatedly. Witnesses representing differing views on military justice were invited, came to testify, and were unfailingly given a sympathetic ear. Many of these men came from familiar organizations: CoMA, the JAG's, members of service and bar associations. But Ervin also heard from a number of independents, such as law Professor Kenneth A. Pye, the ACLU's Lawrence Speiser, and the ubiquitous Frederick Wiener.

Ervin's personal approach was also temperate. For example, in his opening remarks, he asserted that obviously great improvement had been made in court-martial law since the days when Blackstone wrote that soldiers occupied a "state of servitude in the midst of a nation of freemen" and intimated that much of this was because of the guardianship of the Court of Military Appeals. But later, when General Harmon, no supporter of the court, implied that CoMA was responsible for some of the lax law enforcement in the services, the Senator agreed at least to the extent that "enough has been done for those who murder, rape and rob, and it is time that somebody was concerned about doing something for those who do not wish to be murdered, raped or robbed."[3]

His desire to tread the line between retaining protective guarantees for the accused and establishing methods for swift and sure punishment of offenders continued to mark Ervin's efforts in military justice. The Senator intended that the hearings be more than a superficial glance at the problem. He marked out four subject areas of his inquiry: unfair command control of courts-martial, the extent of a defendant's right to legally trained counsel, the ways military justice continued to vary from service to service, and the effectiveness of UCMJ due process.

In addition to questions concerning the code itself, the subcommittee was interested in a number of items ancillary to the court-martial system, such as the administrative discharge, correction of military records, and a Navy JAG Corps. The hearings, consequently, were broad and comprehensive and when published filled a volume fully three-quarters the size of the combined House and Senate hearings and reports on the original code.[4]

Ervin's hearings were undertaken during the same Congressional session that enacted the Article 15 reforms. As we have seen, the military decided that it was best to focus on a few specific areas of reform, rather than spreading the effort and interest over a wide field. But others clung to the old tactics. During the Ervin hearings, testimony supporting the now fragmented H.R. 3387 was heard from the American Bar Association, and the American Legion came to argue for its generally opposing but equally comprehensive plan. Ervin's own approach as the result of this first exposure to problems of military justice was a mixture of the two methods. Like the Code Committee's, his recommendations were contained in a series of bills, each of which contained only one or two proposals. But the total package included ideas for sweeping reform of all aspects of the code and was in scope much more like the omnibus and American Legion bills.[5]

The proposal consisted of eighteen bills. Several of them, such as permitting single officer courts-martial, widening the ban of illicit influence over a court to include all persons, not just commanders, and extending to two years the time for a petition for a new trial, were the same measures the Code Committee had been urging on Congress since 1953. But the fact that Ervin plowed some new ground is illustrated by the number of innovations his package contained.[6]

First of all, the program was heavily weighted towards correcting shortcomings in administrative board procedures and results. Strictly speaking, the administrative discharge is outside the realm of military justice. But ever since General Harmon's 1958 speech in Los Angeles, observers had increasingly acknowledged that the administrative separation provided a too readily available escape from the strictures of the Uniform Code. Ervin listened intently as Harmon, by then retired, described how the inadequacies of the UCMJ led necessarily to the abuses of the undesirable discharge. Ervin's interest in the administrative discharge problem was not merely fleeting. Following the hearings, he sent to the JAG offices of all the services a detailed questionnaire, probing into their administrative elimination methods, trends, and workloads.[7]

Out of the eighteen bills submitted to Congress, five dealt with administrative discharges. One of them would give a serviceman the right to elect a court-martial whenever faced with an administrative board. Another would extend double jeopardy protection to the administrative procedure so that a man could not be subsequently tried for an offense first taken to a board nor be administratively separated for an offense originally referred to court-martial. The same bill would prohibit a second administrative board from awarding a more severe "sentence" than the first. A third bill would establish Court of Military Appeals review over the work of discharge and records correction boards. The fourth bill would require open hearings, a law officer to preside over them, confrontation between the serviceman and hostile witnesses, and a preboard warning of rights similar to those in Article 31 of the code. The final proposal would establish a Board for the Correction of Military Records in the Office of the Secretary of Defense rather than at the service level as it then existed. These bills, although scattered among the eighteen proposals, presented the first indication of an idea only then beginning to germinate in Senator Ervin's mind: a kind of Uniform Code for Administrative Boards.

Other parts of the Ervin package dealt with more orthodox points of military justice. The old Powell idea of eliminating the summary court was included, but as a part of an entirely different *quid pro quo*. Rather than being coupled to an increase in commander's punishment, which was already on the books by the time the Ervin plan was submitted, this abolition bill was tied to a formalization of the special court-martial, the development most feared by the Powell committee. Under Ervin's proposal, special courts would have a law officer and would be prohibited from awarding punitive discharges unless trained lawyer defense counsel was provided the accused. Except for its size, and perhaps the rank of its members, the special court would be identical in rules, procedures, and formalities to the general court. With the elimination of the summary court-martial, there would no longer be a "line-officer" tribunal. Everything in the Uniform Code, except for nonjudicial punishment, would be in the hands of the lawyers, if Ervin's plan passed.

This expansion of the role of military lawyers was the goal of other Ervin bills. Pretrial sessions dealing with admissibility of evidence or special motions could be conducted by the law officer alone, even before the court itself had met. Single-officer general and special courts, an idea long recommended by the Code Committee, were proposed. In the view of the JAG's, the single officer courts would save the valuable time of line officers who otherwise would have to sit for long hours and days as a jury. The Court of Military Appeals thought of the measure as a way to make findings and sentences more consistent and to protect the individual by fore-stalling possible command influence. But, while Ervin no doubt believed in those goals, in the context of his total program the single-officer courts were a way of bestowing greater confidence, power, and prestige on the military lawyers who would serve in them.

Lawyers would proliferate not only at courts-martial under the Ervin plan. They would be required at administrative discharge boards and probably also at Article 32 pretrial investigations. Finally, new symbols of respect would be conferred by changing the title "law officer" to "military judge" and "board of review" to "Court of Military Review." Under Ervin's plan, the court-martial and administrative discharge systems would become almost the sole province of military lawyers, who would receive, along with the greater responsibility, an increase in power and independence sufficient to discharge it.

Nowhere in the package was this made more clear than in the bill which called for a Navy JAG Corps, an idea whose time had come. With the end in the 1950s of the dominance of men like Admiral Nunn who were sailors first and lawyers second, the in-house opposition to a corps dwindled. By the time of the Ervin hearings, Admiral Mott could claim that there was no serious opposition to the JAG Corps anywhere in the government. Mott himself endorsed the idea heartily, saying it would help recruiting and retention and provide better service for the client, thus promoting Ervin's goals of greater justice in the service. No one argued in rebuttal that officers restricted to legal work might not have enough to do, as Admiral Russell had in 1949. Nor did anyone claim that JAG Corps might produce men whose primary goal was something other than the winning of wars, as Admiral Nunn believed would be true of professional lawyers in uniform.[8]

A JAG Corps would enhance recruiting, it was hoped, since it would help cure a morale problem among Navy law specialists regarding their identity. Because they wore line insignia, but were not competent mariners, naval lawyers were regarded by sea-going officers as something rather inferior. A corps, with its own distinctive markings and separate promotions, would alleviate that.[9]

Admiral Mott was mystified as to why there had been no Congressional action on the JAG Corps bill already before Congress. He was probably more baffled that it was not passed finally until almost six years later. Part of the reason for the delay, no doubt, was the simple fact of Capitol Hill inertia. But another reason was the lack of service harmony on the issue. The Army's JAG Corps was almost an accidental creation, due mainly to the legislative coup engineered by Senator Kem in 1948. The Navy opposed the idea then and had been joined by the Air Force. But the sea service's change of heart on this question was not matched by a similar conversion on the part of the Air Force. Well into the second decade of supposed "unification" there were still wide differences of opinion on this point.

Air Force judge advocates have a unique Military Occupation Specialty number which effectively limits them to legal work. Ever since the 1952 directive took them off flight status, Air Force lawyers have faced no problem analogous to the Navy line-law confusion. Air Force JA's are assigned by the office of the JAG, not by the Personnel Department, and they wear on their uniform chests a miniature scales emblem. In those respects they are members of a *de facto* JAG Corps, despite official opposition to the concept. But lawyers are on the same promotion lists with other Air Force officers; in that regard they are integrated with the general service members. Their status does not seem to have made an adverse impact on their legal performance. During his testimony before Ervin's subcommittee, the Air Force Judge Advocate General, Albert M. Kuhfeld, cited some statistics that illustrated the excellence of at least one phase of the job his lawyers were doing. Despite the fact that the Air Force had not adopted the independent judiciary system, and despite its lack of a JAG Corps, Air Force convictions before the Court of Military Appeals had been reversed less frequently than the others during the most recent six-year period. While such a small sample for a rather brief period cannot stand alone as proof, it is consistent with the other forward-looking aspects of the Air Force legal program we have already discussed. The service seemed on solid ground in rejecting both the circuit judiciary and the corps plans. The fact that the Air Force was able to do as well as the others in the quality of its legal work despite its rejection of these innovations seems ample proof that the Navy's goal in establishing a JAG Corps would be primarily symbolic and prestige-seeking.[10]

But these were not unworthy aims; increased lawyer status was a way to end the chronic shorthandedness in the JAG departments, which actually had worsened during the 1960s. The Vietnam War, of course, involved not merely a redeployment of American forces but an expansion of them as well. Just the sheer numbers would seem to promise an increase in legal problems. But ironically, no such thing happened. In fact, court-martial business declined, both in volume and in the number of serious or complex cases. The Army, for example, expanded from an average strength of 1,015,287 in fiscal 1964 to 1,430,009 in fiscal 1967. But while the Army convened 43,118 courts-martial in 1964, that figure rose only to 49,943 in 1967. Put another way, the rate of courts per capita actually decreased, from 1 court per 28.5 soldiers to 1 per 23.5. No single reason can be given for this decline. Maybe a higher quality of recruit was taken into the services. The administrative discharges were being used in many cases that in the earlier period would have gone to court. Perhaps the 1963 reforms in nonjudicial punishment had really taken effect. And, it should be remembered, the figures given come from a year before the presumed dip in GI morale set in as the war dragged on.[11]

Despite these surprising statistics, the requirement for officer lawyers continued to mount. One reason was the impact of the *Miranda* and *Tempia* decisions. These cases established doctrines that forced the services to provide lawyer counsel for an accused at every stage of an investigation and trial. Following *Tempia*, the Navy's "Muse report" urged the appointment of about 120 more lawyers in the Navy and 70 more in the Marine Corps. Only a fraction of that number was actually approved, leading the Judge Advocate General to encourage extra effort on the part of all hands to carry out new policies.[12]

In addition, the Armed Forces were increasingly aware that the quality and extent of legal services provided to GI's and their families was part of the total picture a man considered when he decided whether to make the service a career or not. The Navy's Alford board on retention in 1966 urged the creation of "law centers" to provide professional legal assistance in all matters of interest to sailors. This was put into effect in 1967 and 1968; by August 1969 there were thirty such centers in operation. Although collecting the available legal personnel and equipment under one roof like this meant greater efficiency in handling existing work loads, it also led to more business as prospective clients learned of the facilities and their accessibility. It was this effort to better the quality of Navy life by improving legal services that stimulated the need for greater numbers of lawyers. The prestige of a Navy JAG Corps, it was hoped, would help make them available.[13]

Another means of attracting and keeping good lawyers was to pay them. Throughout the 1960s there were continuing efforts to provide supplemental "professional pay" for judge advocates. Many military lawyers left the service because of the low compensation they received as compared to what they might have earned in civilian practice. In 1969, the Air Force estimated that the differential could be expressed as shown in Figure 5. The point was clear: even at the lowest levels, the pay was second-rate, but as the man got older, his financial situation grew relatively much worse.[14]

Swords and Scales

FIGURE 5. MILITARY LAWYER'S SALARY POTENTIAL
COMPARED WITH HIS CIVILIAN COUNTERPART

Age	*Military Lawyer Earns*	*Civilian Lawyer Earns*
25 – 34	$x per year	$x + 1200 per year
60	$y per year	$y + 17000 per year

As early as 1957, a bill was introduced to pay the GI lawyers something extra to help cushion the expected loss. Arguing strenuously on behalf of the proposal was the Judge Advocates Association, essentially a JAG alumni group. But lawyer incentive pay lacked the broad support from a variety of sources that is usually required for military justice laws, and none of the bills containing the proposal was enacted.[15]

Neither were the ones submitted by Ervin in 1963. His bills fell victim to the death-by-study that Felix Larkin had successfully avoided with the UCMJ. As Ervin remembered later, the proposals were "subjected to intensive study" in the Pentagon and elsewhere, and a number of "alternative suggestions and revised language" were proposed to him.[16] What the Senator meant was that the bills got lost in the bureaucracy. This was the first of the old lessons that Ervin had to learn for himself.

The rejection of his plan by the JAG's was not surprising. They had their own ideas, many of which did not agree with Ervin's. Following the tactics that had brought success to the bad-check law and Article 15 increases, the Code Committee submitted to Congress new abbreviations of the old omnibus bill. Bill "B," now providing only for single-officer courts, was one. Bill "D" was proposed in 1962, asking for law-officer authority to conduct out-of-court hearings. In 1963, these were combined into a single bill "C," to which was added the prohibition against a special court's handing down a punitive discharge unless the accused had been provided with lawyer counsel. There seems to have been no bill "E," but "F" would modify the procedure for executing certain sentences. "H" would give a convict two years to petition for a new trial and increase the power of the Judge Advocate General in those cases he reviewed under Article 69.[17]

Although these proposals (which, it should be remembered, were made jointly by the Court of Military Appeals and the JAG's) had many points in common with Ervin's eighteen, Defense still withheld its support of his package. It was not until 1966 that the Code

Committee and Ervin got together, when he introduced, with the Pentagon's approval, bills "G" and "H." The Senator thought that these bills by themselves were inadequate answers to the need for reform in military justice. But military approval of both the bills and his sponsorship of them were critically important for they gave Ervin a lever with which to move the Armed Services Committee into action. Beforehand, Defense opposition to his plan had forced him to conduct hearings in his Judiciary Committee capacity, although it was well known that without the concurrence of the Armed Services Committee there could be no serious legislative action. Even with the Pentagon's endorsement of Ervin's work, Armed Services was not enthusiastic. The best Ervin could extract was permission to hold joint hearings under the rubric of both Judiciary and Armed Services. At that, the latter expressly reserved for itself the power to veto the bills being discussed.[18]

The 1966 hearings were largely *déjà vu*. The cast of witnesses was much the same as had testified in 1962, and the subject material was also very similar. But the Senator and his guests all claimed to have learned much. For example, in 1962, there were several frank admissions of ignorance about administrative discharges. The New York City Bar Association representative, the Navy Judge Advocate General, and both Judges Kilday and Ferguson all confessed to know little or nothing of the practice. But by 1966 everyone had an answer. Kilday offered remedies even while expressing some lingering ignorance. Judge Ferguson, moreover, seemed to have become an expert in the interim. He went so far as to charge that General Harmon, the first to expose and publicly condemn the practice, was guilty of encouraging the administrative route around courts-martial![19]

Senator Ervin's increased expertise was more genuine. It is perhaps best indicated by comparing the questionnaire sent to the services in 1966 with the one sent in 1962. The earlier one dealt mainly with administrative discharges, and when it did go into purely court-martial matters, it did so only superficially. But in 1966, the questions appropriately gave more weight and space to the UCMJ itself. They were also tied to specific bills in the Ervin package, thus indicating a coherence in planning that was lacking in 1962. So detailed was this inquiry that the most frequent answer given by each of the services was "statistics are not kept on this matter" or words to that effect.[20]

If the 1966 hearings resembled the earlier ones, so did the effects;

they were nil. In fact, Ervin's tactics regressed. Following his 1966 hearings, he redrafted the proposals and submitted them in one massive bill, called "The Military Justice Act of 1967."The title was no overstatement. The bill was a consolidation of all the ingredients that had gone into the earlier eighteen proposals, but this time there was only one bill, composed of five "Titles." Title I, a completely new chapter for the U.S. Code, would make statutory and uniform all the protections Ervin wanted to build into the administrative discharge procedure. The new chapter was fully as detailed and comprehensive in its field as the UCMJ was in its. Title II of the bill would have established a Navy JAG Corps. Title III incorporated all the various improvements in the status and powers of the law officer. Title IV dealt with review procedures. And Title V envisioned a Defense Department Board for the Correction of Military Records.[21]

After all that had been learned in the 1950s about the impossibility of enacting omnibus military justice legislation, the fate of this bill could be predicted. Why Ervin even bothered is difficult to say, but the best guess is that he was new at the game and simply had not yet learned how it was played. On the other hand, perhaps he reasoned that since the military had already declared its opposition to many of his ideas, he might as well put them down in one coherent package. Certainly he had major hopes for Title I, whatever the fate of the rest of the bill, and this may have led him to put the proposal forward, as a way of beginning discussion that would ultimately lead to success. The Senator may have simply been holding out obstinately, trying to secure passage of all of his ideas.[22]

The way the bill was drafted also thwarted the possibility of agreement between Ervin and the Pentagon. Although there were many areas of similarity, they could not easily be segregated from more controversial aspects. Even before the consolidation in 1966, there were a number of points where the services agreed only in part with many of the individual Ervin proposals. The solution was obvious: cull out the sections on which they agreed. In an attempt to do just that, Defense representatives submitted to the 1966 subcommittee substitutes for some of the Senator's eighteen bills. These alternates were nearly identical to the old "G" and "H" bills, however, and Ervin was not yet ready for that sort of "compromise" and as a result moved into an even more inflexible position by drafting the omnibus legislation mentioned above. Once that was done, the points of agreement were more inextricably mixed in with the controversial ones than ever before.

There were, however, encouraging signs during this period that all the forces were moving towards a mutually acceptable reform. After almost two decades of study and argument, all parties had come to know each other well, and all positions and demands were clearly understood on all sides. By 1966, for example, there was virtually complete agreement between two such dissimilar groups as the ACLU and the American Legion in their views on the Ervin program. Likewise, all the parties, except perhaps Senator Ervin, had learned the methods by which success was most likely. The old tactic of going it alone, which the military had tried in 1956, was so discredited by this time that the proposals of a Defense Department study group were not even given the courtesy of formal Congressional introduction.[23]

In 1967, a half-dozen bills dealing with military justice matters were submitted to Congress. There was some duplication of effort. Congressman Charles Bennett introduced a bill to establish a Navy JAG Corps that differed only in form from the proposal included in Ervin's consolidation. Each house had a bill that would emphasize the status of the Court of Military Appeals as a federal court and improve some of the administrative aspects of the institution. It proved relatively easy to pass the JAG Corps bill finally, and most of the CoMA bill was approved, too. But the major legislation had to wait until Senator Ervin and the Pentagon could settle their differences.[24]

As reported later by a high-ranking Navy official, a compromise was worked out in early 1968. The basic concept of the deal was to permit the services some flexibility in complying with the new measures. For example, the law would require law officers at special courts, but the convening authority had the option of dispensing with a law officer if "military exigencies" demanded it. Similarly, counsel would be provided at the special courts, but only if the accused asked for one.[25]

Armed now with general Pentagon approval of important parts of his package, Ervin got the Senate Armed Services Committee to clear a new bill, H.R. 15971, which had already been passed by the House. After that it was easy, and final enactment came in October 1968. This was "The Military Justice Act of 1968," which became effective in August 1969.[26]

The name of the new law was somewhat overstated. Ervin's omnibus bill had originally been called "The Military Justice Act of 1967," and the title apparently endured after the compromise with the military. But the 1968 act was only a pale reflection of the earlier resolution. Some of the provisions were merely common sense revisions of old practices, designed to make things easier for operators in the field. For example, verbatim transcripts which under the original code were required for all general courts (including those which ended in acquittals), would now be mandatory only in cases involving certain severe sentences. A so-called "bail system" was another instance; this was little more than legislative reinstatement of the technical suspension whereby the convening authority in some cases could defer execution of a sentence pending completion of review without putting the man into a probationary status.[27]

On the other hand, the main thrust of the new law was to make the court-martial system as completely as possible the responsibility of lawyers. Single-officer courts, military judges with powers very nearly identical to those possessed by their civilian counterparts, and trained counsel at special courts were all aspects of this reform, and all were enacted.

And yet, nothing whatever became of Ervin's proposals on the administrative discharge. Like the bar association reformers in 1950, the Senator had to be happy with what he could get. The report which accompanied the bill out of committee frankly admitted that it included only those provisions which were "noncontroversial." This was misleading, of course. What was noncontroversial in 1968 was the result of seventeen years of hammering debate. But the administrative discharge had still not reached the point where there was sufficient unanimity and pressure to accomplish any legislative reforms.[28]

Again, though, there were signs that day was beginning to dawn. Many of the changes most urgently desired were beginning to be incorporated into the administrative board procedure by regulation. The system was regarded with such disfavor by the end of the decade that practically all writers on military justice criticized the administrative elimination machinery. And a number of Congressmen introduced what they considered solutions to the problem. These events were the genesis of reform; the separation of "undesirables" by administrative means will be a major issue in the future.[29]

18 Epilogue

At this point, it seems fair to ask the questions, "Where are we now?" and "Where do we go from here?" Historians should avoid crystal-ball gazing, but there are certain elements from the past that may serve as indicators of a probable future.

To begin, the Military Justice Act of 1968 got a magnificent test in the trial of Lieutenant William Calley. While the world tried to comprehend the horror of My Lai, students of the Uniform Code focused on the performance of the military judge, Colonel Reid W. Kennedy. Early in the pretrial stages, defense lawyers let it be known that they would seek to put the blame for the massacre on the Army itself.[1] Calley was merely following orders, they argued, and what he did in that hamlet that morning was at worst an extreme example of common U.S. Army practice in Vietnam. Moreover, they asserted, many people up and down the chain of command knew about it and failed to see in it anything worth reporting or investigating.

This sort of defense would have been unthinkable twenty years before.[2] Even under the original code it is doubtful that it would have been allowed. The law officer, a colonel in the Army, appointed from the local staff judge advocate's office where he was normally subject to the convening authority, would risk his career if he permitted a defense such as the one Calley used. But because the 1968 law had made military judges independent of possible command pressure, Kennedy was free to admit any defense Calley and his lawyers selected. The results were that the Army was maneuvered into the dock along with the lieutenant defendant and

199

that Calley got an undeniably fair trial. Whether Kennedy will have to pay the price later for his courageous handling of these difficult issues is something that will be worth watching.[3]

The enhancement of the military judge answers one of the complaints levelled by the Supreme Court in *O'Callahan*. A serviceman does get a trial before an "independent judge" now. Although there is still no provision for trial by a jury of peers, the right to elect a trial by an independent judge alone in lieu of the multimember court-martial has alleviated the worst part of the potential unfairness of being tried before a panel of officers selected by the commander who preferred charges in the first place.

Justice Douglas' remaining complaint, about lack of grand jury protection in the service, was nothing less than frivolous. The military is specifically exempted from that requirement by the Fifth Amendment to the Constitution. Unless he was implying dissatisfaction with the Constitution, Douglas is therefore guilty of deviousness in charging that the absence of grand jury indictment is a weakness in military law. Moreover, it is not altogether clear to the author just what protection a grand jury gives the accused. The recent Kent State and Hobart College grand juries seem to have been creatures of blind hatred and ignorant fear.[4]. Admittedly, Article 32 proceedings, the closest thing to an indictment process in military law, are subject to tampering, and their recommendations may even be rejected by the convening authority.[5] But a civilian grand jury has at least equally weak aspects and can hardly be held up as a paragon of effective judicial practice.

If the 1968 law established freedom for military judges, thus guaranteeing new protections for the accused, it did absolutely nothing about the role of the commanding officer, the same now as it was in 1951, except for the appointment of the military judge. There is, then, ample room still for him to manipulate a jury if he desires. But that sort of injustice had been made largely academic since the creation of the Court of Military Appeals. Whenever that court even suspects command tampering, it reverses.[6] Commanders who fail to heed this do not act prudently and stand a good chance of having convictions thrown out, with a consequent loss of their own time and energy. Here is a good example of an abuse that may not be eliminated but at least is rectifiable. This is not to say that commanders cannot tamper with the lower courts, which do not ordinarily enjoy CoMA perusal. But with the extension of all-writs power to the special court-martial, CoMA has served implicit notice that it will look into command irregularities even there.[7]

A more subtle command power over courts-martial is the discretionary power *not* to refer a case to trial. This is at the root of the administrative discharge problem. It seems generally agreed among all but the most hostile critics that once a GI's case reaches a point where the Uniform Code takes over, he will be treated about as fairly as he might be in any other jurisdiction.[8] Therefore, if it were required that a court-martial be convened whenever an offense is committed, many of the abuses now condemned would be curtailed. And so would the discrepancy which still exists between the treatment given senior officers and that received by lower-ranking personnel. The "West Point Protective and Benevolent Association." which may have been at work in the exoneration of most of Calley's superiors, and its analogs in the other services, would go out of business if trials were somehow made mandatory.[9]

A final comment on arbitrary power is perhaps in order. Following the Presidio "mutiny" in 1968, there was a great deal of commentary on the shocking conditions in military prisons. Much of the criticism was valid, as the Army's own blue-ribbon commission itself pointed out.[10] But it is singularly inappropriate to argue that it is the military "mentality" that is the cause of these brutalities. Lord Acton's aphorism that "all power corrupts, and absolute power corrupts absolutely" applies here. Whenever one human being is given great authority over another, there is an excellent chance that he will abuse it and in so doing violate the basic human rights of his subject. This is, however, a universal phenomenon; similar conditions exist in prisons across the country, if not the world.[11] It is foolish to contend that it exists in its worst form in the Armed Forces of the United States.[12]. But, barring the onset of the millennium, the best one can hope for within a judicial system is that coercion and brutality will, when uncovered, lead either to rulings that evidence so procured is inadmissible or to writs of habeas corpus. The guardians of American military justice seem to be doing this as well as the officials of any other judicial system.

Foremost among those guardians, of course, is the Court of Military Appeals. Having enjoyed some eighteen years of relative personnel stability, the court is now in a period of great flux. In addition to the recent changes involving Judges Darden and Duncan, there is the great possibility that Judge Quinn may retire soon. He is now almost eighty years old and in 1968 did offer to resign if President Johnson wanted to appoint a younger man.[13] But Quinn, whose term does not expire until 1981, is a loyal party man, and would probably like to hang on long enough for the Democrats to elect a man to the White House, so that his seat would not pass to a Republican. What effect changes of this sort would have on the substance of the court's work remains to be seen.

On the question of future reform, it seems obvious that something will happen soon about the administrative discharge. With the increase in narcotics usage in the services, a large number of GI's are candidates for the lifetime sentence of an undesirable discharge, or if they are fortunate, the only slightly tainted general discharge. Senator Ervin's complex bill, however, had all the ingredients which led to failure in the past, so the solution will probably be something less rigorous. Perhaps continued regulatory reform will prove the ultimate solution. At the very least, one would hope that the services would stop awarding administrative discharges for conduct which is more properly triable by court-martial.

There are a number of prominent national political figures jumping on the military justice bandwagon. Senators Birch Bayh, of Indiana, and Mark Hatfield, of Oregon, have each submitted major bills in a recent Congress.[14] What the outcome will be is anybody's guess. But, again using history as a guide, neither package seems likely to be successful. They are both too sweeping and too complicated, and they have little support from within the military justice establishment. The services want time to adjust to the new requirements of the code and to settle the *O'Callahan* problem.[15] There is, therefore, the likelihood that the near future will be a period of regulatory, as opposed to statutory, reform. The Air Force, for example, is now supplying lawyer counsel at summary courts and at nonjudicial punishment proceedings to insure compliance with *Miranda*. The Army has put its military judges into robes to increase their prestige and, presumably, performance. And the Navy has turned over most of its shipboard casework to dockside courts. None of these developments is required by law. They, and others like them, should be permitted to evolve with a minimum of outside interference for a few years. If it then becomes necessary to legislate anew, it can be done advisedly.

In any case, there is no great chance that major changes can be forced onto the services against their will. If a generalization about the course of military justice since V-J Day can be made, it is that it is in a world of its own. One scholarly observer asserted that during the 1950s there was a fairly widespread concern in civilian as well as military circles for the declining prestige of the military career and the shaky morale of the officer corps [and that therefore a number] of proposals were submitted to restore the authority of commanding officers to punish minor infractions without court-martial.[16]

This is a compelling syllogism, but there is no evidence to support it. At every turn, the major forces in American politics and society have been uninterested in military justice. The Article 15 reforms in 1962-1963 may have *followed* a period of "widespread concern," but they were not *caused* by it. Their enactment was the result of forces within the system and was not whipped up by winds of popular opinion in the country at large. Even at moments of genuine public uproar, such as the immediate post-World War II period, the ultimate legislative action was the work of a handful of men. Their success, in fact, depended on the relative isolation they were able to create. The outcry, it is true, helped to create a milieu in which change was possible, but it had very little to do with the actual reforms that resulted.

On the other hand, the Vietnam War has created an atmosphere of distrust about everything military which is unparalleled in American history. Unlike the agitation in the late 1940s, this repugnance extends to all aspects of the Armed Forces, not just their court-martial practices. Such a revolutionary situation could have an unforeseeably comprehensive impact on the services. Included, of course, might be military justice. There is no way to tell whether what has proven to be a general truth in the past will stand up in the near future. Therefore, should a thorough reform of the defense establishment be undertaken, it might extend to courts-martial.

The past quarter-century has been an era of unprecedented activity in this highly specialized field. There is only one reason: the existence for the first time in American history of a huge peacetime standing military force composed mostly of draftees and others who enlist solely to avoid conscription. The above-mentioned handful of men who have had the opportunity to influence the pattern of military justice have almost without exception been motivated by one idea: it is grossly unfair to force a man into uniform and then make him subject to a law code totally foreign to his previous experience.[17]

Given this, two questions must be asked. First, what happens if an all-volunteer force is created? Does military justice return to the "rocks and shoals" that existed before the code? Will GI's once more become trapped in a "state of servitude in the midst of a nation of free men?" The author is keenly apprehensive about the volunteer service for a number of reasons—its probable ethnic makeup, the chance that it may become an irresponsible tool for ambitious and adventurous foreign policy makers, and its elimination of the "service to country" philosophy—but another point that must be considered by Congress during the debate is whether it will not also return servicemen to the same helpless position they held *vis à vis* the unlimited power of courts-martial before the post-World War II reforms.

The second question is almost contradictory, more bothersome, but unlikely to be debated. It is, in fact, atavistic: has the "advance" of military justice during the period studied been beneficial for society at large? With the formalization of the special court-martial, there is in fact no significant difference between the way the military must, by law, treat the man who has been AWOL for thirty days and the other man who has committed a horrible sex-murder. There is great incongruity in this. The Armed Forces are, after all, supposed to be fighting battles, not lawsuits. Under the Uniform Code, one cannot always be sure. The recent case of Army Captain Jeffrey R. MacDonald, whose family was killed in a crime superficially similar to the Tate-LaBianca murders in Los Angeles for which Charles Manson and his "family" were convicted, is an example of this point. The formal procedures required by the Uniform Code in this instance took more than nine months, involved hundreds of people fulltime, cost untold amounts of the taxpayer's money, and yet the case never got to trial.[18] Fine; money and time are no obstacle if an innocent man is freed. But the time and money expended were supposed to be for national defense, not felony litigation.

In the continuing debate over military justice that is a part of the Vietnam era inquiry into all segments of the defense establishment, it should be asked whether the "lawyerization" of court-martial law that has occurred since 1950 in the United States was really worthwhile. The Code Committee is not a suitable forum for this discussion because its most important member, the Court of Military Appeals, is too inextricably a part of the Uniform Code. But perhaps Congress should ask whether the experiment of the past twenty years had demonstrated the viability of an autonomous legal system within the military, or whether it has shown that such a thing is counter-productive or irrelevant to what should be the first goal of a military force, defending the country.

The history related in these pages suggests that the Uniform Code had been a failure in a number of important ways. Despite the unending efforts of its supporters to make it closely parallel to contemporary civilian law, the Supreme Court has rejected the UCMJ as unsuitable for the trials of all classes of civilians and has even prohibited courts-martial for servicemen under certain conditions. Moreover, Richard Nixon's early announcement that he would exercise the final review of the case of William Calley, convicted murderer in the "My Lai massacre," implies that the President, as chief spokesman for the American people, himself has little faith in the military system's ability to render justice.

And finally, the increasing complexity of the UCMJ over the years has engendered great hostility among those most responsible for its proper operation. Commanders everywhere have sought a variety of ways to avoid using it. Too often, the victims in such cases have been the same draftees or reluctant enlistees the code was originally designed to protect. Many men have been eliminated from the service with an undesirable discharge because commanders would not spare the time, effort, or personnel to try them under the code. Others have received NJP so many times that they are candidates for the tainted general discharge when it is finally time for them to get out. Within the services, the code has created large legal bureaucracies, connected to the defense effort only tangentially, if at all. Within these organizations, and between them, there is a level of squabbling, politicking, and rivalry that may be customary in things pertaining to the military but is unseemly in things pertaining to the law. And the men who run the machinery are often forced by the nature of the code to make statements and assume positions that they believe to be fully sincere but which outsiders regard as disingenuous, thus further disgracing the entire system. Finally, Senator Ervin, the one man on Capitol Hill generally thought to be an expert in court-martial affairs, would like to multiply the complexities and expand the bureaucracies, thus doubtlessly worsening the problems.

If a debate into the worth of the Uniform Code is ever undertaken, perhaps the following ideas might be found to have merit:

(1) completely separate courts-martial from civilian justice, including the Court of Military Appeals, except for *Dynes v. Hoover* inquiry; and

(2) let the military handle its offenses as it sees fit; but

(3) limit maximum sentences within the military system to three

years confinement or the expiration of a defendant's obligated service, whichever comes first; and

(4) eliminate all distinctions among types of discharges.

If this were adopted, an offender would be treated along the following lines. The service might decide he is useless, in which case he could be separated with an utterly nondescript discharge, just like the ones given to everyone else. If his commanders wanted to punish him but retain him, they could try him formally or informally as they chose, but could imprison him only to the end of his enlistment, or (for indefinite enlistments) for three years. The man belongs to the military for that length of time anyway; let him be used as a tank driver, electronics technician, or prisoner. Considerations of morale and dissent, it is to be hoped, would keep to a minimum whatever injustices are possible within this limited power to punish.[19] And even should a case of tyranny emerge, the accused would be able to litigate in the federal courts for habeas corpus. If, on the other hand, the crime was serious enough to merit greater punishment and was not covered by a Status of Forces Agreement, the services would have to let the civilian courts take jurisdiction. There the defendant would have all the protections guaranteed to him by the Constitution, and the military would not be tied down with the expense and effort of a trial. The civilian courts, it is true, are already heavily burdened, but the human and material resources now expended on the UCMJ can be diverted to relieve them at least to the extent of the increase in work. Modern technical advances, particularly in transportation, make this plan possible to a degree unknown even as recently at the *Toth* days.[20]

This suggestion might be a simple solution to some of the thorny problems of military justice. Its major drawback is that it is too nearly a return to the discredited past and for that reason alone is not likely to gain much attention. And besides, the author is outside that small circle of men who can actually do things about court-martial law.

Notes

Notes to Chapter 1

[1] For example, Item 394, or Item 480. [Throughout this work, citations to most source materials will refer the reader to the number of the Item as it appears in the Bibliography, and will include only such other publication information as is necessary to enable the reader to find the source.]

[2] Item 480, p. 38; "War GI Justice Gripes Win 'Fair' Military Code," Veterans' Edition, *Army Times*, June 9, 1951. [Army Times, Inc., also publishes *Navy Times* and *Air Force Times*; its clipping service was the source of much material used by the author. But since the service does not record page citations, such information will not usually be given herein.]

[3] See the file of complaints in Item 10, Vol. VI.

[4] Item 295, p. 251; Item 215, pp. 68-69.

[5] Item 332, p. 2; Item 268, p. 202.

[6] Item 268, p. 202; Item 480, pp. 15-16; Item 347, p. 241; Act of August 29, 1916, 39 Stat. 650-71.

[7] Item 480, p. 15; Item 172, p. 1342; Act of June 23, 1874, 18 Stat. 244; Item 332, pp. 6-9.

[8] Item 268, pp. 203-04; Item 172, pp. 1367-68.

[9] Item 332, pp. 8, 43; Item 432, pp. 21, 30; *Washington Post*, Mar. 7, 1919, 1:1

[10] Item 295, pp. 53-54 [emphasis in original]. The judicial history of Winthrop's assertion is given in Chapter XVI.

[11] S. 64, 66th Cong., 1st Sess. (1919). A companion measure in the House was H.R. 365.

[12] Item 172, pp. 1372-95. The prosecutor at courts-martial has been referred to by a variety of titles during the period covered by this history. He is today called the "trial counsel," but to avoid confusion, this text will uniformly refer to him as "prosecutor."

[13] Item 172, pp. 1373, 1379-80.

[14] Item 433, pp. 67-72. Although it was not specified in S. 64 Morgan thought that the judges on the court of military appeals would probably be civilians. See Item 432, p. 29.

[15] *New York Times*, Aug. 4, 1919, 2:4.

[16] Item 316, pp. 1, 1n, 14, 16.

[17] Act of June 4, 1920, 41 Stat. 787-812. Other revisions since 1776 were in 1806, 1874, and 1916, which in the main were all merely rearrangements or modernizations of the older machinery. See Item 466.

[18] 34 USC §1200 (1946).

[19] Item 446, p. 197; Item 289, p. 107; Item 118, pp. 8, 24.

[20] Item 114, §346, §471.

[21] *Dynes v. Hoover*, 61 U.S. (20 How.) 65 (1857).

207

[22] Item 90 (AW 50), p. 7. [The chapters in Item 90 are named after the Articles of War they discuss and are each separately paged. See p. 37 for a description of the function of these books.] See Item 295, pp. 51-64, for a history of the Army's three courts.

[23] Item 116, § 469(3), § 443 ¶10.

[24] Item 432, p. 21. We have only Morgan's report that this was a boast. It could have been a complaint, or a simple statement of fact.

[25] Item 114, §469. Only the Secretary of the Navy could commute naval sentences. See Item 114, §481.

[26] See Chapter XVI for a discussion of this point.

[27] Item 129, p. 190; Item 386, p. 87; Item 90 (AW 8), p. 22.

[28] In the years following World War II, a man named Burt Drummond surfaced in various letters-to-the-editor columns, claiming he was a former Navy chief petty officer who in the early 1920s had fought to change some of the aspects of World War I court-martial law and had suffered the loss of his career for his efforts. *Buffalo Evening News,* June 21, 1949, letter-to-the-editor clipping; *New York Times,* May 1950, letter-to-the-editor clipping; Drummond, letter to Richard Wels, Jan. 21, 1951; and Drummond, letter to Hanson Baldwin, Feb. 12, 1951; all in Item 14. [Copies of these clippings and letters are in the author's possession.] See also Drummond, letters to the editors of the *Syracuse Post-Standard,* July 19, 1947, the *New York Herald Tribune,* Aug. 3. 1947, and the *Saturday Evening Post,* May 17, 1952; clippings all in Item 14. Letters written to various addresses given by Mr. Drummond are returned by the postal service with the notation that he is dead. Because his story cannot be corroborated, or fully deciphered from the materials available, the views expressed in the text that the Navy had no analog to Gen. Ansell must stand. In any case, Mr. Drummond claimed to have worked only on *Navy Regulations* not the AGN. See *Buffalo Evening News,* June 21, 1949, clipping in Item 14.

[29] Similar appraisals are given in Item 506, p. 12; and in Item 155, p. 17.

Notes to Chapter 2

[1] Item 393.

[2] Item 129, p. 14; Item 510, p. 200.

[3] *New York Times,* Jul. 13, 1947, IV, 8:3; Gibson, letter to Morgan, Nov. 18, 1948, Item 10, Vol. VI; Item 260; Riter's review of Item 260 in Item 298 (June 1954), pp. 27-31; *U.S. v. Slovik,* 15 BR (ETO) 151 (1944); *Providence Journal,* May 23, 1951, 5:6; Item 256, pp. 57, 65-66.

[4] Item 147, p. 1948; Item 149, p. 681. While there were many such reports from men hostile to the old system, even more interesting and convincing is that some men who defended the old ways told similar stories, although they usually began, "In all of my experience, I came across only one incident, etc." E.g., Item 57.

[5] About 80 percent of the wartime Navy cases were AWOL's. See Item 307, Feb. 20, 1953. Statistics prepared for an Army official in 1949 show that during the period 1941-1948, absence offenses accounted for a little over one-third of the Army's court-martial business. See Item 117, p. 50.

[6] Item 119; Item 120; Item 490; Item 128; Items 124, 125, and 126; Item 136.

[7] Item 104; Item 105; Item 155.

[8] Item 105, pp. 2-5.

[9] Item 104, p. 1; Item 155, p. 18. There was a disparity between officers and EM's in the Navy, too, where 97.6 percent of enlisted men tried were found guilty, while only 81.1 percent of the officer defendants were convicted. See Item 117, p. 568.

[10] Item 119; Item 341, p. 202. Apparently the House Naval Affairs Committee investigated naval justice during the war, too. The study was done secretly, and there appears to be no existing record of its findings, although it is referred to in an eleven-page carbon copy of the minority report to Item 120, p. 6.

[11] Item 490, pp. 860, 1211.

[12] Item 120, pp. 6-7.

[13] Item 124, p. 8; Item 394, p. 40; Secretary of the Navy, "Precept," 24 June 1946, in Item 126, p. 16; Item 90 (AW 47, AW 51, AW 52 in part), p. 23, Item 90 (AW 8), p. 20.

[14]Item 119, minority report, p. 6.

[15]The GCMSRB included one Navy admiral, two Navy captains, a Coast Guard captain, a Marine lieutenant colonel, and a Navy commander, in addition to Keeffe, Larkin and Robert Pasley.

[16]Secretary of the Navy, letter to the Navy JAG, June 25, 1946, in Item 120; Item 90 (AW 47, AW 51, AW 52 in part), p. 26.

[17]One major exception to this contention is that the Vanderbilt report proposed that commanders be removed from the court-martial system altogether, but the suggestion was flatly rejected by Secretary of War Patterson. See Item 497, p. 72.

[18]For example, the Acting Chief of the Army JAG's Legislative Projects Branch from 1969 to 1971 was a young Reserve captain with decidedly "liberal" views, who claimed to have great influence over Army policy regarding new legislation.

[19]Smith, letter to Maj. Gen. Myron C. Cramer, Aug. 3, 1945, in War Department memo SPJGJ 1945/13773, Item 4. For his pains, Col. Smith received a tongue-lashing. Cramer, letter to Smith, Aug. 9, 1945, Item 4.

[20]Item 90 (AW 47, AW 51, AW 52 in part), pp. 15, 26, 29.

[21]Item 66. In 1946, Homer A. Walkup was a young naval lawyer in the Bureau of Naval Personnel. He recalls that most of the officers he knew then shared Nunn's opinion of the studies. See Item 71.

Notes to Chapter 3

[1]Item 510, p. 207; Item 149, p. 825.

[2]*New York Times,* June 26, 1945, 20:3.

[3]Howard E. Crouch, letter to Edmund M. Morgan, August 14, 1948, Item 10, Vol. VI.

[4]Item 148, p. 4160.

[5]Item 148, p. 4160; Item 145; H.R. 576, 80th Cong., 1st Sess. (1947).

[6]S. 1338, 80th Cong., 1st Sess. (1947); Item 148, p. 4160; Item 37.

[7]Item 185, p. 10; Dickson, letter to Gen. Harry Vaughan, Feb. 8, 1948, and undated "Reprint from the *Courier-Journal*," both in OF 303-303A, Item 12.

[8]George A. Spiegelberg [City Bar Association], letter to Robert W. Smart, June 16, 1947 [telling Smart that Spiegelberg is the expert on the Articles of War and that Wels, of the County Association, is the man to see on the AGN]; "Notes" from the meeting of the Comm . on Military Justice, City Bar Assn., Dec. 8, 1947 [announcing a joint meeting of the County and City groups]; Smart, letter to Wels, Oct. 30, 1947 [giving confidential information on certain legislation]; Frederick V.P. Bryan [City Bar Assn.], letter to Sen. Chan Gurney, Jan. 29, 1948 [recounting a meeting Bryan and Gurney had in Washington the week before]; and "Notes" from the meeting of the Comm. on Military Justice, City Bar Assn., Dec. 8, 1947 [announcing that Prof. Keeffe and Felix Larkin will attend the next joint meeting]; all in Item 14. The effort to separate command and court-martial will be described later in the text.

[9]Robert Lee Benson, pamphlet mailed to Truman, "Re Crooked Courts-Martial"; Mildred Earsley, letter to Truman, Apr. 15, 1945; and George H. Hall, letter to Mr. Ross [?], Jan. 8, 1946, all in OF 303-303A, Item 12; Robert L. Dressley, "A Plan for the Reorganization of the Naval Court-Martial," Item 10, Vol. VI.

[10]Item 147, p. 1947; Item 140, p. 6. According to one observer, the Elston subcommittee believed that enlisted membership was an unsound idea, but that public demand was too great not to include it in the new articles. See Wels, memo to Bryan, Farmer, Spiegelberg, Wallstein, and Paul DeWitt, June 28, 1947, Item 14. Of course, Wels and all of his addressees wanted very much to believe that the enthusiasm they were trying to whip up was succeeding.

[11]"Nonjudicial punishment" is summary punishment levied by a commanding officer; the topic is covered in detail in Chapter XII below. To the author's knowledge, no officer was ever tried by special court under this or successor legislation.

[12]The wording of AW 50 is nearly incomprehensible, and the specific powers of the Judicial Council are not clear to me, if they ever were to anyone else.

[13]Item 298 (Oct. 1954), p. 11.

[14]Item 516, p. 30. No prudent general was likely to express these sentiments, but Wiener has frequently proved to be in tune with the prevailing ideas at the Pentagon, and it is a fair assumption that he was echoing here what many in the Army felt. See note 6 of Chapter XVIII and page 205 for President Nixon's intervention in the Calley case.

[15]Item 149, p. 618, 654, and 658.

[16]Item 166, p. 316; Item 57.

[17]*New York Times*, March 12, 1948, 22:3. The idea here was to prevent chiefs of staff from interfering with the communications between the staff judge advocate and the commander.

[18]*New York Times*, Jul. 16, 1947, 11:1, and Jul. 9, 1947, 1:7, 15:2; Item 140, p. 9.

[19]The ABA proposals are summarized in Item 147, p. 2002. The ABA became quite conservative in its military justice posture in the 1960's, but so long as George A. Spiegelberg was the motive force behind the special committee, as he was in 1947 and for the next several years, the association remained in step with the most advanced reform ideas current in the civilian community.

[20]Wels, memo to Bryan, Spiegelberg, Wallstein, and Arthur E. Farmer, Jul. 17, 1947; and Smart, letter to Wels, Oct. 30, 1947; both in Item 14.

[21]Gurney, letter to Forrestal, May 3, 1948, Item 10, Vol. I; *Congressional Record*, Feb 2, 1950, S. 1354.

[22]Item 62; *New York Times,* Jul. 29, 1947, 20:1.

[23]*Ibid.*, Jul. 16, 1947, 11:1, and June 10, 1948, 2:6.

[24]Item 299, p. 24.

[25]See page 9.

[26]Item 485, p. 522.

[27]For a general treatment of the history of unification, see Item 286. The author of that work, Mr. Tarr, was Director of the Selective Service System until 1972. Crowder, Kem, Tarr. . . .; one cannot talk long about military justice without tripping over the draft.

[28]PL 775, Act of June 25, 1948, 62 Stat. 1014; Item 97, p. 63. For an account of the confusion over the two *Manuals for Courts-Martial* in 1969, see Chapter XVII, note 26.

[29]Item 298 (Oct. 1949), p. 9; Item 129, p. 184; Item 57; Item 149, p. 636.

[30]*Stock v. Department of the Air Force, et al.*, 186 F 2d 968 (1950). By the time this case was decided, the question had been made moot by successor legislation.

Notes to Chapter 4

[1]Forrestal, letter to Gurney, May 14, 1948, Item 10, Vol. I; Item 149, p. 597; Item 406, p. 8; Item 62.

[2]Forrestal, memo to the Committee on a UCMJ, "Precept and Terms of Reference," Item 10, Vol. I.

[3]Arthur E. Farmer, letter to Forrestal, Jan. 22, 1948, Item 14; Item 62. The UCMJ was one of the Secretary's last acts; he testified before the House subcommittee on March 7, 1949, and then, apparently under some pressure from the President, perhaps because of Truman's fears for his health, resigned on March 28. See Item 218, pp. xi, 552.

[4]Item 10, Vol. I; Item 27.

[5]Larkin, memo to Morgan, Feb. 8, 1949; Larkin, letter [at the direction of Morgan] to Ansell, Feb. 8, 1949, both in Item 10, Vol. IV; Item 15. It seems certain that no one on the UCMJ Committee, except for Morgan, ever met Ansell. Item 62; Item 34.

[6]Item 49.

[7]Item 432.

[8]Item 89, frontispiece.

[9]Item 406, pp. 8-9. The AW's and the AGN are printed side by side in Item 139, pp. 41-76.

[10]Several of the "Notebooks" survive. I have found copies in Item 10, Vol. II; and in Item 3, Item 6, and Item 11.

[11]Item 432, p. 10.

[12]Edmund M. Morgan, letter to _____, March 31, 1949, copy in the possession of Felix E. Larkin. The name of the addressee is known to the author but withheld at Mr. Larkin's request.

[13]Both Morgan and Larkin were first introduced to military justice as members of clemency

boards; Larkin on the Keeffe Commission, and Morgan on an Army panel in the office of the JAG during World War I.

[14] Larkin, memo to the UCMJ Committee Oct. 11, 1948; Minutes of the Oct. 14, 1948 meeting, both in Item 10, Vol. I: Forrestal, memo to Morgan, Jan. 17, 1948, Item 117. p. 339. Before this provision became law, it went through numerous changes, many of which are discussed below.

[15] Item 62; Item 406, pp. 8-9.

[16] The B-36 controversy and the "revolt of the admirals" were still almost a year in the future at this time.

[17] Minutes of the Sep. 17-18, 1948 meetings, Item 10, Vol. I.

[18] Larkin, memo to Forrestal, Jan. 5, 1949, *ibid.*, Vol. IV.

[19] This seems to be interservice rivalry of the "what's-mine-is-best-even-if-I-don't-like-it-myself" genre. The Army tried earnestly to water down the enlisted member provision during the Elston Bill debates. See page 24, but by this time, even before the Elston Articles were in effect, the Army was a fervent advocate of the measure.

[20] Larkin, memo to Forrestal, Jan. 5, 1949, Item 10, Vol. I.

[21] Item 406, p. 9; Item 62.

[22] The nonjudicial punishment question was decided within the Morgan committee. See Larkin, memo to Forrestal, and memo to the UCMJ Committee, both of Jan. 5, 1949; and memo to the UCMJ Committee, Jan. 31, 1949, all in Item 10, Vol. IV. See also Morgan, letter to Forrestal, Feb. 7, 1949, *ibid.*, Vol. V.

[23] H.R. 2498 and S. 857, 81st Cong., 1st Sess. (1949).

[24] See Item 201.

[25] Item 139, pp. 7-8; Item 149, pp. 600-01.

[26] The assistance provided the court by the law officer was a legacy from the law member days when that officer was a part of the court.

[27] Item 129, pp. 209, 211. Kefauver was another former student of Morgan when the latter was at Yale in the 1920's.

[28] Item 86, §39.

[29] "Minor" cases were those not involving a general or admiral or not resulting in a sentence which included one of the following: death, dismissal, punitive discharge, or confinement of one year or more.

[30] Item 149, pp. 1277-78; Gray, statement to supplement the minutes of the Oct. 28 meeting, Item 10, Vol. IV; proposed Art. 57, draft bill dated 11/26/48, Item 10, Vol. I; Larkin, memo to Forrestal, Jan. 5, 1949, Item 10, Vol. IV. Congressman Mendel Rivers wanted to omit Senate confirmation from the draft in order to ensure that there would be a House-Senate conference. See Item 149, p. 1271.

[31] Item 149, p. 1271; Item 166, pp. 311-14; Item 69; Item 159, p. 6; Item 144, p. 4.

[32] Item 149, p. 1275; Item 166, pp. 313-14; Item 129, p. 30.

[33] Item 149, pp. 718-19; Spiegelberg, letter to Brooks, Mar. 14, 1949, Item 10, Vol. VI.

[34] Item 149, pp. 626-27, 630.

[35] *Ibid.*, pp. 647, 651.

[36] Item 149, pp. 597, 656; Item 129, pp. 10, 16.

[37] Memo of telephone conversation between Spiegelberg and Wallstein, Feb. 23, 1949; Spiegelberg, Bryan, Wels, and Farmer, letter to Brooks, March 31, 1949; Farmer, letter to Sen. Morse, May 23, 1949; Wels, letter to the editor of the *New York Times*, June 21, 1949; Farmer, letter to Morse, May 23, 1949; Wels, letter to Rear Adm. George Russell [Navy JAG], Oct. 9, 1951; all in Item 14. This last letter is an astonishing document, in which a conciliatory Wels told Russell that their views are really "much closer" than Russell thought.

[38] Item 149, pp. 778-79.

[39] Item 129, p. 20; Item 149, p. 780.

[40] Item 149, p. 794. The second point was rebutted by Mr. Elston, who reminded his colleagues that CoMA would rule only on matters of law. See *ibid.*, 795.

[41] Item 166, p. 129.

[42] Item 149, pp. 800, 806. Some months later, George Spiegelberg wrote that Wiener's argument "would of course make me conclude that the same officer should operate on those of his men who were wounded." Spiegelberg, letter to Wels, Apr. 9, 1951, Item 14. The rebuttal to that would probably be that offenses tend to diminish a unit's discipline,

whereas wounds do not usually do so.
[43] Item 256, p. 43; Item 166, pp. 132-37, 311-12.
[44] Item 129, pp. 237, 258, 292; *Congressional Record* (Feb. 3. 1950), D60. Morse himself favored life tenure for the CoMA judges and supported Spiegelberg's idea on convening authority.
[45] Item 129, p. 119.
[46] Item 149, pp. 582, 624, 642, 650, 673; Item 139, p. 96.
[47] In Morgan's own papers, for example, there are several law articles dealing with military justice over which he himself pored, underlining and making marginal notes. See Item 10, Vol. III.
[48] Item 166, pp. 304-05; Item 432, p. 34; Item 149, p. 605.
[49] Item 62; Item 149, p. 606.
[50] Item 139, pp. 5, 83. See pages 171-172.
[51] Item 81 (1960), CoMA 5. [The 1960 reports of each member of this committee were separately paged.]
[52] Item 432, p. 22; Item 62.

Notes to Chapter 5

[1] Item 312 (June 1950), p. 16.
[2] Col. Wiener thought the abridgement itself was the cause of much World War II difficulty. Those commands which had the 1921 *MCM*, with its detailed explanations and directions, had much less trouble, he said. Item 73.
[3] Item 118, p. 25.
[4] Item 339, p. 592.
[5] Item 90 (AW 38), pp. 1-2.
[6] Army memo JAGJ 1950/6956, Item 4.
[7] Item 316, p. 12.
[8] Item 85, p. v. Unless otherwise specified, the next several paragraphs are based on an historical note written by Col. Decker in the introduction to Item 85.
[9] Edmund Morgan drafted the sections on evidence, scattered throughout the *Manual*. See Item 315, pp. 14-15.
[10] Item 502, p. 187.
[11] Executive Order 10214, Feb. 8, 1951, in 16 *Federal Register*, pp. 1303-1469.
[12] Item 506, p. 13; Farmer, letter to the City Bar Association, Jul. 6, 1950, Item 14.

Notes to Chapter 6

[1] Item 62; George C. Marshall, memo for the President, Feb. 16, 1951, File #5, Item 2. There were, by the author's count, 104 candidates. Not included among them were Morgan, Larkin, or Robert E. Quinn, who will appear in a few pages. See OF 303, Item 12.
[2] Drew Pearson, "Washington-Merry-Go-Round," June 19, 1951. This article was based on conversations between Pearson and Richard Wels, who maintained in 1970 that it was an accurate presentation of the facts. Item 45.
[3] Minutes of the City Bar Ass'n Committee on Military Justice, Oct. 5, 1950, Item 14 [Patterson is the same gentleman earlier vilified by these organizations for emasculating the Vanderbilt Report, which goes to show how carefully they kept their lines of communications open even with opponents]; John F. Brosnan [N.Y. County Lawyers Ass'n], letter to the editor, *New York Times*, Jan. 22, 1951, 23:1; Wels, letter to the editor of the *New York Herald Tribune*, Jan. 21, 1951, edition, clipping in Item 14; Pearson, "Merry-Go-Round." The Pearson column charged that there was a conspiracy between presidential advisor Gen. Harry Vaughan and Attorney-General J. Howard McGrath, to select the court. This is clearly what Wels thought then, and continued to think. Item 45. Vaughan's denial of his own alleged role appears in a letter to Mr. Toney East, June 25, 1951, OF 303, Item 12. Vaughan and McGrath played key roles in the nominations, as the text shows, below. But I do not think this constituted anything out of the ordinary; after all, one was the President's military advisor, the other the chief of the federal Department of Justice.

[4] S.J.S. [?], memo to Clark Clifford, June 6, 1949, OF 303-303A, Item 12; Sec. 5, Item 201. The major part of the code was to become effective on "the last day of the twelfth month after approval." Excepted were the provision for World War II offense retrials (Sec. 12), and the CoMA appointments (Sec. 5), which could be made three months earlier in order to allow for Senate confirmation and the details necessary to establish the new institution.

[5] Marshall, memo for Truman, Feb. 15, 1951, File #5, Item 2; George M. Elsey, memo for Donald Dawson, Mar. 20, 1951, and unsigned memo for Mr. Connelly, Apr. 5, 1951, both in OF 303, Item 12. Bosone's candidate was not named but was probably George Latimer.

[6] *Congressional Directory* (1953), pp. 518-19; Item 256, p. 57. There was at least one serious woman candidate, Mary Agnes Brown of the Veterans' Board of Appeals. See OF 303, Item 12. The first black man was appointed to the court in 1971. See Chapter XV.

[7] Item 256, pp. 61-64. The notation "self-endorsement to Harry Vaughn [*sic*]" appears in Latimer's file, OF 303, Item 12. And on May 16, Vaughan wired Latimer: "YOU WILL RECEIVE GOOD NEWS WITHIN TWENTY-FOUR HOURS HOPE YOU ARE IN POSITION TO MAKE HURRIED TRIP TO WASHINGTON ADVISE YOU MAKE NO STATEMENT[.]" OF 303, Item 12.

[8] *Providence Journal*, May 23, 1951, 5:6; Item 69.

[9] Item 57; Item 20; *New York Times*, May 23, 1951, 30:2-3.

[10] *New York Times*, June 17, 1951, 17:4.

[11] Wels, letter to Burt Drummond, June 20, 1951, Item 14, citing Zechariah Chaffee, Jr., "State House against Pent-House." The correct title of this work is given in Item 246. Chaffee, a Rhode Islander and Harvard Law School professor, argued (1) that Quinn sought by martial law to overturn the rulings of the State Supreme Court, (2) that the martial law proclamation was probably invalid, and (3) that Quinn was arbitrary and unfair in dealing with the Narragansett Racing Commission. All of this was done, he wrote, in pursuit of crushing a potential political foe, the major of Pawtucket. Wels thought this an inauspicious background for the man who would be charged with proctecting the legal rights of several million GI's.

Notes to Chapter 7

[1] *New York Times*, May 8, 1950, 22:3. Given Truman's earlier apathy about the code, this was a surprising statement.

[2] Item 149, pp. 837ff.; Item 397; Item 394.

[3] Item 126; Item 62; Item 90 (AW 4), p. 7. See page 17-18.

[4] Item 397, pp. 270-282.

[5] Item 470, p. 283; Item 253, pp. 243-44; Item 149, p. 691.

[6] Chapter XVI covers this topic in detail.

[7] Item 397, p. 283; Keeffe, dissent from the report of the ABA's Special Committee on Military Justice, Jan. 29, 1949, Item 14; Item 396, p. 487; Item 149, p. 383; Item 394, p. 44.

[8] Keeffe has admitted that he would have like Morgan's job on the UCMJ Committee. Item 60. But he nevertheless graciously inscribed one of his articles to "Eddie Morgan, the greatest court-martial reformer of us all." Item 10, Vol. III.

[9] Item 298 (Oct. 1949), p. 5; *ibid.* (June 1949), pp. 1, 39.

[10] Item 298 (Oct. 1954), p. 3; *ibid.* (Oct. 1958), p. 6.

[11] Item 97, pp. 1, 15, 38-40.

[12] Item 193; Item 54. See the O'Brien to Tibbs letter, page 136, as an example of JAG School brainpower.

[13] *Army Times*, Jan. 27, 1951.

[14] Item 59.

[15] Department of the Navy, CNO message 061606Z June 1950 (Navop 12-50). Navy inferior courts had never before had jurisdiction over officers, and were limited to two months confinement.

[16] Item 312 (Jul. 1950), p. 9.

[17] Item 66; Item 71. This was a view held, ironically, by Richard Wels, who thought that the deficiencies of the AGN were largely overcome by the excellence of the men who used it. Item 506, p. 12. The Navy is fond of boasting that its last execution took place in 1842,

when a midshipman and a petty officer were hanged summarily for fomenting a mutiny. Because the middie was the son of the Secretary of War, a major furor developed, and the memory of it probably acted as an incentive against future hangings. Item 217. Some death sentences, however, have been handed down since then by Navy courts-martial, *e.g., U.S. v. Henderson*, 11 USCMA 556, 29 CMR 373 (1960), although there have been no executions. On the other hand, until the early 1960s, Army courts frequently condemned men who actually died as a result; 141 soldiers were executed during World War II and ten more in the 1950s. See Item 260, p. 5; and *Army Times*, Oct. 9, 1963.
[18] Item 122, enclosure, p. 1.
[19] Item 123, p. 4; Item 66.
[20] Item 66. The Navy's conservatism is illustrated by Adm. Russell's statement to the press deploring the omission in the UCMJ of the old AGN condemnation of a sailor who "pusillanimously cries for quarter." See *New York Times*, May 31, 1951, 9:4. There is also the provision regarding a commanding officer's "good example of virtue," and the requirement for shipboard divine services, both taken bodily from the AGN and tacked onto the new code, in Sec. 7(c) and (d).

Notes to Chapter 8

[1] Item 82, pp. 47-55; Item 79; Item 68.
[2] Quinn, letter to Truman, Jan. 15, 1952, OF 380, and Quinn, letter to Truman, Nov. 19, 1952. PPF. 66-A "Q", both in Item 12; McGrath, letter to Quinn, Aug. 16, 1951, File "Q," Item 9.
[3] Item 82, p. 50; Robert A. Lovett, letter to Jess Larson [General Services Administration[, June 15, 1951, File 83, Item 9. This letter directed GSA to make permanent space available for the court soon, since it was "contrary to the wishes of Congress and the judicial character of the Court" for it to be located at the Pentagon. The fears implied in this letter and in the actions of the court were well-founded; as late as 1956, Congressman Brooks, whose Armed Services subcommittee had drafted the UCMJ legislation, was surprised to learn that CoMA was not situated in the Pentagon. See Item 150, p. 8572.
[4] Item 190; Item 68.
[5] Supreme Court cases are cited as volume U.S. page; the other two reporters mentioned in the text are cited volume F. 2d page, and volume F. Supp. page. Complete citations for these works are in Item 181, Item 175, and Item 176, respectively. "Reported" as used here is synonomous with "published."
[6] Item 57. The Army reports were no more than bound reproductions of board opinions, arranged roughly chronologically, without index. To find a case, one had to know the approximate date of review and then search the volume containing cases about that time. This is what the author did to find the *Slovik* decision [Chap. II, note 3], and Gen. Harman says there is no easier method.
[7] Item 128. p. 9. Wels said that the Navy's were the only judicial reports in America that were kept secret. See Item 506, p. 12.
[8] The reports are cited volume USCMA page (year). The complete citation is given in Item 174.
[9] Item 80, §1800.3, §1800, 14-27, §§1800.28-30. Revisions occurred in March 1952, May 1953, and January 1959, and a complete overhaul was put into effect in January 1962. See Item 80, p. iii.
[10] Item 149, p. 1286; Item 129, p. 219.
[11] "Mandatory" review for cases involving generals, admirals, and death sentences; "certified" review for those cases certified by the JAG of a service; and "petitions" from defendants who ask for court review of their cases. The precise figures were supplied the author by the chief commissioner of the court.
[12] Years selected reflect wartime and peacetime, and years when there was a full Court of Military Appeals; 1966 is the last year for U.S. court data; CoMA data supplied by the chief commissioner; U.S. court data from Item 476, p. 253. Calculations for CoMA loads per judge by the author.
[13] Item 168, p. 3.
[14] Item 461, p. 5. In mandatory or certified cases there is no question of deciding whether they should be heard, of course.

[15] Item 53.

[16] The court has occasionally changed its decision even after this point, as it did in *U.S. v. Flood*, 2 USCMA 114, 6 CMR 114 (1952).See Item 307, Nov. 14, 1952, p. 206.

[17] Item 330, pp. 167-69; Item 452, pp. 161-62; Item 411, p. 148.

[18] "Federal Rules of Criminal Procedure," 18 USC, Rule 52; Item 407, p. 66; Item 89, p. 84. The last cited source is the booklet the drafters of the code sent to Congress to explain the provisions of H.R. 2498. It may therefore be assumed that Forrestal, Morgan, and Larkin also approved of this interpretation of harmless error.

[19] *Lucas*, 1 USCMA 19, 1 CMR 19 (1951). In a special court, where there was no law officer, the senior officer on the court exercised most of the law officer's duties. See Item 86, §40(b)2.

[20] *Clay*, 1 USCMA 74, 1 CMR 74 (1951). The controversy can be seen in Item 522, and Item 493.

[21] *Lee*, 1 USCMA 212, 2 CMR 118 (1952).

[22] *Berry*, 1 USCMA 235, 2 CMR 141 (1952).

[23] *Keith*, 1 USCMA 493, 4 CMR 85 (1952). In courts-martial, the "court," even though it acts as a jury, remains in the courtroom during deliberations, and all others leave the room.

[24] *McConnell*, 1 USCMA 508, 4 CMR 100 (1952): *Woods and Duffer*, 2 USCMA 203, 8 CMR 2 (1952).

[25] Latimer apparently thought that since the law officer's information to the court was correct, the defendant profited by it.

[26] "Bipartite" means having a judge and a jury, a concept Brosman thought revolutionary in court-martial law since the adoption of the UCMJ. See Item 331; p. 1607.

[27] *Gibson*, 3 USCMA 512, 13 CMR 68 (1953); *Albee*, 5 USCMA 448, 18 CMR 72 (1955).

[28] *McCluskey*, 6 USCMA 545, 20 CMR 261 (1955), 553, citing *Bound*, 1 USCMA 224, 2 CMR 130 (1952).

[29] Item 63.

[30] This forthright position apparently led to a thaw in the relations between the bar association reformers and the court. In early 1953, at the peak of general prejudice (*Woods and Duffer* was handed down in February 1953), the civilians undertook to have Arthur Farmer, who had recently died, memorialized at the court. See Wels, letter to Brosman, Jan. 16, 1953, and Paul B. DeWitt, letter to .Wels, Feb. 5, 1953, both in Item 14. Brosman seemed to favor the idea. See Brosman, letter to Wels, Jan. 30, 1953, Item 14. But nothing came of it, except perhaps a new mutual respect. Wels ultimately thought that "Brosman turned out to be the finest judge of the lot," and that Quinn "turned out to be a good administrator, and . . . has shown a great deal of independence of the Defense Department." See Item 45. General prejudice was at least part of the cause of this reevaluation, although the bar members customary refusal to bear grudges may also have contributed.

Notes to Chapter 9

[1] Another important question along these lines was: to what degree did CoMA have to accept the conclusions of the "triers of fact," *viz.*, the trial court, the convening authority, and the board of review? This was the debate over "substantial evidence," in the *McCrary-O'Neal* line of cases. See Item 404, pp. 491-508; Item 289, pp. 380-85; Item 245, pp. 172-76.

[2] It was not included among the seventeen proposals made in the 1953 report. See Item 81 (1953), pp. 4-11. During the days when the UCMJ and *MCM* were being drafted, the Navy had suggested that capital punishment authority be given to the special court-martial. See Item 85, p. 18.

[3] Item 149, p. 964.

[4] Item 149, p. 1084; Item 85, p. 25; SR 22-1451, Mar. 6, 1952; Item 67.

[5] Item 97, pp. 8-9; Item 81 (1959), p. 34; Item 81 (1966), p. 59; *U.S. v. Culp*, 14 USCMA 199, 33 CMR 41 (1963); *U.S. v. Tempia*, 16 USCMA 629, 37 CMR 249 (1967).

[6] Item 149, p. 1084; Item 364, p. 3; Item 313 (Mar. 1962), p. 13.

[7] Some familiar names on the Seymour committee included Felix Larkin, George Spiegelberg, and Arthur Sutherland. See Item 81 (1953), p. 16.

[8] "Report of the Judge Advocates General of the Army, Navy and Air Force and the General Counsel, Department of the Treasury concerning Recommended Changes to the Uniform Code of Military Justice, August 21, 1953," in Item 81 (1953), pp. 30-33; Whitney North Seymour, "Report of the Court Committee," Item 81 (1953), pp. 23-27.

[9] Item 123, p. 29.

[10] Item 135, pp. 24-25, 66; Item 134, pp. 1-2, 6.

[11] Item 66.

[12] Item 81 (1953), pp. 4-10.

[13] The Judge Advocates Association endorsed the package in Item 298 (June 1954), pp. 15-16. So did the New York State Bar Association; see Knowlton Durham, letter to the Committee on the Administration of Military Justice, May 18, 1956, Item 14.

[14] Item 312 (June 1954), p. 10.

[15] It is worth noting here that the debate evoked some divergent views within the bar associations. George M. Welch, a colonel in the Army Reserve, delivered a paper, "Some Thoughts on the Uniform Code of Military Justice," to the City Bar Association's Committee on Military Justice, May 23, 1955, that favorably endorsed most of the positions taken by the JAG's. See Item 14. Although they only surfaced at this time, these views had probably existed within the association since the beginning, which is additional evidence of the essential pluralism of the politics of military justice reforms.

[16] Item 66; Item 324; Item 325; Spiegelberg, letter to Wels, Apr. 15, 1955, Item 14; *New York Daily News*, May 17, 1956, 4:1-2; H.R. 6583 and S. 2133, 84th Cong., 1st. Sess. (1955). Richard Wels believed that Baldwin was responsible for the suppression by the *Times* of opposing views on the Nunn amendments. See Wels, letter to Brosman, Jul. 20, 1955, Item 14.

[17] Item 150, pp. 8569-90, 8620-47; Item 81 (1955), p. 3. Judge Brosman died before these hearings were begun; his successor claimed ignorance of the issues and declined to testify. See Item 150, p. 8554. Some of the civilian reformers were also fooled by the superficial similarities between H.R. 6583 and the Code Committee proposals. See *ibid.*, p. 8648.

[18] *Ibid.*, pp. 8415, 8445, 8557.

[19] Item 81 (1953), p. 33; *U.S. v. Wilson and Harvey*, 2 USCMA 248, 8 CMR 48 (1953); Item 150, pp. 8585-89.

[20] Item 150, pp. 8593-8605; *Navy Times*, April 21, 1956, 8:1. Another factor leading to the death of the bills was the unfavorable light cast on military authority in general by the tragic drownings of a number of Marine recruits at Parris Island, which occurred while the hearings were in progress. See *New York Times*, May 2, 1956, 1:8; Knowlton Durham, letter to Wels, Aug. 22, 1956, Item 14.

[21] H.R. 8395, 82d Cong., 2d Sess. (1952).

[22] See Item 200.

[23] Public Law 896, Act of Aug. 1, 1956, 70 Stat. 911.

Notes to Chapter 10

[1] Quinn, letter to Eisenhower, June 17, 1953, and penciled note in the margin, PPF 1-EE, Item 1; undated, unsigned slip attached to Bureau of the Budget, memo for Bernard Shanley, June 2, 1954, OF 100D, Item 1. Eisenhower had been very much interested in military justice in 1948, during the debate over the Elston Bill, but that was when he was Army Chief of Staff. See page 26-28.

[2] Shanley, letter to Vanderbilt, May 1, 1954, OF 100D, Item 1; Item 274, pp. 158-59.

[3] Edward D. Tait, memo for "Mr. Seaton [?]," Dec. 29, 1955; Tait, memo for Seaton, Jan. 4, 1956; both in OF 100D, Item 1. The first memo suggests that Tait did not know of Brosman's passing, although it had occurred eight days earlier. The second memo is identical, except for mention of the judge's death. The White House was officially notified of the death by Quinn, letter to Eisenhower, Dec. 27, 1955, PPF 21B, Item 1, and it is possible that Tait learned about Brosman only when that letter was routed to him, presumably sometime after he wrote the Dec. 29 memo. In any case, the staffwork for the first memo was too far advanced to have begun only after the 21st. Mr. Tait can no longer recall the details of this matter. Item 40.

[4] Art Minnich, note to "Ann," Dec. 29, 1955, PPF 21B, Item 1.

[5]*Navy Times*, Jan. 14, 1956; Wilton B. Persons [White House], letter to John Slinkman [editor, *Navy Times*], Jan. 5, 1956, and Bryce N. Harlow [White House], letter to Slinkman, Jan. 5, 1956, both in OF 4-I, Eisenhower Papers. Clerk of the Court Proulx says of Tedrow and Smart, "They may have been running, but they weren't candidates."

[6]*Congressional Directory* (1962), p. 616; Mary B. Keedick, memo for Mr. Greunther, Mar. 5, 1956, OF 100D, Item 1; Item 82, pp. 55-56.

[7]*New York Times*, Sep. 8, 1940, IV, 8:3-4; Item 158 [Ferguson first appears in part 18 of this source, in March 1943]; Item 156, pp. 493-505, 572. Ferguson's career as a Michigan judge was not all brilliant. The *New York Times* called him a "crusading grand juror," on Nov. 4, 1942, 10:3. But his "crusading" earned him the wrath of the Supreme Court in a case where, based solely on his acceptance of one witness' testimony over another's, he imprisoned a man for contempt. See *In re Oliver*, 333 U.S. 206 (1948).

[8]Item 455, p. 16; Item 55; *U.S. v. Carey*, 4 USCMA 112, 15 CMR 112 (1954); Item 166, p. 312.

[9]In the novel, Sears was promised a federal judgeship before he went to "Sarkhan." This might lend credence to the idea that the Eisenhower Administration was casting about to replace Brosman before he died, assuming, of course, that Sears was based on Ferguson, and that Lederer and Burdick had sources of information not available to me. Both Lederer and Ferguson deny my hypothesis. Item 26, Item 55.

[10]See Chapter XVI below.

[11]*Sutton*, 2 USCMA 220, 11 CMR 220 (1953). Other cases on this point are *U.S. v. Valli*, 7 USCMA 60, 21 CMR 186 (1956), and *U.S. v. Drain*, 4 USCMA 646, 16 CMR 220 (1954).

[12] *Parrish*, 1 USCMA 337, 22 CMR 27 (1956); Item 55.

[13]*Jacoby*, 11 USCMA 428, 29 CMR 244 (1960).

[14]Two of the most important Supreme Court cases relating to this point were *Toth v. Quarles*, and *Reid v. Covert*, discussed in detail in Chapter XVI below.

[15]Item 419, p. 45.

[16]Item 106, p. 193.

[17]*Wappler*, 2 USCMA 393, 9 CMR 23 (1953); Item 86, § 125; Item 201, Art. 15(a)(2)(f); *Lucas*, 1 USCMA 19, 1 CMR 19 (1951); *Villasenor*, 6 USCMA 3, 19 CMR 129 (1955).

[18]Item 410, p. 51; *Simmons*, 1 USCMA 691, 5 CMR 119 (1952).

[19]*Boswell*, 8 USCMA 145, 23 CMR 369 (1957).

[20]*Rinehart*, 8 USCMA 402, 24 CMR 212 (1957); *Deain*, 5 USCMA 44, 17 CMR 44 (1954). For other cases along this line, see the list at *Boswell*, p. 148.

[21]Courts could overrule law officers in insanity issues, for example. Item 201, Art. 51(b).

[22]Latimer acknowledged his isolation in *U.S. v. Haynes*, 9 USCMA 792, 22 CMR 60 (1958), 797.

[23]*Cothern*, 8 USCMA 158, 23 CMR 382 (1957).

[24]*Nowling*, 9 USCMA 100, 25 CMR 362 (1958).

[25]*Curtin*, 9 USCMA 427, 26 CMR 207 (1958); Item 86, §171(b).

[26]Item 86, §171(a) and (b); *Lambert v. California*, 355 U.S. 225 (1957).

[27]*Varnadore*, 9 USCMA 471, 26 CMR 251 (1958); *Holt*, 9 USCMA 476, 26 CMR 256 (1958); Item 86, §127(b); *Brasher*, 2 USCMA 50, 6 CMR 50 (1952). Latimer boxed himself in in praising *Brasher*; he had dissented there, too.

[28]*Cecil*, 10 USCMA 371, 27 CMR 445 (1959); *May*, 10 USCMA 358, 27 CMR 432 (1959); Army message DA 443496, Aug. 6, 1956; undated unsigned carbon copy of an Army memo, "By Order of Wilber M. Brucker [Secretary of the Army]," addressed to the Commander-in-Chief, U.S. Army Europe, Item 4 [rather abruptly inquired why USAREUR suspension rates were so low; the carbon copy is stamped "Not Used," but a similar one, though more chummy, addressed to "Dear Hank," was sent]. See *May*, pp. 364-65, for a description of various types of technical suspensions. The offensive *Manual* paragraph was Item 86, §88e (2)(b).

[29]Item 295, pp. 17, 30-31; *U.S. v. Armbruster*, 11 USCMA 596, 29 CMR 412 (1960), p. 598.

[30]It seems likely that the same thing happened to Ferguson in *U.S. v. Smith*, 10 USCMA 153, 27 CMR 227 (1959). Because of the arithmetic of the court, Ferguson was obliged in that case to concur with Quinn on a principle which he had earlier rejected in *U.S. v.*

Horowitz, 10 USCMA 120, 27 CMR 194 (1955). Had he maintained his oppositon to the point, Ferguson might have been joined by Latimer (who reluctantly concurred with the result, too, as it turned out), in a majority that would have effectively overturned the *Varnadore-Holt* doctrine. Ferguson was able conveniently to claim *stare decisis*, and let it go at that. The author is no lawyer, but this sort of tight spot CoMA judges frequently found themselves facing does not seem likely, at least as often, on larger courts, where there is more room to maneuver, philosophically speaking. On Quinn's sense of special responsibility for the enhancement of military justice in general and the Court of Military Appeals in particular, see his dissenting opinions in *U.S. v. Tempia*, 16 USCMA 629, 37 CMR 249 (1966), and *U.S. v. Borys*, 18 USCMA 547, 40 CMR 259 (1969).
[31]*Rinehart*, p. 408.

Notes to Chapter 11

[1]Item 339, p. 589.
[2]Item 312 (July 1950), p. 12; Item 81 (1952), p. 18; Item 166, p. 281; Item 97, p. 57.
[3]Item 149, p. 1292.
[4]Item 127, pp. 10-11; Item 496, p. 15; Item 66. This problem was a cause of the secret House Naval Affairs Committee investigation mentioned above. See Chapter II, note 10.
[5]Item 166, p. 120; Forrestal, letter to JAG, June 25, 1946, Item 120; Item 127, pp. 10-11.
[6]Item 81(1952), p. 18; Item 298 (Oct. 1953), p. 10.
[7]Item 81 (1958), p. 61; *ibid.* (1960), Air Force 4; *ibid.* (1961), p. 68. In 1959, the Air Force enjoyed a net gain of 29 JA's. See *ibid.* (1960), Air Force 4.
[8]*Ibid.* (1958), p. 45; Item 298 (Oct. 1957), p. 18. In 1953, in round numbers, the Navy had 480 lawyers, the Army and Air Force about 1200 each. Item 502, p. 210. By 1959, a year the Air Force concluded with 1232 lawyers, the Navy still had only 465. See Item 81 (1960), Air Force 4; *ibid.* (1959), p. 56.
[9]Item 81 (1962), p. 103; Item 308, Jan. 11, 1961, p. 1.
[10]Item 81 (1963), p. 71; *ibid.* (1964), p. 62.
[11]Item 189; Item 149, p. 680. Nunn was the judge advocate on the court of inquiry that investigated the typhoon that nearly wrecked Admiral Halsey's fleet in 1945. See Item 273, Vol. XIV, p. 308n. Biographies of all the Navy JAG's appear in Item 496, pp. 1-29.
[12]Item 120, pp. 10-11; Item 127, p. 11; Item 185, p. 13; Item 117, p. 93; Item 149, p. 1128.
[13]Item 157, p. 2; Wels, letter to Sen. Richard B. Russell, May 12, 1952; Vinson, letter to Wels, Apr. 2, 1952; Sen. John Stennis, letter to Wels, May 28, 1952; all in Item 14. This is rightly claimed as a victory by the bar association men. But it does not contradict the author's contention that their efforts were generally futile. The civilians could not block Nunn's confirmation and had to settle for promises from Stennis.
[14]Item 496, p. 24.
[15]Item 81 (1960), Navy 5; H.R. 12347, 86th Cong., 2d Sess. (1960).
[16]Item 81 (1953), p. 51; Item 57.
[17]Item 309, 29/55, p. 7; *ibid.*, 36/55, p. 7; Item 81 (1966), p. 64; Item 475, p. 150.
[18]Item 298 (Oct. 1953), p. 13; *ibid.* (Oct. 1954), p. 13. Each issue of the *Judge Advocate Journal* contains this statement of purpose: "[The JAA] seeks to explain to the organized bar the disciplinary needs of the armed forces, . . . [and] to non-lawyers . . . that the American tradition requires . . . at least those minimal guarantees of fairness which go to to make up the attainable ideal of 'Equal Justice under Law.' "
[19]Item 166, p. 271; Item 81 (1955), p. 23.
[20]Item 313, Dec. 2, 1963, pp. 7-10; Item 81 (1958), p. 56; Item 503, pp. 9-10.
[21]Item 81 (1958), p. 53.
[22]For example, Forrestal's acceptance of the Ballantine report (see page 19); the sweeping reforms included in S. 1338 (see pages 29-31); and the adoption of Father White's 1953 recommendations (Mack K. Greenberg, undated memo [1963?] filed with Item 135.)
[23]Item 501, p. 12; Item 54; Item 307, Sep. 4, 1953, p. 183; Item 424, p. 104; Item 378, p. 11.
[24]SECNAVINST 5811. 1, Sept. 11, 1957; SECNAVINST 5811. 2, Dec. 11, 1957; Item 81 (1964), p. 87; Item 171, p. 177; Air Force Manual 111-1 (July 17, 1969), §§4-8; Item 72.

²⁵*Hamill*, 8 USCMA 464, 25 CMR 274 (1957); *Allen*, 8 USCMA 504, 25 CMR 8 (1957); *Walker*, 8 USCMA 647, 25 CMR 151 (1958); *Watkins*, 11 USCMA 611, 29 CMR 427 (1960).
²⁶Item 307, Sep. 4, 1953, p. 183. Civilian bar reformers also generally approved of the negotiated pleas. See minutes of the Nov. 14, 1955 meeting of the City Bar Association Committee on Military Justice, Item 14.
²⁷Army JAGO Memo 10-4, Jul. 5, 1963, §2, Item 4.
²⁸Item 308, Dec. 14, 1960, p. 18; Item 512, pp. 1181-82.
²⁹SECNAVNOTE 5450, Dec. 6, 1950; Item 81 (1961), p. 74.
³⁰Item 81 (1961), p. 60; Item 20.
³¹Item 170, p. 299.
³²Item 171, p. 196; Item 55.
³³Item 512, pp. 1181-82.
³⁴The oldest of the publications was the Navy's *JAG Journal*, first published in 1948; the Army *Military Law Review* appeared in 1958, and a year later the Air Force issued its *JAG Bulletin*, which became the *JAG Law Review* in 1964. The Coast Guard published no law journal, but included legal notes of interest in the *Coast Guard Bulletin*; all the services have unofficial newsletters. The Navy Justice School, now at Newport, R.I., actually antedates Decker's JAG's School, since it was founded in 1947 in Port Hueneme, Cal., where a military government training school had been located during the war. See Item 81 (1957), p. 67; *ibid.*, (1954), p. 56; Wels, "Naval Justice," unpublished manuscript in Item 14, pp. 12-13.
³⁵SECNAVINST 1640, 5, Oct. 1961; Item 501, p. 17.
³⁶Item 171, p. 157; Item 53. Statistics provided the author by CoMA show that the Air Force has consistently certified far fewer cases to the court than the other services. Harmon is remembered for sending "hard" or important cases.
³⁷Item 171, pp. 167-68; Item 196, pp. 1-5, 11, 16-17, 24. The 3320th moved to Lowry AFB, Colo., in the summer of 1967.
³⁸Item 30; Item 263, pp. 51-52. The sociological study is flawed by the small size of the sample; there were only eighty-seven cases studied.
³⁹Item 196, pp. 5, 9, 20; Item 107, p. 3; Item 108, pp. 15-18.
⁴⁰Item 108, p. 6; Item 112; p. 68. One unusual correctional technique CTF uses is to transport successfully retrained men to the Kansas City airport by way of the Army prison at Fort Leavenworth. This is done ostensibly for the convenience of lunch after the 130-mile trip from Fort Riley, but the real reason is to show the CTF "graduates" what happens if they fail on their second chance. See Item 107, pp. 64-65.
⁴¹The Navy has no rehabilitation facility like the two described here. Navy retraining, it is said, is done at the local brig level. See Item 170, p. 1023. This is another example of the Navy's *ad hoc* approach to criminal affairs.

Notes to Chapter 12

¹Item 429, pp. 37-44; Item 114, p. 455; Item 313, Apr. 15, 1963, p. 5. NJP is common to the armed forces of all nations. See Item 462.
²Item 90 (AW 104), p. 13.
³Item 429, p. 99n; Item 281, pp. 71-72.
⁴Item 149, p. 924. Oddly sailors could refuse to submit to deck courts, although a soldier could not opt out of a summary court, the analogous Army trial. This was probably to put a check on the Navy CO who might convene a deck court just to avail himself of the greater powers of punishment. See Item 312 (Mar. 1948), pp. 11-12, for reports of such abuses.
⁵Item 149, p. 932; *ibid.*, pp. 927-928.
⁶Item 149, pp. 932, 945-48. The Navy expert at the hearings told the Congressman that the Navy opposed the forfeiture provision. See *ibid.*, p. 948. In view of the other evidence, he must have erred.
⁷One penalty for officers that did not have to be spelled out in the statute was the shame of being punished. Officers are usually corrected privately and unofficially to avoid smearing their record with the professionally fatal notation that NJP has been administered.
⁸Item 149, p. 932.

[9] Item 117, insert following p. 148.
[10] Larkin, memo to Forrestal, Jan. 5, 1949, Item 10, Vol. IV; Morgan, letter to Forrestal, Feb. 7, 1949, Item 10, Vol. V. See page 40-42.
[11] Item 149, p. 753; Item 253, p. 128; Item 397, p. 151.
[12] Item 122, enclosure, p. 12.
[13] Item 81 (1954), pp. 22, 52.
[14] Item 509, p. 24; Item 135, p. 47.
[15] Item 153, pp. 8413-17, 8453; Item 81 (1954), pp. 32-33, 53.
[16] 10 USC §§3811, 6291, 8811; DOD Directive 1332.14 series; SECNAVINST 1910.3 series; AFM 39-12; AR 635-208.
[17] *U.S. v. Phipps*, 12 USCMA 14, 30 CMR 14 (1960); Item 171, pp. 11-12; DOD Directive 1132.14, Jan. 14, 1959. A table of federal and state veterans' benefits is printed in Item 303 (Apr. 1962), pp. 34-42.
[18] In 1961, only a little over four percent of the Army's separatees were given the general discharge. See Item 171, pp. 11-12. The small number indicates that, despite the "under honorable conditions" tag, there is something wrong with the service rendered by these men. A general discharge does not entitle a veteran to New York state GI benefits. *Schustack v. Herren,* 234 F. 2d 134 (1960), 135n.
[19] Item 171, p. 160; item 356, p. 85n.
[20] There is now an Exemplary Rehabilitation Certificate available from the Labor Department for holders of less than honorable discharges, to indicate that the veteran has overcome the failure which caused his separation. See PL 89-690, Act of October 15, 1966, 80 Stat. 1016.
[21] Item 307, Jan. 2, 1953, p. 1; Item 251, p. 147.
[22] Item 341, p. 199; Item 66.
[23] Item 501, p. 15; Item 398, pp. 819-21, 872-74; Item 399, p. 19; Item 204.
[24] Item 200, Art. 50(b); Item 135, p. 64; Item 112, p. xx.
[25] Wolff, letter to Wels, Sep. 11, 1951; Wels letter to Abraham S. Robinson, Oct. 28, 1958; and Wels, letter to Keeffe, same date; all in Item 14; Item 150, p. 8580.
[26] H.R. 5116, 82d Cong., 1st Sess. (1951); Item 151, p. 14; Item 185, pp. 37-39.
[27] Item 298 (Oct. 1958), pp. 5-6, Judge Ferguson and Col. Wiener have each on occasion stated that Harmon's speech was meant to encourage the use of the administrative discharge loophole. See Item 170, p. 300, and Item 171, p. 796. But the original account of the speech, and Harmon's testimony at Item 171, p. 165, make it clear that they were wrong.
[28] Wels, letter to Robinson, Oct. 28, 1958, Item 14; Item 81 (1958), p. 68; *ibid.* (1960), CoMA 12.

Notes to Chapter 13

[1] Item 81 (1959), p. 49; *ibid.* (1958), pp. 43-44; *ibid.* (1957), p. 42. Among the cases singled out for attack were *Cothern, Rinehart, Varnadore-Holt, Curtin, Nowling,* and *Cecil-May.* See pp. 101-105.
[2] Item 81 (1958), p. 44.
[3] Item 375, p. 13; Item 57.
[4] The Air Force proposal is included in JAGJ 1958/8622, Jan. 5, 1959, Item 4.
[5] Navy Office of the JAG, memo for Maj. Gen. Harmon, 2 January 1959, copy attached to JAGJ 1958/8622, p. 2, Item 4.
[6] O'Brien, letter to Richard B. Tibbs, Dec. 30, 1958, enclosure 7, JAGJ 1958/8622, pp. 1, 6, 9, Item 4.
[7] "Report of the Ad Hoc Committee . . . ," JAGJ 1958/8622, pp. 1-4, Item 4.
[8] *Air Force Times,* Jan. 18, 1958 and Dec. 27, 1958; H.R. 3387, S. 2259, and H.R. 3455, 86th Cong., 1st Sess. (1959).
[9] Item 185, pp. 7-10.
[10] Item 436, p. 302; Item 81 (1960), Army 203-04.
[11] Item 333, p. 844.
[12] Item 59; Item 54.
[13] Item 59; Item 54.
[14] Item 67.

[15]Item 106, pp. 29-30, 54-54, Item 67. The abolition of the lowest court-martial was proposed as early as 1945, when the McGuire committee found the Navy "deck" court rife with possible injustices. See Item 90, AW 10, p. 3. But the Harmon and Powell recommendations were the first to tie such an elimination to increases in non judicial powers.
[16]*Miranda v. Arizona*, 384 U.S. 436 (1966), p. 489.
[17]The citations given below are only to cases heard during the first decade of the court, and at that merely scratch the surface of the topic of Article 31 litigation; *U.S. v. Doyle*, 1 USCMA 545, 4 CMR 137 (1952); *U.S. v. Haynes*, 9 USCMA 792, 27 CMR 60 (1958), dealing with the "fruit of the poison tree" doctrine; *U.S. v. Noce*, 5 USCMA 715, 19 CMR 11 (1955), wiretapping; *U.S. v. Villasenor*, 6 USCMA 3, 19 CMR 129 (1955), corroboration of confessions; *U.S. v. Jewson*, 1 USCMA 652, 5 CMR 80 (1952), and *U.S. v. Rock*, 9 USCMA 503, 26 CMR 283 (1958), both on entrapment; *U.S. v. Morse*, 9 USCMA 799, 26 CMR 67 (1958), and *U.S. v. Rosato*, 3 USCMA 143, 11 CMR 43 (1953), distinguishing "statement" from "evidence."
[18]*Jordan*, 7 USCMA 452, 22 CMR 242 (1957).
[19]*Minnifield*, 9 USCMA 373, 26 CMR 153 (1958). In the line of cases marked by *Breithaupt v. Abram*, 352 U.S. 432 (1957), and *Schmerber v. California*, 384 U.S. 757 (1966), the Supreme Court has consistently held that the Fifth Amendment ban on compelled self-incrimination is applicable only to verbal statements, not handwriting samples, blood tests, voice analyses, footprints, and the like. See pages 180-181.
[20]See page 103.
[21]The cases cited were *Jordan, Nowling*, and *U.S. v. Musquire*, 9 USCMA 67, 25 CMR 329 (1958), a blood-test case. Without trying to make too much of this, it is interesting that the Powell report cites cases only by their CMR location, and not by the USCMA citation, a breach of unswerving custom, and in this case perhaps of courtesy, too.
[22]Item 81 (1960), CoMA 4, 6-7, 10-11.
[23]Item 313, May 23, 1961, p. 1; Item 436, pp. 303-04.

Notes to Chapter 14

[1]Kenneth J. Hodson, memo for the record, Jan. 4, 1961, p. 1, Item 3.
[2]Phillip S. Hughes (Executive Office of the President), letter to Secretary of Defense Thomas S. Gates, Jan. 4, 1961; and Hodson, memo "for the record," Jan. 4, 1961, 1, 3; both in Item 3. Under previous authority, the Air Force resubmitted the omnibus bill in January 1961. See Item 81 (1961), p. 1. But the main thrust was now behind the new plan.
[3]In October 1961, Paul J. Kilday of Texas joined the court, replacing Judge Latimer, whose term expired in May 1961. See Chapter XV. Quinn had been a Rhode Island state senator, Ferguson a U.S. Senator, and Kilday a Congressman from Texas. Among them, they had accumulated almost forty years legislative experience.
[4]PL 87-385, Act of Oct. 4, 1961, 75 Stat. 814.
[5]See Bill "A" in Item 81 (1961), pp. 7-10.
[6]Item 167, pp. 11, 27; Item 313, Aug. 24, 1962, p. 2; Item 165, pp. 1-2. The American Legion endorsed the new bill once the right of election was included, leaving thereafter no organized resistance to passage. See Item 143, pp. 5-7; Item 167, p. 30.
[7]PL 87-648, Act of Sept. 7, 1962, 76 Stat. 447.
[8]Compare Bill "B" as it appears in Item 81 (1961) and Item 81 (1962). See also JAGJ memo 1962/8445, June 26, 1962, from Lt. Col. Bruce C. Babbitt to Judge Jack A. Falk, Miami, Fla.; "Sectional Analysis of a Bill 'B' [labelled "Mastercopy GGA 12/5/62"], in Item 3, a copy of which is in the author's possession. This last source has the typed paragraphs relating to the summary courts heavily crossed out.
[9]Minutes of the Mar. 3, 1961 meeting, JAGJ 1961/8291, Item 3; Item 106, p. 32; Item 171, pp. 250-51; Item 170, p. 115; Powell, letter to Gen. Earle Wheeler, Jan. 30, 1963, Item 3.
[10]Item 81 (1962), pp. 99, 117; *ibid.* (1964), pp. 57, 76; Item 313, Nov. 10, 1961, enclosure p. 1.
[11]Item 313, Dec. 2, 1963, pp. 2-5; *ibid.*, Apr. 8, 1964, pp. 3-4.
[12]Item 81 (1964), p. 76; *ibid.* (1967), p. 30.

[13]There were 22,000 forfeitures, 24,400 extra duties, and 24,600 restrictions. See Item 308, May 20, 1964, p. 6.
[14]Item 106, pp. 25-28; Item 81 (1963), p. 72; Item 67. As director of Ford Foundation National Defender Project, Decker promotes the idea of "Neighborhood Courts," which closely resemble Article 15 sessions.
[15]See comments to this effect in Item 313, Dec. 2, 1963; *Army Times*, June 5, 1963; and *Air Force Times*, June 26, 1963.

Notes to Chapter 15

[1]Item 59; Item 68; Item 62; Item 63.
[2]*New York Times*, June 2, 1961, 10:5.
[3]*New York Times*, June 2, 1961, 10:5; Item 68; Item 170, p. 293. Johnson was elected by 87 votes out of nearly one million cast. See Item 252, p. 24.
[4]The data were compiled for the author by the Staff of Col. John C. Wasson, Chief of the Air Force Division of Military Justice, by interrogating the Defense Department's computer system, dubbed LITE—Legal Information Through Electronics—and are contained in Item 43. Not included are those decisions where the judge dissented in part and concurred in part. The "total decisions" figures were calculated by the author from figures provided by the chief commissioner of the Court, Mr. Carney.
[5]*Culp*, 14 USCMA 199, 33 CMR 411 (1963); other scholarly Kilday opinions include *U.S. v. Smith*, 13 USCMA 105, 32 CMR 105 (1962), dealing with Presidential power to promulgate rules of evidence and procedure; *U.S. v. Kauffman*, 14 USCMA 283, 34 CMR 63 (1963), a spy case; *U.S. v. Carter* 16 USCMA 277, 36 CMR 433 (1966), on search and seizure; and *U.S. v. Howe*, 17 USCMA 165, 37 CMR 429 (1967), a civil liberties test.
[6]*Wimberley*, 16 USCMA 3, 36 CMR 159 (1966); *Lewandowski*, 17 USCMA 51, 37 CMR 315 (1967).
[7]*Smith*, 17 USCMA 55, 37 CMR 319 (1967); *Erb*, 12 USCMA 524, 31 CMR 110 (1961); *U.S. v. Manuel*, 16 USCMA 357, 36 CMR 513 (1966).
[8]*Navy Times*, Nov. 11, 1961 and Feb. 1, 1963; *Army Times*, May 3, 1967; *Air Force Times*, March 22, 1967 and May 8, 1968; *O'Such*, 16 USCMA 537, 37 CMR 157 (1967).
[9]*Breen*, 15 USCMA 658, 16 CMR 156 (1966); Item 86, sample 174, p. 494.
[10]All emphasis is Judge Quinn's. Inner quotes cited the language of *U.S. v. Adams*, 5 USCMA 563, 18 CMR 187 (1955).
[11]*Navy Times*, Feb. 23, 1966.
[12]Item 81 (1966), p. 5.
[13]*Navy Times*, May 11, 1966. There was a slight hitch in Senate confirmation, however, as Sen. Stephen Young, of Ohio, demonstrated his displeasure at President Johnson's refusal to appoint a Young protégé because he was too old at 62. The Senator forced *a pro forma* committee hearing, a rarity in such cases, but then enthusiastically backed Quinn's nomination. See Item 168, pp. 1, 5-6.
[14]Item 149, pp. 1211-13.
[15]*Ferguson*, 5 USCMA 68, 17 CMR 68 (1954); 28 USC §1651(a).
[16]*Tavares*, 10 USCMA 282, 27 CMR 356 (1959); *Taylor*, 12 USCMA 427, 31 CMR 13 (1961); *U.S. v. Bennet*, 11 USCMA 799 (1960); *U.S. v. Davies*, 13 USCMA 716 (1962); *U.S. v. Randall*, 14 USCMA 700 (1963); *U.S. v. St. Thomas*, 15 USCMA 705 (1964). There was one habeas corpus petition, similarly rejected: *U.S. v. Swisher*, 14 USCMA 700 (1963).
[17]*Frischholz*, 16 USCMA 150, 36 CMR 306 (1966); *ibid.* 12 USCMA 727.
[18]*Gale*, 17 USCMA 40, 37 CMR 304 (1967); 17 USCMA x; 16 USCMA ix; Item 81 (1967), p. 5.
[19]*Levy v. Resor*, 17 USCMA 135, 37 CMR 399 (1967). Levy's petition was for habeas corpus and mandamus.
[20]*Jackson*, 17 USCMA 681 (1968); *Bevilacqua*, 18 USCMA 10, 39 CMR 10 (1968).
[21]*Noyd v. Bond*, 395 U.S. 683 (1969). There are indications that the boards of review may soon exercise extraordinary powers; *U.S. v. Dolby*, CM 419804 (U.S. Army Court of Military Review, Sept. 19, 1969), unreported.
[22]Judge Kilday viewed the military as a new federal jurisdiction in *U.S. v. Tempia*, 16 USCMA 629, 37 CMR 249 (1967), especially at 641. Judge Quinn argued that the growth of

this new "district" was appropriate since there were more people in it than in 22 of the states of the Union. See Item 453, p. 1.
[23]A "recess appointment" is one made while Congress is not in session; this one came on election day, Nov. 5, 1968. Senate confirmation was given Jan. 14, 1969, only six days before Richard Nixon took office. Considering the trouble Mr. Johnson had with his Fortas and Thornberry nominations, Darden's acceptance was no mean accomplishment.
[24]LITE has not yet been programmed to include the recent CoMA decisions and no statistics are yet available either on the Quinn-Ferguson-Darden court, or on the Darden-Quinn-Duncan one. Item 43. See *U.S. v. Borys*, 18 USCMA 547. 40 CMR 259 (1969), for recent Quinn and Ferguson views.
[25]*Navy Times*, Oct. 6, 1971, 12:1; *New York Times*, Nov. 30, 1971, 53:4.

Notes to Chapter 16

[1]*Dynes*, 61 U.S. (20 How.) 65 (1857); emphasis in original.
[2]Item 295, pp. 53-55; Item 504, p. 187.
[3]Item 432, p. 170.
[4]*Decatur*, 39 U.S. (14 Pet.) 497 (1840).
[5]*Abelman*, 62 U.S. (21 How.) 506 (1858); *Tarble*, 80 U.S. (13 Wall.) 397 (1871); *Vallandigham*, 68 U.S. (1 Wall.) 243 (1863); *Milligan*, 71 U.S. (4 Wall.) 2 (1866).
[6]*Nielsen* 131 U.S. 176 (1889); *Grimley*, 137 U.S. 147 (1890); *Swaim*, 165 U.S. 553 (1897); *Grafton*, 206 U.S. 333 (1907).
[7]Item 295, pp. 131-32, 138, 146, 829.
[8]*Reaves*, 219 U.S 296 (1911).
[9]*Johnson*, 304 U.S. 438 (1938).
[10]*Billings*,327 U.S. 542 (1944); *Quirin*, 317 U.S. 1 (1942); *Yamashita*, 327 U.S. 1 (1946); *Hirabayashi*, 320 U.S. 81 (1943); *Korematsu*, 323 U.S. 214 (1944). With the growing interest in the question of American war crimes in Vietnam, the Yamashita case has become the topic of new study recently. See Item 479, p. 34.
[11]*Schita v. King*, 133 F. 2d 283 (1943); *Schita v. Cox*, 139 F. 2d 971 (1944). In the rehearing, the Army presented its case more vigorously and proved that Schita's claims were baseless.
[12]*Innes*, 141 F. 2d 664 (1944); *Hicks*, 64 F. Supp. 238 (1946). The Supreme Court handling of the latter case is given below, page 173.
[13]*Hunter*, 169 F. 2d 973 (1948).
[14]*Shapiro*, 69 F. Supp. 205 (1947).
[15]Back-pay litigation has been used by victims of alleged arbitrary treatment at the hands of administrative discharge boards. An outstanding example is *Clackum v. U.S.*, 296 F. 2d 226 (1960); see also summaries of other cases in Item 171, pp. 926-27, 961-64.
[16]Item 133, p. 1.
[17]Item 85, pp. 2-3; Item 149, pp. 865-69, 872-74; Item 139, pp. 10-11.
[18]*Durant v. Hironimus*, 73 F. Supp. 79 (1947); *Hironimus v. Durant*, 168 F. 2d 288 (1948); cert. den., 335 U.S. 818 (1948).
[19]*U.S. ex rel. Hirshberg v. Cooke*, 336 U.S. 210 (1949). The charge that military courts discriminated between officers and enlisted men (see page 17) may be confirmed by the acquittal of Lt. Comdr. Edward Little, who was tried in secret by a Navy court on charges very similar to those of which Hirshberg was convicted; *New York Times*, Nov. 26, 1947, 5:1.
[20]34 USC §855 (1934); Item 149, pp. 567, 880-884.
[21]Item 149, p. 881; AW 94 (1948); Item 117, pp. 176, 380; Item 166, p. 256; Item 85, p. 11.
[22]Item 117, p. 176; Item 129, p. 112; Item 149, p. 624. See Gen. Green's testimony in Item 166, p. 256, and Col. Wiener's in Item 170, pp. 315-18, both citing the precedent of *U.S. v. Bowman*, 260 U.S. 94 (1922), and *U.S. v. Blackmer*, 284 U.S. 421 (1932).
[23]A W 53 (1948).
[24]Item 289, p. vii; Item 420, p. 176; Item 484, pp. 294-95; *Hiatt v. Brown*, 339 U.S. 103 (1950). The lower court handling of the *Hiatt* case is discussed on page 169.
[25]*Gusik*, 340 U.S. 128 (1950); *Whelchel*, 340 U.S. 122 (1950), 126.

[26] *Burns v. Wilson*, 346 U.S. 137 (1953).

[27] E.g., *U.S. v. Marker*, 1 USCMA 393, 3 CMR 127 (1952), where it held that civilians were not presumed amenable to court-martial, so government had to prove such status positively; *U.S. v. Solinsky*, 2 USCMA 153, 7 CMR 29 (1953), where it distinguished the discharge technique employed in *Hirshberg*; and *U.S. v. Garcia*, 5 USMCA 88, 17 CMR 88 (1954), and *U.S. v. Long*, 5 USCMA 572, 18 CMR 196 (1955), where it dealt with questions of waiver in jurisdictional disputes.

[28] *Toth v. Quarles*, 350 U.S. 11 (1955); *Air Force Times*, May 30, 1953; *New York Times*, Nov. 8, 1955, 26:5. Although the Air Force later did select a test case for an important legal point (see page 182), it apparently did not do so here according to Gen. Harmon in Item 21.

[29] *Toth v. Talbott*, 113 F. Supp. 330 (1953); *Talbott v. U.S. ex rel. Toth*, 215 F. 2d 22 (1954).

[30] For a sample of views on the statutory gap created by *Toth*, see Item 514, pp. 1127-1130; Item 170, p. 334; *Navy Times*, June 26, 1963; and *Washington Post*, May 30, 1963, A18:1-3. One of the proposals advanced by the National Commission on Reform of Federal Criminal Laws would cover the gap. See *New York Times*, Jan. 17, 1971, IV, 8:4. The invalidation of UCMJ Art. 3(a) was the reason that those members of Lt. Calley's platoon who were no longer in the Army could not be tried for their part in the My Lai massacre, when that incident finally came to light.

[31] *Gallagher*, 7 USCMA 506, 22 CMR 296 (1957); *Gallagher v. Quinn,. et al.*, 303 F. 2d 301 (1966), pet. den., 385 U.S. 881 (1966). The respondent here was Chief Judge Quinn; Gallagher complained that Article 67(b)(1) was unconstitutional in that it provided mandatory review in the case of generals and admirals, but not for other ranks, a point originally raised by Arthur John Keeffe in 1950. See page 66. The courts disagreed. *Martin*, 10 USCMA 636, 28 CMR 202 (1959) [Ferguson dissenting] ; *Wheeler*, 10 USCMA 646, 28 CMR 212 (1959); *Wheeler v. Reynolds*, 164 F. Supp. 951 (1958).

[32] *Smith*, 5 USCMA 314, 17 CMR 314 (1954); *Sauer v. U.S.*, 241 F. 2d 640 (1957), 646-647, and *U.S. v. Currens*, 290 F. 2d 751 (1961), 771; both refer to Brosman's "excellent opinion" in the *Smith* decision.

[33] Item 73; *U.S. v. Covert*, 6 USCMA 483, 19 CMR 174 (1955); *Kinsella v. Krueger*, 351 U.S. 470 (1956); *Reid v. Covert*, 351 U.S. 487 (1956). Wiener represented Mrs. Covert, too; her case was also considered primarily on insanity. questions by CoMA.

[34] Item 73; *Reid v. Covert*, 352 U.S. 901 (1956). The court's growing interest in courts-martial is further indicated by the fact that between 1937 and 1958, it invalidated only four acts of Congress, but two of them, Arts 2(11) and 3(a) of the *UCMJ*, were in military justice. See Item 270, p. 212.

[35] Item 81 (1956), p. 44; Item 298 (Mar. 1957), p. 47.

[36] *Reid v. Covert*, 354 U.S. 1 (1957).

[37] *U.S. ex rel. Singleton v. Kinsella*, 361 U.S. 234 (1960); *U.S. ex rel. Guagliardo v. McElroy* and *Wilson v. Bohlender*, 361 U.S. 281 (1960); and *Grishman v. Hagan*, 361 U.S. 278 (1960).

[38] *Jencks v. U.S.*, 353 U.S. 657 (1957); a few months later, Congress reinstated the FBI practice by legislation, PL 85-269, Act of Sep. 2, 1957, 71 Stat. 595; *U.S. News and World Report* (June 28, 1957), p. 30; *Watkins v. U.S.*, 354 U.S. 178 (1957); *Sweezy v. New Hampshire*, 354 U.S. 234 (1957); *Yates v. U.S.*, 354 U.S. 298 (1957); *Service v. Dulles et al.*, 354 U.S. 363 (1957).

[39] Item 92; Item 93; Item 298 (Oct. 1953), p. 3; Item 326; H.R. 8957, 85th Cong., 1st Sess. (1957); *Girard*, 354 U.S. 524 (1957). In his trial before the Japanese, Girard was defended by Charles Decker. The trial was scrupulously fair, but he was convicted and imprisoned. See *Air Force Times*, Aug. 10, 1957. For reports on GI's in foreign jails, see *Army Times*, June 17, 1961 and Oct. 16, 1968. The terms of the agreement between the State and Defense Departments curiously resemble the mandate laid down 14 years later in the historic *O'Callahan v. Parker* decision, discussed below, on pp. 183-185.

[40] The most and least restrained of this genre of literature are Item 438 and Item 398.

[41] *Breithaupt*, 352 U.S. 432 (1957); *Minnifield*, 9 USCMA 373, 26 CMR 153 (1958).

[42] *Miranda v. Arizona*, 384 U.S. 436 (1966). Other cases in the line included *Mallory v. U.S.*, 354 U.S. 449 (1957); *Gideon v. Wainwright*, 372 U.S. 335 (1963); and *Escobedo v. Illinois* 378 U.S. 478 (1964).

[43]Item 308, Jul. 6, 1966, pp. 18-19; Navy message ALNAV 40 (1966); Item 313 (Oct. 1966), pp. 11-13; Item 504, p. 189.

[44]Item 81 (1966), p. 60; *Tempia*, 16 USCMA 629, 37 CMR 249 (1967). The Navy has been more agreeable in complying with CoMA decisions. It accepted *Rinehart* without protest and, in contrast to the Army's outrage at *Cothern*, seemed sincerely enthusiastic about the result in that case. See Navy messages ALNAV 28 and 57 (1957).

[45]*O'Callahan*, 395 U.S. 258 (1969), 272. A replacement for Justice Fortas had not yet been appointed to the Court. An irony in *O'Callahan* was that Frederick Wiener was retained as a consultant by the Justice Department for the government's case but was not permitted by the solicitor to argue, despite the fact that the latter's inexperience in military justice caused him to make a number of errors that may have hurt the government's argument. *Navy Times*, Feb. 12, 1969. There can be no doubt that Wiener would have been more competent.

[46]The idea of "open and operating" civilian courts has been important throughout this history; it accounted for the geographic limits of AGN 6 and AW 92 and for the boundaries in Article 2(11) of the UCMJ.

[47]*U.S. v. Snyder*, 20 USCMA 102, 42 CMR 294 (1970).

Notes to Chapter 17

[1]*Congressional Directory*, 91st Cong., 1st Sess. (1969), 128; Item 252, pp. 84-85; *New York Times*, July 17, 1968, 24:4 and July 18, 1968, 20:1; *San Francisco Sunday Examiner and Chronicle*, June 14, 1970, A19:1-8; *Time*, Mar. 8, 1971, pp. 38-39; Item 377, p. 107; Item 417; Item 81 (1963), p. 51.

[2]Item 171, pp. 1-2. See page 180.

[3]Item 170, pp. 2, 169.

[4]*Ibid.*, pp. 4-5; Item 356, p. 79n.

[5]Item 170, pp. 343-54, 403-96. It is no wonder that the ABA supported the DOD proposal; its Military Justice Committee was served by an "advisory committee" composed of the three service JAG's, the Coast Guard general counsel., and a high-ranking Marine lawyer! Item 35. What is surprising is that the ABA continued to press for H.R. 3387 after the JAG's had given up on omnibus legislation.

[6]S. 2002 through S. 2019, 88th Cong., 1st Sess. (1963); S. 2009: S. 2002; S. 2004.

[7]Item 171, pp. 165, 169-75, 827-964.

[8]Item 171, p. 401; Item 149, pp. 1298-1301; Item 66. Two bills not mentioned in the text would provide federal district court jurisdiction over persons formerly triable by court-martial under Arts. 2(11) and 3(a) of the code before the *Toth* and *Covert* decisions. The real issue after the invalidation of those two articles was not whether jurisdiction existed, but how in practice to try such people in the face of the overwhelming logistics problems of procuring witness, or transporting juries to and from overseas sites and American courtrooms.

[9]Item 169, pp. 61-62.

[10]Item 171, p. 134. Detracting from the validity of Kuhfeld's argument is the fact that the Army and Navy convened vastly more courts-martial during the period cited. Comparing the figures used by Kuhfeld with the totals given in Item 81 (1962), pp. 99, 109, and 117, it would seem that the Army's *rate* of reversals before the court was the best, while the Navy's and Air Force's were about the same. This destroys Kuhfeld's contention that Air Force lawyers were the best, but it supports mine that the existence of a JAG Corps made no substantial difference.

[11]Item 81 (1964), p. 57; *ibid.* (1967), p. 19; *ibid.* (1967), p. 15; *ibid.* (1964), p. 51.

[12]Item 313, Nov. 24, 1967, pp. 12, 21-23. The Muse report covered the whole range of the Navy's legal problems and recommended, among other things, an excess leave program like the Army's (see page 109) and authorization for NRTOC graduates to go to law school before entering active duty.

[13]Item 115, "Summary," p. 52; Item 81 (1969), p. 28; Item 475, p. 148.

[14]Item 313, Nov. 30, 1965, p. 1; Item 298 (May 1958), p. 6; *ibid.* (Mar. 1969), pp. 11-12.

[15]S. 1165, 86th Cong., 1st Sess. (1957); Item 298 (Oct. 1957), p. 15. Two recent bills containing the measure have been H.R. 4296 and H.R. 9567, 90th Cong., 1st Sess. (1967).

[16]Item 356, p. 79.
[17]Item 81 (1962), p. 2; *ibid.* (1963), pp. 3-4.
[18]S. 2906 and 2907, 89th Cong., 1st Sess. (1966); Item 356, p. 79; Item 170, p. 1.
[19]Item 171, pp. 193, 206, 256, 400; Item 170, pp. 295-96, 300. Ferguson did not mention Harmon by name, but the reference was clear.
[20]Item 171, pp. 827-967; Item 170, part 3.
[21]S. 2009, 90th Cong., 1st Sess. (1967).
[22]The author asked Ervin to explain his reasoning in a letter, March 7, 1971, but the Senator did not reply.
[23]Item 170, pp. 168-172, 340-43, 873.
[24]H.R. 12910, H.R. 6044, and S. 2634, 90th Cong., 1st Sess. (1967); PL 90-179, Act of Dec. 8, 1967, 81 Stat. 545-549; PL 90-340, Act of June 15, 1968, 82 Stat. 178-179. There was still no life tenure for CoMA judges.
[25]Item 469, p. 129.
[26]PL 90-632, Act of Oct. 24, 1968, 82 Stat. 1335-1343. The vote in both Houses was unanimous, certainly an ironic ending to nearly twenty years of often bitter debate. One of the more humorous, if wasteful, moments in military justice history occurred in conjunction with the new *Manual*. The services had labored long to develop an official revision to *MCM '51*. They finally did get together, and after several years of work, produced a shiny new *Manual*, just in time to see it made obsolete by the 1968 law. An even newer *MCM*, identified as the "Revised Edition," was published in June 1969, in time to accompany the new law into the field. See Item 87 and Item 88.
[27]This new provision gave President Nixon statutory authority to release Lt. Calley from close confinement pending the completion of his appeal, although it is not clear whether the President based his action in doing so on that part of the new code or on some "intrinsic power" of his office. On technical suspensions, see pp. 104-105.
[28]Item 356, p. 97; Item 142, p. 2.
[29]Compare DOD directive 1332.14, "Administrative Discharges," dated Dec. 20, 1965, with the same directive dated Jan. 14, 1959; see also Item 415, pp. 150-58; Item 438, p. 139; H.R. 843 and S. 1226, 91st Cong., 1st Sess. (1969).

Notes to Chapter 18

[1]*New York Times*, Nov. 11, 1970, 1:6. Calley's chief defense counsel was George W. Latimer, Jr., former judge of the Court of Military Appeals.
[2]Going back a century, a good example of this point was the military trial of Capt. Henry Wirz, ex-commandant of the Andersonville prisoner-of-war camp. He tried a defense similar to Calley's, and even though his target was the defeated Confederate high command, the Union Army tribunal refused to hear it. See Item 266, pp. 38-40; Item 247, p. 362.
[3]Another benefit of the 1968 law that was underscored in the Calley case was the excellence of the prosecutor and the military defense counsel. All of these junior officers, Capt. Aubrey McDaniel for the government and Maj. Kenneth W. Raby and Capt. Brooks Doyle for the defense, turned in highly competent performances. In the view of at least one observer, Calley's fate was partly the result of George Latimer's sorry exhibition as compared to his young military colleagues and adversary. See Item 465, and the preceding footnotes.
[4]*New York Times*, Oct. 17, 1970, 1:1 and Feb. 9, 1971, 1:1.
[5]Item 257, p. 106.
[6]The cases that prove this point are many; for example, the court took a hard line on apparent command influence in the following cases: *U.S. v. Gordon*, 1 USCMA 255, 2 CMR 161 (1952); *U.S. v. Littrice*, 3 USCMA 487, 13 CMR 43 (1953); *U.S. v. Whitely*, 5 USCMA 786, 19 CMR 82 (1955); *U.S. v. Hawthorne*, 7 USCMA 293, 22 CMR 83 (1956); *U.S. v. Lackey*, 8 USCMA 718, 25 CMR 222 (1958); *U.S. v. Kitchens*, 12 USCMA 589, 31 CMR 175 (1961); *U.S. v. Donati*, 14 USCMA 235, 34 CMR 15 (1963); *U.S. v. Fraser*, 15 USCMA 28, 34 CMR 474 (1964); *U.S. v. DuBay*, 17 USCMA 147, 37 CMR 411 (1967); there are many more. CoMA has no power over the subtle sort of command influence exercised by President Nixon in pronouncing that he would conduct the final review in the Calley case;

no one can question the President's right to do so, but the timing of the announcement could place extreme pressure on the appellate courts. See also page 205.

[7] See page 162.

[8] Item 329, pp. 33-34; Item 422.

[9] The WPPBA is the informal organization supposedly based on the loyalty of all Academy men towards all others, which prevents them from acting harshly with each other. See *Newsweek*, Nov. 16, 1970, p. 54. The author knows personally of a Navy case that was kept from trial apparently by the influence of the "Green Bowlers," who are supposed to perform roughly the same function in the Navy. See Item 279, p. 260; *Arnheiter v. Ignatius*, 292 F. Supp. 911 (1968).

[10] Item 112.

[11] The nation's prisons are criticized in Item 477; the California system is unfavorably described in Item 363; and the District of Columbia's jails are condemned in an editorial, *The [Washington] Star*, Oct. 16, 1970, A8:1.

[12] As, for example, it is heavily implied in Item 280.

[13] *Navy Times* Jul. 3, 1968; Item 69.

[14] S. 4168 through 4178 and S. 4191, 91st Cong., 2d Sess. (1970).

[15] It was not until 1972 that the Supreme Court made the "service-connected" guide-line retroactive. *New York Times,* March 29, 1972, 46:2-3. The litigation that results from that action could overwhelm the entire military justice system.

[16] Item 261, pp. 460-61.

[17] This is apparently not just an American experience; most of the major nations of the world had important overhauls of their military justice systems in the years immediately following World War II. See Item 352, p. 6; Item 355, p. 65; Item 372, p. 2; Item 381, p. 87; Item 402, p. 128n; Item 441, p. 113; Item 444, p. 307; Item 462, pp. 276-85.

[18] *New York Times,* Oct. 29, 1970, 17:1.

[19] Such factors were at work in the Army's recent alterations regarding nonjudicial punishment in the wake of complaints that discrepancies existed between treatment afforded white soldiers and blacks. *San Francisco Sunday Examiner and Chronicle*, Mar. 21, 1971, A19:1; Item 191.

[20] I have been told that one serious flaw in this plan is that it provides no suitable way to punish a man who commits a serious "military" offense, such as absenting himself from his unit in order to avoid combat, sleeping on watch in a war zone, or disobeying an order under fire, all of which would imperil the other men in his outfit. Such crimes would not be recognizable in a civilian court, and under my proposal the military would have scant power to punish the offenders. While tentatively conceding the validity of this charge, I hasten to point out that stiff court-martial sentences handed down in time of war for military offenses are usually cut after the war to terms which approximate the limits here suggested. For example, after the Roberts board finished its clemency work for the Army in 1947 (see pp. 16-17), the median sentences for wartime AWOL and desertion were, respectively, 3.4 years and 5.0 years. See Item 104, p. 3. In the long run, then, it would seem that these offenses do not merit much more punishment than my plan proposes.

Bibliography

Collections

1. Eisenhower, Dwight D., Papers Eisenhower Library, Abilene, Kans.
2. Friedman, Martin L., Papers. Truman Library. Independence, Mo.
3. Judge Advocate General of the Army, Files on Bills "A," "B," and "C." Division of Military Justice. The Pentagon.
4. ————, Miscellaneous JAGJ Memoranda. Division of Military Justice. The Pentagon.
5. ————. Collections. JAG Library. The Pentagon.
6. Judge Advocate General of the Navy, Collections. JAG Library. Arlington, Va.
7. Larkin, Felix E., Military Justice Files. 3 Hanover Square, New York City.
8. Law Center Library, Collections. U.S. Naval Station, Treasure Island, Calif.
9. McGrath, J. Howard, Papers. Truman Library. Independence, Mo.
10. Morgan, Edmund M., Papers on the Uniform Code of Military Justice. Treasure Room, Harvard Law School Library. Cambridge, Mass.
11. Stanford University, Government Depository. Stanford, Calif.
12. Truman Harry S, Papers. Truman Library. Independence, Mo.
13. U.S. Sixth Army, Judge Advocate Library. Collections. The Presidio of San Francisco, Calif.
14. Wels, Richard H., Military Justice File. 18 E. 48th Street. New York City.

Letters to the Author including historical information

15. Ansell, Samuel T., Jr., Washington, D.C. March 1, 1971.
16. Decker, Charles L., Washington, D.C. Feb. 4, 1971.
17. DeWitt, Paul B., New York. Dec. 29, 1970.
18. Ferguson, Homer., Washington, D.C. Dec. 30, 1970.
19. Halloran, Norbert A. [Administrative Offices of the U.S. Courts], Washington, D.C. Feb. 10, 1971.
20. Harmon, Reginald C., Arlington, Va. Dec. 4, 1970.
21. ————, Feb. 19, 1971.
22. Keeffe, Arthur John, Washington, D.C. Dec. 23, 1970.
23. Larkin, Felix E., New York. Nov. 24, 1970.
24. ————, Dec. 3, 1970.
25. ————, Dec. 28, 1970.

26. Lederer, William J.,   Peacham, Vermont. Dec. 7 [?], 1970.
27 Leva, Marx,   Washington, D.C. Nov. 16, 1970.
28. ————,   Nov. 23, 1970.
29. McCafferty, James A. [Administrative Offices of the U.S. Courts],   Washington, D.C. Feb. 18, 1971.
30. McGillen, John L. [Army Correctional Training Facility],   Fort Riley, Kans. Dec. 28, 1970.
31. Norton, Francis E., Jr. [3320th Rtrng Grp, USAF], Lowry AFB, Colo. Nov. 4, 1970.
32. Ohly, John Hallowell,   MacLean, Va. Nov. 24, 1970.
33. ————, Jan. 3, 1971.
34. Pasley, Robert S.,   Ithaca N.Y. Jan. 18. 1971.
35. Raske, Elma [American Bar Association Military Justice Committee], Chicago. Dec. 24. 1970.
36. Sappenfield, G.K. [Clerk, Iowa Supreme Court],   Des Moines. Nov. 3, 1970.
37. Smart, Robert W.,   Washington, D.C. Feb. 8, 1971.
38. Sobeloff, Simon E. [Fourth Circuit U.S. Court of Appeals],   Baltimore. Nov. 2, 1970.
39. Spiegelberg, George A.,   Hillsdale, N.Y. Dec. 2, 1970.
40. Tait, Edward T.,   Washington, D.C. Feb. 3, 1971.
41. Tedrow, Richard L.,   No. Myrtle Beach, So. Car. Oct. 26 [?], 1970.
42. ————,   Nov. 5 [?], 1970.
43. Wasson, John C.,   Washington, D.C. Jan. 27, 1971.
44. ————,   Feb. 9, 1971.
45. Wels, Richard H.,   New York. Nov. 27, 1970.
46. ————,   Jan. 7, 1971.
47. ————,   Jan. 20, 1971.
48. ————,   Feb. 9, 1971.
49. Wiener, Frederick Bernays,   Washington, D.C. Nov. 6, 1970.
50. ————,   Nov. 20, 1970.
51. ————,   Feb. 3, 1971.
52. Zillman, Donald [*Military Law Review*],   Charlottesville, Va. Jan. 5, 1971.

Interviews
(* indicates tape-recorded)

53. *Carney, Daniel F.,   Washington, D.C. Oct. 22, 1970.
54. Decker, Charles L., Washington, D.C. Oct. 20, 1970.
55. *Ferguson, Homer,   Washington, D.C. Oct. 22, 1970.
56. Gormley, Patricia [Military judge, USMC],   Treasure Island, Calif. Aug. 3, 1970.
57. *Harmon, Reginald C.,   Arlington, Va. Oct. 23, 1970.
58. ————,   January 15, 1971. [By telephone]
59. *Hickman, George W., Jr.,   Solano Beach, Calif. Sept. 3, 1970.
60. Keeffe, Arthur John,   Washington, D.C. Jan. 16, 1971.
61. Kenny, Joseph P. [District Legal Officer],   Treasure Island, Calf. Aug. 3, 1970.
62. *Larkin, Felix E.,   New York, Nov. 11, 1970.
63. *Latimer, George W.,   Salt Lake City. Sept. 15, 1970.
64. Love, Richard H. [Judge Advocates Association],   Washington, D.C. Oct. 1, 1970.
65. Machabee, James D. [Legal Center Yeoman],   Treasure Island, Calif. Aug. 3, 1970.
66. *Nunn, Ira H.,   Washington, D.C. Oct. 7, 1970.
67. *Parker, Harold E.,   The Pentagon. Oct. 21, 1970.
68. *Proulx, Alfred C.,   Washington, D.C. Oct. 14, 1970.
69. *Quinn, Robert E.,   Washington, D.C. Oct. 14, 1970.
70. *Sugarman, Myron C. [Military Justice Division, Army],   The Pentagon. Oct. 19, 1970.
71. Walkup, Homer A.,   Arlington, Va. Oct. 8. 1970.
72. *Wasson, John C.,   Washington, D.C. Oct. 16, 1970.
73. Weiner, Frederick Bernays,   Washington D.C. Jan 15, 1971.
74. Wilson, James R., Jr. [American Legion],   Washington, D.C. Oct. 6, 1970.

Government Documents–United Kingdom

75. *First Report of the Committee Appointed to Consider the Administration of Justice under the Naval Discipline Act 1950.* London. H.M. Stationery Office. 1950.
76. *Report of the Army and Air Force Courts-Martial Committee 1946.* London. H.M. Stationery Office. 1949.
77. *Second Report of the Committee Appointed to Consider the Administration of Justice Under the Naval Discipline Act 1950.* London. H.M. Stationery Office. 1951.

Government Documents–United States

Court of Military Appeals

78. "Interim Report." Submitted to the Committees on Armed Services of the Senate and of the House of Representatives and to the Secretary of Defense and the Secretaries of the Departments Pursuant to the Uniform Code of Military Justice for the period May 31, 1951 to March 1, 1952.
79. Pamphlet. "The United States Court of Military Appeals."
80. "Rules of Practice and Procedure." Revised Jan. 1, 1962.
81. (And the Judge Advocates General of the Armed Forces). *Annual Report Pursuant to the Uniform Code of Military Justice.* 1952-1969.
82. Hanlon, Frederick R., "Ten-Year Chronology of the United States Court of Military Appeals." Published in Item 81 [above] (1961), pp. 47-61.

Department of Defense

83. *Addendum to the Manual for Courts-Martial, United States 1951.* January 1963.
84. *Annotation to the Manual for Courts-Martial, United States 1951.* USAF Pocket Part. 1957.
85. *Legal and Legislative Basis, Manual for Courts-Martial, United States 1951.*
86. *Manual for Courts-Martial, United States 1951.*
87. *Manual for Courts-Martial, United States 1968.*
88. *Manual for Courts-Martial, United States 1969* (rev. ed.).
89. "Uniform Code of Military Justice: Text, References and Commentary, based on the Report of the Committee on a Uniform Code of Military Justice to the Secretary of Defense." Unpublished. 1949 [?].
90. Committee on a Uniform Code of Military Justice, "Comparative Studies Notebook."
91. Judge Advocates General of the United States, *Digest of Opinions.* 1951-——.

Department of Justice

92. Release. "Memorandum of Understanding Between the Departments of Justice and Defense relating to the Investigation and Prosecution of Crimes over which the Two Departments have concurrent Jurisdiction." Nov. 25, 1955.

Department of State

93. Public Services Division. "Questions and Answers No. 6." July 1954.

Department of the Air Force

94. *Manual for Courts-Martial, U.S. Air Forces, 1949.*
95. "Supplement to 'Air Force Summary of Changes in the Manual for Courts-Martial, 1969.'"
96. Continental Air Commander Hq., "Jag Reserve Newsletter." Oct. 1, 1954.

97. Judge Advocate General, "Conference of the JAG, USAF." April 9-10, 1951. Bolling AFB. Copy of report on file in the Stanford University Library Government Documents collection.
98. ————, *Digest.* 3 vols. 1948-1951.
99. 3320th Retraining Group, "The Air Force's Prisoner Retraining Program: 1961 Evaluation Report." 1962.
100. ————, "Follow-Up Study of Returnees of the 3320th Retraining Group." 1970.
101. ————, "Semi-Annual Report: Follow-Up Study of Restorees of the 3320th Retraining Group." October 1962.
102. ————, "Statistical Report: Annual Trend Analysis of Retrainee Population." 1970.

Department of the Army

103. *Manual for Courts-Martial, U.S. Army, 1949.*
104. Advisory Board on Clemency [the so-called "Roberts board," established by the War Department], "Final Report." Unpublished, unpaged report, dated May 19, 1947, on file in the Records Section, Research Office, Army Judge Advocate General, The Pentagon.
105. Advisory Committee on Military Justice [the so-called "Vanderbilt committee," established by the War Department], "Report. . . to the Honorable Secretary of War." Unpublished report, dated Dec. 13, 1946, on file in the Army JAG Library. The Pentagon.
106. Committee on the Uniform Code of Military Justice, Good Order, and Discipline in the Army, "Report to Honorable Wilber M. Brucker, Secretary of the Army." Jan. 18, 1960. [The so-called "Powell report."]
107. Correctional Training Facility, Fort Riley, Kansas, "Annual Report Fiscal Year 1970."
108. ————, "Annual Report and Statistical Analysis Fiscal Year 1969."
109. Judge Advocate General, "Conference at the JAG's School, U.S. Army, Charlottesville, Va., Sept. 9-12, 1963."
110. ————, *Military Laws of the United States (Army) 1949.*
111. ————, "Report of Conference Proceedings: Judge Advocate General Conference." 1954.
112. Special Committee for the Study of the United States Army Confinement System, "Report." May 15, 1970.

Department of the Navy

113. *General Order 21.* May 1, 1963.
114. *Naval Courts and Boards, 1937.* Reprinted 1945, including changes No.1 and No. 2.
115. *Report of the Secretary of the Navy's Task Force on Navy/Marine Corps Personnel Retention.* Jan. 25, 1966. 9 vols. plus Summary.
116. *United States Navy Regulations, 1920.* Washington, Government Printing Office. 1920.
117. Advisory Group on the Uniform Code of Military Justice, *Recommendations.* Unpublished, bound-volume collection of memos on file at the Navy JAG Library, Arlington, Va.
118. Anonymous, "Summary of the Development of the American System of Naval Justice." Unpublished, undated mimeographed typescript on file at the Law Center Library, Treasure Island, Calif.
119. Ballantine, Arthur A., "Organization, Methods and Procedure of Naval Courts." Letter to the Secretary of the Navy, Sep. 24, 1943, on file at the Navy JAG Library, Arlington, Va.
120. ————, "Report of the Board convened by precept of the Secretary of the Navy Dated November 15, 1945." Unpublished. April 24, 1946. On file at the Navy JAG Library, Arlington, Va.

121. Bureau of Naval Personnel, "A Seminar on the Uniform Code of Military Justice, 23-24 May 1951." Unpublished report on file at the Navy JAG Library, Arlington, Va.

122. Commander-in-Chief, U.S. Pacific Fleet, letter, serial 6733. Oct. 1, 1952. On file in the Navy JAG Library, Arlington, Va.

123. Commander, Service Force, U.S. Atlantic Fleet, "Seminar: Discipline and the Code." U.S. Naval Base, Norfolk, Va., Dec. 1953 and Jan. 1953. Unpublished report on file at the Navy JAG Library, Arlington, Va.

124. General Court Martial Sentence Review Board,   "Final Report with Respect to Cases Reviewed, 29 April to 19 Sept. 1946." Unpublished report on file at the Navy JAG Library, Arlington, Va.

125. ――――, "Report and Recommendations." Unpublished, undated (1947[?]) report on file at the Navy JAG Library, Arlington, Va.

126. ――――, "Synopsis of Report on Court-Martial Procedures and Policies." Unpublished, undated (1947[?]) report on file at the Navy JAG Library, Arlington, Va.

127. Hensley, Roy W.   "Evolution of the Office of the Judge Advocate General." Unpublished, undated paper on file at the Law Center Library, Treasure Island, Calif.   .

128. McGuire, Matthew F.,   Holtzoff, Alexander, and Snedeker, James M., "Articles for the Government of the Navy and Courts-Martial Procedure." Unpublished report, dated Nov. 21, 1945, on file at the Navy JAG Library, Arlington, Va.

129. Judge Advocate General,   *Congressional Floor Debates on the Uniform Code of Military Justice.* 1950.

130. ――――,   "Index and Legislative History of the Uniform Code of Military Justice." 1950.

131. ――――,   "Index to Naval Legal and Quasi-Legal Directives." Oct. 1, 1966.

132. ――――,   "JAG Anniversary Ball Souvenir Program." April 25, 1970.

133. ――――,   "Synopsis of Recommendations for the Improvement of Naval Justice." Unpublished, 1947 report, on file at the Navy JAG Library, Arlington, VA.

134. White, Robert J.   "An Interim Report of the Board for the Study of Certain Disciplinary Practices and Procedures of the Navy." Unpublished (dated Jan. 23, 1953). On file at the Navy JAG Library, Arlington, Va.

135. ――――,   "Report of the Board for the Study of Certain Disciplinary Practices and Procedures of the Navy." Unpublished (1953 [?]). On file at the Navy JAG ·Library, Arlington, Va.

136. ――――,   "A Study of Five Hundred Naval Prisoners and Naval Justice." Unpublished. (1946[?]) report on file at the Navy JAG Library, Arlington, Va.

House of Representatives

137. *Report 388.*   86th Cong., 1st Sess. (1959).
138. *Report 439.*   88th Cong., 1st Sess. (1963).
139. *Report 491.*   81st Cong., 1st Sess. (1949).
140. *Report 1034.*   80th Cong., 1st Sess. (1947).
141. *Report 1480.*   90th Cong., 1st Sess. (1967).
142. *Report 1481.*   90th Cong., 2d Sess. (1968).
143. *Report 1612.*   87th Cong., 2d Sess. (1962).
144. *Report 1946.*   81st Cong., 2d Sess. (1950).
145. *Report 2722.*   79th Cong., 2d Sess. (1946).
146. Appropriations Committee,   *Hearings before a Subcommittee . . . on Department of Defense Appropriations, 1961.* 86th Cong. 2d Sess. 1960.
147. Armed Services Committee,   *Subcommittee Hearings on H.R. 2575, to Amend the Articles of War.* 80th Cong. 1st Sess. 1947.
148. ――――,   *Full Committee Hearings on H.R. 774 and H.R. 2575.* 80th Cong. 1st Sess. 1947.
149. ――――,   *Hearings before a Subcommittee. . . . on H.R. 2498: A Bill to unify, consolidate, revise, and codify the Articles of War, the Articles for the*

Government of the Navy, and the Disciplinary Laws of the Coast Guard, and to enact and establish a Uniform Code of Military Justice. 81st Cong. 1st Sess. 1949.

150. ———, Subcommittee Hearings on H.R. 6583, to Amend the Uniform Code of Military Justice. 84th Cong. 2d Sess. 1956.

151. ———, Hearings on H.R. 16646 and H.R. 15053, before the Special Subcommittee on Discharges and Dismissals. 89th Cong. 2d Sess. 1966.

152. ———, Subcommittee No. 1 Hearings on H.R. 12705 to Amend Chapter 47 (UCMJ) of Title 10, U.S. Code. 90th Cong. 1st Sess. 1967.

153. ———, Subcommittee No. 1 Hearing on Title IV (To Establish a Navy Judge Advocate General's Corps) of H.R. 226. . . . 90th Cong. 1st Sess. 1967.

154. Ways and Means Committee, Hearings before a Subcommittee . . . on Traffic in and Control of, Narcotics, Barbiturates, and Amphetamines. 84th Cong. 1st Sess. 1955.

Senate

155. Document 196. 79th Cong., 2d Sess. 1946. [The so-called "Doolittle report."]
156. Document 244. 79th Cong., 2d Sess. (1946).
157. Executive Report 9. 82d Cong., 2d Sess. (1952).
158. Investigation of the National Defense Program: Hearings before a Special Committee Investigating the National Defense Program . . . Pursuant to S. Res. 71, 77th Cong., 1st Sess. [and other legislation], 77th through 80th Congresses, 43 Parts: 1941-1947.
159. Report 486. 81st Cong., 1st Sess. (1949).
160. Report 806. 90th Cong., 1st Sess. (1966).
161. Report 940. 66th Cong., 1st Sess. (1919).
162. Report 1601. 90th Cong., 2d Sess. (1968).
163. Report 1669. 89th Cong., 2d Sess. (1966).
164. Report 1876. 87th Cong., 2d Sess. (1962).
165. Report 1911. 87th Cong., 2d Sess. (1962).
166. Armed Services Committee, Hearings before a Subcommittee . . . on S. 857 and H.R. 4080. 81st Cong. 1st Sess. 1949.
167 ———, Non-Judicial Punishment: Hearing before a Subcommittee . . . on H.R. 11257. 87th Cong. 2d Sess. 1962.
168. ———, Hearing before the Committee . . . on Nomination of Judge Robert Emmett Quinn, of Rhode Island, for Reappointment as a Judge of the United States Court of Military Appeals. 89th Cong. 2d Sess. 1966.
169. ———, Hearing before the Committee . . . on S. 1036 . . . [and] H.R. 12910. 90th Cong. 1st Sess. 1967.
170. ——— and Judiciary Committee, Joint Hearings on S. 745 through S. 762, S. 2906 and S. 2907, Bills to Improve the Administration of Justice in the Armed Services, before the Subcommittee on Constitutional Rights of the Committee on the Judiciary and a Special Subcommittee of the Committee on Armed Services. 89th Cong. 2d Sess. 3 Parts. 1966.
171. Judiciary Committee, Constitutional Rights of Military Personnel: Hearings before the Subcommittee on Constitutional Rights of the Committee . . . Pursuant to S. Res. 260. 87th Cong. 2d Sess. 1962.
172. Military Affairs Committee, Hearings on S. 64 on the Establishment of Military Justice before a Subcommittee. . . . . 66th Cong. 1st Sess. 1919.

Judicial Reports

173. Court-Martial Reports: Holdings and Decisions of the Judge Advocates General Boards of Review and United States Court of Military Appeals. Rochester N.Y. Lawyers Co-operative Publishing Company. 1951–.

174. Decisions of the United States Court of Military Appeals with Headnotes, Tables, Index and Parallel References. Rochester, N.Y. Lawyers Co-operative Publishing Company. 1951–.

175. *Federal Reporter: Cases Argued and Determined in the United States Courts of Appeals, United States Court of Claims, and United States Court of Customs and Patents Appeals.* Second Series. St. Paul, Minn. West Publishing Company. Irregularly.

176. *Federal Supplement: Cases Argued and Determined in the District Courts of the United States [and the] Court of Claims.* St. Paul, Minn. West Publishing Company. Irregularly.

177. U.S. Department of the Air Force,   *Court-Martial Reports of the Judge Advocate General of the Air Force: Holdings and Opinions of the Judge Advocate General, Judicial Council and Boards of Review.* 4 vols. Rochester, N.Y. Lawyers Co-operative Publishing Company. 1949-1951.

178. U.S. Department of the Army,   *Judge Advocate General's Corps. Board of Review and Judicial Council Holdings, Opinions,. and Reviews.* 12 vols. Washington. GPO. 1949-1951.

179. U.S. Department of the Navy,   *Compilation of Court Martial Orders for the Years 1916-1937.* 2 vols. Washington. GPO. 1941.

180. —————,   *Court-Martial Orders for the Year*   Washington. GPO. Annual.

181. *United States Reports: Cases Adjudged in the Supreme Court.* Washington. GPO. Irregularly.

Other Printed Sources

182. American Bar Association,   "Canons of Professional Ethics. Canons of Judicial Ethics. Together with Rules of Procedure of the Committee on Professional Ethics and Grievances and Rules and Standards Adopted as to Law Lists." Chicago. 1954.

183. —————,   Criminal Law Section program. "Is there Justice in the Military?" St. Louis. Aug. 11, 1970.

184. American Law Institute,   "Model Penal Code. " Philadelphia, 1961.

185. The American Legion,   National Legislative Bulletin #6. Oct. 2, 1967.

186. —————,   National Security Div. "Report on the Uniform Code of Military Justice." Indianapolis. 1956.

187. —————,   "National Security Report to the 52nd National Convention." Portland, Ore. Sept. 1-3, 1970.

188. —————,   "Summary of Proceedings of the Annual National Convention." 1961-1969.

189. "Biographical Sketch: Ira H. Nunn."   1970. Provided the author by the National Restaurant Association, Washington, D.C.

190. Brosman, Paul W.,   "Address at the Opening Exercises of the Entering Class (Basic Course), The JAG's School." June 15, 1953. *JAG Chronicle* (June 26, 1953), p. 129.

191. Columbia Broadcasting System, TV News, "60 Minutes." Vol. III, Number 7 (Dec. 8, 1970). Transcript in author's possession.

192. *Congressional Directory (1953-69).* Washington. Government Printing Office. Annual.

193. Decker, Charles L.,   "Personal Resume." Author's possession.

194. The Federal Bar Association,   "A Symposium on Military Justice—Present and Pros-pective." Washington, D.C. Sept. 16, 1970.

195. Hippchen, Leonard J.,   "Methodological Problems in Assessing Ex-Prisoners: Experiences of the 3320th Retraining Group." April 1962..

196. Kennedy, Floyd C.,   "The USAF Prisoner Retraining Program." Revised 1970.

197. The National Archives,   *The Federal Register.* 1950-1969.

198. National Conference of Commissioners on Uniform State Laws,   Model Defender Act. 1959 [?].

199. O'Donnell, Robert D.,   "Research Program Activities of the 3320th Retraining Group." April 1962.

200. Snee, Joseph M.,   "Uniform Code of Military Justice and Rules of Military Criminal Procedure." Undated [1960?], proposal submitted to the Committee on Military Law, District of Columbia Bar Association. Copy provided the author by Mr. Felix Larkin.

201. "The Uniform Code of Military Justice." (The original code is printed in several places. It is PL 506, Act of May 5, 1950, 64 Stat. 108; and 50 USC § §551-736 (1946). This was recodified by PL 1028, Act of Aug. 10, 1956, 70A Stat. 1, which is 10 USC § §801-940 (1964). The original code is also found in Item 86 [above], pp. 411-58, and in16 *Federal Register* pp.1303-1469. The most recent version of the code is in Item 88 [above], pp. A2-1 through A2-37.

202. *U.S. Code.* 1946. 1964.

203. *U.S. Statutes at Large.* 1830. 1855. 1865. 1880. 1902. 1909. 1916. 1920. 1934. 1939-43. 1946-69.

204. Westmoreland, William C., "Remarks." Panel Program of the Section of Criminal Law, American Bar Association Annual Meeting. August 11, 1970.

Newspapers and Magazines

205. *Air Force Times.* 1958-1970. Washington.

206. *Army Times.* 1948-1970. Washington.

207. *Navy Times.* 1954-1970. Washington.

208. *Newsweek.* 1969-1972. Washington.

209. *New York Times.* 1919-1921. 1940-1942. 1945-1972. New York.

210. *Providence Journal.* May-July 1951. Providence, Rhode Island.

211. *San Francisco Chronicle.* 1968-1971. San Francisco.

212. *Time.* 1969-1972. New York.

213. *U.S. News and World Report.* 1957. Washington.

214. *Washington Post.* 1950-1970. Washington.

Collected Documents, Diaries, Memoirs

215. Adams, Charles Francis, *The Works of John Adams, Second President of the United States: with a Life of the Author, Notes and Illustrations.* 3 vols. Boston. Little, Brown. 1865.

216. Bernstein, Barton, and Matusow, Allen W., *The Truman Administration: A Documentary History.* New York. Harper Colophon. 1966.

217. Harford, Harrison, *The Somers Mutiny Affair.* Englewood Cliffs, N.J. Prentice-Hall. 1959.

218. Millis, Walter, ed., with the collaboration of Duffield, E. S., *The Forrestal Diaries.* New York. Viking. 1951.

219. Truman, Harry S. *Memoirs.* 2 vols. Garden City, N.Y. Doubleday. 1955-1956.

Bibliographies

220. Allport, Dorothy V., *Bibliography on Military Justice and Military Law.* Washington. GPO. 1960.

221. ————, *Supplement No. 1.* Washington. GPO. 1962.

222. ————, *Supplement No. 2.* Washington. GPO. 1964.

223. American Bar Foundation, "Index to Legal Theses and Research Projects." Chicago. Irregularly.

224. Hartnett, John E., Jr., "Survey Extended—the Literature of Military Law Since 1952." 12 *Vanderbilt Law Review* (1959), 369-93.

225. Mott, William C., Hartnett, John E., Jr., and Morton, Kenneth B., "A Survey of the Literature of Military Law—A Selective Bibliography." 6 *Vanderbilt Law Review* (1953), 333-69.

226. U.S. Court of Military Appeals Law Library, *A Bibliography of Articles Concerning: U.S. Court of Military Appeals, UCMJ, Military Justice, and Related Miscellaneous Subjects.* Washington. GPO. 1956.

227. U.S. Department of the Air Force, Pamphlet 110-1-2. "Military Legal Bibliography." November 1955.

228. U.S. Department of the Army, The JAG's School. "Catalog of Advanced (Career) Class Theses." Unpublished. Undated.

229. _____, *Military Law Review.* "Ten-Year Index." *Military Law Review* (April 1968).
230. U.S. Department of the Navy, *JAG Journal.* "Topical Index." I. 1947-1956. II. 1957-1960. III. 1961-1964.

Reference Works

231. *Citators and Index to Court-Martial Reports.* Rochester. Lawyers Co-operative Publishing Co. 1959.
232. Dahl, Richard C., *The Military Law Dictionary.* New York. Oceana Publications. 1960.
233. Hamilton, James, *Citer to United States Court of Military Appeals Opinions.* Dallas. American Guild Press. 1956.
234. Holtzoff, Alexander, Ed., *Federal Rules of Criminal Procedure.* New York. New York University School of Law. 1946.

235. Lawyers Co-operative Publishing Company, *Military Jurisprudence: Cases and Materials Selected and Edited by the Editorial Staff of the Publisher Together with the Advice and Counsel of a Group of Officers of the JAG Corps, USA.* Rochester, N.Y. Lawyers Co-operative Publishing Co. 1951.
236. _____, *Scheme Book for Classification of Military Law, with Scope Notes and Instructions.* Rochester, N.Y. Lawyers Co-operative Publishing Co. 1955.
237. Schiller, A. Arthur, *Military Law and Defence [sic] Legislation.* 4th Ed. New York. Columbia Law School. 1968.
238. Shapiro, Irving, *Dictionary of Legal Terms.* New York. Gould Publications 1969.
239. Tedrow, Richard L., *Digest: Annotated and Digested Opinions U.S. Court of Military Appeals, w/1969 Pocket Part.* Washington. GPO. 1966. 1969.
240. Tillotson, Lee Stephen, *Index-Digest and Annotations to the Uniform Code of Military Justice.* 4th Ed. Harrisburg. Military Service Pub. Co. 1956.
241. *Words and Phrases.* Permanent Ed. 45 vols. St. Paul, Minnesota. West Publishing Co. 1952.

Books, Pamphlets, Monographs

242 Alyea, Louis F., *Military Justice Under the 1948 Amended Articles of War.* New York. Oceana Publications. 1949.
243. Andreski, Stanislav, *Military Organization and Society.* 3d Enl. Ed. Berkeley. Univ. of California Press. 1968.
244. Avins, Alfred, *The Law of AWOL.* New York. Oceana Publications. 1957.
245. Aycock, William B., and Wurfel, Seymour W., *Military Law under the Uniform Code of Military Justice.* Chapel Hill, N.C. Univ. of No. Carolina Press. 1955.
246. Chafee, Zechariah, Jr., *State House versus Pent House: Legal Problems of the Rhode Island Race-Track Row.* Providence. The Book Shop. 1937.
247. Chipman, N.P., *The Tragedy of Andersonville: Trial of Captain Henry Wirz the Prison Keeper.* San Francisco. Privately printed. 1911.
248. Curtis, Charles Pelham, *It's Your Law.* Cambridge. Harvard Univ. Press. 1954.
249. Donovan, James A., *Militarism, USA.* New York. Scribner's. 1970.
250. Dougherty, Thomas E., Kellett, Thomas E., and McKenney, James B., "The United States Court of Military Appeals." Unpublished J.D. dissertation. Univ. of Minnesota Law School. 1952.
251. Edwards, Morris Oswald, and Decker, Charles L., *The Serviceman and the Law.* 6th Ed., Rev. Harrisburg. Military Service Publishing Co. 1955.
252. Evans, Rowland, and Novak, Robert., *Lyndon B. Johnson: The Exercise of Power.* New York. New American Library. 1966.
253. Everett, Robinson O., *Military Justice in the Armed Forces of the United States.* Harrisburg. Military Service Publishing Co. 1956.
254. Federal Bar Association, "Symposium on Military Justice: Present and Prospective." Unpublished. 1970 [?].
255. Feld, Benjamin, *A Manual of Courts-Martial Practice and Appeal.* New York. Oceana Press. 1957.

256. ————, "The United States Court of Military Appeals: A Study of the Origin and Early Development of the First Civilian Tribunal for Direct Review of Courts-Martial, 1951-1959." Unpublished Ph.D. dissertation. Georgetown Univ. Department of Government. 1960.

257. Gardner, Fred, *The Unlawful Concert: An Account of the Presidio Mutiny Case.* New York. Viking. 1970.

258. Guttmacher, Manfred S., and Weihofen, Henry, *Psychiatry and the Law.* New York. W.W. Norton. 1952.

259. Hersh, Seymour M., *My Lai 4: A Report on the Massacre and Its Aftermath.* New York. Random House. 1970.

260. Huie, William Bradford, *The Execution of Private Slovik: The Hitherto Secret Story of the Only American Soldier Since 1864 to be Shot for Desertion.* New York. Duell, Sloan and Pearce. 1954.

261. Huntington, Samuel P., *The Soldier and the State: The Theory and Politics of Civil-Military Relations.* New York. Random House. 1957.

262. Kinkead, Eugene, *In Every War But One.* New York. W.W. Norton. 1959.

263. Krise, Edward Fisher, "Role Conflict and Social Diagnosis of the Military Offender." Unpublished Ph.D. dissertatation. Univ. of Chicago Department of Sociology. 1958.

264. Larkin, Murl A., and Munster, Joe H., *Military Evidence.* Indianapolis. Bobbs-Merrill Co:,Inc. 1959.

265. Lederer, William J., and Burdick, Eugene, *The Ugly American.* [A Novel.] New York. Fawcett Crest. 1958.

266. Levitt, Saul, *The Andersonville Trial.* New York. Random House. 1960.

267. Llewelyn, Karl Nickerson, *The Common Law Tradition: Deciding Appeals.* Boston. Little, Brown. 1960.

268. Lockmiller, David A., *Enoch H. Crowder: Soldier, Lawyer and Statesman.* Columbia, Mo. Univ. of Missouri Studies. 1955.

269. Maguire, Robert F., "Pre-Trial Protections Against Compulsory Self-Incrimination Under Military Law." Unpublished thesis. The Judge Advocate General's School, Charlottesville, Va. 1957.

270. Mason, Alpheus Thomas, *The Supreme Court from Taft to Warren.* New York. W.W. Norton. 1958.

271. Mayers, Lewis, *The American Legal System: The Administration of Justice in the United States by Judicial, Administrative, Military, and Arbitral Tribunals.* Rev. ed. New York. Harper and Row. 1964.

272. Millis, Walter, *Arms and Men: A Study in American Military History.* New York. Capricorn. 1956.

273. Morison, Samuel Eliot, *History of United States Naval Operations in World War II.* 15 vols. Boston. Little, Brown. 1947-62.

274. Neustadt, Richard E., *Presidential Power: The Politics of Leadership.* New York. John Wiley & Sons. 1960.

275. Philos, Conrad D., *Handbook of Court-Martial Law.* Rev. ed. Chicago. Callaghan. 1951.

276. Prescott, Arthur Taylor, *Drafting the Federal Constitution: A Rearrangement of Madison's Notes Giving Consecutive Developments of Provisions in the Constitution of the United States, Supplemented by Documents Pertaining to the Philadelphia Convention and to Ratification Processes, and Including Insertions by the Compiler.* New York. Greenwood Press. 1968.

277. Robinson, William M., Jr., *Justice in Grey: A History of the Judicial Systems of the Confederate States of America.* Cambridge. Harvard Univ. Press. 1941.

278. Scott, Robert N., comp., *An Analytical Digest of the Military Laws of the United States: A Compilation of the Constitutional and Statutory Provisions Concerning the Military Establishment in All its Branches and Relations, Accompanied by Judicial and Executive Decisions Explanatory of the Text.* Philadelphia. Lippincott. 1873.

279. Sheehan, Neil. *The Arnheiter Affair.* New York. Random House. 1972.

280. Sherrill, Robert, *Military Justice Is to Justice As Military Music Is to Music.* New York. Harper and Row. 1969.

281. Snedeker, James, *Military Justice Under the Uniform Code.* Boston. Little, Brown. 1953.
282. Sowle, Claude R., *Police Power and Individual Freedom: The Quest for Balance.* Chicago. Aldine Publishing Co. 1962.
283. Spratt, James L., *Military Trial Techniques.* Dallas. American Guild Press. 1957.
284. Stewart, William Scott, *Federal Rules of Criminal Procedure.* Chicago. The Flood Co. 1945.
285. Sullivan, Charles S., Jr., *The Basic Principles of Military Law.* Handbook ed. Washington. McGregor and Werner, Inc. 1952.
286. Tarr, Curtis W., "Unification of America's Armed Forces: a Century and a Half of Conflict, 1798-1947." Unpublished Ph.D. dissertation. Stanford Univ. Department of History. 1962.
287. Ulmer, S. Sidney, *Military Justice and the Right to Counsel.* Lexington, Ky. The University Press of Kentucky. 1970.
288. U.S. Naval Institute, *Military Law.* 2d ed. rev. Annapolis. U.S. Naval Institute. 1963.
289. Walker, Daniel, ed., *Military Law.* New York. Prentice-Hall. 1954.
————, *Rights in Conflict: Convention Week in Chicago, August 25-29, 1968.* E.P. Dutton, 1968.
290. Weaver, John Downing, *Warren: The Man, the Court, the Era.* Boston. Little, Brown. 1967.
291. Wiener, Frederick Bernays, *Military Justice for the Field Soldier.* 2d & rev. ed. Washington. The Infantry Journal. 1944.
292. ————, *The Uniform Code of Military Justice: Explanation, Comparative Text, and Commentary.* Washington. Combat Forces Press. 1950.
293. Wigmore, John Henry, *Code of the Rules of Evidence in Trials at Law.* 3d ed. Boston. Little, Brown. 1942.
294. Williams, Thomas Harry, *Americans at War: The Development of the American Military System.* Baton Rouge, La. Louisiana State Univ. Press. 1960.
295. Winthrop, William, *Military Law and Precedents.* 2d ed., rev. & enl. 2 vols. Boston. Little, Brown. 1896.
296. Woolfolk, William, *Opinion of the Court.* [A Novel.] Garden City, N.Y. Doubleday. 1966.
297. Wouk, Herman, *The Caine Mutiny.* [A Novel.] New York. Dell. 1951.

Journals on the Military

298. *Judge Advocate Journal.* Bulletins 2-41. 1948-1969. Washington.
299. *The Reserve Officer.* November 1948. Washington.
300. U.S. Department of the Air Force, *JAG Bulletin.* 1959-1964.
301. ————, *JAG Law Review.* 1964-1970.
302. U.S. Department of the Army, *Army Information Digest.* 1947-1966.
303. ————. *Military Law Review.* 1958-1970.
304. ————, *Military Review.* 1943-1968.
305. ————, *Officer's Call.* 1949[?]-1954[?].
306. ————, Judge Advocate General, *Bulletin.* 1942-1951.
307. ————, Judge Advocate General, *Chronicle.* 1952-1954.
308. ————, Judge Advocate General, *Judge Advocate Legal Service.* 1958-.
309. ————, *JAGS 250.* 1954-1958.
310. ————, *Military Affairs: Judge Advocate Legal Service.* 1959-1969.
311. U.S. Department of the Navy, *All Hands: Bureau of Naval Personnel Information Bulletin.* 1945-1969.
312. ————, Judge Advocate General. *JAG Journal.* 1948-1970.
313. ————, Judge Advocate General, "Off the Record." 1959-1969.

Articles
(not including the contents of
"Journals on the Military," except for
those articles cited in footnotes)

314. Ackroyd, Gilbert G., "The General Articles, Articles 133 and 134 of the Uniform Code of Military Justice." 35 *St. John's Law Review* (1961), 264-99.

315. ————, "Professor Morgan and the Drafting of the Manual for Courts-Martial." *Military Law Review* (April 1965), 14-16.

316. Ansell, S.T., "Military Justice." 5 *Cornell Law Quarterly* (November 1919), 1-17.

317. Arnow, Arthur E., "The Uniform Code of Military Justice: It Should Be Improved Now. 48 *American Bar Association Journal* (1962), 647-48.

318. Avery, Paul, "A Presidio 'Mutiny' Reversal." *San Francisco Chronicle,* June 17, 1970, 1:3-30:4-5.

319. Avins, Alfred, "The Duty of Military Defense Counsel to an Accused." 58 *Michigan Law Review* (1960), 347-404.

320. ————, "The Joker in Jester—the Parris Island Death March Case." 53 *Northwestern Univ. Law Review* (1958), 33-60.

321. ————, "New Light on the Legislative History of Desertion Through Fraudulent Enlistment: The Decline of the United States Court of Military Appeals." 46 *Minnesota Law Review* (1961), 69-116.

322. Aycock, William B., "The Court of Military Appeals—the First Year." 31 *North Carolina Law Review* (1952), 1-45.

323. Baker, Richard C., "Self-Incrimination: Is the Privilege an Anachronism?" 42 *American Bar Association Journal* (1956), 633-36, 686-89.

324. Baldwin, Hanson W., "Military Justice Code." *New York Times,* March 24, 1955. 16:5,6.

325. ————, "New Military Justice." *New York Times,* March 25, 1955, 12:4,5.

326. Bennett, Oliver P., and Van Kirk, Rolla C., "Tyranny by Treaty." *Judge Advocate Journal* (July 1955), 8-16.

327. Birnbaum, Myron L., "The Effect of Recent Supreme Court Decisions on Military Law." 36 *Fordham Law Review* (1967), 153-74.

328. Bishop, Joseph W., Jr., "Civilian Judges and Military Justice: Collateral Review of Court-Martial Convictions." 61 *Columbia Law Review* (1961), 40-71.

329. ————, "The Quality of Military Justice." *New York Times Magazine,* Feb. 22, 1970, 32-39.

330. Brosman, Paul W., "The Court: Freer Than Most." 6 *Vanderbilt Law Review* (1953), 166-68.

331. ————, "The Uniform Code of Military Justice: Some Problems and Opportunities." 25 *Oklahoma Bar Association Journal* (1954), 1605-10.

332. Brown, Terry W., "The Crowder-Ansell Dispute: The Emergence of General Samuel T. Ansell." *Military Law Review* (January 1967), 1-46.

333. Burns. Arnold I., and Rapson, Donald J., "Sounding the Death Knell of Drumhead Justice." 48 *American Bar Association Journal* (1962), 843-47.

334. Butts, A.B., "The Uniform Code of Military Justice." 22 *Mississippi Law Journal* (1951), 203-11.

335. Byrd, John H., Jr., "Military Law—Failure to Obey Order—Constructive Knowledge of Lawful Order is Insufficient to Sustain Conviction—United States v. Curtin, 9 USCMA 427, 26 CMR 207 (1958)." 27 *George Washington Law Review* (1958-1959), 252-56.

336. Cardozo, Benjamin N., "A Ministry of Justice." 35 *Harvard Law Review* (1921), 113-26.

337. Carl, Clifton S., "Constitutional Law—Separation of Powers—Termination of State of War." 33 *Tulane Law Review* (1959), 668.

338. Christie, James D., "Constitutional Law—Military Personnel—Double Jeopardy—Appeal by Government." 26 *Temple Law Quarterly* (1953), 446-49.

339. Clark, Howard, 2d,   "A Comparison of Civil and Court-Martial Procedure." 4
     Indiana Law Journal (1929), 589-99.
340. "A Code of Trial Conduct: Promulgated by the College of Trial Lawyers." 43
     American Bar Association Journal (1957), 223-26, 283.
341. Colclough, O. S.,   "Naval Justice." 38 *Journal of Criminal Law and Criminology*
     (1947), 198-205.
342. "Constitutional Rights of Servicemen Before Courts-Martial." 64 *Columbia Law
     Review* (1964), 127-49.
343. Cozzi, Adrian,   "Evidence–Military Law–Insanity as a Defense–Durham Rule not
     Acceptable in Military Law." 5 *Catholic Univ. Law Review* (1955), 193-95.
344. Creech, William A.,   "Congress Looks to the Serviceman's Rights." 49 *American
     Bar Association Journal*(1963), 1070-74.
345. "Criminal Jurisdiction Over Civilians Accompanying American Armed Forces
     Overseas." 71 *Harvard Law Review* (1957), 712-27.
346. C.R.M.   "Military Law–Unitary Appellate Review–Military Jeopardy." 21 *George
     Washington Law Review* (1953), 497-500.
347. Currier, Roger M., and Kent, Irvin M.,   "The Boards of Review of the Armed
     Services." 6 *Vanderbilt Law Review* (1953), 241-50.
348. Curtis, Charles P.,   "The Ethics of Advocacy." 4 *Stanford Law Review* (1951),
     3-23.
349. "Discharge from Military Service Does Not Terminate Jurisdiction of Military
     Court." 48 *Journal of Criminology, Criminal Law, and Police Science* (1957),
     455-56.
350. Dixon, Frederick R., and Zadnik, Rudolph S.,   "Military Justice–A Uniform Code
     for the Armed Services." 2 *Western Reserve Law Review* (1950), 147-61.
351. Dougherty, Clifford A., and Lynch, Norman B.,   "The Administrative Discharge:
     Military Justice?" 33 *George Washington Law Review* (1964), 498-528.
352. Draper, G.I.A.D.,   "An Outline of Soviet Military Law." *Military Law Review* (July
     1959), 1-15.
353. Drinker, Henry S.,   "Some Remarks on Mr. Curtis' 'The Ethics of Advocacy.' " 4
     Stanford Law Review (1952), 349-57.
354. Earle, W.K.,   "The Preliminary Investigation in the Army Court-Martial System–
     Springboard for Attacks by Habeas Corpus." 18 *George Washington Law Review*
     (1949), 67-96.
355. Enderby, K.E.,   "Courts-Martial Appeals in Australia." *Military Law Review* (July
     1960), 65-92.
356. Ervin, Sam J., Jr.,   "The Military Justice Act of 1968." *Military Law Review* (July
     1969), 77-98.
357. Everett, Robinson O.,   "Military Administrative Discharge–the Pendulum Swings."
     1966 *Duke Law Journal* (1966), 41-91.
358. ————,   "O'Callahan v. Parker–Milestone or Millstone in Military Justice?"
     1969 *Duke Law Journal* (1969), 853-96.
359. ————,   "Persons Who Can Be Tried by Courts-Martial." 5 *Journal of Public
     Law* (1956), 148-73.
360. Falco, James J.,   "U.S. v. Tempia: The Questionable Application of Miranda to the
     Military." 13 *Villanova Law Review* (1967), 170-86.
361. Feld, Benjamin,   "Courts-Martial Practice: Some Phases of Pretrial Procedure." 23
     Brooklyn Law Review (1956), 25-37.
362. Finan, Robert J., and Vorback, Joseph E.,   "The Court of Military Appeals and the
     Bill of Rights: A New Look." 36 *George Washington Law Review* (1967), 435-46.
363. Findley, Tim, and Howe, Charles,   "Behind Prison Bars." *San Francisco Chronicle*
     (February 22 through March 4, 1971). Front page of each issue.
364. Fitch, Robert A.,   "The Law Specialist Program." *JAG Journal* (June 1957), 3-5.
365. Fontanella, David A.,   "Privileged Communication–The Personal Privileges."
     Military Law Review (July 1967), 155-209.
366. "For Military Justice."   [Editorial.] *New York Times*, March 12, 1948, 22:3-4.
367. Fratcher, William F.,   "Appellate Review in American Military Law." 14 *Missouri
     Law Review* (1949), 15-75.
368. ————,   "Presidential Power to Regulate Military Justice: A Critical Study of

Decisions of the Court of Military Appeals." 34 *New York Univ. Law Review* (1959), 861-90.

369. Gerwig, Robert, "Judicial Control of Administrative Discretion Exercised by Military Authorities." 25 *Mississippi Law Journal* (1954), 217-35.

370. Greenberg, Mack K., "The Dockside Court." *JAG Journal* (December 1957-January 1958), 19-22.

371. "Habeas Corpus, Sentence and Conviction by Courts-Martial." 16 *George Washington Law Review* (1947), 142-47.

372. Halse, Richard C., "Military Law in the United Kingdon." *Military Law Review* (January 1962), 1-22.

373. Hamilton, William C., "Military Law: Drumhead Justice is Dead!" 43 *American Bar Association Journal* (1957), 797-800.

374. Hamlett, Barksdale, "Commander's View of the Army Judge Advocate." 50 *American Bar Association Journal* (1964), 553-36.

375. Harmon, Reginald C., "Progress Under the Uniform Code." *Judge Advocate Journal* (October 1954), 10-14.

376. Henderson, Gordon D., "Courts-Martial and the Constitution: The Original Understanding." 71 *Harvard Law Review* (1957), 293-324.

377. Herbers, John, "Senator Ervin Thinks the Constitution Should Be Taken Like Mountain Whiskey—Undiluted and Untaxed." *New York Times Magazine*, Nov. 15, 1970, 50-52, 207-37, *passim.*

378. Hickman, George W., Jr., "Pleading Guilty for a Consideration in the Army." *JAG Journal* (December 1957-January 1958), 11.

379. Hodges, James W., "The Wayward Serviceman: His Constitutional Rights and Military Jurisdiction." 7 *San Diego Law Review* (1970), 185-236.

380. Hodson, Kenneth J., "Is There Justice in the Military?" *The Army Reserve Magazine* (November-December 1969), 22-24.

381. Hollies, J.H., "Canadian Military Law." *Military Law Review* (July 1961), 69-87.

382. Inbau, Fred E., "Should We Abolish the Constitutional Privilege Against Self-Incrimination?" 45 *Journal of Criminal Law, Criminology, and Police Science* (1954), 180-84.

383. Jackson, Robert H., "The County-Seat Lawyer." 36 *American Bar Association Journal* (1950), 497.

384. Jaffe, Louis L., "The Right to Judicial Review." 71 *Harvard Law Review* (1958), 401-37.

385. James, A. Clayton, Jr., "Military Law—Use of Manual for Courts-Martial by Court-Martial Members Disallowed." 19 *Louisiana Law Review* (1959), 715-21.

386. Johnson, Richard C., "Unlawful Command Influence: A Question of Balance." *JAG Journal* (March-April 1965), 87-94, 110-16.

387. J.T.B., "Military Law—Constitutionality of Special Military Court-Martial Where Defense Counsel is not a Lawyer." 10 *Howard Law Journal* (Winter 1964), 114-20.

388. "Judicial Checks on Command Influence Under the Uniform Code of Military Justice." 63 *Yale Law Journal* (1954), 880, 888.

389. "Judicial Review of Discharge Classifications Determined in Military Administrative Proceedings." 70 *Harvard Law Review* (1957), 533-45.

390. Kamanski, Charles P., "Military Law—Habeas Corpus—Scope of Review by Civil Courts from Decisions of Military Courts-Martial." 27 *So. California Law Review* (1954), 333.

391. Kamisar, Yale, "*Betts v. Brady* 20 Years Later: The Right to Counsel and Due Process Values." 61 *Michigan Law Review* (1962), 219-82.

392. ————, "A Dissent from the *Miranda* Dissents: Some Comments on the 'New' 5th Amendment and the Old 'Voluntariness' Test." 65 *Michigan Law Review* (1966), 59-104.

393. Karlen, Delmar, and Pepper, Louis H., "The Scope of Military Justice." 43 *Journal of Criminal Law, Criminology, and Police Science* (1952), 285-98.

394. Keeffe, Arthur John, "Drumhead Justice: A Look at our Military Courts." *The Reader's Digest* (August 1951), 39-44.

395. ————, "JAG Justice in Korea." 6 *Catholic Univ. Law Review* (1956). 1-55.

396. ———, "Universal Military Training With or Without Reform of Courts-Martial." 33 *Cornell Law Quarterly* (1948), 465-87.
397. ——— and Moskin, Morton. "Codified Military Injustice." 35 *Cornell Law Quarterly* (1949), 151-70.
398. Kent, Irvin M., "The *Jencks* Case: The Viewpoint of a Military Lawyer." 45 *American Bar Association Journal* (1959), 819-21, 872-74.
399. ———, "The Military Justice Branch of a Judge Advocate Office: Pretrial Activities." *Judge Advocate Journal* (June 1962), 17-32.
400. King, Archibald, "Changes in the Uniform Code of Military Justice Necessary to Have It Workable in Time of War." 22 *Federal Bar Journal* (1962), 49.
401. Kiser, Jackson L., "Command Control of Courts-Martial." 42 *American Bar Association Journal* (1956), 969.
402. Kock, Gerald L., "An Introduction to Military Justice in France." *Military Law Review* (July 1964), 119-39.
403. Kuhfeld, Albert M., "Prejudicial Error—The Measurement of Reversal by Boards of Review and the U.S. Court of Military Appeals." 35 *St. John's Law Review* (1961), 255-63.
404. Landman, Bernard, Jr., "One Year of the Uniform Code of Military Justice: A Report of Progress." 4 *Stanford Law Review* (1952), 491-508.
405. Langley, Earnest L., "Military Justice and the Constitution—Improvements Offered by the New Uniform Code of Military Justice." 29 *Texas Law Review* (1951), 651-71.
406. Larkin, Felix E., "Professor Edmund M. Morgan and the Drafting of the Uniform Code." *Military Law Review* (April 1965), 7-13.
407. Larkin, Murl A., "When is an Error Harmless?" *JAG Journal* (December 1967-January 1968), 65-70.
408. Latimer, George W., "A Comparative Analysis of Federal and Military Criminal Practice." 29 *Temple Law Quarterly* (1955), 1-25.
409. ———, " 'Good Cause' in Petitions for Review." 6 *Vanderbilt Law Review* (1953), 163-165.
410. *"Improvements and Suggested Improvements in the Administration of Military Justice." Report of Conference Proceedings.* Army Judge Advocate Conference (1954), 49-51.
411. ———, "Military Justice." 45 *Law Library Journal* (1952), 148.
412. "Law Officer's Instructions Under UCMJ." 5 *Stanford Law Review* (1953), 366-69
413. "Let's Not 'Nit-Pick.' " [Editorial.] *Navy Times*, Sept. 15, 1956, 8:1.
414. Lewis, Anthony, "American Lawyers: Gideon's Army." 50 *Cornell Law Quarterly* (1965), 155-60.
415. Lynch, Norman B., "The Administrative Discharge: Changes Needed?" 22 *Maine Law Review* (1970), 141-69.
416. McBratney, William H., "Reform of Military Justice is not Complete." 35 *Journal of the American Judicature Society* (1951), 81-83.
417. McCaffrey, Joseph, "Meet the Member: U.S. Senator Sam Ervin, Jr., Democrat-North Carolina." Originally broadcast on WMAL, Washington; now a pamphlet distributed by Ervin's office.
418. MacCormick, Austin H.,and Evjen, Victor H., "Statistical Study of 24,000 Military Prisoners." 10 *Federal Probation* (April-June 1946), 6-11.
419. McGovern, Peter J., "The Military Oral Deposition and Modern Communications." *Military Law Review* (July 1969), 43-75.
420. McNiece, Harold F., and Thornton, John V., "Military Law from Pearl Harbor to Korea." 22 *Fordham Law Review* (1953), 155-82.
421. Maglin, W. H., "Rehabilitation the Keynote of the Army's Correctional Program." 19 *Federal Probation* (June 1955), 21-28.
422. Martini, Steve, "Belli Heaps Praise on Military Court System." *Los Angeles Daily Journal* (May 1, 1970). Reprinted in Item 254, p. 27.
423. Mayhew, Donald P., "Peacetime Jurisdiction of Courts-Martial over Civilian Components of the Armed Services in Foreign Countries: The Toth and Covert Decisions." 3 *UCLA Law Review* (1956), 279-324.

424. Melhorn, Donald F., Jr., "Negotiated Pleas in Naval Courts-Martial." *JAG Journal* (September 1962), 103-10, 122.
425. Merriam, Harold A., and Thornton, John V., "Double Jeopardy and the Court-Martial." 19 *Brooklyn Law Review* (1953), 63-80.
426. "Military Law." 87 *Washington Law Reporter* (1959), 553-55.
427. "Military Law—Right to Counsel—Sixth Amendment Right to Counsel Applies To Accused in Special Courts-Martial, but its Requirements are Satisfied by Nonlawyer." 49 *Virginia Law Review* (1961), 1581-88.
428. "Military Personnel and the First Amendment: 'Discreditable Conduct' as a Standard for Restricting Political Activity." 65 *Yale Law Journal* (1956), 1207-17.
429. Miller, Harold L., "A Long Look at Article 15." *Military Law Review* (April 1965), 37-119.
430. Miller, Hubert G., "The New Look in Article 15." *Army Information Digest* (June 1963), 2-6.
431. "Misconduct in the Prison Camp: A Survey of the Law and an Analysis of the Korean Cases." 56 *Columbia Law Review* (1956), 709-94.
432. Morgan, Edmund M., "The Background of the Uniform Code of Military Justice." 6 *Vanderbilt Law Review* (1953), 169-85; reprinted at *Military Law Review* (April 1965), 17-36.
433. ————, "The Existing Court-Martial System and the Ansell Articles." 29 *Yale Law Journal* (1919), 52-74.
434. Moskos, Charles C., Jr., "Military Made Scapegoat for Vietnam." *Washington Post,* Aug. 30. 1970, C1:3-6, C2:1-4.
435. "The Most Important Bill." [Editorial.] *Navy Times,* April 21, 1956. 8:1-2.'
436. Mott, William C., "An Appraisal of Proposed Changes in the Uniform Code of Military Justice." 35 *St. John's Law Review* (1961), 300-22.
437. Mounts, James A., Jr., and Sugarman, Myron G., "The Military Justice Act of 1968." 55 *American Bar Association Journal* (1969), 470.
438. Moyer, Homer E., Jr., "Procedural Rights of the Military Accused: Advantages over a Civilian Defendant." 22 *Maine Law Review* (1970), 105-40.
439. Mummey, R.M., and Meagher, T.F., Jr., "Judges in "Uniform: An Independent Judiciary for the Army." 44 *Journal of the American Judicature Society* (August 1960), 46-52.
440. Murphy, Arthur A., "The Army Defense Counsel: Unusual Ethics for an Unusual Advocate." 61 *Columbia Law Review* (1961), 233-53.
441. Myholm, Soren B., "Danish Military Jurisdiction." *Military Law Review* (January 1963), 110-17.
442. Ochstein, Max S., "The Dockside Court: The Dockside Special Court-Martial of COMINLANT." *JAG Journal* (June-July 1959), 13-15.
443. Page, William Herbert, "Military Law—A Study in Comparative Law." 32 *Harvard Law Review* (1919), 349-73.
444. Pasley, Robert S., Jr., "A Comparative Study of Military Justice Reforms in Britain and America." 6 *Vanderbilt Law Review* (1953), 305-32.
445. ————, "The Federal Courts Look at the Court-Martial." 12 *Univ. of Pittsburgh Law Review* (1950), 7-34.
446. ————, and Larkin, Felix E., "The Navy Court-Martial: Proposals for Its Reform." 33 *Cornell Law Quarterly* (1947), 195-234.
447. Pearlstine, Norman, "Military Justice—Trial of Calley Brings Court-Martial System Under New Scrutiny." *The Wall Street Journal,* Dec. 8, 1969, 1, 33.
448. Powers, Robert D., Jr., "Important UCMJ Change." 88 *U.S. Naval Institute Proceedings* (December 1962), 139-44.
449. Price, Arthur L., "Growth in Military Jurisprudence Since World War II." 41 *Illinois Bar Journal* (1952), 56-61.
450. "The Proposed Uniform Code of Military Justice." 62 *Harvard Law Review* (1949), 1377-87.
451. Pye, A. Kenneth, "The Legal Status of the Korean Hostilities." 45 *Georgetown Law Journal* (1956), 45-60.
452. Quinn, Robert Emmett, "The Court's Responsibility." 6 *Vanderbilt Law Review*

(1953), 161-62.
453. ————— ——, "Military Law: A Twenty-Year Metamorphosis." 22 *Cornell Law Forum* (Fall 1969), 1-2.
454. —————, "Some Comparisons Between Courts-Martial and Civilian Practice." 15 *UCLA Law Review* (1968), 1240-59.
455. —————, "The United States Court of Military Appeals." *Army Information Digest* (Oct. 1952), 12-16.
456. —————, "The United States Court of Military Appeals and Individual Rights in the Military Service." 35 *Notre Dame Lawyer* (1960), 491-507.
457. —————, "The United States Court of Military Appeals and the Military Due Process." 35 *St. John's Law Review* (1961), 225-54.
458. Re, Edward D., "The Uniform Code of Military Justice." 25 *St. John's Law Review* (May 1951), 155-187.
459. "Recommended Amendments to the Uniform Code of Military Justice." *JAG Journal* (June 1954), 9-10.
460. Re, Edward D., "The Uniform Code of Military Justice." 25 *St. John's Law Review* (1951), 155-187.
461. Reed, Macon, "Court of Military Appeals." *Navy Times Family Magazine*, July 21, 1965, 4-5, 12.
462. Rheinstein, Max, "Comparative Military Justice." 15 *Federal Bar Association Journal* (1955), 276-85.
463. Richardson, George L., "A State of War and the Uniform Code of Military Justice." 47 *American Bar Association Journal* (1961), 792-98,
464. "The Right to Counsel in Special Courts-Martial." 50 *Minnesota Law Review* (1965), 147-69.
465. Rogers, Warren, "Calley—Caught in a Foulup." *San Francisco Chronicle* (April 5, 1971), 14:2-6.
466. Rollman, Robert O., "Of Crimes, Courts-Martial and Punishment—a Short History of Military Justice." *Air Force JAG Law Review* (Winter 1969), 212-22.
467. Rosenwald, Harold, "Some Reflections on the Rules of Evidence in Military Courts." 43 *Texas Law Review* (1965), 526-36.
468. Ross, Irwin, "Justice Comes to the GI." *Pageant* (August 1955), 156-161.
469. Ross, Joseph R., "The Military Justice Act of 1968: Historical Background." *JAG Journal* (May-June 1969), 25-29.
470. Royall, Kenneth C., "Revision of the Military Justice Process as Proposed by the War Department." 33 *Virginia Law Review* (1947), 269-88.
471. Russell, G.L., "The Uniform Code of Military Justice." 19 *George Washington Law Review* (1951), 233-74.
472. Rydstrom, J.F., "Uniform Courts of Military Justice." 50 *American Bar Association Journal* (1964), 749-51.
473. Schulberg, B., "100,000 Years at Hard Labor." *Saturday Evening Post* (May 25, 1946), 32-33, 59-64, *passim.*
474. Schweikhardt, F.W., "Non-judicial Punishment Under the Uniform Code of Military Justice." 5 *New York Law Forum* (1959), 45-72.
475. Selman, Richard J., "The Military Justice Act of 1968: Some Problems and Practical Solutions." *JAG Journal* (May-June 1969), 147-51.
476. Shafroth, Will., "Survey of the United States Courts of Appeals." 42 *Federal Rules Decisions* (1967), 243-315.
477. "The Shame of the Prisons." [Cover story.] *Time* (Jan. 18, 1971), 48-55.
478. Sheehan, Neil, "The 99 Days of Captain Arnheiter." *New York Times Magazine* (Aug. 11, 1968), 7-75, *passim.*
479. —————, "Should We Have War Crime Trials?" *New York Times Book Review* (March 28, 1971), 1-34, *passim.*
480. Sherman, Edward F., "The Civilianization of Military Law." 22 *Maine Law Review* (1970), 3-103.
481. Sherrill, Robert, "Justice, Military Style." *Playboy* (February 1970), 120-22, 214-28, *passim.*
482. —————, "Trial by Military Court." *San Francisco Sunday Examiner and Chronicle, Sunday Punch*, May 17, 1970, 5:1-3.

483. Smith, John Anthony, "Subterranean Justice." 22 *Cornell Law Forum* (Fall 1969), 9-10.
484. Snedeker James, "Habeas Corpus and Court-Martial Prisoners." 6 *Vanderbilt Law Review* (1953), 288-304.
485. ————, "The Uniform Code of Military Justice." 38 *Georgetown Law Journal* (1950), 521-73.
486. Spiegelberg, George A., and Ackman, Milton, "Court-Martial Vacuum." *The Nation* (Dec. 24. 1960), 499-502.
487. "The Supreme Court–1955 Term (Constitutional Law–Military Jurisdiction)." 70 *Harvard Law Review* (1956), 107-13.
488. Sutherland, Arthur E., "The Constitution, the Civilian, and Military Justice." 35 *St. John's Law Review* (1961), 215-24.
489. Sutton, John F., Jr., "Re-evaluation of the Canons of Professional Ethics: A Revisor's Viewpoint." 33 *Tennessee Law Review* (1966), 132-44.
490. Taussig, J.K., "Naval War-Time Discipline." 70 *U.S. Naval Institute Proceedings* (1944), 859-65, 995-1001, 1207-15.
491. Thode, W. Wayne, "The Ethical Standard for the Advocate." 39 *Texas Law Review* (1961), 575-600.
492. Thornton, John V., "Military Law." *Annual Survey of American Law* (1954), 112.
493. Walker, Daniel, "An Evaluation of the United States Court of Military Appeals." 48 *Northwestern Univ. Law Review* (1954), 714-33.
494. ————, "The United States Court of Military Appeals." 38 *American Bar Association Journal* (1952). 567-70.
495. ———— and Niebank, George, "The Court of Military Appeals–Its History, Organization and Operation." 6 *Vanderbilt Law Review* (1953), 228-40.
496. Walkup, Homer A., "A Summary History of the Office of the Judge Advocate General of the Navy." JAG Anniversary Ball Souvenir Program, 25 April 1970.
497. Wallstein, Leonard M., Jr., "Justice in the Army?" *The Nation* (July 19, 1947), 71-73.
498. Walsh, William F., "Can the Military Cope with Thirteen Books?" 50 *American Bar Association Journal* (1964), 67-69.
499. ————, "Military Law: Return to Drumhead Justice?" 42 *American Bar Association Journal* (1956), 521-25.
500. Waltz, Jon R., "The Court of Military Appeals: An Experiment in Judicial Revolution." 45 *American Bar Association Journal* (1959), 1185-87.
501. Ward, Chester, "Seapower and Survival: Leadership and Law." *JAG Journal* (July-August 1960), 2, 7-8, 11-15, 17-19.
502. ————, "UCMJ–Does It Work? Evaluation at the Field Level, 18 months Experience. I. The Justice Element. H. The Military Element." 6 *Vanderbilt Law Review* (1953), 186-227.
503. Warns, James T., "Task Force Legal Services for Trial by Court-Martial." *JAG Journal* (February 1960), 9-10.
504. Warren, Earl, "The Bill of Rights and the Military." 37 *New York Univ. Law Review* (1962), 181-203.
505. Weiner, Alfred J., "Right of Military Personnel to Have Counsel Present During Investigation Prior to Preferral of General Court Martial Charges." 10 *Syracuse Law Review* (1958), 169-70.
506. "Wels Calls Naval Justice Archaic and Antiquated." *U.S. Navy Magazine* (October 1947), 12-14.
507. West, Luther C., "A History of Command Influence on the Military Judicial System." 18 *UCLA Law Review* (1970), 1-156.
508. "What Remains of Court-Martial Jurisdiction Over Civilians?–The Toth and Kinsella Cases." 51 *New York Univ. Law Review* (1956), 474-86.
509. White, Robert J., "Has the Uniform Code of Military Justice Improved the Courts-Martial System?" 28 *St. John's Law Review* (1953), 19-29.
510. ————, "The Uniform Code of Military Justice: The Background and the Problem." 35 *St. John's Law Review* (1961), 197-214.
511. Wiener, Frederick Bernays, "Are the General Military Articles Unconstitutionally Vague?" 54 *American Bar Association Journal* (1968), 357-63.

512. ————, "The Army's Field Judiciary System." 46 *American Bar Association Journal* (1960), 1178-83.
513. ————, "Courts-Martial and the Bill of Rights: The Original Practice." 72 *Harvard Law Review* (1958), 1-49, 266-304.
514. ————, "History Vindicates the Supreme Court's Rulings on Military Justice." 51 *American Bar Association Journal* (1965), 1127-30.
515. ————, "The Militia Clause of the Constitution." 54 *Harvard Law Review* (1940), 181-220.
516. ————, "The New Articles of War." 63 *Infantry Journal* (September 1948), 24-31.
517. ————, "The Perils of Tinkering with Military Justice." *Army* (November 1970), 22-25.
518. Wigmore, John Henry, "Lessons from Military Justice." 4 *Journal of the American Judicature Society* (1920), 151-57.
519. Willis, William R., Jr., "Toth v. Quarles—For Better or For Worse." 9 *Vanderbilt Law Review* (1956), 534-41.
520. Winship, Blanton, "Court-Martial Procedure Compared with Criminal Procedure in Civil Courts." *Federal Bar Association Journal* (March 1932), 3-14.
521. Witt, Elder, "Nixon Crime Package—A Model or 'Garbage'?" *San Francisco Examiner and Chronicle,* June 14, 1970, A19:1-8.
522. Wurfel, Seymour W., " 'Military Due Process': What Is It?" 6 *Vanderbilt Law Review* (1953), 251-87.
523. ————, "Military Habeas Corpus." 49 *Michigan Law Review* (1951), 493-528, 699-722.
524. Zearfoss, Herbert K., "Military Law—Declaratory Judgment and Injunction Available in Civil Courts for Review of Court-Martial." 6 *The American Univ. Law Review* (1957), 119-21.

Index